T0091921

GPU Pro^6

GPU Pro⁶

Advanced Rendering Techniques

Edited by Wolfgang Engel

CRC Press
Taylor & Francis Group
Boca Raton London New York

CRC Press is an imprint of the
Taylor & Francis Group, an **informa** business

AN A K PETERS BOOK

CRC Press
Taylor & Francis Group
6000 Broken Sound Parkway NW, Suite 300
Boca Raton, FL 33487-2742

Printed in Canada on acid-free paper
Version Date: 20150318

International Standard Book Number-13: 978-1-4822-6461-6 (Hardback)

Library of Congress Cataloging-in-Publication Data

GPU pro 6 : advanced rendering techniques / edited by Wolfgang Engel.
   pages cm
  Includes bibliographical references and index.
  ISBN 978-1-4822-6461-6 (hardback)
   1. Rendering (Computer graphics) 2. Graphics processing units--Programming. 3. Computer graphics. 4. Real-time data processing. 5. Digital video.
I. Engel, Wolfgang.

  T385.G26674 2015
  006.6'6--dc23
                                                2015006268

Visit the Taylor & Francis Web site at
http://www.taylorandfrancis.com

and the CRC Press Web site at
http://www.crcpress.com

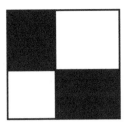

Contents

III   Lighting   181
Michal Valient

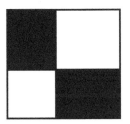

Acknowledgments

The *GPU Pro: Advanced Rendering Techniques* book series covers ready-to-use ideas and procedures that can help to solve many of your daily graphics programming challenges.

The sixth book in the series wouldn't have been possible without the help of many people. First, I would like to thank the section editors for the fantastic job they did. The work of Wessam Bahnassi, Marius Bjørge, Carsten Dachsbacher, Michal Valient, and Christopher Oat ensured that the quality of the series meets the expectations of our readers.

The great cover screenshots were contributed by Ubisoft. They show the game *Assassin's Creed IV: Black Flag.*

The team at CRC Press made the whole project happen. I want to thank Rick Adams, Charlotte Byrnes, Kari Budyk, and the entire production team, who took the articles and made them into a book.

Special thanks goes out to our families and friends, who spent many evenings and weekends without us during the long book production cycle.

I hope you have as much fun reading the book as we had creating it.

—Wolfgang Engel

P.S. Plans for an upcoming *GPU Pro 7* are already in progress. Any comments, proposals, or suggestions are highly welcome (wolfgang.engel@gmail.com).

Web Materials

Example programs and source code to accompany some of the chapters are available on the CRC Press website: go to http://www.crcpress.com/product/isbn/9781482264616 and click on the "Downloads" tab.

The directory structure closely follows the book structure by using the chapter numbers as the name of the subdirectory.

General System Requirements

- The DirectX June 2010 SDK (the latest SDK is installed with Visual Studio 2012).

- DirectX 9, DirectX 10, or even a DirectX 11 capable GPU are required to run the examples. The article will mention the exact requirement.

- The OS should be Microsoft Windows 7, following the requirement of DirectX 10 or 11 capable GPUs.

- Visual Studio C++ 2012 (some examples might require older versions).

- 2GB RAM or more.

- The latest GPU driver.

Updates

Updates of the example programs will be posted on the website.

Geometry Manipulation

The "Geometry Manipulation" section of the book focuses on the ability of graphics processing units (GPUs) to process and generate geometry in exciting ways.

The first article in this section, "Dynamic GPU Terrain" by David Pangerl, presents a GPU-based algorithm to dynamically modify terrain topology and synchronize the changes with a physics simulation.

The next article, "Bandwidth-Efficient Procedural Meshes in the GPU via Tessellation" by Gustavo Bastos Nunes and João Lucas Guberman Raza, covers the procedural generation of highly detailed meshes with the help of the hardware tessellator while integrating a geomorphic-enabled level-of-detail (LOD) scheme.

The third article in this section is "Real-Time Deformation of Subdivision Surfaces on Object Collisions" by Henry Schäfer, Matthias Nießner, Benjamin Keinert, and Marc Stamminger. It shows how to mimic residuals such as scratches or impacts with soft materials like snow or sand by enabling automated fine-scale surface deformations resulting from object collisions. This is achieved by using dynamic displacement maps on the GPU.

The fourth and last article in this section, "Realistic Volumetric Explosions in Games" by Alex Dunn, covers a single-pass volumetric explosion effect with the help of ray marching, sphere tracing, and the hardware tessellation pipeline to generate a volumetric sphere.

—Wolfgang Engel

1

Dynamic GPU Terrain
David Pangerl

1.1 Introduction

Rendering terrain is crucial for any outdoor scene. However, it can be a hard task to efficiently render a highly detailed terrain in real time owing to huge amounts of data and the complex data segmentation it requires. Another universe of complexity arises if we need to dynamically modify terrain topology and synchronize it with physics simulation. (See Figure 1.1.)

This article presents a new high-performance algorithm for real-time terrain rendering. Additionally, it presents a novel idea for GPU-based terrain modification and dynamics synchronization.

Figure 1.1. Dynamic terrain simulation in action with max (0.1 m) resolution rendered with 81,000 tris in two batches.

1.2   Overview

The basic goal behind the rendering technique is to create a render-friendly mesh with topology that can smoothly handle lowering resolution with distance with minimal render calls.

1.3   Terrain Data

Because rendering and manipulation of all the data is performed on a GPU, we need to conserve the amount of data (i.e., reduce the number of rendering and simulation parameters to a minimum) and prepare the data in a GPU-compatible form. Terrain data are saved in a R16G16B16A16 texture format.

Terrain data attributes include

- terrain height—a normalized terrain height,

- texture blend—a texture index and blend parameters,

- flowability—a measure used to simulate condensed cliffs produced by a plow modification,

- compression—a measure used to simulate wheel compression.

Flowability. Terrain flowability is used to simulate terrain particles' ability to spread to neighboring particles. A flowability parameter is fundamental in dynamic erosion modification for cliff creation.

1.4   Rendering

Rendering terrain was one of the most important parts of the algorithm development. We needed a technique that would require as few batches as possible with as little offscreen mesh draw as possible.

We ended up with a novel technique that would render the whole terrain in three or fewer batches for a field of view less than 180 degrees and in five batches for a 360-degree field of view.

This technique is also very flexible and adjustable for various fields of view and game scenarios.

1.4.1   Algorithm

It all starts with the render mesh topology and vertex attributes. A render mesh is designed to discretely move on per level resolution grid with the camera field of view in a way that most of the mesh details are right in front of the camera view. A GPU then transforms the render mesh with the terrain height data.

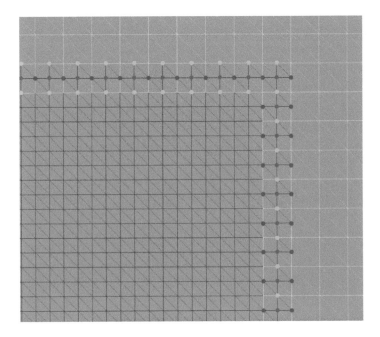

Figure 1.2. The two neighboring levels showing the intersection and geomorphing attributes.

Render mesh topology. As mentioned before, the terrain mesh topology is the most important part of the algorithm.

Terrain render mesh topology is defined by quad resolution R, level size S, level count L, and center mesh level count L_c:

- R, the quad resolution, is the edge width of the lowest level ($Level_0$) and defines the tessellation when close to the terrain.

- S, the level size, defines the number of edge quads. Level 0 is a square made of $S \times S$ quads, each of size $R \times R$.

- L, the level count, defines the number of resolution levels.

- L_c, the center mesh level count, is the number of levels (from 0 to L_c) used for the center mesh.

Each resolution level R is doubled, which quadruples the level area size. Levels above 0 have cut out the part of the intersection with lower levels except the innermost quad edge, where level quads overlap by one tile to enable smooth geomorphing transition and per-level snap movement. (See Figure 1.2.)

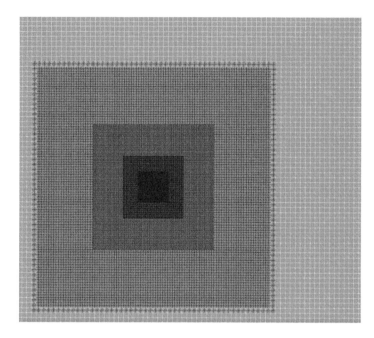

Figure 1.3. A blue center mesh (Mesh 0); green top side mesh (Mesh 1); and white left, bottom, and right side meshes (Mesh 2, Mesh 3, and Mesh 4, respectively). On the intersection of Mesh 0 and Mesh 1, the mesh tri overlap is visible. It is also very important that all mesh rectangles are cut into triangles in the same way (which is why we cannot use the same mesh for Mesh 0 and Mesh 1).

All vertices have a level index encoded in the vertex color G channel. The vertex color channels R and B are used to flag geomorphing X and Z blending factors.

With this method, we get a large tri-count mesh that would, if rendered, have most of the triangles out of the rendering view. To minimize the number of offscreen triangles, we split the render mesh into five parts: the center mesh with L_c levels (Mesh 0) and four-sided meshes with levels from $L_c + 1$ to L (Mesh 1–Mesh 4).

The center mesh is always visible, whereas side meshes are tested for visibility before rendering.

With this optimization, we gain two additional render batches; however, the rendering is reduced by 76% when a field of view is less than 180 degrees. (See Figure 1.3.)

For low field of view angles (60 degrees or less), we could optimize it further by creating more side meshes. For example, if we set L_c to 2 and create eight side meshes, we would reduce the render load by an additional 55% (we would render

58,000 triangles). However, if we looked at the terrain from straight above, we would end up rendering the entire render mesh because the center mesh is so small that it would not fill the screen.

Choosing terrain parameters. Render mesh topology parameters play a very important role in performance, so they should be chosen according to each project's requirements.

Consider a project where we need a landfill with a rather detailed modification resolution and neither big rendering size ($\sim 200 \times 200$ m) nor view distance (~ 500 m).

And now a bit of mathematics to get render mesh numbers:

- View extend (how far will the terrain be visible?)—$V = \frac{R \times S \times 2^{L-1}}{2}$.

- Max level quad resolution—$Q = R \times 2^{L-1}$.

- Level 0 tri count—$T_{L_0} = 2 \times S^2$.

- Level n tri count—$T_{L_n} = 2(S^2 - (\frac{S}{2} - 2)^2)$.

- Total tri count—$T = T_{L_0} + L \times T_{L_n}$.

- Mesh 0 tri count—$T_{M_0} = T_{L_0} + (L_c - 1) \times T_{L_n}$.

- Mesh n tri count—$T_{M_n} = \frac{(L - L_c) \times T_{L_n}}{4}$.

Because we had lots of scenarios where the camera was looking down on the terrain from above, we used a reasonably high center mesh level count (L_c 4), which allowed us to render the terrain in many cases in a single batch (when we were rendering the center mesh only).

We ended up with the quad resolution R 0.1 m, the level size S 100, the level count L 8, and the center mesh level count L_c 4. We used a 2048 × 2048 texture for the terrain data. With these settings we got a 10 cm resolution, a render view extend of ~1 km, and a full tri count of 127,744 triangles. Because we used a field of view with 65 degrees, we only rendered ~81,000 triangles in three batches.

As mentioned previously, these parameters must be correctly chosen to suit the nature of the application. (See Figures 1.4 and 1.5.)

CPU calculations. We calculate per-resolution-level snapping on a CPU. Each resolution level snap value is its edge size. This is the only terrain calculation made directly on the CPU.

A terrain render position is snapped to a double level Q size so that each level is aligned with a higher level. A vertex shader snaps all vertices at $\vec{x}$ and $\vec{z}$ position to a vertex level snap position.

Figure 1.4. Color coded mesh topology for $L = 8$ and $L_c = 4$.

Figure 1.5. Wire frame showing different levels of terrain mesh detail.

The following level shift is used to skip resolution levels that are too small for the camera at ground height:

```
int shift=(int)floor( log( 1 + cameragroundheight / 5 ) );
```

The CPU code is

```
float snapvalue=Q;
float snapmax=2 * snapvalue;
possnap0.x=floor( camerapos.x / snapmax + 0.01f ) * snapmax;
```

```
possnap0.z=floor( camerapos.z / snapmax + 0.01f ) * snapmax;
float levelsnap=snapvalue;

TTerrainRendererParams [0].z=possnap0.x - camerapos.x;
TTerrainRendererParams [0].w=possnap0.z - camerapos.z;

for(int a=1; a<levels; a++)
{
    levelsnap=levelsnap * 2;
    float l=levelsnap * 2;

    TVector lsnap;
    lsnap.x=floor( possnap0.x / l + 0.01f ) * l;
    lsnap.z=floor( possnap0.z / l + 0.01f ) * l;
    TTerrainRendererParams [a].x=lsnap.x - possnap0.x;
    TTerrainRendererParams [a].y=lsnap.z - possnap0.z;
    TTerrainRendererParams [a].z=lsnap.x - camerapos.x;
    TTerrainRendererParams [a].w=lsnap.z - camerapos.z;
}
```

Vertex shader. All other terrain-rendering algorithm calculations are done in the vertex shader:

- perform vertex shader texture fetch,

- calculate world-space position,

- calculate level resolution shift,

- calculate geomorphing parameters and blending factors.

Geomorphing is performed on the inner-level edge where lower-level points lie on edges of a higher level. These points are smoothly shifted onto the edge position while they are closing the distance to where they are hidden and the higher level is shown.

```
float4 pos0=TTerrainRendererParams [16];
float4 siz0=TTerrainRendererParams [17];
//
float4 posWS=input.pos;
//
int level=input.tex1.g;
posWS.xz+=TTerrainRendererParams [ level ].xy;
//
int xmid=input.tex1.r;
int zmid=input.tex1.b;
float geomorph=input.tex1.a;
//
float levelsize =input.tex2.x;
float levelsize2 =input.tex2.y;
//
output.color0=1;
//
float4 posterrain=posWS;
//
posterrain=(posterrain - pos0) / siz0;
```

```
//
output.tex0.xy=posterrain.xz;
//
float4 geo0=posWS;
float4 geox=posWS;
float4 geo1=posWS;
//
geox=(geox - pos0) / siz0;

/////////////////////////////////
// output center geo as tex0
/////////////////////////////////
output.tex0.xy=geox.xz;

/////////////////////////////////
// sample center height
/////////////////////////////////
float heix =tex2Dlod( User7SamplerClamp , float4( geox.x , geox.z,
0 , 0 ) ).r;
//
heix=heix * siz0.y + pos0.y;

/////////////////////////////////
// geomorphing
/////////////////////////////////
if( geomorph > 0 )
{
    float geosnap=levelsize;
    //
    if( xmid )
    {
    geo0.x-=geosnap;
    geo1.x+=geosnap;
    }
    //
    if( zmid )
    {
        geo0.z-=geosnap;
        geo1.z+=geosnap;
    }
    //
    geo0=(geo0 - pos0) / siz0;
    geo1=(geo1 - pos0) / siz0;
    //
    float hei0 =tex2Dlod( User7SamplerClamp ,
                        float4( geo0.x , geo0.z , 0 , 0 ) ).r;
    float hei1 =tex2Dlod( User7SamplerClamp ,
                        float4( geo1.x , geo1.z , 0 , 0 ) ).r;

    // geomorph
    float heigeo=(hei0+hei1) * 0.5 * siz0.y + pos0.y;
    //
    posWS.y=lerp( heix , heigeo , geomorph );
}
else
{
    posWS.y=heix;
}
//
posWS.w=1;
output.pos =mul( posWS , TFinalMatrix );
```

Figure 1.6. A sample of a static render mesh for a dynamic terrain on a small area.

1.4.2 Rendering Terrain for Small Areas

For a small contained dynamic area (e.g., a dump truck cargo area or a dump hole), we use a standard rendering technique with a static mesh (with the level of details) that covers the area. (See Figure 1.6.)

Topology of the mesh in this case is not important because it is small and always rendered as a whole.

1.5 Dynamic Modification

Dynamic terrain modification was the second important aspect of the new algorithm. Previously, we developed several techniques that used CPU terrain modification; however, it was difficult to optimize these techniques and therefore the main target of the new modification algorithm was the one executed on the GPU.

1.5.1 Algorithm Overview

The following is a high-level overview of the algorithm.

As shown in Figure 1.7, we took advantage of the fact that all modifications (red rectangle) in the large main terrain texture (blue rectangle) are mostly done in a very small area (a few meters at the most).

Initially, we created a small temporary modification render texture (black rectangle) that we use as a ping-pong data buffer. While processing, we first selected this temporary modification texture as a render target and the main texture as a source and copied the modified location of the main mesh into the temporary modification texture with a plain data copy shader to maintain the texture pixel size.

Next, we swapped the roles and selected the main texture as a render target and the small temporary modification texture as the texture source. Then we rendered the rectangle only on the modified part of the main texture with the

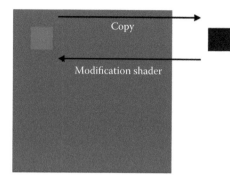

Figure 1.7. Modifications (red rectangle) in the large main terrain texture (blue rectangle) are done in a very small area.

modification shader. Modification shaders can have additional masks to perform the desired modification (e.g., a plow mask, cylinder mask for wheels, or sphere mask).

The temporary texture is sampled in many effects several times around the target pixel to get the final result (e.g., an erosion shader or plow shader).

We use a 128×128 temporary modification texture (covering 12.8×12.8 m changes).

1.5.2   Plow

A plow modification shader is the most complex terrain modification that we do. The idea is to displace the volume moved by the plow in front of the plow while simulating the compression, terrain displacement, and volume preservation.

We use the texture query to measure how much volume the plow would remove (the volume displaced from the last plow location). Then we use the special plow distribution mask and add the displaced volume in front of the plow.

Finally, the erosion simulation creates a nice terrain shape.

1.5.3   Erosion

Erosion is the most important terrain modification. It is performed for a few seconds everywhere a modification is done to smooth the terrain and apply a more natural look.

Erosion is a simple function that sums target pixel height difference for neighboring pixels, performs a height adjustment according to the pixel flowability parameter, and adds a bit of a randomization for a natural look.

Unfortunately, we have not yet found a way to link the erosion simulation with the volume preservation.

1.5.4 Wheels

Wheel modification is a simulation of a cylindrical shape moving over a terrain. It uses a terrain data compression factor to prevent oversinking and to create a wheel side supplant.

We tried to link this parameter with the terrain data flowability parameter (to reduce the texture data), but it led to many problems related to the erosion effect because it also changes the flowability value.

1.6 Physics Synchronization

One drawback of GPU-only processing is that sometimes data needs to be synchronized with the physics, which is in the CPU domain. To do that, we need to transfer data from the GPU memory to the CPU memory to perform synchronization.

1.6.1 Collision Update

Because upon downloading a full terrain data texture (2000×2000 in our case) every frame would be a performance killer, we have to collect and localize eventual terrain changes.

These changes are copied from the main texture into a smaller one for every few frames and downloaded into the main memory and used to update collision mesh information.

We found out that using a 64×64 texture (capturing 6.4×6.4 m) was totally adequate for our needs. Preparation, downloading, and synchronizing in this manner takes less than 0.1 ms.

1.7 Problems

1.7.1 Normals on Cliffs

Normals are calculated per pixel with the original data and with a fixed offset (position offset to calculate slope). This gives a very detailed visual terrain shape even from a distance, where vertex detail is very low. (See Figure 1.8.)

The problem occurs where flowability is very low and the terrain forms cliffs. What happens is that the triangle topology is very different between high and low details, and normals, which are calculated from the high-detailed mesh, appear detached. (See Figure 1.9.)

One way of mitigating this would be to adjust normal calculation offset with the edge size, where flowability is low, but with this we could lose other normal details.

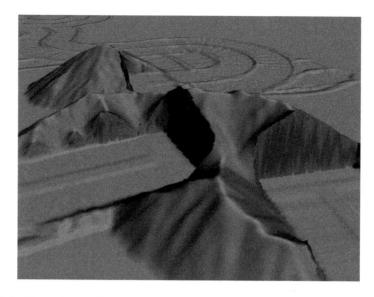

Figure 1.8. Normal on cliffs problem from up close. High-detail topology and normals are the same, and this result is a perfect match.

1.7.2   Physics Simulation on Changing Terrain

Physics simulation (currently we are using Physx 3.3) is very temperamental about changing the cached contact point collision, which we are constantly doing by changing the terrain topology below wheels. If the ground penetrates a collision too deeply, it usually causes a dynamic object to be launched into orbit.

To remedy this behavior we have to adjust the physics solver to limit the maximum penetration depth.

1.7.3   Inconsistent Texture Copy Pixel Offset

When we are performing a dynamic terrain modification, we need to copy from the main texture into the smaller temporary modification texture and back again. With the bilinear texture filtering, this can cause a minor texture shift that is very noticeable when performed repeatedly. Somehow, the per-pixel texture offset is linked to the device resolution even if the texture size is the same.

We have to make an initialization calibration to find an appropriate pixel offset whenever the resolution is changed.

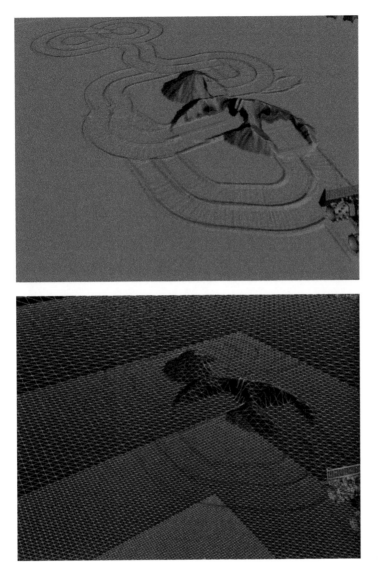

Figure 1.9. Normal on cliffs problem from a distance. Low-detail topology (clearly visible in the bottom wire frame image) and per-pixel normals are not the same.

1.8   Conclusion

1.8.1   Future Work

At the moment, the algorithm described here uses a single texture for the whole terrain and as such is limited by either the extend or the resolution. By adding a

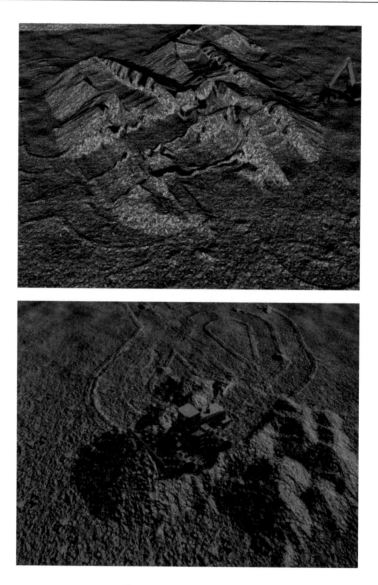

Figure 1.10. Examples.

texture pyramid for coarser terrain detail levels, we could efficiently increase the render extend and not sacrifice the detail.

Mesh 0 and Mesh 2 (as well as Mesh 1 and Mesh 2) are theoretically the same, so we could reuse them to optimize their memory requirements.

Only one level quad edge makes a noticeable transition to a higher level (a lower-lever detail) at a close distance. By adding more overlapping quad edges on lower levels, we would be able to reduce the effect and make smoother geomorphing.

Currently, we have not yet found a way to maintain the terrain volume, so the simulation can go into very strange places (e.g., magically increasing volume).

Because we have already downloaded change parts for collision synchronization, we could also use this data to calculate the volume change and adjust simulation accordingly.

1.8.2 Summary

This paper presents a novel algorithm for terrain rendering and manipulation on a GPU.

In Section 1.4, "Rendering," we showed in detail how to create and efficiently render a very detailed terrain in two or three render batches.

In Section 1.5, "Dynamic Modification," we demonstrated how the terrain can be modified in real time and be synchronized with the CPU base collision.

Figure 1.10 provides an example of the algorithm at work.

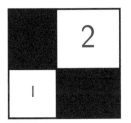

Bandwidth-Efficient Procedural Meshes in the GPU via Tessellation

Gustavo Bastos Nunes and João Lucas Guberman Raza

2.1 Introduction

Memory bandwidth is still a major bottleneck in current off-the-shelf graphics pipelines. To address that, one of the common mechanisms is to replace bus consumption for arithmetic logic unit (ALU) instructions in the GPU. For example, procedural textures on the GPU mitigate this limitation because there is little overhead in the communication between CPU and GPU. With the inception of DirectX 11 and OpenGL 4 tessellator stage, we are now capable of expanding procedural scenarios into a new one: procedural meshes in the GPU via parametric equations, whose analysis and implementation is the aim of this article.

By leveraging the tessellator stage for generating procedural meshes, one is capable of constructing a highly detailed set of meshes with almost no overhead in the CPU to GPU bus. As a consequence, this allows numerous scenarios such as constructing planets, particles, terrain, and any other object one is capable of parameterizing. As a side effect of the topology of how the tessellator works with dynamic meshes, one can also integrate the procedural mesh with a geomorphic-enabled level-of-detail (LOD) schema, further optimizing their shader instruction set.

2.2 Procedural Mesh and the Graphics Pipeline

To generate a procedural mesh in the GPU via the tessellator, this article proposes leveraging parametric meshes. The points of a parametric mesh are generated via a function that may take one or more parameters. For 3D space, the mathematical function in this article shall be referenced as a parametric equation of $g(u, v)$, where u and v are in the $[0, 1]$ range. There are mechanisms other than parametric surface equations, such as implicit functions, that may be used to generate procedural meshes. However, implicit functions don't map well to tessellator use, because its results imply if a point is in or out of a surfaces mesh, which is best used in the geometry shader stage via the marching cubes algorithm [Tatarchuk et al. 07]. Performance-wise, the geometry shader, unlike the tessellator, was not designed to have a massive throughput of primitives.

Although the tessellator stage is performant for generating triangle primitives, it contains a limit on the maximum number of triangle primitives it can generate. As of D3D11, that number is 8192 per patch. For some scenarios, such as simple procedural meshes like spheres, that number may be sufficient. However, to circumvent this restriction so one may be able to have an arbitrary number of triangles in the procedural mesh, the GPU must construct a patch grid. This is for scenarios such as terrains and planets, which require a high poly count. Each patch in the grid refers to a range of values within the $[0, 1]$ domain, used as a source for u and v function parameters. Those ranges dissect the surface area of values into adjacent subareas. Hence, each one of those subareas that the patches define serve as a set of triangles that the tessellator produces, which themselves are a subset of geometry from the whole procedural mesh.

To calculate the patch range p we utilize the following equation:

$$p = \frac{1}{\sqrt{\alpha}},$$

where α is the number of patches leveraged by the GPU. Because each patch compromises a square area range, p may then serve for both the u and the v range for each produced patch. The CPU must then send to the GPU, for each patch, a collection of metadata, which is the patches u range, referenced in this article as $[p_{u_{\min}}, p_{u_{\max}}]$, and the patches v range, referenced in this article as $[p_{v_{\min}}, p_{v_{\max}}]$. Because the tessellator will construct the entire geometry of the mesh procedurally, there's no need to send geometry data to the GPU other than the patch metadata previously described. Hence, this article proposes to leverage the point primitive topology as the mechanism to send metadata to the GPU, because it is the most bandwidth-efficient primitive topology due to its small memory footprint. Once the metadata is sent to the GPU, the next step is to set the tessellation factors in the hull shader.

2.3   Hull Shader

The hull shader's purpose is to receive geometry data, which in this article would be one control point per patch. With that geometry data, the hull shader may then set the tessellation factor per domain edge as well as the primitive's interior. The tessellation factor determines the number of triangle primitives that are generated per patch. The higher the tessellation factor set in the hull shader for each patch, the higher the number of triangle primitives constructed. The hull shader's requirement for this article is to produce a pool of triangle primitives, which the tessellator shader then leverages to construct the mesh's geometry procedurally. Hence, the required tessellation factor must be set uniformly to each patch edges and interior factors, as exemplified in the code below:

```
HS_CONSTANT_DATA_OUTPUT  BezierConstantHS (InputPatch<VS_
CONTROL_POINT_OUTPUT,
INPUT_PATCH_SIZE> ip,  uint PatchID : SV_PrimitiveID)
{
        HS_CONSTANT_DATA_OUTPUT Output;
        Output.Edges[0] = g_fTessellationFactor;
        Output.Edges[1] = g_fTessellationFactor;
        Output.Edges[2] = g_fTessellationFactor;
        Output.Edges[3] = g_fTessellationFactor;
        Output.Inside[0] = Output.Inside[1]= g_fTessellationFactor;
        return Output;
}
```

Because the patch grid will have primitives that must end up adjacent to each other, the edges of each patch must have the same tessellation factor, otherwise a patch with a higher order set of tessellation might leave cracks in the geometry. However, the interior of the primitive might have different tessellation factors per patch because those primitives are not meant to connect with primitives from other patches. A scenario where altering the tessellation factor may be leveraged is for geomorphic LOD, where the interior tessellation factor is based from the distance of the camera to the procedural mesh. The hull shader informs the tessellator how to constructs triangle primitives, which the domain shader then leverages. This LOD technique is exemplified in the high poly count procedural mesh shown in Figures 2.1 and 2.2, with its subsequent low poly count procedural mesh in Figures 2.3 and 2.4.

2.4 Domain Shader

The domain shader is called for each vertex generated by the tessellator. It also receives a pair (u, v) of parametric coordinates for each generated vertex. For this article, we shall reference that coordinate pair as d_u and d_v. Because these parametric coordinates are in domain space, the domain shader must then map them into patch grid space. To do so, we do a linear interpolation:

$$p_u = p_{u_{\min}} + d_u * p_{u_{\max}},$$
$$p_v = p_{v_{\min}} + d_v * p_{v_{\max}},$$

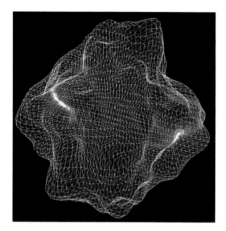

Figure 2.1. A high poly count mesh with noise.

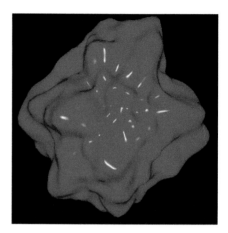

Figure 2.2. The same mesh in Figure 2.1, but shaded.

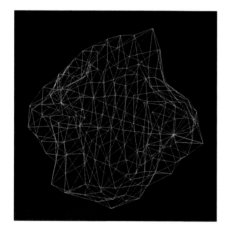

Figure 2.3. The same mesh in Figure 2.1, but with a lower tessellation factor.

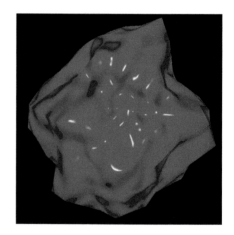

Figure 2.4. The same mesh in Figure 2.3, but shaded.

where p_u and p_v are the parameters to be leveraged in a parametric equation of the implementer's choice. The example in Figure 2.5 uses the following code snippet:

```
float3 heart(float u, float v)
{
    float pi2 = 2 * PI;
    float pi = PI;
    float x, y, z;
    float s = u;
```

Figure 2.5. Parametric heart generated in the GPU.

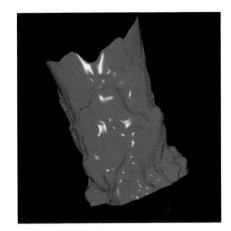

Figure 2.6. Deformed cylinder generated in the GPU.

```
    float t = v;
    x = cos(s * pi) * sin(t * 2 * pi) -
      pow(abs(sin(s * pi) * sin(t * 2 * pi)), 0.5f) * 0.5f;
    y = cos(t * 2 * pi) * 0.5f;
    z = sin(s * pi) * sin(t * 2 * pi);
    float3 heart = float3(x, y, z);
    return heart;
}
```

2.5   Noise in Procedural Meshes

Noise with procedural meshes allows applications to generate a myriad of different mesh outputs based on a common factor. For example, with the algorithm proposed in this article for a sphere, noise may allow an application to construct several different types of planets, asteroids, rocks, etc., by altering the generated vertices of the mesh. A possible effect is exemplified in Figure 2.6, as it displays the deformation of a cylinder with Perlin noise as described in [Green 05].

2.6   Performance Optimizations

Because all the primitives are being generated in the GPU, primitives won't be subject to frustum culling. To optimize this aspect, clients should determine if the triangles generated from a patch will be in the frustum or not. This can be done by a heuristic that verifies if the points of the given patch are within a volume that intersects with the frustum. Once that's done, the application can adjust the patch's parametric range or cull the patch altogether from being sent to further states in the GPU. Depending on the optimization, the former can be done on the client or in the GPU hull shader via setting the tessellation factor to 0.

Another set of optimizations relates to normal calculations when using noise functions. Calculating the normal of the produced vertices might be one of the main bottlenecks, because one needs to obtain the nearby positions for each pixel (on per-pixel lighting) or per vertex (on per-vertex lighting). This circumstance becomes even further problematic when leveraging a computationally demanding noise implementation. Take the example in the proposal by [Perlin 04]. It calculates the new normal $(\overrightarrow{N_n})$ by doing four evaluations of the noise function while leveraging the original noiseless normal $(\overrightarrow{N_o})$:

$$F_0 = F(x, y, z),$$
$$F_x = F(x + \epsilon, y, z),$$
$$F_y = F(x, y + \epsilon, z),$$
$$F_z = F(x, y, z + \epsilon),$$
$$\overrightarrow{dF} = \left| \frac{F_x - F_0}{\epsilon}, \frac{F_y - F_0}{\epsilon}, \frac{F_z - F_0}{\epsilon} \right|,$$
$$\overrightarrow{N_n} = \text{normalize}(\overrightarrow{N_o} + \overrightarrow{dF}).$$

However, given that the domain shader for each vertex passes its coordinates (u, v) in tangent space, in relation to the primitive that each vertex belongs to, one might be able to optimize calculating the normal vector $(\overrightarrow{N})$ by the cross product of the tangent $(\overrightarrow{T})$ and binormal $(\overrightarrow{B})$ vectors (which themselves will also be in tangent space) produced by the vertices in the primitive:

$$F_0 = g(u, v) + \text{normalize}(\overrightarrow{N_o}) \times F(g(u, v)),$$
$$F_x = g(u + \epsilon, v) + \text{normalize}(\overrightarrow{N_o}) \times F(g(u + \epsilon, v)),$$
$$F_y = g(u, v + \epsilon) + \text{normalize}(\overrightarrow{N_o}) \times F(g(u, v + \epsilon)),$$
$$\overrightarrow{T} = F_x - F_0,$$
$$\overrightarrow{B} = F_y - F_0,$$
$$\overrightarrow{N} = T \times B,$$

where the parametric function is $g(u, v)$, the noise function that leverages the original point is $F(g(u, v))$, and the original normal is $\overrightarrow{N_o}$. This way, one only does three fetches, as opposed to four, which is an optimization in itself because noise fetches are computationally more expensive than doing the cross product.

Lastly, in another realm of optimization mechanisms, the proposed algorithm produces a high quantity of triangles, of which the application might not be able to have a predefined understanding of its output topology. Deferred shading could then be used to reduce the number of operations done in the resulting fragments.

2.7 Conclusion

For the proposed algorithm, the number of calculations linearly increases with the number of vertices and patches, thus making it scalable into a wide range of scenarios, such as procedural terrains and planets. An example of such a case would be in an algorithm that also leverages the tessellation stages, such as in [Dunn 15], which focuses on producing volumetric explosions. Other domains of research might also be used to extend the concepts discussed herein, due to their procedural mathematical nature, such as dynamic texture and sounds. Lastly, as memory access continues to be a performance bottleneck, especially in hardware-constrained environments such as mobile devices, inherently mathematical processes that result in satisfactory visual outputs could be leveraged to overcome such limitations.

2.8 Acknowledgments

João Raza would like to thank his family and wife for all the support they've provided him. Gustavo Nunes would like to thank his wife and family for all their help. A special thanks goes to their friend F. F. Marmot.

Bibliography

[Green 05] Simon Green. "Implementing Improved Perlin Noise." In *GPU Gems 2*, edited by Matt Farr, pp. 409–416. Reading, MA: Addison-Wesley Professional, 2005.

[Owens et al. 08] J. Owens, M. Houston, D. Luebke, S. Green, J. Stone, and J. Phillips. "GPU Computing." *Proceedings of the IEEE* 96:5 (2008), 96.

[Perlin 04] Ken Perlin. "Implementing Improved Perlin Noise." In *GPU Gems*, edited by Randima Fernando, pp. 73–85. Reading, MA: Addison-Wesley Professional, 2004.

[Tatarchuk et al. 07] N. Tatarchuk, J. Shopf, and C. Decoro. "Real-Time Isosurface Extraction Using the GPU Programmable Geometry Pipeline." In *Proceedings of SIGGRAPH 2007*, p. 137. New York: ACM, 2007.

[Dunn 15] Alex Dunn. "Realistic Volumetric Explosions in Games." In *GPU Pro 6: Advanced Rendering Techniques*, edited by Wolfgang Engel, pp. 51–62. Boca Raton, FL: CRC Press, 2015.

Real-Time Deformation of Subdivision Surfaces on Object Collisions

Henry Schäfer, Matthias Nießner, Benjamin Keinert, and Marc Stamminger

3.1 Introduction

Scene environments in modern games include a wealth of moving and animated objects, which are key to creating vivid virtual worlds. An essential aspect in dynamic scenes is the interaction between scene objects. Unfortunately, many real-time applications only support rigid body collisions due to tight time budgets. In order to facilitate visual feedback of collisions, residuals such as scratches or impacts with soft materials like snow or sand are realized by dynamic decal texture placements. However, decals are not able to modify the underlying surface geometry, which would be highly desirable to improve upon realism. In this chapter, we present a novel real-time technique to overcome this limitation by enabling fully automated fine-scale surface deformations resulting from object collisions. That is, we propose an efficient method to incorporate high-frequency deformations upon physical contact into dynamic displacement maps directly on the GPU. Overall, we can handle large dynamic scene environments with many objects (see Figure 3.1) at minimal runtime overhead.

An immersive gaming experience requires animated and dynamic objects. Such dynamics are computed by a physics engine, which typically only considers a simplified version of the scene in order to facilitate immediate visual feedback. Less attention is usually paid to interactions of dynamic objects with deformable scene geometry—for example, footprints, skidmarks on sandy grounds, and bullet impacts. These high-detail deformations require a much higher mesh resolution, their generation is very expensive, and they involve significant memory I/O. In

Figure 3.1. Our method allows computation and application of fine-scale surface deformations on object collisions in real time. In this example, tracks of the car and barrels are generated on the fly as the user controls the car.

most real-time applications, it is thus too costly to compute fine-scale deformations on the fly directly on the mesh. Instead, good cost-efficient approximations are deformations on a template as decal color textures, bump maps, or displacements.

Recently, we have introduced a more flexible approach to this problem [Schäfer et al. 14]. We dynamically generate and store displacements using tile-based displacement maps—that is, deformations are computed, stored, and applied individually on a per-patch level. While low-frequency dynamics are still handled by the CPU physics engine, fine-detail deformations are computed on the fly directly on the GPU. Every frame, we determine colliding objects, compute a voxelization of the overlap region, and modify displacements according to the resulting deformations. Deformed patches are then rendered efficiently using the hardware tessellator. As our algorithm runs entirely on the GPU, we can avoid costly CPU–GPU data transfer, thus enabling fine-scale deformations at minimal runtime overhead.

In this chapter, we describe the implementation of our system, which is available on GitHub as part of this publication[1]. The input to our deformation framework are large scenes composed of quadrilateral subdivision meshes.

---

[1]https://github.com/hsdk/DeformationGPU

More specifically, we process Catmull-Clark subdivision surfaces, which we render using feature-adaptive subdivision and the GPU hardware tessellator [Nießner et al. 12]. Deformations are realized by analytic displacements, which can be efficiently updated at runtime without a costly normal map re-computation [Nießner and Loop 13]. In order to keep GPU storage requirements at a minimum, we use dynamic memory management, thus only allocating space for displacements of surface patches affected by deformations.

3.2   Deformable Surface Representation

We represent deformable objects as displaced subdivision surfaces, where the base mesh is a Catmull-Clark mesh [Catmull and Clark 78], and high-frequency detail is stored in displacement offsets. On modern hardware, these high-quality surface representations are efficiently evaluated and rendered using the hardware tessellation unit [Nießner et al. 12]. Catmull-Clark surfaces are defined by a coarse set of control points, which are refined at render time and converge to a limit surface that is C^2 continuous everywhere except at non–valence-four vertices, where it is C^1. On top of this surface, displacements are applied along the analytic surface normal of the subdivided mesh.

If we detect object collisions causing deformations, we update the displacement data accordingly (see Section 3.4). When rendering this surface, the normals resulting from these displacements are required. If displacements are static, these normals can be precomputed and stored in a high-resolution normal map, yet in our case we have to update these normals on the fly, which is costly. We thus employ analytic displacements [Nießner and Loop 13], where normals are analytically obtained from scalar surface offsets, allowing for efficient displacement updates without costly normal re-computations (see Section 3.4.3).

3.2.1   Analytic Displacements

The key idea of analytic displacements is the combination of a C^2 base surface $s(u, v)$ with a C^1 offset function $D(u, v)$. As a result, the displaced surface $f(u, v) = s(u, v) + N_s(u, v)D(u, v)$ is C^1 everywhere and provides a continuous normal field $\frac{\partial}{\partial u}f(u, v) \times \frac{\partial}{\partial v}f(u, v)$; $s(u, v) \in \mathbb{R}^3$, $D(u, v) \in \mathbb{R}^1$, and $f(u, v) \in \mathbb{R}^3$. $D(u, v)$ is a scalar-valued, biquadratic B-spline with Doo-Sabin connectivity and special treatment at extraordinary vertices. The connectivity is dual with respect to the base Catmull-Clark surface, which provides a one-to-one mapping between base patches and the subpatches of the displacement function.

Tile-based texture format.   We store scalar-valued displacement offsets (i.e., control points of the biquadratic B-spline) in a tile-based texture format similar to PTex [Burley and Lacewell 08] (see Figure 3.2). The key advantage of a tile-based format is the elimination of seam artifacts at (u, v)-boundaries because texels are

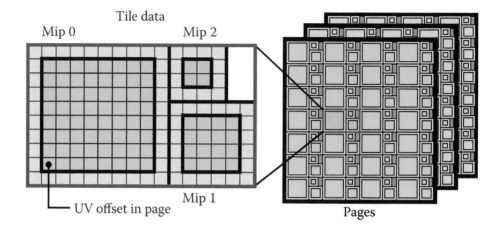

Figure 3.2. The tile-based texture format for analytic displacements: each tile stores a one-texel overlap to avoid the requirement of adjacency pointers. In addition, a mipmap pyramid, computed at a tile level, allows for continuous level-of-detail rendering. All tiles are efficiently packed in a large texture array.

aligned in parameter space; that is, the parametric domain of the tiles matches with the Catmull-Clark patches, thus providing consistent (u, v)-parameters for $s(u, v)$ and $D(u, v)$. In order to evaluate the biquadratic function $D(u, v)$, 3×3 scalar control points (i.e., subpatch; see Figure 3.3) need to be accessed (see Section 3.2.1). At base patch boundaries, this requires access to neighboring tiles.

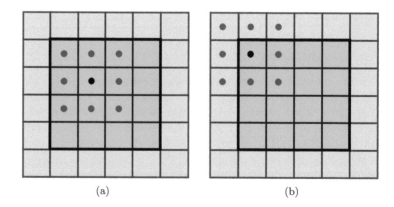

Figure 3.3. (a) A 3×3 control point array of a scalar-valued biquadratic B-spline subpatch of a texture tile storing displacement data. (b) Another set of control points of the same tile where the one-texel boundary overlap is used; overlap data is redundant with adjacent tiles. Each tile corresponds to a Catmull-Clark base patch.

```
struct TileDescriptor
{
  int page;     // texture slice
  int uOffset;  // tile start u
  int vOffset;  // tile start v
  uint size;    // tile width, height
  uint nMipmap; // number of mipmaps
};

TileDescriptor GetTile(Buffer<uint> descSRV, uint patchID)
{
  TileDescriptor desc;
  uint offset    = patchID * 4;
  desc.page      = descSRV[offset];
  desc.uOffset   = descSRV[offset + 1];
  desc.vOffset   = descSRV[offset + 2];
  uint sizeMip   = descSRV[offset + 3];
  desc.size      = 1 << (sizeMip >> 8);
  desc.nMipmap   = (sizeMip & 0xff);
  return desc;
}
```

Listing 3.1. Tile descriptor: each tile corresponds to a Catmull-Clark base face and is indexed by the face ID.

This access could be done using adjacency pointers, yet pointer traversal is inefficient on modern GPUs. So we store for each tile a one-texel overlap, making tiles self-contained and such pointers unnecessary. While this involves a slightly larger memory footprint, it is very beneficial from a rendering perspective because all texture access is coherent. In addition, a mipmap pyramid is stored for every tile, allowing for continuous level of detail. Note that boundary overlap is included at all levels.

All tiles—we assume a fixed tile size—are efficiently packed into a large texture array (see Figure 3.2). We need to split up tiles into multiple pages because the texture resolution is limited to $16,000 \times 16,000$ on current hardware. Each page corresponds to a slice of the global texture array. In order to access a tile, we maintain a buffer, which stores a page ID and the (u, v) offset (within the page) for every tile (see Listing 3.1). Entries of this buffer are indexed by corresponding face IDs of base patches.

Efficient evaluation. In order to efficiently render the displaced objects, we use the GPU hardware tessellation unit. The Catmull-Clark base surface $s(u, v)$ and the corresponding normal $N_s(u, v)$ are exactly evaluated using feature-adaptive subdivision [Nießner and Loop 13]. Because there is a one-to-one mapping between the Catmull-Clark base patches and texture tiles, displacement data can be retrieved by the patch ID, $u, v \in [1, 0] \times [1, 0]$ triple. That is, we obtain the 3×3 array of scalar-valued biquadratic displacement coefficients $d_{i,j}$ of the subpatch corresponding to the base patch u, v. For each base patch, the scalar displacement function $D(u, v)$ is then evaluated using the B-spline basis functions B_i^2:

$$D(u, v) = \sum_{i=0}^{2} \sum_{j=0}^{2} B_i^2(T(u)) B_j^2(T(v)) d_{i,j},$$

where the subpatch domain parameters $\hat{u}, \hat{v}$ are given by the linear transformation T,

$$\hat{u} = T(u) = u - \lfloor u \rfloor + \frac{1}{2} \quad \text{and} \quad \hat{v} = T(v) = v - \lfloor v \rfloor + \frac{1}{2}.$$

In order to obtain the displaced surface normal $N_f(u, v)$, the partial derivatives of $f(u, v)$ are required:

$$\frac{\partial}{\partial u} f(u, v) = \frac{\partial}{\partial u} s(u, v) + \frac{\partial}{\partial u} N_s(u, v) D(u, v) + N_s(u, v) \frac{\partial}{\partial u} D(u, v).$$

In this case, $\frac{\partial}{\partial u} N_s(u, v)$ would involve the computation of the Weingarten equation, which is costly. Therefore, we approximate the partial derivatives of $f(u, v)$ (assuming small displacements) by

$$\frac{\partial}{\partial u} f(u, v) \approx \frac{\partial}{\partial u} s(u, v) + N_s(u, v) \frac{\partial}{\partial u} D(u, v),$$

which is much faster to compute. The computation of $\frac{\partial}{\partial v} f(u, v)$ is analogous.

Rendering implementation. The rendering of subdivision surfaces with analytic displacements can be efficiently mapped to the modern graphics pipeline with the hardware tessellation unit. The Catmull-Clark base surface $s(u, v)$ is converted into a set of regular bicubic B-spline patches using DirectX Compute Shaders [Nießner et al. 12]—that is, all regular patches, which have only valence-four vertices, are directly sent to the tessellation unit as they are defined as bicubic B-splines. Irregular patches, which have at least one non–valence-four vertex, are adaptively subdivided by a compute kernel. Each refinement step turns an irregular patch into a set of smaller regular patches and an irregular patch next to the extraordinary vertex. After only a few adaptive subdivision steps, the size of irregular patches is reduced to just a few pixels and can be rendered as final patch filling quads; no further tessellation is required.

All generated regular patches are sent to the hardware tessellation unit, where the domain shader takes the 16 patch control points to evaluate $s(u, v)$ and $N_s(u, v)$ using the bicubic B-spline basis functions. In addition, the domain shader evaluates a displacement function $D(u, v)$ and computes the displaced vertices $f(u, v) = s(u, v) + N_s(u, v) D(u, v)$. Generated vertices are then passed to the rasterization stage. In the pixel shader, the shading normals $N_f(u, v)$ are computed based on the partial derivatives of the displacement function; i.e., $\frac{\partial}{\partial u} D(u, v)$ and $\frac{\partial}{\partial v} D(u, v)$ are evaluated. Code for the evaluation of analytic displacements is shown in Listing 3.2, the domain shader part in Listing 3.3, and the

```
Texture2DArray<float> g_displacementData : register(t6);
Buffer<uint>          g_tileDescriptors  : register(t7);

float AnalyticDisplacement(in uint patchID, in float2 uv,
                           inout float du, inout float dv)
{
  TileDescriptor tile = GetTile(g_tileDescriptors, patchID);

  float2 coords = float2( uv.x * tile.size + tile.uOffset,
                          uv.y * tile.size + tile.vOffset);

  coords -= float2(0.5, 0.5);
  int2 c = int2(round(coords));

  float d[9];
  d[0] = g_displacementData[int3(c.x-1, c.y-1, tile.page)].x;
  d[1] = g_displacementData[int3(c.x-1, c.y-0, tile.page)].x;
  d[2] = g_displacementData[int3(c.x-1, c.y+1, tile.page)].x;
  d[3] = g_displacementData[int3(c.x-0, c.y-1, tile.page)].x;
  d[4] = g_displacementData[int3(c.x-0, c.y-0, tile.page)].x;
  d[5] = g_displacementData[int3(c.x-0, c.y+1, tile.page)].x;
  d[6] = g_displacementData[int3(c.x+1, c.y-1, tile.page)].x;
  d[7] = g_displacementData[int3(c.x+1, c.y-0, tile.page)].x;
  d[8] = g_displacementData[int3(c.x+1, c.y+1, tile.page)].x;

  float evalCoord = 0.5 - (float(c) - coords);
  float displacement = EvalQuadricBSpline(evalCoord, d, du, dv);

  du *= tile.size;
  dv *= tile.size;
  return displacement;
}
```

Listing 3.2. Analytic displacement lookup and evaluation.

pixel shader computation in Listing 3.4. Note that shading normals are obtained on a per-pixel basis, leading to high-quality rendering even when the tessellation budget is low.

Evaluating $f(u,v)$ and $N_f(u,v)$ for regular patches of the Catmull-Clark patch is trivial because tiles correspond to surface patches. Regular patches generated by feature-adaptive subdivision, however, only correspond to a subdomain of a specific tile. Fortunately, the feature-adaptive subdivision framework [Nießner et al. 12] provides local parameter offsets in the domain shader to remap the subdomain accordingly.

Irregular patches only remain at the finest adaptive subdivision level and cover only a few pixels. They require a separate rendering pass because they are not processed by the tessellation stage; patch filling quads are rendered instead. To overcome the singularity of irregular patches, we enforce the partial derivatives of the displacement function $\frac{\partial}{\partial u}D(u,v)$ and $\frac{\partial}{\partial v}D(u,v)$ to be 0 at extraordinary vertices; i.e., all adjacent displacement texels at tile corners corresponding to a non–valence-four vertex are restricted to be equal. Thus,

```
void ds_main_patches(in HS_CONSTANT_FUNC_OUT input,
                     in OutputPatch<HullVertex, 16> patch,
                     in float2 domainCoord : SV_DomainLocation,
                     out OutputVertex output )
{
  // eval the base surface s(u,v)
  float3 worldPos = 0, tangent = 0, bitangent = 0;
  EvalSurface(patch, domainCoord, worldPos, tangent, bitangent);
  float3 normal = normalize(cross(Tangent,BiTangent));

  float du = 0, dv = 0;
  float displacement = AnalyticDisplacement(patch[0].patchID,
                 domainCoord, du, dv);
  worldPos += displacement * normal;

  output.pos       = mul(ProjectionMatrix, float4(worldPos, 1.0));
  output.tangent   = tangent;
  output.bitangent = bitangent;
  output.patchCoord = domainCoord;
}
```

Listing 3.3. Analytic displacement mapping evaluation in the domain shader.

```
float4 ps_main(in OutputVertex input) : SV_TARGET
{
  // compute partial derivatives of D(u,v)
  float du = 0, dv = 0;
  float displacement = AnalyticDisplacement(input.patchID,
                  input.patchCoord, du, dv);
  // compute base surface normal N_s(u,v)
  float3 surfNormal = normalize(cross(input.tangent,
                                      input.bitangent));
  float3 tangent   = input.tangent   + surfNormal * du;
  float3 bitangent = input.bitangent + surfNormal * dv;
  // compute analytic displacement shading normal N_f(u,v)
  float3 normal    = normalize(cross(tangent, bitangent));

  // shading
  ...
}
```

Listing 3.4. Analytic displacement mapping evaluation in the pixel shader.

$N_f(u,v) = N_s(u,v) \; \forall(u,v)_{\text{extraordinary}}$. A linear blend between this special treatment at extraordinary vertices and the regular $N_f(u,v)$ ensures a consistent C^1 surface everywhere.

3.3 Algorithm Overview

Our aim is to provide highly detailed deformations caused by object-object collisions. To achieve instant visual feedback, we approximate collisions and apply

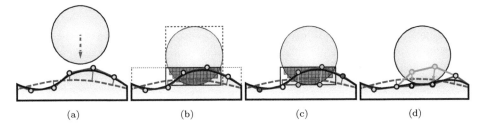

Figure 3.4. Algorithm overview: (a) Subdivision surfaces with quadratic B-spline displacements are used as deformable object representation. (b) The voxelization of the overlapping region is generated for an object penetrating the deformable surface. (c) The displacement control points are pushed out of the voxelization, (d) creating a surface capturing the impact.

deformations by updating displacement data. This is much more cost efficient than a physically correct soft body simulation and also allows for visually plausible results. In this section, we provide an overview of our algorithm as outlined in Figure 3.4. A detailed description of our implementation can be found in Section 3.4.

For simplicity, we first assume collisions only between a rigid penetrating object and a deformable one. We represent deformable objects as displaced subdivision surfaces (see Section 3.2). The penetrating object can be either a subdivision surface or a regular triangle mesh (see Figure 3.4(a)). For all colliding *deformable-penetrating* object pairs, we compute the deformation using the following algorithm:

- Approximate the penetrating object by computing a solid voxelization using an improved variant of the real-time binary voxelization approach by Schwarz [Schwarz 12] (see Figure 3.4(b)).

- From the voxelization, determine displacement offsets of deformable objects to match the shape of the impact object (Figure 3.4(c) and (d)). This is achieved by casting rays from the deformable object's surface and modifying the displacements accordingly.

In the case that both objects are deformable, we form two collision pairs, with each deformable acting as a rigid penetrating object for the other deformable and only applying a fraction of the computed deformations in the first pass.

3.4 Pipeline

In this section, we describe the implementation of the core algorithm and highlight important details on achieving high-performance deformation updates.

3.4.1 Physics Simulation

Our algorithm is designed to provide immediate visual feedback on collisions with
deformable objects made of soft material such as sand or snow. Because a full soft
body simulation would be too expensive in large scene environments, we interpret deformable objects as rigid bodies with fine-scale dynamic surface detail. We
handle rigid body dynamics using the Bullet physics engine [Coumans et al. 06].
All dynamic objects are managed on the CPU and resulting transformation matrices are updated every frame. In theory, we could also process low-frequency
deformations on base meshes if allowed by the time budget; however, we have not
explored this direction.

After updating rigid bodies, we search for colliding objects and send pairs
that hit a deformable to our deformation pipeline on the GPU.

3.4.2 Voxelization

Once we have identified all potential deformable object collisions (see above),
we approximate the shape of penetrating objects using a variant of the binary
solid voxelization of Schwarz [Schwarz 12]. The voxelization is generated by a
rasterization pass where an orthogonal camera is set up corresponding to the
overlap region of the objects' bounding volumes. In our implementation, we
use a budget of 2^{24} voxels, requiring about 2 MB of GPU memory. Note that
it is essential that the voxelization matches the shape as closely as possible to
achieve accurate deformations. We thus determine tight bounds of the overlap
regions and scale the voxelization anisotropically to maximize the effective voxel
resolution.

Intersecting volume. In order to determine the voxelization space, we intersect the
oriented bounding boxes (OBBs) of a collision pair. The resulting intersecting
volume is extended such that it forms a new OBB that conservatively bounds
the overlapping region (see Figure 3.5). We precompute all OBBs in model space
during loading and transform OBBs at runtime using the physics rigid transformations. Exceptions are skinned animations, for which we apply skinning in a
compute shader and recompute the OBB each frame.

Efficient GPU implementation. The voxelization of objects is generated by performing a simple rasterization pass using an orthographic camera. The voxel
grid is filled in a pixel shader program using scattered `write` operations (see Listing 3.5). We determine the voxelization direction—i.e., the camera direction—
according to the major axis of the intersection volume. Clipping an object against
the intersecting volume results in nonclosed surfaces, which cannot be handled
in all cases by the original voxelization approach by Schwarz. However, the voxelization will be correct if we guarantee that front-faces are always hit first—i.e.,
they are not being clipped. Therefore, we construct intersecting OBBs such that

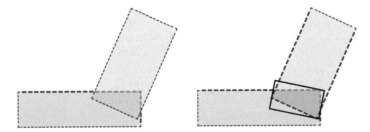

Figure 3.5. Generation of the OBB for voxelization: a new OBB is derived from the intersecting OBBs of the deformable and the penetrating object.

at least one of the faces is completely outside of the penetrating object OBB. The voxelization is then performed toward the opposite direction of the face, which is on the outside. We use either of two kernels to perform the voxelization and fill the adaptively scaled voxel grid forward or backward, respectively, as shown in Listing 3.5.

```
RWByteAddressBuffer g_voxels : register(u1);

float4 PS_VoxelizeSolid(in OutputVertex input) : SV_TARGET
{
    // transform fragment position to voxel grid
    float3 fGridPos = input.posOut.xyz / input.posOut.w;
    fGridPos.z *= g_gridSize.z;
    int3 p = int3(fGridPos.x, fGridPos.y, fGridPos.z + 0.5);

    if (p.z > int(g_gridSize.z))
        discard;

    // apply adaptive voxel grid scale
    uint address =  p.x * g_gridStride.x
                  + p.y * g_gridStride.y
                  + (p.z >> 5) * 4;

#ifdef VOXELIZE_BACKWARD
    g_voxels.InterlockedXor(address,
                            ~(0xffffffffu << (p.z & 31)));
    // flip all voxels below
    for (p.z = (p.z & (~31)); p.z > 0; p.z -= 32) {
        address -= 4;
        g_voxels.InterlockedXor(address, 0xffffffffu);
    }
#else
    g_voxels.InterlockedXor(address, 0xffffffffu << (p.z & 31));
    // flip all voxels below
    for(p.z = (p.z | 31) + 1; p.z < g_gridSize.z; p.z += 32) {
        address += 4;
        g_voxels.InterlockedXor(address, 0xffffffffu);
    }
#endif
}
```

Listing 3.5. Pixel shader implementation of the binary voxelization using atomic operations.

3.4.3 Ray Casting

In the previous stage, we generated a voxelization of the penetrating object into the space of the intersecting volume. Now, all patches of the deformable surface within the intersecting volume are to be displaced such that they no longer intersect with the (voxelization of the) penetrating object. Our implementation of this process is shown in Listing 3.6. First, we evaluate the surface at all control points of the displacement B-spline (patch parameter-space position of the displacement map texels) and compute their corresponding world-space positions. More precisely, these are Catmull-Clark surface points, evaluated at the knot points of the displacement B-spline, with applied displacement (see Figure 3.4(b)). Hence, we account for the previous surface offset in case the surface at this position is already displaced.

If such a control point lies within the penetrating object, we move it in the negative base surface normal direction until it leaves the penetrating object (the red control points in Figure 3.4). Therefore, we cast a ray that originates at the control points' corresponding world-space position pointing along the negative base surface normal. This step involves evaluating the Catmull-Clark surface. Fortunately, this evaluation is very fast using the regular B-spline patches obtained by adaptive subdivision.

We now traverse the rays through the binary voxelization using a 3D digital differential analyzer (DDA) (see Listing 3.7). We also make sure that the ray can actually hit the voxel volume by first intersecting the ray with the voxel grid's OBB. Thereby, control points outside the voxelization (e.g., the yellow one in Figure 3.4) and outside the overlap region (the red ones) are left unchanged. In case the ray can hit the voxel volume but the surface position and thus the ray originates outside the voxel volume, the initial ray distance is updated such that it lies on the intersection point with the voxel grid. Then, we trace the ray through the voxel grid and on each set voxel encountered we update the displacement distance until we leave the voxel volume. It is important to trace the ray until it leaves the voxelization, otherwise concave objects would result in an incorrect deformation, as depicted in Figure 3.6.

After ray traversal, we update the displacement by applying the negative traveled distance to account for the deformation and write the result into the displacement map.

3.4.4 Overlap Update

Once surface deformations are computed, we need to update the analytic displacement map tile overlap in order to enforce fast, watertight, and consistent evaluation during rendering. This requires copying B-spline coefficients (displacement values) from the boundary to the overlap region of the adjacent patches. To this end, we precompute patch adjacency in a preprocessing step. More precisely, per patch we store the indices of the four neighboring patches and the

```
#define NUM_BLOCKS (TILE_SIZE/DISPLACEMENT_DISPATCH_TILE_SIZE)
[numthreads(DISPLACEMENT_DISPATCH_TILE_SIZE ,
            DISPLACEMENT_DISPATCH_TILE_SIZE , 1)]
void ComputeDisplacementCS( uint3 blockIdx  : SV_GroupID ,
                            uint3 threadIdx : SV_GroupThreadID )
{
  uint patchID = blockIdx.x + g_PrimitiveIdBase ;

  TileDescriptor tile = GetTile(g_TileInfo , patchID);
  if(threadIdx.x >= tile.size || threadIdx.y >= tile.size)
    return ;

  int patchLevel = GetPatchSubDLevel(patchID);

  // threadIdx to tile coord
  float2 tileUV  = ComputeTileCoord( patchID , tile ,
                                     blockIdx , threadIdx );
  // threadIdx to (sub-) patch coord
  float2 patchUV = ComputePatchCoord(patchID , patchLevel ,
                                     blockIdx , threadIdx );

  int3 coord = int3(tile.uvOffset + tileUV.xy * tile.size ,
                    tile.page );

  float disp = g_displacementUAV[coord];

  // eval surface and apply displacement
  float3 worldPos = 0;
  float3 normal   = 0;

  float3 controlPoints[16] = ReadControlPoints(patchID);
  EvalPatch(controlPoints , patchUV , worldPos , normal );
  worldPos += disp * normal ;

  // traverse ray until leaving solid
  float3 rayOrigin = mul((g_matWorldToVoxel ),
                         float4(worldPos ,1.0)).xyz ;
  float3 rayDir = normalize(mul((float3x3)g_matWorldToVoxel ,
                                -normal.xyz ));

  float distOut = 0;
  if(! VoxelDDA(rayOrigin , rayDir , dist));
    return ;

  float3 p = rayDir * distOut ;
  p = mul((float3x3)(((g_matNormal))), p);
  disp = disp - length(p);

  g_displacementUAV[coord] = disp ;
}
```

Listing 3.6. Implementation of displacement update using voxel ray casting.

```
bool IsOutsideVolume(int3 voxel) {
  return (any(voxel < 0) || any(voxel > int3(g_gridSize)))
}
bool VoxelDDA(in float3 origin, in float3 dir, out float dist)
{
  PreventDivZero(dir);
  float3 dt = abs(1.0 / dir);

  float tEnter,tExit;
  if (!intersectRayVoxelGrid(origin, dir, tEnter, tExit))
    return false;

  // start on grid boundary unless origin is inside grid
  tEnter = max( 0.0, tEnter - 0.5 * min3(dt.xyz);

  float3 p = origin + tEnter * dir;
  int3 gridPos = floor(p);

  // check if ray is starting in voxel volume
  if(IsOutsideVolume(gridPos))
    return false;

  float3 tMin = INFINITY;
  // update step, dir components are != 0 (PreventDivZero)
  tMin.x = (dir.y < 0.0) ? (p.x-gridPos.x) : (gridPos.x-p.x+1);
  tMin.y = (dir.y < 0.0) ? (p.y-gridPos.y) : (gridPos.y-p.y+1);
  tMin.z = (dir.z < 0.0) ? (p.z-gridPos.z) : (gridPos.z-p.z+1);
  tMin *= dt;

  int3 step = 1;
  if (dir.x <= 0.0) step.x = -1;
  if (dir.y <= 0.0) step.y = -1;
  if (dir.z <= 0.0) step.z = -1;

  uint maxSteps = g_gridSize.x + g_gridSize.y + g_gridSize.z;
  [allow_uav_condition]
  for(uint i = 0; i < maxSteps; i++) {
    t = min(tMin.x, min(tMin.y, tMin.z));

    if(tEnter + t >= tExit) break;

    if (IsVoxelSet(gridPos))
        dist = t;

    if(tMin.x <= t) { tMin.x += dt.x; gridPos.x += step.x; }
    if(tMin.y <= t) { tMin.y += dt.y; gridPos.y += step.y; }
    if(tMin.z <= t) { tMin.z += dt.z; gridPos.z += step.z; }

    if(IsOutsideVolume(gridPos)) break;
  }
  return (dist > 0);
}
```

Listing 3.7. Implementation of the voxel digital differential analyzer (DDA) algorithm for ray casting.

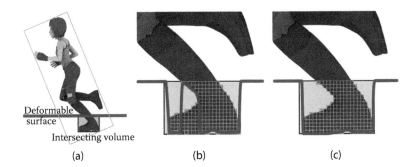

(a)   (b)   (c)

Figure 3.6. (a) Illustration of the ray casting behavior when tracing from the surface of the deformable through the voxelized volume. (b) The incorrect deformations that occur when using the distance of the first exit of the ray. (c) Tracing the ray throughout the complete volume yields correct deformations.

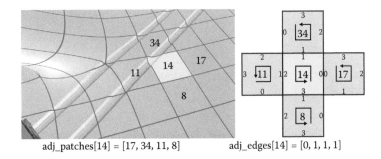

adj_patches[14] = [17, 34, 11, 8]   adj_edges[14] = [0, 1, 1, 1]

Figure 3.7. Example of the adjacency information storage scheme: for the green patch, we store all neighboring patch indices and indices of the shared edges in the neighboring patches in counterclockwise order.

shared edges' indices oriented with respect to the respective neighboring patch as depicted in Figure 3.7.

In our implementation, we handle the edge overlap separately from the corner overlap region, as the corners require special treatment depending on whether the patch is regular or connected to an irregular vertex.

Edge overlap. Using the precomputed adjacency information, we first update the edge overlap by scattering the boundary displacements coefficients to the adjacent neighbors overlap region. This process is depicted in Figure 3.8 for a single patch.

Corner overlap. Finally, we have to update the corner values of the overlap region to provide a consistent evaluation of the analytic displacement maps during rendering. The treatment of the corner values depends on the patch type. For

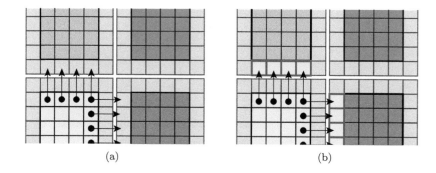

(a)   (b)

Figure 3.8. Edge overlap update for a single patch: (a) The direction of the overlap updates originates from the blue patch. (b) The two adjacent patches (red and yellow) receive their resulting overlap data by gathering the information from the blue patch.

Catmull-Clark subdivision surfaces two patch types are possible:

- Regular patches: All vertices of a patch have exactly four incoming edges.

- Irregular patches: At least one vertex of the patch has a valence different from four.

In the regular case, the corner values of a patch can simply be copied to the diagonal patch's boundary corner (see Figure 3.9(a)). In our implementation, we do not store the patch index of the diagonal adjacent patch. However, after the edges are updated, we can achieve exactly the same result by copying the correct

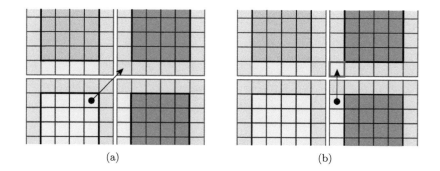

(a)   (b)

Figure 3.9. Corner overlap update at regular vertices. (a) The direction of the corner overlap update originates from the blue patch. The required information is also stored in the direct neighbors of the green patch after the edge overlap update pass. (b) The resulting corner overlap update is gathered from the overlap of the adjacent yellow patch.

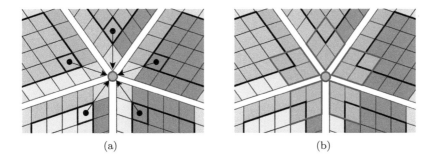

(a) (b)

Figure 3.10. Corner overlap update at irregular vertices: (a) texels to be gathered and (b) the result of scattering the resulting average value to the adjacent tiles.

coefficient from the adjacent patch's edge to the boundary corner as depicted in Figure 3.9(b).

In order to provide a watertight and consistent evaluation in the irregular case, all four corner coefficients must contain the same value. Therefore, we run a kernel per irregular vertex and average the interior corner coefficients of the connected patches (see Figure 3.10(a)). Then, we scatter the average to the four corner texels of the analytic displacement map in the same kernel.

In the end, the overlap is updated and the deformed mesh is prepared for rendering using displacement mapping.

3.5 Optimizations

3.5.1 Penetrated Patch Detection

The approach described in the previous sections casts rays for each texel of each patch of a deformed object: a compute shader thread is dispatched for each texel to perform the ray casting in parallel. This strategy is obviously inefficient since only a fraction of the patches of a deformed object will be affected. This can be prevented by culling patches that are outside the overlap regions. To this end, we compute whether the OBB of the penetrating object and the OBB of each patch of the object to be deformed do overlap. For this test, we extend the OBBs of the patches by the maximum encountered displacement to handle already displaced patches' surfaces properly. In case an overlap is detected, the patch (likely to be intersected by the penetrating object) is marked, and its patch index is enqueued for further processing. Also, the update of tile overlaps is only necessary for these marked patches.

Intersection. The patch intersection detection stage is implemented entirely on the GPU using a compute shader. One dispatch detects the collision of a single penetrating object's OBB with all patches of the scene. For each patch, a thread is dispatched. In the compute shader the OBB of the patch is computed on the fly from the patches' control points and overlap tested against the OBB of the penetrating object. If an overlap is found, the patch index is appended to the list to be handled for further processing.

Intersection batching. The previously depicted intersection stage implementation dispatches threads for each penetrating object sequentially, thus causing unnecessary and redundant memory accesses because the same patch control points have to be read over multiple kernel dispatches. This memory I/O overhead can significantly be reduced by batching multiple penetrating objects into a single dispatch. Batching the intersection testing of multiple penetrating objects into a single dispatch additionally reduces the number of total compute shader dispatches required. For patches requiring memory allocation, their index is appended to a global append buffer. In addition, we use further append buffers for each penetrating object. If a patch is possibly affected by a penetrating object, the patch index is appended to the penetrating object's append buffer for ray casting. Finally, the overlap is updated only once per deformable object after all penetrating collisions are processed.

3.5.2   Memory Management

Because we want to support deformation on scenes with a large number of patches at high tile resolutions, statically preallocating tile memory for each possibly deformed patch would require unreasonably large amounts of GPU memory. Therefore, we preallocate a predefined number of tiles and manage a table of tile descriptors pointing to these unused tiles. In addition, we use an atomic index i for memory allocation, which points to the end of the free memory table when no tiles are in use.

If memory allocation is required for a patch, this is implemented using an atomic decrement operation on i and fetching the tile descriptor of the tile it pointed to before decrementation. (See Listing 3.8.)

3.5.3   Optimized Pipeline

Our final deformation pipeline, including the proposed optimizations, is depicted in Figure 3.11.

3.6   Results

In this section, we provide several screenshots showing the qualitative results of our real-time deformations pipeline. The screenshots in Figure 3.12 are taken from our example scene (see Figure 3.1) consisting of a snowy deformable terrain

```
Buffer<uint>       g_isctResults      : register(t0);
Buffer<uint3>      g_memoryTable      : register(t1);
RWBuffer<uint4>    g_tileDescriptors  : register(u0);
RWBuffer<int>      g_atomicIndex      : register(u1);

void allocTile(uint tileID) {
    int i = 0;
    InterlockedAdd(g_atomicIndex[0], -1, i);

    // copy page ID and start offsets (u, v)
    g_tileDescriptors[tileID].xyz = g_memoryTable[i].xyz;
}

[numthreads(ALLOCATOR_BLOCKSIZE, 1, 1)]
void AllocateTilesCS(uint3 DTid: SV_DispatchThreadID) {
    uint tileID = DTid.x;
    if (tileID >= g_NumTiles) return;

    if (IsTileIntersected(tileID) && IsNotAllocated(tileID))
        allocTile(tileID);
}
```

Listing 3.8. Compute shader for tile memory allocation with atomic operations.

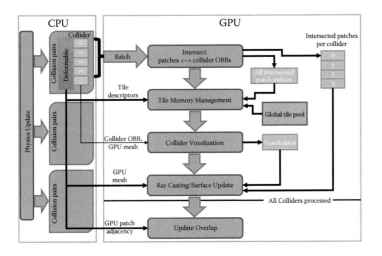

Figure 3.11. Overview of deformation pipeline with optimizations.

subdivision surface, dynamic objects like the car and barrels, and static objects such as trees and houses.

We start by presenting the parameters that impact the overall quality of the deformations.

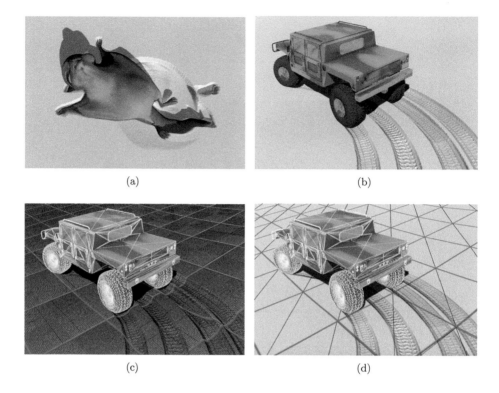

Figure 3.12. Results of the proposed deformation pipeline on snowy surface: (a) an example of animated character deforming the surface; (b) high-quality geometric detail including shadows and occlusion; and (c) wireframe visualization of a deformed surface. (d) Even at low tessellation densities, the deformation stored in the displacement map can provide visual feedback in shading.

3.6.1   Influence of Tile Resolution

The first parameter is the tile resolution for storing the per-patch displacement coefficients. Figure 3.13 shows a comparison of the deformation quality for different tile resolutions ((a) 32×32 and (b) 128×128). Obviously, the lower resolution tiles (a) cannot represent the impact of the collider on the surface well. Employing our tile memory allocation scheme (Section 3.5.2) enables very high tile resolution (b) on the deformed patches and thus highly detailed deformations. These tile resolutions would not be possible using static preallocation for all patches without memory management due to the limited GPU memory.

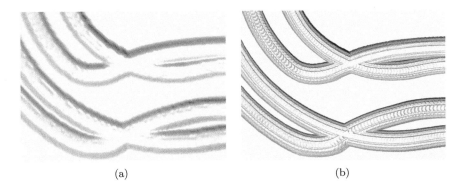

(a) (b)

Figure 3.13. Comparison of deformation quality using different tile resolutions per patch: (a) The higher resolution (128×128) captures high-frequency detailwhile (b) the lower (32×32) does not.

3.6.2 Influence of Voxelization

The second parameter that influences the overall quality most is the approximation of the penetrating object shape. The quality of the voxelization is limited by the chosen voxel grid size. Choosing too low a voxel grid resolution results in a low-quality deformation as shown in the example in Figure 3.14. In our implementation, we use a single voxel grid per penetrating object. Voxelizing the object only in the overlapping region as described in Section 3.4.2 results in a much better utilization of the available voxel space in the region of interest compared to voxelizing the entire object.

Figure 3.14. Choosing too coarse a voxel grid cannot capture the shape of the penetrating object (wheel) well and results in a low-quality deformation.

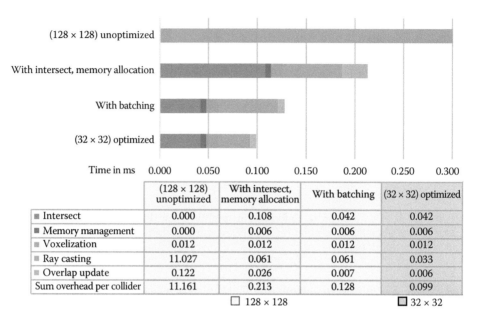

Figure 3.15. Timings in milliseconds on an NVIDIA GTX 780 for the different optimizations. The first three bars (from top to bottom) show the effects of our optimizations for a tile resolution of 128×18 texels, while the last bar shows the timings for a 32×32 tile resolution with all optimizations enabled.

3.6.3 Performance

In this section we provide detail timings of our deformation pipeline, including the benefits of the optimizations presented in Section 3.5. While we use the standard graphics pipeline for rendering and the voxelization of the models, including hardware tessellation for the subdivision surfaces, we employ compute shaders for patch-OBB intersection, memory management, ray casting (DDA), and updating the tile overlap regions.

Figure 3.15 summarizes the performance of the different pipeline stages and the overall overhead per deformable-penetrator collision pair measured on an NVIDIA GTX 780 using a default per-patch tile size of 128×128.

The measurements in Figure 3.15 show that ray casting is the most expensive stage of our algorithm. With a simple patch–voxel volume intersection test we can greatly improve the overall performance by starting ray casting and overlap updates only for the affected patches. This comes at the cost of spending additional time on the intersection test, which requires reading the control points of each patch. Because fetches from global memory are expensive, we optimize the intersection stage by computing the intersection with multiple penetrating objects after reading the control points, which further improves overall performance.

The chosen displacement tile size—as expected—only influences the ray casting and overlap stage. Because the computational overhead for the higher tile resolution is marginal, the benefits in deformation quality easily pay off.

3.7 Conclusion

In this chapter, we described a method for real-time visual feedback of surface deformations on collisions with dynamic and animated objects. To the best of our knowledge, our system is the first to employ a real-time voxelization of the penetrating object to update a displacement map for real-time deformation. Our GPU deformation pipeline achieves deformations in far below a millisecond for a single collision and scales with the number of deforming objects since only objects close to each other need to be tested. We believe that this approach is ideally suited for complex scene environments with many dynamic objects, such as in future video game generations. However, we emphasize that the deformations aim at a more detailed and dynamic visual appearance in real-time applications but cannot be considered as a physical simulation. Therefore, we do not support elasticity, volume preservation, or topological changes such as fractures.

3.8 Acknowledgments

This work is co-funded by the German Research Foundation (DFG), grant GRK-1773 Heterogeneous Image Systems.

Bibliography

[Burley and Lacewell 08] Brent Burley and Dylan Lacewell. "Ptex: Per-Face Texture Mapping for Production Rendering." In *Proceedings of the Nineteenth Eurographics Conference on Rendering*, pp. 1155–1164. Aire-la-Ville, Switzerland: Eurographics Association, 2008.

[Catmull and Clark 78] E. Catmull and J. Clark. "Recursively Generated B-Spline Surfaces on Arbitrary Topological Meshes." *Computer-Aided Design* 10:6 (1978), 350–355.

[Coumans et al. 06] Erwin Coumans et al. "Bullet Physics Library: Real-Time Physics Simulation." http://bulletphysics.org/, 2006.

[Nießner and Loop 13] Matthias Nießner and Charles Loop. "Analytic Displacement Mapping Using Hardware Tessellation." *ACM Transactions on Graphics* 32:3 (2013), article 26.

[Nießner et al. 12] Matthias Nießner, Charles Loop, Mark Meyer, and Tony DeRose. "Feature-Adaptive GPU Rendering of Catmull-Clark Subdivision Surfaces." *ACM Transactions on Graphics* 31:1 (2012), article 6.

[Schäfer et al. 14] Henry Schäfer, Benjamin Keinert, Matthias Nießner, Christoph Buchenau, Michael Guthe, and Marc Stamminger. "Real-Time Deformation of Subdivision Surfaces from Object Collisions." In *Proceedings of HPG'14*, pp. 89–96. New York: ACM, 2014.

[Schwarz 12] Michael Schwarz. "Practical Binary Surface and Solid Voxelization with Direct3D 11." In *GPU Pro 3: Advanced Rendering Techniques*, edited by Wolfgang Engel, pp. 337–352. Boca Raton, FL: A K Peters/CRC Press, 2012.

Realistic Volumetric Explosions
in Games
Alex Dunn

4.1 Introduction

In games, explosions can provide some of the most visually astounding effects. This article presents an extension of well-known ray-marching [Green 05] techniques for volume rendering fit for modern GPUs, in an attempt to modernize the emulation of explosions in games

Realism massively affects the user's level of immersion within a game, and previous methods for rendering explosions have always lagged behind that of production quality [Wrennige and Zafar 11]. Traditionally, explosions in games are rendered using mass amounts of particles, and while this method can look good from a static perspective, the effect starts to break down in dynamic scenes with free-roaming cameras. Particles are camera-facing billboards and, by nature, always face the screen; there is no real concept of rotation or multiple view angles, just the same texture projected onto the screen with no regard for view direction. By switching to a volumetric system, explosions look good from all view angles as they no longer depend on camera-facing billboards. Furthermore, a single volumetric explosion can have the same visual quality as thousands of individual particles, thus, removing the strain of updating, sorting, and rendering them all—as is the case with particle systems.

By harnessing the power of the GPU and the DirectX 11 tessellation pipeline, I will show you that single-pass, fully volumetric, production-quality explosions are now possible in the current generation of video games. We will be exploring volumetric rendering techniques such as ray marching and sphere tracing, as well as utilizing the tessellation pipeline to optimize these techniques.

There are certain drawbacks to the technique, such as it not being as generic a system as particles. It's more of a bespoke explosion system and like particles, the effect is generally quite pixel heavy from a computational perspective.

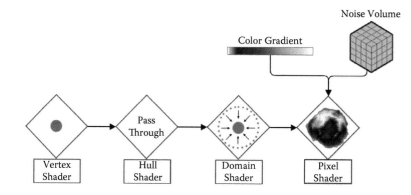

Figure 4.1. Pipeline flow overview of the technique.

4.2 Rendering Pipeline Overview

Explosions are represented by a single volumetric sphere with detail layered on top. The explosion is rendered by first generating a hemisphere mesh of a radius equal to the maximum radius of the explosion. (The explosion won't have a uniform radius, so instead we define a *maximum radius*, which is the distance from the explosion at its most extended point, to its core.) Then, shrink the hemisphere around the explosion to form a tight-fitting semi-hull. This is done in order to decrease the amount of degenerate fragments when later performing ray marching in the pixel shader. An overview of the technique is shown in Figure 4.1.

4.3 Offline/Preprocessing

First, we must create a 3D volume of noise, which we can use later to create some nice noise patterns. We can do this offline to save precious cycles later in the pixel shader. This noise is what's going to give the explosions their recognizable cloud-like look. In the implemention described here, simplex noise was used—however, it should be noted that it isn't a requirement to use simplex noise; in fact, in your own implementation you are free to use whatever type of noise you want, so long as it tiles correctly within our volume. In order to conserve bandwidth and fully utilize the cache, size, and format of this texture is detrimental to the performance of the technique. The implementation demonstrated here uses a $32 \times 32 \times 32$ sized volume with a 16-bit floating point format, `DXGI_FORMAT_R16_FLOAT`. The noise is calculated for each voxel of the volume using its UVW coordinate as the position parameter for the noise function.

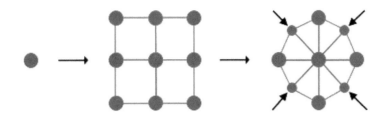

Figure 4.2. The life of a vertex. In an actual implementation, the level of subdivision should be much higher than shown in the diagram.

4.4   Runtime

As the effect will be utilizing the tessellation pipeline of the graphics card for rendering, it is required to submit a draw call using one of the various patch primitive types available in Direct X. For this technique, the `D3D11_PRIMITIVE_TOPOLOGY1_CONTROL_POINT_PATCHLIST` primitive type should be used as we only need to submit a draw call that emits a single vertex. This is because the GPU will be doing the work of expanding this vertex into a semi-hull primitive. The life of a vertex emitted from this draw call throughout this technique is shown in Figure 4.2.

4.4.1   Semi-Hull Generation

The GPU starts rendering our explosion with the vertex shader. This is run once per explosion. Its job is to read values from some data buffer, which stores position, radius, and "time lived" in seconds, and passes them down to the next shader in the pipeline, the hull shader. For your own implementation, it's entirely up to you how this information is stored, so long as it's accessible by the GPU.

The next stage of the pipeline is the hull shader. It runs once for each point of the input primitive and outputs control points for the next stage. This hull shader will be using the quad domain. When using this domain, the shader will load in a single vertex patch and the data associated with it (loaded in by the vertex shader previously) and output the four corner vertices of a quad (control points), each with its own copy of the data.

The tessellator stage is fixed function in DirectX 11. Its main purpose is to accept the control points generated by the hull shader as inputs and subdivide them. While programming the subdivision of control points is out of our reach in DirectX 11, we do have control over the level of subdivision. For the purposes of this article, we will just use a constant tessellation level. However, there is scope to adaptively tessellate your primitives based on the onscreen size of the explosions. A higher tessellation level can provide a tighter fitting hull around the explosion and thus decrease the amount of fragments rendered, which can make a big difference for high-quality, close-up explosions. The performance gains vary from case to case though, so I'd suggest profiling to find the best fit for your own implementations.

Once the patch has been subdivided, the next stage of the tessellation pipeline takes over. With the domain shader, we first transform the vertices into a screen-aligned hemisphere shape, with the inside of the sphere facing the camera and the radius set to that of the explosion. Then we perform a technique called *sphere tracing* [Hart 94] to shrink wrap the hemisphere around the explosion to form a tight-fitting hull. Sphere tracing is a technique not unlike ray marching, where starting at an originating point (a vertex on the hemisphere hull), we move along a ray toward the center of the hemisphere. Normally, when ray marching, we traverse the ray at fixed size intervals, but when sphere tracing, we traverse the ray at irregular intervals, where the size of each interval is determined by a distance field function evaluated at each step. A distance field function represents the signed distance to the closest point on an implicit surface from any point in space. (You can see an example of a signed distance function for an explosion in Listing 4.1).

4.4.2   Pixel Shading

The last programmable stage required for the effect is the pixel shader. This shader is invoked for each visible pixel of the explosion on screen; it is here where the bulk of the work will be done. For each pixel, it is required to step, or "march," through our explosion and evaluate the color at each step. The stepping will take place along a per-pixel ray, calculated using the world-space position of the pixel. The ray is then marched from front to back. At each step along the ray, a distance field function is evaluated. This function is the distance function for a sphere, perturbed by the value stored in the noise texture for the current position. A source code snippet is provided in Listing 4.1. The function `DrawExplosion`, will return the distance to the explosion from a point in world space and provide the amount of displacement caused by noise at that point. If the distance returned from this function is less than some epsilon, then this step is inside the explosion and contributes to the final color of this pixel. (For a great primer on this technique, see [Green 05].)

The method `FractalNoise`, used in Listing 4.1, calculates how perturbed the surface of the explosion will be at a given point in world space. The inner mechanics of this function can be seen in Listing 4.2.

The `FractalNoise` function uses the noise volume we created offline earlier. The volume is sampled multiple times. The location of each sample is calculated from the original sampling position by applying a constant frequency factor. Each sample read in this fashion is known as an *octave*. Once we have completed reading all the samples, the values from each are summed to give the final noise value. We found that four octaves provided a fairly reasonable visual experience.

```
// Returns the distance to the surface of a sphere.
float SphereDistance(float3 pos, float3 spherePos, float radius)
{
  float3 relPos = pos - spherePos;
  return length( relPos ) - radius
}

// Returns the distance to the surface of an explosion.
float DrawExplosion
  (
    float3 posWS,
    float3 spherePosWS,
    float radiusWS,
    float displacementWS,
    out float displacementOut
  )
{
  displacementOut = FractalNoise( posWS );

  float dist = SphereDistance(posWS, spherePosWS, radiusWS);

  return dist - displacementOut * displacementWS;
}
```

Listing 4.1. HLSL source: Distance field function for explosion.

```
// How many octaves to use when calculating the fractal noise.
static const uint kNumberOfNoiseOctaves = 4;

// Returns a noise value by texture lookup.
float Noise( const float3 uvw )
{
  return _NoiseTexR0.Sample( g_noiseSam, uvw, 0 );
}

// Calculates a fractal noise value from a world-space position.
float FractalNoise( const float3 posWS )
{
  const float3 animation = g_AnimationSpeed * g_time;

  float3 uvw = posWS * g_NoiseScale + animation;
  float amplitude = 0.5f;
  float noiseValue = 0;

  [unroll]
  for( uint i=0 ; i<kNumberOfNoiseOctaves ; i++ )
  {
    noiseValue += amplitude * Noise( uvw );
    amplitude *= g_NoiseAmplitudeFactor;
    uvw *= g_NoiseFrequencyFactor;
  }

  return noiseValue;
}
```

Listing 4.2. HLSL source: the noise function.

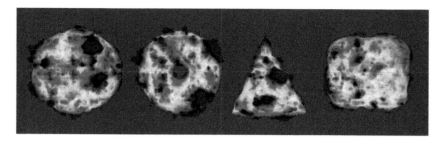

Figure 4.3. A collection of explosions rendered using different primitive types.

The color of the explosion at each step is calculated by performing a lookup into a gradient texture using the `displacementOut` parameter (from Listing 4.1) as a texture coordinate. This color is then blended with the other samples gathered from previous steps before the next step of the ray.

This process is repeated either until we hit the exit point of our ray or, as a further optimization, until the output color has reached full opacity and no further steps would contribute to the final color of the pixel. (It is important to note that this optimization will only work when marching through the explosion from front to back.)

4.5   Visual Improvements

4.5.1   Primitives

While this article has so far only demonstrated how to create an explosion based on the sphere primitive shape, it's possible to extend the technique to handle a variety of shapes, as you can see in Figure 4.3.

In Listing 4.1, there is a method called `SphereDistance`, which calculates the distance to the closest point on a sphere from some point in world space. In order to render an explosion with a different underlying primitive type, this method can be swapped for one that calculates the distance to another primitive, or even a collection of primitives. See Listing 4.3 for a list of basic primitive functions written in HLSL.

Rendering an explosion with one of the customized primitives above can be useful in situations where explosions are formed from explosive containers. For example, the cylinder primitive type would be useful when modeling an explosion that's to be associated with an old game developer favorite, the exploding barrel.

4.5.2   Extra Step

When the number of steps used to render an explosion is low, and when the explosion intersects some of the scene geometry, certain view angles relative to

```
float Sphere(float3 pos, float3 spherePos, float radius)
{
  float3 relPos = pos - spherePos;
  return length( relPos ) - radius
}

float Cone( float3 pos, float3 conePos, float radius )
{
  float3 relPos = pos - conePos;

  float d = length( relPos.xz );
  d -= lerp( radius * 0.5f, 0, 1 + relPos.y/radius );

  d = max( d,-relPos.y - radius );
  d = max( d, relPos.y - radius );

  return d;
}

float Cylinder( float3 pos, float3 cylinderPos, float radius )
{
  float3 relPos = pos - cylinderPos;

  float2 h = radius.xx * float2( 1.0f, 1.5f ); // Width, Radius
  float2 d = abs( float2( length( relPos.xz ), relPos.y ) ) - h;

  return min( max( d.x, d.y ), 0.0f) + length( max( d, 0.0f) );
}

float Box( float3 pos, float3 boxPos, float3 b )
{
  float3 relPos = pos - boxPos;
  float3 d = abs( relPos ) - b;

  return min( max( d.x, max( d.y, d.z ) ), 0.0f )
         + length( max( d, 0.0f ) );
}

float Torus( float3 pos, float3 torusPos, float radius )
{
  float3 relPos = pos - boxPos;

  float2 t = radius.xx * float2( 1, 0.01f );
  float2 q = float2( length( relPos.xz ) - t.x , relPos.y );

  return length( q ) - t.y;
}

// Rendering a collection of primitives can be achieved by
// using multiple primitive distance functions, combined
// with the 'min' function.
float Cluster( float3 pos )
{
  float3 spherePosA = float3(-1, 0, 0);
  float3 spherePosB = float3( 1, 0, 0);
  float sphereRadius = 0.75f;

  return min( Sphere(pos, spherePosA, sphereRadius),
              Sphere(pos, spherePosB, sphereRadius) );
}
```

Listing 4.3. HLSL source: a collection of distance functions for various primitives.

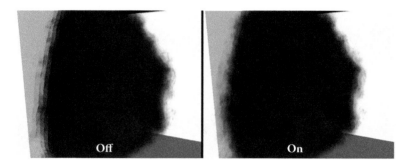

Figure 4.4. The extra step trick in action.

the intersection geometry can produce an ugly banding artifact in which the slices of the volume are completely visible.

The extra step trick [Crane et al. 07] attempts to minimize this artifact by adding one final step at the end of the ray marching, passing in the world-space position of the pixel instead of the next step position. Calculating the world-space position of the pixel can be done any way you see fit; in the approach demonstrated here, we have reconstructed world-space position from the depth buffer. (See Figure 4.4.)

4.5.3   Lighting

Lighting the explosion puffs from a directional light is possible by performing a similar ray-marching technique to the one seen earlier while rendering the explosion [Ikits et al. 03]. Let's go back to when we were rendering via ray marching. In order to accurately calculate lighting, we need to evaluate how much light has reached each step along the ray. This is done at each rendering step by ray marching from the world-space position of the step toward the light source, accumulating the density (in the case of the explosion this could be the opacity of the step) until either the edge of the volume has been reached or the density has reached some maximum value (i.e., the pixel is fully shadowed).

Because this is rather expensive, as an optimization you don't need to calculate the lighting at every step. Depending on the amount of steps through the volume and the density of those steps, you can just calculate the lighting value for one in every x steps and reuse this value for the next steps. Use best judgement and check for visual artifacts while adjusting the x variable.

4.6   Results

The screenshots in Figures 4.5–4.7 were rendered using 100 steps (but only a few rays will actually use this much) with the shrink wrapping optimization enabled.

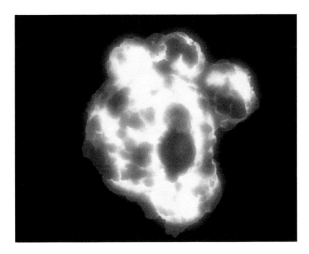

Figure 4.5. A shot of a clustered volumetric explosion. Here, a collection of spheres has been used to break up the obvious shape of a singular sphere.

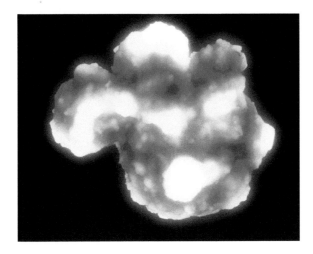

Figure 4.6. Varying the displacement to color gradient over time can provide a powerful fourth dimension to the effect.

4.7 Performance

The performance of this explosion technique is certainly comparable to that of a particle-based explosion. With the shrink wrapping optimization, rendering times can be significantly reduced under the right circumstances. In Figure 4.8, you'll see a visual comparison of the shrink wrapping technique and the effect it

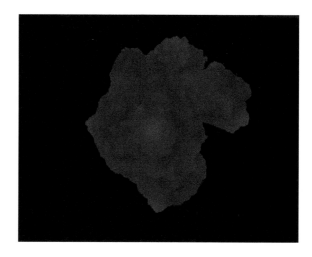

Figure 4.7. As the life of an explosion comes to an end, the entire effect turns more smoke than flame.

Figure 4.8. Here you can see the amount of rays required to step through the explosion (more red means more steps are required): with no shrink wrapping optimizations (left), with shrink wrapping and early out for fully opaque pixels (middle), and the final rendering (right).

has on the number of steps required to render a volumetric explosion. Following this, Figure 4.9 shows a graph detailing the amount of time taken to render the same explosion with shrink wrapping on and off across a range of rendering steps. For both datasets, the exact same GPU and driver were used (NVIDIA GTX980 with driver v344.11) and the time taken has been calculated by recording an average over 200 frames.

4.7.1 Further Optimizations

Half-resolution up-sampling. With a slight modification to [Cantlay 07], we can significantly reduce the pixel workload by reducing the size of the rendering buffer. This technique works by binding a low-resolution render target in place of the

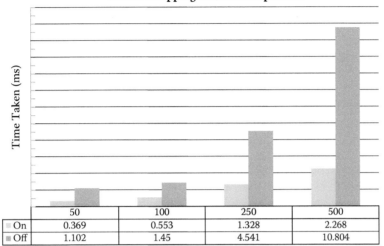

Shrink Wrapping-On/Off Comparison

	50	100	250	500
On	0.369	0.553	1.328	2.268
Off	1.102	1.45	4.541	10.804

Figure 4.9. See how the shrink wrapping optimization improves the render time. All numbers were captured using a GTX980 (driver v344.11). Timings were averaged over 200 frames.

back buffer just before rendering an explosion, then, once the explosions have been rendered, up-sampling the texture associated with the low-resolution render target by rendering it to the full-resolution back buffer.

There are several corner cases to be aware of—depth testing and edge intersections to name a couple—that are out of the scope of this article. I recommend reading [Cantlay 07], in which these are thoroughly explained.

Depth testing. Currently, when rendering an explosion, we do so by rendering the back faces (front-face culling) of the sphere geometry. The upside of this is that we can still see the back faces while inside the explosion, which allows us to keep rendering. The downside is that we can't perform hardware depth testing for early exiting pixels, which are occluded by nearer geometry but have to resort to performing a texture read-dependent branch in the pixel shader.

It's possible, with very little tweaking, to render the explosion by using the front faces (back face culling) which will allow the correct use of hardware depth testing on a read-only depth buffer (we still need to read from the depth buffer in the shader to figure out the depth of the scene, so the DSV bound must be readonly, that is, created with 'flags = 0'). The only downside is that once the camera moves inside the explosion, the front faces are no longer visible, and the explosion disappears. The solution to this is to switch to the back faces once the camera enters the volume.

4.8   Conclusion

Volumetric explosions undoubtedly provide a much richer visual experience over particle-based techniques, and as I've shown, it's possible to use them now in the current generation of games. This article has demonstrated how to best utilize the modern graphics pipeline and DirectX, taking full advantage of the tessellation pipeline. The optimization methods described allow for implementing this effect with a minimal impact on frame times.

4.9   Acknowledgments

The techniques described in this article are an extension of the previous works of Simon Green in the area of real-time volume rendering.

Bibliography

[Cantlay 07] Iain Cantlay. "High-Speed, Off-Screen Particles." In *GPU Gems 3*, edited by Hubert Nguyen, pp. 535–549. Reading, MA: Addison-Wesley Professional, 2007.

[Crane et al. 07] Keenan Crane, Ignacio Llamas, and Sarah Tariq. "Real-Time Simulation and Rendering of 3D Fluids." In *GPU Gems 3*, edited by Hubert Nguyen, pp. 653–694. Reading, MA: Addison-Wesley Professional, 2007.

[Green 05] Simon Green. "Volume Rendering For Games." Presented at Game Developer Conference, San Francisco, CA, March, 2005.

[Hart 94] John C. Hart. "Sphere Tracing: A Geometric Method for the Antialiased Ray Tracing of Implicit Surfaces." *The Visual Computer* 12 (1994), 527–545.

[Ikits et al. 03] Milan Ikits, Joe Kniss, Aaron Lefohn, and Charles Hansen. "Volume Rendering Techniques." In *GPU Gems*, edited by Randima Fernando, pp. 667–690. Reading, MA: Addison-Wesley Professional, 2003.

[Wrennige and Zafar 11] Magnus Wrennige and Nafees Bin Zafar. "Production Volume Rendering." SIGGRAPH Course, Vancouver, Canada, August 7–11, 2011.

Rendering

This is an exciting time in the field of real-time rendering. With the release of new gaming consoles comes new opportunities for technological advancement in real-time rendering and simulation. The following articles introduce both beginners as well as expert graphics programmers to some of the latest trends and technologies in the field of real-time rendering.

Our first article is "Next-Generation Rendering in Thief" by Peter Sikachev, Samuel Delmont, Uriel Doyon, and Jean-Normand Bucci in which a number of advanced rendering techniques, specifically designed for the new-generation of gaming consoles, are presented. The authors discuss real-time reflections, contact shadows, and compute-shader-based postprocessing techniques.

Next is "Grass Rendering and Simulation with LOD" by Dongsoo Han and Hongwei Li. In this article, the authors present a GPU-based system for grass simulation and rendering. This system is capable of simulating and rendering more than 100,000 blades of grass, entirely on the GPU, and is based on earlier work related to character hair simulation.

"Hybrid Reconstruction Antialiasing" by Michał Drobot provides the reader with a full framework of antialiasing techniques specially designed to work efficiently with AMD's GCN hardware architecture. The author presents both spatial and temporal antialiasing techniques and weighs the pros and cons of many different implementation strategies.

Egor Yusov's "Real-Time Rendering of Physically Based Clouds Using Precomputed Scattering" provides a physically based method for rendering highly realistic and efficient clouds. Cloud rendering is typically very expensive, but here the author makes clever use of lookup tables and other optimizations to simulate scattered light within a cloud in real time.

Finally, we have "Sparse Procedural Volume Rendering" by Doug McNabb in which a powerful technique for volumetric rendering is presented. Hierarchical data structures are used to efficiently light and render complex volumetric effects in real time. The author also discusses methods in which artists can control volumetric forms and thus provide strong direction on the ultimate look of volumetric effects.

The new ideas and techniques discussed in this section represent some of the latest developments in the realm of real-time computer graphics. I would like

to thank our authors for generously sharing their exciting new work and I hope
that these ideas inspire readers to further extend the state of the art in real-time
rendering.

—Christopher Oat

Next-Generation Rendering in Thief

Peter Sikachev, Samuel Delmont, Uriel Doyon, and Jean-Normand Bucci

1.1 Introduction

In this chapter we present the rendering techniques used in *Thief*, which was developed by Eidos Montreal for PC, Playstation 3, Playstation 4, Xbox 360, and Xbox One. Furthermore, we concentrate solely on techniques, developed exclusively for the next-generation platforms, i.e., PC, Playstation 4, and Xbox One.

We provide the reader with implementation details and our experience on a range of rendering methods. In Section 1.2, we discuss our reflection rendering system. We describe each tier of our render strategy as well as final blending and postprocessing.

In Section 1.3, we present a novel contact-hardening shadow (CHS) approach based on the AMD CHS sample. Our method is optimized for Shader Model 5.0 and is capable of rendering high-quality large shadow penumbras at a relatively low cost. Section 1.4 describes our approach toward lit transparent particles rendering.

Compute shaders (CSs) are a relatively new feature in graphics APIs, introduced first in the DirectX 11 API. We have been able to gain substantial benefits for postprocessing using CSs. We expound upon our experience with CSs in Section 1.5.

Performance results are presented in the end of each section. Finally, we conclude and indicate further research directions in Section 1.6.

1.2 Reflections

Reflections rendering has always been a tricky subject for game engines. As long as the majority of games are rasterization based, there is no cheap way to get correct reflections rendered in the most general case. That being said, several methods for real-time reflection rendering produce plausible results in special cases.

1.2.1 Related Methods

One of the first reflection algorithms used for real-time applications, was real-time planar reflection (RTPR) rendering [Lengyel 11]. This method yields an accurate solution for geometry reflected over a plane and is typically used for water or mirror reflections. The method involves rendering objects, or proxies of them, as seen through the reflection plane. Depending on the number of things rendered in the reflection scene, it is possible to balance performance and quality, but the technique is generally considered to be expensive. The main drawback of this method is that in practice, several planes of different heights and orientations would be required to model correctly the environment view surrounding the player, which would be unacceptably expensive to process. This prevents the technique from being used across a wide range of environments.

Cube map reflections are another approach that has been used for many years [NVIDIA Corporation 99]. Though they are very fast and they can handle nonplanar objects, cube maps have their limitations, too. They usually lack resolution and locality compared to other techniques. One also usually needs to precompute cube maps in advance, as it is usually prohibitively expensive to generate cube maps dynamically at runtime. This could additionally complicate an asset pipeline. Precomputed cube maps will not reflect a change in lighting or dynamic objects. Moreover, cube maps do not produce high-quality reflections when applied to planar surfaces, which was one of our main scenarios.

Screen-space reflection (SSR) is a relatively new technique that has grown quickly in popularity [Uludag 14]. It has a moderate performance cost and is easy to integrate. Moreover, it provides great contact reflections (i.e., reflections that occur when an object stands on a reflecting surface; these reflections "ground" an object) hardly achieved by other techniques. However, SSR is prone to numerous artifacts and fails to reflect invisible (or offscreen) parts of a scene. Therefore, it is usually used in combination with some backup technique.

Image-based reflection (IBR) is a method that utilizes planar proxies in order to approximate complex geometries to accelerate ray tracing [Wright 11]. It was developed and shown off in the Unreal Engine 3 *Samaritan* demo. IBR can achieve good results in reflection locality and allows an arbitrary orientation of a reflector. However, the complexity grows linearly with the number of proxies, which could become prohibitive for large scenes.

Figure 1.1. From left to right: cube map reflections only, SSR + cube maps, IBR + cube maps, and SSR + IBR + cube maps. [Image courtesy Square Enix Ltd.]

Numerous variations of the methods discussed above have been proposed and used in real-time rendering. For instance, localized, or parallax-corrected cube maps [Lagarde and Zanuttini 13] are arguably becoming an industry standard. In the next sections, we will describe the reflection system we used in *Thief*.

1.2.2 Thief Reflection System Overview

Creating a reflection system that perfectly handles every surface type, in real time, is a very difficult problem. Therefore, together with the art department, we developed a specification of requirements and limitations for the *Thief* reflection system. Given that *Thief* was originally designed for the Xbox 360 and Playstation 3 generation of platforms, we had quite a generous performance budget for the reflection system on the next-generation platforms: 5 ms. Beforehand, we implemented the real-time planar reflection method, which ran at 10 ms. This running time was obviously unacceptable; moreover, this technique could render reflections for only one plane.

The majority of reflections in the game world come from the ground (wet spots, tile, etc.), therefore we limited ourselves to quasi-horizontal surfaces. However, since *Thief* is a multilevel game (e.g., you can make your way across rooftops instead of streets), unlike [Lagarde and Zanuttini 13], we could not be limited to a single reflection plane. As mentioned above, we performed tests with PRTR and the single reflection plane limitation was insufficient for our assets.

The target was to accurately capture human-sized objects and contact reflections. In addition, we also wanted to capture principal landmarks (e.g., large buildings). Finally, as torches and bonfires are a typical light source in the world of *Thief*, we needed a way to render reflection from certain transparent geometry as well.

To achieve these goals, we came up with a multitier reflection system, outlined in Figure 1.1. The reflection system of *Thief* consists of the following tiers:

- screen-space reflections (SSR) for opaque objects, dynamic and static, within a human height of a reflecting surface;

- image-based reflections (IBR) for walls and far away landmarks;

- localized cube map reflections to fill the gaps between IBR proxies;

- global cube map reflections, which are mostly for view-independent sky-boxes.

Each tier serves as a fallback solution to the previous one. First, SSR ray-marches the depth buffer. If it does not have sufficient information to shade a fragment (i.e., the reflected ray is obscured by some foreground object), it falls back to image-based reflection. If none of the IBR proxies are intersected by the reflection ray, the localized cube map reflection system comes into play. Finally, if no appropriate localized cube map is in proximity, the global cube map is fetched. Transition between different tiers is done via smooth blending, as described in Section 1.2.6.

1.2.3 Screen-Space Reflections

SSR is an image-based reflection technique based on ray-marching through the depth buffer [Kasyan et al. 11]. We use the lit color buffer, the normal buffer, and the depth buffer from the current frame. SSR is applied before rendering translucent geometry in order to avoid perspective artifacts.

At each fragment we reconstruct the camera-space position, using the screen uv-coordinates, the fetched depth, and the projection matrix. Afterward, we ray-march with a constant step along the reflected ray until the analytical depth of the fetch along the ray is more than the depth buffer fetch from the same screen-space position. Finally, the intersection location is refined with several binary search steps, as shown in Figure 1.2.

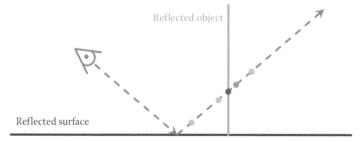

Figure 1.2. Screen-space reflections linear steps (green) and binary search steps (orange and then red).

This method yields very accurate reflections at the contact of a reflective surface and a reflected object. There are, however, several major issues with SSR. First, this method is very expensive: at each fragment we need to make several potentially uncoalesced (due to the discrepancy of reflection rays) texture fetches, some of which are even view-dependent (binary search). Second, reflected information is often missing: it's either out of screen or obscured by a closer object.

We address the first issue with several optimization techniques, described below in this subsection. The second issue is addressed by falling back to the subsequent tier of the reflection system.

We decrease the memory traffic by approximating the normal at the fragment with a normal pointing vertically up. This dramatically increases the number of texture fetches at neighboring fragments that might be coalesced and processed within a single dynamic random-access memory (DRAM) burst. However, this naturally results in ideal mirror-like reflections without any normal perturbation. We address this issue further in Section 1.2.7.

Moreover, we use dynamic branching to employ early exit for the constant step loop when the first intersection with the depth buffer is found. Although it might result in false ray-depth buffer collision detection, we compromise on accuracy in order to further save on bandwidth.

Another optimization is decreasing the number of samples for the distant fragments. We came up with an empirical formula that decreases the number of steps proportional to the exponent of the distance:

$$N_{\text{linear samples}} = \max(1, k_1 e^{-k_2 d}),$$

where depth is denoted with d, k_1 is the linear factor, and k_2 is the exponential factor.

Additionally, we use a bunch of early-outs for the whole shader. We check if the surface has a reflective component and if a reflection vector points to the camera. The latter optimization does not significantly deteriorate visual quality, as in these situations SSR rarely yields high-quality results anyway and the reflection factor due to the Fresnel equation is already low. Moreover, this reduces the SSR GPU time in the case when IBR GPU time is high, thus balancing the total.

However, one should be very careful when implementing such an optimization. All fetches inside the `if`-clause should be done with a forced mipmap level; all variables used after should be initialized with a meaningful default value, and the `if`-clause should be preceded with a `[branch]` directive. The reason is that a shader compiler might otherwise try to generate a gradient-requiring instruction (i.e., `tex2D`) and, therefore, flatten a branch, making the optimizations useless.

1.2.4 Image-Based Reflections

Image-based reflections are a reflection technique implemented in [Wright 11]. The key idea is to introduce one or more planar quad reflection proxies and pre-render an object of interest into it. During fragment shading, we just ray-trace the reflected ray against an array of proxies in the pixel shader. A similar idea is utilized in [Lagarde and Zanuttini 13]. However, in the latter, the reflections are rendered only for planes at a single height. Therefore, we were unable to use optimizations proposed in [Lagarde and Zanuttini 13].

In *Thief*, our ambition was to have around 50 IBR proxies per scene. IBR back-face culling effectively reduces the visible proxy count by half. A straightforward approach resulted in well over 8 ms of GPU time at the target configuration, which was totally unacceptable. Therefore, we employed a series of acceleration techniques, described below.

First, we utilized the same approach for normal approximation as for SSR to increase memory coalescing. This allowed the following optimizations:

- rejecting planes not facing the player,

- rejecting planes behind the player,

- tile-based IBR rendering (discussed below).

Bump perturbation was then performed for SSR and IBR together.

Second, we introduced tile-based IBR. Because we have limited ourselves to quasi-horizontal reflections, we divided the entire screen space into a number of vertical tiles. Our experiments have proven 16 tiles to be an optimal number. After that, for each reflection proxy, we calculate the screen-space coordinates for each vertex. If a vertex is in front of the near clip plane, we flip the w sign before perspective divide in order to handle close proxies. Then x-coordinates of the transformed vertices might be used as minimum and maximum values to determine the tiles covered by the proxy's reflection.

However, due to perspective projection, this method would result in reflections being cut, especially when a proxy approaches the screen borders. To fix that, we introduce the following workaround. For each of two vertical sides of the proxy, we extend them to the intersections with top and bottom screen borders as shown in Figure 1.3. The resultant x-coordinates are used to decrease the minimum and/or increase the maximum. The pseudocode of this method is shown in Algorithm 1.1.

The above mentioned optimization decreases GPU time dramatically; however, if a player looks straight down, all the proxies start occupying almost all tiles due to high perspective distortions. To alleviate performance drops in this case, we use a bounding sphere test in the pixel shader for an early-out before the actual high-cost tracing. While this check deteriorates the performance in the most common cases, it increases GPU performance in the worst cases, resulting in a more consistent frame rate.

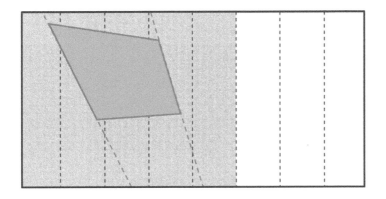

Figure 1.3. IBR tile-based rendering optimization. IBR proxy is shown in orange. Tiles are shown in dotted blue lines, and vertical sides extensions are shown in orange dotted lines. The affected tiles are shaded with thin red diagonal lines.

1: $x_{min} = 1$
2: $x_{max} = -1$
3: **for all** IBR proxies in front of player and facing player **do**
4:      find AABB of the current proxy
5:      **for all** vertices of AABB **do**
6:          calculate vertex coordinate in homogeneous clip space
7:          $w := |w|$
8:          calculate vertex coordinate in screen clip space
9:          $x_{min} := min(x, x_{min})$
10:         $x_{max} := max(x, x_{max})$
11:     **end for**
12:     **for all** vertical edges of AABB in screen space **do**
13:         calculate intersections x_1 and x_2 with top and bottom of the screen
14:         $x_{min} := min(x_1, x_2, x_{min})$
15:         $x_{max} := max(x_1, x_2, x_{max})$
16:     **end for**
17:     **for all** IBR tiles **do**
18:         **if** the tile overlaps with $[x_{min}, x_{max}]$ **then**
19:             add the proxy to the tile
20:         **end if**
21:     **end for**
22: **end for**

Algorithm 1.1. Algorithm for finding affected tiles for an IBR proxy.

Additionally, in order to limit the number of active IBR proxies in the frame, we introduced the notion of *IBR rooms*. Essentially, an IBR room defines an AABB so that a player can see IBR reflections only from the IBR proxies in

Figure 1.4. Non-glossy reflection rendering (left) and CHGR (right). [Image courtesy Square Enix Ltd.]

the same room. Moreover, the lower plane of an IBR room's AABB defines the maximum *reflection extension* of each of the proxies inside it. This allowed us to drastically limit the number of reflections when a player is looking down.

As a side note, *Thief* has a very dynamic lighting environment. In order to keep the IBR reflection in sync with the dynamic lights, IBR had to be scaled down based on the light intensity. This makes the IBR planes disappear from reflection when lights are turned off. Although this is inaccurate since the IBR textures are generated from the default lighting setup, it was not possible to know which parts of the plane were actually affected by dynamic lighting.

Also, IBRs were captured with particles and fog disabled. Important particles, like fire effects, were simulated with their own IBRs. Fog was added accordingly to the fog settings and the reflection distance after blending SSR and IBR.

1.2.5 Contact-Hardening Glossy Reflections

Because the majority of the reflecting surfaces in *Thief* are not perfect mirror reflectors, we decided to simulate glossy reflections. Glossy SSR reflections are not a new feature, having been first implemented in [Andreev 13]. We decided to take SSR a step further and render contact-hardening glossy reflections (CHGRs). An example of a CHGR is shown in Figure 1.4.

The main phenomena we wish to capture is that a reflection is sharpest near the contact point of the reflected object and the reflecting surface. The reflection grows more blurry as these two surfaces get farther away from each other.

The algorithm for CHGR rendering is as follows. First, we output the distance between the reflecting surface and the point where the reflected ray hits the reflected object. Because we want to limit the size of the render targets, we

```
//World—space  unit  is  1  centimeter
int  distanceLo  =  int(worldSpaceDistance)  %  256;
int  distanceHi  =  int(worldSpaceDistance)  /  256;

packedDistance  =  float2(float(distanceLo)  /  255.0f,
                          float(distanceHi)  /  255.0f);
```

Listing 1.1. Reflection distance packing.

```
float3  reflectedCameraToWorld  =
    reflect(cameraToWorld,  worldSpaceNormal);
float  reflectionVectorLength  =
    max(length(reflectedCameraToWorld),  FP_EPSILON);
float  worldSpaceDistance  =  255.0f  *  (packedDistance.x  +
                         256.0f  *  packedDistance.y)  /
                         reflectionVectorLength;
...
//Reflection  sorting  and  blending
...
float4  screenSpaceReflectedPosition  =
    mul(float4(reflectedPosition,  1),  worldToScreen);
screenSpaceReflectedPosition  /=  screenSpaceReflectedPosition.w;

ReflectionDistance  =  length(screenSpaceReflectedPosition.xy  —
                         screenSpaceFragmentPosition.xy);
```

Listing 1.2. Reflection distance unpacking.

utilize R8G8B8A8 textures for color and depth information. As 8 bits does not
provide enough precision for distance, we pack the distance in two 8-bit channels
during the SSR pass, as shown in Listing 1.1.

The IBR pass unpacks the depth, performs blending, and then converts this
world-space distance into screen-space distance as shown in Listing 1.2. The
reason for this is twofold. First, the screen-space distance fits naturally into the
$[0, 1]$ domain. As we do not need much precision for the blurring itself, we can
re-pack it into a single 8-bit value, ensuring a natural blending. Second, the
screen-space distance provides a better cue for blur ratio: the fragments farther
away from the viewer should be blurred less than closer ones, if both have the
same reflection distance.

The second step is to dilate the distance information. For each region, we
select the maximum distance of all the pixels covered by the area of our blur
kernel. The reason for this is that the distance value can change suddenly from one
pixel to the next (e.g., when a close reflection proxy meets a distant background
pixel). We wish to blur these areas with the maximum blur coefficient from
the corresponding area. This helps avoid sharp silhouettes of otherwise blurry
objects. This problem is very similar to issues encountered with common depth-

of-field rendering algorithms. In order to save on memory bandwidth, we apply a two-pass, separable dilation maximum filter. This provides us with an acceptable approximation.

Finally, we perform the blur with the adjustable separable kernel. In addition to selecting the Gaussian parameters based on the distance value, we also apply the following tricks. First, we ignore the samples with zero specular intensity in order to avoid bleeding at the silhouette of an object. This requires on-the-fly adjustment of the kernel in the shader. Second, we follow the same heuristic as in [Andersson 13], so we blur the image more in the vertical direction than in the horizontal direction, achieving more plausible visual results.

1.2.6 Reflection Blending

As our reflection system consists of several tiers, we need to define how we blend between them. In addition to the distance factor, our SSR pass also outputs a blending factor. This factor depends on the following:

- height (the longer we cast a reflection ray, the less contribution it makes),

- tracing accuracy (depth delta between the ray coordinate and the fetched depth),

- surface tilt (the more the surface normal diverges from vertical, the less SSR should contribute),

- Reflection ray going toward camera or out of screen.

Afterward, IBR is merged on top, outputting a cumulative blending factor. Finally, the cube map is applied. Figure 1.5 shows seamless blending between SSR and IBR.

Figure 1.5. SSR only (left) and SSR blended with IBR (right). [Image courtesy Square Enix Ltd.]

Figure 1.6. Reflection blending without sorting (left) and with sorting (right). [Image courtesy Square Enix Ltd.]

However, this approach causes certain problems in cases when a transparent IBR proxy is in front of the object that could be potentially reflected with SSR. Figure 1.6 shows the issue. To address this problem, instead of simply blending SSR and IBR, we perform layer sorting beforehand. We create a small (three to four entries) array of reflection layers in the IBR shader and inject SSR results into it as the first element. The array is kept sorted when we add every subsequent IBR trace result. Thus, we end up with the closest intersections only.

1.2.7 Bump as a Postprocess

As mentioned above, we assume that the normal is pointing up for SSR and IBR rendering in order to apply acceleration techniques. Furthermore, in order to reduce memory bandwidth, we render reflection at half resolution. Together, this diminishes high-frequency details, which are crucial for reflections, especially on highly bumped surfaces. To alleviate this, we apply a *bump* effect as a postprocess when upscaling the reflection buffer to full resolution.

The main idea is very similar to the generic refraction approach [Sousa 05]. We use the difference between the vertical normal and the per-pixel normal to offset the UV in the rendered reflection texture. To fight reflection leaking, we revert to the original fetch if the new fetch is significantly closer than the old one. Figure 1.7 shows the benefits of applying reflection bump.

1.2.8 Localized Cube Map Reflections

In the SSR, IBR, and cube map reflection strategies, the cube map would ideally only contain the skybox and some far away geometry since the playable environment would be mapped by IBR planes. In this situation, only one cube map would be required. In practice, the IBR planes have many holes and do not connect perfectly to each other. This is a consequence of how our IBR planes are generated using renderable textures.

Figure 1.7. Reflection without bump (left) and with bump as a postprocess (right). [Image courtesy Square Enix Ltd.]

When a reflected ray enters into one of these cracks and hits the skybox, it results in a bright contrast pixel because most *Thief* scenes typically use a skybox that is much brighter than the rest of the environment. To fix this, we used localized cube maps taken along the playable path. Any primitive within reach of a localized cube map would then use it in the main render pass as the reflected environment color.

Technically, the cube map could be mapped and applied in screen space using cube map render volumes, but we chose to simply output the cube map sample into a dedicated render target. This made the cube map material-bound and removed its dependency with the localized cube map mapping system.

The main render pass in *Thief* would output the following data for reflective primitives:

- material lit color (sRGB8),

- environment reflection color + diffuse lighting intensity (sRGB8),

- world normal + reflectivity (RGB8).

After generating the IBR and SSR half-resolution reflection texture, the final color is computed by adding SSR, IBR, and finally the environment reflection color (i.e., cube map color). If the material or platform does not support IBR/SSR, the color would simply be added to the material-lit color and the extra render targets are not needed.

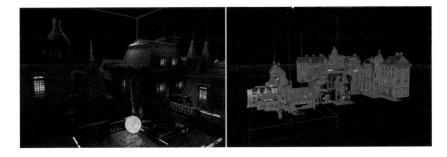

Figure 1.8. Creation of the multiple volumes for covering the whole environment. [Image courtesy Square Enix Ltd.]

Note here that we needed the diffuse lighting intensity to additionally scale down the IBR and cube map color because they were captured with the default lighting setup, which could be very different from the current in-game lighting setup. This scale was not required for the SSR because it is real-time and accurate, while the IBR proxies and cube maps are precomputed offline.

1.2.9 Art Pipeline Implications

For each level in *Thief*, we set a default cube map. This one is used by all the geometry that has reflective materials. This cube map is pretty generic and reflects the most common area of the level.

We then identify the areas where we require a more precise cube map definition. The decision is often based on lighting conditions or the presence of water puddles. For an area that could benefit from a more precise cube map, artists add a localized cube map, which comes with its own scene capture preview sphere. This is shown in the Figure 1.8.

We then built our entire environment using these volumes that enhance the look of the level. After using a build process, we generated all the cube maps for the volumes created. Figure 1.9 shows the additional build process created with the different resources generated.

Thief's reflection systems strongly enhanced the visual quality and next-generation look of the game. It was deeply embedded into the artistic direction of the title. The water puddles, in particular, helped create the unique look our artists wanted for the game. This also contributed to the gameplay of *Thief*. Because light and shadows are so important to our gameplay, the reflective water puddles became an additional challenge the player must manage when trying to stay hidden in the shadows.

For *Thief*, we dedicated a budget of 5 ms for the reflection pipeline. Given the allocated budget and the production stage at which we pushed the data in, we had to make clever choices, sometimes using all available techniques and other times

Figure 1.9. Build process generating the individual cube map captures. [Image courtesy Square Enix Ltd.]

using only one, given the rendering stresses of an environment. For example, certain environment condition might force us to use only one technique. Poor lighting condition could be a good example where you do not want to pay the extra cost of an expensive cube map or IBR planes.

We found that screen-space reflections were very easy for our art team to integrate. For this reason, we used SSR as our base tool for most of our reflection needs. This would then dictate where some of our IBR planes should go; it was a fallback solution when SSR failed.

1.2.10 Results

We came up with a robust and fast reflection system that is ready for the next-generation consoles. Both SSR and IBR steps take around 1–1.5 ms on Playstation 4 (1080p) and Xbox One (900p). However, these are worst case results, i.e., taken on a synthetic scene with an SSR surface taking up the whole screen and 50 IBR proxies visible. For a typical game scene, the numbers are usually lower than that. Reflection postprocessing is fairly expensive (around 2 ms). However, we did not have time to implement it using compute shaders, which could potentially save a lot of bandwidth.

Figure 1.10. Shadow with ordinary filtering (left) and with contact-hardening shadows (right). [Image courtesy Square Enix Ltd.]

Our reflection system does not support rough reflections. Taking into account the emerging interest in physically based rendering solutions, we are looking into removing this limitation. Reprojection techniques also look appealing both for quality enhancement and bandwidth reduction.

1.3 Contact-Hardening Shadows

Contact-hardening shadows (CHSs), similar to percentage-closer soft shadows (PCSSs) [Fernando 05], are a shadow-mapping method to simulate the dynamic shadows from area lights. The achieved effect is a sharper shadow as the shadow caster and the receiver are closer to each other and a blurrier (softer) shadow as the caster and the receiver are farther from each other (see Figure 1.10). The implementation in *Thief* is based on the method from the AMD SDK [Gruen 10].

This method is easy to integrate because it uses the shadow map generated by a single light source and can just replace ordinary shadow filtering. One of the main drawbacks in this technique is the extensive texture fetching, and in *Thief* we implemented an optimized method for Shader Model 5.0 that drastically limits the access to the shadow map. The CHS process is divided into three steps, which are the blocker search, the penumbra estimation, and the filtering.

1.3.1 Blocker Search

The first step consists of computing the average depth of the blockers inside a search region around the shaded point (that we will reference as *average blocker depth*). A kernel grid of $N \times N$ texels centered at the shaded point covers this search region. A blocker is a texel in the shadow map representing a point closer to the light than the currently computed fragment, as shown in Figure 1.11. This average-blocker-depth value will be used in the penumbra estimation.

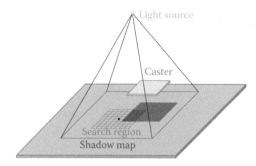

Figure 1.11. Blockers in a 8×8 search grid.

Shader Model 5.0's new intrinsic `GatherRed()` accelerates this step by sampling four values at once. In *Thief*, we decided to use a 8×8 kernel size, which actually performs 16 samples instead of 64 for a Shader Model 4.0 implementation (see Listing 1.4). Increasing the size of the kernel will allow a larger penumbra, since points that are farther from the shaded one can be tested, but it obviously increases the cost as the number of texture fetches grows.

Because the penumbra width (or blurriness) is tightly related to the size of the kernel, which depends on the shadow map resolution and its projection in world space, this leads to inconsistent and variable penumbra width when the shadow map resolution or the shadow frustum's FOV changes for the same light caster/receiver setup. Figure 1.12 shows the issue.

To fix this issue in *Thief*, we extended the CHS by generating mips for the shadow map in a prepass before the CHS application by downsizing it iteratively. Those downsizing operations are accelerated with the use of the `GatherRed()` intrinsic as well. Then, in the CHS step, we dynamically chose the mip that gives

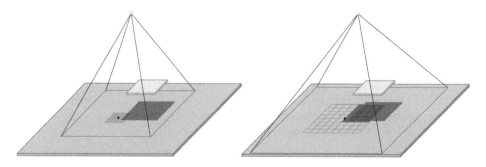

Figure 1.12. For the same 8×8 search grid, a smaller search region due to higher resolution shadow map (left) and a bigger search region due to wider shadow frustum (right).

```
#define KERNEL_SIZE 8
float wantedTexelSizeAt1UnitDist =
   wantedPenumbraWidthAt1UnitDist / KERNEL_SIZE;
float texelSizeAt1UnitDist =
   2*TanFOVSemiAngle/shadowMapResolution;
float MaxShadowMip =
   -log(texelSizeAt1UnitDist/wantedTexelSizeAt1UnitDist)/log(2);
MaxShadowMip = min(float(MIPS_COUNT-1),max(MaxShadowMip,0.0));
// both BlkSearchShadowMipIndex and MaxShadowMip are passed
// to the shader as parameters
int BlkSearchShadowMipIndex = ceil(MaxShadowMip);
```

Listing 1.3. Algorithm for choosing a mip from a user-defined penumbra width, the shadow map resolution, and the FOV angle of the shadow frustum.

Figure 1.13. Shadow-map mips layout. [Image courtesy Square Enix Ltd.]

a kernel size in world space that is closer to a user-defined parameter. Listing 1.3 shows how the mip index is computed from this user-defined parameter, the shadow map resolution, and the FOV angle of the shadow frustum. This process can be done on the CPU and the result is passed to a shader as a parameter.

Unfortunately, the `GatherRed()` intrinsic does not allow mip selection. Therefore, the mips are stored in an atlas, as shown in Figure 1.13, and we offset the texture coordinates to sample the desired mip. This is achieved by applying a simple offset scale to the coordinates in texture space (see Listing 1.4).

In order to save on fragment instructions, the function returns, as an early out, a value of 0.0 (fully shadowed) if the average blocker depth is equal to 1.0 (found a blocker for all samples in the search region) or returns 1.0 (fully lit) if the average blocker depth is equal to 0.0 (no blocker found). Listing 1.4 shows the details of the average-blocker-depth compute.

```
#define KERNEL_SIZE 8
#define BFS2 (KERNEL_SIZE - 1) / 2

float3 blkTc = float3(inTc.xy, inDepth);
// TcBiasScale is a static array holding the offset-scale
in the shadow map for every mips.
float4 blkTcBS = TcBiasScale[BlkSearchShadowMipIndex];
blkTc.xy = blkTcBS.xy + blkTc.xy * blkTcBS.zw;
// g_vShadowMapDims.xy is the shadow map resolution
// g_vShadowMapDims.zw is the shadow map texel size
float2 blkAbsTc = ( g_vShadowMapDims.xy * blkTc.xy );
float2 fc = blkAbsTc - floor( blkAbsTc );
blkTc.xy = blkTc.xy - ( fc * g_vShadowMapDims.zw );
float blkCount = 0; float avgBlockerDepth = 0;
[loop]for( int row = -BFS2; row <= BFS2; row += 2 )
{
  float2 tc = blkTc.xy + float2(-BFS2*g_vShadowMapDims.z,
              row*g_vShadowMapDimensions.w);
  [unroll]for( int col = -BFS2; col <= BFS2; col += 2 )
  {
    float4 depth4 = shadowTex.GatherRed(pointSampler, tc.xy);
    float4 blk4 = (blkTc.zzzz <= depth4)?(0).xxxx:(1).xxxx;
    float4 fcVec = 0;
    if (row == -BFS2)
    {
      if (col == -BFS2)
        fcVec = float4((1.0-fc.y) * (1.0-fc.x),
                       (1.0-fc.y), 1, (1.0-fc.x));
      else if (col == BFS2)
        fcVec = float4((1.0-fc.y), (1.0-fc.y) * fc.x, fc.x, 1);
      else
        fcVec = float4((1.0-fc.y), (1.0-fc.y), 1, 1);
    }
    else if (row == BFS2)
    {
      if (col == -BFS2)
        fcVec = float4((1.0-fc.x), 1, fc.y, (1.0-fc.x) * fc.y);
      else if (col == BFS2)
        fcVec = float4(1, fc.x, fc.x * fc.y, fc.y);
      else
        fcVec = float4(1, 1, fc.y, fc.y);
    }
    else
    {
      if (col == -BFS2)
        fcVec = float4((1.0-fc.x), 1, 1, (1.0-fc.x));
      else if (col == BFS2)
        fcVec = float4(1, fc.x, fc.x, 1);
      else
        fcVec = float4(1,1,1,1);
    }
    blkCount += dot(blk4, fcVec.xyzw);
    avgBlockerDepth += dot(depth4, fcVec.xyzw*blk4);
    tc.x += 2.0*g_vShadowMapDims.z;
  }
}
if( blkCount == 0.0 ) // Early out - fully lit
  return 1.0f;
else if (blkCount == KERNEL_SIZE*KERNEL_SIZE) // Fully shadowed
  return 0.0f;
avgBlockerDepth /= blkCount;
```

Listing 1.4. Average-blocker-depth compute.

$$\text{width}_{\text{penumbra}} = \frac{(\text{depth}_{\text{receiver}} - \texttt{avgBlockerDepth}) \cdot \text{width}_{\text{light}}}{\texttt{avgBlockerDepth}}$$

Algorithm 1.2. Algorithm for computing the penumbra estimation.

1.3.2 Penumbra Estimation

Based on the average-blocker-depth value from the previous step and the user-defined light width, a factor (the penumbra estimation) is computed. Algorithm 1.2 is pretty straightforward and is the same as many other PCSS implementation.

1.3.3 Filtering

The final CHS step consists of applying a dynamic filter to the shadow map to obtain the light attenuation term. In this step, we also take advantage of the shadow-map mips. The main idea is to use higher-resolution mips for the sharp area of the shadow and lower-resolution mips for the blurry area. In order to have a continuous and unnoticeable transition between the different mips, we use two mips selected from the penumbra estimation and perform one filter operation for each mip before linearly blending the two results (see Figure 1.14). Doing so

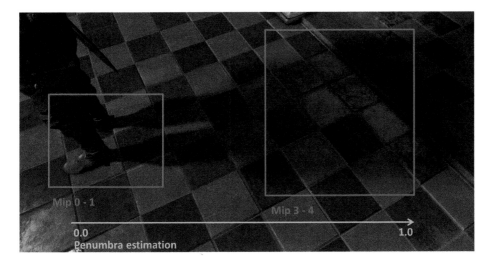

Figure 1.14. Mips used for the filtering, depending on the user-defined region search width and the penumbra estimation. [Image courtesy Square Enix Ltd.]

```
#define KERNEL_SIZE 8
#define FS2 (KERNEL_SIZE − 1) / 2

float Ratio = penumbraWidth;
float clampedTexRatio = max(MaxShadowMip − 0.001, 0.0);
float texRatio = min(MaxShadowMip * Ratio, clampedTexRatio);
float texRatioFc = texRatio − floor(texRatio);
uint textureIndex = min(uint(texRatio), MIPS_COUNT −2);
float4 highMipTcBS = TcBiasScale[textureIndex]; // higher res
float4 lowMipTcBS = TcBiasScale[textureIndex+1]; // lower res
// Pack mips Tc into a float4, xy for high mip, zw for low mip
float4 MipsTc = float4(highMipTcBS.xy + inTc.xy*highMipTcBS.zw,
                       lowMipTcBS.xy + inTc.xy*lowMipTcBS.zw);
float4 MipsAbsTc = (g_vShadowMapDims.xyxy * MipsTc);
float4 MipsFc = MipsAbsTc − floor(MipsAbsTc);
MipsTc = MipsTc − (MipsFc * g_vShadowMapDims.zwzw);
...
//Apply the same dynamic weight matrix to both mips
//using ratio along with the corresponding MipsTc and MipsFc
...
return lerp(highMipTerm, lowMipTerm, texRatioFc);
```

Listing 1.5. Shadow mips filtering and blending.

gives a realistic effect with variable levels of blurriness, using the same kernel size (8×8 in *Thief*) through the whole filtering. The highest mip index possible (which corresponds to a penumbra estimation of 1.0) is the same one used in the blocker search step.

As described above, we need to get the attenuation terms for both selected mips before blending them. A dynamic weight matrix is computed by feeding four matrices into a cubic Bézier function, depending only on the penumbra estimation, and used to filter each mip (not covered here; see [Gruen 10] for the details). Like the previous steps, this is accelerated using the `GatherCmpRed()` intrinsic [Gruen and Story 09]. Listing 1.5 shows how to blend the filtered mips to obtain the final shadow attenuation term.

The number of shadow map accesses for the blocker search is 16 (8×8 kernel with the use of `GatherCmpRed()`) and 2×16 for the filter step (8×8 kernel for each mip with the use of `GatherCmpRed()`), for a total of 48 texture fetches, producing very large penumbras that are independent from the shadow resolution (though the sharp areas still are dependent). A classic implementation in Shader Model 4.0 using a 8×8 kernel with no shadow mipmapping would perform 128 accesses for smaller penumbras, depending on the shadow resolution.

Performance-wise, on an NVIDIA 770 GTX and for a 1080p resolution, the CHS takes 1–2 ms depending on the shadow exposure on the screen and the shadow map resolution. The worst case corresponds to a shadow covering the whole screen.

Figure 1.15. Old-generation *Thief* particles rendering (left) and next-generation version (right). Notice the color variation of the fog due to different lighting. [Image courtesy Square Enix Ltd.]

1.4 Lit Particles

Another addition made for the next-generation version of *Thief* was the support for lit particles. Prior to this, our particle system colors had to be tweaked by hand, and this meant that particles could not react to lighting changes. With lighting support, particles look much more integrated into the environment and they appear to react more dynamically to changes in lighting.

The lighting feature set for particles included static light maps, static shadow maps, projected textures, and up to four dynamic lights. We experimented with having dynamic shadow maps, but it revealed too much about the geometry used to render the visual effects (it made it obvious that we were using camera-aligned sprites). Each sprite would have a well-defined shadow mapped as a plane, while the texture used for the particle is usually meant to fake a cloud-like shape. This issue was not visible with static light maps and shadow maps because they were mapped as 3D textures across the particle bounds. Figure 1.15 shows a comparison between old- and next-generation versions of particle rendering in *Thief*.

1.5 Compute-Shader-Based Postprocessing

One of the major novelties of the DirectX 11 API and the next-generation consoles' hardware is the support of compute shaders. One particular feature of compute shaders is the introduction of local data storage (LDS), a.k.a. thread group shared memory (TGSM). LDS is a cache-like on-chip memory, which is generally faster than VRAM but slower than register memory. One can use LDS to exchange data between shader threads running within the same thread group.

Figure 1.16. Gaussian-based DoF with circular bokeh (top) and DoF with hexagonal bokeh (bottom). [Image courtesy Square Enix Ltd.]

This functionality can be used for numerous applications. One obvious use case is decreasing bandwidth for postprocesses, which computes a convolution of a fairly large radius. In *Thief*, we used this feature for depth-of-field (DoF) computations, as will be described below.

1.5.1 Depth-of-Field Rendering

For our DoF algorithm we used two approaches: Gaussian blur for the round-shaped bokeh and [White and Barré-Brisebois 11] for hexagonal bokeh. Figure 1.16 shows examples of these techniques. Both approaches result in two separable filter passes. DoF is texture-fetch limited, as kernels take a big number of samples to accommodate a large radius bokeh.

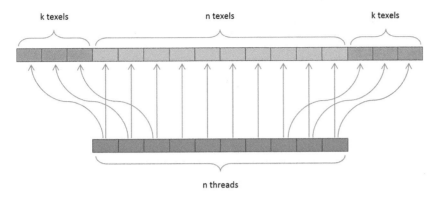

Figure 1.17. Fetching of texels with a filter kernel using local data storage.

1.5.2 Improving Bandwidth by Using Local Data Storage

In order to reduce the texture bandwidth for the DoF pass, we use LDS. The main idea is for a filter of radius k and n threads to prefetch $2k + n$ samples as shown in Figure 1.17. Each of the n threads loads a texel; additionally, every thread close to the thread group boundaries loads another texel. Then, each thread stores the values it loaded into LDS. Finally, to compute the kernel, each thread reads values from LDS instead of DRAM, hence the bandwidth reduction.

Initially, we used the code from Listing 1.6 to load and store from LDS. However, this resulted in even worse performance than not using LDS at all. The reason for this is a four-way LDS memory bank conflict, which we introduced. As bank size on the majority of the video cards is 32-bits wide, each thread will make a strided access with $stride = 4$. To fix that, we needed to de-vectorize our code, as shown in Listing 1.7.

1.5.3 Results

To understand the LDS win, we tested different implementations of the DoF kernel filters. For a DoF pass using a kernel with $radius = 15$ for a FP16 render target, we got 0.15 ms without LDS, 0.26 with vectorized LDS structure, and 0.1 ms for de-vectorized LDS on AMD HD7970. Both next-generation consoles have shown a speedup with a similar factor. In contrast, using LDS on NVIDIA GPUs (GeForce 660 GTX) resulted in no speedup at all in the best case. As a result, on AMD GPUs (which include next-generation consoles), using compute shaders with LDS can result in a significant (33%) speedup if low-level performance considerations (e.g., banked memory) are taken into account.

```
groupshared float4 fCache[NR_THREADS + 2 * KERNEL_RADIUS];

Texture2D inputTexture : register(t0);
RWTexture2D<float4> outputTexture : register(u0);

[numthreads(NR_THREADS, 1, 1)]
void main(uint3 groupThreadID : SV_GroupThreadID,
        uint3 dispatchThreadID : SV_DispatchThreadID)
{
    //Read texture to LDS
    int counter = 0;
    for (int t = groupThreadID.x;
            t < NR_THREADS + 2 * KERNEL_RADIUS;
            t += NR_THREADS, counter += NR_THREADS)
    {
        int x = clamp(
            dispatchThreadID.x + counter - KERNEL_RADIUS,
            0, inputTexture.Length.x - 1);
        fCache[t] = inputTexture[int2(x, dispatchThreadID.y)];
    }
    GroupMemoryBarrierWithGroupSync();

    ...
    //Do the actual blur
    ...

    outputTexture[dispatchThreadID.xy] = vOutColor;
}
```

Listing 1.6. Initial kernel implementation. Notice a single LDS allocation.

1.6 Conclusion

In this chapter, we gave a comprehensive walkthrough for the rendering techniques we implemented for the next-generation versions of *Thief*. We presented our reflection system, the contact-hardening shadow algorithm, particles lighting approach, and compute shader postprocesses. Most of these techniques were integrated during the later stages of *Thief* production, therefore they were used less extensively in the game than we wished. However, we hope that this postmortem will help game developers to start using the techniques, which were not practical on the previous console generation.

1.7 Acknowledgments

We would like to thank Robbert-Jan Brems, David Gallardo, Nicolas Longchamps, Francis Maheux, and the entire *Thief* team.

```
groupshared float fCacheR[NR_THREADS + 2 * KERNEL_RADIUS];
groupshared float fCacheG[NR_THREADS + 2 * KERNEL_RADIUS];
groupshared float fCacheB[NR_THREADS + 2 * KERNEL_RADIUS];
groupshared float fCacheA[NR_THREADS + 2 * KERNEL_RADIUS];

Texture2D inputTexture : register(t0);
RWTexture2D<float4> outputTexture : register(u0);

[numthreads(NR_THREADS, 1, 1)]
void main(uint3 groupThreadID : SV_GroupThreadID,
        uint3 dispatchThreadID : SV_DispatchThreadID)
{
    //Read texture to LDS
    int counter = 0;
    for (int t = groupThreadID.x;
            t < NR_THREADS + 2 * KERNEL_RADIUS;
            t += NR_THREADS, counter += NR_THREADS)
    {
        int x = clamp(
            dispatchThreadID.x + counter - KERNEL_RADIUS,
            0, inputTexture.Length.x - 1);
        float4 tex = inputTexture[int2(x, dispatchThreadID.y)];
        fCacheR[t] = tex.r;
        fCacheG[t] = tex.g;
        fCacheB[t] = tex.b;
        fCacheA[t] = tex.a;
    }
    GroupMemoryBarrierWithGroupSync();

    ...
    //Do the actual blur
    ...

    outputTexture[dispatchThreadID.xy] = vOutColor;
}
```

Listing 1.7. Final kernel implementation. Notice that we make a separate LDS allocation for each channel.

Bibliography

[Andersson 13] Zap Andersson. "Everything You Always Wanted to Know About mia_material." Presented in Physically Based Shading in Theory and Practice, SIGGRAPH Course, Anaheim, CA, July 21–25, 2013.

[Andreev 13] Dmitry Andreev. "Rendering Tricks in Dead Space 3." Game Developers Conference course, San Francisco, CA, March 25–29, 2013.

[Fernando 05] Randima Fernando. "Percentage-Closer Soft Shadows." In *ACM SIGGRAPH 2005 Sketches*, p. article 35. New York: ACM, 2005.

[Gruen and Story 09] Holger Gruen and Jon Story. "Taking Advantage of Direct3D 10.1 Features to Accelerate Performance and Enhance Quality." Presented at AMD sponsored session, Eurographics, Munich, Germany, March 30–April 3, 2009.

[Gruen 10] Holger Gruen. "Contact Hardening Shadows 11." AMD Radeon SDK, http://developer.amd.com/tools-and-sdks/graphics-development/amd-radeon-sdk/archive/, 2010.

[Kasyan et al. 11] Nick Kasyan, Nicolas Schulz, and Tiago Sousa. "Secrets of CryENGINE 3 Graphics Technology." SIGGRAPH course, Vancouver, Canada, August 8, 2011.

[Lagarde and Zanuttini 13] Sébastien Lagarde and Antoine Zanuttini. "Practical Planar Reflections Using Cubemaps and Image Proxies." In *GPU Pro 4: Advanced Rendering Techniques*, edited by Wolfgang Engel, pp. 51–68. Boca Raton, FL: CRC Press, 2013.

[Lengyel 11] Eric Lengyel. *Mathematics for 3D Game Programming and Computer Graphics*, Third edition. Boston: Cengage Learning PTR, 2011.

[NVIDIA Corporation 99] NVIDIA Corporation. "Cube Map OpenGL Tutorial." http://www.nvidia.com/object/cube_map_ogl_tutorial.html, 1999.

[Sousa 05] Tiago Sousa. "Generic Refraction Simulation." In *GPU Gems 2*, edited by Matt Farr, pp. 295–305. Reading, MA: Addison-Wesley Professional, 2005.

[Uludag 14] Yasin Uludag. "Hi-Z Screen-Space Cone-Traced Reflections." In *GPU Pro 5: Advanced Rendering Techniques*, edited by Wolfgang Engel, pp. 149–192. Boca Raton, FL: CRC Press, 2014.

[White and Barré-Brisebois 11] John White and Colin Barré-Brisebois. "More Performance! Five Rendering Ideas from *Battlefield 3* and *Need For Speed: The Run*." Presented in Advances in Real-Time Rendering in Games, SIGGRAPH Course, Vancouver, August 7–11, 2011.

[Wright 11] Daniel Wright. "Image Based Reflections." http://udn.epicgames.com/Three/ImageBasedReflections.html, 2011.

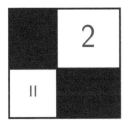

2

II

Grass Rendering and Simulation with LOD
Dongsoo Han and Hongwei Li

2.1 Introduction

Grass rendering and simulation are challenging topics for video games because grass can cover large open areas and require heavy computation for simulation. As an extension of our previous hair technology, TressFX [Tre 13], we chose grass because it has unique challenges. (See Figure 2.1.) Our initial plan was to support rendering many individual grass blades covering a wide terrain and simulating their interactions using rigid bodies and wind.

To satisfy our requirements, we developed an efficient and scalable level-of-detail (LOD) system for grass using DirectX 11. In addition to LOD, a master-and-slave system reduces simulation computation dramatically but still preserves the quality of the simulation.

Figure 2.1. Grass rendering and simulation with balls.

Figure 2.2. Five grass blade types generated by an in-house tool.

2.2   Render Grass Blades

To make the grass look natural, it is vital to acquire a natural shape for the grass blades. We first adopted the method described in [Bouatouch et al. 06], where they generate grass blade in a procedural manner. For each grass blade, its stem is defined as a parabolic curve formed by tracking the motion of a point, shooting from the root vertex, with a random initial speed and angle. This method is simple yet effective, but cannot provide a rich variance in the grass blade geometric appearance as they are always parabolic curves, tall or low, curved or straight. It is difficult to generate complex and natural-looking grass blades using this approach since the blades are poorly described by a quadratic curve alone.

We find instancing can tackle this variance problem very well. First, we generate a few grass blade types, each of which has a fixed number of knots. In our application, the number of knots is 16, which balances the efficiency of simulation and the smoothness of blade shape. Also, we have experimented with different numbers of types and find five is good enough to create a grass lawn with rich variance. More types do not hurt the performance but do not increase the visual quality much either. Figure 2.2 shows five blade types that we created using an in-house tool.

To further increase the variance, when we instantiate these blade types and plant them in the scene (we call it the growing process), we randomize orientations, lengths, widths, and textures of instantiated blades. For example, for the fifth blade type, its length can vary between 0.1 m and 0.15 m. When it is instantiated, its length will be set to a number between 0.1 m and 0.15 m with regards to the normal distribution. Each knot on the blade is linearly scaled to this new length. The range of length for each blade type is hard coded. The variance is further enhanced by distributing blade types unevenly. Some of them will be used more often than others. The probability of instantiating one particular blade type is tweaked for the best look in the final scene.

The grass blade created by hand or tool only describes the blade stem. The stem is expanded to a blade in the runtime so that we can set the width of each blade separately. Each line segment in the stem becomes a quad, i.e., two triangles. There are 16 knots and thus there are 15 quads or 30 triangles. The

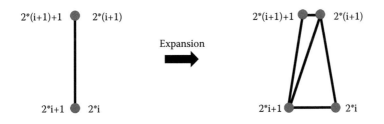

Figure 2.3. Expand the stem to grass blade in vertex shader. The two overlapping vertices from two triangles are dragged to opposite positions in the vertex shader.

expansion direction follows the binormal of the grass blade, and the expansion width is chosen by the user. Moreover, we reduce the expansion width gradually from bottom knots to top in order to make a sharp blade tip. This geometry expansion was firstly implemented in a geometry shader, but the performance was not satisfying. We then adopted the approach presented in TressFX, where they do the geometry expansion in the vertex shader by expanding two degraded triangles to normal, nondegenerate triangles. Figure 2.3 illustrates the process of expanding the degenerate triangles. We also modified our in-house blade modeling tool so that its output became a triangle strip: each knot in the stem is duplicated into two vertices at the same coordinate as the knot, and one line segment becomes two triangles. At runtime, we upgrade triangles by translating two overlapping vertices at the knot position in opposite directions determined by the modulo 2 result of the vertex ID, e.g., `SV_VertexID`.

Regarding the rendering, we do not have much freedom in choosing a shading model for the grass blade for there are thousands of blades to be rendered in one frame. It must be a lightweight shading model that still can create a promising, natural appearance for the grass blade. Under this constraint, we adopt the conventional Phong model and replace its ambient component with Hemispherical Ambient Light [Wilhelmsen 09]. Hemispherical ambient light is a good approximation of the true ambient color of grass in lieu of the more precise ambient occlusion and color, which can be very expensive to generate. It is computed as the sum of sky light and earth light as shown in following equation:

$$ambient = skylight \times ratio + earthlight \times (1 - ratio),$$

where $ratio$ is defined by the dot product between the hemisphere's "up" direction and the vertex normal.

We also investigated screen-space translucency [Jimenez and Gutierrez 10], but the increase in the visual quality is minor, and it added an extra 50 shader instructions, so we did not use it.

Besides the lighting model, a grass blade has both a front and a back face, and thus we cannot disable face culling on the GPU. We rely on DirectX's semantic

`SV_IsFrontFace` to tell us whether the current pixel is now facing forward or backward. If it is the back face, we invert the normal and use the back surface texture in the shading computation.

2.3   Simulation

Like hair simulation in TressFX, each grass blade is represented as vertices and edges. We usually use 16 vertices for each blade and 64 for the thread group size for compute shaders, but it is possible to change the thread group size to 32 or 128.

For hair simulation in TressFX, three constraints (edge length, global shape, and local shape) are applied after integrating gravity. The TressFX hair simulation includes a "head" transform. This is required in a hair simulation since the character's head can change its position and orientation, but we do not require this transform for grass. We can also skip applying the global shape constraint because grass gets much less force due to the absence of head movement. For the edge length constraint and the local shape constraint, two to three iterations are usually good enough.

The last step of simulation before going to LOD is to run a kernel to prevent grass blades from going under the ground. This can be done simply by moving each vertex position above the position of the blade root vertex position.

2.3.1   Master-and-Slave System

Master blades are the grass blades that are actively simulated. During the process of growing blades procedurally, we arrange master blade vertex positions followed by slave vertex positions. In our demo, we typically use a 1:4 ratio of master to slave blades, but that ratio can be easily changed during the growing process.

After simulating master blades, we copy the master vertex positions to their slaves. The important part of this process is that we should add perturbations so that slave blades are not exactly showing the same motion of their master. The perturbations become larger along the vertices toward the tip so that blades can be separated wider between tips and avoid parallel patterns. It is also possible to increase or decrease the perturbations based on the master blade's velocity so that if the master moves faster, the slaves will be farther behind.

2.3.2   Distance-Based Sorting

For LOD, two new read/write buffers (`QuantizedLODDistance` and `LODSortedStrand Index`) were added to TressFX. `QuantizedLODDistance` is to store the distances from the camera to each blade. `LODSortedStrandIndex` is to store the blade index for `QuantizedLODDistance`. Basically, these two buffers make key and value pairs for sorting.

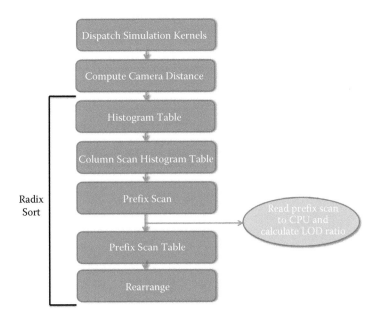

Figure 2.4. Kernel execution flow chart of radix sort.

The sorting algorithm we choose must run on the GPU efficiently and support key and value pairs. Also, we need to count how many keys are less than a given distance threshold so that we can determine the work item size for dispatch. Choosing radix sort could give us an extra benefit that, if we quantize the distance value in 8 bits, we need only one pass. Normally, radix sort needs four passes to sort 32-bit keys with an 8-bit radix; see Figure 2.4.

After simulating master blades and updating slave vertices, `ComputeCamera Distance` in Listing 2.1 calculates the distance from the camera position to each blade. Also, frustum culling is performed here, and a negative distance value will be assigned if the blade is outside of the camera's frustum. We quantize the distance values to 8 bits using the maximum distance given as user input.

Listings 2.2, 2.3, and 2.4 show the full code of radix sort. The inputs of radix sort are `QuantizedLODDistance` and `LODSortedStrandIndex`. `PrefixScan` performs a prefix scan of all the elements of `QuantizedLODDistance`. Before running the next kernels of radix sort, we read the prefix scan data on the CPU and compute the LOD ratio, which is a ratio of the number of valid blades to the number of total blades. We use this LOD ratio to compute the thread group size for simulation during the next frame.

Listing 2.5 shows how we can use a prefix scan to get the LOD ratio. We first calculate the quantized distance threshold and simply read the value of the prefix-scan array using the quantized distance threshold as an index; the prefix scan stores counts of values.

```
#define THREAD_GROUP_SIZE 64

RWStructuredBuffer<uint> QuantizedLODDistance : register(u6);
RWStructuredBuffer<uint> LODSortedStrandIndex : register(u7);

// cameraPos, cameraDir, and maxDist are given through
// const buffer.

[numthreads(THREAD_GROUP_SIZE, 1, 1)]
void ComputeCameraDistance(uint GIndex : SV_GroupIndex,
                uint3 GId : SV_GroupID,
                uint3 DTid : SV_DispatchThreadID)
{
  uint globalBladedIndex, globalRootVertexIndex;

  // Calculate indices above here.

  float4 pos = g_HairVertexPositions[globalRootVertexIndex+1];
  float dist = dot((pos.xyz - cameraPos.xyz), cameraDir.xyz);

  // Perform frustum culling and assign negative distance
  // if this blade is out of frustum here.

  // Quantize distance into 8 bits (0 ~ 2^8-1)
  // so that radix sort can sort it in one pass.
  if ( dist < 0 || dist > maxDist )
    dist = maxDist;

  uint quantizedDist = (uint)((dist/maxDist) * 255.f);

  QuantizedLODDistance[globalBladedIndex] = quantizedDist;
  LODSortedStrandIndex[globalBladedIndex] = globalBladedIndex;
}
```

Listing 2.1. Compute camera distance kernel.

```
#define RADIX 8                        // 8 bit
#define RADICES (1 << RADIX)      // 256 or 0x100
#define RADIX_MASK (RADICES - 1)  // 255 or 0xFF
#define THREAD_GROUP_SIZE RADICES

cbuffer CBRadixSort : register( b0 )
{
  int numElement;
  int bits;
  float dummy[2];
}

// UAVs
RWStructuredBuffer<uint> QuantizedLODDistance : register(u0);
RWStructuredBuffer<uint> histogramTable : register(u1);
RWStructuredBuffer<uint> particiallySortedData : register(u2);
RWStructuredBuffer<uint> prefixScan : register(u3);
RWStructuredBuffer<uint> LODSortedStrandIndex : register(u4);
RWStructuredBuffer<uint> particiallySortedValue : register(u5);

groupshared uint sharedMem[RADICES];
groupshared uint sharedMemPrefixScan[RADICES];
```

```
uint pow2(uint a)
{
  return ( ((uint)1) << a);
}

// Each thread (work item) works on one element.
[numthreads(THREAD_GROUP_SIZE, 1, 1)]
void HistogramTable(uint GIndex : SV_GroupIndex,
                    uint3 GId : SV_GroupID,
                    uint3 DTid : SV_DispatchThreadID)
{
  uint localId = GIndex;
  uint groupId = GId.x;
  uint groupSize = RADICES;
  uint globalId = groupSize * groupId + localId;

  // Initialize shared memory.
  sharedMem[localId] = 0;
  GroupMemoryBarrierWithGroupSync();

  particiallySortedData[globalId]
                          = QuantizedLODDistance[globalId];
  particiallySortedValue[globalId]
                          = LODSortedStrandIndex[globalId];

  uint value = particiallySortedData[globalId];
  value = (value >> bits) & RADIX_MASK;
  InterlockedAdd(sharedMem[value], 1);
    GroupMemoryBarrierWithGroupSync();

  uint index = RADICES * groupId + localId;
  histogramTable[index] = sharedMem[localId];
}
```

Listing 2.2. Constant buffer, UAVs, and histogram table kernels in radix sort.

```
// There is only one thread group and the each thread
// (work item) works on each column on histogram table.
[numthreads(THREAD_GROUP_SIZE, 1, 1)]
void ColumnScanHistogramTable(uint GIndex : SV_GroupIndex,
            uint3 GId : SV_GroupID,
            uint3 DTid : SV_DispatchThreadID)
{
  uint localId = GIndex;
  uint numHistograms = numElement / THREAD_GROUP_SIZE;
  uint sum = 0;

  for ( uint i = 0; i < numHistograms; i++ )
  {
    sum += histogramTable[RADICES * i + localId];
    histogramTable[RADICES * i + localId] = sum;
  }
}

// There is only one thread group.
[numthreads(THREAD_GROUP_SIZE, 1, 1)]
void PrefixScan(uint GIndex : SV_GroupIndex,
            uint3 GId : SV_GroupID,
```

```
                       uint3 DTid : SV_DispatchThreadID )
{
  uint localId = GIndex;

  uint numHistograms = numElement / THREAD_GROUP_SIZE;
  sharedMemPrefixScan[localId]
     = histogramTable[RADICES * (numHistograms - 1) + localId];
  sharedMem[localId] = sharedMemPrefixScan[localId];
  GroupMemoryBarrierWithGroupSync();

  uint iter = (uint)(log2(256));
  uint k = localId;

  for ( uint i = 0; i < iter; i++ )
  {
    if ( k >= pow2(i) )
      sharedMem[k] = sharedMemPrefixScan[k]
                     + sharedMemPrefixScan[k-pow2(i)];

    GroupMemoryBarrierWithGroupSync();
    sharedMemPrefixScan[k] = sharedMem[k];
    GroupMemoryBarrierWithGroupSync();
  }

  if ( localId > 0 )
    prefixScan[localId] = sharedMemPrefixScan[localId-1];
  else
    prefixScan[localId] = 0;
}
```

Listing 2.3. Column scan histogram table and prefix scan kernels in radix sort.

```
// Each thread (work item) works on one element.
[numthreads(THREAD_GROUP_SIZE, 1, 1)]
void PrefixScanTable(uint GIndex : SV_GroupIndex,
                uint3 GId : SV_GroupID,
                uint3 DTid : SV_DispatchThreadID )
{
  uint localId = GIndex;
  uint groupId = GId.x;

  uint index = RADICES * groupId + localId;
  sharedMem[localId] = histogramTable[index];
  GroupMemoryBarrierWithGroupSync();

  sharedMem[localId] += prefixScan[localId];
  histogramTable[index] = sharedMem[localId];
}

// One thread (work item) works on one element.
[numthreads(THREAD_GROUP_SIZE, 1, 1)]
void Rearrange(uint GIndex : SV_GroupIndex,
                uint3 GId : SV_GroupID,
                uint3 DTid : SV_DispatchThreadID )
{
  uint localId = GIndex;
  uint groupId = GId.x;

  if ( localId == 0 )
```

```
{
  for ( int i = 0; i < RADICES; i++ )
  {
    uint element = particiallySortedData [ groupId
                                  * RADICES + i ];
    uint value = ( element >> bits ) & RADIX_MASK ;
    uint index ;

    if ( groupId == 0 )
    {
      index = prefixScan [ value ];
      prefixScan [ value ]++;
    }
    else
    {
      index = histogramTable [ RADICES * ( groupId −1) + value ];
      histogramTable [ RADICES * ( groupId −1) + value ]++;
    }

    QuantizedLODDistance [ index ] =
                particiallySortedData [ groupId * RADICES + i ];
    LODSortedStrandIndex [ index ] =
                particiallySortedValue [ groupId * RADICES + i ];
  }
}
}
```

Listing 2.4. Prefix scan table and rearrange kernels in radix sort.

```
// distThresholdLOD is a distance threshold for LOD
// and maxDistanceLOD is the maximum distance for quantization.
unsigned int quantizedDistThresholdLod =
    ( unsigned int )(( distThresholdLOD / maxDistanceLOD ) * 255.f );

int count = prefixScan [ quantizedDistThresholdLod +1 ];
LODRatio = ( float ) count / ( float ) numMasterBlades ;
```

Listing 2.5. Calulating the LOD ratio.

2.3.3 Wind

There are two kinds of wind motions: local ambient and global tidal motions. Local ambient motion is small scale and is independent of neighboring blades. In TressFX, wind was applied to each vertex by calculating the force from the wind and edge vectors. In grass, we simplified this by grabbing the tip vertex and moving it along the wind vector. This simple method works as well as the force-based approach. The amount of displacement is controlled by the magnitude of the wind. To prevent a visible directional pattern, perturbations are added into the wind directions and magnitudes.

Global tidal motion is also simple. This is wavy motion and neighbor blades should work together. In our grass, we simply sweep the grass field with large cylindrical bars and the collision handling system generates the nice wave motion.

2.4   Conclusion

With 32,768 master blades and 131,072 slave blades, simulating an entire grass field takes around 2.3 ms without LODs. Because radix sort takes around 0.3 ms, we see that simulation time can easily drop by more than 50% with LODs using reasonable distance thresholds.

In our test, we applied only one distance threshold. However, it is also possible to use multiple distance thresholds. This would allow us to smoothly change between LOD regions and reduce popping problems during camera movement.

Bibliography

[Bouatouch et al. 06] Kadi Bouatouch, Kévin Boulanger, and Sumanta Pattanaik. "Rendering Grass in Real Time with Dynamic Light Sources." Rapport de recherche RR-5960, INRIA, 2006.

[Jimenez and Gutierrez 10] Jorge Jimenez and Diego Gutierrez. "Screen-Space Subsurface Scattering." In *GPU Pro: Advanced Rendering Techniques*, edited by Wolfgang Engel, pp. 335–351. Natick, MA: A K Peters, Ltd., 2010.

[Tre 13] "TressFX 2.0." http://developer.amd.com/tools-and-sdks/graphics -development/amd-radeon-sdk/, accessed November 13, 2013.

[Wilhelmsen 09] Petri Wilhelmsen. "Hemispheric Ambient Light." http:// digitalerr0r.wordpress.com/2009/05/09/xna-shader-programming-tutorial -19-hemispheric-ambient-light/, accessed May 9, 2009.

Hybrid Reconstruction Antialiasing
Michał Drobot

3.1 Introduction

In this article, we present the antialiasing (AA) solution used in the Xbox One and Playstation 4 versions of *Far Cry 4*, developed by Ubisoft Montreal: hybrid reconstruction antialiasing (HRAA). We present a novel framework that utilizes multiple approaches to mitigate aliasing issues with a tight performance budget in mind.

The Xbox One, Playstation 4, and most AMD graphics cards based on the GCN architecture share a similar subset of rasterizer and data interpolation features. We propose several new algorithms, or modern implementations of known ones, making use of the aforementioned hardware features. Each solution is tackling a single aliasing issue: efficient spatial super-sampling, high-quality edge antialiasing, and temporal stability. All are based around the principle of data reconstruction. We discuss each one separately, identifying potential problems, benefits, and performance considerations. Finally, we present a combined solution used in an actual production environment. The framework we demonstrate was fully integrated into the Dunia engine's deferred renderer. Our goal was to render a temporarily stable image, with quality surpassing 4× rotated-grid super-sampling, at a cost of 1 ms at a resolution of 1080p on the Xbox One and Playstation 4 (see Figure 3.1).

3.2 Overview

Antialiasing is a crucial element in high-quality rendering. We can divide most aliasing artifacts in rasterization-based rendering into two main categories: temporal and spatial. Temporal artifacts occur as flickering under motion when details fail to get properly rendered due to missing the rasterization grid on certain

Figure 3.1. The crops on the right show no AA (top), SMAA (middle), and the presented HRAA (bottom) results. Only HRAA is capable of reconstructing additional details while providing high-quality antialiasing.

frames. Spatial artifacts result from signal under-sampling when dealing with a single, static image. Details that we try to render are just too fine to be properly resolved at the desired resolution, which mostly manifests itself as jagged edges.

Both sources of aliasing are directly connected with errors of signal under-sampling and occur together. However, there are multiple approaches targeting different aliasing artifacts that vary in both performance and quality. We can divide these solutions into analytical, temporal, and super-sampling–based approaches.

In this article, we present a novel algorithm that builds upon all these approaches. By exploring the new hardware capabilities of modern GPUs (we will base our findings on AMD's GCN architecture), we optimize each approach and provide a robust framework that shares the benefits of each algorithm while minimizing their shortcomings.

3.3 Related Work

A typical antialiasing solution used in offline rendering is to super-sample (SSAA) the image; render at a higher resolution and then perform a resolve step, which is a down-sampling filter into the desired final resolution [Burley 07]. If enough samples are used, then this type of antialiasing tackles all the aliasing problems mentioned earlier. Unfortunately, it requires effectively rendering the image multiple times and is of limited usefulness for real-time rendering.

An optimized version of super-sampling is provided by graphics hardware in the form of multi-sampled antialiasing (MSAA) [Kirkland et al. 99]. Instead of shading all pixels at higher resolution, only samples along triangle edges are rasterized multiple times (but only shaded once), which is followed by an optimized resolve. MSAA proves to be a valid solution to spatial aliasing issues, but is strictly limited to triangle edges. All samples need to be stored in an additional framebuffer until they are resolved, therefore making this method very expensive in terms of memory consumption. As a result, not many games use it as the main antialiasing solution on performance-limited platforms.

It is worth noting that the number of gradient steps on antialiased edges is strictly correlated to the number of samples that MSAA or SSAA uses (i.e., 4×MSAA can provide a maximum of five gradients depending on the sampling pattern and edge orientation).

On the previous generation of consoles (Xbox 360 and Playstation 3), we observed a rise in popularity of image-based, postprocessing, morphological antialiasing solutions such as FXAA [Lottes 09], MLAA [Reshetov 09], and SMAA [Jimenez et al. 11]. These algorithms provided excellent results, with perceptual quality comparable to extremely high levels of MSAA rendering at a fraction of the cost of MSAA. A typical morphological filter derives visually perceivable edges from the current image and performs edge re-vectorization. Unfortunately the result still relies only on the final rasterized image data, which can suffer from temporal and spatial aliasing. In practice, static images that are processed with these algorithms look much better than what the hardware-based MSAA can achieve. Unfortunately the quality degrades dramatically under motion, where spatial and temporal under-sampling result in "wobbly" edges and temporal flicker of high-contrast details.

It is clear that morphological methods alone will not achieve the high-quality spatio-temporal results of super-sampling. This sparked research in two different directions: analytical- and temporal-based antialiasing. Several researchers experimented with postprocessing methods, augmented by additional information, derived from actual triangle-edge equation. Probably the most well known is GBAA [Persson 11], which calculates per-pixel signed distance to the closest triangle edge. This information is stored in an additional buffer and is used later during a postprocessing pass to effectively rerasterize triangle edge-pixel intersections analytically. This method can provide a high level of quality and perfect temporal stability of triangle edges. Unfortunately, due to its use of a geometry shader pass to gather triangle information, it exhibits poor performance and thus never gained widespread adoption. It is also hindered by multiple other issues that we will discuss in-depth in Section 3.5.

Another approach gaining popularity is based on temporal algorithms that try to perform filtering using previously rendered frames utilizing image temporal coherency [Nehab et al. 07]. This effectively allows multi-sampled algorithms to be amortized over time [Yang et al. 09]. Several titles use temporal resolves to augment SSAO [Bavoil and Andersson 12, Drobot 11] or to stabilize the final image in motion [Sousa 13]. Some engines experiment with temporal super-sampling [Malan 12]; however, due to a lack of robust sample rejection methods, those approaches are rather conservative, i.e., accumulating only two frames using a limited subset of visible pixels [Sousa 11].

Recently *Killzone: Shadow Fall* used a robust temporal up-sampling method, effectively rendering images with $2\times$ super-sampling. It also used previously reconstructed frames to stabilize images in motion in order to avoid image flickering [Valient 14].

Several researchers have tried to combine the benefits of hardware-based MSAA, temporal sampling and morphological filtering into one combined solution. This resulted in $4\times$SMAA [Jimenez et al. 12], which combines the quality of SMAA edge gradients with the temporal stability of $2\times$MSAA and $2\times$temporal super-sampling. Unfortunately, not many console titles can afford this due to the use of expensive $2\times$MSAA.

One more research direction has been toward optimizing sampling patterns for multi-sampled approaches [Akenine-Möller 03]. Unfortunately, this approach didn't get much traction in the real-time rendering field due to a lack of hardware and software support for custom sampling patterns. Only a few predefined sampling patterns are supported in hardware-based MSAA modes.

Another hardware-based solution involves augmenting the standard MSAA pipeline with coverage samples that can be evaluated with minimal performance and memory overhead. This solution was, up to this point, a part of the fixed GPU pipeline in the form of EQAA [AMD 11] and CSAA [Young 06].

3.4 Hybrid Antialiasing Overview

Our antialiasing solution can be divided into several components. Each one can stand on its own and can be freely mixed with any other approach.

The aim of each component is to tackle a different source of aliasing, so each algorithm can be used to its best effect in limited use-case scenarios.

Our framework is built around the following components:

- temporally stable edge antialiasing,

- temporal super-sampling,

- temporal antialiasing.

3.5 Temporally Stable Edge Antialiasing

The aim of this component is to provide perceptually plausible gradients, for geometric edges, that remain stable under motion. We do not need to worry about pixel discontinuities that come from texture data or lighting, as that source of aliasing will be taken care of by a different framework component.

In Section 3.3, we briefly discussed potential algorithms that would suit our needs for high-quality edge rendering: morphological and analytical. However, only the latter can provide temporally stable antialiasing. Unfortunately, all purely analytical methods exhibit problems, including performance issues.

We would like to propose a new implementation based on AMD's GCN architecture that makes analytical edge antialiasing virtually free. In Section 3.5.1, we propose several extensions as well as real production issues connected with the method itself. Section 3.5.2 offers a brief introduction to EQAA's inner workings. It also introduces a new algorithm—coverage reconstruction antialiasing—that uses coverage samples from hardware-based EQAA to analytically estimate the edge orientation as well as triangle spatial coverage, building upon previous analytical-only algorithms.

3.5.1 Analytical Edge Antialiasing (AEAA)

The original GBAA algorithm relies on a geometry shader to pass down geometry information to the pixel shader. Interpolators are used to store the distance to the edge in the major direction. Then, the pixel shader selects the closest signed distance to the currently rasterized pixel and outputs it into an additional offscreen buffer. Distance data needs to contain the major axis and the actual signed distance value in range $[-1, 1]$, where 0 is considered to be at the rasterized pixel center. Later, a fullscreen postprocessing pass searches for each pixel's immediate neighbor's closest edges. After an edge crossing the pixel is found, we use its orientation and distance to blend the two nearest pixels accordingly (see Figure 3.2).

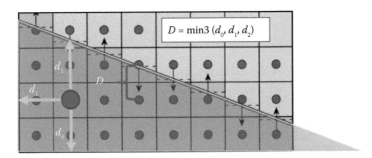

Figure 3.2. In analytical distance-to-edge techniques, every triangle writes out the distance to the closest edge used to antialias pixels in a postprocessing pass.

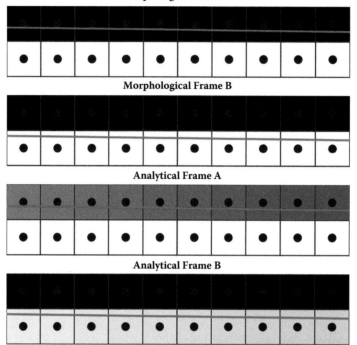

Figure 3.3. Antialiased edge changes in motion when using analytical data. Note that every morphological solution will fail as no gradient change will be detected due to the same results of rasterization. This gets more problematic with shorter feature search distance.

Such methods provide temporally stable edge antialiasing, as the blend factor relies on continuous triangle information rather than discrete rasterization results (see Figure 3.3).

Gradient length is limited only by storage. In practice, it is enough to store additional data in 8 bits: 1 bit for the major axis and 7 bits for signed distance, providing 64 effective gradient steps.

This algorithm also deals efficiently with alpha-tested silhouettes, if a meaningful distance to an edge can be estimated. This proves to be relatively easy with nonbinary alpha channels. Alpha test derivatives can be used to estimate the distance to a cutout edge. A better solution would be to use signed distance fields for alpha testing and directly output the real distance to the edge.

Both methods are fast and easy to implement in practice. It is worth noting that the final distance to the edge should be the minimum of the geometric distance to the triangle edge and the edge derived from the alpha channel.

We implemented GBAA and optimized it to take advantage of the benefits of the new hardware features found in modern GPUs. AMD's GCN architecture allows pixel shaders to sample vertex data from the triangle descriptors used to rasterize the current pixel. This means that we no longer need the expensive geometry-shader stage to access vertex data in order to calculate the distance to the edge as shown by [Drobot 14].

The snippet in Listing 3.1 shows the improved GBAA algorithm with offsets directly evaluated in the pixel shader. The final postprocess resolve step remains unchanged from the original algorithm.

```
// Calculate closest axis distance between point X
// and line AB. Check against known distance and direction
float ComputeAxisClosestDist(float2 inX,
float2 inA,
float2 inB,
inout uint      ioMajorDir,
inout float     ioAxisDist)
{
float2 AB          = normalize(inB - inA);
float2 normalAB = float2(-AB.y, AB.x);
float dist         = dot(inA, normalAB) - dot(inX, normalAB);
bool majorDir      = (abs(normalAB.x) > abs(normalAB.y));
float axisDist     = dist * rcp(majorDir? normalAB.x : normalAB.y)↩
    ;

if(axisDist < ioAxisDist) ioAxisDist = axisDist;
if(axisDist < ioAxisDist) ioMajorDir = majorDir;
}

void GetGeometricDistance(float2 inScreenCoord,
out float oDistance,
out bool oMajorDir)
    {
    // GetParameterX are HW implementation dependant
float2 sc = GetParameterInterpolated( inScreenCoord );
    float2 sc0 = GetParameterP0( inScreenCoord )
    float2 sc1 = GetParameterP1( inScreenCoord );
    float2 sc2 = GetParameterP2( inScreenCoord );
oDistance = FLT_MAX;

ComputeAxisClosestDist(sc, sc0, sc1, oMajorDir, oDistance);
ComputeAxisClosestDist(sc, sc1, sc2, oMajorDir, oDistance);
ComputeAxisClosestDist(sc, sc2, sc0, oMajorDir, oDistance);
}

// inAlpha is result of AlphaTest,
// i.e., Alpha - AlphaRef
// We assume alpha is a distance field
void GetSignedDistanceFromAlpha(float inAlpha,
out float oDistance,
out bool oGradientDir)
{
    // Find alpha test gradient
float xGradient = ddx_fine(inAlpha);
float yGradient = ddy_fine(inAlpha);
oGradientDir = abs(xGradient) > abs(yGradient);
// Compute signed distance to where alpha reaches zero
oDistance = -inAlpha * rcp(oGradientDir ? xGradient : yGradient);
```

```
    }

    void GetAnalyticalDistanceToEdge(float inAlpha,
    float2 inScreenCoord,
    out float oDistance,
    out bool oMajorDir )
    {
    bool alphaMajorAxis; float alphaDistance;
    GetSignedDistanceFromAlpha(inAlpha,
    alphaDistance,
    alphaMajorAxis)
    GetGeometricDistance(inScreenCoord,
    oDistance,
    oMajorDir);
    if(alphaDistance < oDistance) oDistance = alphaDistance;
    if(alphaDistance < oDistance) alphaMajorAxis = alphaMajorAxis;
    }
```

Listing 3.1. Optimized GBAA distance to edge shader. This uses direct access to vertex data from within the pixel shader.

In terms of quality, the analytical methods beat any morphological approach. Unfortunately, this method proves to be very problematic in many real-world scenarios. Malan developed a very similar antialiasing solution and researched further into the practical issues [Malan 10].

The main problem stems from subpixel triangles, which are unavoidable in a real game production environment. If an actual silhouette edge is composed of multiple small or thin triangles, then only one of them will get rasterized per pixel. Therefore, its distance to the edge might not be the actual distance to the silhouette that we want to antialias. In this case, the resulting artifact will show up as several improperly smoothed pixels on an otherwise antialiased edge, which tends to be very visually distracting (see Figure 3.4 and Figure 3.5).

Malan proposed several ways of dealing with this problem [Malan 10]. However, none of these solutions are very practical if not introduced at the very beginning of the project, due to complex mesh processing and manual tweaking.

Another issue comes again from the actual data source. Hints for antialiasing come from a single triangle, therefore it is impossible to correctly detect and process intersections between triangles. Many assets in a real production scenario have intersecting triangles (i.e., a statue put into the ground will have side triangles intersecting with the terrain mesh). GPU rasterization solves intersections by depth testing before and after rendering a triangle's pixels. Therefore, there is no analytical information about the edge created due to intersection. In effect, the distance to the closest edge does not represent the distance to the intersection edge, which results in a lack of antialiasing.

3.5.2 Coverage Reconstruction Antialiasing (CRAA)

In order to improve upon the techniques and results shared in Section 3.5.1, we would like to find a way to determine more information about a triangle's actual

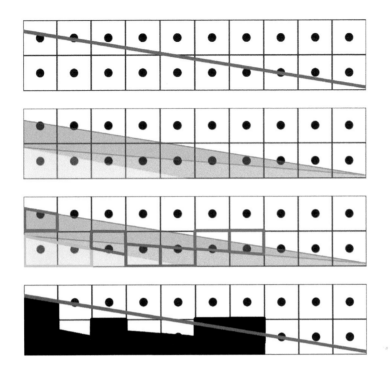

Figure 3.4. False distance to a silhouette edge due to subpixel triangles. Taking a single triangle into account would result in rerasterization of a false edge (blue) instead of the real silhouette edge (red).

Figure 3.5. Top to bottom: a visualization of analytical distance to edge, rasterized edge, analytically antialiased edge, an edge using 5-bit gradients, and an edge showing minor artifacts when multiple triangles intersect one pixel.

intersections and edges within a pixel. With this information, we could partially address most of the aforementioned issues. Fortunately, EQAA provides exactly the information we are interested in by using AMD's hardware EQAA.

EQAA overview. The enhanced quality antialiasing (EQAA) framework augments the standard MSAA color/depth resolve with coverage samples. The rasterizer, while processing triangles, can do cheap analytical sample coverage tests within a triangle. The results of such tests are saved into a compressed buffer called a *fragment mask* (FMask). The FMask acts as an indirection table that associates sample locations with color fragments that were rasterized and stored in the fragment buffer (as in normal MSAA). The number of samples can be higher than the number of stored fragments. In order to accomidate this, a sample in FMask may be marked as "unknown" if it is associated with a fragment that cannot be stored in the fragment buffer (see Figure 3.6).

An important aspect of coverage rendering is correct depth testing. Normally, incoming coverage samples need to be tested against depth fragments stored in the MSAA depth buffer. In order to get correct coverage information, normal MSAA would require a depth buffer that stores of the same number of depth fragments as the number of coverage samples (we can get away with storing fewer color fragments because FMask allows us to associate a single fragment with multiple samples). Fortunately, one feature of AMD's GCN architecture is an ability to work with a compressed depth buffer, which is stored as a set of plane equations. When this mode is enabled, EQAA uses these plane equations to do correct depth testing by analytically deriving depth values for all coverage samples. This means that it is possible to get correct coverage information, even if depth and color information is evaluated and stored as a single fragment (thus MSAA is effectively turned off for all render targets).

Another important requirement for correctly resolving coverage is to sort triangles from front to back. Otherwise, due to the rules of rasterization, it is possible for a triangle to partially overlap a pixel and not get rasterized. If that happens, then that pixel's coverage value might not get updated. Therefore, it is essential to sort objects from front to back (which most rendering engines do already). Fragment sorting is mostly taken care of by GCN hardware. Unfortunately, it is still possible to get incorrect results due to subpixel triangles that won't get rasterized and therefore can't correctly update pixel coverage information.

The memory footprint of FMask is directly proportional to number of unique fragments and samples used. For every sample, we need enough bits to index any of the fragment stored for that pixel and also an additional flag for an unknown value. For the sake of this article, we will focus on use cases with one fragment and eight samples (1F8S)—which require 1 bit per sample, thus 8 bits per pixel total (see Figure 3.7). Such a setup proved to be optimal with regard to EQAA performance as well as the FMask's memory footprint.

CRAA setup. Our goal is to use part of the EQAA pipeline to acquire coverage information at a high resolution (8 samples per pixel) without paying the computational and memory overhead of full MSAA rendering. We would like to use

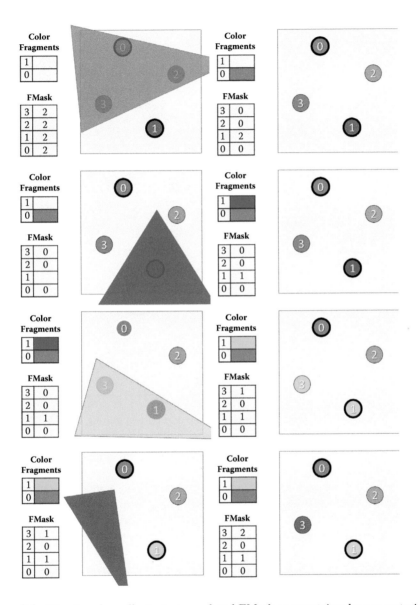

Figure 3.6. The steps here illustrate an updated FMask as new triangles are rasterized. Important note: in the last step, the red triangle does not need to evict Sample 3 if it would fail a Z-test against the sample. (This, however, depends on the particular hardware setup and is beyond the scope of this article.)

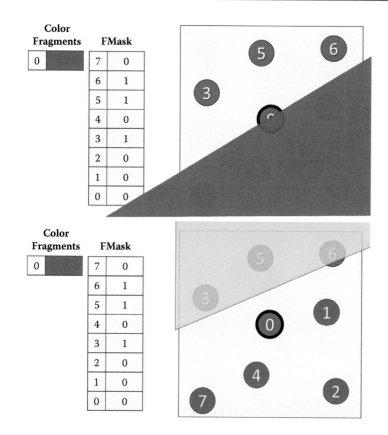

Figure 3.7. Simple rasterization case and corresponding FMask.

information recovered from the coverage data to derive blending hints in a similar fashion to AEAA.

In our simplified case of 1F8S we know that FMask will be an 8-bit value, where the nth bit being set to 0 represents the nth sample being associated with the rasterized fragment (therefore it belongs to the current pixel's triangle and would pass depth testing), while 1 informs us that this sample is unknown—i.e., it was occluded by another triangle.

We can think of FMask as a subset of points that share the same color. If we were to rasterize the current pixel with this newly acquired information, we would need to blend the current pixel's fragment weighted by the number of its known coverage samples, with the other fragment represented by "unknown" coverage samples. Without adding any additional rendering costs, we could infer the unknown color fragments from neighboring pixels. We assume that the depth buffer is working in a compressed mode and that EQAA is using analytical depth testing, thus providing perfectly accurate coverage information.

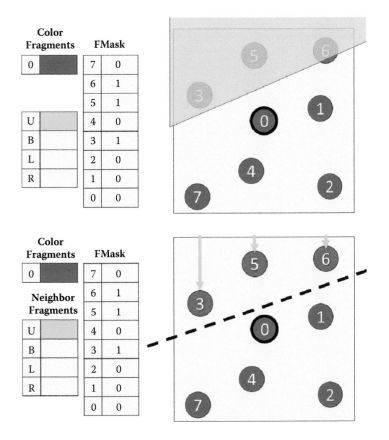

Figure 3.8. Here we illustrate the process of finding an edge that divides a set of samples into "known" and "unknown" samples. Later, this half plane is used to find an appropriate neighboring pixel for deriving the unknown color value.

Single edge scenario. We can apply the same strategy behind AEAA to a simple case in which only a single edge has crossed the pixel. In this case, the pixel's FMask provides a clear division of coverage samples: those that passed will be on one side of the edge, while failed samples will be on the other side. Using a simple line-fitting algorithm, we can find an edge that splits our set of samples into two subsets—passed and failed. This edge approximates the real geometric edge of the triangle that crossed the pixel. In the same spirit of the GBAA algorithm, we find the major axis of the edge as well as its distance from the pixel's center. Then we just need to blend the nearest neighboring pixel color with the current fragment using the edge distance as a weight. Thus, this technique infers the unknown samples from the pixel closest to the derived half plane (see Figure 3.8).

```
float4 CRAA( Texture2DMS<float4> inColor,
             Texture2D<uint2> inFMask,
             uint2 inTexcord )
{
    // Read FMask / HW dependant
    uint iFMask = inFMask.Load( uint3( viTexcoord, 0 ) );
    uint unknownCov = 0;
    float2 hP = 0.0;

    // Average all directions to unknown samples
    // to approximate edge halfplane
    for( uint iSample = 0; iSample < NUM_SAMPLES; ++iSample )
        if( getFMaskValueForSample(iFMask, iSample) == UNKNOWN_CODE )
        {
            hP += TexColorMS.GetSamplePosition(iSample);
            unknownCoverage++;
        }

    // Find fragment offset to pixel on the other side of edge
    int2 fOff = int2( 1, 0);
    if(abs(hP.x) > abs(hP.y) && hP.x <= 0.0) fOff = int2(-1, 0);
    if(abs(hP.x) <= abs(hP.y) && hP.x > 0.0) fOff = int2( 0, 1);
    if(abs(hP.x) <= abs(hP.y) && hP.x <= 0.0) fOff = int2( 0,-1);

    // Blend in inferred sample
    float knownCov = NUM_SAMPLES - unknownCoverage;
    float4 color = inColor.Load( viTexcoord, 0 ) * knownCov;
    color += inColor.Load( viTexcoord + fOff, 0 ) * unknownCov;
    return color /= NUM_SAMPLES;
}
```

Listing 3.2. A simple shader for finding the half plane that approximates the orientation of the "unknown" subset of samples. The half plane is then used to find the closest pixel on the other side of the edge in order to infer the unknown sample's color.

The resolve we have described is akin to GBAA with a limited number of gradient steps (the number of steps is equal to the number of samples used by EQAA). An important thing to note is that our resolve does not need to know anything about the neighboring geometric data (all the information that is needed for reconstruction is contained within the pixel). This is an important difference, because we can reconstruct an edge that was created as the result of rasterizating multiple overlapping triangles; GBAA can only recreate the edge of a single triangle.

Our resolve can be efficiently implemented at runtime by approximating the half plane (see Listing 3.2) while still providing quality comparable to MSAA with the same sampling ratio (see Figure 3.9).

Complex scenario. Following what we learned about resolving simple edges using FMask, we would now like to apply similar ideas to resolving more complex situations in which multiple edges cross a given pixel. In order to achieve this, we would like to be able to group together "failed" samples from different triangles

Figure 3.9. A challenging rendering scenario for antialiasing (top left). Rasterization grid and edge layout (top right). Simple 8×CRAA resulting in edge antialiasing comparable to 8×MSAA apart from pixels that are intersected by multiple triangles (bottom left). The results of 8×MSAA (bottom right).

into multiple disconnected sets. For every disconnected set, we find edges (up to two edges in our implementation) that split it off from other sets. Then we use the acquired edges to find major directions that should be used for subset blending. For every subset of unknown fragments, we blend in a color from the neighboring fragment associated with that subset and weighted by the subset's area coverage within the pixel. Finally, we sum all the color values for each subset and blend this with the current fragment's known color weighted by the percentage of passing coverage samples. This way, we can partially reconstruct the subpixel data using the current pixel's surrounding neighborhood (see Figure 3.10).

Using precomputed LUT. Clearly, our algorithm could be rewritten to provide a set of weights for blending colors from the surrounding 3×3 pixel neighborhood. The blend weights rely only on the data present in FMask, and thus our blend weights can be precomputed and stored in a look up table (LUT), which is indexed directly by a pixel's FMask bit pattern.

In our 1F8S case, the LUT would only need 256 entries. Our implementation uses only top, bottom, left, and right neighboring pixels and uses only 4-bit gradients or blend weights. Therefore, the whole LUT requires $256 \times 4 \times 4 = 512$-byte array, which easily fits entirely within the cache.

We also experimented with more complex LUT creation logic. FMask can be evaluated in a morphological fashion to distinguish shapes, thus calculating more accurate and visually plausible gradients. Unfortunately, due to our project's time constraints, we did not have time to properly pursue this direction of research. We believe that a significant quality improvement can be gained from smarter

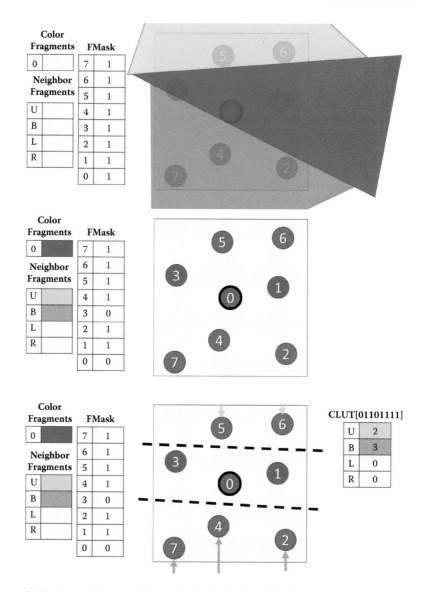

Figure 3.10. One of the possible methods for finding blend weights for sample subsets. The bottom image illustrates a blend weight resolve using a lookup table.

FMask analysis. Using 1F16S would also provide significantly better precision and subpixel handling.

It is worth noting that even the simple logic presented in this section allows for significant aliasing artifact reduction on thin triangles. Figure 3.11 illustrates a

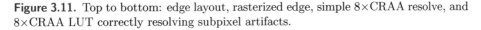

Figure 3.11. Top to bottom: edge layout, rasterized edge, simple 8×CRAA resolve, and 8×CRAA LUT correctly resolving subpixel artifacts.

problematic case for AEAA, where our simple CRAA resolve correctly antialiased the edge. Unfortunately, when there are too many subpixel triangles that don't pass rasterization, CRAA may also fail due to incorrect coverage information. In practice, this heavily depends on the exact rendering situation, and still CRAA has much more relaxed restrictions than AEAA.

The code snippet in Listing 3.3 illustrates the CRAA LUT resolve properly resolving minor subpixel details (see Figure 3.10).

```
float4 CRAA_LUT( Texture2DMS<float4> inColor,
                 Texture2D<uint2> inFMask,
                 Texture1D<uint> inCRAALUT,
                 uint2 inTexcord )
{
  // Read FMask / HW dependant
  uint iFMask      = inFMask.Load( uint3( viTexcoord, 0 ) );
  uint LUTREsult = inCRAALUT[iFMask];
  float wC, wN, wE, wS, wW;

  // LUT is packed as 8bit integer weights
  // North 8b | West 8b | South 8b | East 8b
  // Can also pack whole neighborhood weights in 4 bits
  ExctractLUTWeights(LUTResult, wC, wN, wE, wS, wW);

  float4 color = inColor.Load( viTexcoord + int2( 0, 0) * wC;
         color += inColor.Load( viTexcoord + int2( 0,-1) * wN;
         color += inColor.Load( viTexcoord + int2( 0, 1) * wE;
         color += inColor.Load( viTexcoord + int2( 0, 1) * wS;
         color += inColor.Load( viTexcoord + int2(-1, 0) * wW;
         return color;
}
```

Listing 3.3. CRAA LUT implementation.

3.6   Temporal Super-Sampling

3.6.1   Overview

Temporal super-sampling can be succinctly described by the following simple algorithm:

1. Every frame, offset the projection matrix by a subpixel offset.

2. Use the current frame's N motion vectors to reproject data from frame $N - k$ to time step N.

3. Test if the reprojected data is valid:

   - No occlusion occurred.

   - The data comes from the same source (i.e., object or triangle).

   - The data is not stale (i.e., due to lighting changes).

4. Accumulate data from frame N with data reprojected from frame $N - k$.

5. Repeat steps 2–4 for k frames back in time.

The number k dictates the number of unique subpixel offsets used for jitter in order to get spatially unbiased results after converging by accumulation of all the k samples. However, it is easy to see that by increasing the number k of frames of history, the algorithm has a much higher complexity and therefore a much higher chance of failure.

The most proper (and expensive) approach would be to hold the last k frames in memory along with their motion vectors and additional data required to verify sample validity. Then we would need to evaluate a series of dependent reads and checks to verify if reprojected pixels were valid back in both the spatial and temporal domains. For a given pixel, we could only accumulate as many samples as managed to pass these checks until we encountered the first failure. This approach would guarantee a very high-quality result [Yang et al. 09], however the cost when $k > 1$ is prohibitively expensive for real-time, performance-oriented scenarios, such as games.

Other solutions rely on a so-called *history buffer* that holds all the accumulated samples, thus simplifying the previously described method to the $k = 1$ case. Unfortunately, this solution can't guarantee convergence as it is impossible to remove stale samples from the history buffer without discarding it totally. Also, the validation functions need to be much more conservative in order to prevent incoherent samples from entering the history buffer. This approach, when used for super-sampling, results in a somewhat unstable image with possible "fizzing" high-contrast pixels since they can't converge [Malan 12]. Very similar approaches can be used to stabilize the image over time (instead of super-sampling), as shown in [Sousa 13] and [Valient 14]. We will be discussing this more in Section 3.7.

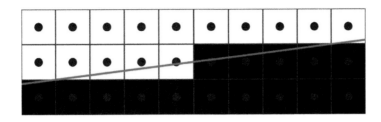

Figure 3.12. One sample centroid rasterization pattern.

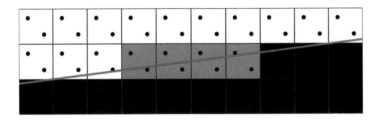

Figure 3.13. Two rotated samples from a standard 2×MSAA pattern.

Taking all pros and cons into account, we decided to pursue the highest possible quality with $k = 1$. This means that we are only dealing with one frame of history, and for every single frame we have two unique samples at our disposal (assuming that our history sample was accepted as valid); we would like to get as much data from them as possible.

3.6.2 Sampling Patterns

A single sample resolve can't provide any gradients (see Figure 3.12 for a baseline reference).

As discussed in Section 3.6.1, we want to maximize the resolve quality while using only two unique samples. One possible way to achieve this is through a more complex resolve and sampling pattern. Currently, common implementations of 2× super-sampling use the 2×MSAA sampling pattern (see Figure 3.13).

One possible improvement upon this is to use a quincunx sampling pattern [NVIDIA 01]. This pattern relies on sharing a noncentral sample with adjacent pixels; thus, the resolve kernel needs to sample corner data from neighboring pixels (see Figure 3.14).

In practice, quincunx sample positions are not very beneficial. Having sampling points on regular pixel rows and columns minimizes the number of potential edges that can be caught. In general, a good pattern should be optimized for maximum pixel row and column coverage. The 4× rotated-grid pattern is a good example (see Figure 3.15).

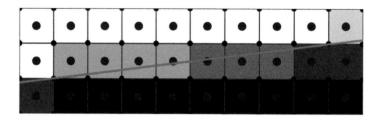

Figure 3.14. Quincunx sampling and resolve pattern guarantees higher-quality results than 2×MSAA while still keeping the sample count at 2.

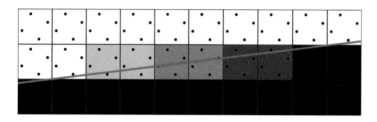

Figure 3.15. The 4× rotated-grid super-sampling pattern maximizes row and column coverage.

3.6.3 FLIPQUAD

[Akenine-Möller 03] proposed several other low-sample-cost patterns such as FLIP-TRI and FLIPQUAD. We will focus on FLIPQUAD as it perfectly matches our goal of using just two unique samples. This sampling pattern is similar to quincunx in its reuse of samples between pixels. However, a massive quality improvement comes from putting sampling points on pixel edges in a fashion similar to the rotated-grid sampling patterns. This provides unique rows and columns for each sample, therefore guaranteeing the maximum possible quality.

The FLIPQUAD pattern requires a custom per-pixel resolve kernel as well as custom per-pixel sampling positions (see Figure 3.16). An important observation is that the pattern is mirrored, therefore every single pixel quad is actually the same.

The article [Laine and Aila 06] introduced a unified metric for sampling pattern evaluation and proved FLIPQUAD to be superior to quincunx, even surpassing the 4× rotated-grid pattern when dealing with geometric edges (see Figure 3.17 and Table 3.1).

We can clearly see that the resolve kernel is possible in a typical pixel shader. However, the per-pixel sampling offsets within a quad were not supported in hardware until modern AMD graphic cards exposed the EQAA rasterization pipeline extensions. This feature is exposed on Xbox One and Playstation 4, as well as through an OpenGL extension on PC [Alnasser 11].

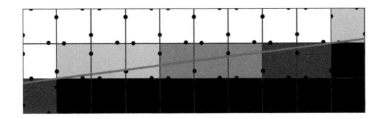

Figure 3.16. FLIPQUAD provides optimal usage of two samples matching quality of 4× rotated-grid resolve.

Figure 3.17. Left to right: single sample, FLIPQUAD, and quincunx. [Image courtesy [Akenine 03].]

The implementation of the FLIPQUAD pattern is fairly straightforward using 2×MSAA. The snippets in Listings 3.4 and 3.5 give sampling positions for pixels within a quad and the reconstruction kernel.

3.6.4 Temporal FLIPQUAD

In Section 3.6.3 we discussed implementing FLIPQUAD sampling and reconstruction on modern hardware. However, in the context of temporal super-sampling, we need to adapt our pattern and resolve kernel. We decided to split the pattern into two subsets—one that will be used to render even frames (blue) and one used on odd frames (red) (see Figure 3.18).

Pattern	E
1× Centroid	> 1.0
2 × 2 Uniform Grid	0.698
2 × 2 Rotated Grid	0.439
Quincunx	0.518
FLIPQUAD	0.364

Table 3.1. Error metric (E) comparison against a 1024-sample reference image as reported by [Laine and Aila 06] (lower is better).

```
// Indexed [SAMPLES LOCATIONS] in n/16 pixel offsets
int2 gFQ_Q00[2] = { int2 (-8,-2), int2 ( 2,-8) };
int2 gFQ_Q10[2] = { int2 (-8, 2), int2 (-2,-8) };
int2 gFQ_Q01[2] = { int2 (-8, 2), int2 (-2,-8) };
int2 gFQ_Q11[2] = { int2 (-8,-2), int2 ( 2,-8) };
```

Listing 3.4. FLIPQUAD sample array.

```
s0 = CurrentFrameMS.Sample(PointSampler, UV, 0);
s1 = CurrentFrameMS.Sample(PointSampler, UV, 1);
s2 = CurrentFrameMS.Sample(PointSampler, int2( 1, 0), 0);
s3 = CurrentFrameMS.Sample(PointSampler, int2( 0, 1), 1);

return 0.25 * (s0 + s1 + s2 + s3);}
```

Listing 3.5. FLIPQUAD reconstruction kernel.

To resolve this sampling scheme properly, we need two resolve kernels—one
for even and one for odd frames (see Listings 3.6 and 3.7). Due to the alternating
patterns, in each frame the kernel will be guaranteed to properly resolve horizontal
or vertical edges. If data from the previous frame is accepted, a full pattern will
be properly reconstructed.

It is worth noting that an incorrect (or missing) FLIPQUAD reconstruction
pass will result in jigsaw edges, which are a direct result of a nonuniform sampling
grid (see Figure 3.19).

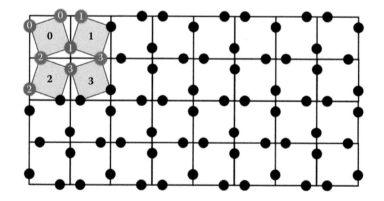

Figure 3.18. Temporal FLIPQUAD pattern. Red samples are rendered on even frames.
Blue samples are rendered on odd frames.

```
// Indexed [FRAME] [SAMPLES LOCATIONS] in n/16 pixel offsets
// BLUE RED
int2 gTempFQ_Q0 [2][1]    = { int2 (-8,-2), int2 ( 2,-8) };
int2 gTempFQ_Q1 [2][1]    = { int2 (-8, 2), int2 (-2,-8) };
int2 gTempFQ_Q2 [2][1]    = { int2 (-8, 2), int2 (-2,-8) };
int2 gTempFQ_Q3 [2][1]    = { int2 (-8,-2), int2 ( 2,-8) };
```

Listing 3.6. Temporal FLIPQUAD sample array.

```
#if defined (ODD_FRAME) // RED
// Horizontal pattern for frame [1]
int2 offset0 = int2 (0, 1);
int2 offset1 = int2 (1, 0);
#else if defined (EVEN_FRAME) // BLUE
int2 offset0 = int2 (1, 0);
int2 offset1 = int2 (0, 1);
#endif

s0 = CurrentFrame . Sample (PointSampler , UV);
s1 = CurrentFrame . Sample (PointSampler , UV, offset0);
s2 = PreviousFrame . Sample (LinearSampler , previousUV);
s3 = PreviousFrame . Sample (LinearSampler , previousUV , offset1);

return 0.25 * (s0 + s1 + s2 + s3);}
```

Listing 3.7. Temporal FLIPQUAD reconstruction kernel.

Rasterization should happen at sample locations in order to take full advantage of FLIPQUAD. This can be easily achieved by using the `sample` prefix in HLSL's interpolator definition. This way, texture data will be offset properly, resulting in a correctly super-sampled image.

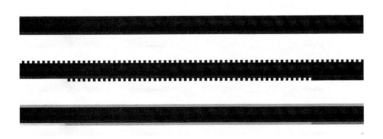

Figure 3.19. Top to bottom: edge rasterized on an even frame and then an odd frame and the final edge after temporal FLIPQUAD reconstruction kernel.

```
// Quad defined as (sample positions within quad)
// s00 s10
// s01 s11
DDX[f(s00)] = [f(s00) -- f(s10)]/dx, dx = |s00 -- s10|
DDY[f(s00)] = [f(s00) -- f(s01)]/dy, dy = |s00 -- s01|

// Hardware assumes dx = dy = 1
// In case of sampling pattern from Listing 6. dx != dy
// Footprint-based sampling picks base mip level
// Based on max(ddx, ddy)
// Frame A max(ddx, ddy) != Frame B max(ddx, ddy)
// Implies non temporarily coherent mip selection

// Calculated in 1/16th of pixel
// Frame A (BLUE)
dx = |-8 -- (16 + (-8))| = 16
dy = |-2 -- (16 + ( 2))| = 20
baseMip ~ max(dx, dy) = 20

// Frame B (RED)
dx = | 2 -- (16 + (-2))| = 12
dy = |-8 -- (16 + (-8))| = 16
baseMip ~ max(dx, dy) = 16}
```

Listing 3.8. Default method for derivative calculation.

3.6.5 Temporal FLIPQUAD and Gradients

One side effect of using the temporal FLIPQUAD pattern is a nonuniform distance between samples within a quad. This causes problems for the gradient calculation and mipmap selection. Graphics cards rely on calculating per-pixel (or per-quad) derivatives using differentials within a quad. This process is fairly straightforward (see Listing 3.8).

As an optimization, spatial distances, used to normalize the differential, are assumed to be 1. However, if we look at our temporal FLIPQUAD pattern, we clearly see that distances between samples are different between the x- and y-axes, and we alternate from frame to frame (see Listing 3.8).

Nonuniform distances will result in a biased mipmap level-of-detail calculation, as $ddx(uv)$ or $ddy(uv)$ will be increasing faster than it should. In effect, the textures will appear sharper or blurrier than they should be. In the worst case, a single texture can select different mipmap levels, under the same viewing direction, when rendering even and odd frames. This would lead to temporal instability since bilinear filtering picks the mipmap based on $\max(ddx, ddy)$, which, in this case, would result in differences between frames (see Figure 3.20).

One way to solve this issue would be to switch all texture samples to a gradient-based texture read (i.e., tex2Dgrad in HLSL) and to calculate the gradients analytically taking sample distance into account. Unfortunately, this complicates all shaders and can have significant performance overhead.

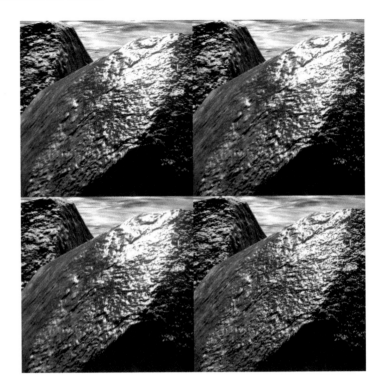

Figure 3.20. The top row shows even and odd frames of the reordered Temporal FLIPQUAD pattern. The bottom row shows the default temporal FLIPQUAD pattern clearly suffering from mipmap level mismatches. (The bottom right represents an oversharpened odd frame).

Another option is to change the pattern in order to minimize frame-to-frame sample distance variance. While this will not provide correct results, the error may not be noticeable in practice as long as it is temporarily stable (see Figure 3.20). Please note that this also requires different offsets (kernel and projection matrix offsets) to shift samples outside the pixel window (see Listings 3.9 and 3.10 for details).

```
// Indexed [FRAME][SAMPLES LOCATIONS] in n/16 pixel offsets
int2 gTempFQ_Q0 [2][1] = { int2 ( 0,-2), int2 (-2, 0) };
int2 gTempFQ_Q1 [2][1] = { int2 ( 0, 2), int2 ( 2, 0) };
int2 gTempFQ_Q2 [2][1] = { int2 ( 0, 2), int2 ( 2, 0) };
int2 gTempFQ_Q3 [2][1] = { int2 ( 0,-2), int2 (-2, 0) };
int2 gProjMatOff [2][1] = { int2 (-8, 0), int2 ( 0, 8) };}
```

Listing 3.9. Reordered temporal FLIPQUAD with additional projection matrix offsets.

```
#if defined(ODD_FRAME)  // RED
// Horizontal pattern for frame [1]
int2 offset0 = int2(0,-1);
int2 offset1 = int2(1, 0);
#else if defined(EVEN_FRAME)  // BLUE
int2 offset0 = int2(1, 0);
int2 offset1 = int2(0,-1);
#endif

s0 = CurrentFrame.Sample(PointSampler, UV);
s1 = CurrentFrame.Sample(PointSampler, UV, offset0);
s2 = PreviousFrame.Sample(LinearSampler, previousUV);
s3 = PreviousFrame.Sample(LinearSampler, previousUV, offset1);

return 0.25 * (s0 + s1 + s2 + s3);}
```

Listing 3.10. Reordered temporal FLIPQUAD reconstruction kernel.

3.6.6 History Sample Acceptance Method

Our acceptance method for history samples is based on the algorithm used in
Killzone: Shadow Fall [Valient 14].

The history sample from frame $N - 1$ is valid only if

- the motion flow between frame N and $N - 1$ is coherent,

- the color flow between frames N and $N - 2$ is coherent. (Note that $N - 2$
  and N have the same subpixel jitter.)

The first constraint guarantees that a sample was not occluded and was moving
in a similar direction. The second constraint guarantees that there was no major
change in lighting conditions between frames with the same subpixel jitter. Both
tests use a 3×3 neighborhood using the sum of absolute differences to estimate
the degree of similarity between frames. It is possible to achieve reasonable
results using a smaller neighborhood, however, testing might need to be more
conservative.

If any constraint fails, then we fall back to clamping history samples to the
current frame color bounding box, as described in Section 3.7. This guarantees no
ghosting and enhanced temporal stability. It is worth noting that the color flow
constraint is very important in a real production environment. It enables the
unrestricted usage of animated textures and particle effects as well as lighting
changes. Another important benefit is that it grants convergence in the event
that the viewport becomes fixed.

3.6.7 Resampling

Any reprojection method is prone to numerical diffusion errors. When a frame
is reprojected using motion vectors and newly acquired sampling coordinates do

not land exactly on a pixel, a resampling scheme must be used. Typically, most methods resort to simple bilinear sampling. However, bilinear sampling will result in over-smoothing. If we would like to use a history buffer in order to accumulate multiple samples, we will also accumulate resampling errors, which can lead to serious image quality degradation (see Figure 3.22). Fortunately, this problem is very similar to well-researched fluid simulation advection optimization problems.

In fluid simulation, the advection step is very similar to our problem of image reprojection. A data field of certain quantities (i.e., pressure and temperature) has to be advected forward in time by a motion field. In practice, both fields are stored in discretized forms; thus, the advection step needs to use resampling. Assuming that the operation is a linear transform, this situation is equal to the problem of reprojection.

Under these circumstances, a typical semi-Lagrangian advection step would be equal to reprojection using bilinear resampling. A well-known method to prevent over-smoothing is to use second order methods for advection. There are several known methods to optimize this process, assuming that the advection operator is reversible. One of them is the MacCormack scheme and its derivation: back and forth error compensation and correction (BFECC). This method enables one to closely approximate the second order accuracy using only two semi-Lagrangian steps [Dupont and Liu 03].

BFECC is very intuitive. In short, we advect the solution forward and backward in time using advection operator A and its reverse, A^R. Operator error is estimated by comparing the original value against the newly acquired one. The original value is corrected by error $(\frac{\varphi^n - \widehat{\varphi}^n}{2})$ and finally advected forward into the next step of the solution (see Algorithm 3.1 and Figure 3.21 for an illustration).

In the context of reprojection, our advection operator is simply a bilinear sample using a motion vector offset. It is worth noting that the function described by the motion vector texture is not reversible (i.e., multiple pixels might move to same discretized position).

A correct way to acquire a reversible motion vector offset would be through a depth-buffer–based reprojection using an inverse camera matrix. Unfortunately, this would limit the operator to pixels subject to camera motion only. Also, the operator would be invalid on pixels that were occluded during the previous time step.

$$
\begin{aligned}
&1\text{: } \widehat{\varphi}^{n+1} = A(\varphi^n). \\
&2\text{: } \widehat{\varphi}^n = A^R(\widehat{\varphi}^{n+1}). \\
&3\text{: } \bar{\varphi} = \varphi^n + \frac{\varphi^n - \widehat{\varphi}^n}{2}. \\
&4\text{: } \varphi^{n+1} = A(\bar{\varphi}).
\end{aligned}
$$

Algorithm 3.1. Original BFECC method.

$$1: \; \widehat{\varphi}^{n+1} = A(\varphi^n).$$
$$2: \; \widehat{\varphi}^n = A^R(.\widehat{\varphi}^{n+1}).$$
$$3: \; \varphi^{n+1} = \widehat{\varphi}^{n+1} + \frac{\varphi^n - \widehat{\varphi}^n}{2}.$$

Algorithm 3.2. Simplified BFECC method.

Another option is to assume a high-coherency motion vector field (texture) and just use a negative motion vector for the reverse operator. However, this approach would break under perspective correction (i.e., high slopes) as well as with complex motion.

In practice, we used a mix of both approaches. The reverse operator is acquired through depth-based reprojection for static pixels and reversing motion vectors for pixels from dynamic objects. For us, this proved to be both efficient and visually plausible (even if not always mathematically correct).

Another important optimization we used was inspired by the simplified BFECC method by [Selle et al. 08]. In this approach, it is proven that the error is not time dependent; therefore the results from frame $n+1$ can be directly compensated by an error estimate. This simplifies the original BFECC by one full semi-Lagrangian (see Algorithm 3.2).

Unfortunately, the proposed method requires reading $\widehat{\varphi}^n$, φ^n, and $\widehat{\varphi}^{n+1}$ in order to evaluate φ^{n+1}. However, as we already assumed that the error estimate is time invariant, we can as use the values from step $n+1$ to estimate the error. Therefore, we can calculate φ^{n+1} using only $\widehat{\varphi}^{n+1}$ and $\widehat{\widehat{\varphi}}^{n+1}$, where $\widehat{\widehat{\varphi}}^{n+1}$ is easy to acquire in a shader (see Algorithm 3.3, Listing 3.11, and Figure 3.21 for details).

One last thing worth mentioning is that BFECC, by default, is not unconditionally stable. There are multiple ways of dealing with this problem, but we found bounding by local minima and maxima to be the most practical [Dupont and Liu 03, Selle et al. 08]. Listing 3.11 presents the simplest implementation of our optimized BFECC, and Figure 3.22 demonstrates the results.

$$1: \; \widehat{\varphi}^{n+1} = A(\varphi^n).$$
$$2: \; \widehat{\varphi}^n = A^R(\widehat{\varphi}^{n+1}).$$
$$3: \; \widehat{\widehat{\varphi}}^{n+1} = A(\widehat{\varphi}^n).$$
$$4: \; \varphi^{n+1} = \widehat{\varphi}^{n+1} + \frac{\widehat{\varphi}^{n+1} - \widehat{\widehat{\varphi}}^{n+1}}{2}.$$

Algorithm 3.3. Shader optimized simplified BFECC method.

```
// Pass outputs phiHatN1Texture
// A() operator uses motion vector texture
void GetPhiHatN1(float2 inUV, int2 inVPOS)
{
    float2 motionVector = MotionVectorsT.Load(int3(inVPOS, 0)).xy;
    float2 forwardProj = inUV + motionVector;
    // Perform advection by operator A()

    return PreviousFrameT.SampleLevel(Linear, forwardProj, 0).rgb;
}

// Pass outputs phiHatTexture
// AR() operator uses negative value from motion vector texture
// phiHatN1 texture is generated by previous pass GetPhiHatN1()
void GetPhiHatN(float2 inUV, int2 inVPOS)
{
    float2 motionVector = MotionVectorsT.Load(int3(inVPOS, 0)).xy;
    float2 backwardProj = inUV - motionVector;

    // Perform reverse advection by operator AR()
    return phiHatN1T.SampleLevel(Linear, backwardProj, 0).rgb;
}

// Final operation to get correctly resampled phiN1
// A() operator uses motion vector texture
// phiHatN1 and phiHatN textures are generated by previous passes
void GetResampledValueBFECC(float2 inUV, int2 inVPOS)
{
    float3 phiHatN1 = phiHatN1T.Load(int3(inVPOS, 0)).rgb;

    // Find local minima and maxima
    float3 minima, maxima;
    GetLimitsRGB(phiHatN1Texture, inUV, minima, maxima);

    float2 motionVector = MotionVectors.Load(int3(inVPOS, 0)).xy;
    float2 A = inUV + motionVector;

    // Perform advection by operator A()
    float3 phiHatHatN1 = phiHatT.SampleLevel(Linear, A, 0).rgb;

    // Perform BFECC
    float3 phiN1          = 1.5 * phiHatN1 - 0.5 * phiHatHatN1;

    // Limit the result to minima and maxima
    phiN1                 = clamp(phiN1, minima, maxima);
    return phiN1;
}
```

Listing 3.11. Reordered temporal FLIPQUAD reconstruction kernel.

3.7 Temporal Antialiasing (TAA)

3.7.1 Overview

In Sections 3.5 and 3.6, we presented methods for improving spatial and temporal stability and resolution of antialiased images. However, even when using $4\times$ rotated-grid super-sampling and dedicated edge antialiasing, disturbing temporal

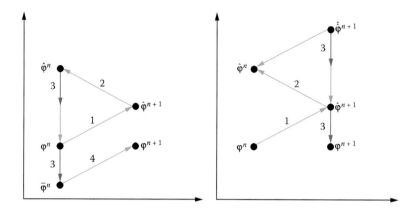

Figure 3.21. Conceptual scheme of the original BFCE method (left) and of the shader optimized BFCE used for texture resampling (right).

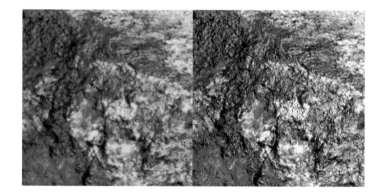

Figure 3.22. Continuous resampling of 30 frames using a history buffer. The camera is in motion, panning from left to right. Using bilinear sampling shows numerical diffusion errors resulting in a blurry image (left). Using optimized linear BFCE helps to minimizes blurring (right).

artifacts may occur. Ideally we would like to accumulate more frames over time to further improve image quality. Unfortunately, as described in Sections 3.6.1 and 3.6.6, it is very hard to provide a robust method that will work in real-world situations, while also using multiple history samples, without other artifacts. Therefore, several methods rely on super-sampling only in certain local contrast regions of an image [Malan 12, Sousa 13, Valient 14]. These approaches rely on visually plausible temporal stabilization (rather than super-sampling). We would like to build upon these approaches to further improve our results.

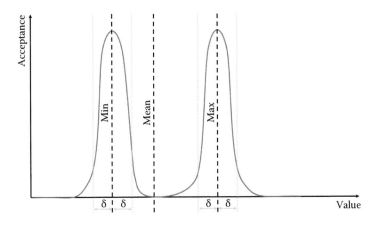

Figure 3.23. Frequency-based acceptance function plot.

3.7.2 Frequency-Based Acceptance Metric

A simple temporal antialiasing scheme can be described as a cumulative blend between the current frame and an accumulation buffer of previous frames (history data). However, finding the correct blend factor is difficult. We would like to stabilize the data such that we avoid fluctuations over time and enhance the image quality by accumulating new information. On the other hand, we need to detect when data becomes stale or invalid.

We build a color bounding box of fresh data by sampling the 3×3 spatial neighborhood from the current frame. From this data we evaluate the local minima, maxima, and mean value per RGB channel.

We follow a reasoning grounded in signal frequency analysis. If our history data is too similar to the local mean, it does not bring much new information to the current frame and might even diffuse the result if it contains accumulated errors (i.e., due to sampling errors). The more "different" the data is from mean, the more important it is. However, certain information might just be a fluctuation that skews the data. With all of this in mind, we can treat information that is in close proximity to fresh data's local minima and maxima as valid (to a degree). Therefore, we could plot our function of history data acceptance as two peaks centered at a local minima and maxima, with a slope curve steered by a user controlled δ value (see Figure 3.23).

To reduce incorrectly accepted samples even further, we utilize motion-based constraints as described in Section 3.6.6. This combination method minimizes the possible reprojection artifacts to a 3×3 pixel neighborhood (i.e., ghosting) while still guaranteeing a very high level of temporal stabilization. It's worth noting that this method can't provide convergence in the context of super-sampling (or jittered rendering), as sample acceptance relies on local data changes. See Listing 3.12 for details.

```
// curMin, curMax, curMean are estimated from 3x3 neighborhood
float3 getTAA(float2 inCurtMotionVec,
              float2 inPrevMotionVec,
              float3 inCurtMean,
              float3 inCurtMin,
              float3 inCurtMax,
              float3 inCurtValue,
              float3 inPrevValue)
{
  // Motion coherency weight
  float motionDelta = length(inCurMotionVec - inPrevMotionVec);
  float motionCoherence = saturate(c_motionSens * motionDelta));

  // Calculate color window range
  float3 range = inCutMin - inCurMax;

  // Offset the window bounds by delta percentage
  float3 extOffset = c_deltaColorWindowOffset * range;
  float3 extBoxMin = max(inCurMin - extOffset.rgb, 0.0);
  float3 extdBoxMax = inCurMax + extOffset;

  // Calculate deltas between previous and current color window
  float3 valDiff = saturate(extBoxMin - inPrevValue);
  valDiff += saturate(inPreviousValue - extBoxMax);
  float3 clampedPrevVal = clamp(inPrevValue, extBoxMin, extBoxMax);

  // Calculate deltas for current pixel against previous
  float3 meanWeight = abs(inCurValue - inPreValue);
  float loContrast = length(meanWeight)* c_loWeight;
  float hiContrast = length(valDiff) * c_hiWeight;

  // Calculate final weights
  float denom = max((loContrast - hiContrast), 0.0);
  float finalWeight = saturate(rcp(denom + epsilon));

  // Check blend weight against minimum bound
  // Prevents the algorithm from stalling
  // in a 'saddle' due to numerical imprecision
  // Regulates minimum blend of current data
  finalWeight= max(c_minLimiter, w);

  // Correct previous samples according to motion coherency weights
  finalWeight = saturate(finalWeight - motionCoherence);
  // Final value blend
  return lerp(inCurValue, clampedPrevVal, finalWeight);
}
```

Listing 3.12. Temporal antialiasing using our frequency-based acceptance metric.

3.8 Final Implementation

Our final framework's implementation can be split into two main stages:

- temporally stable edge antialiasing, which includes

  ○ SMAA,

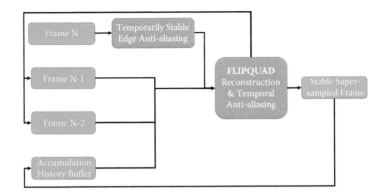

Figure 3.24. Data flow graph in our implementation of the HRAA pipeline.

- ○ CRAA,
- ○ AEAA (GBAA);

• Temporal FLIPQUAD reconstruction combined with temporal antialiasing (TAA) (see Listing 3.13).

Figure 3.24 illustrates the data flow inside the framework.

During production, we implemented and optimized all three approaches to temporally stable edge antialiasing.

SMAA was implemented with geometric edge detection based on depth and normal buffers. Edges were refined by a predicated threshold based on the luminescence contrast. Our edge-detection algorithm choice was dictated by making the resolve as temporally stable as possible.

CRAA and AEAA used the implementations described in Sections 3.5.1 and 3.5.2. Our EQAA setup used a 1F8S configuration, while our AEAA offset buffer was compressed down to 5 bits (utilizing the last remaining space in our tightly packed G-buffer).

The results of either edge antialiasing pass were used as N, $N-1$, and $N-2$ frame sources in the last pass. The history buffer used by TAA at frame N was the output buffer of TAA from frame $N-1$.

3.9 Results Discussion

Our packing/performance scheme resulted in fairly low-quality gradients coming out of edge antialiasing (only 3 bits for steps). However, FLIPQUAD reconstruction provided two to four times the edge gradients virtually for free. In practice, the whole system provided excellent results, matching a 4× rotated-grid super-sampled reference while providing much higher-quality edge antialiasing and temporal stability at minimal cost.

```
// Unoptimized pseudocode for final
// Temporal FLIPQUAD reconstruction & TAA
// Frames N & N−2 are assumed
// To have same jitter offsets
float3 getFLIPQUADTaa()
{
  float3 curMin, currMax, curMean;
  GetLimits(currentValueTexture, curMin, curMax, curMean);

  float3 prevVal = Resample(prevValueTexture);
  float3 prevPrevVal = Resample(prevPrevValueTexture);

  // Get sums of absolute difference
  float3 curSAD = GetSAD(curValueTexture);
  float3 prevPrevSAD = GetSAD(prevPrevValueTexture);

  // Motion coherency weight
  float moCoherence = GetMotionCoherency(curMotionTexture,
                                         prevMotionTexture);

  // Color coherency weight
  float colCoherence = GetColorCoherency(curSAD, prevPrevSAD);

  // FLIPQUAD parts
  float3 FQCurPart = GetCurFLIPQUAD(curValueTexture);
  float3 FQPrevPart = GetPrevFLIPQUAD(prevValueTexture);
  float FQCoherency = motionCoherence + colorCoherence;
  float3 clampFQPrev = clamp(FQPrevPart, curMin, curMax);

  // This lerp allows full convergance
  // If color flow (N−2 to N) is coherent
  FQPrevPart = lerp(FQPrevPart, clampFQPrev, colCoherence);

  // Final reconstruction blend
  float3 FLIPQUAD = lerp(FQCurPart, FQPrevPart, 0.5*moCoherence);

  float3 historyVal = Resample(historyValueTexture);

  return getTAA(curMotionTexture, prevMotionTexture,
                curMin, curMax, curMean,
                FLIPQUAD, historyVal)
}
```

Listing 3.13. Pseudocode for the combined temporal FLIPQUAD reconstruction and temporal antialiasing.

While temporal FLIPQUAD and TAA remained stable and reliable components of the framework, the choice of the edge antialiasing solution proved to be problematic.

SMAA provided the most visually plausible results on static pixels under any circumstances. The gradients were always smooth and no edge was left without antialiasing. Unfortunately, it sometimes produced distracting gradient wobble while in motion. The wobble was partially mitigated by the FLIPQUAD and TAA resolves. Unfortunately, SMAA had the highest runtime cost out of the whole framework.

AEAA provided excellent stability and quality, even in close-ups where triangles are very large on screen. Unfortunately, objects with very high levels of tessellation resulted in very objectionable visual noise or even a total loss of antialiasing on some edges. Even though this was the fastest method for edge antialiasing, it proved too unreliable for our open world game. It is worth noting that our AEAA implementation required us to modify every single shader that writes out to the G-buffer. This might be prohibitively expensive in terms of developer maintainability and runtime performance.

CRAA mitigated most of the issues seen with AEAA and was also the easiest technique to implement. Unfortunately, on the current generation of hardware, there is a measurable cost for using even a simple EQAA setup and the cost scales with the number of rendered triangles and their shader complexity. However, in our scenario, it was still faster than SMAA alone. Even though we were able to solve multiple issues, we still found some finely tessellated content that was problematic with this technique and resulted in noisy artifacts on edges. These artifacts could be effectively filtered by temporal FLIPQUAD and TAA. Unfortunately the cost of outputting coverage data from pixel shaders was too high for our vegetation-heavy scenarios. We did not experiment with manual coverage output (i.e., not hardware based).

At the time of writing, we have decided to focus on two main approaches for our game: SMAA with AEAA used for alpha-tested geometry or CRAA with AEAA used for alpha-tested geometry. SMAA with AEAA is the most expensive and most reliable while also providing the lowest temporal stability. CRAA with AEAA provides excellent stability and performance with medium quality and medium reliability. The use of AEAA for alpha-tested objects seems to provide the highest quality, performance, and stability in both use cases; therefore, we integrated its resolve filter into the SMAA and CRAA resolves. See the performance and image quality comparisons of the full HRAA framework in Figure 3.25 and Table 3.2.

3.10   Conclusion

We provided a production proven hybrid reconstruction antialiasing framework along with several new algorithms, as well as modern implementations of well-known algorithms. We believe that the temporal FLIPQUAD super-sampling as well as temporal antialiasing will gain wider adoption due to their low cost, simplicity, and quality. Our improvements to distance-to-edge–based methods might prove useful for some projects. Meanwhile, CRAA is another addition to the temporally stable antialiasing toolbox. Considering its simplicity of implementation and its good performance, we believe that with additional research it might prove to be a viable, widely adopted edge antialiasing solution. We hope that the ideas presented here will inspire other researchers and developers and provide readers with valuable tools for achieving greater image quality in their projects.

Figure 3.25. Comparison of different HRAA setups showing different scenarios based on actual game content. From left to right: centroid sampling (no antialiasing), temporal FLIPQUAD (TFQ), AEAA + TFQ, CRAA + TFQ, and SMAA + TFQ.

Single Pass	Timing (ms)	G-Buffer Overhead (%)
BFECC single value	0.3	N/A
Temporal FLIPQUAD (TFQ)	0.2	N/A
AEAA	0.25	< 1% C
8×CRAA	0.25	< 8% HW/C
SMAA	0.9	N/A
TAA	0.6	N/A
TFQ + TAA	0.62	N/A
AEAA(alpha test) + 8×CRAA + TFQ + TAA	0.9	< 3% HW/C
SMAA + TFQ + TAA	1.4	N/A

Table 3.2. Different HRAA passes and timings measured on an AMD Radeon HD 7950 at 1080p resolution, operating on 32-bit image buffers. "C" means content dependent and "HW" means hardware type or setup dependent.

Bibliography

[Akenine-Möller 03] T. Akenine-Möller. "An Extremely Inexpensive Multisampling Scheme." Technical Report No. 03-14, Ericsson Mobile Platforms AB, 2003.

[AMD 11] AMD Developer Relations. "EQAA Modes for AMD 6900 Series Graphics Cards." http://developer.amd.com/wordpress/media/2012/10/EQAAModesforAMDHD6900SeriesCards.pdf, 2011.

[Alnasser 11] M. Alnasser, G. Sellers, and N. Haemel. "AMD Sample Positions." *OpenGL Extension Registry*, https://www.opengl.org/registry/specs/AMD/sample_positions.txt, 2011.

[Bavoil and Andersson 12] L. Bavoil and J. Andersson. "Stable SSAO in Battlefield 3 with Selective Temporal Filtering." Game Developer Conference Course, San Francisco, CA, March 5–9, 2012.

[Burley 07] B. Burley. "Filtering in PRMan." *Renderman Repository*, https://web.archive.org/web/20130915064937/http:/www.renderman.org/RMR/st/PRMan_Filtering/Filtering_In_PRMan.html, 2007. (Original URL no longer available.)

[Drobot 11] M. Drobot. "A Spatial and Temporal Coherence Framework for Real-Time Graphics." In *Game Engine Gems 2*, edited by Eric Lengyel, pp. 97–118. Boca Raton, FL: CRC Press, 2011.

[Drobot 14] M. Drobot. "Low Level Optimizations for AMD GCN Architecture." Presented at Digital Dragons Conference, Kraków, Poland, May 8–9, 2014.

[Dupont and Liu 03] T. Dupont and Y. Liu. "Back and Forth Error Compensation and Correction Methods for Removing Errors Induced by Uneven Gradients of the Level Set Function." *J. Comput. Phys.* 190:1 (2003), 311–324.

[Jimenez et al. 11] J. Jimenez, B. Masia, J. Echevarria, F. Navarro, and D. Gutierrez. "Practical Morphological Antialiasing." In *GPU Pro 2: Advanced Rendering Techniques*, edited by Wolfgang Engel, pp. 95–114. Natick, MA: A K Peters, 2011.

[Jimenez et al. 12] J. Jimenez, J. Echevarria, D. Gutierrez, and T. Sousa. "SMAA: Enhanced Subpixel Morphological Antialiasing." *Computer Graphics Forum: Proc. EUROGRAPHICS 2012* 31:2 (2012), 355–364.

[Kirkland et al. 99] Dale Kirkland, Bill Armstrong, Michael Gold, Jon Leech, and Paula Womack. "ARB Multisample." *OpenGL Extension Registry*, https://www.opengl.org/registry/specs/ARB/multisample.txt, 1999.

[Laine and Aila 06] S. Laine and T. Aila. "A Weighted Error Metric and Optimization Method for Antialiasing Patterns." *Computer Graphics Forum* 25:1 (2006), 83–94.

[Lottes 09] T. Lottes. "FXAA." NVIDIA white paper, 2009.

[Malan 10] H. Malan. "Edge Anti-aliasing by Post-Processing." In *GPU Pro: Advanced Rendering Techniques*, edited by Wolfgang Engel, pp. 265–290. Natick, MA: A K Peters, 2010.

[Malan 12] H. Malan. "Realtime global illumination and reflections in Dust 514." Advances in Real-Time Rendering in Games: Part 1, SIGGRAPH Course, Los Angeles, CA, August 5–9, 2012.

[NVIDIA 01] NVIDIA Corporation. "HRAA: High-Resolution Antialiasing Through Multisampling". Technical report, 2001.

[Nehab et al. 07] D. Nehab, P. V. Sander, J. Lawrence, N. Tararchuk, and J. R. Isidoro. "Accelerating Real-Time Shading with Reverse Reprojection Caching." In *Proceedings of the 22nd ACM SIGGRAPH/EUROGRAPHICS Symposium on Graphics Hardware*, edited by Dieter Fellner and Stephen Spencer, pp. 25–35. Aire-la-Ville, Switzerland: Eurographics Association, 2007.

[Persson 11] E. Persson. "Geometric Buffer Antialiasing." Presented at SIGGRAPH, Vancouver, Canada, August 7–11, 2011.

[Reshetov 09] A. Reshetov. "Morphological Antialiasing." In *Proceedings of the Conference on High Performance Graphics*, edited by S. N. Spencer, David McAllister, Matt Pharr, and Ingo Wald, pp. 109–116. New York: ACM, 2009.

[Selle et al. 08] A. Selle, R. Fedkiw, B. Kim, Y. Liu, and J. Rossignac. "An Unconditionally Stable MacCormack Method." *J. Scientific Computing* 35:2–3 (2008), 350–371.

[Sousa 11] T. Sousa. "Anti-aliasing Methods in CryENGINE3." Presented at SIGGRAPH 2011, Vancouver, Canada, August 7–11, 2011.

[Sousa 13] T. Sousa T. "CryENGINE 3 Graphics Gems." Presented at SIGGRAPH 2013, Anaheim, CA, July 21–25, 2013.

[Valient 14] M. Valient. "Taking *Killzone Shadow Fall* Image Quality into the Next Generation." Presented at Game Developers Conference, San Francisco, CA, March 17–21, 2014.

[Yang et al. 09] L. Yang, D. Nehab, P. V. Sander, P. Sitthi-Amorn, J. Lawrence, and H. Hoppe. "Amortized Supersampling." Presented at SIGGRAPH Asia, Yokohama, Japan, December 17–19, 2009.

[Young 06] P. Young. "Coverage Sampled Antialiasing." Technical report, NVIDIA, 2006.

Real-Time Rendering of Physically Based Clouds Using Precomputed Scattering

Egor Yusov

4.1 Introduction

Rendering realistic clouds has always been a desired feature for a variety of applications, from computer games to flight simulators. Clouds consist of innumerable tiny water droplets that scatter light. Rendering clouds is challenging because photons are typically scattered multiple times before they leave the cloud. Despite the impressive performance of today's GPUs, accurately modeling multiple scattering effects is prohibitively expensive, even for offline renderers. Thus, real-time methods rely on greatly simplified models.

Using camera-facing billboards is probably the most common real-time method [Dobashi et al. 00, Wang 04, Harris and Lastra 01, Harris 03]. However, billboards are flat, which breaks the volumetric experience under certain conditions. These methods have other limitations: lighting is precomputed resulting in static clouds [Harris and Lastra 01], multiple scattering is ignored [Dobashi et al. 00], or lighting is not physically based and requires tweaking by artists [Wang 04]. Volume rendering techniques are another approach to render clouds [Schpok et al. 03, Miyazaki et al. 04, Riley et al. 04]. To avoid aliasing artifacts, many slices usually need to be rendered, which can create a bottleneck, especially on high-resolution displays. More physically accurate methods exist [Bouthors et al. 06, Bouthors et al. 08], which generate plausible visual results, but are difficult to reproduce and computationally expensive.

We present a new physically based method to efficiently render realistic animated clouds. The clouds are comprised of scaled and rotated copies of a single particle called the *reference particle*. During the preprocessing stage, we precompute optical depth as well as single and multiple scattering integrals describing the light transport in the reference particle for all possible camera positions and view directions and store the results in lookup tables. At runtime, we load the data from the lookup tables to approximate the light transport in the cloud in order to avoid costly ray marching or slicing. In this chapter, we elaborate upon our previous work [Yusov 14b]. In particular, the following improvements have been implemented:

- a better real-time shading model based on precomputed lookup tables,

- an improved method to calculate light attenuation in the body of the cloud using a 3D grid,

- a new particle generation algorithm,

- performance optimization, including GPU-based particle sorting.

We briefly review the main concepts of this method, but we will concentrate on implementation details and improvements. Additional information can be found in the original paper [Yusov 14b].

4.2 Light Transport Theory

Now we will briefly introduce the main concepts of the light transport in a participating medium. More information can be found in [Riley et al. 04, Bouthors 08]. There are three phenomena that can be found in a participating medium: scattering, absorption, and emission. Scattering only changes the direction of a photon traveling through the medium. Absorption eliminates the photon by transforming its energy into other forms, while emission does the opposite. The intensity of these processes is described by scattering, absorption, and emission coefficients β_{Sc}, β_{Ab}, and β_{Em}, respectively. Absorption and scattering both reduce the intensity of light traveling through the medium. The extinction coefficient $\beta_{Ex} = \beta_{Ab} + \beta_{Sc}$ describes the net attenuation. In the cloud body, emission and absorption are negligible: $\beta_{Em} = \beta_{Ab} = 0$. As a result, both scattering and extinction can be described by the same coefficient: $\beta_{Sc} = \beta_{Ex} = \beta$.

The intensity of light traveling from point $\mathbf{A}$ to point $\mathbf{B}$ inside the cloud is reduced by a factor of $e^{-\tau(\mathbf{A},\mathbf{B})}$. $\tau(\mathbf{A},\mathbf{B})$, called *optical depth*, is the integral of the extinction coefficient over the path from $\mathbf{A}$ to $\mathbf{B}$:

$$\tau(\mathbf{A},\mathbf{B}) = \int_{\mathbf{A}}^{\mathbf{B}} \beta(\mathbf{P}) \cdot ds, \qquad (4.1)$$

where $\mathbf{P} = \mathbf{A} + \frac{\mathbf{B}-\mathbf{A}}{||\mathbf{B}-\mathbf{A}||} \cdot s$ is the current integration point.

To determine the intensity of single scattered light, we need to step along the view ray and accumulate all the differential amounts of sunlight scattered at

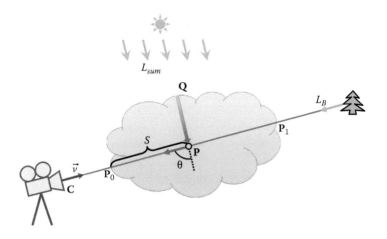

Figure 4.1. Single scattering.

every point toward the camera:

$$L_{In}^{(1)}(\mathbf{C}, \vec{v}) = \int_{\mathbf{P}_0}^{\mathbf{P}_1} \beta(\mathbf{P}) \cdot L_{Sun} \cdot e^{-\tau(\mathbf{Q},\mathbf{P})} \cdot e^{-\tau(\mathbf{P},\mathbf{P}_0)} \cdot P(\theta) \cdot ds. \qquad (4.2)$$

In this equation, $\mathbf{C}$ is the camera position and $\vec{v}$ is the view direction. $\mathbf{P}_0$ and $\mathbf{P}_1$ are the points where the view ray enters and leaves the cloud body, L_{Sun} is the intensity of sunlight outside the cloud, and $\mathbf{Q}$ is the point through which the sunlight reaches the current integration point $\mathbf{P}$ (Figure 4.1). $P(\theta)$ is the phase function that defines how much energy is scattered from the incident direction to the outgoing direction, with θ being the angle between the two. Note that the sunlight is attenuated twice before it reaches the camera: by the factor of $e^{-\tau(\mathbf{Q},\mathbf{P})}$ on the way from the entry point $\mathbf{Q}$ to the scattering point $\mathbf{P}$, and by the factor of $e^{-\tau(\mathbf{P},\mathbf{P}_0)}$ on the way from the scattering point to the camera.

The phase function for cloud droplets is very complex [Bohren and Huffman 98]. In real-time methods, it is common to approximate it using the Cornette-Shanks function [Cornette and Shanks 92]:

$$P(\theta) \approx \frac{1}{4\pi} \frac{3(1-g^2)}{2(2+g^2)} \frac{(1+\cos^2(\theta))}{(1+g^2-2g\cos(\theta))^{3/2}}. \qquad (4.3)$$

Using the intensity $L_{In}^{(1)}$ of single scattering, we can compute secondary scattering $L_{In}^{(2)}$, then third-order scattering $L_{In}^{(3)}$, and so on. The nth-order scattering intensity measured at point $\mathbf{C}$ when viewing in direction $\vec{v}$ is given by the following integral:

$$L_{In}^{(n)}(\mathbf{C}, \vec{v}) = \int_{\mathbf{P}_0}^{\mathbf{P}_1} J^{(n)}(\mathbf{P}, \vec{v}) \cdot e^{-\tau(\mathbf{P},\mathbf{P}_0)} \cdot ds. \qquad (4.4)$$

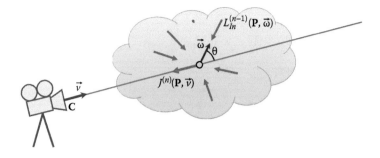

Figure 4.2. Multiple scattering.

In Equation (4.4), $J^{(n)}(\mathbf{C}, \vec{v})$ is the net intensity of order $n-1$ light $L_{In}^{(n-1)}(\mathbf{C}, \vec{v})$ that is scattered in the view direction:

$$J^{(n)}(\mathbf{P}, \vec{v}) = \beta(\mathbf{P}) \cdot \int_{\Omega} L_{In}^{(n-1)}(\mathbf{P}, \vec{\omega}) \cdot P(\theta) \cdot d\omega, \qquad (4.5)$$

where integration is performed over the whole sphere of directions Ω, and θ is the angle between $\vec{\omega}$ and $\vec{v}$ (see Figure 4.2).[1]

The total in-scattering intensity is found by calculating the sum of all scattering orders:

$$L_{In}(\mathbf{C}, \vec{v}) = \sum_{n=1}^{\infty} L_{In}^{(n)}(\mathbf{C}, \vec{v}). \qquad (4.6)$$

The final radiance measured at the camera is the sum of in-scattered intensity and background radiance L_B (see Figure 4.1) attenuated in the cloud:

$$L(\mathbf{C}, \vec{v}) = L_{In}(\mathbf{C}, \vec{v}) + e^{-\tau(\mathbf{P}_0, \mathbf{P}_1)} \cdot L_B. \qquad (4.7)$$

4.3   Precomputed Solutions

Equations (4.1)–(4.7) are very complex and cannot be solved at runtime. Our solution to this problem is to model the light transport in a reference volumetric particle at preprocess time and to solve all the equations for that particle. We store the resulting information in lookup tables and use it at runtime to compute shading.

4.3.1   Optical Depth

Consider some inhomogeneous volumetric particle with known density distribution (Figure 4.3 (left)). Our goal is to precompute the optical depth integral in

---

[1]Strictly speaking, θ is the angle between the incident direction $-\vec{\omega}$ and the outgoing direction $-\vec{v}$, which is the same.

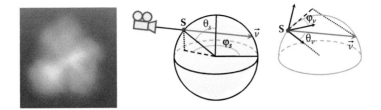

Figure 4.3. Volumetric particle (left) and 4D parameterization (middle and right).

Equation (4.1) through the particle for every camera position and view direction. To describe every ray piercing the particle, we need 4D parameterization.[2] The first two parameters are the azimuth $\varphi_S \in [0, 2\pi]$ and zenith $\theta_S \in [0, \pi]$ angles of the point **S** where the view ray enters the particle's bounding sphere (Figure 4.3 (middle)). The other two parameters are the azimuth $\varphi_v \in [0, 2\pi]$ and zenith $\theta_v \in [0, \pi/2]$ angles of the view ray in the tangent frame constructed at the entry point **S** (Figure 4.3 (right)). The z-axis of this frame is pointing toward the sphere center. Note that we only need to consider the rays going inside the sphere; thus, the maximum value for θ_v is $\pi/2$.

To precompute the optical depth integral, we go through all possible values of φ_S, θ_S, φ_v, and θ_v and numerically evaluate the integral in Equation (4.1). Section 4.5.1 provides additional details.

4.3.2 Single Scattering

In contrast to optical depth, we cannot precompute scattering inside the inhomogeneous particle. The reason for this is that we also need to account for the light direction, and this would require five parameters, which is impractical. So we precompute scattering in a homogeneous spherical particle. We assume that the light is shining in the positive z direction. Due to the symmetry of the problem, the light field is symmetrical with respect to the light direction, so the φ_S parameter can be dropped. On the other hand, to compute Equation (4.5), we need to know the light field in the entire volume, not only on the sphere's surface. We thus use the distance from the sphere center to the start point as the fourth parameter. Our parameterization for computing single scattering is then $\theta_S \in [0, \pi]$, $\varphi_v \in [0, 2\pi]$, $\theta_v \in [0, \pi]$, $r \in [0, 1]$. Note that because we now need to cover the entire sphere of directions, the maximum value for θ_v is π.

Precomputing single scattering is then implemented by going through all the parameter values and numerically evaluating Equation (4.2). Since the particle is assumed to be homogeneous, $\beta(\mathbf{P}) \equiv \beta$. Sun intensity, L_{Sun}, and phase function, $P(\theta)$, are factored out and evaluated separately. Additional details can be found in Section 4.5.1.

---

[2]We assume that the camera is always located outside the particle's bounding sphere.

4.3.3 Multiple Scattering

We use the same parameterization for the multiple scattering lookup table as for
the single scattering. To precompute multiple scattering, we process scattering
orders one by one, and for every order we perform three steps:

1. compute the $J^{(n)}$ term using the previous order $L^{(n-1)}$ for all parameter
    values according to Equation (4.5);

2. compute the current order $L^{(n)}$ according to Equation (4.4);

3. accumulate the current scattering order.

Implementation details are given in Section 4.5.1.

After each scattering order is processed, we retain only the light field on the
surface, discarding the rest of the data. It must be noted that in contrast to
optical depth, scattering is not linear with respect to density and particle radius.
In our original method, we precomputed scattering for a number of densities and
encoded the resulting information in a 4D lookup table with the fourth parameter
being the particle density scale. This, however, required additional storage and
two fetches from a 3D texture. We found out that using just one density still
works reasonably well and simplifies the algorithm.

Computing cloud shading using the precomputed lookup tables is discussed
in Section 4.5.3.

4.4   Volume-Aware Blending

Our clouds consists of a collection of individual particles and we need to merge
them together into a continuous medium. A typical way to achieve this would be
using alpha blending. This method, however, is primarily intended for blending
"thin" objects such as glass or tree leaves. Our particles are volumetric entities, and there is no way to account for their intersections using standard alpha
blending. To solve the problem, we propose a new technique, which we call
volume-aware blending. The key idea of this technique is to keep track of the
volumetric element closest to the camera, for each pixel, and blend every new
particle against this representation.

The algorithm starts by clearing the closest element buffer and the back buffer.
It then renders all volumetric particles back to front. Each particle's extent is
tested against the current closest element. If the particle is closer to the camera,
then the closest element's color is written into the back buffer using alpha blending
and the new particle replaces the closest element (see Figure 4.4). If the particle
is located farther from the camera, then its color is blended into the back buffer
and the closest element is retained.

If the particle extent intersects the current closest element, then things become a bit more involved. First, the tail is alpha-blended into the back buffer

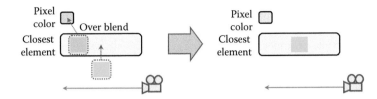

Figure 4.4. Volume-aware blending when the new particle does not intersect the closest element.

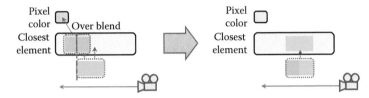

Figure 4.5. Volume-aware blending when the new particle intersects the closest element.

(Figure 4.5). Next, the color of the intersection is computed using the density-weighted average:

$$T_i = e^{-(\rho_0 + \rho_1) \cdot d_i \cdot \beta}, \tag{4.8}$$

$$C_i = \frac{C_0 \cdot \rho_0 + C_1 \cdot \rho_1}{\rho_0 + \rho_1} \cdot (1 - T_i), \tag{4.9}$$

where C_0, C_1, ρ_0, and ρ_1 are non–alpha-premultiplied colors and densities, and d_i is the intersection length. The color of the front part is then alpha-blended with the resulting color C_i, and the new merged element is written back as shown in Figure 4.5 (right). Section 4.5.4 provides additional details.

4.5   Implementation

We implemented our method in C++ using the Direct3D 11 API. The full source code can be found in the supplemental materials to this book. It is also available at https://github.com/GameTechDev/CloudsGPUPro6.

4.5.1   Precomputing Light Transport

Our precomputed data constitute a 4D and a 3D lookup table. The optical depth integral is stored in a $32 \times 16 \times 32 \times 16$ ($N_{\varphi_S} = 32$, $N_{\theta_S} = 16$, $N_{\varphi_v} = 32$, $N_{\theta_v} = 16$) 8-bit lookup table. Multiple scattering is stored in a $32 \times 64 \times 16$ ($N_{\theta_S} = 32$, $N_{\varphi_v} = 64$, $N_{\theta_v} = 16$) 16-bit float lookup table. The first table requires 0.25 MB of storage, while the latter requires 64 KB. Note that in contrast to our base

method, we use a different approach to approximate single scattering that does
not rely on a precomputed lookup table.

Because current graphics hardware does not natively support 4D textures, we
implement them with 3D textures, such that a $X \times Y \times Z \times W$ 4D texture is
stored as a $X \times Y \times Z \cdot W$ 3D texture. We perform manual filtering for the fourth
coordinate as shown below:

```
#define SAMPLE_4D(tex3DLUT, LUT_DIM, f4LUTCoords, fLOD, Result) \
{                                                               \
  float3 f3UVW0;                                                \
  f3UVW0.xy = f4LUTCoords.xy;                                   \
  float fQSlice = f4LUTCoords.w * LUT_DIM.w - 0.5;             \
  float fQ0Slice = floor(fQSlice);                             \
  float fQWeight = fQSlice - fQ0Slice;                         \
  f3UVW0.z = (fQ0Slice + f4LUTCoords.z) / LUT_DIM.w;           \
  /* frac() assures wraparound filtering of w coordinate*/      \
  float3 f3UVW1 = frac(f3UVW0 + float3(0,0,1/LUT_DIM.w));      \
  Result = lerp(                                                \
    tex3DLUT.SampleLevel(samLinearWrap, f3UVW0, fLOD),         \
    tex3DLUT.SampleLevel(samLinearWrap, f3UVW1, fLOD),         \
    fQWeight);                                                  \
}
```

Note that φ_S and φ_v coordinates require wraparound filtering to avoid artifacts. We use the `frac()` function to achieve this for the fourth coordinate. Also
note that the z-coordinate cannot be filtered with wraparound mode.

The precomputation process can be summarized as follows:

1. Precompute the optical depth integral.

2. Precompute single scattering in the whole volume and store the data in the
   temporary 32-bit float lookup table.

3. For scattering order n from 2 to N,

   (a) evaluate the $J^{(n)}$ term in the whole volume,

   (b) evaluate $L_{In}^{(n)}$ in the whole volume,

   (c) accumulate $L_{In}^{(n)}$ in the multiple scattering lookup table.

4. Copy multiple scattering radiance on the sphere's surface from the temporary lookup table into the final 16-bit float table

The rest of this subsection gives details on each step.

Optical depth.   Precomputing the optical depth integral as discussed in Section 4.3.1 is implemented by a shader that renders slices of the lookup table one
by one. The shader code is shown in Listing 4.1.

The shader first computes the start position and the ray direction from the
input 4D coordinates using the `OpticalDepthLUTCoordsToWorldParams()` function

```
 1 float2 PrecomputeOpticalDepthPS (SQuadVSOutput In) : SV_Target
 2 {
 3   float3 f3StartPos , f3RayDir;
 4   // Convert lookup table 4D coordinates into the start
 5   // position and view direction
 6   OpticalDepthLUTCoordsToWorldParams(
 7       float4(ProjToUV(In.m_f2PosPS), g_Attribs.f4Param.xy),
 8       f3StartPos , f3RayDir );
 9
10   // Intersect the view ray with the unit sphere
11   float2 f2RayIsecs;
12   // f3StartPos is located exactly on the surface; slightly
13   // move it inside the sphere to avoid precision issues
14   GetRaySphereIntersection (f3StartPos + f3RayDir*1e-4, f3RayDir ,
15                              0, 1.f, f2RayIsecs);
16
17   float3 f3EndPos = f3StartPos + f3RayDir * f2RayIsecs.y;
18   float fNumSteps = NUM_INTEGRATION_STEPS ;
19   float3 f3Step = (f3EndPos - f3StartPos) / fNumSteps;
20   float fTotalDensity = 0;
21   for(float fStepNum=0.5; fStepNum < fNumSteps; ++fStepNum)
22   {
23     float3 f3CurrPos = f3StartPos + f3Step * fStepNum;
24     float fDensity = ComputeDensity(f3CurrPos);
25     fTotalDensity += fDensity;
26   }
27
28   return fTotalDensity/fNumSteps;
29 }
```

Listing 4.1. Precomputing optical depth integral.

(lines 3–8). The first two components come from the pixel position, the other two are stored in the g_Attribs.f4Param.xy uniform variable. The shader then intersects the ray with the unit sphere (lines 11–15) and finds the ray exit point (line 17). The GetRaySphereIntersection() function takes the ray start position and direction, sphere center (which is 0), and radius (which is 1) as inputs and returns the distances from the start point to the intersections in its fifth argument (the smallest value always go first). Finally, the shader performs numerical integration of Equation (4.1). Instead of storing the integral itself, we store the normalized average density along the ray, which always lies in the range $[0, 1]$ and can be sufficiently represented with an 8-bit UNorm value. Optical depth is reconstructed by multiplying that value by the ray length and extinction coefficient. The ComputeDensity() function combines several 3D noises to evaluate density at the current point.

Single scattering. Precomputing single scattering (Section 4.3.2) is performed by a pixel shader as presented in Listing 4.2. Note that single scattering is computed inside the entire volume, not only on the surface, and a temporary 4D lookup table is used to store it. The fourth coordinate of this table encodes the distance from the sphere center and is provided by the uniform variable g_Attribs.f4Param.y.

```
1 float PrecomputeSingleSctrPS(SQuadVSOutput In) : SV_Target
2 {
3   float3 f3EntryPoint, f3ViewRay, f3LightDir;
4   ScatteringLUTToWorldParams(
5     float4(ProjToUV(In.m_f2PosPS), g_Attribs.f4Param.xy),
6     g_Attribs.f4Param.z, f3EntryPoint, f3ViewRay, f3LightDir);
7
8   // Intersect the view ray with the unit sphere
9   float2 f2RayIsecs;
10  GetRaySphereIntersection(f3EntryPoint, f3ViewRay,
11                           0, 1.f, f2RayIsecs);
12  float3 f3EndPos = f3EntryPoint + f3ViewRay * f2RayIsecs.y;
13
14  float fNumSteps = NUM_INTEGRATION_STEPS;
15  float3 f3Step = (f3EndPos - f3EntryPoint) / fNumSteps;
16  float fStepLen = length(f3Step);
17  float fCloudMassToCamera = 0;
18  float fParticleRadius = g_Attribs.RefParticleRadius;
19  float fInscattering = 0;
20  for(float fStepNum=0.5; fStepNum < fNumSteps; ++fStepNum)
21  {
22    float3 f3CurrPos = f3EntryPoint + f3Step * fStepNum;
23    GetRaySphereIntersection(f3CurrPos, f3LightDir,
24                             0, 1.f, f2RayIsecs);
25    float fCloudMassToLight = f2RayIsecs.x * fParticleRadius;
26    float fAttenuation = exp(
27      -g_Attribs.fAttenuationCoeff *
28      (fCloudMassToLight + fCloudMassToCamera) );
29
30    fInscattering += fAttenuation * g_Attribs.fScatteringCoeff;
31    fCloudMassToCamera += fStepLen * fParticleRadius;
32  }
33
34  return fInscattering * fStepLen * fParticleRadius;
35 }
```

Listing 4.2. Precomputing single scattering.

The shader numerically integrates Equation (4.2). Note that the phase function $P(\theta)$ and the sun intensity L_{Sun} are omitted. Thus, at every step, the shader needs to compute the following integrand: $\beta(\mathbf{P}) \cdot e^{-\tau(\mathbf{Q},\mathbf{P})} \cdot e^{-\tau(\mathbf{P},\mathbf{P_0})}$. The scattering/extinction coefficient $\beta(\mathbf{P})$ is assumed to be constant and is provided by the g_Attribs.fScatteringCoeff variable. We use $\beta = 0.07$ as the scattering/extinction coefficient and a reference particle radius of 200 meters. Extinction $e^{-\tau(\mathbf{Q},\mathbf{P})}$ from the current point to the light entry point is evaluated by intersecting the ray going from the current point toward the light with the sphere (lines 23–25). Extinction $e^{-\tau(\mathbf{P},\mathbf{P_0})}$ toward the camera is computed by maintaining the total cloud mass from the camera to the current point in the fCloudMassToCamera variable (line 31).

Multiple scattering. After single scattering, we compute up to $N = 18$ scattering orders. During this process, we use three temporary 4D 32-bit float lookup tables:

one to store the $J^{(n)}$ term, the other to store the current order scattering $L_{In}^{(n)}$, and the third to accumulate higher-order scattering. Note that these intermediate tables cover the entire volume.

Computing every scattering order consists of three steps, as discussed in Section 4.3.3. The first step is evaluating the $J^{(n)}$ term according to Equation (4.5). This step is implemented by the shader shown in Listing 4.3.

The first step in this shader, like the prior shaders, retrieves the world-space parameters from the 4D texture coordinates (lines 3–6). In the next step, the shader constructs local frame for the ray starting point by calling the `ConstructLocalFrameXYZ()` function (lines 8–10). The function gets two directions as inputs and constructs orthonormal basis. The first direction is used as the z-axis. Note that the resulting z-axis points toward the sphere center (which is 0).

The shader then runs two loops going through the series of zenith θ and azimuth φ angles (lines 18–19), which sample the entire sphere of directions. On every step, the shader constructs a sample direction using the (θ, φ) angles (lines 23–25), computes lookup coordinates for this direction (lines 26–28), and loads the order $n-1$ scattering using these coordinates (lines 29–31). Remember that the precomputed single scattering does not comprise the phase function and we need to apply it now, if necessary (lines 32–34). `g_Attribs.f4Param.w` equals 1 if we are processing the second-order scattering and 0 otherwise. After that, we need to account for the phase function $P(\theta)$ in Equation (4.5) (line 35). For single scattering, we use anisotropy factor $g = 0.9$, and for multiple scattering we use $g = 0.7$ to account for light diffusion in the cloud. Finally, we need to compute the $d\omega = d\theta \cdot d\varphi \cdot sin(\theta)$ term (lines 37–40).

After the $J^{(n)}$ term is evaluated, we can compute nth scattering order according to Equation (4.4). The corresponding shader performing this task is very similar to the shader computing single scattering (Listing 4.4). The difference is that in the integration loop we load $J^{(n)}$ from the lookup table (lines 19–23) instead of computing sunlight attenuation in the particle. We also use trapezoidal integration to improve accuracy.

In the third stage, the simple shader accumulates the current scattering order in the net multiple scattering lookup table by rendering every slice with additive blending.

4.5.2 Particle Generation

We wanted to efficiently control the level of detail and provide high fidelity for close clouds, while still being able to render distant clouds. To do this, we use a nested grid structure inspired by the geometry clipmaps method [Losasso and Hoppe 04]. The grid consists of a number of rings. Particles in each next outer ring are twice the size of particles in the inner ring and have twice the spacing interval. We refer to this structure as a *cell grid* (Figure 4.6 (left)). Each cell

```
1 float GatherScatteringPS(SQuadVSOutput In) : SV_Target
2 {
3   float3 f3StartPos, f3ViewRay, f3LightDir;
4   ScatteringLUTToWorldParams(
5     float4(ProjToUV(In.m_f2PosPS), g_Attribs.f4Param.xy),
6              f3StartPos, f3ViewRay, f3LightDir);
7
8   float3 f3LocalX, f3LocalY, f3LocalZ;
9   ConstructLocalFrameXYZ(-normalize(f3StartPos), f3LightDir,
10                          f3LocalX, f3LocalY, f3LocalZ);
11
12  float fJ = 0;
13  float fTotalSolidAngle = 0;
14  const float fNumZenithAngles = SCTR_LUT_DIM.z;
15  const float fNumAzimuthAngles = SCTR_LUT_DIM.y;
16  const float fZenithSpan = PI;
17  const float fAzimuthSpan = 2*PI;
18  for(float Zen = 0.5; Zen < fNumZenithAngles; ++Zen)
19    for(float Az = 0.5; Az < fNumAzimuthAngles; ++Az)
20    {
21        float fZenith = Zen/fNumZenithAngles * fZenithSpan;
22        float fAzimuth = (Az/fNumAzimuthAngles - 0.5) * fAzimuthSpan;
23        float3 f3CurrDir =
24          GetDirectionInLocalFrameXYZ(f3LocalX, f3LocalY, f3LocalZ,
25                                      fZenith, fAzimuth);
26        float4 f4CurrDirLUTCoords =
27          WorldParamsToScatteringLUT(f3StartPos, f3CurrDir,
28                                     f3LightDir);
29        float fCurrDirSctr = 0;
30        SAMPLE_4D(g_tex3DPrevSctrOrder, SCTR_LUT_DIM,
31                  f4CurrDirLUTCoords, 0, fCurrDirSctr);
32        if( g_Attribs.f4Param.w == 1 )
33          fCurrDirSctr *= HGPhaseFunc( dot(-f3CurrDir, f3LightDir),
34                          0.9 );
35        fCurrDirSctr *= HGPhaseFunc( dot(f3CurrDir, f3ViewRay), 0.7 );
36
37        float fdZenithAngle = fZenithSpan / fNumZenithAngles;
38        float fdAzimuthAngle = fAzimuthSpan / fNumAzimuthAngles *
39                               sin(ZenithAngle);
40        float fDiffSolidAngle = fdZenithAngle * fdAzimuthAngle;
41        fTotalSolidAngle += fDiffSolidAngle;
42        fJ += fCurrDirSctr * fDiffSolidAngle;
43    }
44
45  // Total solid angle should be 4*PI. Renormalize to fix
46  // discretization issues
47  fJ *= 4*PI / fTotalSolidAngle;
48
49  return fJ;
50 }
```

Listing 4.3. Computing J term.

in the grid contains a predefined number of layers. Each voxel of a resulting 3D structure can potentially contain a particle. We refer to this structure as a *particle lattice* (Figure 4.6 (right)). To facilitate particle generation and lighting,

```
1 float ComputeScatteringOrderPS(SQuadVSOutput In) : SV_Target
2 {
3    // Transform lookup coordinates into the world parameters
4    // Intersect the ray with the sphere, compute
5    // start and end points
6    ...
7
8    float fPrevJ = 0;
9    SAMPLE_4D(g_tex3DGatheredScattering, SCTR_LUT_DIM,
10             f4StartPointLUTCoords, 0, fPrevJ);
11   for(float fStepNum=1; fStepNum <= fNumSteps; ++fStepNum)
12   {
13      float3 f3CurrPos = f3StartPos + f3Step * fStepNum;
14
15      fCloudMassToCamera += fStepLen * fParticleRadius;
16      float fAttenuationToCamera = exp( -g_Attribs.fAttenuationCoeff *
17                                        fCloudMassToCamera );
18
19      float4 f4CurrDirLUTCoords =
20          WorldParamsToScatteringLUT(f3CurrPos, f3ViewRay, f3LightDir);
21      float fJ = 0;
22      SAMPLE_4D(g_tex3DGatheredScattering, SCTR_LUT_DIM,
23               f4CurrDirLUTCoords, 0, fJ);
24      fJ *= fAttenuationToCamera;
25
26      fInscattering += (fJ + fPrevJ) / 2;
27      fPrevJ = fJ;
28   }
29
30   return fInscattering * fStepLen * fParticleRadius *
31          g_Attribs.fScatteringCoeff;
32 }
```

Listing 4.4. Computing order-n scattering.

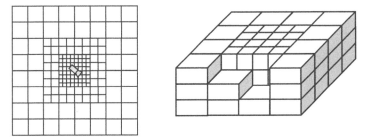

Figure 4.6. Cell grid (left) and 3D lattice (right).

we maintain two additional 3D structures: *cloud density 3D lattice* and *light attenuation 3D lattice*. These two structures have twice the resolution of the particle lattice in each dimension and are implemented as 3D textures.

The steps for particle generation and processing are as follows:

1. Process the 2D cell grid to build a list of valid nonempty cells, and compute the cell attributes.

2. Compute the density for each voxel of the cloud density lattice located in the nonempty cells.

3. Process the visible voxels of the light attenuation lattice located in the nonempty cells and compute attenuation for each voxel.

4. Process the particle lattice and generate particles for visible cells whose density is above the threshold.

5. Process the particles and store lighting information.

6. Sort the particles.

Every step mentioned above is implemented by a compute shader. We use a GPU-based implementation, thus the CPU does not know how many GPU threads need to be executed for each compute kernel. We use the Dispatch Indirect() function to let the GPU assign work to itself. This function takes the same arguments as the regular Dispatch() function, but these arguments are stored in a GPU buffer. What is important is that other compute kernels can write data to that buffer, thus allowing the GPU to control itself. We discuss each step in detail below.

Processing cell grid. The processing cell grid is performed by a compute shader that executes one thread for every cell. It computes the cell center and size based on the camera world position and the location of the cell in the grid. Using the cell center, the shader then computes the base cell density by combining two 2D noise functions. If the resulting value is above the threshold, the cell is said to be *valid* (Figure 4.7). The shader adds indices of all valid cells to the append buffer (g_ValidCellsAppendBuf), which at the end of the stage contains an unordered list of all valid cells. If a cell is also visible in the camera frustum, the shader also adds the cell to another buffer (g_VisibleCellsAppendBuf) that collects valid visible cells.

Processing cloud density lattice. In the next stage, we need to process only those voxels of the lattice that are located within the valid cells of the cloud grid. To compute the required number of GPU threads, we execute a simple one-thread compute shader:

```
RWBuffer<uint> g_DispatchArgsRW  :  register( u0 );
[numthreads(1, 1, 1)]
void ComputeDispatchArgsCS ()
```

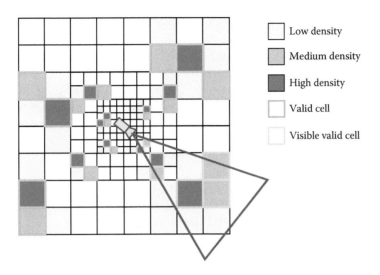

Figure 4.7. Valid cells.

```
{
    uint s = g_GlobalCloudAttribs.uiDensityBufferScale;
    g_DispatchArgsRW[0] = (g_ValidCellsCounter.Load(0) * s*s*s *
        g_GlobalCloudAttribs.uiMaxLayers + THREAD_GROUP_SIZE-1) /
        THREAD_GROUP_SIZE;
}
```

The number of elements previously written into the append buffer can be copied into a resource suitable for reading (`g_ValidCellsCounter`) with the `CopyStructure Count()` function. The buffer previously bound as UAV to `g_DispatchArgsRW` is then passed to the `DispatchIndirect()` function to generate the required number of threads. Each thread then reads the index of the valid cell it belongs to from `g_ValidCellsUnorderedList`, populated at the previous stage, and finds out its location within that cell. Then the shader combines two 3D noise functions with the cell base density to create volumetric noise. The noise amplitude decreases with altitude to create typical cumulus cloud shapes with wider bottoms and narrower tops.

Light attenuation. Light attenuation is computed for every voxel inside the *visible* grid cells. To compute the required number of threads, we use the same simple compute shader used in the previous stage, but this time provide the number of valid *and* visible cells in the `g_ValidCellsCounter` variable. Light attenuation is then computed by casting a ray from the voxel center toward the light and ray marching through the density lattice. We perform a fixed number of 16 steps. Instead of storing light attenuation, we opt to store the attenuating cloud mass because it can be properly interpolated.

Particle generation. The next stage consists of processing valid and visible voxels of the cloud lattice and generating particles for some of them. To generate the required number of threads, we again use the simple one-thread compute shader. The particle generation shader loads the cloud density from the density lattice and, if it is not zero, it creates a particle. The shader randomly displaces the particle from the voxel center and adds a random rotation and scale to eliminate repeating patterns. The shader writes the particle attributes, such as position, density, and size, into the particle info buffer and adds the particle index into another append buffer (`g_VisibleParticlesAppendBuf`).

Processing visible particles. This is required to compute lighting information. In particular, we compute the color of the sunlight reaching the center of the particle, ignoring occlusion by the cloud and the intensity of ambient skylight. We also sample the light-attenuating mass texture to compute the light occlusion. We use the value on the particle surface to compute attenuation for multiple scattering and the value in the particle center for single scattering. Moreover, we scale the light-attenuating mass by a factor of 0.25 to account for strong forward scattering when computing attenuation for multiple scattering.

Sorting. Sorting particles back to front is the final stage before they can be rendered and is necessary for correct blending. In our original work, we sorted all the voxels of the particle lattice on the CPU and then streamed out only valid visible voxels on the GPU. This approach had a number of drawbacks. First, it required active CPU–GPU communication. Second, due to random offsets, particle order could slightly differ from voxel order. But the main problem was that all voxels were always sorted even though many of them were actually empty, which resulted in significant CPU overhead.

We now sort particles entirely on the GPU using the merge sort algorithm by Satish et al. [Satish et al. 09] with a simplified merge procedure. We begin by subdividing the visible particle list into subsequences of 128 particles and sorting each subsequence with a bitonic sort implemented in a compute shader. Then we perform a number of merge stages to get the single sorted list. When executing the binary search of an element to find its rank, we directly access global memory. Because the number of particles that need to be sorted is relatively small (usually not greater than 50,000), the entire list can fit into the cache and merging is still very efficient even though we do not use shared memory.

An important aspect is that we do not know how many particles were generated on the GPU and how many merge passes we need to execute. Thus, we perform enough passes to sort the maximum possible number of particles. The compute shader performs an early exit, with very little performance cost, when no more work needs to be done.

4.5.3 Rendering

After visible particles are generated, processed, and sorted, they are ready for rendering. Since only the GPU knows how many particles were generated, we use the `DrawInstancedIndirect()` function. It is similar to `DrawInstanced()`, but reads its arguments from a GPU buffer. We render one point primitive per visible particle. The geometry shader reads the particle attributes and generates the particle bounding box, which is then sent to the rasterizer.

In the pixel shader, we reconstruct the view ray and intersect it with the ellipsoid enclosed in the particle's bounding box. If the ray misses the ellipsoid, we discard the pixel. Otherwise, we apply our shading model based on the precomputed lookup tables, as shown in Listing 4.5.

Our first step is to compute the normalized density along the view ray using the optical depth lookup table (lines 2–10). We randomly rotate the particle around the vertical axis to eliminate repetitive patterns (line 6). `f3EntryPoint USSpace` and `f3ViewRayUSSpace` are the coordinates of the entry point and the view ray direction transformed into the particle space (which is unit sphere space, thus the US suffix). Next, we compute the transparency (lines 14–17).

Our real-time model consists of three components: single scattering, multiple scattering, and ambient light. We compute single scattering in lines 20–27. It is a product of a phase function, sunlight attenuation (computed as discussed in Section 4.5.2), and the sunlight intensity. Because single scattering is most noticeable where cloud density is low, we multiply the value by the transparency.

Next, we evaluate multiple scattering by performing a lookup into the precomputed table (lines 30–39). We multiply the intensity with the light attenuation. Since multiple scattering happens in dense parts of the cloud, we also multiply the intensity with the opacity (`1-fTransparency`).

Finally, we use an ad hoc approximation for ambient light (lines 42–52). We use the following observation: ambient light intensity is stronger on the top boundary of the cloud and decreases toward the bottom. Figure 4.8 shows different components and the final result.

Figure 4.8. From left to right, single scattering, multiple scattering, ambient, and all components.

```
1  // Compute lookup coordinates
2  float4 f4LUTCoords;
3  WorldParamsToOpticalDepthLUTCoords(f3EntryPointUSSpace,
4                                     f3ViewRayUSSpace, f4LUTCoords);
5  // Randomly rotate the sphere
6  f4LUTCoords.y += ParticleAttrs.fRndAzimuthBias;
7  // Get the normalized density along the view ray
8  float fNormalizedDensity = 1.f;
9  SAMPLE_4D_LUT(g_tex3DParticleDensityLUT, OPTICAL_DEPTH_LUT_DIM,
10               f4LUTCoords, 0, fNormalizedDensity);
11
12 // Compute actual cloud mass by multiplying the normalized
13 // density with ray length
14 fCloudMass = fNormalizedDensity * fRayLength;
15 fCloudMass *= ParticleAttrs.fDensity;
16 // Compute transparency
17 fTransparency = exp( -fCloudMass * g_Attribs.fAttenuationCoeff );
18
19 // Evaluate phase function for single scattering
20 float fCosTheta = dot(-f3ViewRayUSSpace, f3LightDirUSSpace);
21 float PhaseFunc = HGPhaseFunc(fCosTheta, 0.8);
22
23 float2 f2Attenuation = ParticleLighting.f2SunLightAttenuation;
24 // Compute intensity of single scattering
25 float3 f3SingleScattering =
26   fTransparency *  ParticleLighting.f4SunLight.rgb *
27   f2Attenuation.x * PhaseFunc;
28
29 // Compute lookup coordinates for multiple scattering
30 float4 f4MultSctrLUTCoords =
31   WorldParamsToScatteringLUT(f3EntryPointUSSpace,
32   f3ViewRayUSSpace, f3LightDirUSSpace);
33 // Load multiple scattering from the lookup table
34 float fMultipleScattering =
35   g_tex3DScatteringLUT.SampleLevel(samLinearWrap,
36   f4MultSctrLUTCoords.xyz, 0);
37 float3 f3MultipleScattering =
38   (1-fTransparency) * fMultipleScattering *
39   f2Attenuation.y * ParticleLighting.f4SunLight.rgb;
40
41 // Compute ambient light
42 float3 f3EarthCentre = float3(0, -g_Attribs.fEarthRadius, 0);
43 float fEnttryPointAltitude = length(f3EntryPointWS - f3EarthCentre);
44 float fCloudBottomBoundary =
45   g_Attribs.fEarthRadius + g_Attribs.fCloudAltitude -
46   g_Attribs.fCloudThickness/2.f;
47 float fAmbientStrength =
48   (fEnttryPointAltitude - fCloudBottomBoundary) /
49   g_Attribs.fCloudThickness;
50 fAmbientStrength = clamp(fAmbientStrength, 0.3, 1);
51 float3 f3Ambient = (1-fTransparency) * fAmbientStrength *
52                    ParticleLighting.f4AmbientLight.rgb;
```

Listing 4.5. Real-time shading.

4.5.4   Volume-Aware Blending

Blending is the final stage after all particle shading attributes are computed. To implement the volume-aware blending technique described in Section 4.4, we use an unordered access view, which enables the pixel shader to read and write to arbitrary memory locations. For each pixel on the screen, we store the following information about the closest element: minimal/maximal distance along the view ray, optical mass (which is the cloud mass times the scattering coefficient), and color:

```
struct SParticleLayer
{
    float2 f2MinMaxDist;
    float  fOpticalMass;
    float3 f3Color;
};
```

The pixel shader implements the merging scheme described in Section 4.4 and is shown in the code snippet given in Listing 4.6. The shader creates an array of two layers. The properties of one layer are taken from the attributes of the current particle (lines 8–10). The other layer is read from the appropriate position in the buffer (lines 12–17). Then the layers are merged (lines 20–23), and the merged layer is written back (line 26) while color f4OutColor is passed to the output merger unit to be blended with the back buffer.

```
1  // Init extensions
2  IntelExt_Init();
3  ...
4  // Process current particle and compute its color f3NewColor,
5  // mass fCloudMass, and extents fNewMinDist/fNewMaxDist
6
7  SParticleLayer Layers[2];
8  Layers[1].f2MinMaxDist = float2(fNewMinDist, fNewMaxDist);
9  Layers[1].fOpticalMass = fCloudMass * g_Attribs.fAttenuationCoeff;
10 Layers[1].f3Color = f3NewColor;
11
12 uint2 ui2PixelIJ = In.f4Pos.xy;
13 uint uiLayerDataInd =
14    (ui2PixelIJ.x + ui2PixelIJ.y * g_Attribs.uiBackBufferWidth);
15 // Enable pixel shader ordering
16 IntelExt_BeginPixelShaderOrdering();
17 Layers[0] = g_rwbufParticleLayers[uiLayerDataInd];
18
19 // Merge two layers
20 SParticleLayer MergedLayer;
21 float4 f4OutColor;
22 MergeParticleLayers(Layers[0], Layers[1], MergedLayer,
23                     f4OutColor.rgb, f4OutColor.a);
24
25 // Store updated layers
26 g_rwbufParticleLayers[uiLayerDataInd] = MergedLayer;
```

Listing 4.6. Volume-aware blending.

Particle info buffer `g_rwbufParticleLayers` is declared as a read/write buffer:

```
RWStructuredBuffer<SParticleLayer> g_rwbufParticleLayers;
```

It must be noted that the algorithm described above would not work as expected on standard DirectX 11–class graphics hardware. The reason is that we are trying to read from the same memory in parallel from different pixel shader threads, modify data, and write it back. There is no efficient way on DirectX 11 to serialize such operations. Intel graphics chips, starting with the Intel HD Graphics 5000, can solve this problem. They contain a special extension, called *pixel shader ordering*. When it is enabled, it guarantees that all read–modify–write operations from different pixel shader instances, which map to the same pixel, are performed atomically. Moreover, the pixel shader instances are executed in the same order in which primitives were submitted for rasterization. The second condition is very important to ensure temporally stable results. In DirectX 11, the extensions are exposed through two functions. `IntelExt_Init()` tells the compiler that the shader is going to use extensions, and after the call to `IntelExt_BeginPixelShaderOrdering()`, all instructions that access UAVs get appropriately ordered. It is worth mentioning that this capability will be a standard feature of DirectX 12, where it will be called rasterizer ordered views.

After all particles are rendered, the closest volume buffer needs to be merged with the back buffer. We render a screen-size quad and perform the required operations in the pixel shader.

During rendering, we generate three buffers: cloud color, transparency, and the distance to the closest cloud. To improve performance, we render the clouds to a quarter resolution buffers $(1/2 \times 1/2)$ and then upscale to the original resolution using a bilateral filter.

4.5.5 Integration with Atmospheric Effects

To render the earth's atmosphere, we use the method described in our earlier work [Yusov 14a]. To create the effect of light shafts, we employ a light-space cloud transparency buffer. This buffer is populated by projecting the 2D noise (Section 4.5.2) onto the light projection plane. The buffer has the same structure as a cascaded shadow map. We use this buffer to attenuate the sunlight. We assume that the cloud altitude is fixed. Then, at each step, we check if the current sample on the ray is below or above this altitude. If it is, we sample the light-space attenuation texture to get the amount of light that reaches the point through the cloud. We use the same minimum–maximum structure to accelerate the ray traversal. To eliminate artifacts, we reduce the step size to one texel when crossing the cloud altitude. We also use screen-space cloud transparency

Figure 4.9. Sample refinement takes cloud transparency into account.

and distance to the cloud to attenuate the light samples along the view ray (please refer to [Yusov 14b] for more details).

One important missing detail is sample refinement (see [Yusov 14a]), which needs to account for screen-space cloud transparency. When computing coarse unoccluded in-scattering, we take the screen-space cloud transparency and distance to attenuate the current sample. This automatically gives the desired effect (Figure 4.9) with a minimal increase in performance cost.

4.6 Results and Discussion

Figure 4.10 shows some images generated using our method under different lighting conditions. To evaluate the performance, we used two test platforms. The first platform is an Ultrabook powered by an Intel Core i5 CPU and an Intel HD Graphics 5200 GPU (47 W shared between CPU and GPU). Our second test platform is a desktop workstation powered by an Intel Core i7 CPU and an NVIDIA GeForce GTX 680 GPU (195 W TDP). The viewport resolution was set to 1280 × 720 on the first platform and to 1920 × 1080 on the second. Note also that the NVIDIA GPU does not support pixel shader ordering, so images were rendered with volume-aware blending disabled. Also note that this feature is going to be exposed in DirectX 12, so it will soon be available on a wide range of graphics hardware.

We used four quality settings: low, medium, high, and highest (Table 4.1). Figure 4.11 compares images rendered by our algorithm in each setting.

Table 4.2 summarizes the performance of different stages of the algorithm on our first test platform.

Rendering particles takes the most time, about 70% of the rendering time, in all cases. The main sticking point is sampling the precomputed optical depth texture. Reducing its resolution can significantly improve performance at the

Figure 4.10. Images generated by our algorithm.

Profile	Num. rings	Ring dimension	Num. layers	Num. particles
Low	4	120	3	2919
Medium	5	136	4	7103
High	5	168	6	15,725
Highest	5	216	8	33,702

Table 4.1. Quality profiles.

Profile	Clearing	Processing	Sorting	Rendering	Total
Low	0.62	0.63	0.24	4.22	5.71
Medium	1.31	1.00	0.31	8.72	11.34
High	2.98	2.07	0.48	15.73	21.26
Highest	6.53	4.62	0.83	26.5	28.48

Table 4.2. Performance of the algorithm on Intel HD Graphics 5200, 1280 × 720 resolution (times in ms).

Figure 4.11. Test scene rendered in different quality profiles: highest (top left), high (top right), medium (bottom left), and low (bottom right).

Profile	Processing	Sorting	Rendering	Total
Low	0.38	0.1	1.74	2.22
Medium	0.65	0.11	3.73	4.49
High	1.39	0.14	6.53	8.06
Highest	2.97	0.24	10.72	13.93

Table 4.3. Performance of the algorithm on NVIDIA GeForce GTX 680, 1920 × 1080 resolution (times in ms).

cost of lower quality. The processing stage includes all the steps discussed in Section 4.5.2 except sorting, which is shown in a separate column. The clearing column shows the amount of time required to clear the cloud density and light attenuation 3D textures to initial values. This step takes almost the same time as processing itself. This is because of the low memory bandwidth of the GPU. Rendering light scattering effects takes an additional 5.8 ms. In the medium-quality profile, the total required time is less than 20 ms, which guarantees real-time frame rates.

Performance results on our high-end test platform are given in Table 4.3. Because our second GPU has much higher memory bandwidth, the performance of the algorithm is significantly better. It takes less than 2.3 ms to render the clouds in low profile and less than 4.5 ms to render in medium profile at full HD resolution. Since clearing the 3D textures takes much less time, we do not separate this step in Table 4.3. Computing atmospheric light scattering takes an additional 3.0 ms of processing time. Also note that the GTX 680 is a relatively old GPU. Recent graphics hardware provides higher memory bandwidth, which will improve the performance of our method.

4.6.1 Limitations

Our method is physically based, not physically accurate. We make two main simplifications when approximating shading: scattering is precomputed in a homogeneous spherical particle, and energy exchange between particles is ignored. Precomputing the scattering inside an inhomogeneous particle would require a 5D table. It is possible that some degrees of that table can allow point sampling, which would reduce the lookup into the table to two fetches from a 3D texture. This is an interesting direction for future research.

The other limitation of our method is that our volume-aware blending can precisely handle the intersection of only two particles. When more than three particles intersect, the method can fail. However, visual results are acceptable in most cases. We also believe that our method gives a good use-case example for the capabilities of upcoming GPUs.

4.7 Conclusion

In this chapter we presented a new method for rendering realistic clouds. The key idea of our approach is to precompute optical depth and single and multiple scattering for a reference particle at preprocess time and to store the resulting information in lookup tables. The data is then used at runtime to compute cloud shading without the need for ray marching or slicing. We also presented a new technique for controlling the level of detail as well as a method to blend the particles accounting for their volumetric intersection. We believe that our idea of precomputing scattering is promising and can be further improved in future research. The idea of precomputing transparency can also be used for rendering different kinds of objects such as distant trees in forests.

Bibliography

[Bohren and Huffman 98] C. Bohren and D. R. Huffman. *Absorption and Scattering of Light by Small Particles.* Berlin: Wiley-VCH, 1998.

[Bouthors et al. 06] Antoine Bouthors, Fabrice Neyret, and Sylvain Lefebvre. "Real-Time Realistic Illumination and Shading of Stratiform Clouds." In *Proceedings of the Second Eurographics Conference on Natural Phenomena,* pp. 41–50. Aire-la-Ville, Switzerland: Eurographics Association, 2006.

[Bouthors et al. 08] Antoine Bouthors, Fabrice Neyret, Nelson Max, Eric Brune-ton, and Cyril Crassin. "Interactive Multiple Anisotropic Scattering in Clouds." In *SI3D*, edited by Eric Haines and Morgan McGuire, pp. 173–182. New York: ACM, 2008.

[Bouthors 08] Antoine Bouthors. "Real-Time Realistic Rendering of Clouds." PhD thesis, Université Joseph Fourier, 2008.

[Cornette and Shanks 92] W.M. Cornette and J.G. Shanks. "Physical Reason-able Analytic Expression for the Single-Scattering Phase Function." *Applied Optics* 31:16 (1992), 3152–3160.

[Dobashi et al. 00] Yoshinori Dobashi, Kazufumi Kaneda, Hideo Yamashita, Tsuyoshi Okita, and Tomoyuki Nishita. "A Simple, Efficient Method for Realistic Animation of Clouds." In *Proceedings of the 27th Annual Con-ference on Computer Graphics and Interactive Techniques*, pp. 19–28. New York: ACM Press/Addison-Wesley, 2000.

[Harris and Lastra 01] Mark J. Harris and Anselmo Lastra. "Real-Time Cloud Rendering." *Comput. Graph. Forum* 20:3 (2001), 76–85.

[Harris 03] Mark Jason Harris. "Real-Time Cloud Simulation and Rendering." Ph.D. thesis, The University of North Carolina at Chapel Hill, 2003.

[Losasso and Hoppe 04] Frank Losasso and Hugues Hoppe. "Geometry Clipmaps: Terrain Rendering Using Nested Regular Grids." *ACM Trans. Graph.* 23:3 (2004), 769–776.

[Miyazaki et al. 04] Ryo Miyazaki, Yoshinori Dobashi, and Tomoyuki Nishita. "A Fast Rendering Method of Clouds Using Shadow-View Slices." In *Proceed-ing of Computer Graphics and Imaging 2004, August 17–19, 2004, Kauai, Hawaii, USA*, pp. 93–98. Calgary: ACTA Press, 2004.

[Riley et al. 04] Kirk Riley, David S. Ebert, Martin Kraus, Jerry Tessendorf, and Charles Hansen. "Efficient Rendering of Atmospheric Phenomena." In *Pro-ceedings of the Fifteenth Eurographics Conference on Rendering Techniques*, pp. 375–386. Aire-la-Ville, Switzerland: Eurographics Association, 2004.

[Satish et al. 09] Nadathur Satish, Mark Harris, and Michael Garland. "Design-ing Efficient Sorting Algorithms for Manycore GPUs." In *Proceedings of the 2009 IEEE International Symposium on Parallel&Distributed Process-ing, IPDPS '09*, pp. 1–10. Washington, DC: IEEE Computer Society, 2009.

[Schpok et al. 03] Joshua Schpok, Joseph Simons, David S. Ebert, and Charles Hansen. "A Real-time Cloud Modeling, Rendering, and Animation System." In *Proceedings of the 2003 ACM SIGGRAPH/Eurographics Symposium on*

Computer Animation, pp. 160–166. Aire-la-Ville, Switzerland: Eurographics Association, 2003.

[Wang 04] Niniane Wang. "Realistic and Fast Cloud Rendering." *J. Graphics, GPU, and Game Tools* 9:3 (2004), 21–40.

[Yusov 14a] Egor Yusov. "High Performance Outdoor Light Scattering using Epipolar Sampling." In *GPU Pro 5: Advanced Rendering Techniques*, edited by Wolfgang Engel, pp. 101–126. Boca Raton, FL: CRC Press, 2014.

[Yusov 14b] Egor Yusov. "High-Performance Rendering of Realistic Cumulus Clouds Using Pre-computed Lighting." In *Proceedings of High-Performance Graphics 2014*, edited by Ingo Wald and Jonathan Ragan-Kelley, pp. 127–136. Lyon, France: Eurographics Association, 2014.

Sparse Procedural
Volume Rendering
Doug McNabb

5.1 Introduction

The capabilities and visual quality of real-time rendered volumetric effects disproportionately lag those of film. Many other real-time rendering categories have seen recent dramatic improvements. Lighting, shadowing, and postprocessing have come a long way in just the past few years. Now, volumetric rendering is ripe for a transformation. We now have enough compute to build practical implementations that approximate film-style effects in real time. This chapter presents one such approach.

5.2 Overview of Current Techniques

There are many different kinds of volumetric effects, and games render them with several different techniques. We cover a few of them here.

Many games render volumetric effects with 2D billboard sprites. Sprites can produce a wide range of effects, from smoke and fire to water splashes, froth, and foam. They have been around for years, and talented artists are constantly getting better at using them. But, the sprite techniques have limits and are beginning to show their age. The growing excitement for virtual reality's stereoscopic rendering is particularly difficult because the billboard trick is more apparent when viewed in stereo, challenging the illusion. We need a better approximation. The techniques presented here help improve the illusion. (See the example in Figure 5.1.)

There have been several recent advancements in rendering light scattering in homogeneous media, enabling effects like skies, uniform smoke, and fog. These techniques leverage the volume's uniformity to simplify the light-scattering approximations. They're now fast enough to approximate multiple scattering in

Figure 5.1. Sparse procedural volume rendering example.

real time with amazing visual quality [Yusov 14]. Light scattering in heterogeneous participating media is the more-general problem, and correspondingly is more expensive. Our technique approximates single scattering in heterogeneous media and can look very good. It is worth noting that our scattering model is simpler than the typical homogeneous counterparts to accommodate the added complexity from heterogeneous media.

Fluid simulation is another mechanism for generating volumetric effects. The results are often stunning, particularly where accuracy and realism are required. But, the costs can be high in both performance and memory. Developers typically use these simulations to fill a volume with "stuff" (e.g., smoke, fire, water, etc.), and then render that volume by marching rays originating from the eye's point of view. They periodically (e.g., every frame) update a 3D voxel array of properties. Each voxel has properties like pressure, mass, velocity, color, temperature, etc. Our technique fills the volume differently, avoiding most of the traditional simulation's computation and memory costs. We can use less memory than typical fluid simulations by directly populating the volume from a small set of data. We can further reduce the memory requirements by filling the volume on demand, processing only the parts of the volume that are covered by volume primitives. This volume-primitive approach is also attractive to some artists as it gives good control over sculpting the final effect.

5.3   Overview

Our goal for rendering the volume is to approximate efficiently how much light propagates through the volume and reaches the eye. We perform a three-step process to produce our results:

1. Fill a volume with procedural volume primitives.

2. Propagate lighting through the volume.

3. Ray-march the volume from the eye's point of view.

Before we compute how much light propagates through a volume, we need to know the volume's contents; we need to fill the volume with interesting stuff. Volume primitives are an inexpensive, expressive option for describing a volume's contents [Wrennige and Zafar 11]. Different volume primitive types are characterized by their different mechanisms for describing and controlling the contents. Procedural volume primitives describe the contents with algorithms controlled by a set of parameters (e.g., size, position, radius, etc.). We can populate a volume with multiple primitives, sculpting more-complex results. There are many possible volume primitive types. Our system implements a single "displaced sphere" procedural volume primitive. We often refer to them interchangeably as *particles* and *displaced spheres*.

Rendering a single volume primitive is interesting, but a system that can render many and varied overlapping volume primitives is much more useful. We need to render many volume primitives within a unified volume; they need to correctly shadow and occlude each other. Supporting translucent volume primitives is particularly useful. We satisfy these requirements by decoupling the volume "filling" step from the light propagation step. We fill a metavoxel with all relevant volume primitives before we propagate lighting by ray-marching through the volume. We simplify light propagation by supporting only a single directional light (e.g., the sun), allowing us to orient the volume to align with the light's direction. This enables us to traverse trivially the volume one voxel at a time along the light's direction. Each light propagation step illuminates the current voxel with the current light intensity. At each step, the intensity is attenuated to account for absorption and scattering. Note that we propagate only the light intensity. This process can be extended (at additional cost) to accommodate colored light by independently propagating each of the red, green, and blue wavelength intensities.

We capture the volume's lit color and density (or opacity) at each voxel. Note that our model doesn't include light scattered from the neighboring volume. This could presumably be added at additional cost in time and complexity. Our model does account for shadows cast by the rest of the scene onto the volume, and for casting the volume's shadow onto the rest of the scene.

When the eye sees the lit volume, the amount of light it sees at each voxel is reduced by any other voxels between the lit volume and the eye. This is similar to propagating light through the volume with a couple of important differences. The eye view is a perspective view, in contrast to the directional light's orthographic view. And, each voxel along the eye ray can both occlude more-distant voxels and contribute light (if the voxel is emissive, or lit by the light).

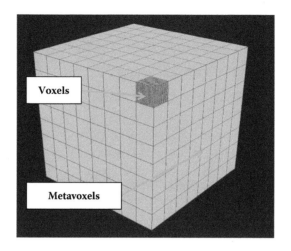

Figure 5.2. A large volume composed of metavoxels, which are composed of voxels.

The volume may also occlude the background; the amount of light from the background that reaches the eye can be absorbed and scattered by the volume. Our approach separates these two eye-view contributions. We determine the lit volume's contribution with a pixel shader and attenuate the background's contribution with alpha blending.

5.4   Metavoxels

The key point of our approach is that we can gain efficiency by avoiding unoccupied parts of the volume. Each of our tasks can be made significantly less expensive: we can fill fewer voxels, propagate light through fewer voxels, and ray-march fewer voxels. We accomplish this by logically subdividing the volume into a uniform grid of smaller volumes. Each of these smaller volumes is in turn a collection of voxels, which we call a *metavoxel*. (See Figure 5.2.)

The metavoxel enables us to efficiently fill and light the volume. Most importantly, it allows us to avoid working on empty metavoxels. It also allows processing multiple metavoxels in parallel (filling can be parallel; lighting has some dependencies). It allows us to switch back and forth between filling metavoxels and ray-marching them, choosing our working set size to balance performance against memory size and bandwidth. Using a small set improves locality. Reusing the same memory over many metavoxels can reduce the total memory required and may reduce bandwidth (depending on the hardware). It also improves ray-marching efficiency, as many rays encounter the same voxels.

Figure 5.3 shows a few variations of a simple scene and the related metavoxels. The first pane shows a few stand-in spheres, a camera, and a light. The second

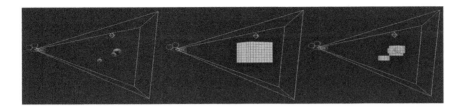

Figure 5.3. A simple scene (left), with all metavoxels (middle) and with only interesting/occupied metavoxels (right).

Figure 5.4. Multiple spheres and the metavoxels they cover.

pane shows a complete volume containing the spheres. The third pane shows the scene with only those metavoxels covered by one or more spheres. This simplified example shows a total volume of $512(8^3)$ metavoxels. It requires processing only 64 of them, culling 7/8 of the volume.

Figure 5.4 shows a stream of simple spheres and a visualization of the metavoxels they cover. Note how the metavoxels are tilted toward the light. Orienting the volume this way allows for independently propagating light along each voxel column. The lighting for any individual voxel depends only on the voxel above it in the column (i.e., the next voxel closer to the light) and is unrelated to voxels in neighboring columns.

Computers get more efficient every year. But memory bandwidth isn't progressing as rapidly as compute efficiency. Operating on cache-friendly metavoxels

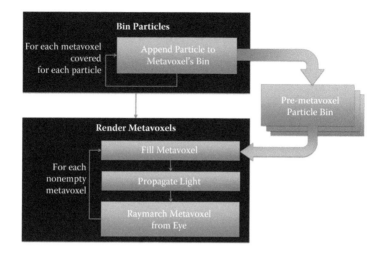

Figure 5.5. High-level algorithm.

may be more useful in the coming years as compute efficiency will almost certainly continue to outpace bandwidth efficiency. Ray-marching multiple metavoxels one at a time can be more efficient than ray-marching a larger volume. The metavoxel localizes the sample points to a relatively small volume, potentially improving cache hit rates and minimizing expensive off-chip bandwidth.

We fill a metavoxel by testing its voxels against the set of particles that cover the metavoxel. For each of the voxels covered by a particle, we compute the particle's color and density at the covered location. Limiting this test to the metavoxel's set of voxels is more efficient than filling a much larger volume; choosing a metavoxel size such that it fits in the cache(s) can reduce expensive off-chip bandwidth. Processing a single voxel multiple times, e.g., once for each particle, can also be more efficient if the voxel's intermediate values are in the cache. Populating the metavoxel with one particle type at a time allows us to maintain separate shaders, which each process different particle types. Note that we currently populate the volume with only a single particle type (displaced sphere). But, composing an effect from multiple particle types is a desirable feature and may be simplified through sharing intermediate results versus a system that requires that a single shader support every particle type.

5.5   Algorithm

Our goal is to render the visible, nonempty metavoxels. Figure 5.5 shows that we loop over each of these interesting metavoxels, filling them with particles (i.e., our displaced sphere volume primitive), and then ray-marching them from the

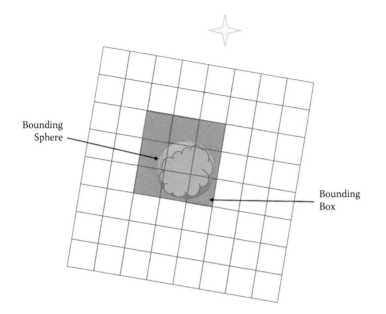

Figure 5.6. Visualization of binning rules.

eye. It's worth noting that "visible" here means visible either from the eye's view or the light's view. We consider the light's view when culling because even if a metavoxel lies outside the eye view, it may still lie between the light and the eye's view such that the metavoxels that are within the eye's view may receive its shadows. We need to propagate lighting through all parts of the volume that contribute to the final scene.

5.5.1 Binning

We determine the interesting metavoxels using a binning process. Binning adds a small amount of extra work but it reduces the overall workload. We can quickly generate a list for each metavoxel containing the indices for the particles that cover the metavoxel, and only those particles. It also allows us to completely avoid metavoxels that aren't covered by any particles.

Each bin holds a list of particle indices. We populate the bin with an index for every particle that covers the metavoxel. We maintain an array of bins—one bin for every metavoxel. (For example, were we to subdivide our total volume into $32 \times 32 \times 32$ metavoxels, then we would have a $32 \times 32 \times 32$ array of bins.) A typical sparsely populated volume will involve a small fraction of these, though the algorithm does not inherently impose a limit.

We bin a particle by looping over the metavoxels covered by the particle's bounding box. (See Figure 5.6.) We refine the approximation and improve overall

```
// Determine the particle's extents
min = particleCenter − particleRadius
max = particleCenter + particleRadius

// Loop over each metavoxel within the extents
// Append the particle to those bins for the
// metavoxels also covered by the bounding sphere
for Z in min.Z to max.Z
    for Y in min.Y to max.Y
        for X in min.X to max.X
            if particleBoundingSphere covers metavoxel[Z,Y,X]
                append particle to metavoxelBin[Z,Y,X]}
```

Listing 5.1. Binning pseudocode.

efficiency by testing each of these metavoxels against the particle's bounding sphere. If the particle's bounding sphere covers the metavoxels, then we append the particle to the metavoxel's bin.

Listing 5.1 shows simple pseudocode for binning a particle.

5.5.2 Filling Metavoxels

Our goal is to ray-march the metavoxels from the eye's point of view. Before we can do that, we need a metavoxel through which to march rays. We populate a metavoxel by testing each of its voxels against each volume-primitive particle. We say the voxel is covered by the particle if and only if the voxel is inside the volume primitive.

We reduce the number of tests by testing each metavoxel only against the particles that cover it; many more particles may participate in the system, but they may cover only other metavoxels. There are many more potential optimizations for reducing the total number of tests (e.g., progressive/hierarchical traversal). Some of these strategies can be explored within this framework, but some of them encourage fundamental changes. We look forward to future improvements.

Our task for filling the metavoxel has two goals:

1. a final density value for every voxel,

2. a final color value for every voxel.

We use a simple model for combining particle densities and colors:

$$\text{density}_{\text{final}} = \sum_{1}^{n} \text{density}_n,$$

$$\text{color}_{\text{final}} = \max(\text{color}_0 \ldots \text{color}_n).$$

The final density is given by a simple sum of the densities for every particle that covers the voxel. Color is more complex. We could blend colors together

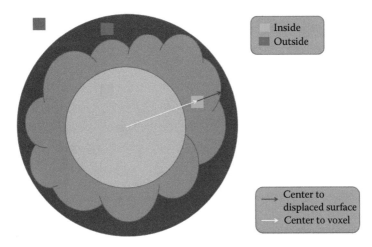

Figure 5.7. Determining coverage.

proportionally to particle density (i.e., a dense particle affects the final color more than a less-dense particle). In practice, simply accepting the maximum between two colors produces plausible results and is computationally inexpensive. This won't work for every effect, but it efficiently produces good results for some.

Different color components may be required for different effects. For example, fire is emissive with color ranging from white through yellow and orange to red, then black as the intensity drops. Smoke is often constant color and not emissive. The diffuse color is modulated by light and shadow, while the emissive color is not.

We compute the density by performing a coverage test. Figure 5.7 shows our approach. We determine the particle's density at each voxel's position. If a voxel is inside the displaced sphere, then we continue and compute the particle's color and density. Voxels outside the displaced sphere are unmodified. Note that the displacement has a limited range; there are two potentially interesting radii— inner and outer. If the voxel is inside the inner radius, then we can be sure it's inside the displaced sphere. If the voxel is outside the outer radius, then we can be sure that it's outside the displaced sphere. Coverage for voxels that lie between these two points is defined by the displacement amount.

We radially displace the sphere. The position of each point on the displaced sphere's surface is given by the length of the vector from the sphere's center to the surface. If the vector from the sphere's center to the voxel is shorter than this displacement, then the voxel is inside the sphere; otherwise it's outside.

Note a couple of optimizations. First, the dot product inexpensively computes length^2: $\mathbf{A} \cdot \mathbf{A} = \text{length}^2(\mathbf{A})$. Using distance^2 allows us to avoid the potentially expensive square-root operations. The second optimization comes from storing

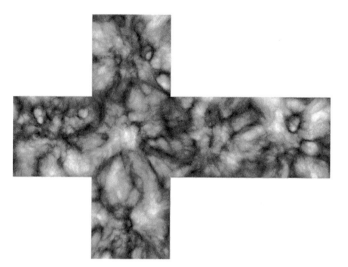

Figure 5.8. Example cube map: 3D noise sampled at sphere surface, projected to cube map faces.

our displacement values in a cube map. The cube map, like the displacement is defined over the sphere's surface. Given a voxel at position (X, Y, Z) and the sphere's center at $(0, 0, 0)$, the displacement is given by cubeMap$[X, Y, Z]$.

We don't currently support dynamically computed noise. We suspect that a dynamic solutions would benefit from using a cube map for intermediate storage as an optimization; the volume is 3D while the cube map is 2D (cube map locations are given by three coordinates, but they project to a flat, 2D surface as seen in Figure 5.8). The number of expensive dynamic-noise calculations can be reduced this way.

We determine each voxel's lit color by determining how much light reaches it and multiplying by the unlit color. We propagate the lighting through the volume to determine how much light reaches each voxel. (See Figure 5.9.)

There are many possible ways to compute the color: constant, radial gradient, polynomial, texture gradient, cube map, noise, etc. We leave this choice to the reader. We note a couple of useful approximations: Figure 5.10 shows the results of using the displacement map as an ambient occlusion approximation and using the radial distance as a color ramp (from very bright red-ish at the center to dark gray further out). The ambient occlusion approximation can help a lot to provide form to the shadowed side.

Many of the displaced sphere's properties can be animated over time: position, orientation, scale, opacity, color, etc. This is a similar paradigm to 2D billboards, only with 3D volume primitives.

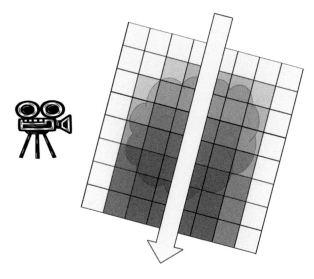

Figure 5.9. Propagating light through a metavoxel's voxels.

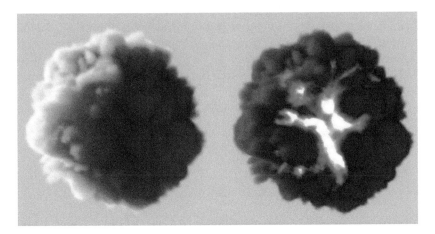

Figure 5.10. Procedural colors.

5.5.3 Light Propagation

We propagate light through the metavoxel with a simple loop. We use the rasterizer and pixel shader to perform the work. We draw one pixel for each of the metavoxel's voxel columns—i.e., a two-triangle quad covering one pixel for each of our voxel columns (e.g., for a $32 \times 32 \times 32$ metavoxel, we draw a 32×32 pixel square). Our pixel/fragment shader loops over each voxel in the corresponding voxel column.

```
// 100% light propagates to start
propagatedLight = 1

// Loop over all voxels in the column
for Z in 0 to METAVOXEL_HEIGHT
    // Light this voxel
    color[Z] *= propagatedLight

    // Attenuate the light leaving this voxel
    propagatedLight /= (1 + density[Z])
```

Listing 5.2. Light propagation pseudocode.

Listing 5.2 shows pseudocode for propagating lighting through the metavoxel. At each step, we light the current voxel and attenuate the light for subsequent voxels.

5.5.4 Eye-View Ray March

We march along the eye rays, through the metavoxel, accumulating color from the metavoxel's lit voxels and attenuating according to the voxel's density.

We implement the eye-view ray march by drawing a cube (i.e., 6 quads = 12 triangles) with the rasterizer from the eye's point of view. The pixel shader executes once for each pixel covered by the cube. Listing 5.3 gives pseudocode for the pixel shader. It loops along a ray from the eye through the pixel, sampling the

```
// The ray starts at the eye and goes through the
// near plane at the current pixel
ray = pixelPosition - eyePosition

// Compute the start and end points where the ray
// enters and exits this metavoxel
start = intersectFar( ray, metavoxel )
end = intersectNear( ray, metavoxel )

// Clamp the ray to the eye position
end = max( eyePosition, end )

// Start assuming volume is empty
// == black, and 100% transmittance
resultColor = 0
resultTransmittance = 1

// step along the ray, accumulating and attenuating
for step in start to end
    color = volume[step].rgb
    density = volume[step].a
    blendFactor = 1/(1 + density)
    resultColor = lerp( color, resultColor, blendFactor )
    resultTransmittance *= blendFactor
```

Listing 5.3. Ray march pseudocode.

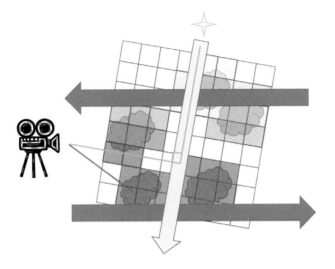

Figure 5.11. Metavoxel sort order.

volume as a 3D texture at each step. It accumulates lighting from the sample's color and attenuates it by the sample's alpha (i.e., density). The end result is a color and an alpha we can use with alpha blending to composite with our back buffer.

Note that we draw this box with front-face culling. If the eye is inside the box, then it sees only back faces. If we were to use back-face culling, then the pixels wouldn't draw and no ray marching would occur. We also don't want to draw without culling because that would potentially cause our pixels to unnecessarily draw twice.

5.5.5 Metavoxel Sort Order

Lastly, we need to render the metavoxels in the correct order for the alpha blending to be correct. We render the metavoxels one at a time, propagating light and ray-marching each one. The results blend to a shared render target. Because the metavoxels can contain semitransparent voxels, order matters.

Figure 5.11 demonstrates why we need to process our metavoxels from the top to bottom (with respect to the light) and back to front (with respect to the eye). Light propagation dictates the top-to-bottom order because an individual metavoxel's final colors depend on how much light propagates through any metavoxels nearer the light. Similarly, we need to blend each metavoxel's eye-view ray march results with those of previously rendered metavoxels.

There's a twist, however. Rendering from top to bottom and back to front can produce incorrect results for those metavoxels below the perpendicular (the green line from the camera). The eye is looking down on those metavoxels. So, the eye can see through some previously rendered metavoxels. In this case, we need to render the more-recent metavoxel behind the previously rendered metavoxel. The solution is to process all of the metavoxels above the perpendicular before processing those below. We also switch sort order and render those metavoxels below the line sorted front to back.

The different sort orders require different alpha-blending modes. We render back to front with *over blending*. We render front to back with *under blending* [Ikits et al. 04].

It is possible to render all metavoxels sorted front to back with under blending. That requires maintaining at least one column of metavoxels. Light propagation requires processing from top to bottom. Sorting front to back can require rendering a metavoxel before those above it have been processed. In that case, we would still propagate the lighting through the entire column before ray-marching them. Consistently sorting front to back like this could potentially allow us to "early out," avoiding future work populating and ray-marching fully occluded voxels.

5.6 Conclusion

Computers are now fast enough for games to include true volumetric effects. One way is to fill a sparse volume with volume primitives and ray-march it from the eye. Efficiently processing a large volume can be achieved by breaking it into smaller metavoxels in which we process only the occupied metavoxels that contribute to the final image. Filling the metavoxels with volume primitives allows us to efficiently populate the volume with visually interesting contents. Finally, sampling the metavoxels from a pixel shader as 3D textures delivers an efficient ray-marching technique.

Bibliography

[Ikits et al. 04] Milan Ikits, Joe Kniss, Aaron Lefohn, and Charles Hansen. "Volume Rendering Techniques." In *GPU Gems*, edited by Randima Fernando, Chapter 39. Reading, MA: Addison-Wesley Professional, 2004.

[Wrennige and Zafar 11] Magnus Wrennige and Nafees Bin Zafar "Production Volume Rendering Fundamentals." SIGGRAPH Course, Vancouver, Canada, August 7–11, 2011.

[Yusov 14] Egor Yusov. "High Performance Outdoor Light Scattering using Epipolar Sampling" In *GPU Pro 5: Advanced Rendering Techniques*, edited by Wolfgang Engel, pp. 101–126. Boca Raton, FL: CRC Press, 2014.

III

Lighting

Lighting became one of the most active areas of research and development for many of the game teams. Ever increasing speed of the GPUs in Playstation 4, Xbox One, and new PCs finally give programmers enough power to move beyond the Phong lighting model and rudimentary shadow algorithms. We're also seeing solutions for in-game indirect diffuse or specular lighting, be it prerendered or real-time generated.

The chapter "Real-Time Lighting via Light Linked List" by Abdul Bezrati discusses an extension to the deferred lighting approach used at Insomniac Games. The algorithm allows us to properly shade both opaque and translucent surfaces of a scene in an uniform way. The algorithm manages linked lists of lights affecting each pixel on screen. Each shaded pixel then can read this list and compute the appropriate lighting and shadows.

This section also includes two chapters about techniques used in *Assassin's Creed IV: Black Flag* from Ubisoft. "Deferred Normalized Irradiance Probes" by John Huelin, Benjamin Rouveyrol, and Bartłomiej Wroński describes the global illumination with day–night cycle support. The authors take time to talk about various tools and runtime optimizations that allowed them to achieve very quick turnaround time during the development.

"Volumetric Fog and Lighting" by Bartłomiej Wroński focuses on volumetric fog and scattering rendering. The chapter goes beyond screen-space ray marching and describes a fully volumetric solution running on compute shaders and offers various practical quality and performance optimizations.

The next chapter, "Physically Based Light Probe Generation on GPU" by Ivan Spogreev, shows several performance optimizations that allowed the generation of specular light probes in *FIFA 15*. The algorithm relies on importance sampling in order to minimize the amount of image samples required to correctly approximate the specular reflection probes.

The last chapter in this section is "Real-Time Global Illumination Using slices" by Hugh Malan. Malan describes a novel way of computing single-bounce indirect lighting. The technique uses slices, a set of 2D images aligned to scene surfaces, that store the scene radiance to compute and propagate the indirect lighting in real time.

I would like to thank all authors for sharing their ideas and for all the hard work they put into their chapters.

—Michal Valient

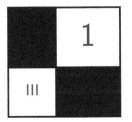

Real-Time Lighting via Light Linked List

Abdul Bezrati

1.1 Introduction

Deferred lighting has been a popular technique to handle dynamic lighting in video games, but due to the fact that it relies on the depth buffer, it doesn't work well with translucent geometry and particle effects, which typically don't write depth values. This can be seen in Figure 1.1, where the center smoke effect and the translucent water bottles are not affected by the colorful lights in the scene.

Common approaches in deferred engines have been to either leave translucent objects unlit or apply a forward lighting pass specifically for those elements. The forward lighting pass adds complexity and an extra maintenance burden to the engine.

At Insomniac Games, we devised a unified solution that makes it possible to light both opaque and translucent scene elements (Figure 1.2) using a single path. We have named our solution Light Linked List (LLL), and it requires unordered access views and atomic shader functions introduced with DirectX 10.1–level hardware.

The Light Linked List algorithm shares the performance benefits of deferred engines in that lighting is calculated only on the pixels affected by each light source. Furthermore, any object not encoded in the depth buffer has full access to the lights that will affect it. The Light Linked List generation and access is fully GPU accelerated and requires minimal CPU handholding.

1.2 Algorithm

The Light Linked List algorithm relies on a GPU-accessible list of light affecting each pixel on screen. A GPU Linked List has been used in the past to implement

Figure 1.1. Smoke effect and translucent water bottles don't receive any scene lighting in a traditional deferred lighting engine.

Figure 1.2. Smoke effects and translucent water bottles receive full-scene lighting via the LLL.

Order Independent Transparency as well as Indirect Illumination [Gruen and Thibieroz 10].

For each new frame in the game, we populate the linked list of lights and we later access it to evaluate lighting at each pixel.

1.2.1   GPU List Structure

For efficient lighting using the Light Linked List, we need to store each light's minimum and maximum depths so we can quickly reject any pixel that is outside of the light's boundaries. We also store the index of the light into a global array, where we keep each light's attributes such as colors, radii, intensities, etc.

Finally, we store a link to the next light at the current screen pixel: The Light Linked List algorithm follows a LIFO convention, where the last linked element stored is evaluated first.

```
struct LightFragmentLink
{
    float m_MinDepth;  // Light minimum depth at the current pixel
    float m_MaxDepth;  // Light maximum depth at the current pixel

    uint m_LightIndex; // Light index into the full information array
    uint m_Next;       // Next LightFragmentLink index
};
```

1.2.2   GPU Structure Compressed

Because memory can be scarce on some systems and in an effort to reduce bandwidth usage, we chose to compress the LightFragmentLink structure and shave off half of the original memory requirements.

Both minimum and maximum light depths were converted to half precision and packed into a single unsigned integer uint. HLSL provides the useful intrinsic f32tof16 to convert from full precision to half precision float. The light index was compressed from 32 to 8 bits, which puts an upper limit of 256 maximum visible lights at any frame. In practice, we found out that our scenes rarely ever exceed 75 lights per shot, but if the need for more than 256 lights ever comes up, we can either allocate more bits for the index or place it back in its own unsigned integer.

The link to the next fragment bits were reduced from 32 down to 24 bits in order to fit with the 8-bit light index. A 24-bit unsigned integer allows for more than 16 million actively linked fragments at once. The compressed LightFragmentLink structure stands at 8 bytes, whereas previously it required 16 bytes of memory.

```
struct LightFragmentLink
{
    uint m_DepthInfo; // High bits min depth, low bits max depth
    uint m_IndexNext; // Light index and link to the next fragment
};
```

1.2.3 Required Resources

To generate the Light Linked List, we use a total of four buffers, though the algorithm can easily be modified to require only three.

The first buffer is a pool of all the `LightFragmentLinks` that can be allocated and linked during a single frame. This resource is a read and write structured buffer:

$$\text{RWStructuredBuffer} < \text{LightFragmentLink} > \text{g\_LightFragmentLinkedBuffer}$$

The `LightFragmentLink` minimum and maximum depth values will be generated in separate draw calls, and thus we need a buffer to temporarily store one value while waiting for the matching depth to render. The second required buffer is a read and write byte address buffer:

$$\text{RWByteAddressBuffer} \qquad \text{g\_LightBoundsBuffer}$$

The third buffer is also a read and write byte address buffer that will be used to track the index of the last `LightFragmentLink` placed at any given pixel on screen:

$$\text{RWByteAddressBuffer} \qquad \text{g\_LightStartOffsetBuffer}$$

The final buffer is an optional depth buffer that will be used to perform software depth testing within a pixel shader. We chose to store the depth as linear in a FP32 format instead of the typical hyper values.

1.2.4 Light Shells

To render the dynamic lights into the LLL buffers, we represent the lights as geometry: Point lights are represented by spheres (Figure 1.3), spotlights are represented by cones, and area lights are represented by boxes.

To perfectly represent a sphere or a cone in 3D space with polygons, we need an extremely well-tessellated mesh, which places a heavy burden on both memory resources and GPU rendering time. To work around the tessellation problem, we resort to creating coarsely tessellated geometry that is oversized enough to fully contain the original high-resolution mesh.

1.3 Populating the Light Linked List

The pixel shader that generates the light linked list can be described in three steps. The first step is to perform a software depth test to reduce the number of `LightFragmentLinks` allocated in a single frame. The depth test is followed by collecting the light's minimum and maximum depth, before moving forward with the allocation of a `LightFragmentLink` element.

Figure 1.3. The light shell displayed in gray is used to describe a point light in the scene.

1.3.1 Software Depth Test

The Light Linked List algorithm allocates and links `LightFragmentLink` elements when the back faces of the light geometry get rasterized and sent to the pixel shader. In the common scenario where the scene geometry intersects the light sources, the hardware depth test can let the front faces pass through but occlude the back faces and thus interfere with the allocation of a `LightFragmentLink` (Figure 1.4).

To guarantee that back faces get processed by the pixel shader, we disable the hardware depth test and only perform the software test against the front faces; this will be explained in detail in the next section.

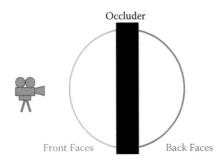

Figure 1.4. Front faces in green pass the hardware depth test, whereas back faces fail.

1.3.2   Depth Bounds

The LightFragmentLink structure stores both minimum and maximum light depth; however, those two values are rasterized by the hardware and sent to the pixel shaders at different times: The minimum depth will be carried through by the light geometry's front faces, whereas the maximum depth will be provided by the geometry's back faces.

We first draw the light geometry with back-ace culling turned on to allow rasterization of only the front faces. A pixel is determined to belong to a front- or back-facing polygon by the use of the HLSL semantic SV_IsFrontFace.

We perform a software depth test by comparing the light depth against the scene's depth. If the test fails, we turn the light depth into a negative value. If the test passes, we leave the target value unaltered.

The light's incoming depth is stored in an unsigned integer's lower 16 bits, the global light index in the upper 16 bits, and this value is then written to the g_LightBoundsBuffer resource.

```
// Detect front faces
if( front_face == true )
{
    // Sign will be negative if the light shell is occluded
    float depth_test = sign( g_txDepth[vpos_i].x - light_depth );

    // Encode the light index in the upper 16 bits and the linear
    // depth in the lower 16
    uint bounds_info = (light_index << 16) | f32tof16( light_depth*
        depth_test );

    // Store the front face info
    g_LightBoundsBuffer.Store( dst_offset, bounds_info );

    // Only allocate a LightFragmentLink on back faces
    return;
}
```

Once we have processed the front faces, we immediately rerender the light geometry but with front-face culling enabled.

We fetch the information previously stored into g_LightBoundsBuffer, and we decode both the light ID and the linear depth. At this point, we face two scenarios.

In the first scenario, the ID decoded from the g_LightBoundsBuffer sample and the incoming light information match. In this case, we know the front faces were properly processed and we proceed to check the sign of the stored depth: if it's negative we early out of the shader since both faces are occluded by the regular scene geometry.

The second scenario occurs when the decoded ID doesn't match the light information provided by the back faces. This scenario can happen when the

frustum near clip intersects the light geometry. In this case, the minimum depth
to be stored in the `LightFragmentLink` is set to zero.

```
// Load the content that was written by the front faces
uint bounds_info = g_LightBoundsBuffer.Load( dst_offset );

// Decode the stored light index
uint stored_index = (bounds_info >> 16);

// Decode the stored light depth
float front_depth = f16tof32( bounds_info >> 0 );

// Check if both front and back faces were processed
if(stored_index == light_index)
{
    // Check the case where front faces rendered but were occluded
    // by the scene geometry
    if(front_depth < 0)
    {
        return;
    }
}
// Mismatch, the front face was culled by the near clip
else
{
    front_depth = 0;
}
```

1.3.3   Allocation of LightFragmentLink

Now that we know both minimum and maximum light depths are available to
us, we can move forward with the allocation of a `LightFragmentLink`. To allocate a `LightFragmentLink`, we simply increment the internal counter of our
`StructuredBuffer` containing all the fragments. To make the algorithm more robust and to avoid driver-related bugs, we must validate our allocation and make
sure that we don't overflow:

```
// Allocate
uint   new_lll_idx = g_LightFragmentLinkedBuffer.IncrementCounter();

// Don't overflow
if(new_lll_idx >= g_VP_LLLMaxCount)
{
    return;
}
```

Once we have allocated a `LightFragmentLink`, we need to update our second
`RWByteAddressBuffer` to keep track of the last inserted LLL element. Again, we
make use of the HLSL atomic function `InterlockedExchange`:

```
uint        prev_lll_idx;

// Get the index of the last linked element stored and replace
// it in the process
g_LightStartOffsetBuffer.InterlockedExchange( dst_offset, new_
    lll_idx, prev_lll_idx );
```

At this point, we have all four of the required values to populate and store a valid **LightFragmentLink**:

```
// Encode the light depth values
uint light_depth_max = f32tof16( light_depth );// Back face depth
uint light_depth_min = f32tof16( front_depth );// Front face depth

// Final output
LightFragmentLink element;

// Pack the light depth
element.m_DepthInfo = (light_depth_min << 16) | light_depth_max;

// Index/Link
element.m_IndexNext = (light_index << 24) | (prev_lll_idx &
    0xFFFFFF);

// Store the element
g_LightFragmentLinkedBuffer[ new_lll_idx ] = element;
```

1.4   Accessing the Light Linked List

Accessing the Light Linked List is the same whether your engine uses a deferred or a forward renderer.

The first step is to convert the incoming pixel position from viewport space to an LLL index, and we do so by first converting the vPos to the LLL resolution, as shown below.

```
uint lll_x     = uint( (vpos_f.x / g_VP_Width ) * g_VP_LLLWidth );
uint lll_y     = uint( (vpos_f.y / g_VP_Height) * g_VP_LLLHeight );
uint src_index = lll_y * g_VP_LLLWidth + lll_x;
```

With the LLL index calculated, we fetch our first link from the unordered access view resource **g_LightStartOffsetView** and we start our lighting loop; the loop stops whenever we find an invalid value.

```
uint src_index    = ScreenUVsToLLLIndex( screen_uvs );
uint first_offset = g_LightStartOffsetView[ src_index ];

// Decode the first element index
uint element_index = (first_offset & 0xFFFFFF);
```

```
// Iterate over the Light Linked List
while( element_index != 0xFFFFFF )
{
    // Fetch
    LightFragmentLink element    = g_LightFragmentLinkedView [↩
        element
    _index];

    // Update the next element index
    element_index          = (element.m_IndexNext & 0xFFFFFF);
    ...
}
```

Once we have acquired a valid **LightFragmentLink**, we decode the stored light depths and we perform a simple bounds test against the incoming pixel: if the pixel lies outside the light's bounds, we skip the rest of the lighting loop.

```
// Decode the light bounds
float light_depth_max     = f16tof32( element.m_DepthInfo >> 0 );
float light_depth_min     = f16tof32( element.m_DepthInfo >> 16 );

// Do depth bounds check
if( (l_depth > light_depth_max) || (l_depth < light_depth_min) )
{
    continue;
}
```

If our pixel lies within the light's bounds, we decode the global light index stored in the **LightFragmentLink** and we use it to read the full light information from a separate global resource.

```
// Decode the light index
uint light_idx = (element.m_IndexNext >> 24);

// Access the light environment
GPULightEnv light_env = g_LinkedLightsEnvs [ light_idx ];
```

1.5   Reduced Resolution

One way to reduce the memory footprint of the algorithm is to shrink the resolution at which the Light Linked List is stored. Running at a full resolution of 1080p and assuming an even light distribution of 32 lights per pixel, the total memory required for the linked list would be

$$1920 \times 1080 \times 32 \times \texttt{LightFragmentLink} = 506.25 \text{ MB}.$$

In practice, generating the Light Linked List at one quarter of the native game resolution, or even one eighth, is largely sufficient and reduces the required memory footprint by a significant amount:

$$(1920 \div 8) \times (1080 \div 8) \times 32 \times \texttt{LightFragmentLink} = 7.91 \text{ MB}.$$

1.5.1 Depth Down-Sampling

For engines that perform either a depth prepass or have a G-buffer, layer we need
to down-sample the depth buffer to match the resolution of the LLL.

Scaling down the depth buffer must be done via point sampling and the use
of the function max to avoid missing light information due to aggressive Z-culling.
To speed up the down-sampling of the depth buffer, we make extensive use of the
GatherRed function, which allows us to read four depth samples at once. Below
is an example of how to down-sample a full-resolution depth buffer down to one
eighth across the width and height:

```
float4 d4_max;

{
  float4 d4_00 = g_txDepth.GatherRed(g_samPoint, screen_uvs, int2↵
    (-3, -3));
  float4 d4_01 = g_txDepth.GatherRed(g_samPoint, screen_uvs, int2↵
    (-1, -3));
  float4 d4_10 = g_txDepth.GatherRed(g_samPoint, screen_uvs, int2↵
    (-3, -1));
  float4 d4_11 = g_txDepth.GatherRed(g_samPoint, screen_uvs, int2↵
    (-1, -1));
        d4_max = max(d4_00, max( d4_01, max( d4_10, d4_11)));
}

{
  float4 d4_00 = g_txDepth.GatherRed(g_samPoint, screen_uvs, int2↵
    (-3, 3));
  float4 d4_01 = g_txDepth.GatherRed(g_samPoint, screen_uvs, int2↵
    (-1, 3));
  float4 d4_10 = g_txDepth.GatherRed(g_samPoint, screen_uvs, int2↵
    (-3, 1));
  float4 d4_11 = g_txDepth.GatherRed(g_samPoint, screen_uvs, int2↵
    (-1, 1));
        d4_max = max(d4_max, max(d4_00, max( d4_01, max( d4_10, ↵
            d4_11))));
}

{
  float4 d4_00 = g_txDepth.GatherRed(g_samPoint, screen_uvs, int2↵
    (3, -3));
  float4 d4_01 = g_txDepth.GatherRed(g_samPoint, screen_uvs, int2↵
    (1, -3));
  float4 d4_10 = g_txDepth.GatherRed(g_samPoint, screen_uvs, int2↵
    (3, -1));
  float4 d4_11 = g_txDepth.GatherRed(g_samPoint, screen_uvs, int2↵
    (1, -1));
        d4_max = max(d4_max, max(d4_00, max( d4_01, max( d4_10, ↵
            d4_11))));
}

{
```

```
    float4 d4_00 = g_txDepth.GatherRed(g_samPoint, screen_uvs, int2(←
        3, 3));
    float4 d4_01 = g_txDepth.GatherRed(g_samPoint, screen_uvs, int2(←
        1, 3));
    float4 d4_10 = g_txDepth.GatherRed(g_samPoint, screen_uvs, int2(←
        3, 1));
    float4 d4_11 = g_txDepth.GatherRed(g_samPoint, screen_uvs, int2(←
        1, 1));
        d4_max = max(d4_max, max(d4_00, max( d4_01, max( d4_10, ←
            d4_11))));
}

// Calculate the final max depth
float depth_max = max(d4_max.x, max( d4_max.y, max(d4_max.z, ←
    d4_max.w)));
```

1.6 Conclusion

The Light Linked List algorithm helped us to drastically simplify our lighting
pipeline while allowing us to light translucent geometry and particle effects, which
were highly desirable. With Light Linked List, we were able to match or improve
the performance of our deferred renderer, while reducing memory use. Additionally, the flexibility of Light Linked List allowed us to easily apply custom lighting
for materials like skin, hair, cloth, and car paint.

In the future, we intend to further experiment with a more cache-coherent
layout for the `LightFragmentLink` buffer, as this seems likely to yield further performance improvements.

Bibliography

[Gruen and Thibieroz 10] Holger Gruen and Nicolas Thibieroz. "Order Independent Transparency and Indirect Illumination Using Dx11 Linked Lists." Pre-
sentation at the Advanced D3D Day Tutorial, Game Developers Conference,
San Francisco, CA, March 9–13, 2010.

2
III

Deferred Normalized Irradiance Probes
John Huelin, Benjamin Rouveyrol, and Bartłomiej Wroński

2.1 Introduction

In this chapter we present deferred normalized irradiance probes, a technique developed at Ubisoft Montreal for *Assassin's Creed 4: Black Flag*. It was developed as a cross-console generation scalable technique and is running on all of our six target hardware platforms: Microsoft Xbox 360, Microsoft Xbox One, Sony Playstation 3, Sony Playstation 4, Nintendo WiiU, and PCs. We propose a partially dynamic global illumination algorithm that provides high-quality indirect lighting for an open world game. It decouples stored irradiance from weather and lighting conditions and contains information for a whole 24-hour cycle. Data is stored in a GPU-friendly, highly compressible format and uses only VRAM memory. We present the reasoning behind a higher achieved quality than what was possible with other partially baked solutions like precomputed radiance transfer (under typical open-world game constraints).

We also describe our tools pipeline, including a fully GPU-based irradiance baking solution. It is able to generate bounced lighting information for a full-day cycle and big game world in less than 8 minutes on a single PC machine. We present multiple optimizations to the baking algorithm and tools that helped achieve such performance and high productivity.

We provide details for both CPU and GPU runtime that stream and generate data for a given world position, time of day, and lighting conditions.

Finally, we show how we applied the calculated irradiance information in a fullscreen pass as part of our global ambient lighting and analyze the performance of whole runtime part of the algorithm. We discuss achieved results and describe how this technique affected art pipelines.

In the last section of our chapter, we propose potential improvements to developed solutions: analysis of pros and cons of different irradiance data storage basis and possible next-generation runtime extensions to improve the quality even more.

2.1.1 Overview

Achieving realistic, runtime lighting is one of biggest unsolved problems in real-time rendering applications, especially in games. Simple direct lighting achieved by analytical lights is quite easy to compute in real time. On the other hand, indirect lighting and effects of light bouncing around the scene and its shadowing are very difficult to compute in real time. Full-scene lighting containing both direct and indirect lighting effects is called *global illumination* (GI), and full runtime high-quality GI is the Holy Grail of rendering.

A full and proper solution to the light transport equation is impossible in the general case—as it is an infinite integral and numerical solutions would require an infinite number of samples. There are lots of techniques that approximate results, but proper GI solutions are far from being close to real time (they achieve timing of seconds, minutes, or even hours).

In games and real-time rendering, typically used solutions fall into three categories:

1. static and baked solutions,

2. dynamic crude approximations,

3. partially dynamic, partially static solutions.

The first category includes techniques like light mapping, radiosity normal mapping [McTaggart 04], or irradiance environment mapping [Ramamoorthi and Hanrahan 01]. They can deliver very good final image quality, often indistinguishable from ground truth for diffuse/Lambertian lighting. Unfortunately, due to their static nature, they are not usable in games featuring very dynamic lighting conditions (like changing time of day and weather).

The second category of fully dynamic GI approximation is gaining popularity with next-generation consoles and powerful PCs; however, it still isn't able to fully replace static GI. Current dynamic GI algorithms still don't deliver a comparable quality level as static solutions (light propagation volumes [Kaplanyan 09]), rely on screen-space information (deep screen-space G-buffer global illumination [Mara et al. 14]), or have prohibitive runtime cost (voxel cone tracing [Crassin 11]).

There are some solutions that try to decouple some elements of the light transport equation—for example, shadowing like various screen-space ambient occlusion techniques—but they capture only a single part of the phenomenon.

The final category containing partially dynamic and partially static solutions is the most interesting one thanks to a variety of different approaches and solutions working under different constraints. Usually in computer games we can assume that some of scene information is static (like placements of some objects and scene geometry) and won't change, so it is possible to precompute elements of a light transport integral and apply them in the runtime. In our case, some constraints were very limiting—very big open world size, previous generations of consoles as two major target platforms, dynamic weather, and dynamic time of day. On the other hand, due to the game setting, we didn't need to think about too many dynamic lights affecting GI and could focus only on sky and sun/moon lighting.

An example of partially dynamic solutions is precomputed radiance transfer [Sloan et al. 02]. It assumes that shaded scene is static, and lighting conditions can be dynamic but are fully external (from faraway light sources). Under such constraints, it is possible to precompute radiance transfer, store it using some low-frequency basis, and then in runtime compute a product integral with similar representation of lighting in the scene. Using orthonormal storage functions like spherical harmonics, the product integral is trivial and very efficient, as it simplifies to a single dot product of basis functions coefficients. The biggest problem of typical partially resident texture (PRT) solutions is a long baking time and large memory storage requirements (if stored per vertex or in PRT texture maps). Interesting and practical variations and implementations of this technique for an open-world game with dynamic weather, sky, and lighting conditions was presented as *deferred radiance transfer volumes* by Mickael Gilabert and Nikolay Stefanov at GDC 2012 [Gilabert and Stefanov 12].

Its advantages are numerous—relatively small required storage, real-time performance on previous generations of consoles, good quality for open-door rendering scenarios, and full dynamism. For *Assassin's Creed 4*, we tried integrating this technique in our engine. Unfortunately, we found that while it delivered good quality for uninhabited and rural areas, it wasn't good enough in case of dense, colonial towns with complex shadowing. Achieved results were too low of frequency, both in terms of temporal information (indirect lighting direction and irradiance didn't change enough when changing time of day and the main light direction) as well as spatial density (a probe every 4 meters was definitely not enough). We realized that simple second-order spherical harmonics are not able to capture radiance transfer in such complex shadowing of the scene (the result was always a strong directional function in the upper hemisphere, so lighting didn't change too much with changing time of day). We decided to keep parts of the solution but to look for a better storage scheme fitting our project requirements.

2.1.2 Theory and Introduced Terms

In general, rendering an equation for a single point and angle can be expressed as

$$L_o(x, \omega_o) = L_e(x, \omega) + \int_\Omega f(x, \omega_o, \omega) L_i(x, \omega) \underline{(\omega \cdot n)} d\omega,$$

where L_o is outgoing radiance, x is position in space, ω_o is outgoing radiance direction, ω is incoming radiance direction, L_e is radiance emitted by the surface, f is the bidirectional reflectance distribution function, L_i is incident radiance, n is the surface normal, and Ω is the hemisphere centered around the surface normal; $\overline{(\omega \cdot n)}$ is the dot product of the incoming radiance direction and surface normal clamped to positive-only values (and equals 0 for the lower hemisphere).

This equation applies to a single point in space and is recursive (the outgoing radiance of one point becomes part of the incoming radiance to another point in space). Therefore, it's impossible to simply solve it for any generic case or just precompute some of its terms. However, if we are interested in light transport only for diffuse (Lambertian) lighting for nonemissive surfaces, we can simplify this equation a lot:

$$L_o(x, \omega_o) = \frac{c_{diff}}{\pi} \int_{\Omega} L_i(x, \omega) \underline{(\omega \cdot n)} d\omega,$$

where c_{diff} is the albedo color of the shaded surface.

The integral in this equation is called *irradiance*. We introduce the term *normalized irradiance* as the final irradiance of a shaded point caused by a single directional light source of white color and unified brightness. Our key reasoning behind using this term in our algorithm is that because such simplified lighting transport equation is linear, we can compute light transport for the whole scene for such normalized lighting from a single light direction and then de-normalize it for specific lighting conditions by multiplying it by a given color.

2.2 Deferred Normalized Irradiance Probes Algorithm

2.2.1 Requirements

We needed an algorithm that could handle the dynamic and changing time-of-day cycle and multiple weather presets very well.

Due to *Assassin's Creed 4* being shipped on the previous generation of consoles—Microsoft Xbox 360 and Sony Playstation 3—we had quite strict memory and performance budgets: a maximum 1 MB of used memory for relatively large effect ranges (at least several blocks away in colonial towns), preferably using only VRAM (not to take memory away from gameplay systems on Playstation 3) and under 1 millisecond of runtime cost on those consoles over seven years old.

Our game required coherent and simple handling of both static and dynamic objects—the lighting system and renderer should be transparent to this information and light the whole scene in a single pass.

Finally, as we decided to add a global illumination algorithm during actual game production when some levels were almost ready, its impact on the art pipelines had to be minimal. Baking times needed to be short enough to allow the artist to do many lighting iterations per hour, and, in the case of changing scene geometry, lighting shouldn't be completely broken. Therefore, we decided to do the baking on the artists' computers and wanted to allow them to re-bake quickly (within seconds) some parts of levels instead of having to set up lighting server farms and rely on nightly builds.

2.2.2   Assumptions and Limitations

We observed that we can simplify diffuse global illumination in *Assassin's Creed 4* with the following conditions being met and assumptions being made:

1. Game levels are fully static in terms of object placement and diffuse materials.

2. There is no diffuse GI caused by dynamic objects.

3. There is only a single dominant light: sun/moonlight affects GI.

4. Weather affects only light color and intensity, not light direction.

5. Worlds are very big, but only parts of them are fully accessible to the player and need global illumination.

6. We had a good-quality and optimal system for handling direct sky lighting and its occlusion already [St-Amour 13].

Based on this information, we were able to decouple normalized irradiance from dominant light transferred from the weather-modified parameters—weather-specific lighting color and intensity. As sky lighting was a separate term, this was even easier as our algorithm could focus only on diffuse indirect sunlight. It is a low-frequency term, so it allowed us to reduce the temporal and spatial resolution and meet memory requirements.

2.2.3   Algorithm Overview

Our algorithm is based on baking normalized irradiance into a grid of light probes covering world areas that are accessible for players. To support dynamic time of day, we decided to keyframe eight different times of day (spaced three hours apart). Our keyframes are captured at midnight, 3AM, 6AM, 9AM, noon, 3PM, 6PM, and 9PM. In the runtime, we interpolate diffuse normalized irradiance information from textures storing keyframed data, de-normalize the irradiance in the runtime using sun radiance, and then apply it in a deferred manner.

As we are storing only a single layer of information, it must be interpolated correctly with changing height. We do it in the runtime using available height information texture and blend the stored GI with a *neutral* global light probe with irradiance specified by lighting artists.

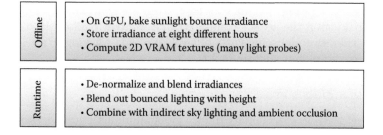

Figure 2.1. Simplified diagram of our algorithm split into two parts.

The whole algorithm is split into two parts: the static, tool-side part and the final runtime part.

The tool-side part consists of the following steps:

1. Spawn a uniform 2.5D grid of light probes, placing them on the lowest point accessible to the player (near the ground).

2. Split the probes into regularly sized *sectors* of 16×16 probes.

3. For each sector, render a cube map with G-buffer information for each probe and a single, high-resolution shadow map for every keyframed hour for the whole sector using calculated light direction.

4. Using pixel shaders, compute normalized irradiance for every light probe and keyframed hour, and store it in a texture.

Having such baked textures storing this information, we are able to use them in the runtime in the following steps:

1. Stream in textures in the sectors around the camera.

2. Determine a probe-snapped 2D viewport of the sectors around the camera.

3. Blend normalized irradiance information from two keyframed hours. Denormalize it while drawing irradiance data from the offscreen buffer.

4. On the CPU or SPU, prepare height information from available gameplay data.

5. In the deferred ambient pass, combine all computed information with sky lighting and SSAO into the final per-pixel ambient lighting.

A simplified diagram showing these steps and split between the editor and runtime parts is shown in Figure 2.1. Both parts will be covered in detail in following sections.

Figure 2.2. A light probe and the four vectors constructed using the irradiance basis.

2.2.4 Data Structure

Our light probes are using the *Far Cry 3* storage basis. The basis is constructed using three vectors pointing up in space (as in the *Half Life 2* irradiance storage basis) and an additional vector that points directly down (shown in Figure 2.2). Every vector stores directly normalized irradiance (irradiance response to unified-intensity white light) information in 8-bit sRGB. Unfortunately, such basis is not normalized, not orthonormal, and prone to ringing, ground color bleeding, and errors. We were aware of such mathematical limitations and improperness, but in our case it didn't produce any artifacts that artists would consider unacceptable. We will discuss this basis usage and propose better alternatives in Section 2.5.2.

Every light probe contains information for eight keyframed hours. Therefore, every probe takes exactly 96 bytes:

$$3 \text{ bytes normalized irradiance} \times 4 \text{ basis vectors} \times 8 \text{ hours.}$$

We store light probes in a uniform 2.5D grid. The grid density is 1 probe every 2 meters, and such assumptions helped us to keep the runtime code very simple. We organized light probes into sectors of 16×16 light probes (32×32 meters). Therefore, such a sector takes 24 kB of memory. We store sectors

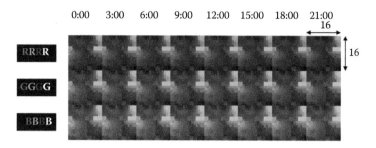

Figure 2.3. Packed normalized irradiance texture for a single sector.

as noncompressed 2D RGBA textures—texture color channels correspond to the different basis vectors (see Figure 2.3). Having our memory budget of 1 MB, we were able to load GI data of up to around 200 meters, but it wasn't necessary and was larger than our engine's regular streaming grid size.

2.3   Tool Side of the Algorithm

Our goal was to generate all this data directly on the artist's computer, provide interactive iterations on the lighting, and not rely on a render farm approach that would generate the GI data overnight.

A typical *Assassin's Creed* world is a square sized approximately 1 km on each 2D axis. Because we had to handle current-generation and next-generation consoles, our target resolution was 1 probe every 2 meters. This meant spawning more than 110,000 probes on just a single layer. Trimming this data as much as possible was a necessity to keep the baking times reasonable.

2.3.1   Probe-Spawning Process

We wanted the transition process in our pipelines between the old system and our new solution to be as fast and transparent for game editor users as possible. Placing probes by hand would mean too much manual work in a project with such a big scope, and we decided that we need some other, automatic solution—even if manual placement would give us better results. We decided to find a probe-placement solution that would require as little artist input as possible.

Using a simple uniform 2.5D grid gave us a few advantages: it not only usually is easy to implement, but it also guarantees a perfect repartition and easy interpolation of the probes. It can be a really good thing to get a good overall quality quickly, but, on the other hand, it means that many probes generated are not adapting to the actual mesh layout and the frequency of GI information. We observed that sometimes we ended up having probes at places we didn't

Figure 2.4. Example probe placement—notice the lack of probes on buildings' rooftops.

need them. And because the number of probes directly drove the generation and baking process times, we had to address the problem of game levels over-sampling.

In order to reduce the number of probes, we had to remove as many unnecessary probes automatically as possible—for instance, probes inside houses, in the ocean, or in unattainable areas. We decided to use the player and AI navigation mesh (navmesh) for that for a few reasons: it gave us a simple representation of our world, easy to query, but it also provided clues to where the player can and, most importantly, can't go.

We also wanted to avoid placing probes on the roofs. We used the navigation mesh in conjunction with another representation of our world called the ground-heights map (usually used for sound occlusion, it stores only the ground height; no roofs or platforms are included in this data). By computing the difference between the navmesh z position and the ground height position, we decided, under a certain threshold, whether to spawn the probe or not—see Figure 2.4 and Figure 2.5.

If included, the probe was spawned on the lowest z position of the navmesh. The xy position was decided by the regular grid. This gave us a 70% reduction of the number of probes spawned in our biggest game world, bringing it down to 30,000 probes.

Because of memory constraints, we couldn't keep all the data for the whole world loaded at the same time on consoles: we split it by sectors of 32×32 meters, aligned on the uniform grid. Therefore, the texture owned by a sector is 16×16 texels.

Figure 2.5. Example probe placement—regular grid.

Probes inside a sector could be moved, deleted, or added by artists to adjust the baking position if the automatic placement was problematic. At the export time, every texel of the deferred normalized irradiance probe (DNIP) texture was taking the closest probe available. During the game's postmortem, we were told that this feature was used very rarely: the original placement heuristic was robust enough.

2.3.2 Baking

For each probe, we needed to get irradiance value for four basis vectors. We didn't have any baking solution in our engine, and writing a dedicated ray tracer or renderer was out of question. We also wanted the lighting artists to be able to iterate directly on their computers (not necessarily DirectX 11 compatible at that point), so it had to be completely integrated inside our world editor.

Due to such constraints, we decided to use cube-map captures. It meant getting one G-buffer cube map and one shadow map for each time of day, lighting them, and integrating them to get the irradiance values. The normalized lighting was done at eight different times of day, with a plain white light, no weather effects enabled (rain, fog) and neutral but still artist-controllable ambient terms (to be able to still capture some bounces in the shadowed areas). To do the integration, for each basis and for each time of day, we computed a weighted integral of normalized irradiance responses against the basis.

The irradiance computation is very similar to that of [Elias 00]: for every single basis vector and for every cube-map texel, we project incoming radiance to diffuse the lighting contribution. To do this efficiently, we have a multiplier map that takes into account both Lambert's cosine law term and the hemicube's shape compensation. This weight map is normalized (the sum of all texel weights for a single basis is 1). Compensation is necessary because different cube-map texels corresponding to different positions subtend a different solid angle on a hemisphere. Once incoming radiance is multiplied by a bidirectional reflectance distribution function (BRDF) and normalization factors for a given basis, we can integrate it by simply adding all texel contributions together.

We faded the integrated radiance smoothly with distance. The reasoning for it was to avoid popping and aliasing artifacts that could happen because of a limited cube-map far plane (for optimization purposes)—in some cases, GI could suddenly appear. Then for every basis vector, we merged whole information from relevant cube-map faces and downscaled the result down to one pixel that represented our normalized irradiance at a given probe position or basis direction. All the data was then packed in our sector textures and added to our loading grid to be streamable at runtime.

Therefore, our first version directly used our renderer to generate each face of each cube map at each time of day independently, integrating the results on the CPU by locking the cube-map textures and integrating radiance in serial loops. Even with efficient probe number reduction like the one mentioned in Section 2.3.1, computing the data for around 30,000 probes for eight different times of day was a lengthy process: at 60 fps and 48 renders for every probe (6 faces × 8 times of day), it would take 400 minutes. This "quick and dirty" prototype generated data for the world in 12 hours. Most of the time was spent on the CPU and GPU synchronization and on the inefficient, serial irradiance integration. The synchronization problem was due to the fact that on PCs it is not uncommon for the GPU to be 2–3 frames behind the CPU and the command buffer being written due to driver scheduling and resource management. Also, sending and copying lots of data between GPU and CPU memory (needed for reading) is much slower than localized, GPU-only operations. Therefore, when we tried to lock the cube-map textures for CPU read-back in the naïve way (after every single cube-map face being rendered), we spent an order of magnitude higher times on synchronization and CPU computations than on the actual rendering. (See Figure 2.6.)

Therefore, the first step was to remove the CPU irradiance calculations part by processing all the downscaling and irradiance calculations on the GPU and reading back only final irradiance values on the CPU. This kind of operation is also trivially parallelizable (using many simple 2 × 2 down-sample steps) and is well suited for the GPU, making the whole operation faster than the CPU version.

But even when the whole algorithm was running on the GPU, we were still losing a lot of time on the CPU when locking the final result (1 lock per probe)

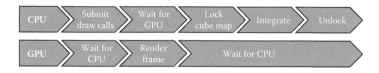

Figure 2.6. Diagram showing the first naïve implementation for the GPU-based baker. Work is done on a per-probe basis.

Figure 2.7. Overview of batched baking rendering pipeline. "Render Sector N" means drawing, lighting, and computing irradiance for each of the 16×16 probes in Sector N.

because the CPU was well ahead of the GPU. We decided to use a pool of textures and lock only when we knew the GPU actually wrote the data and it was ready to be transferred (we checked it using asynchronous GPU queries). Batching also helped: instead of locking texture for every probe, we locked once per sector— each probe was directly writing its data to its own texel inside the sector's texture. At that point, our entire baker was running asynchronously between CPU and GPU and was generating the whole map in around three hours. The GPU cost was still high, but we were mainly CPU traversal bound at that point. (See Figure 2.7.)

To cut some of the CPU cost, we wrote a new occlusion culling system that was much less accurate (it didn't matter for such short rendering distances), but simpler and faster. We used a simple custom traversal per sector (radial distance around the sector) and used also a reduced far-plane distance during the cube-map generation.

To reduce the GPU workload, we also generated only one shadow map per sector, instead of per probe. This helped reduce the GPU cost, as well as the CPU cost of traversing the scene for the shadow geometry pass each time for each time of day.

For each face of the cube map, we were generating the G-buffer only once. We could reuse it for each time of day, as material properties like albedo and normals don't change over time. We could light the cube maps per every keyframed time with the albedo, normal, and depth information we had, plus the sun and shadow-map direction at the requested time of day.

At the end, generating our biggest world was taking 8 minutes on an artist's computer. The baking was so fast that we provided a real-time baking mode. It was collecting the closest probes and computed lighting for them in the background. This way, artists could see the result of their work with GI almost

```
RenderSector
  Draw shadow maps containing sector for the eight times of day
  For each probe in sector
      For each of the six directions
        Render G-buffer centered on probe
        For each time of day
            Use sector shadow map for current time of day
            Perform lighting
                For every basis
                    Compute texels irradiance BRDF contribution
                    Down-sample irradiance contribution until 1x1
```

Listing 2.1. Pseudocode used by the final GPU baker.

immediately, and it updated continuously when they moved meshes or changed lighting parameters.

Listing 2.1 summarizes the final GPU baker.

2.3.3   Debugging Tools

We also created a set of debugging tools for our algorithm and pipeline. The tools were aimed to help visualize the baking process by showing a normalized lighting cube map generated for each probe, the associated depth, the shadow map used, and also the runtime 2D texture used for the rendering later on. So by just selecting a probe, we could see all that information, debug the whole baking process, and pinpoint potential issues immediately. We had many display modes that showed probes placed in the world. Probes could be displayed showing either the stored, normalized data (not multiplied by the final sun color and intensity) or with the full final lighting on. We also provided a mode that showed which probe was selected for each sector texel.

In Figure 2.8, you can see the rendered data on the left and the sector boundaries in pink. Interesting information is shown by the green lines—they connected probes to additional points in the sector texture that didn't have a probe placed, and that probe was used to fill those texels to avoid any potential interpolation artifacts.

2.4   Runtime Details of Algorithm

2.4.1   Streaming

Each texture like the one in Figure 2.3 is embedded inside regular *entities*. These entities are owned by sectors of 32×32 meters, and the textures are streamed in like any other resource. They represent a subrectangle of the final textures that will be used during the final ambient lighting pass.

Figure 2.8. Implemented GI baking debugging tools. Top left inset, from left to right: the six faces of the normalized cube map for the current time of day, the associated depth for those faces, the current sector shadowmap, and the runtime heightmap texture (see Section 2.4.3).

Because all these texture are relatively lightweight (24 kB of VRAM per sector), the impact on the game streaming system was negligible and no additional effort was necessary to improve the loading times.

2.4.2   Resolved DNIP Textures

Having a varying number of textures at runtime (based on what is currently loaded) is not convenient to use for a unified ambient lighting pass: texture arrays are not available on Playstation 3 or Xbox 360, per-pixel dynamic branching is slow, and additional filtering work would be necessary for data between sectors. Therefore, we decided to generate an intermediate set of textures instead: the *resolved DNIP textures.*

These textures encode the irradiance in the same manner as the sector textures, but instead of storing normalized irradiance for multiple times of day, we store the final irradiance based on the current time of day and weather conditions. Figure 2.9 shows these resolved DNIP textures. This way, we have a fixed number of textures that cover the entire space around the camera: no additional work for filtering is needed.

Generating these resolve textures is done on the GPU. Figure 2.10 is a representation of the draw calls that are issued. Each square is a draw call; the one in yellow is currently being issued.

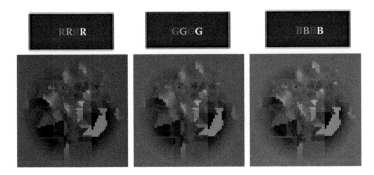

Figure 2.9. Resolved DNIP textures—the circle shape is a radial attenuation of the DNIP to hide popping when streaming data in or out.

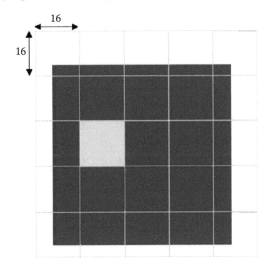

Figure 2.10. Debug representation for the resolved DNIP textures: yellow square—single blitted sector; blue area—whole final irradiance texture; dashed squares—squares only partially blitted into final texture.

Each of these draw calls will interpolate the DNIP data from the two closest stored times of day, and multiply the result by the current lighting condition. Based on the distance to the camera, we fade out the DNIP contribution to a constant color. This allows us to stream in and out the DNIP data that is far away without any discontinuity. This shader is very cheap to evaluate (works on a configuration of three 128×128 render targets): less than 0.1 ms on Playstation 3.

Once these textures are generated, we use them during the ambient lighting pass.

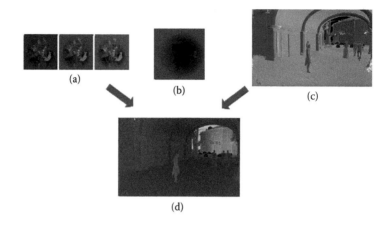

Figure 2.11. Visual summary of DNIP evaluation: (a) resolved DNIP textures, (b) world height-map data, (c) world-space normals buffer, and (d) final indirect sunlight GI contribution.

2.4.3 Ambient Lighting Pass

This pass works at full resolution on all platforms and needs to be as efficient as possible. The goal of this pass is to get the final ambient lighting color based on the pixel normal and position. The resolved DNIP textures contain the current ambient lighting in four directions. We compute the final color for the pixel in a similar manner as [Gilabert and Stefanov 12], but we precomputed the weights of each basis direction in a lookup cube texture: our profiling tools indicated that on a Sony Playstation 3, a better ALU:TEX ratio was achieved this way. Additionally, the packing used for the DNIP textures allows us to get the final color with three dot products per one texture read, because no swizzling is required inside the shader.

As mentioned before, the DNIP data is 2D only. During the resolve pass, we need to fade out the data vertically to a user-specified neutral color. This is done on the CPU by generating a dynamic texture based on height-map data. The difference between the current pixel height and the height stored in the dynamic texture is computed and scaled. This gives a factor to interpolate the DNIP data to a neutral value. Figure 2.11 is a visualization of the whole process. Figures 2.12 and 2.13 show how the final image is composited from different lighting contributions.

Jean-Francois St-Amour described our sky lighting occlusion factor (Figure 2.12(b)) where direct sky lighting gets an occlusion multiplier from a distance field called *world ambient occlusion* [St-Amour 13]. It consists of a low-resolution blurred top-down shadow map that is being sampled to get an estimated occluder height. (See Figure 2.14.)

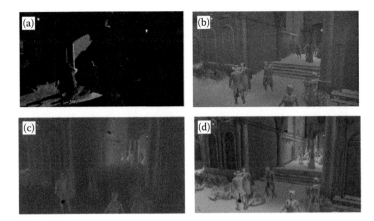

Figure 2.12. Lighting composition: (a) direct sunlight, (b) direct sky lighting, (c) indirect sunlight (exaggerated), and (d) composed ambient lighting buffer.

Figure 2.13. Final composed image with direct sunlight and albedo.

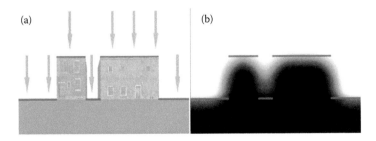

Figure 2.14. World ambient occlusion: (a) source top-down depth map and (b) blurred shadow map used for the runtime evaluation of the world ambient occlusion.

Figure 2.15. Examples of final images using DNIP in *Assassin's Creed 4*.

DNIP results are added to the sky lighting, giving the final ambient color.

On next-generation consoles and PCs, this ambient term gets multiplied by SSAO before being added to the direct lighting. On the previous generation of consoles, because of memory constraints, SSAO was multiplied at the end of the lighting pass (after sunlight and local lights). It was improper, but allowed us to alias some render targets and save a considerable amount of GPU memory.

2.5 Results and Discussion

2.5.1 Performance

The quality offered by the technique, associated with small performance impact at runtime, and the low overhead on production allowed us to ship it on all the maps in *Assassin's Creed 4: Black Flag*. Figure 2.15 shows the final achieved effect, composed with direct and sky lighting.

GPU Performance Cost	1.2 ms Fullscreen Pass 720p (Playstation 3)
Memory cost (probe data)	600 kB (VRAM only)
Memory cost (render targets)	56 kB
CPU cost	0.6 ms (amortized)
Num probes (non-optimized)	~ 110,000
Num probes (optimized)	~ 30,000, 1 probe per 2 meters
Full baking time for game world	8 minutes (GTX 680, one machine)

Table 2.1. Summary of the DNIP technique.

Table 2.1 gives a summary of the important data used by the DNIP technique. The GPU time indicates the total time taken by both the resolved DNIP textures generation and the ambient lighting pass. The 600 kB of VRAM is for a total of 25 DNIP textures of streamed sectors, which covers an area of 160×160 meters around the camera. The render targets are the resolved DNIP textures, which are 64×64 and cover an area of 128×128 meters around the camera.

2.5.2 Limitations and Future Extensions

Even if we are happy with the results we got in *Assassin's Creed 4*, removing support for current-generation consoles together with the additional processing power of Playstation 4 and Xbox One would allow for a lot of improvements.

Increasing the probe density in the X, Y, Z directions is the first easy solution. Having a layered approach like this would require some additional work on the resolve step of the algorithm, but it is definitely doable.

Used storage basis is not perfect, as we are losing any directional bounce coming from the sides and the ground color is bleeding to the sides (Figure **??**). We tried changing the basis used by [Gilabert and Stefanov 12] to a six-axis cube basis. It was giving us definitely superior results, but was eventually dropped because of the performance and memory cost for Playstation 3 and Xbox 360. We decided to keep platform parity on such important topics as the lighting. On next-generation consoles, we could store lighting properly in 16-bit HDR formats. This way we could combine the DNIP data together with the sky lighting and achieve physically based sky occlusion.

Handling multiple light bounces was implemented, but dropped because of the increased baking time and the lack of HDR support in the engine. To do it, we were performing multiple passes of our algorithm iteratively (in the style of radiosity techniques). One-pass results were injected as additional indirect lighting into the second pass. Due to the linear properties of Lambertian lighting, it is mathematically correct. Unfortunately, for it to work properly, we would need to conserve energy to ensure that each additional pass does not add energy to the scene, but rather diffuses it—which was not the case because of our selected lighting basis (energy was lost in some directions but added in the direction of basis vectors).

Thanks to our baking algorithm running only on the GPU and not needing any special data structures, generating the indirect lighting in the runtime for the closest probes could also be another path to explore. This way we could support single- or multi-bounce indirect lighting from various light sources and occluded by dynamic objects, instead of just the key lighting.

Finally, having multiple volumes of GI would allow us to work at multiple content-dependent frequencies and help solve the potential light leaking problem that would happen in any game mixing indoors and outdoors. This was not a problem on *Assassin's Creed 4*, as it was a game based mostly on exteriors—in our case almost no system supported mixed interiors and exteriors, which was solved by game design and in data. All the interiors were already separate areas into which players were teleported instead of being real areas embedded in the world.

2.6 Acknowledgments

We would like to thank the whole *Assassin's Creed 4* team of rendering program-mers, technical art directors, and lighting artists for inspiring ideas and talks about the algorithm and its optimizations. Special thanks go to Mickael Gilabert, author of "Deferred Radiance Transfer Volumes," for lots of valuable feedback and suggestions and to Sebastien Larrue, Danny Oros, and Virginie Cinq-Mars for testing and giving feedback and practical applications of our solution.

Bibliography

[Crassin 11] Cyril Crassin. "Gigavoxels", "GigaVoxels: A Voxel-Based Rendering Pipeline for Efficient Exploration of Large and Detailed Scenes." PhD thesis, Grenoble University, 2011.

[Elias 00] Hugo Elias. "Radiosity." http://freespace.virgin.net/hugo.elias/ radiosity/radiosity.htm, 2000.

[Gilabert and Stefanov 12] Mickael Gilabert and Nikolay Stefanov. "Deferred Radiance Transfer Volumes." Presented at Game Developers Conference, San Francisco, CA, March 5–9, 2012.

[Kaplanyan 09] Anton Kaplanyan. "Light Propagation Volumes in CryEngine 3." SIGGRAPH Course: Advances in Real-Time Rendering in 3D Graphics and Games, SIGGRAPH 2009, New Orleans, LA, August 3, 2009.

[Mara et al. 14] M. Mara, M. McGuire, D. Nowrouzezahrai, and D. Luebke. "Fast Global Illumination Approximations on Deep G-Buffers." Technical Report NVR-2014-001, NVIDIA Corporation, June 16, 2014.

[McTaggart 04] Gary McTaggart. "Half Life 2/Valve Source Shading." *Direct 3D Tutorial,* http://http://www2.ati.com/developer/gdc/D3DTutorial10_Half-Life2_Shading.pdf, 2004.

[Ramamoorthi and Hanrahan 01] Ravi Ramamoorthi and Pat Hanrahan. "An Efficient Representation for Irradiance Environment Maps." In *Proceedings of the 28th Annual Conference on Computer Graphics and Interactive Techniques,* pp. 497–500. New York: ACM, 2001.

[Sloan et al. 02] Peter-Pike Sloan, Jan Kautz, and John Snyder. "Precomputed Radiance Transfer for Real-Time Rendering in Dynamic, Low-Frequency Lighting Environments." *Proc. SIGGRAPH '02: Transaction on Graphics* 21:3 (2002), 527–536.

[St-Amour 13] Jean-Francois St-Amour. "Rendering of Assassin's Creed 3." Presented at Game Developers Conference, San Francisco, CA, March 5–9, 2012.

3

Volumetric Fog and Lighting

Bartłomiej Wroński

3.1 Introduction

This chapter presents *volumetric fog*, a technique developed at Ubisoft Montreal for Microsoft Xbox One, Sony Playstation 4, and PCs and used in *Assassin's Creed 4: Black Flag*. We propose a novel, real-time, analytical model for calculating various atmospheric phenomena. We address the problem of unifying and calculating in a coherent and optimal way various atmospheric effects related to atmospheric scattering, such as

- fog with varying participating media density,

- smoke and haze,

- crepuscular rays or light shafts,

- volumetric lighting and shadows.

This chapter provides a brief introduction to a light-scattering model that includes effects of in- and out-scattering and the Beer–Lambert law. We also describe how scattering can be computed and integrated numerically.

Volumetric fog supports light scattering coming from multiple light sources in a coherent and efficient manner. We include proper light shadowing (for volumetric shadows and light-shaft effects) and in-scattering of lighting coming from any complex ambient and global illumination models. The described technique uses compute shaders and data storage in volume textures. Unlike existing ray-marching solutions, our algorithm doesn't store information for a single depth value from a depth buffer but for all possible depth values for a given camera ray. Using volumetric storage, we are able to decouple multiple stages of atmospheric effects and calculate them in different resolutions. All phases of volumetric fog are independent of screen resolution, and due to use of trilinear filtering, the produced effect is free of edge artifacts.

The presented algorithm is compatible with many different shading models and rendering scenarios. It can be applied in deferred and forward shading models, doesn't require a depth prepass, and supports multiple layers of transparency at no additional cost. It can be computed asynchronously from regular scene geometric rendering on platforms that support such types of rendering (next-generation consoles, new APIs like AMD Mantle, and potentially DirectX 12).

3.2 Overview

Atmospheric scattering is a very important physical phenomenon describing interaction of light and various particles and aerosols in transporting media (like air, steam, smoke, or water). It is responsible for various visual effects and phenomena, like sky color, clouds, fog, volumetric shadows, light shafts, and "god rays."

Computer graphics research tries to reproduce those effects accurately. They not only increase realism of rendered scenes and help to establish visual distinction of distances and relations between objects, but also can be used to create a specific mood of a scene or even serve as special effects. Computer games and real-time rendering applications usually have to limit themselves to simplifications and approximations of the phenomena, including analytical exponential fog [Wenzel 06], image-based solutions [Sousa 08], artist-placed particles and billboards, or, recently, various modern ray-marching–based solutions [Tóth and Umenhoffer 09, Vos 14, Yusov 13].

All of those approaches have their limitations and disadvantages—but ray marching seemed most promising and we decided to base our approach on it. Still, typical 2D ray marching has number of disadvantages:

- Solutions like epipolar sampling [Yusov 13] improve the performance but limit algorithms to uniform participating media density and a single light source.

- The power of current GPUs allows us to calculate effect only in smaller-resolution buffers, which produces visual artifacts like jagged lines. More advanced up-sampling algorithms like bilateral up-sampling can miss some thin geometric features or introduce artifacts for high-contrast source images. Volumetric fog also operates on small-resolution volumes but uses 3D trilinear filtering to prevent edge artifacts from happening due to missing depth information in low-resolution image in 2D solutions.

- Most algorithm variations are not compatible with forward shading and multiple layers of transparent affected objects. A notable exception here is the solution used in *Killzone: Shadow Fall* [Vos 14], which uses low-resolution 3D volumes specifically for particle shading. Still, in this ap-

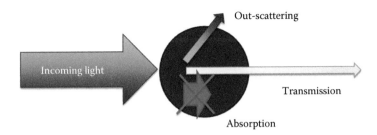

Figure 3.1. Process of atmospheric scattering.

proach, scattering effects for shaded solid objects are computed in an image-based manner.

Therefore, we decided to develop a novel solution that would overcome all those limitations, and we present the solution that we call *volumetric fog*. We used volumetric textures to transform the whole scattering problem into a 3D, easy-to-parallelize, filterable domain.

3.2.1 Atmospheric Scattering

The phenomenon of light scattering is caused by the interaction of photons with particles that form any transporting media. When light traverses any medium that isn't void, photons and light rays may collide with particles that create such a medium. On collision, they may either be diffused or absorbed (and turned into thermal energy). In optics, such a process is usually modeled statistically, and we can define the amount of energy that takes part in the following processes:

- transmittance,

- scattering,

- absorption.

As energy is always conserved, we can write that

$$\mathbf{L}_{\text{incoming}} = \mathbf{L}_{\text{transmitted}} + \mathbf{L}_{\text{absorbed}} + \mathbf{L}_{\text{scattered}}.$$

We can see these processes in Figure 3.1.

Depending on the particles that form the participating medium, the amount of light that takes part in those processes can be different. One example of scattering models is *Rayleigh scattering*. It is scattering of very small particles (like Earth's atmosphere air particles) and it responsible for the blue color of the sky. It is very isotropic and uniform but is wavelength dependent—scattering is stronger for shorter wavelengths and absorption is negligible.

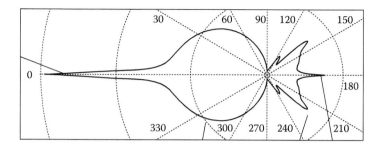

Figure 3.2. Example polar plot of a phase function for clouds [Bouthors et al. 06]. In this plot, we see how much scattering happens in which direction—zero being the angle of the original light path direction.

On the other hand, so-called *Mie scattering* of bigger particles (like aerosols or dust) has a very anisotropic shape with a strong forward lobe and much higher absorption proportion.

In reality, photons may get scattered many times before entering the eye or camera and contributing to the final image. This is called *multi-scattering*. Unfortunately, such effects are difficult and very costly to compute, so for real-time graphics we use a *single-scattering* model. In this model, atmospheric scattering contributes to the final image in two separate phenomena, *in-scattering* and *out-scattering*.

In-scattering is the effect of additional light entering the paths between shaded objects and the camera due to scattering. Therefore, we measure larger radiance values than without the scattering. Out-scattering has the opposite effect—because of scattering, photons exit those paths and radiance gets lost. The physical term describing how much light gets through the medium without being out-scattered is *transmittance*. When in- and out-scattering effects are combined in a single-scattering model, they result in contrast loss in comparison to the original scene.

Characteristics of different scattering types can be modeled using three mathematical objects: scattering coefficient β_s, absorption coefficient β_a, and a *phase function*. A phase function is a function of the angle between an incoming light source and all directions on a sphere describing how much energy is scattered in which direction. We can see an example of a complex phase function (for clouds) in Figure 3.2.

A very common, simple anisotropic phase function that is used to approximate Mie scattering is the Henyey–Greenstein phase function. It is described using the following formula:

$$p(\theta) = \frac{1}{4\pi} \frac{1 - g^2}{(1 + g^2 - 2g\cos\theta)^{3/2}},$$

where g is the anisotropy factor and θ is the angle between the light vector and

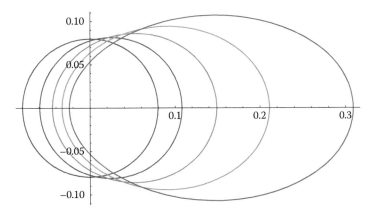

Figure 3.3. Polar plot of Henyey–Greenstein phase function for different g anisotropy coefficients (0.0, 0.1, 0.2, 0.3, and 0.4). In this plot, the positive x-axis corresponds to the original view direction angle.

the view vector (facing the camera). We can see how this phase function looks for different anisotropy factors in Figure 3.3.

The Henyey–Greenstein phase function has two significant advantages for use in a real-time rendering scenario. First, it is very efficient to calculate in shaders (most of it can be precomputed on the CPU and passed as uniforms) for analytical light sources. Second, the Henyey–Greenstein phase function is also convenient to use for environmental and ambient lighting. Very often, ambient lighting, sky lighting, and global illumination are represented using spherical harmonics [Green 03]. To calculate the integral of spherical harmonics lighting with a phase function, one has to calculate the spherical harmonics representation of the given function first. This can be difficult and often requires the expensive step of least-squares fitting [Sloan 08]. Fortunately, the Henyey–Greenstein phase function has trivial and analytical expansion to zonal spherical harmonics, which allows efficient product integral calculation of lighting that is stored in the spherical harmonics (SH). The expansion up to the fourth-order zonal SH is simply $(1, g, g^2, g^3)$.

Finally, the last physical law that is very useful for light scattering calculations is the Beer–Lambert law that describes the extinction of incoming lighting (due to the light out-scattering). This law defines the value of transmittance (proportion of light transported through medium to incoming light from a given direction). It is defined usually as

$$T(A \rightarrow B) = e^{\int_A^B \beta_e(x)dx}$$

where β_e is the extinction coefficient, defined as the sum of scattering and absorption coefficients. We can see from the Beer–Lambert law that light extinction is an exponential function of traveled distance by light in a given medium.

3.3   Volumetric Fog Algorithm

Volumetric fog is an extension of existing ray-marching algorithms like in [Tóth and Umenhoffer 09]. However, by decoupling and splitting typical ray-marching steps and using intermediate storage, we aimed to solve the aforementioned disadvantages of classic 2D ray-marching solutions.

We based our algorithm on existing research on atmospheric scattering used in the CGI industry and movies [Wrennige et al. 10] and computer games algorithms using hardware volumetric 3D textures as an intermediate storage [Kaplanyan 09]. An article by Wrennige et al. describes how 3D textures and grids are used in the VFX industry to compute single- and multi-scattering effects and introduces a solution to scattering by numerical, iterative integration [Wrennige et al. 10]. We used a similar approach, but simplified it and adapted it to GPUs, real-time graphics, and pipelines used by in games. That article also mentions how to handle aliasing and subsampling problems that we faced. While we couldn't apply this part of CGI research directly due to prohibitive computational cost, it inspired our own solutions.

Volumetric fog requires DirectX 11+–level hardware (or OpenGL 4.3+) to work as it relies on compute shaders and random-access writes into volumetric textures using unordered access views.

3.3.1   The Algorithm Steps Overview

The algorithm consists of the following steps, run as separate passes:

1. estimating the density of participating media,

2. calculating in-scattered lighting,

3. ray marching,

4. applying the effect to shaded objects.

All passes compute volumetric information about scattering for the whole space within the camera frustum. We compute and store it for many steps or slices along sparse camera rays. Such information is stored in 3D textures.

3.3.2   Volumetric Texture Storage Format

For storage between multiple passes, volumetric fog uses view-frustum–aligned 3D volumetric textures. Depending on the target hardware platform, *Assassin's Creed 4* used 3D textures sized $190 \times 90 \times 128$ or $190 \times 90 \times 64$ texels. The X and Y dimensions are uniformly aligned with the main screen or viewport X and Y dimensions. The Z dimension is uniformly aligned with screen depth, but uses nonuniform, exponential depth slice distribution to an artist-defined range (in the case of *Assassin's Creed 4*, only 50–100 meters). Depending on

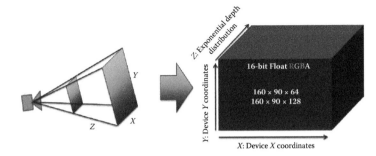

Figure 3.4. Mapping of a camera frustum to a 3D texture with volumetric intermediate storage data layout and format.

performance budgets and target hardware platforms (for example high-end PCs), used resolutions could be larger as the algorithm scales linearly in terms of used compute threads and the arithmetic logic unit (ALU).

We used two of such textures: one for in-scattered lighting at a given point and a density-related extinction coefficient and the second one to store final lookups for integrated in-scattering and transmittance. The used format for those two textures was a four-channel (RGBA) 16-bit floating point. The volumetric texture's layout can be seen in Figure 3.4.

The resolution of volumetric textures may seem very low in the X and Y dimensions, and it would be true with 2D ray-marching algorithms. To calculate information for low-resolution tiles, classic ray-marching approaches need to pick a depth value that is representative of the whole tile. Therefore, many depth values contained by this tile might not be represented at all. Algorithms like bilateral up-sampling [Shopf 09] try to fix it in the up-sampling process by checking adjacent tiles for similar values. However, this approach can fail in case of thin geometric features or complex geometry. Volumetric fog doesn't suffer from this problem because, for every 2D tile, we store scattering values for many depth slices. Even very small, 1-pixel wide objects on screen can get appropriate depth information. Figure 3.5 shows this comparison of 2D and 3D approaches in practice.

Still, even with better filtering schemes, small-resolution rendering can cause artifacts like under-sampling and flickering of higher-frequency signals. Sections 3.3.7 and 3.4.3 will describe our approach to fix those problems.

A significant disadvantage of such low volume resolution rendering is visual softness of the achieved effect, but it can be acceptable for many scenarios. In our case, it did fit our art direction, and in general it can approximate a "soft" multi-scattering effect that would normally have prohibitive calculation cost.

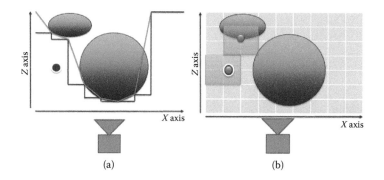

Figure 3.5. Flat XZ scene slice. (a) A smaller-resolution 2D image (black lines represent depth) causes lack of representation for a small object (black dot)—no adjacent tiles contain proper information. (b) All objects, even very small ones, get proper filtered information (3D bilinear filtering shown as green boxes).

3.3.3   Estimation of Participating Media Scattering Coefficients

To be able to calculate scattering coefficients and solve scattering, we need first to calculate participating medium density. Therefore, the first part of our algorithm computes the density of the participating medium at every 3D point corresponding to a volume texture texel and stores it in an intermediate volumetric texture.

In our algorithm implementation, we have support for varying densities of participating media. This allows not only for physically based density distributions, but also artist-authored and dynamically changing ones. Mie scattering is usually modeled using exponential height distributions due to the fact that aerosol particles are heavier than air and tend to gather near the ground. Exponential height density distribution is expressed using the equation

$$d(h) = d_0 \times e^{-hD},$$

where $d(h)$ is the calculated density for height h, d_0 is density at the reference level (literature usually specifies it as ground or sea level), and D is the scaling coefficient describing how fast the density attenuates. Coefficient D depends on the type of aerosols and particles, and in typical in-game rendering scenarios, it probably will be specified by the environment and lighting artists.

The second part of density estimation is purely art driven. We wanted to simulate clouds of dust or water particles, so we decided to use the animated, volumetric GPU shader implementation of Ken Perlin's noise function [Perlin 02, Green 05]. It is widely used in procedural rendering techniques as it has advantage of smoothness, lack of bilinear filtering artifacts, derivative continuity, and realistic results. We can see it in Figure 3.6. Perlin's improved noise can be combined in multiple octaves at varying frequencies to produce a fractal turbulence

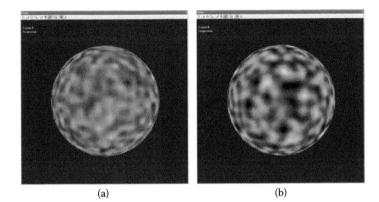

Figure 3.6. (a) Bilinear textured noise compared to (b) volumetric 3D improved Perlin noise [Green 05].

effect similar to clouds. We exposed animation tempo as an editable parameter but connected noise movement direction to the game world wind direction to make medium-density animation coherent with gameplay and particle wind. We tried using 2–3 octaves of noise to achieve a "cloudy" and fractal appearance of noise, but due to art direction preference decided to use only a single, simple octave of noise.

For *Assassin's Creed 4*, we didn't try any other density variation techniques, but we will describe them and ideas for extending controllability of effects in Section 3.4.4.

Due to exponential distribution of Z slices of volumetric texture, we must multiply the final estimated density by a slice length to get the amount of scattering that happens in given slice of space (more particles and more scattering in bigger or longer slices).

3.3.4 In-Scattered Light Calculation

Knowing the participating medium density, we were able to estimate scattering coefficients and calculate in-scattered lighting at every texel of the volumetric texture representing the camera frustum space covered by the volumetric fog effect.

We dispatched a compute shader launched in a 3D group one thread per volume texture texel and used unordered access views to access and write to volumetric texture and store such data. For every texel of our volumetric texture, we reconstructed its world position using corresponding world-space camera vectors. Using reconstructed position, it is possible to calculate shadowing and lighting for given point in space. The efficient and aliasing-free shadowing algorithm that we used for the sunlight will be explained in Section 3.3.7.

In a similar manner, we can calculate a list of dynamic lights (point- and spotlights) affecting the participating medium at a given point. In our case, we had a small number of lights affecting our scene in the camera frustum (between 0 and 4), so we were able to loop over all of them in negligible runtime cost. We performed regular light culling and added information about them to a constant buffer. Our compute shader simply looped over a uniform containing the number of lights and added contributions from them in every loop iteration. This allowed us to have proper, ordered influence of many local lights without any need for sorting.

Having lighting and shadowing information, we can simply multiply it by the scattering coefficient estimated from the participating medium density, the participating medium albedo, and a phase function for the given angle between light direction and the vector facing the camera. Whole computations performed per every texel in this pass of volumetric fog can be seen in HLSL pseudocode at Listing 3.1.

```
//World-space position of volumetric texture texel
float3 worldPosition
    = CalcWorldPositionFromCoords(dispatchThreadID.xyz);

//Thickness of slice — non-constant due to exponential slice
//distribution
float layerThickness = ComputeLayerThickness(dispatchThreadID.z);

//Estimated density of participating medium at given point
float dustDensity = CalculateDensityFunction(worldPosition);

//Scattering coefficient
float scattering = g_VolumetricFogScatteringCoefficient * dustDensity
 * layerThickness;

//Absorption coefficient
float absorption = g_VolumetricFogAbsorptionCoefficient * dustDensity
 * layerThickness;

//Normalized view direction
float3 viewDirection = normalize(worldPosition - g_WorldEyePos.xyz);

float3 lighting = 0.0f;

// Lighting section BEGIN
// Adding all contributing lights radiance and multiplying it by
// a phase function — volumetric fog equivalent of BRDFs

lighting += GetSunLightingRadiance(worldPosition)
    * GetPhaseFunction(viewDirection, g_SunDirection,
    g_VolumetricFogPhaseAnisotropy);

lighting += GetAmbientConvolvedWithPhaseFunction(worldPosition,
    viewDirection, g_VolumetricFogPhaseAnisotropy);

[loop]
for (int lightIndex = 0; lightIndex < g_LightsCount; ++lightIndex)
{
```

```
    float3 localLightDirection =
        GetLocalLightDirection(lightIndex, worldPosition);

    lighting += GetLocalLightRadiance(lightIndex, worldPosition)
        * GetPhaseFunction(viewDirection, localLightDirection,
        g_VolumetricFogPhaseAnisotropy);
}

// Lighting section END

// Finally, we apply some potentially non-white fog scattering albedo
color lighting *= g_FogAlbedo;

// Final in-scattering is product of outgoing radiance and scattering
// coefficients, while extinction is sum of scattering and absorption
float4 finalOutValue = float4(lighting * scattering, scattering
    + absorption);
```

Listing 3.1. Pseudocode for calculating in-scattering lighting, scattering, and absorption coefficients in compute shaders.

The last part of lighting in-scattering that helps to achieve scene realism is including ambient, sky, or indirect lighting. Ambient lighting can be a dominating part of scene lighting in many cases, when analytical lights are shadowed. Without it, the scene would be black in shadowed areas. In a similar way, if ambient lighting is not applied to in-scattering, the final scattering effect looks too dark (due to lighting out-scattering and extinction over the light path). Figure 3.7 shows a comparison of a scene with and without any ambient lighting.

The main difference between direct lighting and ambient lighting is that ambient lighting contains encoded information about incoming radiance from all possible directions. Different engines and games have different ambient terms—e.g., constant term, integrated cube sky lighting, or environment lighting containing global illumination. The main problem for calculating the in-scattering of ambient lighting is that most phase functions have only simple, directional, analytical forms, while ambient contribution is usually omnidirectional but nonuniform.

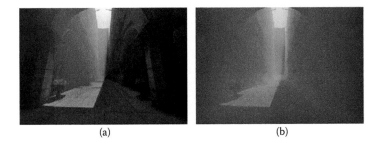

(a)   (b)

Figure 3.7. Effect of adding ambient lighting to volumetric fog in-scattering calculations: (a) Fog without sky lighting or GI = darkening, and (b) Fog with sky lighting and GI.

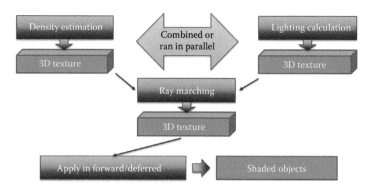

Figure 3.8. Volumetric fog algorithm steps.

In our case, ambient lighting was split into two parts. First, the indirect sunlight was stored and shaded using deferred normalized irradiance probes, described in the previous chapter [Huelin et al. 15]. We used a simple irradiance storage basis constructed from four fixed-direction basis vectors, so it was trivial to add their contribution to volumetric fog and calculate the appropriate phase function. The second part was the cube-map–based sky lighting (constructed in real time from a simple sky model) modulated by the precomputed sky visibility [St-Amour 13]. It was more difficult to add it properly to the fog due to its omnidirectional nature. Fortunately, when we calculated the cube-map representation using CPU and SPU jobs, we computed a second, simpler representation in spherical-harmonics basis as well. As described in Section 3.2.1, this orthonormal storage basis is very simple and often used to represent environment lighting [Green 03]. We used the Henyey–Greenstein phase function due to its very simple expansion to spherical harmonics and calculated its product integral with the sky lighting term in such form.

The optimization that we used in *Assassin's Creed 4* combines density estimation and lighting calculation passes together. As we can see in Figure 3.8, those passes are independent and can be run in serial, in parallel, or even combined. By combining, we were able to write out the values to a single RGBA texture—RGB contained information about in-scattered lighting, while alpha channel contained extinction coefficient (sum of scattering and absorption coefficients).

This way we avoided the cost of writing and reading memory and launching a new compute dispatch between those passes. We also reused many ALU computations—local texture-space coordinates, slice depth, and the texture voxel world position. Therefore, all computations related to in-scattering were performed locally and there was no need for an intermediate density buffer. It's worth noting though that in some cases it may be beneficial to split those passes— for example, if density is static, precomputed, or artist authored, or if we simply can calculate it in lower resolution (which often is the case). Splitting passes can lower effective register count and increase shader occupancy of them as well. It is also impossible to evaluate density in the lighting pass if some dynamic and nonprocedural density estimation techniques are used.

3.3.5 Ray Marching and Solving the Scattering Equation

The final *volumetric* step of our algorithm is an extension of typical ray-marching techniques [Tóth and Umenhoffer 09] that uses already computed values of light in-scattered into the view ray direction. Contrary to the previous pass, this pass is executed as a 2D group and operates serially, slice by slice. Our algorithm launches a 2D dispatch group of $X \times Y$ threads for a slice of our volumetric texture.

This compute shader pass marches along the view rays, accumulating scattering coefficients and the in-scattered lighting. It could be described as the following simple loop:

1. Read in-scattered lighting and extinction coefficients at slice N, starting with zero.

2. Add an extinction coefficient to the extinction accumulation register, and calculate transmittance from it using the Beer–Lambert law.

3. Apply transmittance to in-scattered lighting at a given slice, and add the result to the in-scattering accumulation RGB registers.

4. Write out to another volumetric texture at the same position RGB as the accumulated in-scattering and alpha of the transmittance value.

5. Increase N and proceed back to the Step 1.

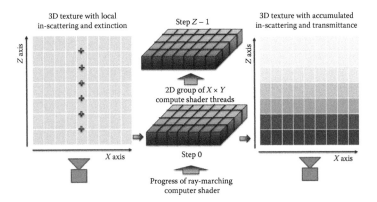

Figure 3.9. Scattering equation integration progress.

The pass progresses with this loop until all Z slices are processed. This process is illustrated in Figure 3.9.

A single step of this process accumulates both in-scattering color as well as the scattering extinction coefficients, which are applied in the Beer–Lambert law. This way, we can calculate transmittance for not only color but also the in-scattered lighting. Lighting in-scattered farther away from camera gets out-scattered by decreasing the transmittance function, just like the incoming radiance of shaded objects. Without it, with very long camera rays, in-scattering would improperly accumulate to infinity—instead, it asymptotically approaches some constant value. The entire code responsible for this is presented on Listing 3.2.

```
// One step of numerical solution to the light
// scattering equation
float4 AccumulateScattering (in float4 colorAndDensityFront,
in float4 colorAndDensityBack)
{
    // rgb = in-scattered light accumulated so far,
    // a = accumulated scattering coefficient
    float3 light = colorAndDensityFront.rgb + saturate(
        exp(-colorAndDensityFront.a)) * colorAndDensityBack.rgb;
    return float4(light.rgb,      colorAndDensityFront.a +
    colorAndDensityBack.a);}
}

// Writing out final scattering values}
void WriteOutput(in uint3 pos, in float4 colorAndDensity)
{
    // final value rgb = in-scattered light accumulated so far,
    // a = scene light transmittance
    float4 finalValue = float4(colorAndDensity.rgb,
        exp(-colorAndDensity.a));
    OutputTexture[pos].rgba = finalValue;
}

void RayMarchThroughVolume(uint3 dispatchThreadID)
{
    float4 currentSliceValue = InputTexture[uint3(dispatchThreadID.
    xy, 0)];

    WriteOutput(uint3(dispatchThreadID.xy, 0), currentSliceValue);

    for (uint z = 1; z < VOLUME{\_}DEPTH; z++)}
{
        uint3 volumePosition =
        uint3(dispatchThreadID.xy, z);}
        float4 nextValue = InputTexture[volumePosition];}
        currentSliceValue =}
            AccumulateScattering(currentSliceValue, nextValue);}
        WriteOutput(volumePosition, currentSliceValue);}
    }
}
```

Listing 3.2. Process of numerical integration of scattering equation.

```
// Read volumetric in-scattering and transmittance
float4 scatteringInformation = tex3D(VolumetricFogSampler,
positionInVolume);
float3 inScattering = scatteringInformation.rgb;
float transmittance = scatteringInformation.a;

// Apply to lit pixel
float3 finalPixelColor = pixelColorWithoutFog * transmittance.xxx
+ inScattering;
```

Listing 3.3. Manual blending for applying the volumetric fog effect.

3.3.6 Applying the Effect on Deferred- or Forward-Shaded Objects

Having scattering values written into a volumetric texture, we can express pixel color of a distant object as

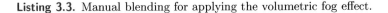

$$\texttt{ShadedPixelColor} = \texttt{ShadedPixelColor} \times \texttt{Transmittance} + \texttt{InScattering},$$

where `InScattering` is described by the RGB value of a texel read from volumetric texture and `Transmittance` is in its alpha.

Because we store 3D information for many discrete points along the view ray (from camera position up to the effect range), it is trivial to apply the effect using trilinear filtering to any amount of deferred- or forward-shaded objects. In the case of deferred shading, we can read the value of the Z-buffer, and using it and the screen position of shaded pixel, we can apply either hardware blending (`Dest` × `SourceAlpha` + `Source`) or manual blending (Listing 3.3).

The sampler we are using is linear, so this way we get piecewise-linear approximation and interpolation of the in-scattering and transmittance functions. It is not exactly correct (piecewise-linear approximation of an exponential decay function), but the error is small enough, and even with the camera moving it produces smooth results.

For the deferred-shaded objects, this step can be combined together with a deferred lighting pass—as lighting gets very ALU heavy with physically based rendering techniques, this could become a free step due to latency hiding. Information for volumetric fog scattering can be read right at the beginning of the lighting shader (it doesn't depend on anything other than screen-space pixel position and depth value). It is not needed (there is no wait assembly instruction that could stall the execution) until writing the final color to the lighting buffer, so the whole texture fetch latency hides behind all the lights calculations.

For forward-lit objects, particles, and transparencies, we can apply scattering in the same way. The advantage of our algorithm is that we can have any number of layers of such objects (Figure 3.10) and don't need to pay any additional cost other than one sample from a volumetric texture and a fused multiplication–addition operation.

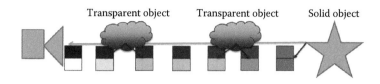

Figure 3.10. Multiple layers of opaque and transparent objects and trilinear 3D texture filtering.

3.3.7   Fighting Low-Resolution Under-Sampling Artifacts and Aliasing Problems

A common rendering problem is aliasing and under-sampling of geometric edges, shading, shadowing, and many other rendering pipeline elements. It happens when trying to sample complex, high-frequency signals in much lower resolution. While volumetric lighting in general is rather low frequency, the volumetric textures we used are so low resolution that some aliasing artifacts are inevitable.

In the case of *Assassin's Creed 4*, the main sources of volumetric fog aliasing were the shadow maps. Our rendering used four 1024×1024 shadow cascades that contained lots of very high-frequency animated details, like palm leaves. When the camera or those shadow-casting objects moved even slightly, the shadowing result, which was originally a binary function, changed a lot, causing unpleasant temporal artifacts. A common solution to any aliasing problem is super-sampling or low-pass filtering the source or target signal. A comparison of binary shadowing with frequencies in signals much higher than the Nyquist frequency and shadowing with proper low-pass filtering applied is shown in Figure 3.10. We applied such a solution and down-pass filtering to the shadowing function of volumetric lighting.

Our first attempt was using 32-tap percentage closer filtering (PCF) [Bunnell and Pellacini 04] of the shadowing test, but its performance was unacceptable for the real-time scenario and our budgets (a few-milliseconds filtering cost). We were noticing very high cache miss ratios due to large source shadow map resolution. We decided to look for other shadowing techniques that would allow us to down-sample shadow maps, do filtering in much cheaper 2D space, and potentially use some form of separable filtering on the signal.

There is ongoing research on the topic of better shadow-mapping techniques with different tradeoffs. There are already many existing shadowing algorithms that transform shadowing information from depth into some other domain and perform shadowing tests using some function that is lower frequency and filterable. Examples of those techniques are variance shadow mapping [Myers 07], convolution shadow maps [Annen et al. 07], exponential shadow maps [Annen et al. 08], transmittance function mapping [Delalandre et al. 11], and Fourier opacity mapping [Jansen and Bavoil 10].

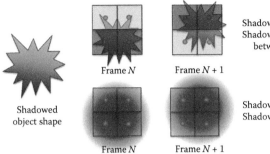

Shadow moving without any filter
Shadowing result changes abruptly
between frames

Shadowed
object shape

Shadow moving without low-pass filter
Shadowing result changes smoothly

Figure 3.11. Under-sampling and aliasing problems without a low-pass filter caused by small changes in the shadow map (top). Correct low-pass filtering helps to mitigate such problems (bottom).

We decided to use exponential shadow mapping [Annen et al. 07] due to its simplicity and low runtime and storage costs. It simplifies shadowing using exponential functions and allows us to perform shadow-map super-sampling, down-scaling, and separable filtering. To perform low-pass filtering, we transform the signal into the exponential domain and then do down-sampling four times for each shadow cascade—we end up with 256×256-sized textures. Then we perform separable Gaussian blur on those textures and end up with much lower frequency signal. The final shadowing test is trivial and is a smooth comparison ramp function of preconvolved values stored in shadow maps and an exponential function of the shadow-space depth of a shaded point in space.

The main disadvantage of exponential shadow maps that makes this algorithm not practical for most cases of regular rendering is the problem of *shadow leaking*. With exponential shadow maps, any fine-scale self-shadowing is impossible and shadows tend to be almost transparent on shadowed surfaces that are near the shadow casters. Shadows get harder farther away from shadow-casting objects, which is nonrealistic (the opposite effect should be visible) and is usually an unacceptable artifact. Fortunately in our case of volumetric shadows, self-shadowing is not really an issue because we perform shadowing tests not of real hard surface points but of the actual participating medium in between the surfaces. Therefore, shadow leaking and hardening artifacts were not visible and exponential shadow maps were good enough in our case.

3.4   Results and Discussion

Technique was implemented in *Assassin's Creed 4* for Microsoft Xbox One, Sony Playstation 4, and Microsoft Windows PC computers. We can see the achieved results (exaggerated, non-photorealistic rendering) in Figure 3.12.

Figure 3.12. Examples of volumetric fog in *Assassin's Creed 4*.

Our performance figures on Microsoft Xbox One are shown in Table 3.1. It is worth noting that we included in this table the cost of a separate fullscreen pass for effect application in deferred rendering—but in typical rendering scenarios this pass would be combined with deferred lighting. We also included the costs of shadow-map down-sampling and blurring—but those passes are not unique to the volumetric fog. They could be reused for particle shadowing or other low-frequency shadowing (translucent object shadowing), and this way the cost would be amortized among multiple parts of the rendering pipeline.

We are satisfied with the achieved results and performance and are already using it in many other projects. Still, it is possible to extend the algorithm and improve the quality and controllability, allowing us to achieve a slightly different visual effect and fit other rendering scenarios. It is also possible to improve performance for games with tighter frame budgets—like 60 fps first-person or racing games.

Total Cost	1.1 ms
Total cost without shadow-map operations and applying as a separate pass	*0.55 ms*
Shadow-map down-sample	0.163 ms
Shadow-map blur	0.177 ms
Lighting volume and calculating scattering	*0.43 ms*
Solving scattering equation	0.116 ms
Applying on screen	0.247 ms

Table 3.1. Algorithm performance numbers on Microsoft Xbox One.

The main area for future improvements is related to the low effect resolution. While most of the shadow aliasing is gone due to the described shadowing algorithm, aliasing from both density calculation and lighting could still be visible with extreme fog and scattering settings. Also, staircase bilinear filtering artifacts can be visible in some high-contrast areas. They come from piecewise linear approximation of bilinear filtering—which is only a C_0-continuous function.

Such strong scattering settings were never used in *Assassin's Creed 4*, so we didn't see those artifacts. However, this algorithm is now an important part of the Anvil game engine and its renderer and we discussed many potential improvements that could be relevant for other projects. We will propose them in the following subsections.

3.4.1 Potential Optimizations

Biggest cost of the algorithm is the in-scattering lighting and density estimation pass. It costs around 0.43 ms, even with very simple lighting models and only a few local lights. In the case of many lights, it could be important to accelerate this pass.

Because our volumetric lighting doesn't depend on the shaded onscreen scene geometry, only on the shadow maps, it is possible to reschedule it. With modern AMD GPU hardware and APIs like Mantle or next-generation console APIs, it is possible to use an *asynchronous compute* and launch the volumetric lighting in parallel with some other raster- and bandwidth-heavy passes.

We also didn't apply any early-out optimization to volumetric fog. Very often the algorithm also performed all calculations (density estimation, in-scattering calculation, and ray marching) for points behind the visible opaque objects. While it made the cost and timing of volumetric fog fixed (which can be desirable when creating frame time performance budgets), it was also a waste of GPU cycles. It is possible to use a hierarchical Z-buffer (which became quite common for forward and clustered lighting [Harada 12, Olsson et al. 12] or a hierarchical Z-buffer culling [Hill and Collin 11]) to reduce the number of unnecessary computations. By using such information, it is possible to perform an early-out exit in all algorithm passes and skip updating the fog texture volumes behind solid objects as this information won't be read and used for the shading of any currently visible object. It doesn't help in the worst case (when viewing distance is very large and the whole screen covers the full fog range), but in an average case (half of the screen is the ground plane or near objects), it could cut the algorithm cost by 30–50% by providing a significant reduction of both used bandwidth and ALU operations. It could also be used for better 3D light culling like in [Olsson et al. 12]. We didn't have hierarchical Z-buffer information available in our engine, and computing it would add some fixed cost, so we didn't try this optimization. On the other hand, relying on the depth buffer would mean that asynchronous compute optimization could not be applied (unless one has a depth prepass). Therefore, it is a tradeoff and its practical usage depends on the used engine, target platforms, and whole rendering pipeline.

3.4.2   Interleaved or Stochastic Sampling

In our implementation of volumetric fog, we used fixed sampling pattern, always sampling the center of the processed 3D texture texel. As literature proves [Tóth and Umenhoffer 09, Vos 14], it can be beneficial to use interleaved or stochastic sampling, alternating the sampling pattern between adjacent pixels and adding some jitter inside pixel cells (Figure 3.13). This way it is possible to reduce aliasing and ringing artifacts and trade them for increased noise. Noise is usually much easier to filter (it's a high-frequency component easily removed by low-pass filters), and the resulting image is more visually pleasant. We didn't try this approach in the shipped game, but it could be trivially extended into our solution—and the demo code for this chapter has it implemented in the most trivial form. It is possible to precompute some 3D sampling patterns that maximize sample variance in the neighborhood and are not biased and read them from a wrapped, low-resolution 3D texture. The process of jittered and stratified sampling and various possible sampling schemes are described very well in [Pharr and Humphreys 10]. It could work especially well to vary those patterns also in time with temporal super-sampling described in the next section.

3.4.3   Temporal Super-Sampling and Reprojection

One of rendering techniques that is gaining popularity is temporal super-sampling and antialiasing using temporal reprojection techniques. Temporal super-sampling and smoothing were used in *Assassin's Creed 4* for regular screen buffer antialiasing, but we also extended them easily to super-sample the screen-space ambient occlusion. As [Vos 14] and [Valient 14] showed in articles and presentations about *Killzone: Shadow Fall* technology, it can be used for many other effects, like screen-space reflections and volumetric lighting. In the case of a 2D image, temporal super-sampling and reprojection are quite difficult, as information for only

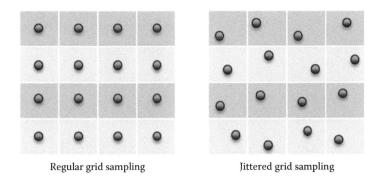

Regular grid sampling   Jittered grid sampling

Figure 3.13. Comparison of regular and jittered sampling patterns.

one layer of objects is stored (the depth buffer acts like a height field—we have no information for objects behind it). Therefore, when reprojecting a dynamic 2D scene, occlusion artifacts are inevitable and there is a need to reconstruct information for pixels that were not present in the previous frame (Figure 3.14).

In the case of volumetric reprojection, it is much easier, as we store information for whole 3D viewing frustum in volumetric textures, as well as for the space behind the shaded objects. Therefore, there are only two cases of improper data after volumetric reprojection:

1. data for space that was occupied by objects that moved away as shading changes,

2. data outside of the volume range.

We can see how much easier the reprojection is in a 3D case in Figure 3.15.

Reprojection itself stabilizes some motion flickering artifacts but isn't the solution for increasing image quality for a static scene or camera. A common

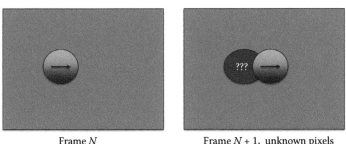

Frame N Frame $N + 1$, unknown pixels
                        Improper reconstruction data

Figure 3.14. Problems with 2D temporal reprojection of a dynamic scene.

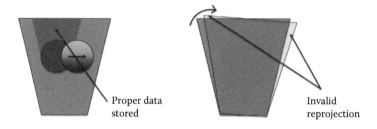

Figure 3.15. Volumetric reprojection (top view of the whole view volume).

technique used as temporal super-sampling is to introduce a temporal jitter—a variation between sampling points between frames. On its own, it would cause serious temporal artifacts like noise or image shaking, but in conjunction with the temporal reprojection and smoothing, it gives high-quality super-sampled images. We prototyped it after shipping *Assassin's Creed 4*, and we can see this technique in use in Figure 3.16. It shows how staircase artifacts appearing due to low resolution are fixed using temporal super-sampling with an accumulation buffer and many alternating, Poisson-distributed samples. We definitely aim to use this temporal super-sampling in future projects using volumetric fog.

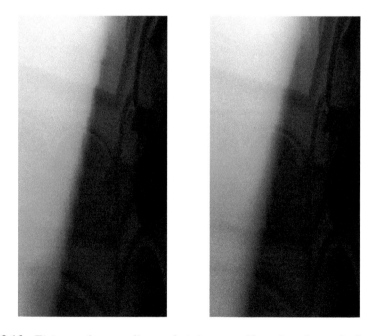

Figure 3.16. Fixing under-sampling and staircase artifacts in volumetric fog without (left) and with (right) temporal jittering and super-sampling.

3.4.4   Artist-Authored Variation of Participating Media Density

In our algorithm implementation, participating medium had a simple, procedurally modeled density using Perlin noise and simple exponential vertical attenuation (Section 3.3.3). We believe that it could be beneficial to add other ways of modeling scattering intensity and varying the participating medium density. We see two potential ways of increasing variety of scattering intensity:

1. baked-on levels and static,

2. dynamic and gameplay influence.

The first option could be useful especially for games with big and varied levels. Some parts of an environment contain lots of mist (plains and forests) or dust (interiors of uninhabited old buildings). Such areas would benefit from having different, larger scattering coefficients and a more pronounced scattering effect. Depending on the game type and level structure, it could be stored in various ways. For mainly outdoor, open-world games it could be stored as a simple, low-resolution 2D world texture with density painted on by artists. For interiors, artists and level designers could define them by adding analytical interior shapes.

Second, a dynamic way could utilize effects systems commonly used in games—particle systems, force fields, analytical dynamic shapes, etc. Effect artists know such tools very well and already use them for simulating scattering effects by alpha blending, so applying such tools in a physically based manner on volumetric fog effects should be easy for them. The article [Wrennige et al. 10] describes how it is possible to do this and counter common under-sampling and aliasing artifacts (used in high-quality, CGI and movie rendering). Regarding games, [Vos 14] describes the use of particles for the injection of scattering intensities based on an alpha particle into volumetric textures in an efficient way.

3.5   Acknowledgments

I would like to thank whole *Assassin's Creed 4* team of rendering programmers, technical art directors, and lighting artists for inspiring ideas and talks about the algorithm and its optimizations. Special thanks go to colleagues at Ubisoft Montreal who were working on similar topics for other games and shared their code and great ideas—Ulrich Haar, Stephen Hill, Lionel Berenguier, Typhaine Le Gallo, and Alexandre Lahaise.

Bibliography

[Annen et al. 07] Thomas Annen, Tom Mertens, Philippe Bekaert, Hans-Peter Seidel, and Jan Kautz. "Convolution Shadow Maps." In *Proceedings of the 18th Eurographics conference on Rendering Techniques*, pp. 51–60. Aire-la-Ville, Switzerland: Eurographics Association, 2007.

[Annen et al. 08] T. Annen, T. Mertens, H.-P. Siedel, E. Flerackers, and J. Kautz. "Exponential Shadow Maps." In *Graphics Interface 2008*, edited by L. Bartram and C. Shaw, pp. 155–161. Toronto: Canadian Human-Computer Communications Society, 2008.

[Bouthors et al. 06] Antoine Bouthors, Fabrice Neyret, and Sylvain Lefebvre. "Real-Time Realistic Illumination and Shading of Stratiform Clouds." Presented at Eurographics, Vienna, Austria, September 4–8, 2006.

[Bunnell and Pellacini 04] Michael Bunnell and Fabio Pellacini. "Shadow Map Antialiasing." In *GPU Gems*, edited by Randima Fernando, Chapter 11. Reading, MA: Addison-Wesley Professional, 2004.

[Delalandre et al. 11] Cyril Delalandre, Pascal Gautron, Jean-Eudes Marvie, and Guillaume François. "Transmittance Function Mapping." Presented at Symposium on Interactive 3D Graphics and Games, San Francisco, CA, February 18–20, 2011.

[Green 03] Robin Green. "Spherical Harmonic Lighting: The Gritty Details." Presented at Game Developers Conference, San Jose, CA, March 4–8, 2003.

[Green 05] Simon Green. "Implementing Improved Perlin Noise." In *GPU Gems 2*, edited by Matt Farr, pp. 409–416. Reading, MA: Addison-Wesley Professional, 2005.

[Harada 12] Takahiro Harada, Jay McKee, and Jason C.Yang. "Forward+: Bringing Deferred Lighting to the Next Level." Presented at Eurographics, Cagliari, Italy, May 13–18, 2012.

[Hill and Collin 11] Stephen Hill and Daniel Collin. "Practical, Dynamic Visibility for Games." In *GPU Pro 2: Advanced Rendering Technicques*, edited by Wolfgang Engel, pp. 329–347. Natick, MA: A K Peters, 2011.

[Huelin et al. 15] John Huelin, Benjamin Rouveyrol, and Bartłomiej Wroński, "Deferred Normalized Irradiance Probes." In *GPU Pro 6: Advanced Rendering Techniques*, edited by Wolfgang Engel, pp. 195–215. Boca Raton, FL: CRC Press, 2015.

[Jansen and Bavoil 10] Jon Jansen and Louis Bavoil. "Fourier Opacity Mapping." Presented at Symposium on Interactive 3D Graphics and Games, Bethesda, MD, February 19–20, 2010.

[Kaplanyan 09] Anton Kaplanyan. "Light Propagation Volumes in CryEngine 3." SIGGRAPH Course: Advances in Real-Time Rendering in 3D Graphics and Games, SIGGRAPH 2009, New Orleans, LA, August 3, 2009.

[Myers 07] Kevin Myers. "Variance Shadow Mapping." Technical report, NVIDIA, January 2007.

[Olsson et al. 12] Ola Olsson, Markus Billeter, and Ulf Assarsson. "Clustered Deferred and Forward Shading." In *Proceedings of the Nineteenth Eurographics Conference on Rendering*, pp. 87-96. Aire-la-Ville, Switzerland: Eurographics Association, 2012.

[Perlin 02] Ken Perlin. "Improving Noise." *ACM Trans. Graphics* 21:3 (2002), 681–682.

[Pharr and Humphreys 10] Matt Phar and Greg Humphreys. *Physically Based Rendering: From Theory to Implementation*, Second Edition. San Francisco: Morgan Kaufmann, 2010.

[Shopf 09] Jeremy Shoph. "Mixed Resolution Rendering." Presented at Game Developers Conference, San Francisco, CA, March 23–27, 2009.

[Sloan 08] Peter-Pike Sloan. "Stupid Spherical Harmonics (SH) Tricks." Presented at Game Developers Conference, San Francisco, CA, February 18–22, 2008.

[Sousa 08] Tiago Sousa. "Crysis Next Gen Effects." Presented at Game Developers Conference, San Francisco, CA, February 18–22, 2008.

[St-Amour 13] Jean-Francois St-Amour. "Rendering of Assassin's Creed 3." Presented at Game Developers Conference, San Francisco, CA, March 5–9, 2012.

[Tóth and Umenhoffer 09] Balázs Tóth, Tamás Umenhoffer, "Real-Time Volumetric Lighting in Participating Media." Presented at Eurographics, Munich, Germany, March 30–April 3, 2009.

[Valient 14] Michal Valient. "Taking *Killzone Shadow Fall* Image Quality into the Next Generation." Presented at Game Developers Conference, San Francisco, CA, March 17–21, 2014.

[Vos 14] Nathan Vos. "Volumetric Light Effects in *Killzone: Shadow Fall.*" In *GPU Pro 5: Advanced Rendering Techniques*, edited by Wolfgang Engel, pp. 127–148. Boca Raton, FL: CRC Press, 2014.

[Wenzel 06] Carsten Wenzel. "Real-Time Atmospheric Effects in Games Revisited." Presented at SIGGRAPH, Boston, MA, July 30–August 3, 2006.

[Wrennige et al. 10] Magnus Wrenninge, Nafees Bin Zafar, Jeff Clifford, Gavin Graham, Devon Penney, Janne Kontkanen, Jerry Tessendorf, and Andrew Clinton. "Volumetric Methods in Visual Effects." SIGGRAPH Course, Los Angeles, CA, July 25–29, 2010.

[Yusov 13] Egor Yusov. "Practical Implementation of Light Scattering Effects Using Epipolar Sampling and 1D Min/Max Binary Trees." Presented at Game Developers Conference, San Francisco, CA, March 28–29, 2013.

Physically Based Light Probe Generation on GPU
Ivan Spogreev

4.1 Introduction

As the quality and complexity of modern real-time lighting has steadily evolved, increasingly more and more advanced and optimal methods are required in order to hit performance targets. It is not merely enough nowadays to have a static ambient term or simple cube-map reflections to simulate indirect light. The environment needs to have lighting that fully matches the surroundings. The shading needs to not only handle and properly process direct lighting coming from the light source, but also lighting that bounces around the environment. Lighting received by a surface needs to be properly reflected toward the camera position as well. By generating and processing our lighting information entirely on the GPU, we were able to achieve dynamic, physically based environment lighting while staying well within our performance targets.

When we started working on *FIFA 15*, we decided that we require a physically based system that can dynamically update indirect lighting for the players on the pitch at runtime. The main goal was to generate the lighting information for the pitch at level load time. Because *FIFA* has a playable loading screen, there is significant latency and performance constraints on these lighting computations. When a player waits for the match to get started, the system cannot result in any frame drops or stuttering. This means that each step of the light-generation procedure needs to complete within a few milliseconds so we can completely render the rest of the frame. The second goal was to give the artist the ability to iterate on the lighting conditions without waiting for a pass of content pipeline to provide the relevant updates in lighting information. Under our approach, each time the artist would change a light direction, color value, or sky texture, he or she would immediately see an updated scene with the proper lighting. Finally, our technique also allowed us to include many area lights directly into the precalculated lighting information.

4.2   Light Probes Theory

Correctly lighting an object is a computationally intensive process. The light that propagates directly from a light source can bounce around the environment before it hits a given object. We will define the light that propagates directly from a light source as direct lighting, and the light that propagates as a result of bounces in the environment as indirect lighting. Direct lighting can be solved in a number of different ways depending on the light source type [Drobot 14] and is not covered in this chapter. Here we will focus on indirect lighting and how to calculate it.

To calculate all lighting coming from an environment we need to solve the general rendering equation:

$$L_o(\omega) = \int_\Omega \text{brdf}(\omega_i, \omega_o) \times L_i(\omega_i) \times (\omega_i \cdot n) d\omega_i, \tag{4.1}$$

where ω_o is the direction of the outgoing light, ω_i is the negative direction of the incoming light, Ω is the unit hemisphere containing all possible values for ω_i, $L_i(\omega_i)$ is radiance coming from direction, and $\omega_i \cdot n$ is the dot product of the incoming direction and normal.

One can think about this integral as gathering all of the lighting information from all possible directions for a given surface point. When the incoming light from any particular direction hits a surface, we translate it to the reflected light toward the direction of the camera. The material function that defines how the light gets transformed and modulated is known as the bidirectional reflectance distribution function (BRDF). There are different types of BRDFs for various materials such as cloth, skin, hair, etc. In our work, we focused on dielectric and electric materials like plastic, metals, wood, concrete, and so on. For such materials, we treat light reflected directly off the surface differently than light refracted into it. Metals, in particular, have the property of absorbing all the refracted light. In contrast, dielectric materials absorb only a small fraction of the refracted light, and usually, after scattering inside the material, the light eventually finds its way back to out the surface and toward the viewer [Hoffman 12]. We define light resulting from scattering as *diffuse reflection* and differentiate it from *specular reflection*, which is light resulting from a pure surface reflection. Thus, the BRDF for such materials can be presented as a combination of the two BRDFs, diffuse and specular:

$$\text{BRDF} = \text{BRDF}_{\text{diffuse}} + \text{BRDF}_{\text{specular}}.$$

This is actually a common approach for representing a large variety of material types found in real-time applications such as video games [Hoffman 12].

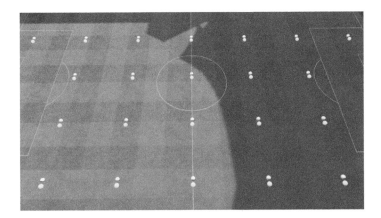

Figure 4.1. Light probes grid on a pitch.

Separating the integral in Equation (4.1) into two parts, we get

$$
\begin{aligned}
L_o(\omega_0) &= \int_\Omega \mathrm{brdf}(\omega_i, \omega_o) \times L_i(\omega_i) \times (\omega_i \cdot n) d\omega_i \\
&= \int_\Omega \mathrm{brdf}D(\omega_i, \omega_o) \times L_i(\omega_i) \times (\omega_i \cdot n) d\omega_i \qquad (4.2) \\
&\quad + \int_\Omega \mathrm{brdf}S(\omega_i, \omega_o) \times L_i(\omega_i) \times (\omega_i \cdot n) d\omega_i.
\end{aligned}
$$

In computer graphics, there are different methods to solve the rendering equation (e.g., path tracing and photon mapping), all of which require the tracing of many rays and performing heavy computations. This is simply not an option for games and real-time 3D graphics. So, instead of computing lighting every frame for every single shading point, we preintegrate it for some base variables and use the results later. Such precomputation should give us the quality we require with the real-time performance we need.

The composition of the preintegrated lighting information for a given position in space is commonly called a *light probe*. (See Figure 4.1.) Again, we introduce a separation. We define two light probes for both parts of the integral in Equation (4.2): diffuse light probes and specular light probes.

4.3 Generating Light Probes on the GPU

As described in the previous section, indirect lighting is light coming from the environment (as opposed to directly from the light source). Environment lighting for a given point in space can easily be represented by rendering the scene into a cube-map texture. For our application, *FIFA 15*, we must do this rendering during level load corresponding to our dynamic lighting conditions for each game match. When rendering into the cube map is complete, we run the preintegration step that will be described in the Sections 4.3.3, 4.3.4, and 4.3.5. After the preintegration step is done for one probe, we move to the next light probe and repeat the process. This process can incidentally increase the loading time of a level because we cannot render dynamic objects using the light probes without the completion of the preintegration step. It was thus important to make this process as performant as possible without making significant quality tradeoffs.

After a cube map gets generated, we need to solve the rendering integral in Equation (4.2). One well-known tool to generate the probes themselves is called CubeMapGen [Lagarde 12]. This tool can be used in the pipeline to generate the lighting information from an environment. It is open source, so it can be modified if need be. However, this tool uses the CPU to prefilter specular cube maps and takes a significant amount of time to process a high resolution environment map.

Because our goal was to generate the light probes in runtime during the level loading and we had graphics cycles to spare, a GPU solution appeared more favorable.

4.3.1 Generating Diffuse Light Probes from an Environment Map

First, we need to define our diffuse BRDF. We use the normalized Lambertian BRDF. It is very simple and easy to preintegrate and also matches the required visual quality:

$$\text{Lambertian BRDF} \quad = \quad \frac{1}{\pi}, \tag{4.3}$$

$$\int_{\Omega} \text{brdf} D(\omega_i, \omega_o) \times L_i(\omega_i) \times (\omega_i \cdot n) d\omega_i \quad = \quad \int_{\Omega} \frac{1}{\pi} \times L_i(\omega_i) \times (\omega_i \cdot n) d\omega_i.$$

The integral in Equation (4.3) depends on two vectors: normal and light direction. While the normal is constant per shading point, the incoming light (L_i) varies across the hemisphere. We treat each pixel in a cube map as a light source. Because the diffuse BRDF does not depend on the view direction, we integrate the rendering equation for every possible normal direction. We do this by integrating and projecting the rendering equation onto spherical harmonic coefficients [Ramamoorthi and Hanrahan 01] in real time using the GPU [King 05]. This method allows us to preintegrate the diffuse part of the integral in 0.5 ms on a GeForce GTX 760.

Spherical harmonics and their usage in real-time 3D graphics is out of the scope of this chapter. For more information, we recommend reading the great article from Peter-Pike Sloan: "Stupid Spherical Harmonics (SH) Tricks" [Sloan 08].

4.3.2 Generating Specular Light Probes from an Environment Map

Similar to diffuse light probe generation, we start by defining our specular BRDF. We use the Cook-Torrance BRDF [Cook and Torrance 81] shown in Equation (4.4) as the specular part with the normalized GGX [Walter et al. 07, Burley 12], and we use Equation (4.5) as the distribution function:

$$\text{Cook-Torrance specular BRDF} = \frac{D \times F \times G}{4 \times (V \cdot N) \times (N \cdot L)}, \qquad (4.4)$$

where D is the microfacet distribution function, F is the Fresnel term, G is the geometric shadowing term, $(V \cdot N)$ is the dot product of the view and normal vectors, and $(N \cdot L)$ is the dot product of the normal and light vectors; and

$$\text{GGX } D(H) = \frac{a^2}{\pi(\cos(\theta_H)^2 \times (a^2 - 1) + 1)^2}, \qquad (4.5)$$

where H is the half vector, $a = \text{roughness}^2$, and $\cos(\theta_H) = (N \cdot H)$.

Using the GGX function (Equation (4.5)) gives us good-looking specular highlights. The function can also be easily integrated (as will be seen later).

For more detailed information on choosing a distribution function, a Fresnel term ,and a masking term, please review the SIGGRAPH courses on physically based rendering [Hill and McAuley 12].

As with diffuse light probes, we need to preintegrate the specular integral. However, while the diffuse BRDF depends only on the normal and light directions, there are more variables in the specular BRDF. To simplify the BRDF for preintegration, we first assume that there are neither Fresnel effects (F) nor shadow masking (G) on the material. This removes the F and G terms from Equation (4.4). We integrate based on the reflected direction R—so for every direction, we store a preintegrated value in the cube map. Furthermore, different mip levels of the cube map correspond to different roughness values. The normal (N) is the only remaining unknown variable (L is the light direction). In order to simplify the integral further, we assume N is equal to V, which means that R is equal to V as well.

The specular BRDF for the preintegration is therefore

$$\text{brdfS}(\omega_i, \omega_o) = \frac{D}{4 \times (N \cdot L)}, \qquad (4.6)$$

$$\int_\Omega \text{brdfS}(\omega_i, \omega_o) \times L_i(\omega_i) \times (\omega_i \cdot n) d\omega_i = \int_\Omega \frac{D}{4 \times (N \cdot L)} \times L_i(\omega_i) \times (\omega_i \cdot n) d\omega_i.$$

Note that $(N \cdot V) = 1$ since $N = V$, as mentioned above.

Assuming N is equal to V obviously produces error (for example, long highlights are lost at grazing angles). Furthermore, we also introduce inaccuracy

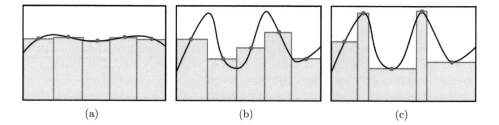

(a)   (b)   (c)

Figure 4.2. (a) When the function is regular, the Monte Carlo integration works well
with a small number of samples. (b) When the function is irregular, it gets harder to
estimate. (c) Importance sampling focuses on the difficult areas and gives us a better
approximation.

by removing the F and G terms. At runtime, we compensate for this error by
multiplying by a Fresnel term.

   This derivation results in a prefiltering that is very similar to the *split-sum*
method introduced by Brian Karis [Karis 13]. The difference is that by splitting
the sum, they take into account the F and G terms, which produces more accurate
results in the final runtime indirect lighting.

Monte Carlo importance sampling. To solve the integral from Equation (4.6), we
use the Monte Carlo importance sampling method [Hammersley and Handscomb
64] shown in Equation (4.7):

$$\int_\Omega f(x)dx \approx \frac{1}{N}\sum_{i=1}^{N}\frac{f(X_i)}{p(X_i)}, \tag{4.7}$$

where $p(x)$ is the probability distribution function (PDF).

   One can think of importance sampling as trying to focus on the most "important" areas of the function. If one can imagine a function that is very smooth
and regular (Figure 4.2(a)), then the sampling position would have little impact on the result. But when the function has local extremes (Figure 4.2(b)),
it will be harder to estimate the integral correctly and many more samples will
be needed. Importance sampling helps to capture samples whose values have a
higher influence on the final result being computed (Figure 4.2(c)).

BRDF importance sampling. Using the BRDF shape as a PDF can result in a
sample distribution that matches the integrand well. For example, with a mirror-
like surface, it would make sense to focus on the directions around the reflection
direction (Figure 4.3) as this would be the area where most of the visible light
rays originate from.

   In order to match the specular BRDF shape closely, we build the PDF based
on the distribution function D and the cosine between the half vector H and the

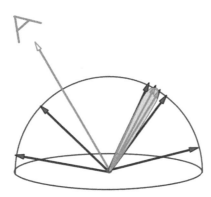

Figure 4.3. Illustration of the BRDF importance sampling. Most of the samples get generated toward the reflection vector, where the specular BRDF commonly has higher values.

normal N (Equation (4.8)) [Burley 12]. This is because D has the most effect on the BRDF's shape. The multiplication by the cosine term will help in further calculations:

$$\text{PDF}(H) = D(H) \times \cos(\theta_H). \tag{4.8}$$

The GGX microfacet distribution gives us the distribution of half vectors around the normal. The PDF (Equation (4.8)) is therefore defined in half-vector space. However, the integration step (Equation (4.6)) requires integrating the light direction against a specific view direction. Therefore, we need to convert the PDF from half-vector space to light space (from $\text{PDF}(H)$ to $\text{PDF}(L)$).

Per [Pharr and Humphreys 04], this PDF conversion is simply

$$\text{PDF}(L) = \frac{\text{PDF}(H)}{4\cos(\theta_H)}.$$

Because we can represent the half-vector in spherical coordinates ϕ, θ, we can also represent the PDF as a multiplication of $\text{PDF}(\phi)$ and $\text{PDF}(\theta)$ [Pharr and Humphreys 04]:

$$\text{PDF}(H) = \text{PDF}(\phi) \times \text{PDF}(\theta).$$

From Equation (4.8) and Equation (4.5), we can see that the $\text{PDF}(H)$ does not depend on the angle ϕ. So we can simply derive [Pharr and Humphreys 04] that $\text{PDF}(\phi)$ becomes constant with a value of $\frac{1}{2\pi}$:

$$\text{PDF}(\phi) = \frac{1}{2\pi}.$$

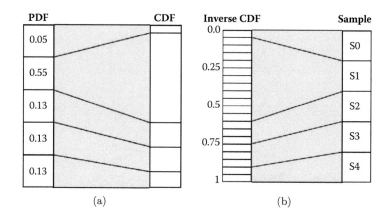

(a)   (b)

Figure 4.4. The illustration of the correlation between PDF and CDF. (a) The sample with the higher PDF value has more space on the CDF. (b) The inverse CDF maps the uniform distributed values to the samples. A given value on the [0 : 1] interval has higher chance to get mapped to the sample S1.

Therefore,

$$\text{PDF}_{(\theta)} = \frac{D(H) \times \cos(\theta_H)}{\text{PDF}(\phi)} = \frac{2 \times a^2 \times \cos(\theta_H)}{(\cos(\theta_H)^2 \times (a^2 - 1) + 1)^2}.$$

By using the Monte Carlo importance sampling, with the PDF(H), we now have all we need to approximate the specular part of the rendering integral:

$$\int_\Omega \frac{D}{4 \times (n \cdot \omega_i)} \times L_i(\omega_i) \times (\omega_i \cdot n) d\omega_i \tag{4.9}$$

$$\approx \frac{1}{N} \sum_{i=1}^{N} \frac{D \times L_i(\omega_i) \times (\omega_i \cdot n)}{4 \times (n \cdot \omega_i) \times \text{PDF}(\omega_i)} = \frac{1}{N} \sum_{i=1}^{N} L_i(\omega_i),$$

where N is the number of samples, ω_i is the sampling light direction, and $L_i(\omega_i)$ is the sampling color in direction ω_i.

The PDF only gives us the probability of a certain direction x. What we actually require is the inverse; we need to be able to generate samples based on a given probability. We start by computing a *cumulative distribution function* (CDF) for our PDF [Papoulis 84, pp. 92–94] (Equation (4.10)). For a value x, the CDF defines the uniformly distributed value ε on the [0 : 1] interval in a proportion to PDF(x) [Papoulis 84, Pharr and Humphreys 04] (Figure 4.4(a)). While the CDF has a uniform unit probability distribution, it is actually the opposite of what we desire. To solve our problem, we simply need to calculate the inverse CDF (Figure 4.4(b)).

The following equations show how to calculate the CDFs ($\text{CDF}(\phi)$ and $\text{CDF}(\theta)$) for the PDF function derived from the original specular BRDF based on the formal definition (Equation (4.10)) of the CDF:

$$\text{CDF}(X) = \int \text{PDF}(x)dx, \tag{4.10}$$

$$\text{CDF}(\phi) = \int_0^\phi \frac{1}{2\pi}dx = \frac{1}{2\pi}\phi,$$

$$\text{CDF}(\theta) = \int_0^q \frac{2 \times a^2 \times x}{(x^2 \times (a^2 - 1) + 1)^2}dx = \frac{1 - q^2}{1 + q^2(a^2 - 1)},$$

where $q = \cos(\theta_H)$.

We now invert our CDF functions to produce mappings from uniform values ε_1 and ε_2 to the angles ϕ and θ, respectively:

$$\phi = \text{Inverse CDF}(\varepsilon_1) = \varepsilon_1 \times 2\pi, \tag{4.11}$$

$$\theta = \text{Inverse CDF}(\varepsilon_2) = \text{acos}\left(\sqrt{\frac{1 - \varepsilon_2}{1 + \varepsilon_{2(a^2 - 1)}}}\right). \tag{4.12}$$

Finally, we can now generate a direction (ϕ, θ) based on Equations (4.11) and (4.12) from uniformly distributed random values $(\varepsilon_1, \varepsilon_2)$ in $[0:1]$.

Putting all this together we get the code in Listing 4.1.

```
//e1, e2 is pair of two random values
//Roughness is the current roughness we are integrating for
//N is the normal
float3 ImportanceSampleGGX ( float e1, float e2, float Roughness,
    float3 N )
{
        float a = Roughness * Roughness;

        //Calculate phi and cosine of theta using Equations (4.14)
        //and (4.15)
        float phi = 2 * PI * e1;
        float cos_theta = sqrt((1 - e2) / ( 1 + (a*a - 1) * e2 ));
        float sin_theta = sqrt( 1 - cos_theta * cos_theta);

        //Build a half vector
        float3 H;
        H.x = sin_theta * cos(phi);
        H.y = sin_theta * sin(phi);
        H.z = cos_theta;

        //Transform the vector from tangent space to world space
        float3 up = abs(N.z) < 0.999? float3(0,0,1): float3(1,0,0);
        float3 right = normalize( cross(up, N ) );
        float3 forward = cross( N, right );

        return right * H.x + forward * H.y + N * H.z;
}
```

```
//For the given Roughness and the View vector function
//samples the environment map using the BRDF importance sampling
//e1, e2 is pair of two random values
//totalWeight the number of the valid samples
float3 SampleBRDF(float e1, float e2, float Roughness, float3 V)
{
        float3 N = V;
        //Calculate the H vector using BRDF importance sampling
        float3 H = ImportanceSampleGGX(e1, e2 , Roughness, N );
        //Calculate the L vector using the standard reflection
        //equation
        float3 L = 2 * dot( V, H ) * H - V;

        float NoL = saturate( dot( N, L ) );

        float3 color = 0;
        //we skip the samples that are not in the same hemisphere
        //with the normal
        if( NoL > 0 )
        {
                        //Sample the cube map in the direction L
                        color += SampleTex(L).rgb;
        }

        return color;
}
```

Listing 4.1. BRDF importance sampling.

We use the Hammersley quasirandom low-discrepancy sequence [Niederreiter 92] to generate the uniformly distributed random values $\varepsilon_1, \varepsilon_2$ on the GPU (Listing 4.2).

Figure 4.5 shows some results. We preintegrate an environment map using 1024 samples per direction. The performance numbers for BRDF Importance Sampling preintegration on a GeForce GTX 760 are shown in Table 4.1 (timings are in milliseconds).

```
float radicalInverse (uint bits)
{
    bits = (bits << 16u) | (bits >> 16u);
    bits = ((bits & 0x55555555u) << 1u)|((bits & 0xAAAAAAAAu)>>1u);
    bits = ((bits & 0x33333333u) << 2u)|((bits & 0xCCCCCCCCu)>>2u);
    bits = ((bits & 0x0F0F0F0Fu) << 4u)|((bits & 0xF0F0F0F0u)>>4u);
    bits = ((bits & 0x00FF00FFu) << 8u)|((bits & 0xFF00FF00u)>>8u);
    return float(bits) * 2.3283064365386963e-10; // / 0x100000000
}

float2 Hammersley (uint i, uint N)
{
    return float2(float(i)/float(N), radicalInverse(i));
}
```

Listing 4.2. The Hammersley function generates a uniformly distributed quasirandom 2D point $(\varepsilon_1, \varepsilon_2)$.

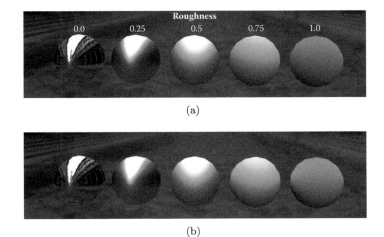

(a)

(b)

Figure 4.5. (a) The preintegrated specular BRDF for different roughness with 1024 samples per pixel. (b) The ground truth integration using 100,000 samples without the importance sampling.

Number of	Preintegrated Cube Map Face Size				
samples	128×128	64×64	32×32	16×16	8×8
64	2.8	0.8	0.2	0.04	0.02
128	6.2	1.6	0.5	0.1	0.08
512	25	6.5	1.7	0.4	0.3
1024	-	13.5	3	1	0.7
4096	-	53.8	15	5	3

Table 4.1. BRDF importance sampling preintegration on GTX 760.

The main problem with BRDF importance sampling (and importance sampling in general) is that a large number of samples are needed in order to reduce noise and get a smooth image (Figure 4.6). This problem gets even worse when

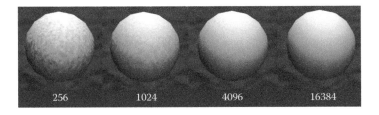

Figure 4.6. Number of samples and noise.

Figure 4.7. Dark environment map with few bright light sources using 1024 samples.

there are high-frequency details in the environment map (Figure 4.7). Some of our nighttime environments have area lights surrounded by dark regions (which introduces a lot of high-frequency details). Having such noisy prefiltered maps is a big issue. We needed some additional methods to help resolve this issue.

4.3.3 Prefiltered Environment Map

As mentioned above, thousands of samples are required for each pixel to keep the noise level low. It might take too much time even on the GPU to prefilter each probe for low roughness values (Table 4.1). We therefore use the following approach [Křivánek and Colbert 08] to reduce noise and keep the number of samples low.

The idea is simple: noise is created when there are high-frequency details in areas with relatively low values in the PDF. In order to combat that, we filter out the high-frequency details by creating a mip chain. This is in a similar vein to using a mip chain to avoid aliasing when down-sampling an image. For higher-probability samples, on the other hand, we still sample from the unfiltered image.

We proceed by using a ratio of the solid angle around a sample direction to the solid angle subtended by one pixel in the environment map [Křivánek and Colbert 08]. In the original paper, they found that biasing the mip level by 1 creates a less noisy result. However, in our case, we did not wish to bias in order to preserve detail for lower roughness. Therefore, we pick the starting mip based on the material roughness, as seen in Listing 4.3.

```
float pdf = a / pow(NoH*NoH * (a-1) + 1, 2);
float area = 2 * PI;

pdf = pdf * NoL / (4 * LoH);
float s_solidangle = 1.0 / (numBRDFSamples * pdf); //sample solid
                                                   //angle
float p_solidangle = area / (1.0 * mapW * mapH); //pixel solid angle
float base_mip = lerp(0,4, Roughness); // pick starting mip based
                                       // on roughness
float mipmapLevel = clamp(0.5 * log2(s_solidangle/ p_solidangle),
  base_mip, 5);
```

Listing 4.3. Choosing a mip level based on the sample PDF.

Figure 4.8. Source environment (left) and ground truth (right), with roughness 0.25 BRDF IS using 128 samples (middle left) and roughness 0.25 BRDF IS using 128 samples with prefiltering (middle right).

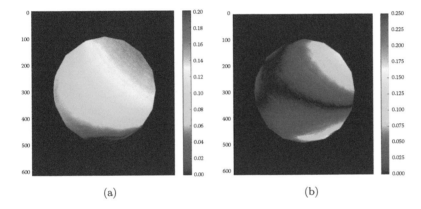

Figure 4.9. Error heat map of the final result using BRDF importance sampling with prefiltering: (a) a result using 128 samples, and (b) a result using 1024 samples.

Prefiltering the environment map solves most of the problems with noise. We found that it works well for daytime environments, where the energy is relatively similar in the local pixel neighborhood. However, for nighttime, although there is no noise in the result, the error is still higher due to the extremely high frequency details (Figure 4.8) that get excessively blurred. For example, a low-probability sample might get a lower energy value than it would have gotten in the ground truth (Figure 4.9).

We are thus faced with a problem. On one hand, if we don't prefilter the environment map, the result is too noisy. On the other hand, prefiltering produces high error with a low number of samples. So we added another technique for the preintegration of probes with high roughness values.

4.3.4 Environment Map Importance Sampling

Previously we discussed BRDF importance sampling where we use the PDF to match the behavior of the BRDF. But that might not always be the best sampling

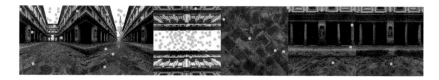

Figure 4.10. Sampling distribution.

Figure 4.11. Unwrapped environment map.

strategy. For example, consider the case of a dark room with very few bright light sources (or in *FIFA 15*'s case, a nighttime stadium with small but bright area light sources). Sampling based on the BRDF distribution might generate many samples that miss the light sources. This will create variance when the samples do hit the light source (especially if the samples had low probability). In that case, it would have been preferable to instead generate samples that tend to point toward light sources (i.e., pixels with high energy values). Environment map importance sampling [Colbert et al. 10] allows us to achieve exactly this. We use environment map importance sampling to focus the sample generation on areas with higher intensity (Figure 4.10).

First, we reduce the number of dimensions that we are working with to simplify calculations. Cube-map texture sampling is based on a 3D vector, yet it really only has a 2D dependency. We instead use spherical surface coordinates to represent a direction. We also need to map our sphere to a linear rectangular texture. In order to do that, we simply stack each cube map face one after the other (Figure 4.11).

In order to generate sample directions with proper probabilities, we need to define the PDF, CDF, and inverse CDF (similarly to the BRDF importance sampling). However, in this case, because the environment map is not analytical, we need to work with discrete versions of these functions.

We start with the PDF. We simply use the luminosity of each pixel as a basis for generating the PDF. This allows us to catch the "brightest" pixels in the image. We also need to define two types of PDFs: marginal and conditional (Figure 4.12). We use the marginal PDF to find which row of pixels we will sample from. The sum of the PDF for a given row is the probability that a random sample will fall within that row; this is the marginal PDF. Then we use the conditional PDF of this row to find which column the sample falls into. The

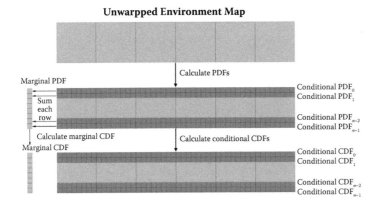

Figure 4.12. The structure of the marginal and conditional PDFs and CDFs. The conditional PDF and CDF are unique for each row and are represented as a 1D array for each row. However, there is only one marginal PDF and one marginal CDF for the image, which are also represented as 1D arrays.

conditional and marginal PDFs can be calculated using the following equations:

$$\text{conditional PDF}_{(i,j)} = \text{luminance}(i,j), \tag{4.13}$$

$$\text{marginal PDF}_j = \sum_{i=0}^{n} \text{luminance}(i,j). \tag{4.14}$$

For each type of PDF we define, there is a corresponding CDF: marginal and conditional CDFs. When a PDF is purely discrete, the CDF can be calculated as the sum of the PDF values from 0 to m for each location m [Pharr and Humphreys 04]:

$$\text{CDF}_m = \sum_{k=0}^{m} \text{PDF}_k. \tag{4.15}$$

The function that represents the summation of the rows' probabilities is the row-wise CDF for the image as a whole; this is the marginal CDF (Figure 4.12). The individual row PDFs are unique and each also has its own column-wise CDF, which is called the conditional CDF (Figure 4.12).

The simple example in Figure 4.13 demonstrates the behavior of the discrete CDF. Samples with high probabilities get mapped to a wide range on the Y axis. For example, if we randomly choose a $[0:1]$ value on the Y axis, the third sample will be picked with a probability of 0.7.

The inverse CDF is thus simply a mapping between a random $[0:1]$ value and its corresponding sample. Since by definition the CDF is a sorted array (Equation (4.15)), we can use a binary search to find the corresponding sample's index. In short the algorithm can be described as follows:

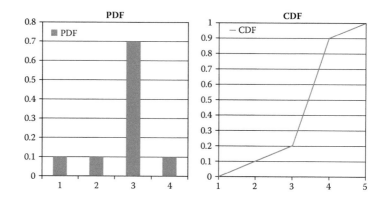

Figure 4.13. PDF and its corresponding CDF.

1. Generate a random number α in the range $[0 : 1]$.

2. Find an i where $\text{CDF}(i) \leq \alpha$.

3. Then, i is the resulting sample with $\text{PDF}(i)$.

Because we have the PDF, CDF, and inverse CDF, we can now generate the environment map samples. It is worth noting that since the samples' locations depend on neither the BRDF nor the shading point location and orientation, the samples can be pregenerated on the CPU. At the GPU stage, we simply integrate using those samples.

The final sample generation process can thus be described as follows:

1. For each pixel in each row of the map, calculate the PDF value using Equation (4.13).

2. For each j, sum the conditional PDF values and store them into marginal $\text{PDF}(j)$ (Equation (4.14)).

3. For each row, build the conditional CDF using Equation (4.15).

4. Build the marginal CDF using the marginal PDFs, using the Equation (4.15).

5. Pregenerate n samples on the CPU and pass them to the GPU.

Listing 4.4 shows the code that generates 128 samples using the stratified sampling method [Niederreiter 92]. We found that in our case 128 samples give the best results, given a required performance level.

Furthermore, we can improve the random sampling by stratifying the samples. Random 2D sampling might sometimes produce bad coverage (Figure 4.14). By

```
//Pregenerate 128 samples on CPU that we will pass to the GPU
for(int j = 0 ; j < 16; j++)
for(int i = 0 ; i < 8; i++)
{
    //Generate random values (e1,e2) using the stratified sampling
    //method
    float e1 = float(i) / 8.0f + randf() / 8.0f;
    float e2 = float(j) / 16.0f + randf() / 16.0f;

    //Find the row for the sample based on the conditional CDF
    int row = lower_bound(marginalCDF,e1);
    //Now, using our row, we find the correct column and therefore
    //sample
    int column = lower_bound(conditionalCDF[row], e2);

    //Get the PDF values of the sample for the further calculation
    //of the integral on the GPU
    float pdfRow = marginalPDF[row];
    float pdfColumn = conditionalPDF[row][column];

    //Save the sample position and PDF values in the array
    uint32_t index = i + 8*j;
    SamplesData[index*4 + 0] = row;
    SamplesData[index*4 + 1] = column;
    SamplesData[index*4 + 2] = pdfRow;
    SamplesData[index*4 + 3] = pdfColumn;
}
```

Listing 4.4. Generating samples based on environment PDF.

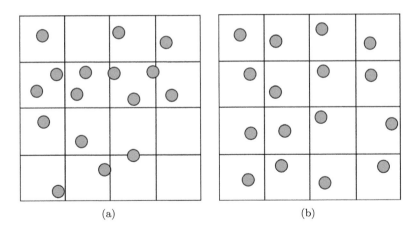

(a)   (b)

Figure 4.14. (a) Random samples might produce bad coverage. (b) Stratified sampling guarantees at least one sample in equally distributed areas.

stratifying the samples, we guarantee that we have at least one sample in equally distributed areas. This reduces the probability of sample "clumping" around a specific location.

We then have an array of samples that we pass on to the GPU. The GPU receives flattened (u, v) coordinates. In order to use those samples, we have to first convert (u, v) coordinates to direction vectors, and transform the PDF from the (u, v) distribution to a distribution over a solid angle [Pharr and Humphreys 04]. The PDF conversion can be derived from the environment map unwrapping where we have six cube-map faces in a row and each face has the field of view equal to $\frac{\pi}{2}$:

$$\text{solid angle PDF}_u = \text{PDF}_u \times 6 \times \frac{\pi}{2},$$

$$\text{solid angle PDF}_v = \text{PDF}_v \times \frac{\pi}{2}.$$

The final GPU code for the environment map importance sampling is shown in Listing 4.5.

```
//Calculate the outgoing radiance for the sample direction L
float3 envMapSample ( float Roughness, float2 uv, float3 L,
                      float3 N, float pdfV, float pdfU)
{
    //Cosine weight
    float NoL = saturate(dot(N, normalize(L)));
    float3 color = unwrapTex.Load( int3(uv.xy, 0 )).rgb;

    float3 V = N;
    float3 H = normalize(L+V);
    float D = GGX(Roughness, H, N);
    float brdf = D / (4*NoL);

    //Calculate the solid angle
    //dA (area of cube) = (6*2*2)/N^2
    //N is a face size
    //dw = dA / r^3 = dA * pow(x*x + y*y + z*z, -1.5)
    float dw = (6*4.0 / (CUBEMAP_SIZE*CUBEMAP_SIZE)) *
               pow(L.x*L.x + L.y*L.y + L.z*L.z, -1.5);

    //pdfV and pdfU is the PDFs for [0;1] range in a cube map face.
    //We need to convert them to a solid angle range.
    //Each face has HALF_PI fov and we have 6 faces.
    //Solid Angle PDFu (saPDFu) = PDFu * 6 * HALF_PI
    //Solid Angle PDFv (saPDFv) = PDFv * HALF_PI

    //E = brdf * color * NoL * dw / (saPDFu * saPDFv)

    return brdf * color * NoL * dw * / (pdfV * pdfU * 6 * PI * PI
        *0.5*0.5);
}

float3 SampleENV(int index, float Roughness, float3 N, float3 V)
{
    //Get the position of the sample
    float2 uv = samples[index].xy;

    //Get the PDF values of the current sample. Note that the final
    //PDF is pdfV* pdfU
    float pdfV = samples[index].z;
    float pdfU = samples[index].w;
```

```
        //Convert the uv sample position to a vector. We need this to
        //calculate the BRDF
        float3 L = normalize(uvToVector( uv ));
        //Sample the light coming from the direction L
        //and calculate the specular BRDF for this direction
        float3 envIS = envMapSample ( Roughness , uv, L, N, pdfV , pdfU );
        return envIS;
}

float3 PreintegrateSpecularLightProbe( float Roughness ,
    int numENVSamples , float3 R )
{
    //For the preintegration , we assume that N=V=R
    float3 N = R;
    float3 V = R;

    float3 finalColor = 0;

    //Sample all of the pregenerated samples
    for(int i = 0; i < numENVSamples; i++)
    {
        finalColor += SampleENV(i, Roughness , N, V);
    }

    //The final color needs to be divided by the number of samples
    //based on the Monte Carlo importance sampling definition
    finalColor /= numENVSamples;

    return finalColor;
}
```

Listing 4.5. Environment map importance sampling.

Using this method helped us to reduce the error for the high roughness values in the nighttime lighting conditions (Figure 4.15). However, using environment map sampling alone isn't necessarily the best solution. Similarly to BRDF sampling, there can be situations where sampling purely based on the environment would generate a lot of noise (or "fireflies") (Figure 4.16). For example, this can occur if the environment samples do not follow the BRDF's specular lobe (much more likely in low roughness materials).

Because all of the samples are pre-generated on CPU, the preintegration computation time on the GPU for the high roughness values is less than 0.05 ms on a GTX 460.

4.3.5 Combining Both Importance Sampling Methods

We now have two independent methods that both work well in different situations (e.g., low roughness and/or high-frequency detail in the environment map). We would like to somehow combine both methods to have a solution that works well in most cases.

This is where multiple (or combined) importance sampling comes in. Multiple importance sampling allows us to combine two sampling techniques. The equation

Figure 4.15. Environment map importance sampling error for the roughness value 1 using 128 samples at the nighttime-specific lighting condition.

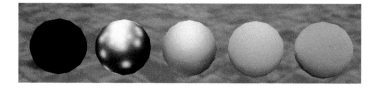

Figure 4.16. Specular light probe using environment map importance sampling. The first probe is black because it is a perfect mirror and none of the samples hit the reflection ray exactly.

for multiple importance sampling (or MIS) is as follows:

$$\frac{1}{n_f + n_g} \left(\sum_{i=1}^{n_f} \frac{f(X_i)g(X_i)w_f(X_i)}{p_f(X_i)} + \sum_{i=1}^{n_g} \frac{f(Y_i)g(Y_i)w_g(Y_i)}{p_g(Y_i)} \right),$$

where n_f is the number of samples taken from the p_f distribution method, n_g is the number of samples taken from p_g, and w_f and w_g are special weighting functions chosen such that the expected value of this estimator is the value of the integral $f(x)g(x)$ [Pharr and Humphreys 04]. In our case, p_f is the BRDF importance sampling distribution and p_g is the environment map importance sampling distribution.

For the weighing variables, w_f and w_g, we use the simplest possible method. We pick w_f to be n_f, and w_g to be n_g. We found that this method gives acceptable results for very low performance costs (as opposed to the balance heuristic; for example, [Pharr and Humphreys 04]).

As for the number of samples for each method, we simply use a hard-coded value that we achieved by trial and error (in our case, 64 for both methods). Fur-

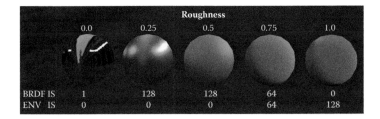

Figure 4.17. Number of samples in each method for a specular probe.

Figure 4.18. The ground truth render using 10,000 samples.

thermore, we only use environment map importance sampling when the roughness is greater than 0.7. With lower roughness values, BRDF importance sampling worked well alone. Figure 4.17 shows the number of samples for both methods with different roughness values.

Listing 4.6 demonstrates the final preintegration function that uses the combination of both methods.

Using the combined importance sampling gives us the required quality result within less than 2 ms of GPU time. (See Figure 4.18.)

4.4 Conclusion

Implementing combined importance sampling on the GPU gave us the ability to generate and prefilter the light probes during level loading. Each probe takes less than 2 ms to preintegrate. (This time does not include the time it takes to generate the environment map itself.) However, we split the light probe generation process across multiple frames in order to prevent frame drops.

Using environment importance sampling helps to reduce preintegration error in nighttime situations with small and bright area lights. It also helped keep the number of samples low in order to stay within performance restrictions. However, we found that BRDF importance sampling works well for the majority of cases. It is only during our specific case of nighttime lighting that BRDF importance sampling (with prefiltering) alone was not enough.

```
//Combined Importance Sampling for the specified roughness and the
//reflection vector R using numBRDFSamples for the BRDF IS
//and numENVSamples for the ENV IS
float3 PreintegrateSpecularLightProbe( float Roughness,
      int numENVSamples, int numBRDFSamples, float3 R )
{
   //For the preintegration we assume that N=V=R
   float3 N = normalize(R);
   float3 V = normalize(R);

   float3 finalColor = 0;
   float3 envColor = 0;
   float3 brdfColor = 0;

   //Solve the integral using environment importance sampling
   for(int i = 0; i < numENVSamples; i++)
   {
         envColor += SampleENV(i, Roughness, N, V);
   }
   //Solve the integral using BRDF importance sampling
   for(int i = 0; i < numBRDFSamples; i++)
   {
      //Generate the uniformly distributed random values using
      //Hammersley quasirandom low−discrepancy sequence
      //(Listing 4.2)
      float2 e1e2 = Hammersley( (i), numBRDFSamples);

      brdfColor += SampleBRDF(e1e2.x, e1e2.y, Roughness, N, V);
   }

   //Divide each results by the number of samples using to
   //compute it
   envColor /= numENVSamples;
   brdfColor /= numBRDFSamples;

   //Combine both method based on the number of samples using to
   //solve each of them
   float envColorWeight = numENVSamples / (numENVSamples +
                                                numBRDFSamples);
   float brdfColorWeight = numBRDFSamples/ (numENVSamples +
                                                numBRDFSamples);

   finalColor = envColor * envColorWeight +
                    brdfColor * brdfColorWeight;

   return finalColor;
}
```

Listing 4.6. Multiple (combined) importance sampling.

One positive side effect of having fast probe generation is quick feedback to the artist. The artist is able to iterate on the lighting setup and see the results almost instantaneously.

For future work, we would like to further optimize the shader code for specular probe generation. This would allow us to place even more probes in the level without affecting loading times.

4.5   Acknowledgments

I would like to express my gratitude to the people who supported me and proof-read this chapter: Peter McNeeley of EA Canada and Ramy El Garawany of Naughty Dog.

I would also like to thank the editors Michal Valient of Guerilla Games and Wolfgang Engel of Confetti FX.

Bibliography

[Burley 12] B. Burley. "Physically-Based Shading at Disney." Practical Physically Based Shading in Film and Game Production, SIGGRAPH Course, Los Angeles, CA, August 8, 2012.

[Colbert et al. 10] Mark Colbert, Simon Premože, and Guillaume François. "Importance Sampling for Production Rendering." SIGGRAPH Course, Los Angeles, CA, July 25–29, 2010.

[Cook and Torrance 81] R. Cook and K. Torrance. "A Reflectance Model for Computer Graphics." *Computer Graphics: Siggraph 1981 Proceedings* 15:3 (1981), 301–316.

[Drobot 14] Michal Drobot. "Physically Based Area Lights." In *GPU Pro 5: Advanced Rendering Techniques*, edited by Wolfgang Engel, pp. 67–100. Boca Raton, FL: CRC Press, 2014.

[Hammersley and Handscomb 64] J. M. Hammersley and D. C. Handscomb. *Monte Carlo Methods*, Methuen's Monographs on Applied Probability and Statistics. London: Methuen, 1964.

[Hoffman 12] N. Hoffman. "Background: Physics and Math of Shading." Practical Physically Based Shading in Film and Game Production, SIGGRAPH Course, Los Angeles, CA, August 8, 2012.

[Křivánek and Colbert 08] Jaroslav Křivánek and Mark Colbert. "Real-Time Shading with Filtered Importance Sampling." *Comp. Graph. Forum: Proc. of EGSR 2008*, 27:4 (20080, 1147–1154.

[Karis 13] Brian Karis. "Real Shading in Unreal Engine 4." SIGGRAPH Course, Anaheim, CA, July 21–25, 2013.

[King 05] Gary King. "Real-Time Computation of Dynamic Irradiance Environment Maps." In *GPU Gems 2*, edited by Matt Farr, pp. 167–176. Reading, MA: Addison-Wesley, 2005.

[Lagarde 12] Sébastien Lagarde. "AMD Cubemapgen for Physically Based Rendering." http://seblagarde.wordpress.com/2012/06/10/amd-cubemapgen-for-physically-based-rendering/, 2012.

[Niederreiter 92] Harald Niederreiter. *Random Number Generation and Quasi-Monte Carlo Methods.* Philadelphia: Society for Industrial and Applied Mathematics, 1992.

[Papoulis 84] A. Papoulis. *Probability, Random Variables, and Stochastic Processes*, Second Edition. New York: McGraw-Hill, 1984.

[Pharr and Humphreys 04] Matt Pharr and Greg Humphreys. *Physically Based Rendering: From Theory to Implementation.* San Francisco: Morgan Kaufmann, 2004.

[Ramamoorthi and Hanrahan 01] Ravi Ramamoorthi and Pat Hanrahan. "An Efficient Representation for Irradiance Environment Maps." In *Proceeding of SIGGRAPH*, pp. 497–500. New York: ACM, 2001.

[Hill and McAuley 12] Stephen Hill and Stephen McAuley, Organizers. "Practical Physically Based Shading in Film and Game Production," SIGGRAPH Course, Los Angeles, CA, August 5–9, 2012. (Available at http://blog.selfshadow.com/publications/s2012-shading-course/.)

[Sloan 08] Peter-Pike Sloan. "Stupid Spherical Harmonics (SH) Tricks." Presented at Game Developers Conference, San Francisco, CA, February 18–22, 2008.

[Walter et al. 07] Bruce Walter, Stephen R. Marschner, Hongsong Li, and Kenneth E. Torrance. "Microfacet Models for Refraction through Rough Surfaces." In *Proceedings of the Eurographics Symposium on Rendering*, pp. 195–206. Aire-la-Ville, Switzerland: Eurographics Association, 2007.

5

III

Real-Time Global Illumination Using Slices

Hugh Malan

5.1 Introduction

In this chapter, we'll present a method for implementing real-time single-bounce global illumination.

In recent years, several practical real-time global illumination techniques have been demonstrated. These have all been voxel-based scene databases.

The common theme of all these approaches is to initialize the data structure using the lit scene geometry. Then, a propagation or blurring step is applied, and after that the structure is ready for irradiance or reflection queries.

The Light Propagation Volumes (LPV) method [Kaplanyan and Dachs -bacher 10] uses a voxel array, where each voxel contains a first-order spherical harmonic representation of the irradiance. The array is initialized using reflective shadow maps; the propagation step is to iteratively transfer irradiance from each cell to its neighbors.

The voxel octrees algorithm [Crassin et al. 2011] converts the scene to an octree representation, where each leaf holds radiance. Non-leaf nodes are calculated to have the average of child node colors. Sharp reflections are computed by ray-tracing the octree and sampling the color from the leaf node hit; blurry reflections and irradiance are found by sampling a parent node, whose generation depends on blurriness.

The cascaded 3D volumes approach [Panteleev 2014] uses a sequence of 3D volumes. They are all the same dimension, but each one's side length doubles. The algorithm is comparable to the octree approach, but it can be updated and queried more efficiently.

Figure 5.1. Example of a single slice.

5.2   Algorithm Overview

Like the voxel approaches described in the introduction, our algorithm works by building a data structure using the lit scene geometry and then querying that structure to evaluate irradiance.

Here, the datastructure is a collection of *slices*. A slice is a scaled and deformed unit square, aligned to some surface of the scene (see Figure 5.1). During the initialization step, it captures the radiance of that part of the scene. It can then be queried to efficiently compute the irradiance due to the light emitted from that surface.

Slices are arranged in an array of distorted cuboids (called *cells*) that are fitted to the scene geometry; an example is shown in Figure 5.2.

To evaluate the irradiance for a particular location and surface normal, we begin by finding the cell containing that location. Then, the six slices making up the faces of that cell are queried to compute their irradiance. The six irradiance values are combined by summing them.

Like the LPV approach, we also need to propagate light from cuboid to cuboid, so a light emitted in one cuboid can illuminate geometry in another. This is done at slice initialization time by allowing light from nearby slices to contribute.

The rest of the chapter will be organized as follows. To begin with, we'll discuss how to efficiently compute irradiance due to an emissive flat surface.

Figure 5.2. Scene geometry with distorted cuboids (cells) fitted to it. The cuboid edges are shown with red lines; dimmer lines indicate hidden edges.

Then, we'll deal with the question of how to support multiple such surfaces, the motivation for the distorted-cuboid approach, and how to set up the array of cells to match the geometry for a given scene.

5.3   Approximating the Irradiance Due to an Emissive Plane

The irradiance at a point p with surface normal $\boldsymbol{n}$ is

$$E(p, \boldsymbol{n}) = \int_{H^+} L_i(p, \boldsymbol{\omega}) \cos \theta \; d\boldsymbol{\omega}, \tag{5.1}$$

where H^+ is the upper hemisphere above p centered on the direction $\boldsymbol{n}$, and $L_i(p, \omega)$ is the incoming radiance reaching p from the direction $\boldsymbol{\omega}$—where $\boldsymbol{\omega}$ can be in spherical polar coordinates as (θ, ϕ).

Imagine a plane at $z = 0$ that emits light, where the radiance is defined by a function $r(x, y)$. We're interested in finding an approximation to the function $E(p, \boldsymbol{n})$ that can be evaluated on the GPU in an efficient manner.

First, notice that evaluating irradiance can be expressed as a convolution of $r(x, y)$ with a kernel that depends on $\boldsymbol{n}$ and $|p_z|$, i.e., the distance from the plane:

$$E(p, \boldsymbol{n}) = \int_{x=-\infty}^{x=+\infty} \int_{y=-\infty}^{y=+\infty} r(x, y) W(x - p_x, y - p_y, -p_z, \boldsymbol{n}) dy \; dx,$$

where W is the convolution kernel

$$W(\Delta x, \Delta y, \Delta z, \boldsymbol{n}) = \frac{\max(0, (\Delta x, \Delta y, \Delta z) \cdot \boldsymbol{n})}{\left(\sqrt{(\Delta x^2 + \Delta y^2 + \Delta z^2)}\right)^3}.$$

Second, the kernel scales up with distance from the plane. If we sample a point k times farther from the plane, then the weighting function scales too:

$$\begin{aligned}
W(\Delta x, \Delta y, k\Delta z, \boldsymbol{n}) &= \frac{\max(0, (\Delta x, \Delta y, \Delta z) \cdot \boldsymbol{n})}{\left(\sqrt{(\Delta x^2 + \Delta y^2 + (k\Delta z)^2)}\right)^3} \\
&= \frac{\max(0, k(\Delta x/k, \Delta y/k, \Delta z) \cdot \boldsymbol{n})}{\left(\sqrt{k^2((\Delta x/k)^2 + (\Delta y/k)^2 + \Delta z^2)}\right)^3} \\
&= \frac{k \cdot \max(0, (\Delta x/k, \Delta y/k, \Delta z) \cdot \boldsymbol{n})}{k^3 \left(\sqrt{((\Delta x/k)^2 + (\Delta y/k)^2 + \Delta z^2)}\right)^3} \\
&= \frac{W(\Delta x/k, \Delta y/k, \Delta z, \boldsymbol{n})}{k^2}.
\end{aligned}$$

So, the convolution kernel scales up in proportion to distance from the plane: for a point twice as far from the plane, the kernel is scaled up by a factor of 2 in the x and y directions.

This fact suggests that for a given $\boldsymbol{n}$, we could store the irradiance for the volume $(x, y, z) : x, y \epsilon [-s, +s], z \epsilon [0, t]$ in an image pyramid, where each level is twice as far from the plane as the previous level and half the resolution. If s is the distance to the first mip level, then

$$\text{distance from emissive plane to layer } m = s \cdot 2^m. \tag{5.2}$$

The increase in texel size at each level corresponds to the increase in the convolution kernel size, so the fidelity can be expected to be consistent for all levels of the image pyramid.

This image pyramid can be implemented on the GPU by using a standard mipmapped texture, sampled using trilinear filtering.

For a given distance d from the emissive plane, the mipmap parameter is

$$\text{mipmap parameter} = \log_2\left(\frac{d}{s}\right) \tag{5.3}$$

5.4   Building the Image Pyramid

Our approach was inspired by the summed-Gaussian approach used in "Advanced Techniques for Realistic Real-Time Skin Rendering" [d'Eon and Luebke 07]—a

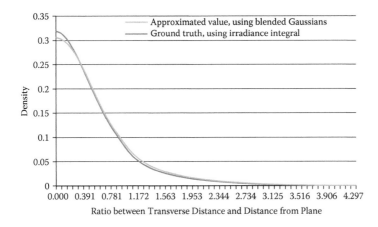

Figure 5.3. Irradiance contribution of a flat plane: cross section of the contribution of each point using the ideal irradiance integral and a paired-Gaussian approximation.

nonseparable function may be approximated by a weighted sum of a series of Gaussian blurs. Like that paper, we used just two Gaussian blurs.

The pair of blended Gaussian blurs were matched to the ideal convolution kernel by minimizing the least-squared error. If d is the distance from the emissive plane, here is the best-fit approximation:

$g_0 =$ blurred radiance image using Gaussian blur with standard deviation $1.368d$;

$g_1 =$ blurred radiance image using Gaussian blur with standard deviation $0.532d$;

approximate irradiance $= 0.54g_0 + 0.46g_1.$ $\hspace{2cm}$ (5.4)

Figure 5.3 shows the comparison between the ideal and approximation.

The naive approach to generate the image pyramid is to consider each mipmap in turn, and for the implied distance from the plane, calculate the Gaussian blur radii, then blur and blend the radiance image correspondingly. Unfortunately, this leads to prohibitively large tap counts for more distant images.

The solution we used is to generate a second image pyramid from the radiance image as a preprocess—this image pyramid is like a mipchain; each layer is constructed by down-sampling the previous layer by a factor of 2 using a box filter.

Then, rather than blurring the full-resolution image, an appropriate mip level is chosen as input to the aforementioned Gaussian blur. The standard deviation of the Gaussian blur is specified in world units, so the number of taps will vary depending which mip level is chosen—though obviously the quality will degrade if the resolution and tap count are too low. This means the tap count for the Gaussian blur can be controlled, and it's possible to use even just 5–10 taps without substantial quality loss.

5.4.1 Putting It All Together

Given an emissive plane, begin by capturing the radiance and opacity in a texture map (R). The image pyramid for irradiance queries is generated from R as follows:

1. Generate a standard mipmap chain for the texture map R. Each mipmap is a half-size boxfiltered down-sample of the previous. Let R' be the resulting image pyramid. It contains radiance in RGB and opacity in A. The opacity value is not used for the irradiance pyramid generated here, but is required for the cell-to-cell propagation step described later in Section 5.8.

2. Allocate the irradiance image pyramid I. It will have the same dimensions and mipmap count as R'. Each mipmap corresponds to a certain distance from the emissive plane, defined by Equation (5.2).

3. For each mip level m of the image pyramid I, we generate the image as described by Equation (5.4).

For the current mip level, compute its distance from the emissive plane, and find the standard deviations of the two Gaussian blurs as a distance in world space. Find the two source mip levels to use as inputs for the blurs. (We found that evaluating the Gaussian out to two standard deviations and using five taps gave acceptable results.) Blur those two input images using the appropriate Gaussian functions, rescale the results so they're the same resolution, and blend the resulting two images to build the mipmap for I.

Note that because the image pyramid I contains RGB only, these image-processing steps can discard the alpha channel.

5.4.2 Sampling the Image Pyramid

With the image pyramid described, it's possible to query the irradiance. However, we're restricted to points that are directly above the planar region where the texture map R is defined. Also, the surface normal must be facing directly toward the emissive plane, as this is the assumption made for the image pyramid construction.

First, we find the relative position of the query point within the image pyramid volume, to obtain the (u, v) for sampling the pyramid. We compute the distance to the plane d. The mipmap we need to sample is determined by Equation (5.3). We sample the image pyramid with the computed (u, v) and mipmap parameter and the resulting value is the irradiance.

As it stands, the restrictions on surface normal and position make this method too limited to be useful. Here's how the restrictions may be lifted.

5.4.3   Supporting Arbitrary Normals

Consider the infinite plane at $z = 0$ radiating a constant color. Since the plane is infinite and radiance constant, the irradiance measured at a particular point will not vary if it's moved (without crossing the plane). The only thing that matters is what part of the visible hemisphere is covered by the emissive plane, and this is unaffected by movement. So in this case, the irradiance depends only on the surface normal.

Let E_0 be the irradiance measured at the point p_{xyz} with $p_z < 0$, facing directly toward the plane. Let E_1 be the irradiance measured at the same point with an arbitrary normal (n_{xyz}; assume it to be normalized). Then

$$\frac{E_1}{E_0} = \frac{1 + n_z}{2}. \tag{5.5}$$

We'll use the relationship from Equation (5.5) to attenuate the value sampled from the image pyramid, to support arbitrary query normals.

Proof: We're interested in computing the irradiance for a scene consisting only of a constant emissive plane. We may assume with no loss of generality that the sample point is at the origin, and the upper hemisphere over which we gather irradiance is $(0, 0, 1)$. The plane is initially at $z = -1$, with surface normal $(0, 0, 1)$; it is rotated around the x axis by the angle θ_{max}, where $\theta_{max} \epsilon [0, 180°]$. If θ_{max} is 180°, then the plane is above the origin with surface normal $(0, 0, -1)$, so the irradiance integral covers the full hemisphere as usual. But if $\theta_{max} < 180°$, then areas on the hemisphere for which $\theta > \theta_{max}$ correspond to rays that will miss the emissive plane. Therefore, the irradiance integral is restricted to directions in the range $[0, \theta_{max}]$.

Figure 5.4 shows the situation. The grid represents the plane; it has been faded out in the middle so it doesn't obscure the rest of the diagram. The gray truncated hemisphere represents the set of directions that intersect the emissive plane.

The integral is identical to Equation (5.1), but expressed in spherical polar coordinates (ϕ and θ) and restricted to directions that intersect the emissive plane. For a given ϕ and θ, the z component is $\sin(\phi)\sin(\theta)$, which is equivalent to the $\cos(\theta)$ term in Equation (5.1). We also scale by $\sin(\phi)$ to compensate for the change in area near the poles. Suppose the constant color radiated by the plane is L_p. Then the integral is as follows:

$$\int_{\theta=0}^{\theta=\theta_{max}} \int_{\phi=0}^{\phi=\pi} L_p \sin(\phi)\sin(\theta)\sin(\phi)d\phi d\theta$$

$$= L_p \int_{\theta=0}^{\theta=\theta_{max}} \sin(\theta)d\theta \cdot \int_{\phi=0}^{\phi=\pi} \sin^2(\phi)d\phi$$

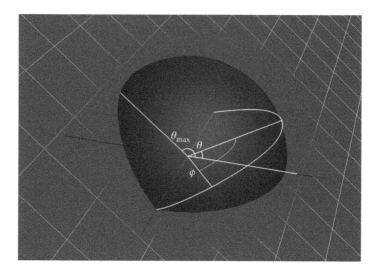

Figure 5.4. Integral variables.

$$= L_p \int_{\theta=0}^{\theta=\theta_{\max}} \sin(\theta) \cdot \frac{\pi}{2} = L_p[-\cos(\theta)]_0^{\theta_{\max}} \cdot \frac{\pi}{2}$$

$$= L_p([-\cos(\theta_{\max})] - [-\cos(0)]) \cdot \frac{\pi}{2} = L_p(1 - \cos(\theta_{\max})) \cdot \frac{\pi}{2}$$

$$= L_p \cdot \pi \cdot \frac{1 - \cos(\theta_{\max})}{2}$$

The irradiance E_0, when the surface normal points directly toward the plane, can be found by substituting $\theta_{\max} = \pi$. This gives $E_0 = L_p\pi$. The ratio E_1/E_0 is therefore

$$\frac{E_1}{E_0} = \frac{1 - \cos(\theta_{\max})}{2}.$$

Substituting $\cos(\theta_{\max}) = \boldsymbol{n} \cdot (0, 0, -1) = \boldsymbol{n}f_z$ gives Equation (5.5). $\square$

5.4.4 Sampling Outside the Depth Pyramid Volume

A reasonable approximation for irradiance outside the image pyramid volume is to clamp the sample point to the border of the image pyramid region, calculate irradiance from the image pyramid using the clamped location, and then scale down the resulting irradiance progressively as the query point moves farther from

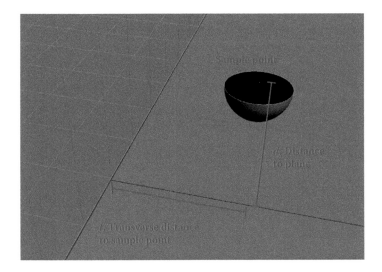

Figure 5.5. Sampling irradiance outside valid region.

the border, using

irradiance outside the valid region

$$= (\text{irradiance at the border}) \cdot \left(1 + \frac{d}{\sqrt{t^2 + d^2}}\right). \quad (5.6)$$

Figure 5.5 shows how the function is defined. The colored region on the left is the valid region, where the image pyramid is defined; we're considering it to be an infinite half-plane for simplicity. The hemisphere indicates the "upper hemisphere" (see Equation (5.1)) around which the irradiance for the sample point is gathered.

For a given sample point, with a surface normal pointing toward the emissive plane, we're interested in how much the valid region contributes to the irradiance. For points above the border, this will be exactly 50%. For points farther from the valid region, this value will tend to 0%.

Figure 5.6 shows a cross section of valid half-plane and irradiance hemisphere. There are strong similarities to the calculation of irradiance for a tilted plane described in Section 5.4.3: in both cases, the irradiance integral is restricted to a subset of the upper hemisphere, which can be expressed as the range $0 \le \theta \le \theta_{\max}$.

Making use of Equation (5.5) means finding the normalized vector to the edge of the valid region (s). Normalizing the vector $s = (t, d)$ gives

$$(t, d) \cdot \frac{1}{\sqrt{t^2 + d^2}}.$$

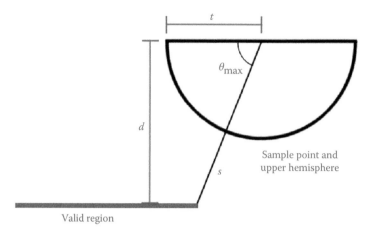

Figure 5.6. Cross section showing contribution of valid region.

Substituting the appropriate component into Equation (5.5) and simplifying it gives

$$\text{fractional contribution of the valid region} = 0.5 + \frac{d}{2\sqrt{t^2 + d^2}}. \qquad (5.7)$$

Dividing by 0.5, which is the value taken on the border, gives Equation (5.6).

Figure 5.7 is a graph of Equation (5.7), showing how the fractional contribution to irradiance changes for points past the border. The reason for using the ratio t/d as an axis is that Equation (5.7) may be rewritten as a function of t/d.

5.4.5   Evaluating Irradiance Using the Image Pyramid

The image pyramid is sampled as follows. For the query point p, with normal n:

1. Find the relative position of p within the image pyramid volume, to obtain the (u, v) for sampling the pyramid. Compute d, the distance to the plane.

2. Find the mipmap parameter using Equation (5.3).

3. Sample the image pyramid using trilinear filtering, with the mipmap parameter calculated at the previous step. Clamp the (u, v) to the image pyramid region. Let c_{RGB} be the color sampled.

4. If the query point is not within the image pyramid volume, attenuate c_{RGB} using Equation (5.6).

5. Attenuate c_{RGB} based on surface normal using Equation (5.5).

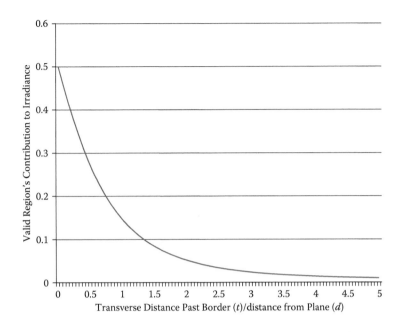

Figure 5.7. Contribution of the valid region to irradiance when sampling beyond the border.

5.4.6 Results

Before moving on, it's useful to compare the approximation that has been described, with the ground truth result.

Figure 5.8 shows the scene. The black square with the cyan circle is the emissive plane, at $y = 0$. We'll evaluate the irradiance at points on the transparent square, which are the points $-32 \le x \le +32$, $-64 \le y \le 0$, $z = 0$. For simplicity, the surface normal used for sampling is $n = (0, 1, 0)$, directly toward the emissive plane.

Figure 5.9 to Figure 5.11 show the resulting irradiance. Figure 5.9 shows the ground truth result where the indirect term at each point was evaluated using 16,000 importance-sampled rays. A lot of rays are needed because there's only a small bright region—even using 1000 rays per pixel gives noisy results.

Figure 5.10 shows the image-pyramid approximation described in this chapter. The image pyramid only covers a subset of this space: $-16 \le x, y \le +16$, between the yellow lines. Note that the values outside this region are still a good approximation because the trilinear sample is attenuated using Equation (5.6). For comparison, Figure 5.11 shows the standard boxfiltered mipchain without the Gaussian blurs or attenuation.

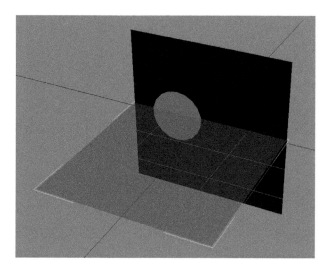

Figure 5.8. Emissive plane and sample area.

Figure 5.9. Ideal result—importance sampled using 16,000 rays.

Figure 5.10. Texture approximation. One trilinear filtered lookup from a 256×256 texture.

Figure 5.11. Comparison—trilinear lookup without Gaussian blurs or attenuation.

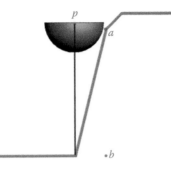

Figure 5.12. Extreme distortions cause significant approximation errors.

5.4.7 Limitations

It's tempting to try using the slice approach with arbitrary heightfields. Unfortunately, this can often give poor results: slices approximate the emissive surface as a flat plane and weight the contributions of each part of the emissive plane accordingly. With a heightfield, it's possible for there to be points quite close to our sample point, which means they should contribute significantly to irradiance—but with the slice approach, they have a very low contribution.

For instance, consider the situation shown in Figure 5.12. The green line is a cross section through a heightfield. Suppose we've distorted a slice to match it exactly, and use the slice to evaluate irradiance. The point p is the location where we'd like to sample irradiance; the semicircle indicates the hemisphere for the gather. The black line running vertically down from p to the heightfield shows the distance to the heightfield; this will be the distance used to calculate the mipmap parameter for the image pyramid lookup.

In Figure 5.12, point a is quite close to p, so it should contribute significantly to irradiance. However, the slice approximation will weight it as if it were at b.

So, if the shape of a slice is distorted too much, the quality of the approximation will suffer.

In conclusion, if we restrict the emissive surfaces to near-planar surfaces, then we can efficiently evaluate the indirect lighting contribution and, in addition, the steps to build the image pyramid are cheap enough to run in real time.

In the next sections of the chapter, we'll describe how to use this approach to support more general scenes.

5.5 Combining Multiple Slices

5.5.1 Irradiance Values May Be Combined Only If the Slices Do Not Occlude Each Other

The value sampled from the image pyramid is an RGB irradiance value.

Figure 5.13. Two emissive squares; one completely occludes the other when irradiance is gathered for the hemisphere indicated.

It's tempting to combine the irradiance values sampled from different slices. Unfortunately, the only way this can be reliably done is if the slices do not obscure each other.

Imagine two nearly coincident squares, one red and one blue, with their irradiance sampled, as shown in Figure 5.13. The red square does not contribute to the irradiance at all when they are combined; it's completely obscured by the blue square.

In this case, occlusion completely changes the result—and occlusion isn't accounted for with the slice approximation. However, it is possible to sum the irradiance and opacity sampled from two slices if they do not obscure each other at all. Recall the irradiance definition from, Equation (5.1):

$$E(p, \boldsymbol{n}) = \int_{H^+} L_i(p, \boldsymbol{\omega}) \cos \theta \; d\boldsymbol{\omega},$$

where $L_i(p, \boldsymbol{\omega})$ is the incoming light falling on p from the direction $\boldsymbol{\omega}$. Define $L_i^A(p, \boldsymbol{\omega})$ to be the incoming light if there was only object A in the scene, and $L_i^B(p, \boldsymbol{\omega})$ similarly. These will give the RGB value $(0, 0, 0)$ for directions that don't hit the corresponding object.

If there are no p and $\boldsymbol{\omega}$ such that $L_i^A(p, \boldsymbol{\omega})$ and $L_i^B(p, \boldsymbol{\omega})$ are simultaneously nonzero—i.e., there is no sample position p and direction $\boldsymbol{\omega}$ from which one of the objects occludes the other—then $L_i(p, \boldsymbol{\omega}) = L_i^A(p, \boldsymbol{\omega}) + L_i^B(p, \boldsymbol{\omega})$. Then,

$$E(p, \boldsymbol{n}) = \int_{H^+} L_i(p, \boldsymbol{\omega}) \cos \theta \; d\boldsymbol{\omega} = \int_{H^+} (L_i^A(p, \boldsymbol{\omega}) + L_i^B(p, \boldsymbol{\omega})) \cos \theta \; d\boldsymbol{\omega}$$

$$= \int_{H^+} L_i^A(p, \boldsymbol{\omega}) \cos \theta \; d\boldsymbol{\omega} + \int_{H^+} L_i^B(p, \boldsymbol{\omega})) \cos \theta \; d\boldsymbol{\omega}$$

$$= [\text{irradiance due to object } A] + [\text{iradiance due to object } B].$$

So, we can sum the irradiance from different objects/slices if they never occlude each other.

However: the relation $L_i(p, \omega) = L_i^A(p, \omega) + L_i^B(p, \omega)$ will still be a reasonable approximation if the amount of overlap is low. If the amount of overlap is high—such as the above example where one object completely occludes another—then it will no longer hold.

5.5.2 An Array of Distorted Cubes

One way to construct a set of slices that never occlude each other is to arrange six slices as faces of a cube, and to allow only sampling from points within the cube. With this arrangement, we could accurately evaluate the irradiance within a cube using slices—but this is, of course, far too restrictive to be generally useful.

However, it's possible to stretch and skew the cube. The restriction that slices never occlude each other is equivalent to requiring that the shape remains convex. Secondly, there is the requirement that the slices not be too distorted from their original square shape—the greater the distortion, the more the irradiance approximation degrades.

A wide variety of shapes can be created that meet these two requirements: cuboids and extruded parallelograms are possible, as are more esoteric shapes created by nonlinear distortions, such as truncated square pyramids. It's even possible to allow a small amount of nonconvexity without the slice approximation failing (see the discussion on occlusion in the previous section) so transformations that lead to a slightly nonconvex result are still valid. An example is a bend or twist operation. Each of these distorted cubes is called a *cell*.

The next step is to fit the cells together. If a particular face is flat, then it could be shared with a neighboring cell: on the shared face, there would be two coincident slices, one associated with each neighbor.

It's possible to extend this even further to create a large group of cells that fill space with no overlaps. In this case, the process of evaluating irradiance is done by finding the cell that contains the query point, calculating the irradiance contributed by each of its six slices, and summing those six values.

Allowing an arbitrary arrangement of cells would be possible, but we imposed some restrictions to make the search for the cell containing the query point more efficient, as well as the transformation to slice space for evaluating irradiance.

5.6 Layered Heightfields

The approach we chose was to define a set of layered heightfields for each axis. For the x axis, we have $x = f_i(y, z)$, where the series of functions f_i define the heightfields; $0 \le i \le n_x$. Figure 5.14 shows an example.

We also require that $f_i(y, z) < f_{i+1}(y, z)$ to enforce the layers to never intersect, and for each successive heightfield to be farther along the x axis. A similar series of functions g_j, h_k are defined for the y and z axes.

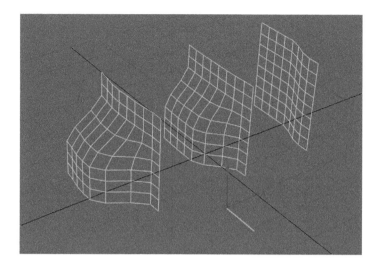

Figure 5.14. Layered heightfields for the x axis.

These heightfields define the split between neighboring cells. They produce a collection of cells that can be indexed using three integers (i, j, k), where $0 \le i \le n_x$, $0 \le j \le n_y$, and $0 \le k \le n_z$. The resulting arrangement of cells are like a distortion of an $n_x \times n_y \times n_z$ array of voxels.

The region covered by the cell (i, j, k) occupies the set of points $(f_i(y, z), g_j(x, z), h_k(x, y))$ where $x \in (i, i+1)$, $y \in (j, j+1)$, and $z \in (k, k+1)$.

Defining the distortion in this way does not allow arbitrary distortions to be represented. For instance, a twist distortion (like the "twirl" distortion in Adobe Photoshop) with an angle of more than 90 degrees cannot be expressed as a series of layered heightfields.

5.6.1   Mapping from World Space to Cell Space

The search for a containing cell is done on an axis-by-axis basis: for a given point (x, y, z), find the identifier (i, j, k) of the containing cell. The value of i is the value for which $f_i(y, z) \le x < f_{i+1}(y, z)$; note that it's independent of j and k and may be done as a simple binary search within the series of heightfields. It specifically avoids the need for a volume texture lookup. (If the layered heightfields are constructed as described in Section 5.7, then the heightfields are restricted to a series of regular intervals, which simplifies the lookup substantially: the value of i can be found by querying two heightfields.) Values for j and k are computed in a similar fashion.

Secondly, we can find the relative position within the cell. This is the point (u, v, w), where $0 \le u, v, w \le 1$. It is found by the relative position between the boundary heightfields:

$$u = \frac{x - f_i(y, z)}{f_{i+1}(y, z) - f_i(y, z)},$$

$$v = \frac{y - g_j(x, z)}{g_{j+1}(x, z) - g_j(x, z)},$$ (5.8)

$$w = \frac{z - h_k(x, y)}{h_{k+1}(x, y) - h_k(x, y)}.$$

The point (u, v, w) can be used directly for evaluating the slice irradiance. For example, to evaluate the contribution of the slice on the f_i side of the cell, the texture coordinate to sample the slice texture is (v, w), and the value u can be directly used to calculate the mipmap paramater (Equation (5.3)) if the distance to the first mipmap is also expressed in that space. The other five slices making up the cell can be evaluated in a similar way.

So at runtime, the full process of evaluating irradiance for a given point in world space involves these steps:

- Search the layered heightfields for each of the three axes to find the cell (i, j, k).

- Find the relative position (u, v, w) within the cell using Equation (5.9).

- Sample the image pyramid of each of the six slices associated with that cell.

- Scale and attenuate those six samples based on surface normal and distance outside border (if need be) to evaluate irradiance using Equations (5.4) and (5.5).

- Sum the resulting six irradiance values.

5.7 Slice Placement

For a given scene, we need a way to build the layered heightfields that divide up the space, and define the cells. The goal is for the cell faces to be coincident with scene geometry wherever possible.

The method we used is intended to be run offline, as a preprocess. It works as follows.

Let the number of slices for each axis be $\boldsymbol{n}_x$, $\boldsymbol{n}_y$, and $\boldsymbol{n}_z$. Each axis will be processed in turn. For each axis, we'll generate the series of layered heightfields described earlier: i.e., for the x axis, the heightfields will be of the form $x_i = f_i(y, z)$, for integer i with $0 \le i \le \boldsymbol{n}_x$; for the y axis, the heightfields will be of the form $y_j = g_j(x, z)$ for integer j with $0 \le j \le \boldsymbol{n}_y$; and similar for the z axis. The collection of heightfields for a particular axis will never intersect each

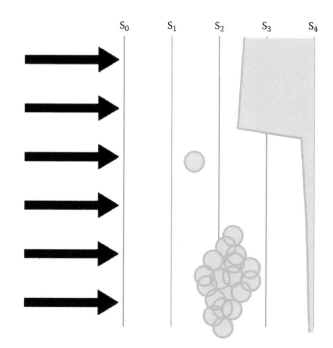

Figure 5.15. Scene divided into equal parts. The geometry is shown in green; the arrows on the left indicate the ray collection.

other—they'll form a series of layers. So $f_i(y, z) < f_{i+1}(y, z)$ always, with similar restrictions for the g and h series.

5.7.1   Generating the Defining Heightfields

The problem is to find a collection of layered heightfields for each axis that matches the significant surfaces of the scene.

This is the process to generate the $x = f_i(y, z)$ heightfield collection. This approach is repeated with obvious modifications to generate the y and z axis collections.

1. Find the scene extent: $(x_{min}, y_{min}, z_{min}) - (x_{max}, y_{max}, z_{max})$. Divide the scene into $\boldsymbol{n}_x$ equal-sized parts along the x axis, i.e., $\boldsymbol{n}_x$ subsets, each covering the region $(\boldsymbol{s}_i, y_{min}, z_{min}) - (\boldsymbol{s}_{i+1}, y_{max}, z_{max})$, where $\boldsymbol{s}_0 = x_{min}, \boldsymbol{s}_1 = x_{min} + k, \ldots, \boldsymbol{s}_i = x_{min} + ik, \ldots, \boldsymbol{s}_{nx} = x_{max}$.

2. Define a collection of rays in the direction $(1, 0, 0)$ that originate from a regular grid of points, i.e., (x, y, z) such that $x = x_{min}, y = y_{min} + p * (y_{max} - y_{min})/p_{max}$, and $z = z_{min} + q * (z_{max} - z_{min})/q_{max}$ for integer p, q. See Figure 5.15.

3. For each ray in turn, trace the ray through the scene, finding each of the surface intersections. Within each of the n_x subset spaces defined at step 1, find the front-facing intersection with the minimum x component, and the back-facing intersection with maximum x. (*Front-facing* means the surface the ray intersected has a surface normal whose x component is < 0—i.e., the ray hit the surface from the front. *Back-facing* means the opposite.) Let S_j be the resulting set of intersection points for ray j. Record the intersection by storing the ray parameter, i.e., the value p for which (ray origin) + (ray direction $\times p$) = intersection point. Figure 5.16 shows the relevant front- and back-faces for each scene subset.

4. We now assign a significance value to each of the points in S; S_j is $\{p_0, p_1, \ldots, p_{k_{max}}\}$, the ordered set of surface intersection points for ray j. Let the significance value of each point default to 0. For each k, if p_k is back-facing and p_{k+1} is front-facing, then the significance value is $|p_{k+1} - p_k|$; assign it to both p_k and p_{k+1}. Figure 5.17 shows red bars for each such interval. Note that there are no significance bars passing through the solid green regions, due to the check for back-face/front-face order. Ideally, the significance value would measure how often that surface point is seen. We're approximating this using the distance between that point and the point it is facing—this line segment is in open space, rather than within an object, so it's a space where the viewer may go, and the longer that line segment, the larger the open space is. Conversely, a surface that is hidden by another surface will be less significant.

5. Build a 2D table of value and weight for each scene subset. Within each of the n_x scene subsets, for each ray i we have up to two intersection points (a front-facing one and a back-facing one) and an associated significance value.

   Compute the pair $\{v * w, w\}$, where v is the sum of the ray parameters and w is the sum of the associated significance value for those intersection points— there will be zero, one, or two of them. Figure 5.18 shows the average positions.

   If there were no intersection points for the ray in this scene subset, let the pair be $\{0, 0\}$.

   Because the rays are defined to be a regular grid, indexed by the integers p and q (see Step 2) assign the pair $\{v, w\}$ to the table entry $T_i(p, q)$, where i indicates the scene subset.

6. Smooth and extrapolate the table associated with each of the scene subsets. Let $O(p, q)$ be the point at which the ray (p, q) originates. Then $T_i'(p, q) = \sum_{0 \le r \le p_{max}, 0 \le s \le q_{max}} T_i(r, s) \cdot c^{-|0(p,q)-o(r,s)|}$, where c is a constant controlling

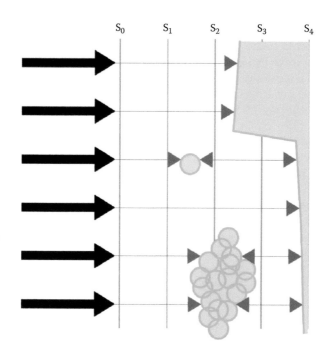

Figure 5.16. Red markers indicate front and back faces for each scene subset.

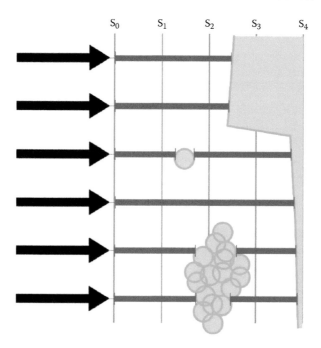

Figure 5.17. Red bars indicate significance.

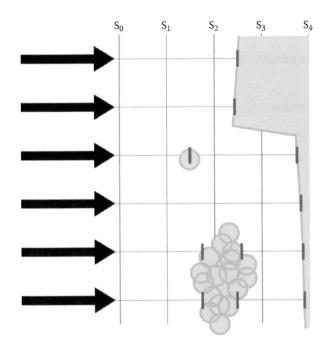

$S_0 \quad S_1 \quad S_2 \quad S_3 \quad S_4$

Figure 5.18. Average position of the intersection points in each scene subset.

the locality of the blur. Note that the values $T(p, q)$ are pairs of real values $\{a, b\}$; they are scaled and added like 2D vectors.

7. Output the heightfield. Define the 2D table U_i with the same dimensions as T_i'. $T_i'(p, q)$ is the pair $\{a, b\}$; the corresponding entry $U_i(p, q)$ is defined to be a/b. Note that b will be zero if and only if the b entry is zero for all entries in table T_i (see Figure 5.19). Note that the heightfields follow the scene geometry where possible, and there is no heightfield in the $s - s_1$ subset.

In short, assign a significance value to the relevant surface intersections in each scene subset, and perform a weighted blur that respects the significance factor to extrapolate and smooth out the heightfield. The parameter and significance pair is encoded as a homogeneous value specifically to support this step.

The heightfield U_i will be contained within scene subset i, thereby meeting the requirement that the heightfields do not cross over.

Note that the input scene may well contain interpenetrating geometry—for example, a ray traveling through the scene may intersect several consecutive front-facing surfaces in a row. Also, there may be "open" or nonmanifold geometry—i.e., a ray passing completely through the scene may encounter a different number

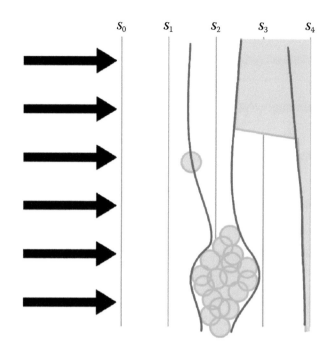

Figure 5.19. Final heightfield for each scene subset.

of front- and back-facing intersections. These problems are unavoidable when working with production scenes. The nearest front-face/last back-face logic in Step 3 is designed to support these situations.

5.7.2   Discussion

This approach works well for scenes which have strong axis-aligned features. That is, scenes where the main surfaces are roughly parallel to the xy, xz, and yz planes. Architectural scenes and game environments built out of prefabs usually meet this requirement.

Large curved surfaces run the risk of problems. If the surface needs to be represented by slices from more than one axis, parts of that surface may be missed (leading to light leakage) or have regions included in two slices (leading to too much indirect light).

These problem cases can usually be fixed by manually editing the distortion function to ensure that the surface always aligns with one and only one slice.

The slice placement step was intended to run offline, as a preprocess, to generate slice geometry that does not change at runtime.

Figure 5.20. Light propagating from one cell to another.

5.8 Propagating Irradiance

While the slice geometry does not change at runtime, the slice image pyramids are intended to be regenerated at runtime in response to lighting changes. Local lighting changes within a cell can be accommodated by recapturing the radiance for those slices and rebuilding the image pyramid as described in Section 5.4.

However, this doesn't allow light to have an effect outside the cell where it was emitted. To achieve this, we use a propagation step, analogous to the light propagation step described by [Kaplanyan and Dachsbacher 10]. For each step, each cell is considered in turn, and light within that cell is propagated to its neighbors. After enough steps, lighting changes will propagate throughout the array of cells.

Figure 5.20 shows a cross section through a collection of cells. The shape of the faces/slices are indicated by red lines—many have been omitted for clarity. We'll only consider some of the vertical slices, by the letters $a-c$. Light is emitted from the slice marked "source," as shown by the arrows.

Light is propagated from cell to cell in two ways. Firstly, it is propagated forward—from source to slice a, in the example image. This is done as follows: when regenerating slice a, the irradiance from *source* is sampled, scaled down by $(1-\text{opacity})$, and added into the radiance of slice a, which is input for generating the image pyramids.

This definition means if a point on slice a is opaque, then the light from *source* will be blocked. If it's transparent, then the irradiance will be continuous—there will be no discontinuity or other artifact.

Secondly, it is propagated laterally—from *source* into slice b in Figure 5.20. This is done when generating the image pyramid for each slice by allowing the blurs to pick up color from neighboring slices, scaled by transparency of the intervening slices (c in the example case).

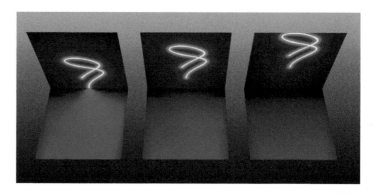

Figure 5.21. Light transport within a single cell.

Again, this definition means that if a slice is opaque, it will block the lateral flow of light. If a slice is transparent, then the light will flow laterally from cell to cell with no discontinuities or artifacts.

With this approach, the light will radiate outward in a plausible fashion, with no discontinuities at the cell borders.

5.9 Results

Figure 5.21 shows the simplest case. Light radiated from a wall is captured by a single slice. The floor plane samples that irradiance. The images demonstrate how the irradiance softens and widens with distance from the emissive surface. It also underlines that the emissive surface can radiate light in any pattern; it's not a point or line but a texture.

Figure 5.22 shows a scene with two cells separated by a perforated wall. This scene shows light propagation from cell to cell and how the attenuation is affected by the occluding wall. Note that the light that passes through the holes and falls on the floor gives a sharper pool of light for the hole near the floor. The farther hole gives a pool of light on the floor that's blurrier and farther from the wall.

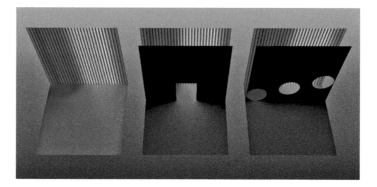

Figure 5.22. Light propagating from one cell to another, with attenuation.

Figure 5.23. Sample scene.

Figure 5.24. Example of changes possible at runtime.

Figure 5.23 shows a production scene where the irradiance is provided using slices. The inset image shows the direct lighting. The blue skylight was created by adding constant blue light into the transparent areas of the topmost layer. For this scene, the cells are roughly 5 m along each side, and each slice is 64×64 resolution.

Figure 5.24 illustrates the sort of changes possible at runtime: the lefthand image shows the a scene with a single light; on the right, a square hole has been cut out of the balcony and the roof above is now lit by bounce light. The slice shapes were not altered in any way: opening the hole in the balcony only changed the transparency of one of the slices, allowing light to propagate from the cell beneath the balcony to the cell above.

5.10   Conclusion

We have presented a method for efficiently evaluating irradiance from a flat surface using an image pyramid, and an efficient method for rebuilding the image pyramid at runtime.

The biggest weakness of this approach is the requirement that the scene be represented by a set of slices. If this requirement can't be met, there will be light leakage and other quality problems. While most architectural and man-made scenes can be adequately represented by slices, more organic environments are a challenge.

In addition, this method won't support dynamic objects moving through the scene. While it can support limited changes to the architecture (e.g., doors opening, a wall collapsing, a roof opening up), it isn't a solution for real-time irradiance effects due to characters moving through the scene.

In conclusion, this best use case for this approach is an architectural or other manmade scene that can be accurately represented by slices; where the lighting is dynamic, the effects of dynamic objects on irradiance is not significant, and the runtime changes to the scene geometry are limited (e.g., doors opening and closing). In this case, it will yield high-quality irradiance that updates in real time.

Bibliography

[Crassin et al. 2011] Cyril Crassin, Fabrice Neyret, Miguel Sainz, Simon Green, and Elmar Eisemann. "Interactive Indirect Illumination Using Voxel Cone Tracing." *Computer Graphics Forum: Proc. of Pacific Graphics 2011* 30:7 (2011), 1921–1930.

[d'Eon and Luebke 07] Eugene d'Eon and David Luebke. "Advanced Techniques for Realistic Real-Time Skin Rendering." In *GPU Gems 3*, edited by Hubert Nguyen, Chapter 14. Reading, MA: Addison-Wesley Professional, 2007. (Available online at http://http.developer.nvidia.com/GPUGems3/gpugems3_ch14.html.)

[Kaplanyan and Dachsbacher 10] Anton Kaplanyan and Carsten Dachsbacher. "Cascaded Light Propagation Volumes for Real-Time Indirect Illumination." In *Proceedings of the 2010 ACM SIGGRAPH Symposium on Interactive 3D Graphics and Games*, pp. 99–107. New York: ACM, 2010.

[Panteleev 2014] A. Panteleev. "Practical Real-Time Voxel-Based Global Illumination for Current GPUs." Presented at SIGGRAPH, Vancouver, CA, August 10–14, 2014. (Available at http://on-demand.gputechconf.com/gtc/2014/presentations/S4552-rt-voxel-based-global-illumination-gpus.pdf.)

Shadows

Shadows are the dark companions of lights, and although both can exist on their own, they shouldn't exist without each other in games. Achieving good visual results in rendering shadows is considered one of the particularly difficult tasks of graphics programmers.

The first article in the section, "Practical Screen-Space Soft Shadows" by Márton Tamás and Viktor Heisenberger, describes how to implement a shadow filter kernel in screen space while preserving the shadow color data in layers.

The next article, "Tile-Based Omnidirectional Shadows" by Hawar Doghramachi, shows how to implement efficient shadows in combination with a tiled deferred shading system by using programmable draw dispatches, the programmable clipping unit, and tetrahedron shadow maps.

The third and last article, "Shadow Map Silhouette Revectorization" by Vladimir Bondarev, utilizes MLAA to reconstruct the shadow penumbra, concealing the perspective aliasing with an additional umbra surface. This is useful for hard shadow penumbras.

—Wolfgang Engel

Practical Screen-Space Soft Shadows

Márton Tamás and Viktor Heisenberger

1.1 Introduction

This article describes novel techniques that extend the original screen-space soft shadows algorithm [Gumbau et al. 10] in order to make sure that the speed of rendering is optimal and that we take into consideration overlapping and translucent shadows. We introduce layers, an essential component to filtering overlapping shadows in screen space. We aim to render near one hundred properly filtered, perceptually correct shadows in real time. We also aim to make this technique easy to integrate into existing rendering pipelines.

1.2 Overview

Shadows are important to establish spatial coherency, establish relationships between objects, enhance composition, add contrast, and indicate offscreen space that is there to be explored. As a gameplay element, they are used to project objects onto walls with the intent to create new images and signs that may tell a story. Shadows are often used to either lead the viewer's eye or obscure unimportant parts of the scene.

In computer graphics, light emitters are often represented as a single point with no definite volume. These kinds of mathematical lights cast only hard-edged shadows (a point is entirely obscured by a shadow caster or not) called an *umbra*. However, in the real world, lights usually have volume (like the sun), and therefore they cast soft-edged shadows that consist of an umbra, *penumbra* (a point is partially obscured by shadow caster), and *antumbra* (the shadow caster appears entirely contained by the light source, like a solar eclipse). Figure 1.1 shows a real-world umbra, penumbra, and antumbra.

Figure 1.1. A real-life umbra, penumbra, and antumbra. The objects are lit by a desk spot lamp.

1.3   History

Traditionally, umbras have been represented by either shadow mapping [Williams 78] or shadow volumes [Crow 77]. Shadow mapping works by rendering the scene depth from the point of view of the light source and later in the lighting pass sampling it and comparing the reprojected scene depth to it to determine if a point is in a shadow. Shadow volumes work by creating shadow geometry that divides space into shadowed and unshadowed regions. However, shadow volumes are often bottlenecked by fill rate, leading to lower performance [Nealen 02]. Thus, we use shadow mapping.

While shadow volumes can achieve pixel-perfect hard shadows, shadow mapping's quality depends on the allocated shadow map's (depth texture's) size. If there's not enough shadow map resolution, under-sampling will occur, leading to aliasing. If there's more than enough shadow map resolution, over-sampling will occur, leading to wasted memory bandwidth. Shadow maps also suffer from projective aliasing, perspective aliasing, and erroneous self-shadowing, which needs to be properly addressed.

To simulate penumbra, shadow mapping is often extended with shadow filtering. In order to render soft shadows, percentage closer filtering (PCF) was introduced by [Reeves et al. 87]. This technique achieves soft shadows by implementing blurring in shadow space. Later, PCF was extended by a screen-space

Figure 1.2. Hard shadows (left), a uniform penumbra rendered using PCF (middle), and a perceptually correct variable penumbra rendered using SSSS. When using a variable penumbra, shadow edges become sharper as they approach the shadow caster.

blurring pass [Shastry 05] that enables the use of large filter kernels. However, these techniques can only achieve uniform penumbras. Figure 1.2 shows a comparison of hard shadows, shadows with uniform penumbras, and shadows with variable-sized penumbras.

Percentage-closer soft shadows (PCSS) was introduced to properly render variable-sized penumbras [Fernando 05]. PCSS works by varying the filter size of the PCF blurring. It does a blocker search in order to estimate the size of the penumbra at the given pixel, then uses that information to do variable-sized blurring. However, PCSS still does the blurring step in shadow space, and, depending on the shadow map and kernel size, this step can be a bottleneck, especially when multiple lights are involved. Screen-space soft shadows (SSSS) [Gumbau et al. 10] aims to combat this by deferring the blurring to a screen-space pass so that it will be independent of the actual shadow map size. In screen space, however, we need to account for the varying view angle and therefore we need to use an anisotropic filter. Because the blocker search is still an expensive step ($O(n^2)$), SSSS was extended by [Gumbau et al. 10] with an alternate way to estimate the penumbra size by doing a $\mathtt{min}$ filter on the shadow map. In addition, this filter is separable and the result only needs to be coarse, so a low-resolution result is acceptable ($O(n + n)$, for much smaller n). [Engel 10] extends SSSS by adding exponential shadow maps and an improved distance function. This allows for self-shadowing, artifact-free soft shadows and better use of the same filter size when viewed from far away.

Mipmapped screen-space soft shadows (MSSSS) [Aguado and Montiel 11] also tries to further improve the speed of filtering. It transforms the shadow map

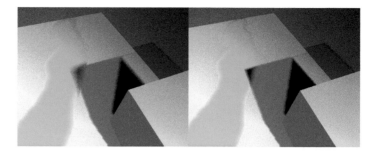

Figure 1.3. Not handling overlapping shadows properly by using layers can lead to artifacts (left), and correct overlapping shadows (right).

blurring problem into the selection of an appropriate mipmap level of a pre-blurred screen-space shadow map based on the estimated size of the penumbra. It also introduces an extension to the algorithm to account for multiple occlusions by using numerous shadow maps.

These screen-space techniques are beneficial because they come with a constant filtering cost, so one does not need to filter the shadows per light source, but the whole screen. Therefore, lights and shadow map filtering are decoupled, and one can employ huge filter kernels resulting in cheap, large penumbras. However, in screen space, another problem surfaces: overlapping shadows of multiple lights. In order to properly account for overlapping shadows, we introduce layered shadow mapping.

The reason we need layers is that if we were to just average the penumbra sizes (storing only one penumbra size per pixel), then we would get incorrect values and artifacts (see Figure 1.3), thus the shadows wouldn't look perceptually correct anymore. With the layers, we can store multiple penumbra sizes and shadow data per pixel, so each light's shadow will be blurred using the correct penumbra size.

In addition, in real-life situations, shadows are often cast by translucent objects, so we also need to take into consideration translucent shadows. The aim of this technique is to render fast, perceptually correct soft shadows with variable penumbra sizes, also accounting for overlapping and translucent shadows. Figure 1.3 shows a comparison between not handling overlapping shadows and handling overlapping shadows.

1.4   Algorithm Overview

1.4.1   G-Buffer Pass

This pass is highly implementation dependent, and while in the original SSSS algorithm this was included in the distances (penumbra) map pass (covered later), we decided to separate this to make sure this technique can be easily integrated into any rendering pipeline. It is possible to go with any G-buffer layout, provided it contains at least the depth buffer and the normals of the scene, as we will need these later. It is important to state that it doesn't matter whether deferred shading or deferred lighting or any of the other popular techniques is being used. We decided to use deferred shading because of its simplicity and speed.

Our G-buffer layout consists of

- D24 depth buffer (stores distance between the viewer and the point being processed),

- RGBA8 view-space normals (RGB channels; alpha channel is free).

1.5 Shadow Map Rendering Pass

In this pass, the standard shadow map rendering is performed, capturing the scene depth from the point of view of the light source. Our technique currently supports spotlights, point lights, and directional lights. Because we are rendering soft shadows, this means that these lights will actually have volume. Note that this will not change the lighting of lit surfaces though.

We consider point lights to be six different shadow casters, and therefore they can be treated the same as spotlights. This means that we can efficiently cull away spotlights, or parts of point lights (that also have shadow maps to be rendered), that do not intersect the camera's frustum as they will not influence the final image. Also, one needs to make sure that projective and perspective aliasing, as well as self-shadowing, is taken care of.

We also extend this pass by considering shadow casters that are not opaque. When this is the case, the shadow caster will allow some light to pass through it, and the shadow may even become colored. Consequently, we need to output an RGBA color per pixel from the point of view of the light. Figure 1.4 shows the contents of a translucency map.

1.6 Introducing Layers and Light Assignment

To allow for multiple overlapping shadows using the original SSSS technique, one could just simply perform all the steps for each light and get correct results. However, this approach is prohibitively expensive, and therefore we looked for a way in which we could perform the screen-space anisotropic blurring for all of the overlapping shadows in one pass.

There was one vital observation (that was also described later in [Anichini 14]): if two lights' volumes don't intersect, their shadows will not overlap either. This means that in screen space, the lights' shadows will not overlap, and because of

Figure 1.4. Contents of the translucency map: a red pole rendered from the point of view of the light source.

this, nonintersecting lights' shadows can be blurred in one pass, independently. However, we also need to consider overlapping shadows from multiple lights.

We observed that this problem (blurring overlapping shadows) is essentially a graph coloring problem, where each graph vertex color represents a shadow layer. In each shadow layer, we store the data of several nonoverlapping lights. In this graph, each light will be a vertex, and there will be an edge between two vertices if the two lights intersect. Because determining the amount of colors needed to color a graph is usually an NP-complete problem, we decided to use a simple greedy algorithm, extended with some rules to help it. For example, since the sun (the directional light) is expected to affect everything, it will be assigned a dedicated layer.

Using the greedy algorithm means that the number of layers (colors) needed equals the maximum vertex degree plus one, and therefore the number of screen-space layers that need to be filtered is only dependent on the maximum number of overlapping shadows produced by different lights (maximum vertex degree). One disadvantage of the greedy vertex coloring is that its quality is highly dependent on the order in which we consider the vertices. Therefore, we use a commonly used vertex ordering scheme, namely, ordering the vertices by their vertex degree in ascending order.

Essentially what we are doing with these layers is trying to minimize the memory and bandwidth costs of overlapping shadows by grouping shadow data into layers instead of storing and filtering them separately for each light source.

It is also advisable to restrict the number of layers for a given scene so that the general coloring problem can be transformed into a k-coloring problem (where k is the predefined number of layers). The shadow filtering will have a predictable cost and artists can be told not to use more overlapping lights than the layer

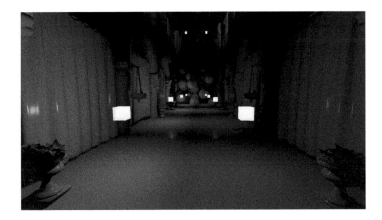

Figure 1.5. Point lights colored according to their respective layer. Each layer is represented by a color (red, green, blue, and yellow). The white cubes illustrate the lights' positions.

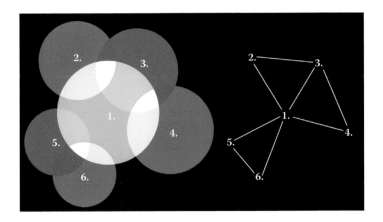

Figure 1.6. Lights are numbered and represented by circles (left), where each color represents a layer (red, green, and blue). Lights and their intersections with each other are represented on a graph (right). We can see that Light 1 has a vertex degree of 5, so we would need a maximum of six layers to render these lights; however, in this case, by using a good graph coloring algorithm, we can reduce the number of needed layers to three.

budget allows for. In addition, in order to speed up the light intersection process, one can use an arbitrary space division data structure such as an octree. The actual layer layout is dependent on the exact technique being used (covered later). Figure 1.5 illustrates the shadow layers and Figure 1.6 illustrates the graph.

1.7 Layered Penumbra Map Pass

In this pass, we calculate all of the needed parameters for the anisotropic Gaussian blur pass, mostly as described in [Gumbau et al. 10]. These parameters include

- distance from the viewer to the point being rendered (scene depth),
- distance of the shadow caster to the point being rendered (penumbra size),
- penumbra mask to determine whether a point needs to be blurred or not,
- shadow buffer (binary value) or exponential shadow buffer (float value, optional),
- translucency map (RGBA values).

1.7.1 Scene Depth

Because we already calculated the scene depth in the G-buffer pass, it is unnecessary to do it again.

1.7.2 Layered Penumbra Map

There are two ways to calculate the penumbra size, as described in [Gumbau et al. 10]:

- using blocker search convolution,
- using a separable `min` filter (covered later).

The first, the blocker search [Fernando 05], is performed by doing a convolution over the shadow map, searching for possible blockers (i.e., where a point is in shadow), then using the average of these blockers' distances (in light projection space) to the light to estimate the penumbra size at a given point. The estimation is done using the following equation, as described in [Gumbau et al. 10]:

$$w_{\mathrm{penumbra}} = \frac{(d_{\mathrm{receiver}} - d_{\mathrm{blocker}})}{d_{\mathrm{blocker}}} \cdot w_{\mathrm{light}},$$

where w_{light} is the size of the light that needs to be tweaked by an artist (empirical value), d_{observer} is the distance to the viewer in light projection space, d_{blocker} is the average blocker distance, and d_{receiver} is the distance to the current point being processed (in light projection space). We can reconstruct the light-projection-space distance (d_{observer}) from a regular depth buffer rendered using a regular OpenGL projection matrix (in Figure 1.7) as shown in Listing 1.1.

It is advisable to store the penumbra size values in at least a 16-bit float value. This means that if we would like to store four layers, we can use an RGBA16F texture. Each of the four layers would be represented by one color channel.

$$\begin{pmatrix} \dfrac{n}{r} & 0 & 0 & 0 \\ 0 & \dfrac{n}{t} & 0 & 0 \\ 0 & 0 & \dfrac{-(f+n)}{f-n} & \dfrac{-2fn}{f-n} \\ 0 & 0 & -1 & 0 \end{pmatrix}$$

Figure 1.7. The (symmetric perspective) OpenGL projection matrix, where n is the near plane distance, f is the far, $t = n \times \tan(\text{fov} \times 0.5)$, and $r = \text{aspect} \times t$

```
//# of bits in depth texture per pixel
unsigned bits = 16;
unsigned precision_scaler = pow(2, bits) - 1;
//generates a perspective projection matrix
mat4 projmat = perspective(radians(fov), aspect, near, far);
//arbitrary position in view space
vec4 vs_pos = vec4(0, 0, 2.5, 1);
//clip-space position
vec4 cs_pos = projmat * vs_pos;
//perspective divide
vec4 ndc_pos = cs_pos / cs_pos.w;
float zranged = ndc_pos.z * 0.5f + 0.5f; //range: [0...1]
//this goes into the depth buffer
unsigned z_value = floor(precision_scaler * zranged);

//helper variables to convert back to view space
float A = -(far + near) / (far - near);
float B = -2 * far * near / (far - near);

//get depth from the depth texture, range: [0...1]
float depth = texture(depth_tex, texcoord).x;
float zndc = depth * 2 - 1; //range: [-1...1]
//reconstructed view-space z
float vs_zrecon = -B / (zndc + A);
//reconstructed clip-space z
float cs_zrecon = zndc * -vs_zrecon;
```

Listing 1.1. Reconstructing clip space z from the depth buffer.

We have two options for generating penumbra information for many lights:

- We can generate them separately and blend them together additively.

- We can batch them and generate all of them at once (covered later).

When generating the penumbra information for each light in a separate pass, at each pixel there will be multiple layers in the penumbra map; therefore, we need to store the penumbra information of each layer separately. We can achieve this by using additive hardware blending.

1.7.3   Layered Penumbra Mask

The penumbra mask essentially stores whether we found a blocker in the blocker search or not. We can notice that the penumbra size calculated previously is in essence just a value that tells us how much we should blur the shadows at a point. In other words, this will scale the effective filter size of the anisotropic Gaussian blurring. Therefore, we can store the penumbra mask in the penumbra size by setting it to zero if the penumbra mask would be zero. Then we can just check when doing the anisotropic blurring if the penumbra size is greater than zero and only blur in that case.

1.7.4   Layered Shadow Buffer

There are two options on what to store in the shadow buffer:

- a binary value that only tells if the point is in shadow or not,

- an exponential shadow map, as described in [Engel 10].

If we are storing the binary shadow value, we can just perform a regular shadow test by sampling the shadow map, reprojecting the scene depth, and comparing the two. This way we can represent each shadow layer in just one bit, so we can store 32 shadow layers in an R32U texture.

Otherwise, if we decide to do exponential shadow mapping, we need to store the result on at least 8 bits so that four layers could fit into an RGBA8 texture. The value that needs to be stored is defined by

$$\text{tex}(z, d, k) = e^{k \cdot (z-d)},$$

where z is the scene depth from the point of view of the viewer, d is the scene depth from the point of view of the light source, and k is an empirical value (scale factor) that is used to tweak the exponential shadow map.

1.7.5   Layered Translucency Map

In order to represent a penumbra in shadows that translucent objects cast, we need to blur the translucency maps computed in the shadow rendering pass, too. Therefore, we accumulate these maps into a layered translucency map. We can represent each layer as an RGBA8 color value that we can pack into an R32F float; so in an RGBA32F texture that has 128 bits, we can store four layers. The packing is done as shown in code Listing 1.2.

1.8   Anisotropic Gaussian Blur Pass

Now we will need to blur the shadows to generate variable-sized penumbras. We will sample the penumbra information generated in the previous pass.

```
//input: float value in range [0...1]
uint float_to_r8( float val )
{
    const uint bits = 8;
    uint precision_scaler = uint(pow( uint(2), bits )) - uint(1);
    return uint(floor( precision_scaler * val ));
}

uint rgba8_to_uint( vec4 val )
{
    uint res = float_to_r8(val.x) << 24;
        res |= float_to_r8(val.y) << 16;
        res |= float_to_r8(val.z) << 8;
        res |= float_to_r8(val.w) << 0;
    return res;
}
```

Listing 1.2. A function to pack an RGBA8 value into an R32F float.

```
float threshold = 0.25;
float filter_size =
    //account for light size (affects penumbra size)
    light_size *
    //anisotropic term, varies with viewing angle
    //added threshold to account for diminishing filter size
    //at grazing angles
    sqrt( max( dot( vec3( 0, 0, 1 ), normal ), threshold ) ) *
    //distance correction term, so that the filter size
    //remains constant no matter where we view the shadow from
    ( 1 / ( depth ) );
```

Listing 1.3. Implementation of the variable filter size.

In order to account for various viewing angles, we need to modify the filter size. To do this, we approximate the filter size by projecting the Gaussian filter kernel into an ellipse following the orientation of the geometry. We used the method described in [Geusebroek and Smeulders 03], which shows how to do anisotropic Gaussian filtering while still keeping the kernel separable. We also need to consider that if we are viewing the shadows from far away, the filter size needs to be decreased to maintain the effective filter width. Because of the nature of the dot product, the filter size can diminish at grazing angles, so we need to limit the minimum filter size. The value that we are comparing to is chosen empirically (usually 0.25 works well). Listing 1.3 shows how this variable filter size is implemented.

Next, all we need to do is evaluate the Gaussian filter. Because this is separable, the blurring will actually take two passes: a horizontal and a vertical. We will modify the filter size by the anisotropy value. We also need to sample all layers at once at each iteration and unpack the individual layers. The layer

```
float unpack_shadow( vec4 shadow, int layer )
{
    //4 layers
    uint layered_shadow = uint(16.0 * shadow.x);
    return ( ( layered_shadow & ( 1 << layer ) ) >> layer );
}

vec4 hard_shadow = texture( layered_shadow_tex, texcoord );
float layer0 = unpack_shadow( hard_shadow, 0 );
```

Listing 1.4. Unpacking shadow data.

```
vec4 uint_to_rgba8( uint val )
{
    uint tmp = val;
    uint r = (tmp & 0xff000000) >> 24;
    uint g = (tmp & 0x00ff0000) >> 16;
    uint b = (tmp & 0x0000ff00) >> 8;
    uint a = (tmp & 0x000000ff) >> 0;
    return vec4( r / 255.0, g / 255.0, b / 255.0, a / 255.0 );
}
```

Listing 1.5. A function to unpack an RGBA8 value from an R32F float.

unpacking is done as shown in Listing 1.4. Because this is a screen-space filter, we need to take into consideration that the shadows might leak light if the filter size is large. Therefore, if the depth difference between the center of the filter and the actual sampled point is greater than a threshold (usually 0.03 works great), then we don't consider the sample.

If we decide to do the Gaussian blurring at half resolution, we can take advantage of the fact that we still have the hard shadow map information available at the original resolution; therefore, if we sample the hard shadow map in a grid pattern (four samples using texture gather), then we can eliminate some of the aliasing artifacts (essentially super-sampling the layered shadow map). We can also decide to use exponential shadow mapping, which will reduce some of the self-shadowing artifacts.

If there are translucent shadow casters, then we need to blur them, too. We need to do the same as for the opaque casters, only the unpacking will be different. The unpacking is done as shown in Listing 1.5.

1.9   Lighting Pass

Finally, we need to apply lighting to the scene. This pass is also highly implementation dependent, but one can still easily integrate SSSS into one's lighting process. We use an optimized tiled deferred shader.

When lighting, one needs to find out which layer the light belongs to, sample the blurred shadow maps accordingly, and multiply the lighting with the shadow value. Note that you only need to sample the screen-space soft shadows once for each pixel and then use the appropriate layer.

1.10   Performance Considerations

There are various ways to speed up the SSSS rendering process. For example, we can do the anisotropic Gaussian blurring at lower (practically half) resolution. This essentially lowers the memory bandwidth requirement of the blurring.

In addition, we can do the penumbra generation at a lower resolution, too; however, this will cause some aliasing near the shadow casters (where the penumbra size is low), which can be eliminated using the super-sampling method described above.

We can also implement the `min`-filter approach. When using this, we need to generate a low-resolution `min`-filtered shadow map, after the shadow-map generation pass. Then we substitute the blocker search result with this value. We can also implement the penumbra mask by checking if this value is below a certain threshold (the anisotropic Gaussian filter width would be negligible anyway). This way we don't need to store the penumbra sizes in screen space in layers, because these `min`-filter maps are small enough to sample each of them in the anisotropic blurring pass, so in the penumbra map pass we only calculate the layered shadow buffer and layered translucency map. The rest of the algorithm remains the same. However, as we observed at 4 layers and 16 lights, this approach is usually around 0.2 ms slower than storing the penumbra size as usual. This may not be the case with more layers, though.

Additionally, instead of generating penumbra information for each light separately and blending them together additively, we can also batch the lights and generate the penumbra information for all of them in one pass. However, if we decide to go this way, then all the shadow map and `min`-filtered shadow map information needs to be available at once. This means that in one pass we need to sample all of the shadow maps of all the visible lights. These can be passed to a shader using texture arrays or texture atlases.

We can also adjust the kernel size of the Gaussian blurring. Usually a 11×11 filter works well, but you can also implement huge filters like a 23×23 filter, which will allow for enormous penumbras, or use an efficient 5×5 filter.

1.11   Results

The tests were run on a PC that has a Core i5 4670 processor, 8-GB DDR3 RAM, and a Radeon 7770 1-GB graphics card. We used an untextured Sponza scene

Figure 1.8. Shadows rendered using SSSS (left), and reference image rendered with Blender (right).

with 16 colored lights each having a 1024×1024 shadow texture to illustrate overlapping shadows.

1.12   Quality Tests

We generated reference images with Blender using path tracing and compared them with the output of the quality tests to make sure that the results were correct. Figure 1.8 shows these comparisons.

As you can see, our results closely match the reference; however, the Gaussian filter size may affect the result. Because the blurring is done in screen space, we can easily afford huge filter sizes. Note that we needed to adjust the light sizes empirically to match the reference images.

Figure 1.9 shows additional examples from the Sponza scene.

1.13   Performance Analysis

Table 1.1 lists the performance results obtained by rendering the Sponza scene with 16 shadow casting lights from the same point of view using our technique, PCSS, PCF, and hard shadows. In the reference image, in our technique, and in the PCSS case, the shadows have variable penumbras. In the PCF version, they have uniform penumbras, and in the hard shadows version, they don't have penumbras.

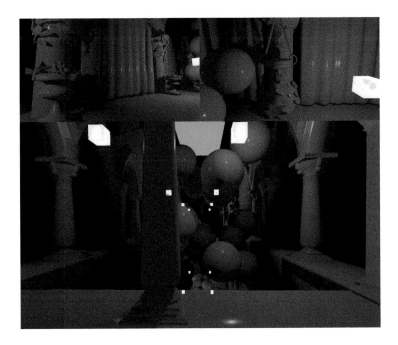

Figure 1.9. Screenshots with light sources rendered over the scene as boxes.

Technique/Resolution	720p	1080p
Lighting only	1.6 ms	3.7 ms
Hard shadows	22.1 ms	25.6 ms
PCF 5×5	25.8 ms	34.1 ms
PCF 11×11	33.9 ms	51.6 ms
PCF 23×23	67.4 ms	126.6 ms
PCSS $5 \times 5 + 5 \times 5$	30.1 ms	43.4 ms
PCSS $5 \times 5 + 11 \times 11$	44.4 ms	75.1 ms
PCSS $5 \times 5 + 23 \times 23$	70.6 ms	133.7 ms
SSSS blocker $5 \times 5 + 5 \times 5$	33.4 ms	50.3 ms
SSSS blocker $5 \times 5 + 11 \times 11$	33.8 ms	51.1 ms
SSSS blocker $5 \times 5 + 23 \times 23$	34.6 ms	52.2 ms
SSSS min *filter* 5×5	26.4 ms	31.7 ms
SSSS min *filter* 11×11	27.0 ms	33.0 ms
SSSS min *filter* 23×23	28.2 ms	35.8 ms
SSSS optimized 5×5	24.7 ms	27.9 ms
SSSS optimized 11×11	24.9 ms	28.4 ms
SSSS optimized 23×23	25.4 ms	29.8 ms

Table 1.1. Performance results (frame times) from the Sponza scene.

We included various versions of our technique, like the `min`-filter optimization and the blocker search variant. We also included an optimized version that uses the `min`-filter optimization, half-resolution Gaussian blurring, and penumbra generation, plus the mentioned super-sampling to maintain the quality. All of the variants use the batching method to generate the layered penumbra data.

You can see that SSSS outperforms PCSS and delivers roughly the same performance as PCF. It can be observed that while the techniques based on shadow-space blurring (PCF and PCSS) took a severe performance hit when increasing the resolution, the SSSS version didn't suffer from this. In addition, increasing the kernel size also had a great impact on the performance of the shadow-space techniques, but the SSSS version still didn't suffer from this problem.

1.14 Conclusion

We showed, that using layered shadow buffers, we can correctly handle overlapping shadows and that we can use layered translucency maps to allow for colored shadows cast by translucent shadow casters. We also showed that this technique can be implemented in real time while still being perceptually correct.

Bibliography

[Aguado and Montiel 11] Alberto Aguado and Eugenia Montiel. "Mipmapped Screen-Space Soft Shadows." In *GPU Pro 2: Advanced Rendering Techniques*, edited by Wolfgang Engel, pp. 257–274. Natick, MA: A K Peters, 2011.

[Anichini 14] Steve Anichini. "Bioshock Infinite Lighting." *Solid Angle*, http://solid-angle.blogspot.hu/2014/03/bioshock-infinite-lighting.html, March 3, 2014.

[Crow 77] Franklin C. Crow. "Shadow Algorithms for Computer Graphics." *Computer Graphics: SIGGRAPH '77 Proceedings* 11:2 (1977), 242–248. 1977

[Engel 10] Wolfgang Engel. "Massive Point Light Soft Shadows." Presented at Korean Game Developer Conference, September 14, 2010. (Available at http://www.slideshare.net/WolfgangEngel/massive-pointlightsoftshadows.)

[Fernando 05] Randima Fernando. "Percentage-Closer Soft Shadows." In *ACM SIGGRAPH 2005 Sketches*, Article no. 35. New York: ACM, 2005.

[Geusebroek and Smeulders 03] Jan M. Geusebroek and Arnold W. M. Smeulders. "Fast Anisotropic Gauss Filtering." *IEEE Transactions on Image Processing* 12:8 (2003), 99–112.

[Gumbau et al. 10] Jesus Gumbau, Miguel Chover, and Mateu Sbert. "Screen Space Soft Shadows." In *GPU Pro: Advanced Rendering Techniques*, edited by Wolfgang Engel, pp. 477–491. Natick, MA: A K Peters, 2010.

[Nealen 02] Andrew V. Nealen. "Shadow Mapping and Shadow Volumes: Recent Developments in Real-Time Shadow Rendering." Project Report for Advanced Computer Graphics: Image-Based Rendering, University of British Columbia, 2002.

[Reeves et al. 87] William T. Reeves, David H. Salesin, and Robert L. Cook. "Rendering Antialiased Shadows with Depth Maps." *Computer Graphics: Proc. SIGGRAPH '87* 21:4 (1987), 283–291.

[Shastry 05] Anirudh S. Shastry. "Soft-Edged Shadows." *GameDev.net*, http://www.gamedev.net/page/resources/_/technical/graphics-programming-and-theory/soft-edged-shadows-r2193, January 18, 2005.

[Williams 78] Lance Williams. "Casting Curved Shadows on Curved Surfaces." *Computer Graphics: Proc. SIGGRAPH '78* 12:3 (1978), 270–274.

Tile-Based
Omnidirectional Shadows
Hawar Doghramachi

2.1 Introduction

Rendering efficiently a massive amount of local light sources had already been solved by methods such as *tiled deferred shading* [Andersson 09], *tiled forward shading* [Billeter et al. 13], and *clustered deferred and forward shading* [Olsson et al. 12]. However, generating appropriate shadows for a large number of light sources in real time is still an ongoing topic. Since accurate shadows from direct lights significantly improve the final image and give the viewer additional information about the scene arrangement, their generation is an important part of real-time rendering.

This chapter will demonstrate how to efficiently generate soft shadows for a large number of omnidirectional light sources where each light casts individual shadows. It will be further shown that this is accomplished without introducing new artifacts, such as shadow flickering. The underlying algorithm is based on *shadow mapping*, introduced in [Williams 78], thus it benefits from the architecture of current rasterizer-based graphics hardware as well as from a wide range of existing techniques to provide high-quality soft shadows.

For this, the concepts of *programmable draw dispatch* [Riccio and Lilley 13] and *tetrahedron shadow mapping* [Liao 10] are combined via a novel usage of the programmable clipping unit, which is present in current consumer graphics hardware. For each light source a separate shadow map is generated, so a hierarchical quad-tree is additionally utilized, which efficiently packs shadow maps of all light sources as tiles into a single 2D texture map. In this way, significantly more shadow maps can be stored in a limited amount of texture memory than with traditional shadow mapping methods.

2.2   Overview

The main target of this work is to utilize recently available features of common consumer graphics hardware, exposed by the OpenGL graphics API, to accelerate the computation of high-quality soft shadows for a high number of dynamic omnidirectional light sources.

Traditional shadow map rendering typically first determines the meshes that are overlapping the volumes of all relevant light sources which is already an $O(nm)$ time complexity task. After this information has been computed, for each relevant mesh and light source, one GPU draw command is dispatched. For omnidirectional lights, the situation is even more problematic: e.g., for a cube map-based approach [Gerasimov 04], we need do the visibility determination for six cube map faces and dispatch up to six GPU draw commands per mesh and light source. The large amount of submitted draw calls can cause a significant CPU overhead. The first part of the proposed algorithm bypasses this problem by using the concept of programmable draw dispatch [Riccio and Lilley 13]. In this way, the entire visibility determination and draw command generation process is shifted to the GPU, avoiding almost the entire CPU overhead of traditional methods.

The second part of the proposed technique makes use of the idea that for omnidirectional light sources it is not necessary to subdivide the 3D space into six view volumes, as done for cube map–based approaches [Gerasimov 04]. According to tetrahedron shadow mapping [Liao 10], it is entirely enough to subdivide the 3D space into four view volumes by a regular tetrahedron to produce accurate shadows for omnidirectional light sources. In this way up to a third of the draw call amount of cube map–based approaches can be saved. In contrast to the tetrahedron shadow mapping algorithm as proposed in [Liao 10], the entire process of creating shadow maps for four separate view directions is efficiently moved to the GPU by introducing a novel usage of the programmable clipping unit, which is part of current consumer graphics hardware. Furthermore, the original method is extended in order to provide soft shadows.

Finally, this work takes advantage of the observation that the required shadow map resolution is proportional to the screen area that the corresponding light source influences—i.e., the smaller the radius of the light source and the larger its distance to the viewer camera, the smaller the required shadow map resolution. After determining the required resolution, the shadow maps of all relevant light sources are inserted as tiles into one large 2D texture map, which will be called the *tiled shadow map*. To make optimal use of the available texture space, a hierarchical quad-tree is used. This concept not only saves memory bandwidth at writing and reading of shadow maps, but further enables the use of a large amount of shadow-casting light sources within a limited texture space.

The entire process of *tile-based omnidirectional shadows* can be subdivided into four distinct steps:

- In a first preparation step, it is determined which meshes and light sources are relevant, i.e., influence the final image. This can be done, for example, by view frustum culling and GPU hardware occlusion queries. For all relevant meshes and light sources, a linear list is written into a GPU buffer that contains information about each mesh and each light source, respectively. This process has an $O(n + m)$ time complexity and is done on the CPU.

- On the GPU, a compute shader takes the previously generated buffers as input and tests each mesh for overlap with each relevant light source. This process has an $O(nm)$ time complexity and thus is spread over a large amount of parallel computing threads. As a result of this overlap test, the corresponding draw commands are written into a GPU buffer, which will be called the *indirect draw buffer*.

- By the use of a single indirect draw call submitted from the CPU, all GPU-generated draw commands within the indirect draw buffer are executed. In this way, shadow maps are generated for all relevant light sources and written into corresponding tiles of the tiled shadow map.

- Finally, the tiled shadow map is sampled during the shading process by all visible screen fragments for each relevant light source to generate soft shadows.

2.3 Implementation

In the following subsections, each step will be described in detail. All explanations assume a column-major matrix layout, right-handed coordinate system with the y axis pointing upward, left-bottom corner as texture and screen-space origin, and clip-space depth-range from -1.0 to 1.0. This work only focuses on generating shadows for point lights, but as will be demonstrated in Section 2.5.2, it can be easily extended to additionally support spotlights.

2.3.1 Preparation

In this step, it is first determined which lights are relevant for further processing. Typically these are all shadow-casting light sources that are visible to the viewer camera—that is, their light volume overlaps the view frustum and is not totally occluded by opaque geometry. This can be accomplished by view frustum culling and GPU hardware occlusion queries.

Tile resolution. After finding all relevant light sources, we need to determine how large the influence of each light source on the final image is. For this, we first compute the screen-space axis-aligned bounding box (AABB) of the spherical light volume. Care must be taken not to clip the AABB against the boundaries

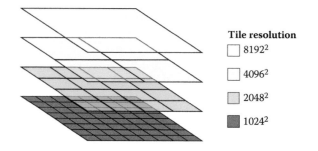

Figure 2.1. First four levels of a quad-tree that manages the tiles of a 8192×8192 tiled shadow map.

of the screen; for example, a large point light that is near to the viewer but only a small portion of which is visible on the screen still requires a high-resolution shadow map tile. After finding the width and height of the AABB, the larger of these two values will be taken as an approximation for the required shadow map tile resolution. However, to avoid extremely small or large values, the acquired resolution should be clamped within a reasonable range. For the case that more shadow-map tiles will be inserted than the tiled shadow map can handle, the lights are sorted relative to their acquired tile resolution. In this way, light sources with the smallest tile resolution will be at the end of the sorted light list and are the first to be excluded from shadow-map rendering when the tiled shadow map runs out of space.

Tile management. A typical texture resolution that should suffice in most cases for a tiled shadow map is 8192×8192. When using a 16-bit depth buffer texture format at this resolution, we can keep the required amount of video memory under 135 MB, which should be a reasonable value on modern graphics cards.

For the quad-tree implementation, a cache-friendly approach is chosen, where all nodes are stored in a preallocated linear memory block. Instead of pointers, indices are used to identify each node. Keeping all nodes in a linear list has the further advantage that resetting the quad-tree is a very fast operation, since we only have to iterate linearly over the node list. Each level of the quad-tree corresponds to a power-of-two shadow map tile resolution and each node holds the texture-space position of a tile in the tiled shadow map (Figure 2.1). To increase runtime performance, the quad-tree nodes are already initialized with the corresponding position values for a user-specified number of levels. The previously acquired tile resolution should be clamped within a reasonable range since, on the one hand, too small values would increase runtime performance for finding an appropriate node and, on the other hand, too large values would rapidly occupy the available texture space.

At runtime, each light source requests, in the order of the sorted light list, a tile inside the quad-tree with the calculated tile resolution. For this, first we must determine the lowest quad-tree level that has a tile resolution that is still higher than the specified value:

$$\text{level} = \log_2(s) - \text{ceil}(\log_2(x)),$$

where s is the resolution of the entire tiled shadow map and x the specified resolution. However, after finding a corresponding free tile node, the initially acquired resolution is used instead of the power-of-two node value. Thus, popping artifacts at shadow edges can be avoided, which would otherwise occur when the distance of the viewer camera to the light source changes. Performance-wise, the costs for the tile lookup are negligible; on an Intel Core i7-4810MQ 2.8 GHZ CPU for 128 light sources, the average required time is about 0.16 ms. Lights that cannot acquire a free tile due to an exaggerated light count are flagged as non–shadow casting and ignored during shadow generation. Because such lights have the smallest influence on the output image anyway, in general, visual artifacts are hard to notice.

Matrix setup. After all relevant lights are assigned to a corresponding shadow map tile, for each light source, the matrices that are used during shadow-map rendering and shading have to be correctly set up. As initially described, a regular tetrahedron is used to subdivide the 3D space for omnidirectional shadows. Because this part of the system builds upon tetrahedron shadow mapping as proposed in [Liao 10], only the modifications introduced here will be described in detail.

First, for each of the four tetrahedron faces, a view matrix needs to be found that consists of a rotational and a translational part. The rotational part can be precomputed since it is equal for all lights and never changes; yaw, pitch, and roll values for constructing these matrices are listed in Table 2.1.

The translational part consists of the vector from the point light center to the origin and must be recalculated whenever the light position changes. Concatenating the translation matrix with each of the rotation matrices yields the final four view matrices.

In the next step, appropriate perspective projection matrices have to be calculated. For this, the far plane is set to the radius of the point light. Table 2.2 shows the horizontal and vertical field of view (FOV) for each tetrahedron face.

Face	Yaw	Pitch	Roll
A	27.36780516	180.0	0.0
B	27.36780516	0.0	90.0
C	−27.36780516	270.0	0.0
D	−27.36780516	90.0	90.0

Table 2.1. Yaw, pitch, and roll in degrees to construct the rotation matrices for the four tetrahedron faces.

Face	Horizontal FOV	Vertical FOV
A	$143.98570868 + \alpha$	$125.26438968 + \beta$
B	$125.26438968 + \beta$	$143.98570868 + \alpha$
C	$143.98570868 + \alpha$	$125.26438968 + \beta$
D	$125.26438968 + \beta$	$143.98570868 + \alpha$

Table 2.2. Horizontal and vertical FOV in degrees to construct the perspective projection matrices for the four tetrahedron faces. As can be seen, faces A and C and, respectively, faces B and D share the same values. In order to provide soft shadows, the values from the original paper have to be adjusted by α and β.

```
vec3 centers[4] = {vec3(-1,0,-1),vec3(1,0,-1),vec3(0,-1,-1),
                   vec3(0,1,-1)};

vec3 offsets[4] = {vec3(-r,0,0),vec3(r,0,0),vec3(0,-r,0),
                   vec3(0,r,0)};
for(uint i=0; i<4; i++)
{
  centers[i] += offsets[i];
  v[i] = normalize(invProjMatrix * centers[i]);
}
dilatedFovX = acos(dot(v[0], v[1])) * 180/PI;
dilatedFovY = acos(dot(v[2], v[3])) * 180/PI;
alpha = dilatedFovX - originalFovX;
beta = dilatedFovY - originalFovY;
```

Listing 2.1. Pseudocode for computing α and β that is used to extend the original FOV values in order to provide soft shadows.

Because the original paper [Liao 10] did not take into account that soft shadows require a slightly larger texture area for filtering, the original horizontal and vertical FOV values must be increased by α and β (Table 2.2). These two angles can be computed by first offsetting the center points of each clip-space edge at the near plane with a dilation radius r. Using $r = 0.0625$ provides in practice enough space for reasonable filter kernels while avoiding an unnecessary reduction of the effective texture resolution. The offset center points are transformed into view space with the inverse projection matrix of tetrahedron face A, which is built with the original FOV values and normalized to form the vectors $\mathbf{v}_0, \ldots, \mathbf{v}_3$ that point from the view-space origin to the transformed points. With the help of these vectors, α and β can be calculated as shown in Listing 2.1.

Fortunately, the projection matrices are equal for all lights and never change; thus, they can be precomputed.

Finally, the texture transformation matrices have to be calculated, which will position the projected tetrahedron views correctly within the tiled shadow map. Because the projected view area of each tetrahedron face correspond to a triangle (Figure 2.2), these areas can be packed together into squared tiles, which

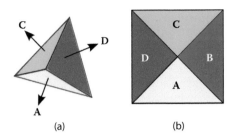

(a)   (b)

Figure 2.2. (a) A perspective view of the used tetrahedron, where face B is facing away from the camera. (b) The triangular-shaped projected views of the four tetrahedron faces packed together into a squared tile.

perfectly fits to the proposed quad-tree–based partitioning scheme. All we need for computing these matrices are the previously computed position coordinates (p_x, p_y) and the size s of each shadow map tile in texture space:

$$
M_A = \begin{pmatrix} s & 0 & 0 & p_x \\ 0 & s/2 & 0 & p_y - s/2 \\ 0 & 0 & 1 & 0 \\ 0 & 0 & 0 & 1 \end{pmatrix}, \quad
M_B = \begin{pmatrix} s/2 & 0 & 0 & p_x + s/2 \\ 0 & s & 0 & p_y \\ 0 & 0 & 1 & 0 \\ 0 & 0 & 0 & 1 \end{pmatrix},
$$

$$
M_C = \begin{pmatrix} s & 0 & 0 & p_x \\ 0 & s/2 & 0 & p_y + s/2 \\ 0 & 0 & 1 & 0 \\ 0 & 0 & 0 & 1 \end{pmatrix}, \quad
M_D = \begin{pmatrix} s/2 & 0 & 0 & p_x - s/2 \\ 0 & s & 0 & p_y \\ 0 & 0 & 1 & 0 \\ 0 & 0 & 0 & 1 \end{pmatrix},
$$

where $M_A, \ldots, M_D$ are the texture transformation matrices for the tetrahedron faces $A, \ldots, D$.

Concatenating the texture, projection and view matrices finally gives the four matrices that are required to render and fetch each shadow map tile and are called *shadow matrices*.

Light buffer. In the order of the sorted light list, the position, radius, and four shadow matrices of each light source have to be uploaded to the GPU, for which a `GL_SHADER_BUFFER_STORAGE` buffer is used.

Mesh-info buffer. Similar as for the light sources, one first needs to determine which meshes are relevant for further processing. Typically these are all shadow-casting meshes that overlap the volumes of the point lights that are found to be visible to the viewer camera. Because the actual light-mesh overlap test will be done later on the GPU, at this stage, only a fast preexclusion of irrelevant meshes should be performed. This could be done for instance by testing the

AABB of the meshes for overlap with the AABB that encloses all relevant light sources. An important prerequisite of the proposed technique is that commonly processed meshes have to share the same vertex and index buffer. However, this is strongly recommended anyway, since frequent switching of GPU resources has a significant impact on the runtime performance due to a driver CPU overhead [Riccio and Lilley 13]. According to the light buffer, the required information for each relevant mesh is written into a GL_SHADER_BUFFER_STORAGE type GPU buffer. For each mesh, its first index into the common index buffer, number of indices required to draw the mesh, and minimum and maximum corners of the enclosing AABB have to be uploaded.

2.3.2   Indirect Draw Buffer Generation

In this step, a compute shader takes the previously generated light and mesh-info buffers as input and generates a command buffer with which the shadow maps of all relevant light sources will be rendered later on. For this, two additional GL_SHADER_BUFFER_STORAGE buffers are created, into which the results are written.

Indirect draw buffer. The first required output buffer is the command buffer itself. The first member of this buffer is an atomic counter variable that keeps track of the number of indirect draw commands that are stored subsequently. The indirect draw command structure is already predefined by the OpenGL specification and contains the number of required mesh indices (count), number of instances to be rendered (instanceCount), first index into the bound index buffer (firstIndex), offset to be applied to the indices fetched from the bound index buffer (baseVertex), and offset for fetching instanced vertex attributes (baseInstance).

Light-index buffer. The second required output buffer stores the indices of all relevant lights that overlap the processed meshes. Corresponding to the indirect draw buffer, an atomic counter variable keeps track of the number of subsequently stored light indices.

Computation. A compute shader is dispatched to generate the indirect draw and light-index buffers, whereby for each relevant mesh one thread group is spawned. For each thread group, a multiple of 32 threads is used.

While each thread group processes one mesh, all threads within a thread group iterate in parallel over all relevant lights and perform a sphere-AABB overlap test between the volume of each point light and the AABB of each mesh. For this, a fast overlap test is used as proposed in [Larsson et al. 07]. Each time an overlap is detected, an atomic counter is incremented and the corresponding light index is written into a light-index list. Both the atomic counter variable as well as the light-index list are located in the fast shared thread group memory of the GPU, thus avoiding frequent atomic writes into the global video memory, which would be more expensive [Harada et al. 13]. After all relevant lights are processed for a mesh, a new indirect draw command is added to the indirect draw buffer, but only if at least one light overlaps the AABB of the processed mesh. This is done by incrementing the atomic counter of the indirect draw buffer and writing the new draw command to the corresponding location. At this point, we additionally increment the atomic counter of the light-index buffer with the number of overlapping lights. This will return a start index into the light-index buffer, which resides in the global video memory, from where the acquired light indices in the shared thread group memory can be copied into the light-index buffer. The copying process is done in parallel by each thread of a thread group at the end of the compute shader.

Besides passing the `firstIndex` and `count` of the current mesh to the new indirect draw command, the number of overlapping lights is forwarded as `instance Count`—i.e., later on, when the indirect draw command is executed, for each light source a new mesh instance will be rendered. However, at that stage it is necessary to acquire for each instance the corresponding light index. For this, we write the obtained start index, which points into the light-index buffer, into the `baseInstance` member of the draw command. This member will be only used by the OpenGL pipeline if instanced vertex attributes are utilized—that is, vertex attributes with a nonzero divisor. Since traditional instancing (e.g., to create multiple instances of the same mesh at various locations) does not make much sense in the proposed method, we can relinquish instanced vertex attributes, which enables the use of the valuable `baseInstance` parameter. Fortunately, in the context of OpenGL 4.4, the `GL_ARB_shader_draw_parameters` extension has been introduced, which allows a shader to fetch various draw command related parameters such as the `baseInstance` one. In this way, when the indirect draw commands are executed later on, for each instance, an offset into the light-index buffer can be retrieved in the vertex shader by summing the OpenGL supplied draw parameters `gl_BaseInstanceARB` and `gl_InstanceID`. At this offset, the corresponding light index can be fetched from the light-index buffer. This approach significantly reduces the required amount of video memory space in contrast to generating for each overlapping light source a new indirect draw command, which requires five times more space than a single light index. Listing 2.2 shows how this can be done for OpenGL in GLSL.

```glsl
#define MAX_NUM_LIGHTS 1024
#define LOCAL_SIZE_X 256

shared uint groupCounter;
shared uint groupLightIndices[MAX_NUM_LIGHTS];
shared uint startLightIndex;

layout(local_size_x=LOCAL_SIZE_X) in;
void main()
```

```
{
  // initialize group counter
  if(gl_LocalInvocationIndex == 0)
    groupCounter = 0;
  barrier();
  memoryBarrierShared();

  // iterate over all relevant light sources
  uint meshIndex = gl_WorkGroupID.x;
  for(uint i=0; i<uniformBuffer.numLights; i+=LOCAL_SIZE_X)
  {
    uint lightIndex = gl_LocalInvocationIndex+i;
    if(lightIndex < uniformBuffer.numLights)
    {
      vec3 lightPosition = lightBuffer.lights[lightIndex].↵
          position;
      float lightRadius = lightBuffer.lights[lightIndex].radius;
      vec3 mins = meshInfoBuffer.infos[meshIndex].mins;
      vec3 maxes = meshInfoBuffer.infos[meshIndex].maxes;

      // perform AABB-sphere overlap test
      vec3 distances = max(mins-lightPosition, 0.0) +
                       max(lightPosition-maxes, 0.0);
      if(dot(distances, distances) <= (lightRadius*lightRadius))
      {
        // For each overlap increment groupCounter and add
        // lightIndex to light-index array in shared thread
        // group memory.
        uint index = atomicAdd(groupCounter, 1);
        groupLightIndices[index] = lightIndex;
      }
    }
  }
  barrier();
  memoryBarrierShared();

  // In case at least one overlap has been detected, add new
  // indirect draw draw command to indirect draw buffer and
  // determine start index into light-index buffer. Both
  // buffers reside in global video memory.
  if(gl_LocalInvocationIndex == 0)
  {
    if(groupCounter > 0)
    {
      uint cmdIndex = atomicAdd(drawIndirectCmdBuffer.counter, ↵
          1);
      startLightIndex = atomicAdd(lightIndexBuffer.counter,
          groupCounter);
      drawIndirectCmdBuffer.cmds[cmdIndex].count =
          meshInfoBuffer.infos[meshIndex].numIndices;
      drawIndirectCmdBuffer.cmds[cmdIndex].instanceCount = ↵
          groupCounter;
      drawIndirectCmdBuffer.cmds[cmdIndex].firstIndex =
             meshInfoBuffer.infos[meshIndex].firstIndex;
      drawIndirectCmdBuffer.cmds[cmdIndex].baseVertex = 0;
      drawIndirectCmdBuffer.cmds[cmdIndex].baseInstance =
          startLightIndex;
    }
  }
  barrier();
  memoryBarrierShared();

  // Copy light indices from shared thread group memory into
  // global video memory.
```

```
for( uint i=gl_LocalInvocationIndex ; i<groupCounter ; i+=↵
    LOCAL_SIZE_X )
{
    lightIndexBuffer . lightIndices [ startLightIndex+i ] =
        groupLightIndices [ i ] ;
}
}
```

Listing 2.2. Compute shader for generating indirect draw buffer.

For the Crytek Sponza scene with 103 meshes and 128 processed light sources, the GPU time taken for this computation task was about 0.02 ms on an NVIDIA GeForce GTX 880 Mobile.

Finally, care must be taken to reset the atomic counters of the indirect draw and light-index buffers at the beginning of each frame, which can be done by using the OpenGL command glClearBufferSubData().

2.3.3 Indirect Shadow Map Rendering

At this stage, the previously generated indirect draw buffer is executed by the OpenGL draw command glMultiDrawElementsIndirectCountARB(). This draw call has been introduced in the context of OpenGL 4.4 with the GL_ARB_indirect_parameters extension and is an improved version of the previously available glMultiDrawElementsIndirect(). Since we have no idea on the host side how many draw commands the GPU has generated and a corresponding query would be very inefficient (since it introduces a synchronization point between CPU and GPU), previously the only possibility was to execute glMultiDrawElementsIndirect() with a maximum number of elements and discard draws by writing zero to the instanceCount member of the indirect draw command. However, discarding draws is not free [Riccio and Lilley 13]. With the new draw call glMultiDrawElements IndirectCountARB(), the number of executed elements will be determined by taking the minimum of the value specified in the draw command itself and a value that is sourced from a GL_PARAMETER_BUFFER_ARB type GPU buffer, for which the atomic counter of the indirect draw buffer is used.

Programmable clipping. There is still one major obstacle that needs to be solved prior to being able to render indirectly all shadow map tiles into the tiled shadow map. As demonstrated, the previously generated shadow matrices will create triangular projected areas that can be theoretically tightly packed as squared tiles, but since we are rendering into a 2D texture atlas, these areas will overlap and cause major artifacts. One possible solution could be the use of a viewport array. However, since the maximum number of simultaneously set viewports is usually limited to a small number, typically around 16, and the viewports are rectangular and not triangular, this approach is not viable. Another possible solution could be to discard in a fragment shader all fragments outside the projected triangular areas, but this would be far too slow to be feasible. Fortunately, with

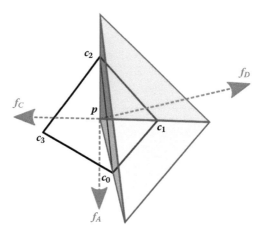

Figure 2.3. The green arrows show the tetrahedron face vectors f_A, f_C, and f_D. Face vector f_B is pointing away from the camera. The four corners of the tetrahedron are marked as $c_0, \ldots, c_3$, and the center of the tetrahedron that coincides with the point light position is shown as p. The three clipping planes that separate the view volume of tetrahedron face D from its neighbors are depicted in blue, green, and yellow.

programmable clipping there exists another hardware-accelerated approach that, to the knowledge of the author, had previously not been used in this context. The clipping unit of current consumer graphics hardware allows the user to insert custom clipping planes inside shaders. This algorithm will take advantage of this feature to efficiently render indirectly all shadow map tiles into the tiled shadow map. Even though on the GPU a triangle setup that uses custom clipping planes is slower than a regular setup, this will not have a significant performance impact since only triangles that are actually clipped at the border of each tetrahedron view volume are affected.

As stated at the beginning of this section, a regular tetrahedron is used to subdivide the 3D space into four view volumes. Hence, each view volume is separated from its neighbors by exactly three planes, as shown in Figure 2.3. In order to clip against these planes, first the plane normals have to be calculated. This can be done by using the four normalized tetrahedron face vectors as given in [Liao 10] (Table 2.3).

With the help of the tetrahedron face vectors $f_A, \ldots f_D$, the vectors $v_0, \ldots, v_3$ can be calculated, which point from the tetrahedron center p to the tetrahedron corners $c_0, \ldots, c_3$ (Figure 2.3):

$$v_0 = -f_A, \quad v_1 = -f_C, \quad v2 = -f_A, \quad v_3 = -f_D.$$

In Listing 2.3, the normal of the yellow clipping plane illustrated in Figure 2.3

Face	x	y	z
A	0.0	−0.57735026	0.81649661
B	0.0	−0.57735026	−0.81649661
C	−0.81649661	0.57735026	0.0
D	0.81649661	0.57735026	0.0

Table 2.3. The x, y, and z components of the four normalized tetrahedron face vectors.

```
normal = normalize(cross(v1, v));
rotationAxis = normalize(cross(fA, fD));

// quat(rotationAxis, alpha) is a quaternion that rotates alpha
// degrees around rotationAxis
rotatedNormal = quat(rotationAxis, alpha) * normal;
```

Listing 2.3. Pseudocode for calculating clipping plane normal.

will be calculated, which separates the view volumes of faces A and D. All other clipping plane normals can be calculated correspondingly.

Since later on it should be possible to generate soft shadows by applying, e.g., *percentage closer filtering* (PCF), the plane normals have to be adjusted appropriately. For this the plane normals are rotated in order to increase the aperture of the tetrahedron view volumes. The angle α used for this is the same as derived in the section "Matrix setup" on page 319; this angle ensures, on the one hand, that a sufficient amount of primitives pass the clipping stage to account for shadow map filtering and, on the other hand, that the projected tetrahedron view areas do not overlap in the effective sampling area. Since the resulting 12 clipping plane normals are equal for all lights and never change at runtime, they can be precalculated and added as constants into the corresponding shader.

At runtime, the precalculated normals are combined each time with the position of the processed light source to construct the appropriate clipping planes.

Vertex processing. To render indirectly the shadow maps, a simple vertex shader is required to fetch the vertex attributes (typically the vertex position), to calculate the light index (as already described in the section "Computation" on page 322), and to pass this value to a subsequent geometry shader.

Primitive processing. After the vertex shader, a geometry shader is invoked to perform clipping with the precalculated plane normals. Depending on which of the four view volumes of the tetrahedron the processed triangle intersects, up to four new primitives have to be generated. Against all expectations, it has proven to be far more performant to run a loop over four primitives in a single geometry shader invocation than using geometry shader instancing and invoking the geometry shader four times. The reasons for this can be that, in a high percentage of cases, less than four primitives have to be emitted and that the light buffer data has to be fetched only once for each incoming primitive in the loop-based approach.

An alternative strategy would be to cull the AABBs of the relevant meshes against the four tetrahedron view volumes for each light in the indirect draw buffer generation step and add for each overlap a new indirect draw command, thus avoiding later the use of the geometry shader. However, it has shown that this approach not only requires more video memory for storing the increased amount of indirect draw commands, but also runs notably slower than the geometry shader approach. A reason for this can be that the geometry shader performs culling on a per-triangle basis, in contrast to culling AABBs of the relevant meshes.

Since back-face culling as implemented by the graphics hardware is performed after the vertex and primitive processing stage, it is done manually at the beginning of the geometry shader. By reducing the amount of processed primitives, runtime performance can be further increased [Rákos 12]. This can be an additional reason why geometry shader instancing is performing more slowly, because the back-face culling code has to be performed four times in contrast to the loop-based solution, where this code is shared for all four primitives.

Though the clip distances are passed via `gl_ClipDistance` to the clipping unit of the graphics hardware, it has proven that additionally culling primitives in the shader further improves runtime performance. This can be done by only emitting a new primitive when at least one of the calculated clip distances of the three processed triangle vertices is greater than zero for all three clipping planes of the processed tetrahedron face.

Finally, transforming the incoming vertices boils down to performing for each relevant tetrahedron face one matrix multiplication with the matching shadow matrix. Listing 2.4 shows the corresponding GLSL geometry shader.

```glsl
float GetClipDist(in vec3 lightPos, in uint vertexIndex, in uint
                  planeIndex)
{
    vec3 normal = planeNormals[planeIndex]; //clipping plane normal
    return (dot(gl_in[vertexIndex].gl_Position.xyz, normal)
            +dot(-normal, lightPosition));
}

layout(triangles) in;
layout(triangle_strip, max_vertices = 12) out;
void main()
{
    const uint lightIndex = inputGS[0].lightIndex;
    const vec3 lightPosition = lightBuffer.lights[lightIndex].position;

    // perform back-face culling
    vec3 normal = cross(gl_in[2].gl_Position.xyz-gl_in[0]
                            .gl_Position.xyz,
                        gl_in[0].gl_Position.xyz-gl_in[1]
                            .gl_Position.xyz);
```

```
vec3 view = lightPosition-gl_in[0].gl_Position.xyz;

if(dot(normal, view) < 0.0f)
    return;

// iterate over tetrahedron faces
for(uint faceIndex=0; faceIndex<4; faceIndex++)
{
    uint inside = 0;
    float clipDistances[9];

    // Calculate for each vertex distance to clipping planes and
    // determine whether processed triangle is inside view
    // volume.
    for(uint sideIndex=0; sideIndex<3; sideIndex++)
    {
        const uint planeIndex = (faceIndex*3)+sideIndex;
        const uint bit = 1 << sideIndex;

        for(uint vertexIndex=0; vertexIndex<3; vertexIndex++)
        {
            uint clipDistIndex = sideIndex*3+vertexIndex;
            clipDistances[clipDistIndex] = GetClipDist(lightPosition,
                vertexIndex, planeIndex);
            inside |= (clipDistances[clipDistIndex] > 0.001) ?
                bit : 0;
        }
    }

    // If triangle is inside volume, emit primitive.
    if(inside == 0x7)
    {
        const mat4 shadowMatrix =
          lightBuffer.lights[lightIndex].shadowMatrices[faceIndex];

        // Transform vertex positions with shadow matrix and
        // forward clip distances to graphics hardware.
        for(uint vertexIndex=0; vertexIndex<3; vertexIndex++)
        {
            gl_Position = shadowMatrix*gl_in[vertexIndex].gl_Position;
            gl_ClipDistance[0] = clipDistances[vertexIndex];
            gl_ClipDistance[1] = clipDistances[3+vertexIndex];
            gl_ClipDistance[2] = clipDistances[6+vertexIndex];
            EmitVertex();
        }
        EndPrimitive();
    }
}
}
```

Listing 2.4. Geometry shader for indirect shadow map rendering.

Tiled shadow map. After the draw commands in the indirect draw buffer are executed, the shadow map tiles of all relevant light sources are tightly packed together into the tiled shadow map. Figure 2.4 shows this texture that was generated for the scene in Figure 2.5.

As can be seen in Figure 2.4, the shadow map tiles of all light sources in the processed scene are tightly packed; thus, shadow maps for significantly more

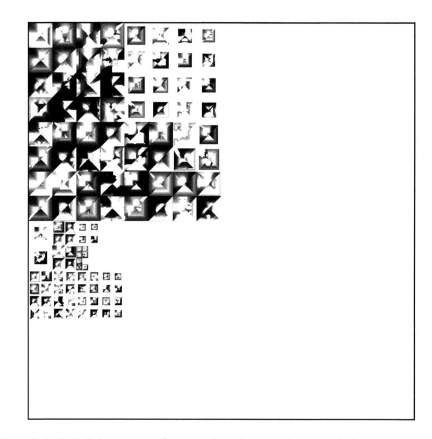

Figure 2.4. A tiled shadow map (generated for the scene in Figure 2.5) with a resolution of 8192 × 8192. The tile size is clamped between 64 and 512. Since the scene is rendered with view frustum culling of invisible light sources, for 117 out of the 128 medium-sized moving point lights, an individual shadow map tile is generated. With this texture and clamped tile resolution, in the worst case, shadow map tiles for 256 light sources can still be stored in the tiled shadow map.

omnidirectional light sources can be stored in a limited texture space than with traditional shadow mapping systems.

2.3.4 Shading

Finally, the tiled shadow map can be used in the shading stage to produce high-quality soft shadows. Shading methods such as tiled deferred shading [Andersson 09], tiled forward shading [Billeter et al. 13], or clustered deferred and forward shading [Olsson et al. 12] require the shadow maps for all relevant light sources to be created prior to the shading process as the proposed algorithm does. How-

```
// matrix of tetrahedron face vectors
mat4x3 faceMatrix;
faceMatrix[0] = faceVectors[0];
faceMatrix[1] = faceVectors[1];
faceMatrix[2] = faceVectors[2];
faceMatrix[3] = faceVectors[3];

// determine face that is closest to specified light vector
vec4 dotProducts = -lightVecN*faceMatrix;
float maximum = max (max(dotProducts.x, dotProducts.y),
           max(dotProducts.z, dotProducts.w));
uint index;
if(maximum == dotProducts.x)
     index = 0;
else if(maximum == dotProducts.y)
     index = 1;
else if(maximum == dotProducts.z)
     index = 2;
else
     index = 3;

// project fragment world-space position
vec4 projPos =
     lightBuffer.lights[lightIndex].shadowMatrices[index]*position;
projPos.xyz /= projPos.w;
projPos.xyz = (projPos.xyz*0.5)+0.5;

// calculate shadow term with HW-filtered shadow lookup
float shadowTerm = texture(tiledShadowMap, projPos.xyz);
```

Listing 2.5. Generating the shadow term with a tiled shadow map.

ever, lighting methods such as deferred shading [Hargreaves and Harris 04] that theoretically can reuse shadow map textures for multiple lights by alternating between shadow map rendering and shading, can profit as well from the proposed method, since frequent switching of render states and GPU resources can be an expensive operation.

Generating shadows with the help of a tiled shadow map is straightforward and follows [Liao 10]. After acquiring the world-space position of the currently shaded screen fragment, for each relevant light source it is first determined inside which of the four tetrahedron view volumes the processed fragment is located. The acquired fragment position is then multiplied with the corresponding shadow matrix to yield the projected fragment position with which a shadow comparison is done. See Listing 2.5 for details.

Besides performing a hardware-filtered shadow comparison, various filtering approaches such as PCF [Reeves et al. 87] or percentage-closer soft shadows (PCSS) [Fernando 05] can be used to produce high-quality soft shadows. Since, as already described earlier in this section, the shadow projection matrices and tetrahedron clipping plane normals are properly adapted, such filtering techniques will not produce any artifacts by sampling outside of the appropriate shadow map areas.

2.4 Results

To capture the results, the Crytek Sponza scene was used, which contains without the central banner 103 meshes and ~280,000 triangles. The test machine had an Intel Core i7-4810MQ 2.8 GHZ CPU and an NVIDIA GeForce GTX 880 Mobile GPU and the screen resolution was set to 1280×720. For the lighting system, tiled deferred shading [Andersson 09] is used.

A layered cube map–based shadowing solution is used as the reference for the proposed technique. For this, the shadow maps of each point light are rendered into a cube map texture array with 128 layer and a 16-bit depth buffer texture format; each cube map face has a texture resolution of 256×256. For each point light, the 3D space is split up into six view frustums that correspond to the six faces of a cube map. Each mesh is tested for overlap with each of the six view frustums. Every time an overlap is detected, a new indexed draw call is submitted to the GPU. To speed up rendering performance, all meshes share the same vertex and index buffer and the cube map face selection is done in a geometry shader. For a large number of light sources, it has proven to be more performant to submit for each overlap a separate draw call rather than always amplifying the input geometry in the geometry shader six times and using one draw call. To improve the quality of the generated shadows, `GL_TEXTURE_CUBE_MAP_SEAMLESS` is enabled, and besides performing hardware shadow filtering, $16\times$ PCF is used for soft shadows. In the remaining part of this section, the reference technique will be referred to as the *cube solution*.

For the proposed method, a 8192×8192 tiled shadow map is used with a 16-bit depth buffer texture format. The tile size is clamped between 64 and 512 (see Figure 2.4). According to the reference method, hardware shadow filtering in combination with $16\times$ PCF is used to produce soft shadows. In the remaining part of this section, this proposed technique will be referred to as the *tiled technique*.

It can be seen in the comparison screenshots in Figure 2.5 that the quality of both images is nearly equal while the proposed method runs more than three times faster than the reference solution. In the close-up comparison screenshots shown in Figure 2.6, we can also see that quality-wise the technique described here comes very close to the reference solution.

For the performance measurements, the same scene configuration was used as in Figure 2.5 with the exception that view frustum culling of invisible lights was disabled; hence, for all 128 point lights in the scene, shadow maps were generated. The measured frame times in Figure 2.7 show that the tiled technique gets significantly faster compared to the reference cube solution as the number of shadow-casting point lights increases. Figure 2.8 shows the number of draw calls that were submitted for each frame from the CPU to render the shadow maps. In the proposed method, the number of draw calls is constantly one due to the indirect shadow map rendering, whereas the number of draw calls rapidly

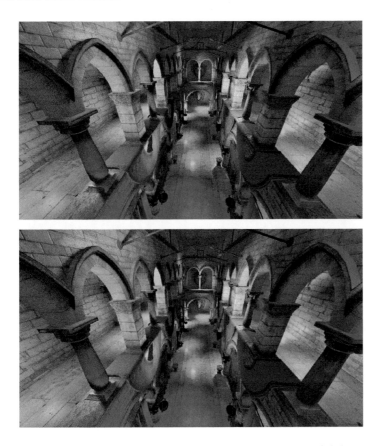

Figure 2.5. Real-time rendering (on an NVIDIA GeForce GTX 880 Mobile at 1280×720 resolution) of the Crytek Sponza scene ($\sim$280,000 triangles) with 128 medium-sized moving point lights, which all cast omnidirectional shadows via shadow maps. The upper image is rendered with the proposed tiled method at 28.44 fps; the lower image is the reference with the cube approach at 8.89 fps. Both methods use hardware shadow filtering in combination with $16\times$ PCF for providing high-quality soft shadows.

increases in the reference technique. Finally, in Table 2.4, CPU and GPU times for shadow map rendering and shading are compared.

According to Table 2.4, the CPU times for rendering shadow maps with the proposed technique are at a constant low value since only one indirect draw call is submitted each frame. However, the CPU times for the reference technique are drastically increasing with the light count due to the rising number of CPU draw calls. When comparing the times taken by the GPU to render the shadow maps, the proposed technique is significantly faster than the reference method, which can be primarily attributed to the reduced number of primitives processed in the

Figure 2.6. One shadow-casting point light is placed directly in front of the lion-head model in the Crytek Sponza scene. The images on the left are rendered with the tiled technique, and the images on the right with the reference cube technique. While the images at the bottom show the final shading results, the images at the top visualize the partitioning of the tetrahedron and cube, respectively, volumes. As can be seen, the shadow quality of the proposed solution comes close to that of the reference method.

tiled solution. Considering the times taken by the GPU to shade all visible screen fragments using tiled deferred shading, it first seems unexpected that the cube solution would have higher execution times than the tiled technique. Though

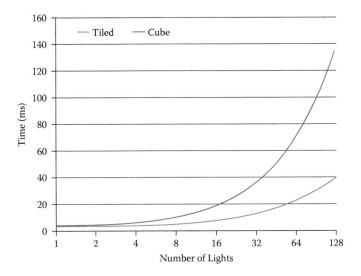

Figure 2.7. Frame times of tiled versus cube technique with an increasing number of shadow-casting point light sources.

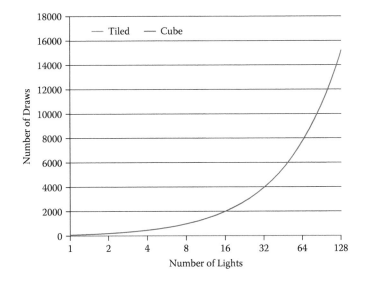

Figure 2.8. Number of CPU submitted draw calls to render shadow maps in tiled and cube technique with an increasing number of shadow-casting point lights.

doing a hardware texture lookup in a cube map is faster than doing the proposed lookup, this is not true for performing PCF to produce soft shadows. While for

| Number | Shadow CPU | | Shadow GPU | | Shading GPU | |
of Lights	Tiled	Cube	Tiled	Cube	Tiled	Cube
1	0.09	0.12	0.49	0.79	0.15	0.18
2	0.09	0.21	0.68	1.45	0.15	0.19
4	0.09	0.41	1.01	3.03	0.16	0.21
8	0.09	0.65	1.65	5.70	0.23	0.35
16	0.09	1.38	3.76	12.98	0.34	0.56
32	0.09	2.89	8.24	29.46	0.70	1.22
64	0.09	5.42	15.59	58.17	1.36	2.52
128	0.09	11.06	33.75	119.94	2.18	4.04

Table 2.4. Comparison of CPU and GPU times (ms) for shadow map rendering and shading with an increasing number of shadow-casting point lights.

the tiled method it is enough to apply 2D offsets to the lookup coordinates, for the cube technique a 3D direction vector, which is used for the texture lookup, has to be rotated in 3D space.

According to the presented performance values, the proposed technique is in all aspects and for all number of shadow-casting point lights faster than the reference technique. On the one hand, the driver CPU overhead, present in the reference method due to the high number of draw calls, can be nearly completely eliminated; on the other hand, the time taken by the GPU to render the shadow maps is significantly reduced.

2.5   Discussion

We now discuss some important aspects related to this technique and relevant for real-time applications such as computer games.

2.5.1   Shadow Map Caching

To further improve runtime performance, it is possible to cache shadow map tiles for certain lights. Every time a light does not move and the shadow-casting geometry in its influence area remains unchanged, the corresponding shadow map tile does not need to be cleared and recomputed. However, this should only be the case when the corresponding tile size does not change significantly in order to avoid popping artifacts at shadow edges and to better utilize the limited amount of available texture space.

To achieve this in the indirect draw buffer generation step, such lights are ignored and the associated tile nodes in the quad-tree are not reset. However, clearing the tiled shadow map can no longer be done by simply calling `glClear()`. One possibility to selectively clear the used texture atlas is to render a list of quadrilaterals that correspond to the tiles of the light sources that are not cached.

2.5.2 Spotlights

Though this chapter focuses on point lights, it is trivial to include support for spotlight shadows as well. Actually, it is easier to handle spotlight sources since only one view volume that corresponds to the view frustum of the spotlight has to be taken into account. However, when clipping the primitives while rendering into the tiled shadow map, the clipping planes must be set to the four side planes of the spotlight view frustum.

2.5.3 Dynamic, Skinned Meshes

Neither CPU- nor GPU-skinned meshes are an issue in the proposed method. For CPU-skinned meshes, the one thing to keep in mind is that the same vertex and index buffers should be used for all meshes. GPU-skinned dynamic meshes are easy to handle as well. In addition to writing the light indices for each light into the light-index buffer when the indirect draw buffer is generated, a unique mesh ID is added prior to the light indices for each relevant mesh. Later on, when the indirect draw commands are executed, according to the light index, the unique mesh ID can be acquired and the corresponding transformation and skinning matrices can be looked up in a GPU buffer. Due to the usage of a geometry shader to render into the four faces of a tetrahedron, each mesh only needs to be transformed and skinned once per point light source.

2.5.4 Alpha Testing

One aspect that needs to be discussed is handling meshes with alpha-tested materials since this involves a texture lookup into an alpha map. This problem can be solved by three different approaches. The first solution is to simply render each alpha-tested mesh separately into the tiled shadow map, hence omitting the indirect draw pipeline but still using the proposed clipping-based geometry shader approach. The second possibility is to pack all alpha maps into a common texture atlas. The third option is to make use of the `GL_ARB_bindless_texture` extension, with which theoretically an arbitrary number of alpha maps can be used simultaneously. However, it should be noted that this extension is not supported by all graphics hardware that otherwise would support the proposed technique.

For the above discussed cases, the indirect draw buffer generation as well as the indirect shadow map rendering step should be handled separately where applicable to avoid dynamic shader branching. In most cases, this only means dispatching the compute shader for generating the indirect draw buffer and submitting an indirect draw call a few times per frame, which will have only a slight negative impact on the driver CPU overhead. Nevertheless, in all cases, one unique tiled shadow map can be used.

2.6 Conclusion

This chapter presented a comprehensive system for generating high-quality soft shadows for a large number of dynamic omnidirectional light sources without the need of doing approximations as merging shadows of multiple lights. It has been demonstrated that this method is competitive quality-wise to a reference cube map–based approach and performs with any tested number of shadow-casting point lights faster. Furthermore, due to the usage of a tiled shadow map, significantly more shadow maps can be stored for point light sources in a limited amount of texture space than with a cube map–based approach.

2.7 Acknowledgments

I would like to thank Nikita Kindt for porting the accompanying demo application to Linux.

Bibliography

[Andersson 09] J. Anderrson. "Parallel Graphics in Frostbite: Current and Future." Beyond Programmable Shading, SIGGRAPH Course, New Orleans, LA, August 3–7, 2009. (Available at http://s09.idav.ucdavis.edu/talks/04-JAndersson-ParallelFrostbite-Siggraph09.pdf.)

[Billeter et al. 13] M. Billeter, O. Olsson, and U. Assarsson. "Tiled Forward Shading." In *GPU Pro 4: Advanced Rendering Techniques*, edited by Wolfgang Engel, pp. 99–114. Boca Raton, FL: CRC Press, 2013.

[Fernando 05] R. Fernando. "Percentage-Closer Soft Shadows." In *ACM SIGGRAPH 2005 Sketches*, Article no. 35. New York: ACM, 2005.

[Gerasimov 04] P. S. Gerasimov. "Omnidirectional Shadow Mapping." In *GPU Gems*, edited by Randima Fernando, pp. 193–203. Reading, MA: Addison-Wesley Professional, 2004.

[Harada et al. 13] T. Harada, J. McKee, and J. C. Yang. "Forward+: A Step Toward Film-Style Shading in Real Time." In *GPU Pro 4: Advanced Rendering Techniques*, edited by Wolfgang Engel, pp. 115–135. Boca Raton, FL: CRC Press, 2013.

[Hargreaves and Harris 04] S. Hargreaves and M. Harris. "Deferred Shading." Presented at NVIDIA Developer Conference: 6800 Leagues Under the Sea, San Jose, CA, March 23, 2004. (Available at http://http.download.nvidia.com/developer/presentations/2004/6800_Leagues/6800_Leagues_Deferred_Shading.pdf.)

[Larsson et al. 07] T. Larsson, T. Akenine-Möller, and E. Lengyel. "On Faster Sphere-Box Overlap Testing." *Journal of Graphics, GPU, and Game Tools* 12:1 (2007), 3–8.

[Liao 10] H.-C. Liao. "Shadow Mapping for Omnidirectional Light Using Tetrahedron Mapping." In *GPU Pro: Advanced Rendering Techniques*, edited by Wolfgang Engel, pp. 455–475. Natick, MA: A K Peters, 2010.

[Olsson et al. 12] O. Olsson, M. Billeter, and U. Assarson. "Clustered Deferred and Forward Shading." In *Proceedings of the Fourth ACM SIGGRAPH/Eurographics Conference on High Performance Graphics*, pp. 87–96. Aire-la-Ville, Switzerland: Eurographics Association, 2012.

[Rákos 12] D. Rákos. "Massive Number of Shadow-Casting Lights with Layered Rendering." In *OpenGL Insights*, edited by Patrick Cozzi and Christophe Riccio, pp. 259–278. Boca Raton, FL: CRC Press, 2012.

[Reeves et al. 87] W. T. Reeves, D. H. Salesin and R. L. Cook. "Rendering Antialiased Shadows with Depth Maps." *Computer Graphics: Proc. SIGGRAPH '87* 21:4 (1987), 283–291.

[Riccio and Lilley 13] C. Riccio and S. Lilley. "Introducing the Programmable Vertex Pulling Rendering Pipeline." In *GPU Pro 4: Advanced Rendering Techniques*. edited by Wolfgang Engel, pp. 21–38. Boca Raton, FL: CRC Press, 2013.

[Williams 78] L. Williams. "Casting Curved Shadows on Curved Surfaces." *Computer Graphics: Proc. SIGGRAPH '78* 12:3 (1978), 270–274.

Shadow Map Silhouette Revectorization

Vladimir Bondarev

Shadow Map Silhouette Revectorization (SMSR) is a two-pass filtering technique inspired by MLAA [Jimenez et al. 11] that aims to improve the visual quality of a projected shadow map by concealing the perspective aliasing with an additional umbra surface. In most cases under-sampled areas result in a higher shadow silhouette edge quality.

SMSR is based on the idea of reducing the perceptual error [Lopez-Moreno et al. 10] by concealing the visible perspective aliasing around the shadow silhouette edge.

3.1 Introduction

Shadow mapping [Williams 78] is known for its compatibility with rasterization hardware, low implementation complexity, and ability to handle any kind of geometry. However, aliasing is also a very common problem in shadow mapping. This chapter introduces a shadow map filtering technique that approximates an additional umbra surface (space completely occluded from the direct light) based on linear interpolation in projected view space.

Projection and *perspective aliasing* [Lloyd et al. 08] are the two main discontinuity types that deteriorate the quality of a projected shadow. Since the introduction of shadow mapping, many algorithms have been developed to reduce or even completely remove shadow map aliasing. Most algorithms that are developed to remove aliasing are not compatible to run in real time [Johnson et al. 05] and in some cases propose additional hardware changes to allow for real-time application [Lloyd et al. 08].

Most real-time shadow-mapping techniques can be divided in two main categories: sample redistribution (PSM, TSM, LiSPSM, and CSM) and filter-based techniques (VSM, PCF, and BFSM). Shadow Map Silhouette Revectorization

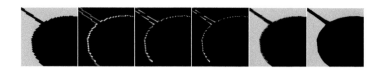

Figure 3.1. From left to right, the shadow silhouette revectorization process.

Figure 3.2. An uncompressed image (left), and the encoded shadow discontinuity buffer (right). See Table 3.1 for color definition.

is a filtering technique that improves upon the conventional two-pass shadow-mapping technique [Williams 78] by concealing the visible aliasing and yet remaining inside an acceptable performance range. In some scenes, SMSR can get away with a much lower shadow-map resolution and at the same time is capable of providing a high-quality umbra.

SMSR achieves a comparable result to shadow silhouette maps (SSM) [Sen et al. 03], however with a very different approach. To generate a silhouette map, SSM rasterizes the edges of all elements as quadrilaterals. In contrast to SMSR, SSM will prove to be more performance intensive with a high polygon-count scene.

3.2 Implementation

The SMSR technique consists of two fullscreen passes and requires access to the depth buffer, shadow map, lighting buffer, view matrix, light matrix, and inverse of the light matrix.

3.2.1 First Pass

The first pass searches for the exterior side of the shadow silhouette edge and compresses the relative edge discontinuity directions into a two-component output vector (Figure 3.1, second image, and Figure 3.2).

In screen space (camera view), we are looking for a shadow discontinuity (edge). The kernel of the first pass compares the current shadow state with the neighboring shadow-map sample state (left, top, right, and bottom). The discontinuity is distinguished into two main types: *exterior discontinuity*, where

Value	Red Channel	Green Channel
0.00	No discontinuity	No discontinuity
0.50	Left	Bottom
0.75	Left and right	Bottom and top
1.00	Right	Top

Table 3.1. Value definition of the two-channel discontinuity encoding.

the current fragment sample is inside the umbra and the next neighboring sample is outside the umbra, and *interior discontinuity*, where the current fragment sample is outside the umbra and the next neighboring sample is inside the umbra.

SMSR is only concerned with the exterior discontinuity of the shadow silhouette edge. When an exterior discontinuity is detected, the direction from the current fragment sample toward the discontinuity is encoded into one of the output channels (used in the second pass to determine discontinuity orientation). Horizontal discontinuities are stored into the red channel and vertical discontinuities are stored into the green channel. Each channel has four possible states: for example, the red channel uses the value 0.0 to indicate no discontinuity, 0.5 discontinuity to the left, 0.75 discontinuity to the left and right, and 1.0 discontinuity to the right. The green channel uses the value 0.0 to indicate no discontinuity, 0.5 discontinuity to the bottom, 0.75 discontinuity to the bottom and top, and 1.0 discontinuity to the top.

To reduce the memory footprint, the discontinuity encoding can be stored in a 4-bit channel. However, for the sake of simplicity, we are not doing it in this implementation.

3.2.2 Second Pass

The second pass consists of five major steps and uses a shadow-map depth buffer, a camera-view depth buffer, and the encoded data gathered by the first pass.

First, we have to find the *discontinuity length* (the length of the exterior discontinuity along the shadow map on the same axis) of the current projected camera-view fragment. To find the discontinuity length, we have to find the relative offset in the projected camera-view space to the neighboring shadow-map sample on the same axis. This is done by transforming the current fragment's world-space position into the light-view space, applying an xy-offset to the neighboring center of the next shadow map sample, replacing the z-vector component by the depth value of the matched shadow map sample and then projecting the coordinate back onto the projected camera-view space.

Second, after we have determined where in the screen space our neighboring shadow-map sample is located, we repeat the step from the new location until we find a break in discontinuity. The discontinuity break is initiated by exceeding the delta-depth threshold, by reaching the maximum search distance, or by find-

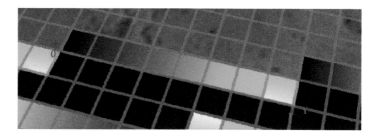

Figure 3.3. Orientated normalized discontinuity space (ONDS) stretches from 0.0 to 1.0 on the y-axis over eight shadow-map samples and on x-axis over just one. The last ONDS sample located near $y = 1.0$ indicates the discontinuity end.

ing a discontinuity on the opposite axis. By performing this iteration in screen space, we approximate the length of the exterior discontinuity along the shadow silhouette.

Third, we need to find a discontinuity contained in both channels (red and green) that indicates a *discontinuity end* (see Figure 3.3). The discontinuity end is used to determine the orientation of the *exterior discontinuity* along the shadow silhouette edge.

Fourth, knowing the discontinuity length and the discontinuity end, we will construct a normalized 2D space that stretches along the exterior discontinuity of the shadow silhouette (*orientated normalized discontinuity space* (ONDS)).

Fifth, after ONDS is constructed, it's normalized coordinate system is used to interpolate a new additional umbra into the lighting buffer.

3.3 Results

SMSR successfully hides the visual perspective aliasing (see Figure 3.1, rightmost image, and Figure 3.4) in under-sampled areas of the shadow map, and the unoptimized version takes less than 1.5 ms to process on GTX 580, regardless of the shadow-map resolution in full HD.

3.3.1 Inconsistencies

SMSR doesn't come without its drawbacks, which are categorized into special cases, absence of data, and mangled silhouette shape.

3.3.2 Special Cases

The technique is unable to handle exterior discontinuities with a parallel umbra spacing of a single shadow-map sample, causing visual artifacts (see Figure 3.5,

Figure 3.4. Configuration of the Crytek Sponza scene with a 1024×1024 shadow map: without SMSR (top) and with SMSR (bottom).

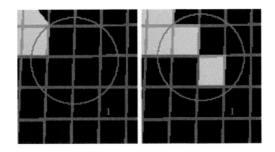

Figure 3.5. A closeup with SMSR (left) and without SMSR (right). Point 1 is the discontinuity in more than two directions, a special case that makes it hard for SMSR to handle. The current solution is to fill those areas completely with an umbra.

right image). SSM suffers from the same problem. The SMSR kernel has a dedicated portion of code that fills all single shadow-map spacing with an additional umbra, yielding less visually noticeable artifacts (see Figure 3.5, left image).

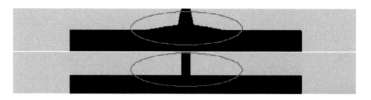

Figure 3.6. A mangled silhouette shape with SMSR (top) and without SMSR (bottom). Due to edge generalization and lack of shape understanding, SMSR changes the desired object shape.

3.3.3 Absence of Data

In this specific scenario, the shadow discontinuity is prematurely interrupted by an occluder or the search function goes outside the viewport boundaries. These cases result in a varying or incorrect edge discontinuity length during the search step, which results in a visible silhouette artifact.

3.3.4 Mangled Silhouette Shape

A typical MLAA approach distinguishes discontinuities into L-, Z-, and U-shaped patterns. Taking the shape pattern into account helps to increase the precision of the edge reapproximation and results in higher image quality. The current approach of SMSR is unable to distinguish shape patterns and processes all discontinuities as L-shaped patterns. This inability to recognize shape patterns leads to a coarse edge approximation and, particularly on low-resolution shadow maps, will often change the shape of the object's shadow (see Figure 3.6).

3.4 Future Work

Shadow Map Silhouette Revectorization effectively reduces the perceptual error by concealing the perspective aliasing of an under-sampled shadow map area. Unfortunately, projection and temporal aliasing remain unaddressed.

By saving the triangle edge data into the shadow map sample [Pan et al. 09], it's possible to approximate a more accurate shadow silhouette edge and at the same time reduce temporal aliasing.

3.5 Conclusion

Shadow Map Silhouette Revectorization particularly shines in scenes with many large polygons, where it has the ability to utilize a lower shadow-map resolution (to reduce the GPU memory footprint) without sacrificing a great portion of visual quality and effectively helps to conserve the GPU fill rate. However, the technique is in its early stage and can be improved in many different areas such as interpolation based on shape patterns (to improve edge revectorization), soft shadows (to improve realism), and temporal aliasing (to reduce jagged edges). It can also be combined with other sample-redistribution techniques such as cascade shadow maps (to optimize the use of shadow sample density where it is needed).

Bibliography

[Jimenez et al. 11] J. Jimenez, B. Masia, J. Echevarria, F. Navarro, and D. Gutierrez. "Practical Morphological Antialiasing." In *GPU Pro 2: Advanced Rendering Techniques*, edited by Wolfgang Engel, pp. 95–114. Natick, MA: A K Peters, 2011.

[Johnson et al. 05] Gregory S. Johnson, Juhyun Lee, Christopher A. Burns, and William R. Mark. "The Irregular Z-Buffer: Hardware Acceleration for Irregular Data Structures." *ACM Transactions on Graphics* 24:4 (2005), 1462–1482.

[Lloyd et al. 08] D. Brandon Lloyd, Naga K. Govindaraju, Cory Quammen, Steven E. Molnar, and Dinesh Manocha. "Logarithmic Perspective Shadow Maps." *ACM Transactions on Graphics* 27:4 (2008), Article no. 106.

[Lopez-Moreno et al. 10] Jorge Lopez-Moreno, Veronica Sundstedt, Francisco Sangorrin, and Diego Gutierrez. "Measuring the Perception of Light Inconsistencies." In *Proceedings of the 7th Symposium on Applied Perception in Graphics and Visualization*, pp. 25–32. New York: ACM Press, 2010.

[Pan et al. 09] Minghao Pan, Rui Wang, Weifeng Chen, Kun Zhou, and Hujun Bao. "Fast, Sub-pixel Antialiased Shadow Maps." *Computer Graphics Forum* 28:7 (2009), 1927–1934.

[Sen et al. 03] Pradeep Sen, Mike Cammarano, and Pat Hanrahan. "Shadow Silhouette Maps." *ACM Transactions on Graphics* 22:3 (2003), 521–526.

[Williams 78] Lance Williams. "Casting Curved Shadows on Curved Surfaces." *Computer Graphics: Proc. SIGGRAPH '78* 12:3 (1978), 270–274.

Mobile Devices

Features of the latest mobile GPUs and the architecture of tile-based GPUs provide new and interesting ways to solve existing rendering problems. In this section we will cover topics ranging from hybrid ray tracing to HDR computational photography.

"Hybrid Ray Tracing on a PowerVR GPU" by Gareth Morgan describes how an existing raster-based graphics engine can use ray tracing to add high-quality effects like hard and soft shadows, reflection, and refraction while continuing to use rasterization as the primary rendering method. The chapter also gives an introduction to the OpenRL API.

"Implementing a GPU-Only Particle-Collision System with ASTC 3D Textures and OpenGL ES 3.0" by Daniele Di Donato shares how the author used OpenGL ES 3.0 and ASTC 3D textures to do bandwidth-friendly collision detection of particles on the GPU. The 3D texture stores a voxel representation of the scene, which is used to do direct collision tests as well as lookup the nearest surface.

"Animated Characters with Shell Fur for Mobile Devices" by Andrew Girdler and James L Jones presents how the authors were able to optimize a high-quality animation system to run efficiently on mobile devices. With OpenGL ES 3.0, they made use of transform feedback and instancing in order to reach the performance target.

"High Dynamic Range Computational Photography on Mobile GPUs" by Simon McIntosh-Smith, Amir Chohan, Dan Curran, and Anton Lokhmotov explores HDR computational photography on mobile GPUs using OpenCL and shares some very interesting results.

I would like to thank all the contributors in this section for their great work and excellent articles.

—Marius Bjørge

Hybrid Ray Tracing on a PowerVR GPU

Gareth Morgan

1.1 Introduction

Ray tracing and rasterization are often presented as a dichotomy. Since the early days of computer graphics, ray tracing has been the gold standard for visual realism. By allowing physically accurate simulation of light transport, ray tracing renders extremely high-quality images. Real-time rendering, on the other hand, is dominated by rasterization. In spite of being less physically accurate, rasterization can be accelerated by efficient, commonly available GPUs and has mature standardized programing interfaces.

This chapter describes how an existing raster-based game engine renderer can use ray tracing to implement sophisticated light transport effects like hard and soft shadows, reflection, refraction, and transparency, while continuing to use rasterization as the primary rendering method. It assumes no prior knowledge of ray tracing.

The PowerVR Wizard line of GPUs adds hardware-based ray tracing acceleration alongside a powerful rasterizing GPU. Ray tracing acceleration hardware vastly improves the efficiency and therefore the performance of the techniques described.

1.2 Review

1.2.1 Conceptual Differences between Ray Tracing and Rasterization

In a ray tracer, everything starts with the initial rays (often called primary rays). Typically, these rays emulate the behavior of a camera, where at least one ray is used to model the incoming virtual light that gives color to each pixel in a framebuffer. The rays are tested against the scene's geometry to find the closest intersection, and then the color of the object at the ray's intersection point is evaluated. More precisely, the outgoing light that is reflecting and/or scattering from the surface in the direction of the ray is computed. These calculations often involve creating more secondary rays because the outgoing light from a surface depends on the incoming light to that surface. The process can continue recursively until the rays terminate by hitting a light-emitting object in the scene or when there is no light contributed from a particular ray path.

Contrast this with rasterization, where the driving action is the submission of vertices describing triangles. After the triangles are projected to screen space, they are broken into fragments and the fragments are shaded. Each datum is processed independently and there is no way for the shading of one triangle to directly influence another unrelated triangle in the pipeline.

Ray tracing enables inter-object visibility, but the tradeoff is that every piece of the scene that could possibly be visible to any ray must be built and resident prior to sending the first ray into the scene.

1.2.2   GPU Ray Tracing

Early 3D games, such as *Quake*, all implemented their own rasterizers in software on the CPU. Eventually, the power of the dedicated hardware in the GPU outweighed the efficiency of the special purpose rasterizer built for the game, and today almost all game renderers take advantage of a hardware abstraction API, such as OpenGL. Today, ray tracing is at a similar stage of evolution. For flexibility and portability, you can implement your own bespoke ray tracer and, performance aside, all of the techniques we describe should work. In this chapter, however, we will use OpenRL.

OpenRL is the ray-tracing API that can take advantage of the dedicated ray tracing hardware in the PowerVR Wizard architecture. OpenRL is conceptually based on OpenGL ES and, like OpenGL ES, is highly configurable by allowing shaders to implement the behavior in certain sections of the process. You can download the OpenRL SDK, including the library, code examples, and documentation at http://community.imgtec.com/developers/powervr/openrl-sdk/.

If you don't want to use OpenRL, you are free to write your own ray tracer and all of these techniques from this chapter will still work. Alternatively, there are several open source ray-tracing projects available, such as LuxRays [LuxRender 14] or Cycles [Blender 14], that take advantage of the GPU for parallel execution. Unfortunately, if you choose to go this route, dedicated ray-tracing hardware acceleration will not provide any speed benefit.

1.2.3   The Simplest Ray Tracer Using OpenRL

To start out, we need to make the geometry available to OpenRL so the rays have something to intersect. This is done by assembling the geometry into primitive

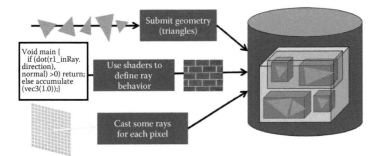

Figure 1.1. Ray tracing overview.

objects. Each primitive object represents a conceptual object within the scene—for example, the glass top of a coffee table could be a primitive object. They are defined in world space, and their state is retained from one frame to the next.

Each primitive object needs to know how to handle rays that intersect it. This is done by attaching a ray shader to the object. The ray shader runs whenever a ray intersects a piece of geometry. It can be used to define the look of the object's material or, more specifically, the behavior of the material when interacting with rays. A ray shader can be thought of as a conceptual analogy to a fragment shader in rasterization. There is, however, one big difference between OpenRL shaders and traditional raster shaders: OpenRL shaders can emit rays, and hence trigger future shader invocations. This feedback loop, where one ray intersection results in secondary rays being emitted, which in turn causes more ray intersections, is a vital part of the ray-tracing process. In OpenRL shaders, this process is implemented via the built-in functions `createRay()` and `emitRay()`. The built-in variable `rl_OutRay` represents the newly created ray. This ray structure is made up of ray attributes, some of which are built-in, such as `direction` and `origin`, and some of which can be user defined.

In the aforementioned glass coffee table example, the ray shader would define the appearance of a glass tabletop by emitting secondary rays based on the material properties stored in the primitive object (such as color and density). Those secondary rays will intersect other objects in the scene, defining how those objects (for example, the base of the table or the floor it is resting on) contribute to the final color of the glass tabletop.

The final step in our simple ray tracer is to create the primary rays. In OpenRL, a frame shader is invoked once for every pixel and is used to programmatically emit the primary rays.

The simplest camera is called a pinhole camera. This name comes from the fact that every light ray passes through the exact same point in space, or pinhole aperture, and therefore the entire scene is in perfect focus.

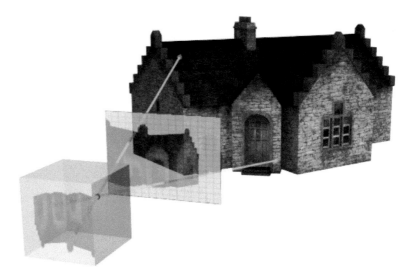

Figure 1.2. Pinhole camera

```
void main() {
  vec3 direction = vec3((rl_FrameCoord/rl_FrameSize-0.5).xy,1.0);
  createRay();
  rl_OutRay.origin        = cameraPosition;
  rl_OutRay.direction     = direction;
  emitRay();
}
```

Listing 1.1. Pinhole camera frame shader.

Simulating a pinhole camera using ray tracing is as easy as emitting a primary ray for every pixel of the image. These rays all share the same origin, which is conceptually the focal point of the light, or the center of the camera's aperture. The direction of the ray is the vector from the ray's origin through the center of the pixel being traced.

1.2.4   Light, Rays, and Rendering

James Kajiya wrote, "All rendering methods are attempting to model the same physical phenomenon, that of light scattering off of various surfaces" [Kajiya 86]. In a pure ray tracer like the example above, rays simulate the light in reverse, starting at the camera and finding a path backward to an illumination source. In this backward propagation model, rays are a means of estimating the incoming light from a specific direction.

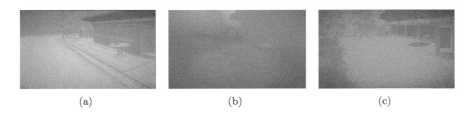

(a)   (b)   (c)

Figure 1.3. G-buffer contents: (a) normals, (b) positions, and (c) material IDs.

Some highly specular materials, like glass, propagate light in a direction that is largely dependent on the direction of the incoming light, while diffuse materials like plaster will scatter incoming light across a whole hemisphere.

A ray is fundamentally a line. It has zero thickness and its intersection with a surface is therefore a point.[1] In order to approximate a diffuse material, renderers often emit many rays to estimate the continuous function of incoming light from all directions.

1.3   Combining Ray Tracing with Rasterization

Raster-based renderers rely on a variety of techniques to calculate the light that is illuminating a surface. Some of these are simplistic, like a universal directional light source that casts no shadows, and some are more complex, like prebaked light maps. Ray tracing adds another tool to your toolbox: the ability to cast rays into the scene to compute light transport and occlusion.

But how do you get a ray tracer, based on a world-space database of the entire scene, to work with a rasterizer that only understands individual screen-space fragments? By taking advantage of the deferred shading architecture used by many modern rasterized renderers [Hargreaves and Harris 04]. In deferred shading, instead of performing the lighting calculations in the fragment shader, the properties of the fragment are simply written into a geometry buffer or *G-buffer*.

After the first pass, this G-buffer contains a 2D screen-space texture for each surface property (such as normal, position, albedo, and material information). Critically, these surface properties are in now in world space. In deferred shading, this G-buffer is then used as an input to a second, screen-space lighting pass. This means lighting calculations are carried out only on the visible fragments.

In our hybrid rendering technique, this screen-space lighting step is replaced by the ray tracer. The G-buffer is used as an input to the frame shader, so rather than emitting rays from a camera, the primary rays are emitted directly

---

[1] OpenRL allows a ray's spread to be tracked as it travels through the scene, and this enables ray shaders to perform mipmapping during texture samples and differential functions within the shader. However, a ray will only intersect one point on one surface.

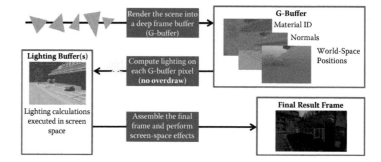

Figure 1.4. Deferred shading pipeline.

```
uniform sampler2D normalTexture;
uniform sampler2D positionTexture;

void main()
{
  vec2 uv = rl_FrameCoord.xy / rl_FrameSize.xy;
  vec4 normal = texture2D(normalTexture, uv);
  vec4 position = texture2D(positionTexture, uv;

  if(normal.w==0.0) return; //No fragment was rendered for this
                            //pixel

  IlluminateSurface(normal, position);
}
```

Listing 1.2. Hybrid frame shader.

from the surface. The results from the ray tracer render are then returned to the rasterizer, where they are composited, along with the albedo color from the original G-buffer, to produce the final frame.

Each G-buffer component is bound to a 2D texture uniform in the frame shader, and those textures are sampled for each pixel. This provides the world-space surface properties required to start tracing rays directly from the surface defined by that pixel, without emitting any camera rays.

On a pixel-by-pixel basis, the frame shader can then decide which effects to implement for that fragment and how many rays each effect uses based on the material properties stored in the G-buffer. This allows the application to use its ray budget on surfaces where raytraced effects will add most to the look or the user experience.

Currently, hybrid ray tracing requires using two different APIs—one for ray tracing (OpenRL) and one for rasterization; a separate OpenRL render context must be created for the ray-tracing operations. Every frame, the contents of the G-buffer must be transferred to the ray tracer, and the results must be returned

```
rlBindTexture(RL_TEXTURE_2D, normalTxt_RL);
rlTexImage2D( RL_TEXTURE_2D,
              0,
        RL_RGBA,
        windowWidth,
        windowHeight,
        0,
        RL_RGBA,
        RL_FLOAT,
        NULL);
normalTxt_EGL = eglCreateImageKHR(
                    dpy,
                    openRLContext,
                    EGL_RL_TEXTURE_2D_IMG,
                    (EGLClientBuffer)normalTxt_RL,
                    NULL);
```

Listing 1.3. Create an EGL image bound to an OpenRL texture.

to the rasterizer for final frame render. On platforms where it is available, EGL can be used to avoid this extra copy by sharing the contents of these textures between the ray tracer and the rasterizer. Listing 1.3 shows how each OpenRL texture object is bound on an EGL image object to achieve this.

The rest of this chapter will discuss some effects that can be added to your raster-based renderer by taking advantage of the light simulation provided by ray tracing.

1.4   Hard Shadows

Shadows are important optical phenomena, caused by objects blocking the path between a light emitter and a surface. The nature of ray tracing, which has an inherent understanding of the world-space layout of the scene, makes it very well suited to shadow rendering.

Rendering physically correct hard shadows simply requires shooting a single ray from the surface to the light. If the ray intersects any scene geometry, it is discarded; if it reaches the light, then the surface is shaded, typically using the traditional Lambertian lighting calculation (the "N dot L" diffuse lighting equation used in 3D graphics for many years).

Ray tracing on PowerVR takes advantage of an optimization that is possible with these kind of rays, referred to as *shadow rays*. As you are not interested in *what* the shadow ray hits, only *whether* it hits anything before reaching its endpoint, an optimization is possible. The intersection algorithm can terminate at the first triangle collision, rather than continuing until it tests all triangles to find the closest collision. In OpenRL shaders, this property is set on the ray using the `occlusionTest` ray attribute. This feature is used in conjunction with the `defaultPrimitive` ray attribute, which defines the ray shader that will be executed

```
vec3 toLight = lightPosition - rl_IntersectionPoint;

createRay();
rl_OutRay.maxT = length(toLight);
rl_OutRay.direction = normalize(toLight);
rl_OutRay.occlusionTest = true;
rl_OutRay.defaultPrimitive = lightPrimitive;
emitRay();
```

Listing 1.4. Emitting a shadow ray.

if the ray fails to hit any geometry. Finally, the distance to the light is calculated and assigned to the ray's `maxT` attribute.[2] These attributes collectively mean that the shader will run when there is no occluding geometry in the way, so light can be accumulated into the framebuffer. If occluding geometry is encountered, the ray is dropped and no light is accumulated. The shader fragment in Listing 1.4 shows how to implement hard shadows using these ray attributes.

1.5   Soft Shadows

In 3D graphics, lights are often approximated as infinitesimally small points. In real life, however, lights are not infinitesimally small. From the point of view of the shadowed surface, lights have a nonzero area. This causes soft shadows with fuzzy edges. These edges are called the *penumbra region*. This phenomenon occurs on parts of the shadowed surface where some of the light area is visible and some is occluded. Scattering media like clouds or dust can also create soft shadows because the light is no longer originating from a single point source.

Rendering soft shadows using ray tracing is also conceptually simple. At each surface point, instead of shooting a single ray, as in the hard shadow case, we shoot multiple rays.

The ray directions are calculated based on a table precomputed on the host CPU. Each ray is shaded identically to the hard shadow case except it is assigned a weight so the total contribution of all the rays is the same as for a single ray. This weight can be encoded in a user-defined ray attribute.

What this technique is actually doing is performing Monte Carlo integration to estimate what percentage of the light is visible at the surface point. The domain we are integrating over is the solid angle representing the total light area visible at the surface, and each ray is in fact a point sample in that domain. The more samples we generate, the better our approximation will be.

---

[2]It is a historical convention in ray tracing to express the distance a ray *travels* between the origin and the intersection point. In OpenRL, `maxT` is a far clipping distance, past which no objects are evaluated for intersection.

```
float weight = 1.0/float(numSamples);
int ii,jj;
for(ii = 0; ii < numLights; ii = ii + 1)
{
  mat4 lightMatrix = lightToWorld[ii];
  for(jj = 0; jj < numSamples; jj = jj + 1)
  {
    vec4 samplePos = lightMatrix * samples[jj];
    vec3 toLight   = samplePos.xyz - rl_IntersectionPoint;

    createRay();
    rl_OutRay.maxT = length(toLight);
    rl_OutRay.direction = toLight/rl_OutRay.maxT;
    rl_OutRay.color = vec3(weight);
    rl_OutRay.occlusionTest = true;
    rl_OutRay.defaultPrimitive = lightPrimitive;
    emitRay();
  }
}
```

Listing 1.5. Emitting multiple shadow rays.

We could use pseudorandom numbers to generate our ray directions, however numerical analysis theory tells us that for small numbers of rays, this will produce a poor approximation of the integral. This is because random numbers will have uneven coverage over the domain. There are a number of other sequences that will be more likely to produce a better distribution over the domain. The book *Physically Based Rendering* by Matt Pharr and Greg Humphreys contains an excellent overview of sampling theory regarding ray tracing [Pharr and Humphreys 04, Chapter 7].

There are many techniques that can be used to reduce the number of rays emitted for each pixel but still produce a good estimate of the lighting integral. One that works well with hybrid ray tracing is interleaved sampling [Keller and Heidrich 01]. This technique takes advantage of the continuity between adjacent pixels so that the final pixel color for one pixel is calculated using the ray tracing results from its neighbors.

1.6 Reflections

Reflections are another optical phenomenon that are well suited for simulation with ray tracing. They are an important aspect of rendering many material types, not just perfectly reflective materials such as chrome and mirrors.

Reflections are caused by light bouncing off of a surface in a manner defined by the law of the reflection. This is an ancient physical law first codified by Euclid in the third century BC. It says that when light hits a perfectly reflective surface, it is reflected at the same angle as the incident angle.

```
void IlluminateSurface(vec4 normal, vec4 position)
{
    float reflectivity = position.w; //Surface reflectivity
    if(reflectivity>0.0)
    DoReflection(normal, position.xyx, reflectivity);
}
```

Listing 1.6. Using surface properties.

Rendering reflections using ray tracing is very simple, and in fact how to do so is suggested by looking at any textbook diagram of the law of reflection. When shading the reflective surface, we simply emit an extra ray from the surface to generate the reflection color. The direction of this reflection ray is calculated by reflecting the direction of the incoming ray about surface normal. When the reflection ray collides with objects in the scene, it should be shaded as if it were a primary ray; in this way, the surface that is visible in the reflection will contribute its color to the original surface.

When rendering reflections using a hybrid approach, there are several additional implementation details that must be handled. Firstly, we have to decide whether the pixel we are shading is reflective. We can do this by encoding our reflectivity in the G-buffer when we rasterize out fragments into it, then reading it back in our frame shader to decide if we need a reflection ray.

Another issue is that we are emitting our primary rays from a surface defined by a G-buffer pixel, so we don't have an incoming ray to reflect. Therefore, we have to calculate a "virtual" incoming ray based on the view frustum used by the rasterizer. In this example, we pass in the corners of the view frustum as four normalized **vec3s**, and then we can calculate the virtual ray's direction by interpolating between the corners based on the pixel position. We then reflect this ray around the normal defined by the G-buffer producing our reflection ray direction. The built-in RLSL function **reflect** is used to perform this calculation.

Finally, when our reflection ray hits a surface, we need to make sure the result is the same as when the same surface is viewed directly. So the output from the ray shader for a reflection ray must match the result of the compositing fragment shader that produces the final color for directly visible surfaces.

1.7   Transparency

Transparency is a fundamental physical property that is not handled well by rasterization. Rasterization approximates transparency using alpha blending. Transparent objects are sorted by distance from the camera and rendered after the opaque objects, in an order starting at the most distant. Transparency is approximated in the raster pipeline by having each fragment combine a percentage of its color with the value already in the framebuffer.

```
vec3 CalcVirtualInRay ()
{
  vec2 uv = rl_FrameCoord.xy/rl_FrameSize.xy;
  vec3 left = mix(frustumRay [0],  frustumRay [1],  uv.y);
  vec3 right = mix(frustumRay [2],  frustumRay [3],  uv.y);
  vec3 cameraRay = mix(left,  right,  uv.x);

  return cameraRay;
}

void DoReflection(vec4 normal,vec3 position, float reflectivity)
{
  vec3 inRay = CalcVirtualInRay ();
  vec3 reflection = reflect(inRay, normal);

  createRay();
  rl_OutRay.direction        = reflection;
  rl_OutRay.origin           = position;
  emitRay();
}
```

Listing 1.7. Reflection in hybrid renderer.

Alpha blending causes many artifacts, as it bares little relation to how transparency works in real life. Transparency is caused by light traveling through a transparent medium, where some wavelengths are absorbed and some are not. Ray tracing can be used to simulate transparency, independent of vertex submission order and without any of the artifacts and problems inherent in alpha blending.

To render a transparent surface, we emit a transparency ray from the back side of the surface, with the same direction as the incoming ray. If the surface is translucent, the ray's color will have its color ray attribute modulated with the color of the surface. This transparency ray is treated exactly the same as a reflection ray. The final color that the transparency ray contributes to the pixel will be modulated by the color of the transparent surface it traveled through. In this example, the surface transparency is stored in the alpha channel of the surface color. If the surface is completely transparent, the ray has 100% intensity, and as the surface becomes opaque, the ray's intensity approaches zero.

Simple ray-traced transparency of this kind does not take into account the behavior of many transparent materials. The physics of what happens when light travels from one transparent medium to another is more complicated than presented above. Some light is reflected off the surface (according the law of reflection discussed earlier) and some light bends, or refracts, changing its direction based on the relative speed of light in the two media.

This too can be represented in a ray tracer using a simple combination of a transparency ray and a reflection ray. The percentage of the light that is reflected versus refracted is defined by Fresnel's equations and can be approximated using a power function.

```
void DoTransparency(vec4 normal,vec3 position, vec4 color)
{
  vec3 inRay = CalcVirtualInRay();

  createRay();
  rl_OutRay.direction  = inRay;
  rl_OutRay.origin     = position;
  rl_OutRay.color      = (1.0-color.a)*rl_InRay.color*color.rgb;
  emitRay();
}
```

Listing 1.8. Emitting a transparency ray.

```
float  incidentDot  = dot(inRay, normal);
vec3   atten = vec3(1.0);
float  powTerm = pow((1.0-abs(incidentDot)), fresnelExp);
float  fres = KrMin+(Kr-KrMin)*powTerm;

if (rl_FrontFacing)
  ior = 1.0 / ior;
else {
  /* Beer's Law to approximate attenuation. */
  atten  = vec3(1.0) - materialColour;
  atten *= materialDensity * -rl_IntersectionT;
  atten  = exp(atten);
}

createRay();
rl_OutRay.direction = refract(rl_InRay.direction, normal, ior);

/* For Total Internal Reflection, reflect() returns 0.0 */
if (rl_OutRay.direction == vec3(0.0)) {
  rl_OutRay.direction = reflect(inRay, normal);
}

rl_OutRay.color *= (1.0 - fres) * atten;
emitRay();
```

Listing 1.9. Refraction shader.

1.8   Performance

Performance in a ray-tracing GPU is a big topic that cannot be covered by one section of this chapter. Hopefully this section contains enough information to provide a framework to begin to optimize your engine.

1.8.1   Rays per Pixel

The most obvious performance metric to measure is how many rays your engine is using. Because each ray can trigger a shader that can potentially emit many more rays, this is not always easy. To address this, OpenRL includes a tool called

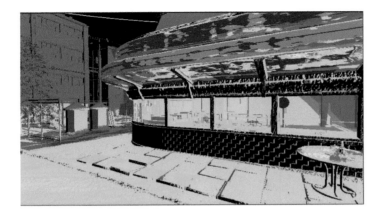

Figure 1.5. A sample heat map showing the most expensive pixels. Note the internal ray bouncing on the refractive glass objects can generate many rays.

Profiler. Profiler can provide a heat mapthat displays a visual representation of the number of rays that were cast for each pixel. This view can be useful to spot a potential shader problem or a problematic interaction between shaders.

Naturally, some effects are just more expensive, so some variation in the heat map is expected. But if some effects require more rays than can be sustained across the entire frame, it is important to design the game so that those pixels never fill the entire frame. Other options are to build in a mechanism to dynamically limit the effect quality up front based on the viewing position, or progressively use more rays until you have consumed the time allotted for the frame. This is sometimes necessary to maintain a stable frame rate.

1.8.2 Bottlenecks within the Ray Tracer

If the number of rays is within the expected ranges, but the performance is not what you had hoped for, then you may have encountered one of several other bottlenecks.

The Wizard architecture has a peak ray flow, measured in rays per second. For the PowerVR GR6500, that is 300 MRays/second. The architecture is not designed to exceed the peak ray flow, so if your measured performance is within 80% of the peak-ray-flow number, the best optimization opportunity is to reduce the number of rays you are casting.

If your performance is substantially below the peak ray flow, the bottleneck is geometry processing, executing shaders, or traversing rays (testing the rays against the scene geometry to find the best hit).

Geometry processing can be ruled out by ensuring that the geometry remains static from one frame to the next. To do this, make sure that no primitive objects

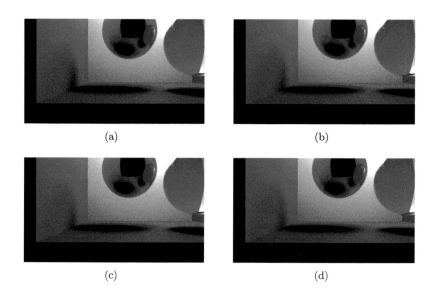

(a)   (b)

(c)   (d)

Figure 1.6. An unfiltered soft shadow computation using (a) one, (b) two, (c) four, and (d) eight rays per pixel. The quality gradually improves as more rays are used.

are created, removed, or modified, and that uniforms that affect a vertex shader are not modified.

The cost of ray traversal is a direct function of the geometric complexity of the scene. If reducing the complexity of your meshes yields a large performance gain, then the ray tracer may be bottlenecked on traversal.

The most difficult factor to isolate is the shader. As in a rasterizer, one valuable test may be to reduce the complexity of the shaders in the scene, for example, by replacing the material ray shaders with a simple shader that visualizes the normal at the ray intersection point. In ray tracing, however, this may also mask the problem by avoiding the emission of secondary rays (and hence less ray traversal).

Keep in mind that, in the Wizard architecture, ray and frame shaders execute on exactly the same shading hardware as the vertex and fragment shaders used in rasterization. Furthermore, they share exactly the same interface to memory. This means that a heavy raster shader could bog down the system for ray tracing or vice versa.

1.9   Results

All of the screenshots in Figures 1.7–1.12 were rendered with between one and four rays per pixel, measured as a frame-wide average.

Figure 1.7. Shadows and ray-traced transparency.

Figure 1.8. Multiple shadow casting lights.

Figure 1.9. Reflections and refraction.

Figure 1.10. High-quality ray-traced shadow from a highly detailed occluder.

Figure 1.11. Soft shadows from multiple lights.

Figure 1.12. Reflections and transparency.

1.10   Conclusion

This chapter described one way of adding the sophisticated light transport simulation of ray tracing to a raster-based renderer. By using ray tracing as a tool like this, the physically accurate rendering techniques that have long been used in ray-tracing production renderers can be added to real-time renderers. As ray-tracing acceleration becomes more wide spread in consumer GPUs, many other techniques will likely be developed as computer graphics developers explore innovative ways to add ray tracing to their products.

Bibliography

[Blender 14] Blender. "Cycles Render Engine." *Blender 2.61 Release Notes*, http://wiki.blender.org/index.php/Dev:Ref/Release_Notes/2.61/Cycles, accessed August 19, 2014.

[Hargreaves and Harris 04] Shawn Hargreaves and Mark Harris. "Deferred Shading." Presented at NVIDIA Developer Conference: 6800 Leagues Under the Sea, San Jose, CA, March 23, 2004. (Available at http://http.download.nvidia.com/developer/presentations/2004/6800_Leagues/6800_Leagues_Deferred_Shading.pdf.).

[Kajiya 86] James T Kajiya. "The Rendering Equation." *Computer Graphics: Proc. SIGGRAPH '86* 20:4 (1986), 143–150.

[Keller and Heidrich 01] Alexander Keller and Wolfgang Heidrich. "Interleaved Sampling." In *Proceeding of the 12th Eurographics Workshop on Rendering Techniques*, edited by S. J. Gortler and K. Myszkowski, pp. 269–176. London: Springer-Verlag, 2001.

[LuxRender 14] LuxRender. "LuxRays." http://www.luxrender.net/wiki/LuxRays, accessed July 19, 2014.

[Pharr and Humphreys 04] Matt Pharr and Greg Humphreys. *Physically Based Rendering*. San Francisco: Morgan Kaufmann, 2004.

2

V

Implementing a GPU-Only Particle-Collision System with ASTC 3D Textures and OpenGL ES 3.0

Daniele Di Donato

2.1 Introduction

Particle simulation has always been a part of games to realize effects that are difficult to achieve in a rasterizer systems. As the name suggests, particles are associated with the concept of small elements that appear in huge numbers. To avoid the complexity of real-world physics, the particles used in graphics tend to be simplified so they can be easily used in real-time applications. One of these simplifications is to consider each particle independent and not interacting with each other, which makes them suitable for parallelization across multiple processors.

The latest mobile GPUs support OpenGL ES 3.0, and the new features added gives us the right tools for implementing this simulation. We also wanted to enable a more realistic behavior, especially concerning collisions with objects in the scene. This can be computationally expensive and memory intensive since the information of the geometry needs to be passed to the GPU and traversed, per simulation step, if we want to parallelize the traditional CPU approach. With the introduction of ASTC [Nystad et al. 12] and its support for 3D textures, we are now able to store voxelized data on mobile devices with huge memory savings. This texture can be used in the OpenGL pipeline to read information about the scene and use it to modify the particle's trajectory at the cost of a single texture access per particle. The following sections describe all the steps of the particle-system simulation in detail (Figure 2.1).

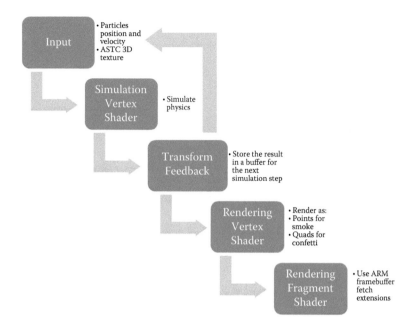

Figure 2.1. Simulation steps.

2.2   GPU-Only Particle System

2.2.1   Gathering Information about the Surroundings

To handle collisions with objects, we need to give the particles knowledge of their surroundings. This is achieved using a 3D texture describing uniform voxels of our 3D scene. For each voxel, we check if it's occupied by parts of the object and we store informations for that location. For voxels that end up on the surface of the mesh, we store a normal direction, while for internal voxels, we store the direction to the nearest surface and the amount of displacement from the current voxel to the nearest voxel on the surface. To achieve this, we used a freely available software called Voxelizer [Morris 13]. Voxelizer uses 32-bit floats for the mentioned values, so we convert them to 16-bit half-floats. This reduces the space needed by the data to be stored in a 3D texture. ASTC allows converting 16-bit per channel values, representing half-floats in our case, for the same memory cost. This gives us a better precision compared to using 8-bit values.

2.2.2   Compression Using ASTC 3D

The ASTC texture compression format is a block-based compression algorithm that is able to compress 2D and 3D textures in LDR or HDR format. Compared to

Block Dimension	Bit Rate (bits per pixel)
$3 \times 3 \times 3$	4.74
$4 \times 3 \times 3$	3.56
$4 \times 4 \times 3$	2.67
$4 \times 4 \times 4$	2.0
$5 \times 4 \times 4$	1.60
$5 \times 5 \times 4$	1.28
$5 \times 5 \times 5$	1.02
$6 \times 5 \times 5$	0.85
$6 \times 6 \times 5$	0.71
$6 \times 6 \times 6$	0.59

Table 2.1. ASTC 3D available block sizes.

other compression algorithms, ASTC offers more parameters to tune the quality of the final image (more details are available in [Smith 14]). The main options are the block size, the quality settings, and an indication of the correlation within the color channels (and the alpha channel if present). For the 3D format, ASTC allows the block sizes described in Table 2.1

Because the block compressed size is always 128 bits for all block dimensions and input formats, the bit rate is simply 128/(number of texels in a block). This specifies the tradeoff between quality and dimension of the generated compressed texture. In Figure 2.2, various ASTC compressed 3D texture have been rendered using slicing planes and various block sizes.

The other parameter to choose is the amount of time spent finding a good match for the current block. From a high-level view, this option is used to increase the quality of the compression at the cost of more compression time. Because this is typically done as an offline process, we can use the fastest option for debug

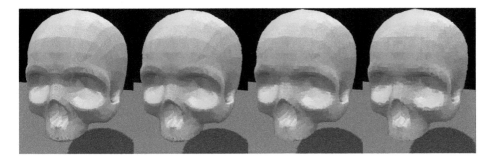

Figure 2.2. From left to right: uncompressed 3D texture, ASTC 3D $3 \times 3 \times 3$ compressed texture, ASTC 3D $4 \times 4 \times 4$ compressed texture, and ASTC 3D $5 \times 5 \times 5$ compressed texture.

purposes and compress using the best one for release. The options supported by
the free ARM ASTC evaluation codec [ARM Mali 15a, ARM Mali 15c] are *very
fast, fast, standard, thorough,* and *exhaustive*. The last parameter to set is the
correlation within the color channels. The freely available tools also allows us to
use various preset configuration options based on the data you want to compress.
For example, the tool has a preset for 2D normal maps compression that treats the
channels as uncorrelated and also uses a different error metric for the conversion.
This preset is not available for 3D textures, so we set the uncorrelation using
the fine-grained options available. Note that the ASTC compression tool used
does not store negative numbers, even in case of half-float format. This is due to
the internal implementation of the ASTC algorithm. Because our data contains
mostly unit vectors, we shifted the origin to be at $[1, 1, 1]$ so that the vectors
resides in the $[0, 0, 0]$ to $[2, 2, 2]$ 3D cube.

2.2.3   Statistics of the Savings

Compressing the 3D texture using ASTC gave us a huge amount of memory
saving, especially thanks to its ability to compress HDR values at the same cost
as LDR values. As can be seen from Table 2.2, the memory saving can reach
nearly 90% with the subsequent reduction of memory read bandwidth, and hence
energy consumption. The memory read bandwidth has been measured using
ARM Streamline profiling tool on a Samsung Galaxy Note 10.1, 2014 edition.
We measured the average read bandwidth from the main memory to the L2
cache of the GPU running the demo for around two minutes for each ASTC
texture format we used. The energy consumption per frame is an approximation
computed using ARM internal reference values for DDR2 and DDR3 memory
modules.

2.3   Physics Simulation

The physics simulation is really simple and tries to approximate the physical
behavior. Each particle will be subject to the force of gravity as well as other
forces we choose to apply. Given an initial state $t = 0$ for the particles, we
simulate the second law of motion and compute the incremental movement after
a Δt. The Δt used in the demo is fixed to 16 ms since we assume the demo will
run at 60 fps. Methods that try to solve ordinary and partial derivative equations
using incremental steps are typically called *explicit methods*.

2.3.1   Explicit Methods

To delegate the physics computation to the GPU, we decided to use an explicit
method of computation for the simulation step, since this methods fits well with

	Sphere	Skull	Chalice	Rock	Hand
Texture Resolution	$128 \times 128 \times 128$	$180 \times 255 \times 255$	$255 \times 181 \times 243$	$78 \times 75 \times 127$	$43 \times 97 \times 127$
Texture Size MB					
Uncompressed	16.78	82.62	89.73	5.94	4.24
ASTC $3 \times 3 \times 3$	1.27	6.12	6.72	0.45	0.34
ASCT $4 \times 4 \times 4$	0.52	2.63	2.87	0.19	0.14
ASTC $5 \times 5 \times 5$	0.28	1.32	1.48	0.10	0.07
Memory Read Bandwidth in MB/s					
Uncompressed	644.47	752.18	721.96	511.48	299.36
ASTC $3 \times 3 \times 3$	342.01	285.78	206.39	374.19	228.05
ASCT $4 \times 4 \times 4$	327.63	179.43	175.21	368.13	224.26
ASTC $5 \times 5 \times 5$	323.10	167.90	162.89	366.18	222.76
Energy consumption per frame DDR2 mJ per frame					
Uncompressed	4.35	5.08	4.87	3.45	2.01
ASTC $3 \times 3 \times 3$	2.31	1.93	1.39	2.53	1.54
ASCT $4 \times 4 \times 4$	2.21	1.21	1.18	2.48	1.51
ASTC $5 \times 5 \times 5$	2.18	1.13	1.10	2.47	1.50
Energy consumption per frame DDR3 mJ per frame					
Uncompressed	3.58	4.17	4.01	2.84	1.66
ASTC $3 \times 3 \times 3$	1.90	1.59	1.15	2.08	1.27
ASCT $4 \times 4 \times 4$	1.82	1.00	0.97	2.04	1.24
ASTC $5 \times 5 \times 5$	1.79	0.93	0.90	2.03	1.24

Table 2.2. ASTC 3D texture compression examples with various block sizes.

the transform feedback feature available through OpenGL ES 3.0. For the purpose of the demo, we implemented a simple Euler integration, and each shader execution computes a step of the integration. This implementation is good enough for the demo, but for advanced purposes, a variable time step can be used and each shader execution can split this time step further and compute a smaller integration inside the shader itself.

So, the physical simulation for step $N + 1$ will be dependent on a function of step N and the delta time (Δt) that occurred between the simulation steps:

$$Y(t + \Delta t) = F(Y(t), \Delta t).$$

Due to the time dependency of position, velocity, and acceleration, this method is suitable for use in our simulation.

```
typedef struct _XFormFeedbackParticle
{
    Vec3   Position;
    Vec3   Velocity;
    Vec4   Attrib;
    float  Life;
} XFormFeedbackParticle;

glGenBuffers( 2, m_XformFeedbackBuffers );

glBindBuffer( GL_ARRAY_BUFFER,
              m_XformFeedbackBuffers[0] );

glBufferData( GL_ARRAY_BUFFER,
              sizeof( XFormFeedbackParticle ) *
              totalNumberOfParticles ,
              NULL,
              GL_STREAM_DRAW );

glBindBuffer( GL_ARRAY_BUFFER,
              m_XformFeedbackBuffers[1] );

glBufferData( GL_ARRAY_BUFFER,
              sizeof( XFormFeedbackParticle ) *
              totalNumberOfParticles ,
              NULL,
              GL_STREAM_DRAW );

//Initialize the first buffer with the particles'
//data from the emitters
unsigned int offset = 0;
for( unsigned int i = 0; i < m_Emitters.Length(); i++ )
{
    glBindBuffer( GL_ARRAY_BUFFER,
                  m_XformFeedbackBuffers[0] );

    glBufferSubData( GL_ARRAY_BUFFER,
                     offset,
                     m_Emitters[i]->MaxParticles() *
                     sizeof( XFormFeedbackParticle ),
                     m_Emitters[i]->Particles() );

    offset += m_Emitters[i]->MaxParticles() *
              sizeof( XFormFeedbackParticle );
}
```

Listing 2.1. Transform feedback buffers initialization.

```
const char* xformFeedbackVaryings[4] = { "oParticlePos",
                                         "oParticleVel",
                                         "oParticleAttrib",
                                         "oParticleLife"  };
glTransformFeedbackVaryings( m_XFormFeedbackShader,
                             4,
                             xformFeedbackVaryings,
                             GL_INTERLEAVED_ATTRIBS );
```

Listing 2.2. Transform feedback output varyings definition.

Position1	Velocity1	Attrib1	Life1	Position2	Velocity2	Attrib2	Life2	...

Table 2.3. Order of `GL_INTERLEAVED_ATTRIBS` attributes.

Position1	Position2	Position3	...
Velocity1	Velocity2	Velocity3	...
Attrib1	Attrib2	Attrib3	...
Life1	Life2	Life3	...

Table 2.4. Order of `GL_SEPARATE_ATTRIBS` attributes.

2.3.2 OpenGL ES Transform Feedback Overview

Transform feedback allows users to store the result of a vertex shader execution into a predefined vertex buffer. This feature fits well with the explicit methods described above, since we can simulate the various steps using two buffers that are swapped at each simulation step (this is usually called ping-ponging). After we generate IDs for the transform feedback buffers using **glGenBuffers**, we initialize them with a set of random particles. If multiple emitters are present, we can store all their particles in the same buffer so that one step of the simulation can actually update multiple emitters in the scene (see Listing 2.1).

Vertex shaders output various results to the subsequent fragment shader, so we need a way to specify which results should also be written to the predefined output buffer. This can be done after we attach the vertex program that will run the simulation to the main program.

The command **glTransformFeedbackVaryings** (see Listing 2.2) will check if the specified strings are defined as output of the vertex shaders, and GL_INTERLEAVED_ATTRIBS will tell OpenGL in which layout to store the data. Possible options are **GL_INTERLEAVED_ATTRIBS** and **GL_SEPARATE_ATTRIBS**. The former will store the result of the vertex shader in a single buffer and in order as specified by the strings passed to the function and the particles' data will look like Table 2.3. The latter stores each attribute in a separate buffer (see Table 2.4).

During the rendering, we do the following:

1. Set which buffer to use as the destination buffer for transform feedback using the specific **GL_TRANSFORM_FEEDBACK_BUFFER** flag.

```
glBindBufferBase ( GL_TRANSFORM_FEEDBACK_BUFFER ,
                   0 ,
                   m_XformFeedbackBuffers [1] );
```

2. Set which buffer is the source buffer and how the data is stored in it.

```
glBindBuffer ( GL_ARRAY_BUFFER , m_XformFeedbackBuffers [0] );
glEnableVertexAttribArray ( m_ParticlePositionLocation );
```

```
glEnableVertexAttribArray ( m_ParticleVelocityLocation );
glEnableVertexAttribArray ( m_ParticleAttribLocation );
glEnableVertexAttribArray ( m_ParticleLifeLocation );

//We store in one buffer the 4 fields that represent a ↩
    particle
//  Position: 3 float values for a total of 12 bytes
//  Velocity: 3 float values for a total of 12 bytes
//  Attrib: 2 float values for a total of 8 bytes
//  life: 1 float value for a total of 4 bytes

glVertexAttribPointer ( m_ParticlePositionLocation ,
                        3 ,
                        GL_FLOAT ,
                        GL_FALSE ,
                        sizeof ( XFormFeedbackParticle ),
                        0) ;

glVertexAttribPointer ( m_ParticleVelocityLocation ,
                        3 ,
                        GL_FLOAT ,
                        GL_FALSE ,
                        sizeof ( XFormFeedbackParticle ),
                        12) ;

glVertexAttribPointer ( m_ParticleAttribLocation ,
                        4 ,
                        GL_FLOAT ,
                        GL_FALSE ,
                        sizeof ( XFormFeedbackParticle ),
                        24) ;

glVertexAttribPointer ( m_ParticleLifeLocation ,
                        1 ,
                        GL_FLOAT ,
                        GL_FALSE ,
                        sizeof ( XFormFeedbackParticle ),
                        40) ;
```

3. Enable transform feedback and disable the rasterizer step. The former is done using the `glBeginTransformFeedback` function to inform the OpenGL pipeline that we are interested in saving the results of the vertex shader execution. The latter is achieved using the `GL_RASTERIZER_DISCARD` flag specifically added for the transform feedback feature. This flag disables the generation of fragment jobs so that only the vertex shader is executed. We disabled the fragment execution since the rendering of the particles required two different approaches based on the scene rendered and splitting the simulation from the rendering gave us a cleaner code base to work with.

```
glEnable ( GL_RASTERIZER_DISCARD );
glBeginTransformFeedback ( GL_POINTS );
```

4. Render the particles as points.

```
glDrawArrays ( GL_POINTS , 0, MaxParticles );
```

5. Disable transform feedback and re-enable the rasterizer.

```
glEndTransformFeedback ();
glDisable ( GL_RASTERIZER_DISCARD );
```

2.3.3 Manage the Physics in the Vertex Shader Using 3D Textures

The attributes of each particle are read in the vertex shader as vertex attributes and used to compute the next incremental step in the physics simulation. First, we compute the total forces acting on the particles. Since this is a very simple simulation, we ended up simulating just the gravity, a constant force, and the air friction. The air friction is computed using the Stokes' drag formula [Wikipedia 15] because the particles are considered to be small spheres:

$$Fd = -6\pi\eta rv,$$

where η is the dynamic viscosity coefficient of the air and is equal to 18.27 μ Pa, r is the radius of the particle (we used 5 μm in our simulation), and v is the velocity of the particle. Since the first part of the product remains constant, we computed it in advance to avoid computing it per particle.

```
//Air friction is given by 6.0 * 3.14 * 5 * 0.000018 = 0.0016956
vec3 totalForce = uConstantForce +
                  ( uParticleMass * gravity ) −
                  0.0016956 * iParticleVel;

vec3 totalAcceleration = totalForce/uParticleMass;

oparticlePos_worldSpace = iparticle_Pos +
                  ( iparticle_Vel * uDeltaT ) +
                  ( totalAcceleration * uDeltaTSquared );
```

The new position is then transformed using the transformation matrix derived by the bounding box of the model. This matrix is computed to have the bounding box minimum to be the origin $(0,0,0)$ of the reference. Also, we want the area of world space inside the bounding box to be mapped to the unit cube space $(0,0,0)$–$(1,1,1)$. Applying this matrix to the particle's position in world space gives us the particle's coordinate in the space with the origin at the minimum corner of the bounding box and also scaled based on the dimension of the model. This means that the particles positioned in bounding box space within $(0,0,0)$

and $(1, 1, 1)$ have a chance to collide with the object, and this position is actually the 3D texture coordinate we will use to sample the 3D texture of the model.

- Host code.

```
uBoundingBoxMatrix = (  (1.0/max.x-min.x,  0.0,0.0,-min.x),
                        (0.0,  1.0/max.y-min.y,  0.0,  -min.y),
                        (0.0,  0.0,  1.0/max.z-min.z,  -min.z),
                        (0.0,  0.0,  0.0,  1.0)  ) *
                     inverse( ModelMatrix );
```

- Vertex shader.

```
vec4 oParticlePos_BBSpace = uBoundingBoxMatrix *
                            vec4( oparticlePos_worldSpace , 1.0 );

vec4 surfaceNormal =  texture( uCollisionTexture , tex3dCoord );
```

The surface's normal will be encoded in a 32-bit field and stored to be used later in the rendering pass to orient the particles in case of collisions. Due to the discrete nature of the simulation, it can happen that a particle goes inside the object. We recognize this event when sampling the 3D texture since we store a flag plus other data in the alpha channel of the 3D texture. When this event happens, we use the gradient direction stored in the 3D texture plus the amount of displacement that needs to be applied and we "push" the particle to the nearest surface. The push is applied to the particles in the bounding-box space, and the inverse of the uBoundingBoxMatrix is then used to move the particles back to the world space. Discrete time steps can cause issues when colliding with completely planar surfaces since a sort of swinging can appear, but at interactive speeds ($\geq$ 30 fps), this is almost unnoticeable. For particles colliding with the surface of the object, we compute the new velocity direction and magnitude using the previous velocity magnitude, the surface normal, the surface tangent direction, and a bouncing resistance to simulate different materials and particle behavior. We use the particle's mass as sliding factor so that heavier particles will bounce while lighter particles such as dust and smoke will slide along the surface. A check needs to be performed for the tangent direction since the normal and the velocity can be parallel, and in that case, the cross product will give an incorrect result (see Listing 2.3).

The velocity is then used to move the particle to its new position. Because we want to avoid copying memory within the GPU and CPU, the lifetime of all the particles should be managed in the shader itself. This means we check if the lifetime reached 0 and reinitialize the particle attributes such as initial position, initial velocity, and total particle duration. To make the simulation more

```
float slidingFactor = clamp( uParticleMass, 0.0,1.0 );
vec3 velocityDir =  normalize( iparticle_Vel );
vec3 tangentDir = cross( surfaceNormal.xyz, velocityDir );

if( length(tangentDir) < 0.0001 )
{
    tangentDir = getRandomTangentDir( surfaceNormal.xyz, 0.0 );
}

iparticle_Vel = length( iparticle_Vel ) *
                ( surfaceNormal.xyz * slidingFactor +
                  tangentDir.xyz * ( 1.0-slidingFactor ) ) *
                uBouncingResistance;
```

Listing 2.3. Particle-collision behavior.

interesting, some randomness can be added while the particles are flowing and no collision occurred. The fragment shader of the simulation is actually empty. This is understandable since we do not need to execute any fragment work for the simulation results. Also, we have enabled the `GL_RASTERIZER_DISCARD` to skip all fragment work from being executed. In a way that differs from the OpenGL standard, OpenGL ES needs a fragment shader to be attached to the program, even if is not going to be used.

2.4   Rendering the Particles

After updating the particles' locations, we can render them as we want. In our demo, we decided to render them as smoke particles and as confetti. The light lamp shape on the floor is procedurally generated using its texture coordinates. The shadows are created using a projected texture that is generated from the light point of view. This texture is used for the shadows of the floor as well the ones on the objects. To achieve this we implement an incremental approach:

1. Render the object without color enabled so that its depth is stored in the depth buffer. We need to do this step to prevent particles behind the object (from the point of view of the light) from casting shadows on the object.

2. Render the particles with depth testing on, but not depth writing.

3. Render the object normally using the texture generated at Step 2 for the shadows.

4. Render the object as shadow in the texture from Step 2.

5. Render the floor with the result of Step 4 for the shadows.

This approach can be optimized. For example, we can use two different frame-buffers for the shadow of the floor and on the object so that we avoid incremental renderings (refer to [Harris 14] for more information). To achieve this, we copy the result of the texture created at the end of Step 2 into the other framebuffer and then render the object as shadow on it.

2.4.1 Smoke Scene

In this scene, the smoke (Figure 2.3) is rendered as point sprites since we always want them to face the viewpoint. The smoke is rendered using a noise texture and some mathematics to compute the final color as if it was a 3D volume. To give the smoke a transparent look, we need to combine different overlapping particles' colors. To do so, we used blending and disabled the Z-test when rendering the particles. This gives a nice result, even without sorting the particles based on the Z-value (otherwise we have to map the buffer in the CPU). Another reason for dis-abling it is to achieve soft particles. From Mali-T600 GPUs onward, we can use a specific extension in the fragment shader called `GL_ARM_shader_framebuffer_fetch` to read back the values of the framebuffer (color, depth, and stencil) without having to render to a texture [Björge 14]. The extension allows us to access a set of built-in variables (`gl_LastFragColorARM`, `gl_LastFragDepthARM`, `gl_LastFrag StencilARM`) from the fragment shader, and for each pixel, the value is based on previous rendering results.

```
#extension GL_ARM_shader_framebuffer_fetch_depth_stencil : enable
#ifdef GL_ARM_shader_framebuffer_fetch_depth_stencil
float dla= (2.0 * uNear) /
           (uFar + uNear - gl_LastFragDepthARM * (uFar - uNear));
#else
    //Texture read fallback
#endif
```

This feature makes it easier to achieve soft particles, and in the demo, we use a simple approach. First, we render all the solid objects so that the Z-value will be written in the depth buffer. Afterward, we render the smoke and we can read the depth value of the object and compare it with the current fragment of the particle (to see if it is behind the object) and fade the color accordingly. This technique eliminates the sharp profile that is formed by the particle quad intersecting the geometry due to the Z-test. During development, the smoke effect looked nice, but we wanted it to be more dense and blurry. To achieve all this, we decided to render the smoke in an offscreen render buffer with a lower resolution compared to the main screen. This gives us the ability to have a blurred smoke (since the lower resolution removes the higher frequencies) as well as lets us increase the number of particles to get a denser look. The current implementation uses a 640×360 offscreen buffer that is up-scaled to 1080p resolution in the final image.

Figure 2.3. Smoke scene.

A naïve approach causes jaggedness on the outline of the object when the smoke is flowing near it due to the blending of the up-sampled low-resolution buffer. To minimize this effect, we apply a bilateral filter. The bilateral filter is applied to the offscreen buffer and is given by the product of a Gaussian filter in the color texture and a linear weighting factor given by the difference in depth. The depth factor is useful on the edge of the model because it gives a higher weight to neighbor texels with depth similar to the one of the current pixel and lower weight when this difference is higher. (If we consider a pixel on the edge of a model, some of the neighbor pixels will still be on the model while others will be far in the background.)

2.4.2 Confetti Scene

In this case, we used quads instead of points since we needed to rotate the particles when they slide along the surfaces (Figure 2.4). Those quads are initialized to `min` $= (-1, -1, 0)$ and `max` $= (1, 1, 0)$. The various shapes are achieved procedurally checking the texture coordinates of the quad pixels. To rotate the quad accordingly, we retrieve the normal of the last surface touched and compute the tangent and binormal vectors. This gives us a matrix that we use to rotate the initial quad position, and afterward we translate this quad into the position of the particle that we computed in the simulation step.

2.4.3 Performance Optimization with Instancing

Even if the quad data is really small, they waste memory because the quads are all initialized with the same values and they all share the same number of vertices and texture coordinates. The instancing feature introduced in OpenGL ES 3.0

Figure 2.4. Confetti scene.

allows us to avoid replication of vertex attribute by defining just one "template" of the mesh we want to render. This template is then instantiated multiple times and the user will vary the parameters (matrices, colors, textures, etc.) to represent multiple meshes with different characteristic with a single draw call (Figure 2.5).

OpenGL ES instancing overview.

1. Bind the buffers that we will use as the template source data.

```
glBindBuffer( GL_ARRAY_BUFFER, m_QuadPositionBuffer );
glEnableVertexAttribArray( m_QuadPositionLocation );
glVertexAttribPointer( m_QuadPositionLocation,
                       3,
                       GL_FLOAT,
                       GL_FALSE,
                       0,
                       (void*)0 );
//Set up quad texture coordinate buffer
glBindBuffer( GL_ARRAY_BUFFER, m_TexCoordBuffer );
glEnableVertexAttribArray( m_QuadTexCoordLocation );
glVertexAttribPointer( m_QuadTexCoordLocation,
                       2,
                       GL_FLOAT,
                       GL_FALSE,
                       0,
                       (void*)0 );
```

2. Set a *divisor* for each vertex attribute array. The divisor specifies how the vertex attributes advance in the array when rendering instances of primitives in a single draw call. Setting it to 0 will make the attribute advance

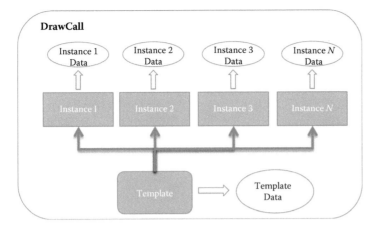

Figure 2.5. OpenGL ES 3.0 instancing.

once per vertex, restarting at the start of each instance rendered. This is what we want to happen for the initial quad position and texture coordinate since they will be the same for each particle (instance) rendered.

```
glVertexAttribDivisor ( m_QuadPositionLocation , 0 );
glVertexAttribDivisor ( m_QuadTexCoordLocation , 0 );
```

3. For the attributes computed in the simulation step, we would like to shift the vertex buffer index for each of the particles (instances) to be rendered. This is achieved using a divisor other than zero. The divisor then specifies how many instances should be rendered before we advance the index in the arrays. In our case, we wanted to shift the attributes after each instance is rendered, so we used a divisor of 1.

```
glVertexAttribDivisor ( m_UpdatedParticlePosLocation , 1 );
glVertexAttribDivisor ( m_UpdatedParticleLifeLocation , 1 );
glVertexAttribDivisor ( m_UpdatedParticleAttribLocation , 1 );
```

4. Bind the buffer that was output from the simulation step. Set up the vertex attributes to read from this buffer.

```
glBindBuffer ( GL_ARRAY_BUFFER , m_XformFeedbackBuffers [1] );

glVertexAttribPointer ( m_UpdatedParticlePosLocation ,
                        3,
                        GL_FLOAT ,
```

```
                                        GL_FALSE ,
                                        sizeof ( XFormFeedbackParticle ) ,
                                        0 ) ;

        glVertexAttribPointer ( m_UpdatedParticleAttribLocation ,
                                 4 ,
                                 GL_FLOAT ,
                                 GL_FALSE ,
                                 sizeof ( XFormFeedbackParticle ) ,
                                 24 ) ;

        glVertexAttribPointer ( m_UpdatedParticleLifeLocation ,
                                 1 ,
                                 GL_FLOAT ,
                                 GL_FALSE ,
                                 sizeof ( XFormFeedbackParticle ) ,
                                 40 ) ;
```

5. Render the particles (instances). The function allows to specify how many vertices belong to each instance and how many instances we want to render. Note that when using instancing, we are able to access a built-in variable `gl_InstanceID` inside the vertex shader. This variable specifies the ID of the instance we are currently rendering and can be used to access uniform buffers.

```
        glDrawArraysInstanced ( GL_TRIANGLE_STRIP , 0 , 4 , MaxParticles ) ;
```

6. Always set back to 0 the divisor for all the vertex attribute arrays since they can affect subsequent rendering even if we are not using indexing.

```
        glDisableVertexAttribArray ( m_QuadPositionLocation ) ;
        glDisableVertexAttribArray ( m_QuadTexCoordLocation ) ;
        glVertexAttribDivisor ( m_UpdatedParticlePosLocation , 0 ) ;
        glVertexAttribDivisor ( m_UpdatedParticleAttribLocation , 0 ) ;
        glVertexAttribDivisor ( m_UpdatedParticleLifeLocation , 0 ) ;
```

2.5   Conclusion

Combining OpenGL ES 3.0 features enabled us to realize a GPU-only particle system that is capable of running at interactive speeds on current mobile devices. The techniques proposed are experimental and have some drawbacks, but the reader can take inspiration from this chapter and explore other options using ASTC LDR/HDR/3D texture as well as OpenGL ES 3.0. In case there is need to sort the particles, the compute shader feature recently announced in the OpenGL ES 3.1 specification will enable sorting directly on the GPU.

An issue derived from the use of a texture is the texture's resolution. This technique can describe a whole 3D static scene in a single 3D texture, but the resolution of it needs to be chosen carefully since too small resolution can cause parts of objects to not collide properly since multiple parts with different normals will be stored in the same voxel. Also, space is wasted if the voxelized 3D scene contains parts with no actual geometry in them but that fall inside the volume that is voxelized. Since we are simulating using a discrete time step, issues can appear if we change the system too fast. For example, we can miss the collision detection in narrow parts of the object if we rotate it too fast.

Bibliography

[ARM Mali 15a] ARM Mali. "ASTC Evaluation Codec." http://malideveloper. arm.com/develop-for-mali/tools/astc-evaluation-codec, 2015.

[ARM Mali 15b] ARM Mali. "Mali Developer Center." http://malideveloper. arm.com, 2015.

[ARM Mali 15c] ARM Mali. "Mali GPU Texture Compression Tool." http://malideveloper.arm.com/develop-for-mali/tools/asset-creation/ mali-gpu-texture-compression-tool/, 2015.

[Björge 14] Marius Björge. "Bandwidth Efficient Graphics with ARM Mali GPUs." In *GPU Pro 5: Advanced Rendering Techniques*, edited by Wolfgang Engel, pp. 275–288. Boca Raton, FL: CRC Press, 2014.

[Harris 14] Peter Harris. "Mali Performance 2: How to Correctly Handle Framebuffers." *ARM Connected Community*, http://community. arm.com/groups/arm-mali-graphics/blog/2014/04/28/mali-graphics -performance-2-how-to-correctly-handle-framebuffers, 2014.

[Morris 13] Dan Morris. "Voxelizer: Floodfilling and Distance Map Generation for 3D Surfaces." http://techhouse.brown.edu/~dmorris/voxelizer/, 2013.

[Nystad et al. 12] J. Nystad, A. Lassen, A. Pomianowski, S. Ellis, and T. Olson. "Adaptive Scalable Texture Compression." In *Proceedings of the Fourth ACM SIGGRAPH/Eurographics Conference on High-Performance Graphics*, pp. 105–114. Aire-la-ville, Switzerland: Eurographics Association, 2012.

[Smith 14] Stacy Smith. "Adaptive Scalable Texture Compression." In *GPU Pro 5: Advanced Rendering Techniques*, edited by Wolfgang Engel, pp. 313–326. Boca Raton, FL: CRC Press, 2014.

[Wikipedia 15] Wikipedia. "Stokes' Law." http://en.wikipedia.org/wiki/Stokes% 27_law, 2015.

Animated Characters with Shell Fur for Mobile Devices
Andrew Girdler and James L. Jones

3.1 Introduction

Fur effects have traditionally presented a significant challenge in real-time graphics. On the desktop, the latest techniques employ DirectX 11 tessellation to dynamically create geometric hair or fur strands on the fly that number in the hundreds of thousands [Tariq and Bavoil 08, Lacroix 13]. On mobile platforms, developers must make do with a much smaller performance budget and significantly reduced memory bandwidth. To compound this, mobile devices are increasingly featuring equal or higher resolution screens than the average screens used with desktop systems.

Many artists are today able to create very detailed models of creatures with advanced animations to be used in 3D applications. This chapter will describe a system to animate and render fully detailed meshes of these creatures with a shell fur effect in real time on mobile platforms. This is made possible by utilizing new API features present in OpenGL ES 3.0, including transform feedback and instancing.

We used this technique in the creation of our *SoftKitty* technical demo, which was first shown at Mobile World Conference 2014. It enabled a high-polygon model of a cat to be animated with 12-bone-per-vertex skinning and then rendered with shell fur at native resolution on an Apple iPad Air. Thanks to the optimizations in this chapter, the device was able to render the cat and a high detail environment in excess of 30 fps.

3.2 Overview

This approach is an optimization of the shell fur technique presented by [Kajiya and Kay 89]. Traditionally, combining a shell fur effect with a skinned mesh

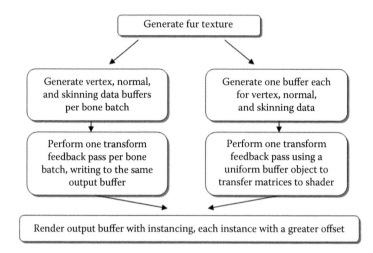

Figure 3.1. Technique overview diagram.

would require the skinned positions to be recomputed for every layer of fur. In addition to this, there would be a separate draw call per layer, resulting in the base mesh being transferred to the GPU multiple times per frame. This is inefficient and, depending on model complexity, possibly not viable on bandwidth-limited platforms.

This approach avoids these issues by first skinning the mesh in a separate transform feedback pass and then using instancing to submit the mesh and create the offset layers of fur with a single draw call. We have also simplified the design of the textures used to create the fur, transitioning from one texture per layer to a single texture for all. There are two approaches to implementing this, the choice of which is decided by model complexity and platform limitations. (See Figure 3.1.)

3.3   Creating a Shell Fur Texture

Traditional shell fur techniques have utilized a separate texture per shell layer to encode the density and length of the strands [Lengyel et al. 01]. An early optimization we used, which was partially necessitated by the use of instancing, was to encode the strand length, and thereby density, onto a single texture. We encoded the length as an integer between 0 (no fur) and the default number of layers and then sampled it in the fur shader to decide whether a strand should be drawn or not. We stored this in the alpha channel of the texture with the intention of storing a color variance (having some strands lighter and some darker than others) in the RGB channels; however, we later removed this as the inherent variance in our diffuse texture was sufficient to give a convincing effect.

```
for (layer < numLayers)
    rand(setSeed)
    length = 1.5f − layer/numLayers
    //hand tuned falloff
    density = inDensity*length
    for i < density
        newxycoords=rand()
        if xycoord.a != layer
            xycoord.a+=1.
```

An alternative approach would be to maintain a single texture per layer and create a 2DTextureArray to pass into the fur instancing shader. This could be explored if more flexibility in the fur was needed, but the single-texture approach was sufficient for our needs and was more bandwidth efficient.

We also created a separate fur length map, using the same UV coordinates as the model's diffuse texture to decide the relative length of the fur for a given location on the model, with white being full length and black being no fur.

3.4 Bone Batches or Single Pass?

We identified two approaches to performing the transform feedback stage for skinning. The first involves performing a separate transform feedback pass for each bone batch, skinning the associated vertices and then appending them into a single output buffer. The second (theoretically more efficient) approach is to export your model with a single batch, pass all the bone matrices into a single pass and skin all the vertices in one go. This avoids the overhead of running multiple transform feedback passes (which may be substantial if the number of batches is high), but depending on the complexity of the model, you may hit an upper limit on the number of uniform matrices that can be passed into a shader. This is an implementation-defined limit that can vary substantially, although we found on several test platforms that using a uniform buffer object (UBO) allowed for a greater number of matrices to be passed in.

Our model had just under 240 bone matrices, as it was designed for offline rendering. If using a model with a near or greater count than this, it would be advisable to use multiple passes, keeping the number of batches to a minimum. If tuning for optimum performance, it would be advisable to test both approaches on your target platform.

3.5 Model Data and Setup

When setting up to performing the transform feedback pass with multiple bone batches, we adopted the approach of having a single output buffer (the size of the entire mesh's vertices and normals) and then two buffers for input—one for

```
glGenTransformFeedbacks (1 , &m_TransformFeedbackObject ) ;
glGenBuffers ( BONE_BATCHES +1, m_ModelDataBuffer ) ;
// m_ModelDataBuffer [0] is output buffer
glGenBuffers ( BONE_BATCHES , m_SkinningDataBuffer ) ;

OutputModelData = new ModelDataStruct [ pMesh . nNumVertex ] ;
for ( unsigned int i = 0; i < pMesh . nNumVertex ; ++i )
{
    //Copy data into OutputModelData
}
glBindBuffer ( GL_ARRAY_BUFFER , m_ModelDataBuffer [0] ) ;
glBufferData ( GL_ARRAY_BUFFER , sizeof ( ModelDataStruct )
    * pMesh . nNumVertex , OutputModelData , GL_STATIC_DRAW ) ;
glBindBuffer ( GL_ARRAY_BUFFER , 0) ;
delete [] OutputModelData ;

//loading each batch of vertices into its own buffer
for ( unsigned int Batch = 0; Batch < BONE_BATCHES ; ++Batch )
{
    //Calculate or retrieve BatchVertexCount
    InputModelData = new ModelDataStruct [ BatchVertexCount ] ;
    for ( int i = 0; i < BatchVertexCount;++i )
    {
        //Copy data into InputModelData
    }
    glBindBuffer ( GL_ARRAY_BUFFER , m_ModelDataBuffer [ Batch +1] ) ;
    glBufferData ( GL_ARRAY_BUFFER , sizeof ( ModelDataStruct )
        * BatchVertexCount , InputModelData , GL_STATIC_DRAW ) ;
    glBindBuffer ( GL_ARRAY_BUFFER , 0) ;
    delete [] InputModelData ;

    InputSkinningData = new BoneDataStruct [ BatchVertexCount ] ;
    for ( int i = 0; i < BatchVertexCount;++i )
    {
        //Copy bone weights and indices into InputSkinningData
    }
    glBindBuffer ( GL_ARRAY_BUFFER , m_SkinningDataBuffer [ Batch ] ) ;
    glBufferData ( GL_ARRAY_BUFFER , sizeof ( BoneDataStruct )
        * BatchVertexCount , InputSkinningData , GL_STATIC_DRAW ) ;
    glBindBuffer ( GL_ARRAY_BUFFER , 0) ;
    delete [] InputSkinningData ;
}
```

Listing 3.1. Creating buffers per bone batch.

vertices and normals and one for skinning data. These input buffers were created per bone batch, containing only the data specific to that bone batch.

If using a single bone batch, the code path in Listing 3.1 can still be used with a batch count of 1. When using the single buffer approach, we created our UBO in the following manner:

```
glGenBuffers (1,& uiUBO ) ;
glBindBuffer ( GL_UNIFORM_BUFFER , uiUBO ) ;
uiIndex = glGetUniformBlockIndex ( ShaderId , szBlockName ) ;
glUniformBlockBinding ( ShaderId , uiIndex , uiSlot ) ;
glBindBufferBase ( GL_UNIFORM_BUFFER , uiSlot , uiUBO ) ;
```

```
glUseProgram(m_TransformFeedback.uiId);
glBindTransformFeedback(GL_TRANSFORM_FEEDBACK, m_TFObject);
glEnable(GL_RASTERIZER_DISCARD);
int iTotalVerts = 0;

for (unsigned int Batch = 0; Batch < BONE_BATCHES; ++Batch)
{ //Calculate or retrieve BatchVertexCount
  glBindBufferRange(GL_TRANSFORM_FEEDBACK_BUFFER,0,
      m_ModelDataBuffer[0],iTotalVerts*sizeof(ModelDataStruct),
      BatchVertexCount*sizeof(ModelDataStruct));
  glBeginTransformFeedback(GL_POINTS);
  //Enable Attrib Arrays
  glBindBuffer(GL_ARRAY_BUFFER, m_ModelDataBuffer[Batch+1]);
  //Set Vertex and Normal Attrib pointers
  glBindBuffer(GL_ARRAY_BUFFER, m_SkinningDataBuffer[Batch]);
  //Set Bone Weight and Index Attrib pointers
  glUniform1i(m_TransformFeedback.uiBoneCount,pMesh.sBoneIdx.n);

#if defined(UBO)
  m_matrixPaletteUBO.UpdateData( m_BoneMatrixPalette[0].ptr() );
#else
  glUniformMatrix4fv(m_TransformFeedback.uiBoneMatrices,
      BONE_PALETTE_SIZE,GL_FALSE, m_BoneMatrixPalette[0].ptr());
#endif

  glDrawArrays(GL_POINTS, 0, BatchVertexCount);
  iTotalVerts += BatchVertexCount;
  glEndTransformFeedback();
  //Disable Attrib Arrays
}
glDisable(GL_RASTERIZER_DISCARD);
```

Listing 3.2. Performing the TF pass.

3.6 Animation with TF

In performing the transform feedback (TF) pass, we transform the vertices to their skinned position and write them all into a single output buffer. We bind the specific range of the output buffer to write to before beginning and ending TF for every batch; we also then bind the batch specific buffers for input data. While the input data refers to specific vertices in each batch, the bone indices are relative to the entire bone matrix palette array; as such, we passed in all the bone matrices for every pass either using a standard uniform or a UBO. (See Listing 3.2.)

We then performed the skinning normally in the shader in Listing 3.3.

3.7 Instancing for Fur Shells

We now submit the output of the transform feedback stage as a single buffer to be drawn with instancing. (See Figure 3.2.) We pass in the shell fur texture and the fur length texture, which governs the offset between layers of the fur. We

```
#if defined(UBO)
layout(std140) uniform BoneMatrixStruct
{ highp mat4 BoneMatrixArray[NUM_BONE_MATRICES]; };

void main()
{
    gl_Position = vec4(inVertex,1.0); //required
    for (int i = 0; i < BoneCount; ++i)
    {
    //perform skinning normally
    }
    oPosition = position.xyz;
    oNormal = normalize(worldNormal);
}
```

Listing 3.3. TF shader.

Figure 3.2. Wireframe view of the final model.

also specify the number of instances to draw, which should be the same as the number of layers used in creating the fur texture. We found with our model, depending on platform and resolution, a count of between 11 and 25 gave good visual results while maintaining workable performance. We bind the `TexCoord` array to a structure that is created when we load our model from disk. (The vertices have not been reordered, so this data is unchanged by the process.) (See Listing 3.4.)

The shell position is then calculated in the shader as shown in Listing 3.5.

Having calculated a base alpha value per layer in the vertex shader, we sample the `StrandLengthTexture` to establish where fur should be drawn and how long it should be. We leave the base layer solid, and we alpha out strands that the random distribution decided should have ended:

```
//Bind Fur Texture, Fur Length Texture, Diffuse Texture
glUniform1i(m_FurShader.uiLayerCount, m_FurLayers);
UpdateShaderMatrices(&m_FurShader,m_WorldFromModel);
glBindBuffer(GL_ARRAY_BUFFER,m_ModelDataBuffer[0]);
//Bind Vertex, Normal Array
glBindBuffer(GL_ARRAY_BUFFER, m_OriginalModelVbo);
//Bind Texcoord Arrays
glEnable (GL_BLEND);
glBlendFunc (GL_SRC_ALPHA, GL_ONE_MINUS_SRC_ALPHA);
glDrawArraysInstanced(GL_TRIANGLES,0,nNumVertex,m_FurLayers);
glDisable(GL_BLEND);
//Disable Attrib arrays
```

Listing 3.4. Submitting the mesh.

```
InstanceID = gl_InstanceID;
oShellDist = (float(InstanceID))/(float(LayerCount)-1.0);
oAlpha = (1.0-pow(oShellDist,0.6)); //tweaked for nicer falloff
shellDist *= texture(ShellHeightTexture,inTexCoord).r;
highp vec3 shellPos = inVertex + inNormal*oShellDist;
gl_Position = ProjectionFromModel *  vec4(shellPos,1.0);
```

Listing 3.5. Instancing shader.

```
highp float alpha = oAlpha;
highp float strandLength = texture(StrandLengthTexture,
                     oTexCoord).a / (float(LayerCount)/255.0);
if(InstanceID > 0 && oShellDist > strandLength) {alpha = 0.0;}
```

3.8 Lighting and Other Effects

In our implementation, we used a minimalist Cook-Torrance BRDF [Schüler 09] to shade the model and fur. (See Figures 3.3 and 3.4 for results.) We experimented with tweaking the alpha values of the fur by hand to achieve a falloff that, when lit, gave a cleaner edge to the fur, avoiding crawling and noise.

For the environment shading, we used a precomputed diffuse reflectance texture and an analytic specular term in the shader. We also stored separate textures for the precomputed shadows so that we could seamlessly merge the shadows cast from the cat into the floor shadow. Having the cat dancing in and out of the shadow was an important part of what we were trying to achieve, and this technique worked well. (See Figure 3.5.) As we were only dealing with a single directional light, we first computed a projected shadow texture for the cat by rendering from outside the window using the preskinned mesh from the transform feedback pass. We then computed the light direction and used this to project the texture to the floor plane situated beneath the cat.

Figure 3.3. Final model lit within the scene.

Figure 3.4. Close-up of fur effect.

Figure 3.5. Model in shadow.

3.9 Conclusion

In moving from skinning every shell individually to using transform feedback, we saw a dramatic performance increase. With a low-polygon early test model on a mobile platform using 18 layers, performance increased from 29 fps to being Vsync limited at 60 fps. We were then able to increase to 30 layers and maintain a framerate above 30 fps. When we later incorporated the changes to the fur texture and incorporated instancing, we saw performance rise to 50 fps. With our final, full-detail model, on a high-performance mobile platform, we were able to run 17 shells on a 1920×1080 display. This gave more than sufficient visual quality and allowed us to render a surrounding scene and other effects, all in excess of 30 fps.

We were able to achieve a pleasing result without the additional use of fins, and our implementation also did not include any force, intersection, or self-shadowing effects. These are all additional avenues that could be explored on higher-performance platforms in the future.

Bibliography

[Kajiya and Kay 89] James T. Kajiya and Timothy L. Kay. "Rendering Fur with Three Dimensional Textures." In *Proceedings of the 16th Annual Conference on Computer Graphics and Interactive Techniques*, pp. 271–180. New York: ACM Press, 1989.

[Lacroix 13] Jason Lacroix.   "Adding More Life to Your Characters with TressFX." In *ACM SIGGRAPH 2013 Computer Animation Festival*, p. 1. New York: ACM Press, 2013.

[Lengyel et al. 01] Jerome Lengyel, Emil Praun, Adam Finkelstein, and Hugues Hoppe. "Real-Time Fur over Arbitrary Surfaces." In *Proceedings of the 2001 Symposium on Interactive 3D Graphics*, pp. 227–232. New York: ACM Press, 2001.

[Schüler 09] Christian Schüler. "An Efficient and Physically Plausible Real-Time Shading Model." In *ShaderX 7*, edited by Wolfgang Engel, pp. 175–187. Boston: Cengage, 2009.

[Tariq and Bavoil 08] Sarah Tariq and Louis Bavoil. "Real Time Hair Simulation and Rendering on the GPU." In *ACM SIGGRAPH 2008 Talks*, p. artcle no. 37. New York: ACM Press, 2008.

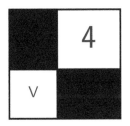

High Dynamic Range Computational Photography on Mobile GPUs

Simon McIntosh-Smith, Amir Chohan, Dan Curran, and Anton Lokhmotov

4.1 Introduction

Mobile GPU architectures have been evolving rapidly, and are now fully programmable, high-performance, parallel-processing engines. Parallel programming languages have also been evolving quickly, to the point where open standards such as the Khronos Group's OpenCL now put powerful cross-platform programming tools in the hands of mobile application developers.

In this chapter, we will present our work that exploits GPU computing via OpenCL and OpenGL to implement high dynamic range (HDR) computational photography applications on mobile GPUs. HDR photography is a hot topic in the mobile space, with applications to both stills photography and video.

We explore two techniques. In the first, a single image is processed in order to enhance detail in areas of the image at the extremes of the exposure. In the second technique, multiple images taken at different exposures are combined to create a single image with a greater dynamic range of luminosity. HDR can be applied to an image to achieve a different goal too: as an image filter to create a range of new and exciting visual effects in real time, somewhat akin to the "radioactive" HDR filter from Topaz Labs [Topaz Labs 15].

These HDR computational photography applications are extremely compute-intensive, and we have optimized our example OpenCL HDR code on a range of GPUs. In this chapter, we shall also describe the approach that was taken during code optimization for the ARM Mali mobile GPUs and give the performance results we achieved on these platforms.

We also share the OpenCL/OpenGL interoperability code we have developed, which we believe will be a useful resource for the reader. Surprisingly little is

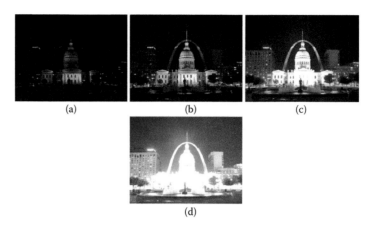

Figure 4.1. Images taken with different exposures: (a) −4 stops, (b) −2 stops, (c) +2 stops, and (d) +4 stops. [Image from [McCoy 08].]

available in the literature on how to efficiently implement HDR pipelines, and even less as real source code. We hope this chapter will address both of these shortcomings.

4.2 Background

Real-world scenes contain a much higher dynamic range of brightness than can be captured by the sensors available in most cameras today. Digital cameras use 8 bits per pixel for each of the red, green, and blue channels, therefore storing only 256 different values per color channel. Real-world scenes, however, can have a dynamic range on the order of about $10^8 : 1$, therefore requiring up to 32 bits per pixel per channel to represent fully.

To compensate for their relatively low dynamic range (LDR), modern digital cameras are equipped with advanced computer graphics algorithms for producing high-resolution images that meet the increasing demand for more dynamic range, color depth, and accuracy. In order to produce an HDR image, these cameras either synthesize inputs taken concurrently from multiple lenses with different exposures, or they take multiple-exposure images in sequential order and combine them into a single scene. Figure 4.1 shows a set of over- and underexposed images of a scene that can be captured in such a way.

The synthesis process produces a 32-bit image encoding the full HDR of the scene. Standard displays, such as computer monitors, TVs, and smartphone or tablet screens, however, only have a dynamic range of around 256 : 1, which means that they are not capable of accurately displaying the rendered HDR image. Therefore, to display HDR images on a standard display, the images first

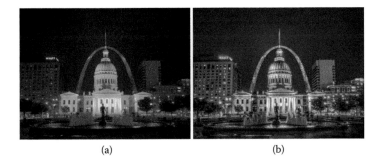

(a)   (b)

Figure 4.2. HDR images obtained using (a) global and (b) local tone-mapping operators. [Image from [McCoy 08].]

need to be compressed to a lower dynamic range in a way that preserves image detail. This process of compressing an HDR image to a lower dynamic range is called *tone mapping*. Once a 32-bit HDR image is tone mapped, the resulting 8-bit HDR image can then be rendered to standard displays. Figure 4.2 shows examples of the outputs of two different tone-mapping operators (TMOs).

4.2.1 Smartphone Photography

Today, nearly all digital cameras embed EXIF (exchangeable image file format) information about each image [Chaney 15]. This information contains dozens of parameters from the time the picture was taken, including camera aperture, exposure, GPS location, etc. Recently, the photo-sharing network Flickr marked a shift in how people take pictures, noting that the majority of images being uploaded to their site were now being taken using smartphones. Smartphone cameras have greatly improved in the last few years, introducing higher megapixel counts, better lenses, and since 2010 an option to take HDR images [GSM Arena 15]. Increasing use of such cameras has led to the emerging field of *high dynamic range imaging* (HDRI).

To obtain an HDR image, a smartphone takes multiple images in quick succession with different exposures. The motivation behind taking multiple-exposure images is to obtain detail in over- and underexposed parts of the image, which is often otherwise lost due to a camera's auto gain control. These images are then synthesized and a TMO is applied to render the HDR image on the screen.

HDRI blends several LDR images taken at different exposures highlighting light and dark parts of a scene (as in Figure 4.1). These multiple-exposure images take a varying amount of time to acquire. For example, an overexposed image that brings out detail in the dark parts of an image needs to leave the camera shutter open for longer to allow for more light to get through. Therefore, in order to acquire HDR images of a scene in real time, multiple lenses are needed looking

(a)   (b)

Figure 4.3. HDR look achieved by Topaz Adjust: (a) original image and (b) HDR image.

at the same scene with the use of a beam splitter. Unfortunately, most mobile phones and other handheld cameras do not yet come with the multiple lenses that would be required to acquire multiple-exposure images in real time. For this reason, the HDR TMOs we present in this chapter not only perform well on 32-bit HDR images but also bring out details in a single-exposure LDR image, giving them a HDR look.

Figure 4.3 shows the results of an HDR effect on a single image as obtained by Topaz Adjust, a plug-in for Adobe Photoshop [Topaz Labs 15]. The plugin is able to enhance local gradients that are hard to see in the original image. Furthermore, photographers often manually apply a pseudo-HDR effect on an LDR image to make it more aesthetically pleasing. One way to achieve such a pseudo-HDR effect, as described by Kim Y. Seng [Seng 10], is to create under- and overexposed versions of a well-exposed LDR image. Seng then uses these artificial under- and overexposed images as the basis for creating a 32-bit HDR image before tone-mapping it using a TMO.

4.2.2   Efficient Smartphone Image Processing Pipelines

Currently, most applications running on mobile devices tend to use the CPU, perhaps exploiting SIMD instructions, to run the compute part of the code and use the GPU just for the graphics part, such as compositing and rendering to the screen. However, today's mobile GPUs are now fully programmable compute units in themselves, and through new languages such as OpenCL, or extensions to existing APIs, such as the latest compute shaders in OpenGL, the GPU can also help with the computationally intensive "heavy lifting" required by the application. Using the GPU in this way can result in higher framerates, but there can be more than just a performance advantage from using the GPU for some of the application's computational needs. An experiment carried out by S. Huang et al. to compare the energy consumptions of a single-core CPU, a multicore CPU, and a GPU showed that using the GPU can result in much more energy-efficient computation [Huang et al. 09]. For mobile devices, this energy saving translates into improved battery life, and thus using general-purpose computing on GPUs (GPGPU) has become a hot topic for mobile applications.

One aim of this chapter is to describe an efficient, open source implementation of a pipeline that can be used to capture camera frames and display output of HDR TMOs in real time. The second aim of the example presented in this chapter is to demonstrate an efficient code framework that minimizes the amount of time taken to acquire the camera frames and render the display to output. The pipeline should be such that it can be used for any image-processing application that requires input from a camera and renders the output to a display. This pipeline should also make it possible to create HDR videos.

We present our example pipeline in OpenCL to serve as a real, worked example of how to exploit GPU computing in mobile platforms. We also exploit OpenCL/OpenGL interoperability with the goal of equipping the reader with a working template from which other OpenCL/OpenGL applications can be quickly developed.

4.3   Tone-Mapping Operators

Tone-mapping operators exist for a range of applications. Some TMOs are designed to focus on producing aesthetically pleasing results, while others focus on reproducing as much image detail as possible or maximizing the image contrast. TMOs can be broadly classified into *global* and *local* operators.

Global operators are nonlinear functions that use luminance and other global variables of an input image to obtain a mapping of all the input pixels to the output pixels. Each individual pixel is then mapped in the same way, independent of any neighboring pixels. This spatially uniform characteristic of global TMOs often results in the unfortunate side effect of local contrast reduction. However, because global TMOs are easy to implement and computationally inexpensive (compared to local TMOs), they are prime candidates for use in digital cameras and other handheld devices that might be computationally limited.

Local TMOs have a different mapping for each pixel in the original image. The function used by these operators changes for each pixel depending on the local features of the image. These spatially varying local operators are much slower to compute and harder to implement than global operators and can often result in artifacts in certain areas of the image, making the output look unrealistic. However, if implemented correctly, they generally provide better results than global TMOs, since human vision is mainly sensitive to local contrast.

Figure 4.2 shows the results of applying global and local TMOs to an HDR image obtained by synthesizing the LDR images in Figure 4.1. Even though the global TMO is able to highlight details from each of the exposures, the results of the local TMO are much more aesthetically pleasing, as there is more local contrast in the image.

Reinhard's global TMO. The tonal range of an image describes the number of tones between the lightest and darkest part of the image. Reinhard et al. implemented one of the most widely used global TMOs for HDRI, which computes the tonal range for the output image [Reinhard et al. 02]. This tonal range is computed based on the logarithmic luminance values in the original images.

The algorithm first computes the average logarithmic luminance of the entire image. This average, along with another parameter, is then used to scale the original luminances. Then, to further allow for more global contrast in the image, this approach lets the high luminances often "burn out" by clamping them to pure white. This burning out step is accomplished by computing the smallest luminance value in the original image and then scaling all of the pixels accordingly.

For many HDR images, this operator is sufficient to preserve details in low-contrast areas, while compressing higher luminances to a displayable range. However for very high dynamic range images, especially where there is varying local contrast, important detail can still be lost.

Reinhard's global TMO uses the key value of the scene to set the tonal range for the output image. The key of a scene can be approximated using the logarithmic average luminance $\bar{L}_w$:

$$\bar{L}_w = \exp\left(\frac{1}{N} \sum_{x,y} \log(\delta + L_w(x,y)) \right),$$

where $L_w(x,y)$ is the luminance of pixel (x,y), N is the total number of pixels in the image, and δ is a very small value to avoid taking the logarithm of 0 in case there are pure black pixels in the image. Having approximated the key of the scene, we need to map this to middle-gray. For well-lit images, Reinhard proposes a value of 0.18 as middle-gray on a scale of 0 to 1, giving rise to the following equation:

$$L(x,y) = \frac{a}{\bar{L}_w} L_w(x,y), \tag{4.1}$$

where $L(x,y)$ is the scaled luminance and $a = 0.18$. Just as in film-based photography, if the image has a low key value, we would like to map the middle-gray value, i.e, $\bar{L}_w$, to a high value of a to bring out details in the darker parts of the image. Similarly, if the image has a high key value, we would like to map $\bar{L}_w$ to a lower value of a to get contrast in the lighter parts of the scene. In most natural scenes, occurrences of high luminance values are quite low, whereas the majority of the pixel values have a normal dynamic range. Equation (4.1) doesn't take this into account and scales all the values linearly.

Reinhard's global TMO can now be defined as

$$L_d(x,y) = \frac{L(x,y)\left(1 + \frac{L(x,y)}{L_{\text{white}}^2}\right)}{1 + L(x,y)}, \tag{4.2}$$

where L_{white} is the smallest luminance that we would like to be burnt out. Although L_{white} can be another user-controlled parameter, in this implementation we will set it to the maximum luminance in the image, L_{max}. This will prevent any burn out; however, in cases where $L_{\mathrm{max}} < 1$, this will result in contrast enhancement, as previously discussed.

The operator has a user-controlled parameter, a. This is the key value and refers to the subjective brightness of a scene: the middle-gray value that the scene is mapped to. Essentially, setting a to a high value has an effect of compressing the dynamic range for darker areas, thus allowing more dynamic range for lighter areas and resulting in more contrast over that region. Similarly, decreasing a reduces the dynamic range for lighter areas and shows more contrast in darker parts of a scene. Since the brightness of a scene is very much subjective to the photographer, in this implementation a will be a controllable parameter that can be changed by the user.

The global TMO is one of the most widely implemented TMOs because of its simplicity and effectiveness. It brings out details in low-contrast regions while compressing high luminance values. Furthermore, Equation (4.1) and Equation (4.2) are performed on each pixel independently, and therefore it is fairly straightforward to implement a data parallel version using OpenCL in order to exploit the compute capability of the GPU.

Reinhard's local TMO. Although the global TMO works well in bringing out details in most images, detail is still lost for very high dynamic range images. Reinhard's local TMO proposes a tone reproduction algorithm that aims to emphasize these details by applying *dodging* and *burning*.

Dodging and burning is a technique used in traditional photography that involves restraining light (dodging) or adding more light (burning) to parts of the print during development. Reinhard et al. extended this idea for digital images by automating the process for each pixel depending on its neighborhood. This equates to finding a local key, i.e., a in Equation (4.1), for each pixel, which can then be used to determine the amount of dodging and burning needed for the region. Along with the key value a, the size of each region can also vary depending on the contrast in that area of the image. This size depends on the local contrast of the pixel. To find the optimal size region over which to compute a, Reinhard's approach uses a *center-surround* function at multiple scales. Center-surround functions are often implemented by subtracting two Gaussian blurred images. For this TMO, Reinhard chose to implement the center-surround function proposed for Blommaert's model for brightness perception [Blommaert and Martens 90]. This function is constructed using Gaussian profiles of the form

$$R_i(x, y, s) = \frac{1}{\pi(\alpha_i s)^2} \exp\left(-\frac{x^2 + y^2}{(\alpha_i s)^2}\right).$$

This circularly symmetric profile is constructed for different scales s around each pixel (x, y) in the image. In Bloommaert's center-surround function, the Gaussian profile is then convolved with the image, resulting in response V_i as a function of scale s and luminance $L(x, y)$ for each pixel (x, y):

$$V_i(x, y, s) = L(x, y) \otimes R_i(x, y, s). \qquad (4.3)$$

Because the response requires convolving two functions, it can either be performed in the spatial domain or they can be multiplied in the Fourier domain for improved efficiency. The example HDR GPU pipeline described in this chapter makes use of mipmaps as an alternative to the Gaussian profile. Equation (4.4) is the final building block required for Bloommaert's center-surround function:

$$V(x, y, s) = \frac{V_1(x, y, s) - V_2(x, y, s)}{2^\phi a / s^2 + V_1(x, y, s)}, \qquad (4.4)$$

where V_1 is the center response function and V_2 is the surround response function obtained using Equation (4.3). The $2^\phi a / s^2$ term in the denominator prevents V from getting too large when V_1 approaches zero. The motive behind having V_1 in the denominator is discussed later. Similarly to the global TMO, a is the key value of the scene, φ is a sharpening parameter, and s is the scale used to compute the response function.

The center-surround function expressed in Equation (4.4) is computed over several scales s to find the optimal scale s_m. This equates to finding the suitably sized neighborhood for each pixel, and therefore plays an important role in the dodging-and-burning technique. An ideal-sized neighborhood would have very little contrast changes in the neighborhood itself; however, the area surrounding the neighborhood would have more contrast. The center-surround function computes the difference between the center response V_1 and surround response V_2. For areas with similar luminance values, these will be much the same, however they will differ in higher-contrast regions. Starting at the lowest scale, the local TMO selects the first scale s_m such that

$$|V(x, y, s_m)| < \epsilon, \qquad (4.5)$$

where ε is a user controlled parameter, which we set to 0.05 in our implementation. Equation (4.5) amounts to finding the largest neighborhood around a pixel such that the luminance in the center area is fairly even. Note that $V_1(x, y, s)$ can serve as a local neighborhood average for that pixel. Therefore, this local logarithmic average luminance can be used in place of the global one in Equation (4.2):

$$L_d(x, y) = \frac{L(x, y)}{1 + V_1(x, y, s_m)}. \qquad (4.6)$$

A dark pixel in a relatively bright area will satisfy $L < V_1$. In such cases, Equation (4.6) will decrease the L_d of that pixel, which will have the effect of contrast enhancement in that area. Similarly, if a pixel is light in a relatively dark area $(L > V_1)$, the local TMO will increase L_d.

$V_1(x, y, s_m)$ plays an important part in controlling the right amount of local contrast in the image. This boils down to choosing the right s_m for each pixel. If s_m is too small, then V_1 will be close to L and Equation (4.6) will reduce to the global operator. However, if s_m is too large, then the resulting tone-mapped image will have halo artifacts around the bright regions.

The set of scale sizes to check can be predetermined. Reinhard's method does not suggest any particular set of scales; however, the implementation proposed by Akyuz [Akyüz 12] suggests using the scale set $\{1, 2, 4, 8, 16, 32, 64\}$. To find the optimal scale s_m, we start from the smallest scale and compute center and surround responses individually for each. To make the algorithm computationally efficient, Reinhard's method suggests setting the center size of the next higher scale to be the size of the current surround. It further suggests maintaining the ratio of 1.6 between the center and surround size; however, since mipmaps are used in this implementation, the next level mipmap can simply be set as the surround.

Just as for the global operator, a is still a user-controlled variable allowing the photographer to obtain more contrast for either dark or light parts of the scene while decreasing the contrast in the other. The local TMO comes with a few more parameters, namely φ and ε. In Equation (4.5), ε serves as a threshold to find the suitable scale s_m for the pixel neighborhood. A small ε causes s_m to be larger and hence results in an increased contrast in the overall image, since there is more contrast at larger scales than smaller ones. On the other hand, φ serves as an edge-enhancing parameter. Increasing φ has more or less the same effects as that of decreasing ε. However, the effects are only noticeable at smaller scales since φ is divided by s^2.

Reinhard's local TMO makes use of traditional photographic techniques to enhance contrast in digital images. The concept behind the local and global operators is more or less the same; however, the local TMO uses information in the pixel's neighborhood to find the suitable "local key" and use that to scale the pixel's luminance. The local TMO is inherently much more compute-intensive due to multiple convolutions required for each pixel to find the suitable neighborhood. This makes the local TMO much more challenging to implement in real time. In this implementation, to minimize the computation required, mipmaps are generated at multiple levels using the OpenGL API instead of using the more compute-intensive Gaussian kernel approach.

Histogram equalization. Contrast enhancement using histogram equalization is one simple way of increasing the global contrast of many images, especially when there isn't much variance between the luminance values in those images. Histogram equalization essentially spreads these densely populated values over the entire luminance range (usually 8-bit), increasing the contrast in low-contrast areas.

The algorithm computes a histogram of the luminance values for an image, calculates its cumulative distribution function (CDF), and then replaces the original histogram with the flattened version of the CDF. The histogram will then have luminance values uniformly distributed over the entire range [UCI iCAMP 10].

Histogram equalization is not an HDR TMO; however, it can be computationally expensive. We include an example of this technique in source code accompanying this chapter (available on the CRC Press website) to demonstrate that our framework is not just limited to HDRI TMOs.

4.4 Related Work

The LDR of cameras has inspired many solutions to produce TMOs for HDR images in recent years. J. Kuang et al. performed a study to compare several existing HDR rendering algorithms [Kuang et al. 07]. In their study, they implemented nine different algorithms and carried out psychophysical experiments whereby they required human observers to evaluate the rendered image. Their results could be useful when selecting an HDR algorithm to implement based solely on the output image. However, the paper does not provide a comparative performance analysis between techniques. In this chapter, we will show results from implementations of several TMOs and compare their performance on various GPUs.

Sing Bing Kang et al. proposed a method to generate an HDR video by taking multiple-exposure images in quick succession [Kang et al. 03]. They did this by automatically determining the temporal exposure bracketing during capture, motion-compensating information between neighboring images, and tone mapping for viewing the results. We take a different approach in this chapter, as we will focus on processing single-exposure images as opposed to multiple images of different exposures. The technique presented by Kang et al. is quite effective, however the frame rate is limited by the rate at which the camera can vary exposures. Motion between exposures can become a problem, and so Kang's method required an algorithm to account for motion between the images. Their implementation was too slow for real-time image processing.

TMOs, in particular local operators, are computationally expensive and therefore currently require a GPU implementation to be able to operate in real time. There have been several proposed real-time implementations of Reinhard's global and local TMOs [Akyüz 12, Krawczyk et al. 05, Chiu et al. 11, Kiser et al. 12]. However, the real-time OpenGL implementation proposed by Akyuz in [Akyüz 12] is most relevant to this research topic. Akyuz presented an HDRI pipeline on the GPU for Reinhard's global and local TMOs. Although the implementation is in OpenGL (as opposed to OpenCL), it provides an insight on how the algorithm can be modified for a GPGPU implementation. We can also use the results from

Akyuz's work as an efficiency benchmark for the OpenCL implementation we present in this chapter.

Perhaps the most closely related work to ours is that by Chris McClanahan [McClanahan 11]. McClanahan created a Linux and Android application that uses a single video camera to create tone-mapped HDR images in real time. The implementation uses OpenCV and OpenMP but does not appear to include a GPGPU implementation. Furthermore, the frame rate of the Linux implementation is very low, even on low-resolution images. Nevertheless, McClanahan's work provides a benchmark against which we can compare.

4.5 GPGPU Using OpenCL

Traditionally, a GPU was designed for one task: speeding up the processing of an image that ends up being rendered to a screen. Today's GPUs are now highly data parallel computational engines, making them really good at performing the same calculation over and over on different data.

Upon evaluating the HDR TMO discussed in this chapter, it should be obvious that often similar operations are applied on each individual pixel in the image. Therefore, these algorithms should benefit from being executed on a GPU. However, in order to take advantage of the highly concurrent nature of a GPU, the algorithms have to be programmed to take advantage of it. Implementing algorithms in such a way is called general purpose computing on GPUs (GPGPU).

This brings us nicely to OpenCL (Open Computing Language). OpenCL is a cross-platform open standard for parallel programming across different kinds of hardware, and can target both CPUs and GPUs, and from embedded SoCs to high-end desktop, workstation, and server GPUs. The framework is standardized by the Khronos Group, which includes ARM, Imagination, Qualcomm, AMD, Intel, NVIDIA, IBM, Samsung, Apple, and most of the other vendors in the CPU/GPU space.

OpenCL 1.0 was released in late 2008, and support by multiple CPU and GPU vendors appeared by mid-2009. Since its initial release, OpenCL has evolved rapidly through two minor releases (OpenCL 1.1 in 2010 and 1.2 in 2011) and a major OpenCL 2.0 release in late 2013. The rapid pace of evolution in the OpenCL standard is challenging for programmers to track and absorb. These modifications to the standard have been necessary, due to the rapid pace of evolution in computer hardware.

This section will now focus on the core features of OpenCL—those that have not changed much since the introduction of the first standard. We explain OpenCL in terms of its key models:

- platform model,

- execution model,

- memory model.

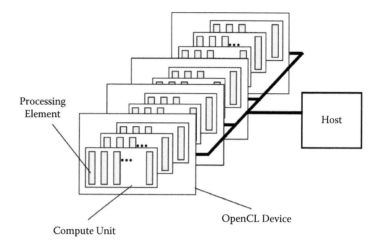

Figure 4.4. The OpenCL platform model with a single host and multiple devices. Each device has one or more compute units, each of which has one or more processing elements.

The *platform* model is presented in Figure 4.4 and consists of a host and one or more devices. The *host* is a familiar CPU-based system supporting file I/O, user interaction, and other functions expected of a system. The *devices* are where the bulk of the computing takes place in an OpenCL program. Example devices include GPUs, many-core coprocessors, and other devices specialized to carry out the OpenCL computations. A device consists of one or more compute units (CUs) each of which presents the programmer with one or more processing elements (PEs). These processing elements are the finest-grained units of computation within an OpenCL program.

The platform model gives programmers a view of the hardware they can use when optimizing their OpenCL programs. Then, by understanding how the platform model maps onto different target platforms, programmers can optimize their software without sacrificing portability.

OpenCL programs execute as a fine-grained SPMD (single program, multiple data) model. The central ideal behind OpenCL is to define an index space of one, two, or three dimensions. Programmers map their problem onto the indices of this space and define a block of code, called a *kernel*, an instance of which runs at each point in the index space.

Consider the matrix multiplication OpenCL kernel in Listing 4.1. Here we have mapped the outermost two loops of the traditional sequential code onto a 2D index space and run the innermost loop (over k) within a kernel function. We then ran an instance of this kernel function, called a *work item* in OpenCL terminology, for each point in the index space.

```
__kernel void mat_mul(const unsigned int Order ,
                      __global const float *A,
                      __global const float *B,
                      __global       float *C)
{
  int i, j, k;
  i = get_global_id(0);
  j = get_global_id(1);
  for (k = 0; k < Order; k++)
    C[i*Order+j] += A[i*Order+k] * B[k*Order+j];
}
```

Listing 4.1. A parallel matrix multiply as an OpenCL kernel.

A more detailed view of how an OpenCL program executes is provided in
Figure 4.5, which summarizes the OpenCL *execution* model. The global index
space, in this case two dimensions each of size 16, implies a set of work items that
execute a kernel instance at each point. These work items are grouped together
into blocks with the same shape as the global index space. Blocks of work items,
called *work groups*, cover the full index space.

Logically, the work items in a single work group run together. Hence, they
can synchronize their execution and share memory in the course of their computation. This is not the case, however, for the work groups. There are no ordering
constraints among the work groups of a single kernel instance; hence, there are
no synchronization constructs among work groups. This limitation has important implications for sharing data, which we will cover as part of the memory
hierarchy discussion.

To a programmer used to the flexibility of programming with threads (e.g.,
Pthreads, Java threads, etc.), these restrictions on synchronization may seem
onerous. They were included in the OpenCL execution model, however, for a good
reason. OpenCL is designed for high-throughput parallel computing typically
associated with highly data parallel algorithms. High performance is achieved
by creating a large internal work pool of work groups that are ready to execute.
A scheduler can then stream these runnable work groups through the compute
units of a device to keep them fully occupied.

Because compute devices such as GPUs may have their own discrete memories,
a heterogeneous platform often cannot provide a single coherent address space.
The *memory* model in OpenCL, therefore, takes this into account by defining
how the memory in OpenCL is decomposed into different address spaces aligned
with the platform model. We present this concept in Figure 4.6.

Starting at the bottom of Figure 4.6, consider the host memory. As the name
implies, *host memory* is defined by the host and only directly visible to the host
(although this is relaxed in OpenCL 2.0). The next layer in the memory hierarchy
is the *global memory*, which includes a read-only memory segment called the

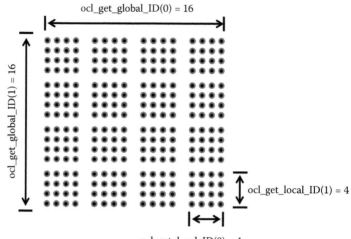

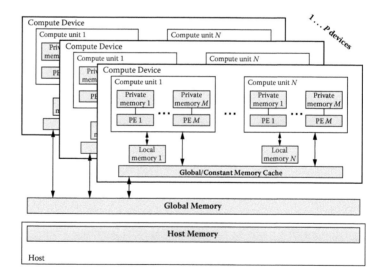

Figure 4.5. A problem is decomposed onto the points of an N-dimensional index space ($N = 1$, 2, or 3), known in OpenCL as an NDRange. A kernel instance runs at each point in the NDRange to define a work item. Work items are grouped together into work groups, which evenly tile the full index space.

Figure 4.6. The memory model in OpenCL 1.X and its relationship to the platform model. Here, P devices exist in a single context and therefore have visibility into the global/constant memory.

constant memory. Global and constant memories hold OpenCL memory objects and are visible to all the OpenCL devices involved in a computation (i.e., within the context defined by the programmer). The onboard DRAM of a discrete GPU or FPGA will typically be mapped as global memory. It is worth noting that, for discrete devices, moving data between host memory and global memory usually requires transferring data across a bus, such as PCI Express, which can be relatively slow.

Within an OpenCL device, each compute unit has a region of memory local to the compute unit called *local memory*. This local memory is visible only to the processing elements within the compute unit, which maps nicely onto the OpenCL execution model, with one or more work groups running on a compute unit and one or more work items running on a processing element. The local memory within a compute unit corresponds to data that can be shared inside a work group. The final part of the OpenCL memory hierarchy is *private memory*, which defines a small amount of per work-item memory visible only within a work item.

Another important OpenCL buffer type for any application that wants to mix OpenCL and OpenGL functionality, is the *textured images* buffer. These are available in 2D and 3D and are a global memory object optimized for image processing, supporting multiple image formats and channels. There is a one-to-one correspondence between an OpenCL textured image and certain OpenGL textures. In fact, as discussed later, this correspondence can be taken advantage of to optimize the framework we will present in this chapter.

Data movement among the layers in the memory hierarchy in OpenCL is explicit—that is, the user is responsible for the transfer of data from host memory to global memory and so on. Commands in the OpenCL API and kernel programming language must be used to move data from host memory to global memory, and from global memory to either local or private memory.

4.6 OpenGL ES and Android

OpenGL is a "cross-platform graphics API that specifies a standard software interface for 3D graphics processing hardware" [Android 15]. OpenGL ES is a subset of the OpenGL specification intended for embedded devices. Although a powerful API in itself, the main use of OpenGL ES in the implemented Android version of our HDR framework is to provide image acquisition and to render the output of our OpenCL TMO kernels to the display. All of the manipulation of the images in our example framework is performed by OpenCL kernels.

4.6.1 OpenCL and OpenGL Interoperability

One of the main hurdles in achieving a real-time implementation of an Android pipeline to process and render camera images is the transfer of image data to and from the GPU's memory. Although the camera input is stored on the GPU, existing image-processing applications tend to transfer the data to the host device (the CPU), where they serially process the data and render it to the display using OpenGL. Clearly this process can cause several inefficient transfers of data back and forth between the CPU and GPU.

What is required is an approach that avoids any unnecessary memory transfers between the GPU's memory and the host's memory. OpenCL/OpenGL interoperability supports this approach. Input from the camera can be acquired in the form of an OpenGL ES texture using Android's `SurfaceTexture` object. OpenCL then allows a programmer to create a textured image from an OpenGL texture, which means that the camera data doesn't need to be transferred to the host, instead staying resident in the GPU from image acquisition all the way to rendering the output of the OpenCL kernels to the screen. Furthermore, even on the GPU, the data doesn't actually move as we switch between OpenCL and OpenGL; instead it just changes ownership from OpenGL to OpenCL and back again. To achieve this pipeline, interoperability between OpenCL and OpenGL ES needs to be established.

4.6.2   EGL

To enable OpenCL and OpenGL ES interoperability, the OpenCL context must be initialized using the current display and context being used by OpenGL ES. OpenGL ES contexts are created and managed by platform-specific windowing APIs. EGL is an interface between OpenGL ES and the underlying windowing system, somewhat akin to GLX, the X11 interface to OpenGL with which many readers might already be familiar.

To avoid unnecessary use of memory bandwidth, the implementation makes use of OpenGL ES to bind the input from the camera to a texture. An OpenGL ES display and context is then created by acquiring a handle to the Android Surface. The context and display are then used to create a shared OpenCL context. This shared context allows OpenCL to have access to the camera texture and therefore to perform computations upon it. Because the Android OS has only recently included support for such APIs, to date not many examples have appeared in this area.

4.7   Implementing an HDR Pipeline Using OpenCL and OpenGL ES

TMOs work best on a 32-bit HDR image obtained by synthesizing multiple LDR images of various exposures. The 32-bit HDR image is then processed to obtain an 8-bit HDR image that combines details from each of the original LDR images.

To achieve a real-time implementation of the HDRI pipeline, multiple cameras are required, with each capturing a different-exposure image and therefore capturing the full dynamic range of the scene among them. However, as discussed earlier, since we are aiming for an implementation on a smartphone with a single camera, we will only have single-exposure images available to us as input for our real-time pipeline. This section discusses the design and implementation details of a GPU pipeline using OpenCL to achieve an HDR look on single-exposure images.

For the example HDR pipeline presented in the rest of this chapter, we used OpenCL v1.1, since this version is supported by all mobile GPU vendors at the time of writing. We also used OpenGL ES 4.2 since this is the version of GL currently supported by the Android OS. We have also written the code in C/C++ in order to achieve the best performance possible (OpenCL/GL bindings for Java, Python, etc. exist, but would not have given the necessary performance).

4.7.1 Pseudo-HDR Pipeline with Image Synthesis

Multiple-exposure images are a set of under- and overexposed LDR images highlighting details in bright and dark regions of a scene, respectively. It's common practice to adjust an image's brightness and contrast to highlight its dark or bright regions. Since here we are limited to using a single-exposure image as the input for our process, we can use a set of such adjusted images as inputs to the pseudo-HDR pipeline.

This is a commonly used approach. For example, Seng manually created a set of over- and underexposed images from a single RAW image using Photomatix [Seng 10]. He then used Photomatix's HDR feature to synthesize and tone-map the pseudo-underexposed and pseudo-overexposed images to create a pseudo-HDR image. This section discusses how this method can be automated. Figure 4.7 shows the modified pipeline to obtain a pseudo-HDR image using single-exposure images.

Step 1: Contrast adjustment. To employ Seng's method for our psuedo-HDR pipeline, we first need to create multiple-exposure images by adjusting the contrast of a well-exposed original image. Here we create multiple images such that each output image brings out details in a certain dynamic range. For our purposes, we used Photomatix to create the under- and overexposed versions of our original input image.

Step 2: Image synthesis. To obtain an HDR image, the multiple-exposure LDR images of a scene are first synthesized. An HDR pixel I_j can be obtained as follows:

$$I_j = \frac{\sum_{i=1}^{N} \frac{p_{ij} w(p_{ij})}{t_i}}{\sum_{i=1}^{N} w(p_{ij})}, \tag{4.7}$$

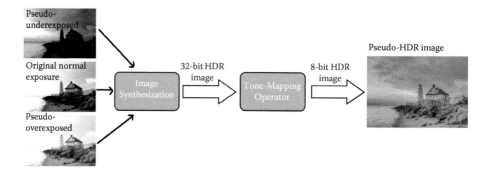

Figure 4.7. Pseudo-HDR pipeline that takes multiple input images with a range of contrasts.

where N is the number of LDR images, $w(p_{ij})$ is the weight of pixel ij, and t_i is the exposure time of the LDR image i.

The serial implementation of Equation (4.7) is straightforward and is therefore not presented here. The algorithm simply iterates over each pixel, computes its luminance and weight, and uses those with the image exposure to calculate the 32-bit HDR pixel color.

Clearly the calculation of each pixel is independent of all the others, and so this natural data parallelism is ideal for a GPU implementation.

Listing 4.2 shows the OpenCL kernel implemented for the image synthesis process. Since the number of LDR images can vary, the kernel is passed a 1D array, `LDRimages`, containing all the images. The 1D array is of type `unsigned char`, which is sufficient to store each 8-bit color value per pixel.

The `if` statement on line 10 ensures that the work items don't access out-of-bound memory. The `for` loop on line 14 uses Equation (4.7) to synthesize the LDR pixels from different images into an HDR pixel. Once an HDR pixel is calculated, it is stored in the 1D array `HDRimage`. The array `HDRimage` is of type `float`, which is sufficient to store the higher dynamic range of the pixel.

Step 3: Automating contrast adjustment. We now have a 32-bit HDR image. The three tone-mapping algorithms we have previously described can now be used to tone map the 32-bit HDR image, producing an 8-bit HDR image that can be rendered on most displays. Their implementation is discussed in more detail later on in this chapter.

4.7.2   HDR Tone-Mapping Operators

This section will describe the OpenCL implementations of the three tone-mapping algorithms.

```
1  //LDRimages contains num_images LDR images
2  //exposures contains num_images exposures, one for each LDR image
3  //HDRimage is the output synthesised 32-bit image.
4  kernel void stitch( __global uchar* LDRimages,
5              __global float* exposures,
6              __global float* HDRimage) {
7
8     int gid = get_global_id(0); //ID in the entire global memory
9
10    if (gid < IMAGE_SIZE) {
11       float weightedSum = 0;
12       float3 hdr, ldr;
13       hdr.x = hdr.y = hdr.z = 0;
14       for (int i=0; i < NUM_IMAGES; i++) {
15          ldr.x = LDRimages[i*IMAGE_SIZE*4 + (gid*4 + 0)];
16          ldr.y = LDRimages[i*IMAGE_SIZE*4 + (gid*4 + 1)];
17          ldr.z = LDRimages[i*IMAGE_SIZE*4 + (gid*4 + 2)];
18
19          float luminance = getPixelLuminance(ldr);
20          float w = weight(luminance);
21          float exposure = exposures[i];
22
23          hdr.x += (ldr.x/exposure) * w;
24          hdr.y += (ldr.y/exposure) * w;
25          hdr.z += (ldr.z/exposure) * w;
26
27          weightedSum += w;
28       }
29
30       HDRimage[gid*4 + 0] = hdr.x/(weightedSum + 0.000001);
31       HDRimage[gid*4 + 1] = hdr.y/(weightedSum + 0.000001);
32       HDRimage[gid*4 + 2] = hdr.z/(weightedSum + 0.000001);
33       HDRimage[gid*4 + 3] = getPixelLuminance(hdr);
34    }
35 }
```

Listing 4.2. OpenCL kernel for image synthesis.

Histogram equalization. The histogram equalization algorithm first computes the brightness histogram of the image. A cumulative distribution function (CDF) of the histogram is then created, which in turn is used to create a new set of brightness values for the image. This process requires several steps, described below.

Brightness histogram. In OpenCL, writes to global memory cannot be synchronized between work items in different work groups. Therefore, a global histogram array can't be used to accumulate the results, as it would result in race conditions between work items. Instead, local histogram arrays are used—one for each work group. The results of these per-work-group histograms are written to global memory, which are then safely merged together into a single histogram by a separate kernel.

The code to perform this partial histogram is included in Listing 4.3 (see kernels partial_hist and merge_hist). These take an LDR image as an

```
 1 const sampler_t sampler = CLK_NORMALIZED_COORDS_FALSE | ↵
       CLK_ADDRESS_NONE | CLK_FILTER_NEAREST;
 2
 3 //Kernel to perform histogram equalization using the modified
 4 //brightness CDF
 5 kernel void histogram_equalisation( read_only image2d_t ↵
       input_image ,
 6                       write_only image2d_t output_image ,
 7                       __global uint* brightness_cdf ) {
 8   int2 pos;
 9   uint4 pixel;
10   float3 hsv;
11   for (pos.y = get_global_id(1); pos.y < HEIGHT; pos.y += ↵
         get_global_size(1)) {
12     for (pos.x = get_global_id(0); pos.x < WIDTH; pos.x += ↵
           get_global_size(0)) {
13       pixel = read_imageui(image , sampler , pos);
14
15       hsv = RGBtoHSV(pixel);   //Convert to HSV to get hue and
16                                //saturation
17
18       hsv.z = ((HIST_SIZE −1)*(brightness_cdf [(int)hsv.z] − ↵
             brightness_cdf [0]))
19             /(HEIGHT*WIDTH − brightness_cdf [0]);
20
21       pixel = HSVtoRGB(hsv);   //Convert back to RGB with the
22                                //modified brightness for V
23
24       write_imageui(output_image , pos , pixel);
25     }
26   }
27 }
```

Listing 4.3. OpenCL kernel to equalize the image histogram.

input and, allocating one pixel to each work item, compute the brightness value for each pixel. Once the brightness value is computed, the index corresponding to that value is incremented in the local histogram array l_hist. To ensure correct synchronization among different work items, a barrier call is made just before writing to the shared l_hist array. Once the l_hist array has been modified, the results are written to the global partial histogram array. The merge_hist kernel then merges the partial histograms together. This kernel is executed with global size of 256, so as to have a one-to-one correspondence between the work items and the indices of the image histogram. For this last kernel, each work item computes the sum over all the partial histograms for the index value corresponding to the work item's ID. Once the sum is computed, the final histogram value for this work item is then set to this sum.

Cumulative distribution function. Computing the cumulative distribution function is an operation that is not so well suited for GPGPU, due to the sequential nature of the algorithm required to compute it. Several OpenCL SDKs provide implementations of a parallel scan, which can be used to compute the cumulative distribution function of a histogram. However, since the histogram is only of size 256, it is not very computationally expensive to compute this sequentially.

Histogram equalization. Once the CDF of the original histogram has been computed, it can be used to compute new brightness values for each pixel; see Listing 4.3. Once the RGB pixel is obtained from the image using an OpenCL image sampler, it is converted to HSV format on line 14. Using the formulation discussed earlier, we then compute the equalized brightness value for this pixel. The HSV value with the modified V is then converted to RGB on line 19, before the results are written to the image.

Unlike previous kernels, this kernel is executed in 2D. This is because the output image is a textured 2D image as opposed to a 1D buffer.

4.7.3 Reinhard Global Tone-Mapping Operator

Reinhard's global TMO iterates over the entire image twice, once to compute $L_{\max}$ and $\bar{L}_w$ and a second time to adjust each pixel according to these values and the key value (a) of the scene.

Computing $L_{\max}$ and $\bar{L}_w$. As discussed previously, the $L_{\max}$ of a scene is the largest luminance value, whereas $\bar{L}_w$ is the average logarithmic luminance of a scene. Calculating these values serially is straightforward; however, to obtain them using an OpenCL kernel, we will need to perform a reduction over the entire image. As described in [Catanzaro 10], the fastest way to perform a reduction is in a two-stage process. Here, each work item i performs reduction operations over the following array indices:

$$\{i + n \times \texttt{global\_size} | i + n \times \texttt{global\_size} < \texttt{array\_size}\}, \forall n \in N.$$

The result from this equation is then stored in the local array, and reduction is then performed over this local array. The output of this stage of the reduction is one partial reduction value for each work group. The second stage of the two-stage reduction requires execution of a separate kernel, which simply performs reduction over these partial results.

The input image to the kernel is a 2D texture image, therefore it's natural to want to run this kernel in 2D. However, this requires implementing a novel 2D version of the above two-stage reduction. The main difference is that now each work item (x, y) performs reduction operations over the image pixels at positions:

$$\{(x + m \times gx, y + n \times gy) \mid (x + m \times gx, y + n \times gy) < (\texttt{imagewidth}, \texttt{imageheight})\},$$
$$\forall m, n \in N,$$

where gx and gy are the global sizes in the x and y dimensions, respectively.

```
 1 const sampler_t sampler = CLK_NORMALIZED_COORDS_FALSE | ←
     CLK_ADDRESS_NONE | CLK_FILTER_NEAREST ;
 2
 3 //This kernel computes logAvgLum by performing reduction
 4 //The results are stored in an array of size num_work_groups
 5 kernel void computeLogAvgLum (    __read_only image2d_t image ,
 6                  __global float* lum ,
 7                  __global float* logAvgLum ,
 8                  __local float* logAvgLum_loc ) {
 9
10    float lum0 ;
11    float logAvgLum_acc = 0.f ;
12
13    int2 pos ;
14    uint4 pixel ;
15    for (pos.y = get_global_id (1); pos.y < HEIGHT; pos.y += ←
        get_global_size (1)) {
16       for (pos.x = get_global_id (0); pos.x < WIDTH; pos.x += ←
           get_global_size (0)) {
17          pixel = read_imageui (image , sampler , pos) ;
18          //lum0 = pixel.x * 0.2126f + pixel.y * 0.7152f + pixel.z * ←
              0.0722f ;
19          lum0 = dot(GLtoCL(pixel.xyz) , (float3)(0.2126f , 0.7152f , ←
              0.0722f)) ;
20
21          logAvgLum_acc += log(lum0 + 0.000001 f) ;
22          lum[pos.x + pos.y*WIDTH] = lum0 ;
23       }
24    }
25
26    pos.x = get_local_id (0) ;
27    pos.y = get_local_id (1) ;
28    const int lid = pos.x + pos.y*get_local_size (0) ;  //Local ID in
29                                                 //one dimension
30    logAvgLum_loc [lid] = logAvgLum_acc ;
31
32    //Perform parallel reduction
33    barrier(CLK_LOCAL_MEM_FENCE ) ;
34
35    for(int offset = (get_local_size (0)*get_local_size (1))/2; offset←
        > 0; offset = offset/2) {
36       if (lid < offset) {
37          logAvgLum_loc [lid] += logAvgLum_loc [lid + offset] ;
38       }
39       barrier(CLK_LOCAL_MEM_FENCE ) ;
40    }
41
42    //Number of workgroups in x dim
43    const int num_work_groups = get_global_size (0)/get_local_size (0)←
        ;
44    const int group_id = get_group_id (0) + get_group_id (1)*←
        num_work_groups ;
45    if (lid == 0) {
46       logAvgLum [group_id] = logAvgLum_loc [0] ;
47    }
48 }
```

Listing 4.4. OpenCL kernel to compute L_{max} and $\bar{L}_w$.

The 2D kernel used to compute such a reduction is shown in Listing 4.4. As described above, first each work item (x, y) computes the sum and maximum of luminances over a range of image pixels (line 17–25). This sum and maximum is then stored in local arrays at an index corresponding to the pixel's position. A wave-front reduction is then performed over these local arrays (lines 36–42), and the result is then stored in the global array for each work group. The `finalReduc` kernel is then used to perform reduction over the partial results, where `num_reduc_bins` is the number of work groups in the execution of the `computeLogAvgLum` kernel. Once the sum over all the luminance values is computed, we take its average and calculate its exponential.

Once we have calculated $L_{\max}$ and $\bar{L}_w$, these values are plugged into Equation (4.7), with $L(x,y) = L_w(x,y)\frac{a}{\bar{L}_w}$, $L_{\text{white}} = L_{\max}$, and $L_w(x,y)$, the luminance of pixel (x,y). Once the values of $L_{\max}$ and $\bar{L}_w$ have been computed, the rest of the computation is fully data parallel, thus benefitting from a GPGPU implementation. Due to limited space, the OpenCL kernel is not presented here as it only requires a simple modification of the serial implementation. The code can be found in the example pipeline source code accompanying this chapter (available on the CRC Press website) .

4.7.4 Reinhard Local Tone-Mapping Operator

Reinhard's local TMO is similar to the global TMO in that it also computes the average logarithmic luminance of the entire image. To do this, the `computeLogAvgLum` and `finalReduc` kernels used for Reinhard's global TMO are modified so that they do not compute $L_{\max}$. Instead, the local TMO computes the average logarithmic luminance over various-sized neighborhoods for each pixel. For greater performance, these kernels are all fused together into one master kernel called `reinhardLocal`, as shown in Listing 4.5.

```
1 const sampler_t sampler = CLK_NORMALIZED_COORDS_FALSE | ←
      CLK_ADDRESS_NONE | CLK_FILTER_NEAREST;
2
3 //Computes the mapping for each pixel as per Reinhard's Local TMO
4 kernel void reinhardLocal( __read_only image2d_t input_image,
5                            __write_only image2d_t output_image,
6                            __global float* lumMips,
7                            __global int* m_width,
8                            __global int* m_offset,
9                            __global float* logAvgLum_acc) {
10
11    float factor = logAvgLum_acc[0];
12
13    //Assumes Phi is 8.0
14    constant float k[7] = {
15       256.f * KEY / ( 1.f*1.f ),
16       256.f * KEY / ( 2.f*2.f ),
17       256.f * KEY / ( 4.f*4.f ),
18       256.f * KEY / ( 8.f*8.f ),
19       256.f * KEY / (16.f*16.f),
20       256.f * KEY / (32.f*32.f),
21       256.f * KEY / (64.f*64.f)
22    };
```

```
23
24 int2 pos, centre_pos, surround_pos;
25 for (pos.y = get_global_id(1); pos.y < HEIGHT; pos.y += ↵
       get_global_size(1)) {
26   for (pos.x = get_global_id(0); pos.x < WIDTH; pos.x += ↵
         get_global_size(0)) {
27     surround_pos = pos;
28     float local_logAvgLum = 0.f;
29     for (uint i = 0; i < NUM_MIPMAPS -1; i++) {
30       centre_pos = surround_pos;
31       surround_pos = centre_pos /2;
32
33       int2 m_width_01, m_offset_01;
34       m_width_01  = vload2(0, &m_width[i]);
35       m_offset_01 = vload2(0, &m_offset[i]);
36
37       int2 index_01 = m_offset_01 + (int2)(centre_pos.x, ↵
           surround_pos.x);
38       index_01 += m_width_01 * (int2)(centre_pos.y, surround_pos↵
           .y);
39
40       float2 lumMips_01 = factor;
41       lumMips_01 *= (float2)(lumMips[index_01.s0], lumMips[↵
           index_01.s1]);
42
43       float centre_logAvgLum, surround_logAvgLum;
44       centre_logAvgLum   = lumMips_01.s0;
45       surround_logAvgLum = lumMips_01.s1;
46
47       float cs_diff = fabs(centre_logAvgLum - surround_logAvgLum↵
           );
48       if (cs_diff > (k[i] + centre_logAvgLum) * EPSILON) {
49         local_logAvgLum = centre_logAvgLum;
50         break;
51       } else {
52         local_logAvgLum = surround_logAvgLum;
53       }
54     }
55
56     uint4 pixel = read_imageui(input_image, sampler, pos);
57
58     float3 rgb = GLtoCL(pixel.xyz);
59     float3 xyz = RGBtoXYZ(rgb);
60
61     float Ld  = factor / (1.f + local_logAvgLum) * xyz.y;
62     pixel.xyz = convert_uint3((float3)255.f * \
63       clamp((pow(rgb.xyz/xyz.y, (float3)SAT)*(float3)Ld), 0.f, ↵
           1.f));
64
65     write_imageui(output_image, pos, pixel);
66   }
67 }
68 }
```

Listing 4.5. OpenCL kernels for Reinhard's local tone-mapping operator.

Computing HDR luminance. To recap, for each pixel the local TMO creates a Gaussian kernel to compute the average logarithmic luminance in a neighborhood. However, Gaussian kernels are expensive to compute, therefore this implementation makes use of OpenGL mipmaps.

Mipmaps of the luminance values are created at different scales and then used as an approximation to the average luminance value at that scale. Using OpenGL's API, mipmaps up to Level 7 are computed. The `reinhardLocal` kernel in Listing 4.5 gets passed these seven mipmaps in the array `lumMips`. The `for` loop on line 29 is the core of this TMO. Each mipmap is iterated over to obtain the average logarithmic luminance at that scale. Lines 37 to 45 compute the center and surround functions V_1 and V_2 used in Equation (4.4). Lines 47 to 53 compute V as in Equation (4.4) and checks whether it is less than ε (Equation (4.5)) to determine the appropriate average logarithmic luminance, $V_1(x, y, s_m)$, for that pixel. Once the optimal center function V_1 is computed, the remaining code implements Equation (4.6) to obtain the HDR luminance for that pixel.

Writing to output. Having computed the HDR luminance array L_d, the local tone-map kernel simply modifies the luminance values to reflect the new dynamic range. We first obtain the original RGB pixel, convert it to (x, y, z), modify its luminance, and convert it back to RGB.

4.8 Android Implementation

One of the contributions of this chapter is the fully working Android Open-CL/OpenGL pipeline, which we will describe in this section. The overall aim of the pipeline is to acquire camera frames, process them in OpenCL, and render the output to the screen using OpenGL. Ideally, the pipeline should be fast enough to allow for real-time image processing. This means that the time between acquiring a camera frame and passing it to OpenCL should be negligible. Our example pipeline achieves this by avoiding the image transfer between the GPU and the host by using OpenCL/OpenGL interoperability. Using this approach, the camera texture is kept on the GPU, and just before the OpenCL kernels are executed, the ownership of the texture is transferred to OpenCL.

To achieve OpenCL–OpenGL interoperability, an OpenCL context must first be initialized using the current OpenGL context as per the OpenCL specification. Then, OpenCL memory objects are created using the OpenGL data objects. Just before enqueing the OpenCL kernels, the ownership of the data objects is passed from OpenGL to OpenCL. Once the OpenCL kernels are executed, the OpenGL objects can be released so that they can be used as the basis for rendering. This section discusses the implementation details of this pipeline.

Java Native Interactive. Our example Android application is written in Java; however, the OpenCL kernel execution code is in C++ for performance reasons. Therefore, to call various C++ functions from the Android application we make use of the Java Native Interface (JNI).

OpenCL. To enable OpenCL and OpenGL ES interoperability, the OpenCL context must be initialized using the current display and context being used by

OpenGL ES. OpenGL ES contexts on Android are created and managed by EGL, the previously described interface between OpenGL ES and the underlying windowing system. Therefore, to create an OpenCL context for interoperability, the properties array must be initialized such that it holds the EGL context and display.

There are two classes in the Android framework API that allow a developer to create and manipulate graphics with the OpenGL ES API: `GLSurfaceView` and `GLSurfaceView.Renderer`.

GLSurfaceView. This class provides a canvas where we can draw and manipulate objects using OpenGL ES API calls. More importantly, `GLSurfaceView` manages an EGL display that enables OpenGL ES to render onto a surface. Therefore, by using `GLSurfaceView`, we don't have to worry about managing the EGL windowing life cycle.

GLSurfaceView.Renderer. This defines the methods required for drawing graphics in `GLSurfaceView`. When `GLSurfaceView` is instantiated, it must be provided with a renderer class that extends `GLSurfaceView.Renderer`. This is further discussed later on in the chapter.

OpenCL texture image. After the OpenCL context has been successfully initialized, OpenCL image textures can be created for the kernels from the camera input.

Convert GL_TEXTURE_EXTERNAL_OES to GL_TEXTURE_2D. A `SurfaceTexture` object can be used to capture frames from the camera as an OpenGL ES texture. The `SurfaceTexture` object is initialized using an OpenGL ES texture ID. However, the texture ID must be bound to the `GL_TEXTURE_EXTERNAL_OES` texture target. Unfortunately, as per the OpenCL specification, when creating an OpenCL texture image from an OpenGL texture, `GL_TEXTURE_EXTERNAL_OES` isn't a valid texture target. Therefore, the `GL_TEXTURE_EXTERNAL_OES` is used instead to create a `GL_TEXTURE_2D` texture.

Then the fragment shader in Listing 4.6 is executed. Note that since we are sampling from `GL_TEXTURE_EXTERNAL_OES`, the directive

```
extensionGL_OES_ EGL_image_external : require
```

must be declared in the fragment shader. This results in the contents of the `GL_TEXTURE_EXTERNAL_OES` target texture being copied to the `GL_TEXTURE_2D` texture rather than being rendered to the display. At this point we now have an OpenGL ES `GL_TEXTURE_2D` texture on the GPU which contains the camera data.

```
1 extension GL_OES_EGL_image_external : require
2
3 precision mediump float;
4 uniform samplerExternalOES sTexture;
5 varying vec2 texCoord
6
7 void main() {
8   gl_FragColor = texture2D(sTexture, texCoord);
9 }
```

Listing 4.6. Fragment shader that samples from a `GL_TEXTURE_ EXTERNAL_OES` texture.

```
1 mem_images[0] = clCreateFromGLTexture2D(m_clContext,
2         CL_MEM_READ_ONLY, GL_TEXTURE_2D, 0, in_tex, &err);
3 err = clEnqueueAcquireGLObjects(m_queue, 1, &mem_images[0], 0, 0, 0);
4     runCLKernels();    //Function to run OpenCL kernels
5 err = clEnqueueReleaseGLObjects(m_queue, 1, &mem_images[0], 0, 0, 0);
```

Listing 4.7. Creating an OpenCL image from an OpenGL texture.

Create an OpenCL image from OpenGL 2D texture. Using JNI, the C++ global state is then instructed to use the previously created OpenCL context to create an OpenCL texture image from the provided input texture ID. Combining OpenCL and OpenGL allows OpenCL kernels to modify the texture image on the GPU, but before the kernels can access the texture data, the host needs to create an OpenCL memory object specifically configured for this purpose (line 1 in Listing 4.7).

4.8.1 Render Output to Display

Having applied TMO to an LDR image, the results now need to be displayed on the Android device. To do so, we create another OpenGL texture and instruct the OpenCL kernels to render the output to that instead. Then, once the OpenCL kernels have been executed, an OpenGL fragment shader can be used to render the contents of the output texture.

One important design point to note is that OpenGL and OpenCL cannot simultaneously access the same data. The OpenCL kernels need to acquire exclusive access to the data, which can be achieved by making a call to `clEnqueue AcquireGLObjects`. Once the data has been acquired, OpenCL kernels to process this data can then be enqueued. Finally, for OpenGL ES to be able to reuse the texture, the OpenCL context must give up the exclusive access to the texture (for example, see line 5 in Listing 4.7).

Once the OpenCL kernels have been executed and access to the textures is given up, the contents of the resulting texture can be rendered to the display in Java (Listing 4.8).

```
precision mediump float;
uniform sampler2D sTexture;
varying vec2 texCoord;
void main() {
  gl_FragColor = texture2D(sTexture, texCoord);
};
```

Listing 4.8. Java code to render the result texture to the display.

4.8.2 GLSurfaceView.Renderer

Extending `GLSurfaceView.Renderer` requires implementation of the following methods.

onSurfaceCreated. This method is called by the Android framework every time the EGL context is created or recreated. Aside from when the application first starts, this typically happens when the Android device wakes up after going to sleep.

Because the OpenCL context relies on the OpenGL ES context created from EGL, it is important to ensure that the OpenCL context is recreated every time this method gets called. Therefore, in **onSurfaceCreated**, we make calls to C++ through JNI to initialize the OpenCL properties. These OpenCL properties are then used to create a new OpenCL context, which in turn is used to execute the OpenCL kernels.

Building OpenCL kernels and initializing OpenCL memory objects every time a new frame is available can be quite expensive. However, these OpenCL objects can't simply be created only when the app starts, as they rely on an active OpenCL context. Therefore, the following tasks are also carried out when **onSurfaceCreated** is called:

- creating OpenCL command queue,

- creating and building the TMO OpenCL program,

- creating all the required kernels,

- creating buffers and textured images,

- setting kernel arguments.

onDrawFrame. This method repeatedly gets called by the **GLSurfaceView.Renderer** API and is responsible for rendering objects to the display. Therefore, this method is the ideal place to execute the tone-mapping process.

First, **updateTexImage** is called to update the camera texture with the latest available frame. An OpenGL ES 2D texture is then created from the camera texture as described earlier. The texture ID of this texture is then passed to the C++ global state, where the OpenCL tone-mapping kernels are executed to create a pseudo-HDR effect on the image. Once the tone-mapping process has finished, the output texture is then rendered to the display.

onSurfaceChanged. This method is called when the surface size changes. However, the method is redundant here as the orientation is locked in our example application.

4.8.3 Mipmap Generation

Mipmaps are used for our implementation of Reinhard's local TMO. OpenGL ES provides built-in functionality to generate the complete chain of mipmaps by making a call to `glGenerateMipmap`. Once generated, the corresponding OpenCL textures can be created by making a call to `clCreateFromGLTexture2D()`. However, executing the said function returns an error, which as per the OpenCL specification is raised when the "OpenGL implementation does not support creating from nonzero mipmap levels" [Khronos 15].

To get around this, an OpenCL kernel (called `channel_mipmap` in the available source code) was implemented, which, when executed, generates the next level mipmap. As discussed previously, for Reinhard's local TMO, we set the number of mipmaps to 8.

4.8.4 Reading from an OpenGL Texture

When called from an OpenCL kernel, `read_imageui` returns the RGBA value of a pixel at a specified coordinate. The returned pixel values represent an 8-bit color each and therefore should be in the range of $\{0, \ldots, 255\}$.

However, while testing our example application, we ran into problems with Qualcomm's OpenCL implementation on their Snapdragon chipset. Their OpenCL implementation (incorrectly) returns values ranging between 0 and 15,359. Moreover, there is no linear mapping between the original 8-bit values and the ones returned by `read_imageui`, making it nontrivial to obtain the original 8-bit color values.

Using linear interpolation on a subset of the reversed mapping, we have managed to generate a suitable polynomial function. However, this polynomial is of a very high degree and therefore is quite computationally expensive to execute. Instead, we have produced a function called `GL_to_CL()`, which is a combination of four linear functions and a quartic function. This work-around code is included in our example pipeline (available on the CRC Press website) for those wishing to try it on a Snapdragon platform (although, of course, this bug may be fixed in their OpenCL implementation at some stage).

| Device | Peak performance | Global Memory | Local |
(32-bit GFLOPS)	Bandwidth (GB/s)	per CU (KB)	Memory
ARM Mali T604	68	12.8	–
NVIDIA GTX 760	2258	192	48
Intel i3-3217U	29	25.6	32
Qualcomm Adreno 330	129	12.8	8

Table 4.1. Specifications for the devices under test.

4.9 Performance of Our HDR Effects

Each of the TMOs we have implemented has been run on images of different sizes to measure their performances. These tests were carried out on a range of devices, as detailed below.

First, we have an ARM Mali-T604–based device: an Arndale development board sporting a Samsung Exynos 5 5250 processor. This processor includes two ARM Cortex A-15 CPU cores and a four-core Mali T604 GPU. A second device in our test is an Android-based Sony Xperia Z Ultra smartphone. This device comes with an embedded Qualcomm Snapdragon 800 quad-core processor and Adreno 330 GPU. Other OpenCL-compatible devices used to analyze the results are an NVIDIA GTX 760 and an Intel i3-3217U CPU. Table 4.1 lists the relevant specifications for each of these devices.

The GFLOPS figure is a measure of peak performance—in this case, billions of single precision floating point operations per second. Global and local memory are the amount of memory resources available to an OpenCL kernel at the time of execution. If an OpenCL kernel exhausts its local memory, then any overspill is typically stored in global memory instead, with correspondingly slower access speeds.

Reinhard global TMO performance. Reinhard's global TMO iterates over the entire image twice; once to compute L_{max} and $\bar{L}_w$, and a second time to adjust each pixel according to these values and the key value (a) of the scene. To achieve a real-time implementation, the kernels need to be executed in less than 33 milliseconds (30 fps). Figure 4.8 compares the execution times of different-sized images, all running the same OpenCL code on the ARM Mali T604 and NVIDIA GTX 760 platforms.

The NVIDIA GTX 760, being a fast, discrete, desktop GPU, executes the OpenCL kernels on all image sizes in less than 2.5 ms, achieving more than 400 fps at 1080p. This is much faster than the equivalent OpenGL implementation by Akyuz, which achieved 103 fps on a 1024×768 image, albeit on much slower hardware. The ARM Mali T604 GPU can process the two smaller images fast enough to render the output in real time. However, processing a 1080p image is slightly borderline, coming in at about 28 fps. With a little more optimization, 30 fps is probably achievable on this platform.

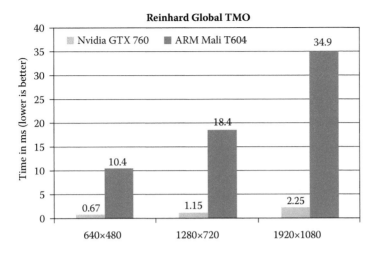

Figure 4.8. Reinhard's global TMO timings (lower is better).

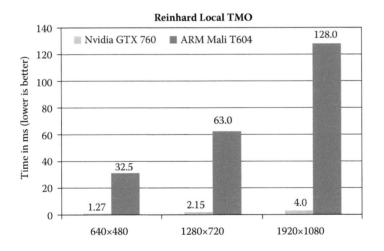

Figure 4.9. Reinhard's local TMO timings (lower is better).

Reinhard local TMO performance. Because Reinhard's Local TMO requires iterating over multiple sizes of neighborhood for each pixel, the algorithm is much more computationally expensive than its global TMO counterpart. Analyzing the results in Figure 4.9, we see that the desktop GPU again processes all the images in less than 33 ms to achieve a real-time implementation. Our OpenCL implementation achieves 250 fps (4.0 ms) on a 1920 × 1080 image compared to Akyuz's OpenGL implementation, which has a frame rate of 103 fps on a slightly smaller (1027 × 768) image.

Reinhard Local TMO

Proportion of time taken by each OpenCL kernel

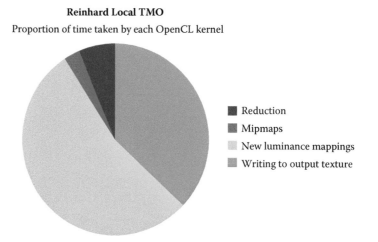

■ Reduction
■ Mipmaps
□ New luminance mappings
■ Writing to output texture

Figure 4.10. The fraction of total time spent in each kernel within Reinhard's local TMO.

For the more data-expensive and computationally expensive local TMO, the ARM Mali T604 GPU achieves real-time performance for the 640×480 image size (30.8 fps), but doesn't exceed our 30 fps goal for the two larger image sizes, instead achieving 15.9 fps on a 1280×720 image and 7.8 fps for the 1920×1080 HD image.

A closer look at the execution time of each kernel shows that most of the time is spent in computing the luminance mappings used to scale each luminance value from the original image (Figure 4.10). These mappings are computed based on the luminance of the scene.

When recording a video or taking a picture, the luminance of the scene doesn't vary much between frames. We could therefore take advantage of this to achieve a higher frame rate by only computing a new set of mappings once every few frames, as opposed to computing them for every frame.

Histogram equalization. Although not an HDR TMO, histogram equalization is a demonstration that our example Android pipeline is not limited to just HDR TMOs and can be used for other classes of image-processing applications that require input from a camera and render the output to a display.

Figure 4.11 shows the execution times of our histogram equalization example OpenCL code, this time on a different set of our target devices. Once again, the desktop GPU is the fastest device. However it is interesting to note that the Intel CPU performs this benchmark much faster than the Adreno 330 GPU, demonstrating that this code is memory bandwidth limited rather than compute limited.

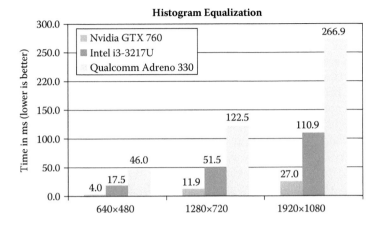

Figure 4.11. Histogram equalization performance results.

4.9.1 Performance Summary

Overall, the example OpenCL kernel implementations presented in this chapter perform better than any previously reported results. Upon closer inspection of the various TMO algorithms we have implemented, Reinhard's global TMO is the least compute intensive. It can achieve real time on 720p images across all the devices we have tested. As expected, the desktop GPU performed best, achieving a frame rate far greater than 30 fps across all the algorithms and all the different-sized images. However, many embedded GPUs are now capable to achieving 30 fps or better for certain image sizes, a very interesting result that shows that real-time HDR pipelines are now within reach for some mobile platforms.

All of this source code is available as a working OpenCL/OpenGL framework, supporting both Linux and Android OSs. We encourage the reader to try the code for themselves and benchmark the hardware platforms of their choice.

4.10 Conclusions

The main contributions of this chapter are

- a description of HDR TMO that can be used to create a pseudo-HDR effect on an image;

- an efficient GPGPU OpenCL/OpenGL implementation of the above algorithms;

- a pipeline that captures camera images, tone-maps them using the above OpenCL implementations, and renders the output to display;

- a demonstration of a working OpenCL–OpenGL interoperability that avoids any unnecessary data transfer in the example pipeline.

For a scene where the overall luminance is very low, Reinhard's TMOs work very well by adjusting the luminance of the image to highlight details in both the dark and the bright regions. The OpenCL implementations of these algorithms have been demonstrated to be efficient and portable. An Android pipeline was also described, which acquired camera frames, tone-mapped them using OpenCL kernels, and rendered the output to a display. Using OpenGL ES and OpenCL interoperability, this pipeline was further optimized to avoid any data transfer of the camera frames. The pipeline can be used for other image-processing applications that require input from the camera. To demonstrate this, an OpenCL histogram equalization program has also been provided.

Bibliography

[Akyüz 12] Ahmet Oğuz Akyüz. "High Dynamic Range Imaging Pipeline on the GPU." *Journal of Real-Time Image Processing: Special Issue* (2012), 1–15.

[Android 15] Android. "OpenGL ES." http://developer.android.com/guide/topics/graphics/opengl.html, accessed May 6, 2015.

[Blommaert and Martens 90] Frans J. J. Blommaert and Jean-Bernard Martens. "An Object-Oriented Model for Brightness Perception." *Spatial Vision* 5:1 (1990), 15–41.

[Catanzaro 10] Bryan Catanzaro. "OpenCL Optimization Case Study: Simple Reductions." *AMD Developer Central*, http://developer.amd.com/resources/documentation-articles/articles-whitepapers/opencl-optimization-case-study-simple-reductions/, August 24, 2010.

[Chaney 15] Mike Chaney. "Understanding Embedded Image Information." *Steve's Digicams*, http://www.steves-digicams.com/knowledge-center/understanding-embedded-image-info.html, 2015.

[Chiu et al. 11] Ching-Te Chiu, Tsun-Hsien Wang, Wei-Ming Ke, Chen-Yu Chuang, Jhih-Siao Huang, Wei-Su Wong, Ren-Song Tsay, and Cyuan-Jhe Wu. "Real-Time Tone-Mapping Processor with Integrated Photographic and Gradient Compression Using 0.13 μm Technology on an ARM SoC Platform." *Journal of Signal Processing Systems* 64:1 (2011), 93–107.

[GSM Arena 15] GSM Arena. "Apple iPhone 4 Specifications." http://www.gsmarena.com/apple_iphone_4-3275.php, 2015.

[Huang et al. 09] Song Huang, Shucai Xiao, and Wu-chun Feng. "On the Energy Efficiency of Graphics Processing Units for Scientific Computing." In *Proceedings of the 2009 IEEE International Symposium on Parallel & Distributed Processing*, pp. 1–8. Washington, CD: IEEE Computer Society, 2009.

[Kang et al. 03] Sing Bing Kang, Matthew Uyttendaele, Simon Winder, and Richard Szeliski. "High Dynamic Range Video. *ACM Transactions on Graphics* 22:3 (2003), 319–325.

[Kiser et al. 12] Chris Kiser, Erik Reinhard, Mike Tocci, and Nora Tocci. "Real-Time Automated Tone Mapping System for HDR Video." In *Proceedings of the IEEE International Conference on Image Processing*, pp. 2749–2752. Piscataway, NJ: IEEE, 2012.

[Krawczyk et al. 05] Grzegorz Krawczyk, Karol Myszkowski, and Hans-Peter Seidel. "Perceptual Effects in Real-Time Tone Mapping." In *Proceedings of the 21st Spring Conference on Computer Graphics*, pp. 195–202. New York: ACM, 2005.

[Khronos 15] Khronos Group. "Khronos OpenCL Standard." http://www.khronos.org/opencl/, accessed May 6, 2015.

[Kuang et al. 07] Jiangtao Kuang, Hiroshi Yamaguchi, Changmeng Liu, Garrett M, and Mark D. Fairchild. "Evaluating HDR Rendering Algorithms." *ACM Trans. Appl. Perception* 4:2 (2007), Article no. 9.

[McClanahan 11] Chris McClanahan. "Single Camera Real Time HDR Tonemapping." *mcclanahoochie's blog*, http://mcclanahoochie.com/blog/portfolio/real-time-hdr-tonemapping/, April 2011.

[McCoy 08] Kevin McCoy. "St. Louis Arch Multiple Exposures." *Wikipedia*, https://en.wikipedia.org/wiki/File:StLouisArchMultExpEV-4.72.JPG, May 31, 2008.

[Reinhard et al. 02] Erik Reinhard, Michael Stark, Peter Shirley, and James Ferwerda. "Photographic Tone Reproduction for Digital Images." *ACM Transactions on Graphics* 21:3 (2002), 267–276.

[Seng 10] Kim Seng. "Single Exposure HDR." *HDR Photography by Captain Kimo*, http://captainkimo.com/single-exposure-hdr/, February 25, 2010.

[Topaz Labs 15] Topaz Labs. "Topaz Adjust." http://www.topazlabs.com/adjust, 2015.

[UCI iCAMP 10] UCI iCAMP. "Histogram Equalization." *Math 77C*, http://www.math.uci.edu/icamp/courses/math77c/demos/hist_eq.pdf, August 5, 2010.

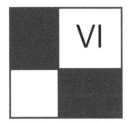

VI

Compute

Short and sweet is this section, presenting three rendering techniques that make intensive use of the compute functionality of modern graphics pipelines. GPUs, including those in new game consoles, can nowadays execute general-purpose computation kernels, which opens doors to new and more efficient rendering techniques and to scenes of unseen complexity. The articles in this section leverage this functionality to enable large numbers of dynamic lights in real-time rendering, more complex geometry in ray tracing, and fast approximate ambient occlusion for direct volume rendering in scientific visualization applications.

"Compute-Based Tiled Culling," Jason Stewart's chapter, focuses on one challenge in modern real-time rendering engines: they need to support many dynamic light sources in a scene. Both forward and deferred rendering can struggle with problems such as efficient culling, batch sizes, state switching, or bandwidth consumption, in this case. Compute-based (tiled) culling of lights reduces state switching and avoids culling on the CPU (beneficial for forward rendering), and computes lighting in a single pass that fits deferred renderers well. Jason details his technique, provides a thorough performance analysis, and deduces various optimizations, all documented with example code.

In "Rendering Vector Displacement-Mapped Surfaces in a GPU Ray Tracer," Takahiro Harada's work targets the rendering of vector displacement-mapped surfaces using ray-tracing–based methods. Vector displacement is a popular and powerful means to model complex objects from simple base geometry. However, ray tracing such geometry on a GPU is nontrivial: pre-tessellation is not an option due to the high (and possibly unnecessary) memory consumption, and thus efficient, GPU-friendly algorithms for the construction and traversal of acceleration structures and intersection computation with on-the-fly tessellation are required. Takahiro fills this gap and presents his method and implementation of an OpenCL ray tracer supporting dynamic tessellation of vector displacement-mapped surfaces.

"Smooth Probablistic Ambient Occlusion for Volume Rendering" by Thomas Kroes, Dirk Schut, and Elmar Eisemann covers a novel and easy-to-implement solution for ambient occlusion for direct volume rendering (DVR). Instead of applying costly ray casting to determine the accessibility of a voxel, this technique employs a probabilistic heuristic in concert with 3D image filtering. This way, ambient occlusion can be efficiently approximated and it is possible to interactively modify the transfer function, which is critical in many applications, such as medical and scientific DVR.

—Carsten Dachsbacher

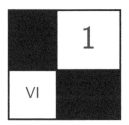

Compute-Based Tiled Culling

Jason Stewart

1.1 Introduction

Modern real-time rendering engines need to support many dynamic light sources in a scene. Meeting this requirement with traditional forward rendering is problematic. Typically, a forward-rendered engine culls lights on the CPU for each batch of scene geometry to be drawn, and changing the set of lights in use requires a separate draw call. Thus, there is an undesirable tradeoff between using smaller pieces of the scene for more efficient light culling versus using larger batches and more instancing for fewer total draw calls. The intersection tests required for light culling can also be a performance burden for the CPU.

Deferred rendering better supports large light counts because it decouples scene geometry rendering and material evaluation from lighting. First, the scene is rendered and geometric and material properties are stored into a geometry buffer or G-buffer [Saito and Takahashi 90]. Lighting is accumulated separately, using the G-buffer as input, by drawing light bounding volumes or screen-space quads. Removing lighting from the scene rendering pass eliminates the state switching for different light sets, allowing for better batching. In addition, CPU light culling is performed once against the view frustum instead of for each batch, reducing the performance cost. However, because each light is now accumulated separately, overlapping lights increase bandwidth consumption, which can decrease GPU performance [Lauritzen 10].

This chapter presents a better method for supporting large light counts: compute-based tiled culling. Modern GPUs, including those in Xbox One and Playstation 4, can execute general-purpose computation kernels. This capability allows light culling to be performed on the GPU. The technique can be used with both forward and deferred rendering. It eliminates light state switching and CPU culling, which helps forward rendering, and it calculates lighting in a single pass, which helps deferred rendering. This chapter presents the technique in detail, including code examples in HLSL and various optimizations. The companion code implements the technique for both forward and deferred rendering and includes a benchmark.

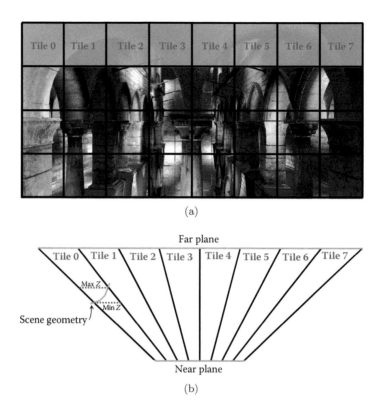

(a)

(b)

Figure 1.1. Partitioning the scene into tiles. (a) Example screen tiles. (b) Fitting view frustum partitions to the screen tiles. For clarity, the tiles shown in this figure are very large. They would typically be 16×16 pixels.

In addition to using the companion code to measure performance, results are presented using Unreal Engine 4, including a comparison of standard deferred rendering versus tiled deferred.

1.2   Overview

Compute-based tiled culling works by partitioning the screen into fixed-size tiles, as shown in Figure 1.1(a). For each tile, a compute shader[1] loops over all lights in the scene and determines which ones intersect that particular tile. Figure 1.1(b) gives a 2D, top-down example of how the tile bounding volume is constructed. Four planes are calculated to represent the left, right, top, and bottom of an

---

[1]This chapter uses Direct3D 11 terminology. In Direct3D 11, the general-purpose computation technology required for tiled culling is called DirectCompute 5.0, and the general-purpose kernel is called a compute shader.

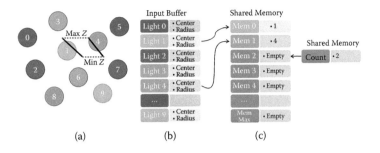

Figure 1.2. Tiled culling overview.

asymmetric partition of the view frustum that fits exactly around the tile. To allow for tighter culling, the minimum and maximum scene depths are calculated for the tile, as shown in Figure 1.1(b) for Tile 0. These depth values form the front and back of the frustum partition. This gives the six planes necessary for testing the intersection between light bounding volumes and the tile.

Figure 1.2 provides an overview of the algorithm. Figure 1.2(a) shows a 2D representation of a tile bounding volume, similar to that shown for Tile 0 in Figure 1.1(b). Several scene lights are also shown. Figure 1.2(b) shows the input buffer containing the scene light list. Each entry in the list contains the center and radius for that light's bounding sphere.

The compute shader is configured so that each thread group works on one tile. It loops over the lights in the input buffer and stores the indices of those that intersect the tile into shared memory.[2] Space is reserved for a per-tile maximum number of lights, and a counter tracks how many entries were actually written, as shown in Figure 1.2(c).

Algorithm 1.1 summarizes the technique.

Referring back to Figure 1.2 as a visual example of the loop in Algorithm 1.1, note from Figure 1.2(a) that two lights intersect the frustum partition: Light 1 and Light 4. The input buffer index (Figure 1.2(b)) of each intersecting light is written to shared memory (Figure 1.2(c)). To make this thread safe, so that lights can be culled in parallel, a counter is stored in shared memory and incremented using the atomic operations available in compute shaders.

1.3 Implementation

This section gives an implementation in HLSL of the compute-based tiled-culling algorithm discussed in the previous section. The three parts of Algorithm 1.1 will be presented in order: depth bounds calculation, frustum planes calculation, and intersection testing.

---

[2]Compute shader execution is organized into thread groups. Threads in the same thread group have access to shared memory.

Input: light list, scene depth
Output: per-tile list of intersecting lights

calculate depth bounds for the tile;
calculate frustum planes for the tile;

for $i \leftarrow$ **thread_index to num_lights do**
   | current_light $\leftarrow$ light_list[i];
   | test intersection against tile bounding volume;
   | **if** *intersection* **then**
   | | thread-safe increment of list counter;
   | | write light index to per-tile list;
   | **end**
   | $i \leftarrow i +$ num_threads_per_tile;
end

Algorithm 1.1. Basic tiled culling.

1.3.1 Depth Bounds Calculation

As mentioned previously (in Footnote 2), compute shader execution is organized into thread groups. You specify the exact organization as part of the compute shader. In HLSL, this is done with the **numthreads** attribute, as shown on line 15 of Listing 1.1. For tiled culling, the thread groups are organized to match the tile size. For example, TILE_RES is defined as 16 in Listing 1.1, and the 16×16-pixel tile size results in a 16×16-thread layout in the compute shader.

Compute shaders are executed with the Dispatch method, which specifies the number of thread groups to launch. For example, a 1920×1080 screen resolution with 16×16-pixel tiles requires 120×68 tiles to cover the screen. Thus, by calling Dispatch(120,68,1) for a compute shader with [numthreads(16,16,1)], each thread maps to a particular screen pixel.

To calculate the depth bounds, each thread simply reads its pixel's depth value from the scene depth buffer and performs a thread-safe atomic minimum and maximum in shared memory. The depth buffer read happens on lines 20–21 of Listing 1.1. The globalIdx variable used to address the depth buffer is the SV_DispatchThreadID value (see line 16), one of the special system-value semantics available to compute shaders. Because the thread group layout from the Dispatch call matches the screen tiles and the thread layout from the numthreads attribute matches the tile size, the SV_DispatchThreadID value corresponds to a screen pixel address and can be used directly with the Load function.

One minor complication with the depth bounds calculation is that the scene depth value is floating point, but the atomic minimum and maximum functions (InterlockedMin and InterlockedMax on lines 43–44) only operate on integer types. Therefore, asuint is used to store the raw bits of the floating point depth value,

```
 1 Texture2D<float> g_SceneDepthBuffer;
 2
 3 // Thread Group Shared Memory (aka local data share, or LDS)
 4 groupshared uint ldsZMin;
 5 groupshared uint ldsZMax;
 6
 7 // Convert a depth value from postprojection space
 8 // into view space
 9 float ConvertProjDepthToView(float z)
10 {
11   return (1.f/(z*g_mProjectionInv._34 + g_mProjectionInv._44));
12 }
13
14 #define TILE_RES 16
15 [numthreads(TILE_RES,TILE_RES,1)]
16 void CullLightsCS(uint3 globalIdx : SV_DispatchThreadID,
17                   uint3 localIdx  : SV_GroupThreadID,
18                   uint3 groupIdx  : SV_GroupID)
19 {
20   float depth = g_SceneDepthBuffer.Load(uint3(globalIdx.x,
21                                               globalIdx.y,0)).x;
22   float viewPosZ = ConvertProjDepthToView(depth);
23   uint z = asuint(viewPosZ);
24
25   uint threadNum = localIdx.x + localIdx.y*TILE_RES;
26
27   // There is no way to initialize shared memory at
28   // compile time, so thread zero does it at runtime
29   if(threadNum == 0)
30   {
31     ldsZMin = 0x7f7fffff;  // FLT_MAX as a uint
32     ldsZMax = 0;
33   }
34   GroupMemoryBarrierWithGroupSync();
35
36   // Parts of the depth buffer that were never written
37   // (e.g., the sky) will be zero (the companion code uses
38   // inverted 32-bit float depth for better precision).
39   if(depth != 0.f)
40   {
41     // Calculate the minimum and maximum depth for this tile
42     // to form the front and back of the frustum
43     InterlockedMin(ldsZMin,z);
44     InterlockedMax(ldsZMax,z);
45   }
46   GroupMemoryBarrierWithGroupSync();
47
48   float minZ = asfloat(ldsZMin);
49   float maxZ = asfloat(ldsZMax);
50
51   // Frustum planes and intersection code goes here
52   ...
53 }
```

Listing 1.1. Depth bounds calculation.

and the minimum and maximum are performed against these unsigned bits. This works because the floating point depth is always positive, and the raw bits of a 32-bit floating point value increase monotonically in this case.

```
 1 // Plane equation from three points, simplified
 2 // for the case where the first point is the origin.
 3 // N is normalized so that the plane equation can
 4 // be used to compute signed distance.
 5 float4 CreatePlaneEquation(float3 Q, float3 R)
 6 {
 7   // N = normalize(cross(Q-P,R-P)),
 8   // except we know P is the origin
 9   float3 N = normalize(cross(Q,R));
10   // D = -(N dot P), except we know P is the origin
11   return float4(N,0);
12 }
13
14 // Convert a point from postprojection space into view space
15 float3 ConvertProjToView(float4 p)
16 {
17   p = mul(p,g_mProjectionInv);
18   return (p/p.w).xyz;
19 }
20
21 void CullLightsCS(uint3 globalIdx : SV_DispatchThreadID,
22                   uint3 localIdx  : SV_GroupThreadID,
23                   uint3 groupIdx  : SV_GroupID)
24 {
25   // Depth bounds code goes here
26   ...
27   float4 frustumEqn[4];
28   { // Construct frustum planes for this tile
29     uint pxm = TILE_RES*groupIdx.x;
30     uint pym = TILE_RES*groupIdx.y;
31     uint pxp = TILE_RES*(groupIdx.x+1);
32     uint pyp = TILE_RES*(groupIdx.y+1);
33     uint width  = TILE_RES*GetNumTilesX();
34     uint height = TILE_RES*GetNumTilesY();
35
36     // Four corners of the tile, clockwise from top-left
37     float3 p[4];
38     p[0] = ConvertProjToView(float4(pxm/(float)width*2.f-1.f,
39         (height-pym)/(float)height*2.f-1.f,1.f,1.f));
40     p[1] = ConvertProjToView(float4(pxp/(float)width*2.f-1.f,
41         (height-pym)/(float)height*2.f-1.f,1.f,1.f));
42     p[2] = ConvertProjToView(float4(pxp/(float)width*2.f-1.f,
43         (height-pyp)/(float)height*2.f-1.f,1.f,1.f));
44     p[3] = ConvertProjToView(float4(pxm/(float)width*2.f-1.f,
45         (height-pyp)/(float)height*2.f-1.f,1.f,1.f));
46
47     // Create plane equations for the four sides, with
48     // the positive half-space outside the frustum
49     for(uint i=0; i<4; i++)
50       frustumEqn[i] = CreatePlaneEquation(p[i], p[(i+1)&3]);
51   }
52   // Intersection code goes here
53   ...
54 }
```

Listing 1.2. Frustum planes calculation.

1.3.2 Frustum Planes Calculation

The frustum planes code appears in Listing 1.2 and is straightforward. The four corners of the tile are constructed in postprojection space and converted to view space. These four corners are then used to calculate the planes for the four sides of the frustum partition. Two corners and the origin give the three points needed for each plane equation.

To calculate the pixel locations of the four corners, the `groupIdx` variable is used, which holds the `SV_GroupID` value (see line 23), another of the special system-value semantics available to compute shaders. Because the thread group layout from the `Dispatch` call matches the screen tiles, the `SV_GroupID` value corresponds to the tile number.

One subtlety happens on lines 33–34. Note that the screen size might not be evenly divisible by the tile size, so the screen width and height cannot be used directly in the four corners calculation. Instead, the code calculates the "whole tile" resolution, which is the closest greater-than (or equal-to) value that is evenly divisible by the tile size.

1.3.3 Intersection Testing

The depth bounds and the four plane equations form the six sides of the tile bounding volume. Light culling is accomplished by testing light bounding volumes for intersection against the tile bounding volume. This is shown in Listing 1.3.

In this example, the light bounding volumes are spheres (a natural fit for point lights), and a standard frustum versus sphere intersection test is performed. That is, the sphere is tested against the six planes of the frustum. If it passes, the index of the light in the input buffer is written to shared memory.

Note on line 28 that each thread starts the loop at a different index and increments the loop counter by `NUM_THREADS`, which is 256 for 16×16-pixel tiles. This allows 256 lights to be culled in parallel for each loop iteration. To make the parallel culling thread safe, `InterlockedAdd` is used on line 44 to increment the output list counter.

As mentioned in the introduction, compute-based tiled culling can be applied to forward rendering [Harada et al. 12] and deferred rendering [Andersson 09]. When used with forward rendering, it is commonly called Forward+ [Harada et al. 12]. When used with deferred rendering, it is called tile-based deferred [Lauritzen 10] or simply tiled deferred [Lauritzen 12]. For Forward+, the compute shader writes the per-tile list to an output buffer (i.e., `RWBuffer`). The forward pixel shader then calculates the tile to which it belongs and uses the list for that tile as input to calculate the lighting. For tiled deferred, the same compute shader that does the light culling can then do the lighting, using the list in shared

```
 1 Buffer<float4> g_LightBufferCenterAndRadius;
 2
 3 #define MAX_NUM_LIGHTS_PER_TILE 256
 4 groupshared uint ldsLightIdxCounter;
 5 groupshared uint ldsLightIdx[MAX_NUM_LIGHTS_PER_TILE];
 6
 7 // Point-plane distance, simplified for the case where
 8 // the plane passes through the origin
 9 float GetSignedDistanceFromPlane(float3 p, float4 eqn)
10 {
11   // dot(eqn.xyz, p) + eqn.w, except we know eqn.w is zero
12   return dot(eqn.xyz, p);
13 }
14
15 #define NUM_THREADS (TILE_RES*TILE_RES)
16 void CullLightsCS(...)
17 {
18   // Depth bounds and frustum planes code goes here
19   ...
20   if(threadNum == 0)
21   {
22     ldsLightIdxCounter = 0;
23   }
24   GroupMemoryBarrierWithGroupSync();
25
26   // Loop over the lights and do a
27   // sphere versus frustum intersection test
28   for(uint i=threadNum; i<g_uNumLights; i+=NUM_THREADS)
29   {
30     float4 p = g_LightBufferCenterAndRadius[i];
31     float  r = p.w;
32     float3 c = mul(float4(p.xyz,1), g_mView).xyz;
33
34     // Test if sphere is intersecting or inside frustum
35     if((GetSignedDistanceFromPlane(c,frustumEqn[0]) < r) &&
36        (GetSignedDistanceFromPlane(c,frustumEqn[1]) < r) &&
37        (GetSignedDistanceFromPlane(c,frustumEqn[2]) < r) &&
38        (GetSignedDistanceFromPlane(c,frustumEqn[3]) < r) &&
39        (-c.z + minZ < r) && (c.z - maxZ < r))
40     {
41       // Do a thread-safe increment of the list counter
42       // and put the index of this light into the list
43       uint dstIdx = 0;
44       InterlockedAdd(ldsLightIdxCounter,1,dstIdx);
45       ldsLightIdx[dstIdx] = i;
46     }
47   }
48   GroupMemoryBarrierWithGroupSync();
49 }
```

Listing 1.3. Intersection testing.

memory directly. Even if lights overlap, the G-buffer is only read once for each pixel, and the lighting results are accumulated into shader registers instead of blended into a render target, reducing bandwidth consumption.

1.4 Optimization

This section covers various optimizations to the compute-based tiled-culling technique. Common pitfalls to avoid are presented first, followed by several optimizations to the basic implementation from the previous section.

1.4.1 Common Pitfalls

Part of optimization is avoiding common pitfalls. Two such pitfalls for compute-based tiled culling are described in this section: forgetting to be cache friendly and choosing a suboptimal tile size. The pitfalls are illustrated by making two seemingly small changes to the code in Section 1.3 and showing that those changes hurt performance dramatically.

For the first change, note that line 1 in Listing 1.3 shows that the light bounding spheres (centers and radii) were stored in a buffer with no other data. However, for convenience and code clarity, developers might decide to include other light data in the same buffer, as shown below.

```
struct LightArrayData
{
    float4  v4CenterAndRadius;
    float4  v4Color;
};
StructuredBuffer<LightArrayData> g_LightBuffer;
```

For the second change, recall that line 14 in Listing 1.1 defines TILE_RES as 16, resulting in 16 × 16 threads per thread group, or 256 threads. For AMD GPUs, work is executed in 64-thread batches called *wavefronts*, while on NVIDIA GPUs, work is executed in 32-thread *warps*. Thus, efficient compute shader execution requires the number of threads in a thread group to be a multiple of 64 for AMD or 32 for NVIDIA. Since every multiple of 64 is a multiple of 32, standard performance advice is to configure the thread count to be a multiple of 64. Because 256 is a multiple of 64, setting TILE_RES to 16 follows this advice. Alternatively, setting TILE_RES to 8 (resulting in 8 × 8-pixel tiles) yields 64 threads per thread group, which is certainly also a multiple of 64, and the smaller tile size might result in tighter culling.

Although these two changes seem minor, both decrease performance, as shown in Figure 1.3. The "unoptimized" curve contains both changes (combined light data in a StructuredBuffer and 8 × 8 tiles). For the cache friendly curve, the

---

[3] All performance data in this chapter was gathered on an AMD Radeon R7 260X GPU. The R7 260X was chosen because its performance characteristics are roughly comparable to the Xbox One and Playstation 4.

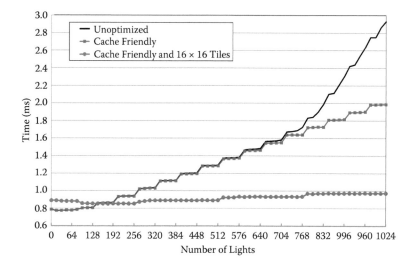

Figure 1.3. Basic optimizations.[3] Tiled-culling compute shader execution time versus number of lights for Forward+ rendering at 1920×1080 using the companion code for this chapter.

`StructuredBuffer` is replaced with the declaration shown in line 1 of Listing 1.3 containing only the data needed for culling. Note that, while performance is similar for much of the chart, performance improves by nearly 1 ms for 1024 lights. Specifically, compute shader execution time decreases from 2.93 ms to 1.99 ms, a 32% reduction.

The "cache friendly" label hints at why this configuration improves performance. Data not needed for culling pollutes the cache during compute shader execution, eventually becoming a bottleneck as light count increases. In general, a structure of arrays (in this case, separate arrays for culling data and light color) is often better for GPU execution than an array of structures, because it allows more cache-friendly memory access.

The "cache friendly and 16×16 tiles" curve keeps the cache-friendly light buffer and changes `TILE_RES` back to 16, resulting in the implementation given in Section 1.3. Because there are now 256 threads, many threads do not have any lights to cull at the lower end of the chart, resulting in a slight performance decrease initially. However, this version scales much better with increasing light counts. At 1024 lights, compute shader execution time is 0.97 ms, a 51% reduction from the previous version and a 67% reduction from the unoptimized version.

The 16×16 configuration is better because more threads per thread group results in more wavefronts/warps in flight per thread group. This allows GPU schedulers to better hide memory latency by switching execution to a new wavefront/warp when the current one hits a high-latency operation.

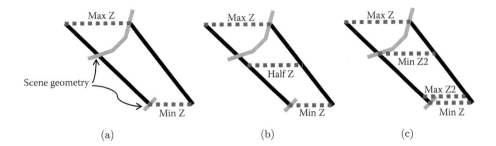

Figure 1.4. Depth discontinuity optimization strategies. (a) Scene depth discontinuities can cause a large depth range in the tile bounding volume. (b) The Half Z method splits the depth range in half and culls against the two ranges. (c) The Modified Half Z method calculates a second minimum and maximum, bounded by the Half Z value.

1.4.2 Depth Discontinuities

Having covered the basic optimizations already present in the code from Section 1.3, additional optimizations will now be presented, starting with those for discontinuities in scene depth.

Figure 1.4 shows 2D representations of a tile bounding volume, similar to that shown for Tile 0 in Figure 1.1(b). As demonstrated in Figure 1.4(a), a foreground object in front of a background object can lead to a large depth range in the tile bounding volume. Lights can intersect the empty space between foreground and background but not actually affect any pixels in the tile. That is, depth discontinuities can lead to an increase in false-positive intersections.

Half Z. Figure 1.4(b) shows a strategy to better handle depth discontinuities called the Half Z method. It simply divides the depth range in two at the midpoint and culls against two depth ranges: one from Min Z to Half Z, and one from Half Z to Max Z. A separate per-tile list is maintained for each depth range. This method requires only two additional plane tests and is a minor change to the code. Listing 1.4 shows the intersection test for this method.

Modified Half Z. Figure 1.4(c) shows a second strategy called the Modified Half Z method. It performs additional atomic operations to find a second maximum (Max Z2) between Min Z and Half Z and a second minimum (Min Z2) between Half Z and Max Z. This can result in tighter bounding volumes compared to the Half Z method, but calculating the additional minimum and maximum is more expensive than simply calculating Half Z, due to the additional atomic operations required.

Light count reduction results. Figure 1.5 shows the reduction in per-tile light count at depth discontinuities from the methods discussed in this section. Note the

```
// Test if sphere is intersecting or inside frustum
if((GetSignedDistanceFromPlane(c,frustumEqn[0]) < r) &&
   (GetSignedDistanceFromPlane(c,frustumEqn[1]) < r) &&
   (GetSignedDistanceFromPlane(c,frustumEqn[2]) < r) &&
   (GetSignedDistanceFromPlane(c,frustumEqn[3]) < r))
{
    if(-c.z + minZ < r && c.z - halfZ < r)
    {
        // Do a thread-safe increment of the list counter
        // and put the index of this light into the list
        uint dstIdx = 0;
        InterlockedAdd(ldsLightIdxCounterA,1,dstIdx);
        ldsLightIdxA[dstIdx] = i;
    }
    if(-c.z + halfZ < r && c.z - maxZ < r)
    {
        // Do a thread-safe increment of the list counter
        // and put the index of this light into the list
        uint dstIdx = 0;
        InterlockedAdd(ldsLightIdxCounterB,1,dstIdx);
        ldsLightIdxB[dstIdx] = i;
    }
}
```

Listing 1.4. Half Z method.

column in the foreground of the left side of the scene in Figure 1.5(a). This causes depth discontinuities for tiles along the column, resulting in the high light counts shown in red in Figure 1.5(c) for the baseline implementation in Section 1.3.

The results for the Half Z method are shown in Figure 1.5(d). Note that the light counts for tiles along the column have been reduced. Then, for the Modified Half Z method, note that light counts have been further reduced in Figure 1.5(e).

Performance results. Figure 1.6 shows the performance of these methods. Note that, while Figure 1.3 measured only the tiled-culling compute shader, Figure 1.6 measures both the compute shader and the forward pixel shader for Forward+ rendering. More time spent during culling can still be an overall performance win if enough time is saved during lighting, so it is important to measure both here.

The "Baseline" curve is from the implementation in Section 1.3. The "Half Z" curve shows this method at a slight performance disadvantage for lower light counts, because the savings during lighting do not yet outweigh the extra cost of testing two depth ranges and maintaining two lists. However, this method becomes faster at higher light counts. The "Modified Half Z" curve starts out with a bigger deficit, due to the higher cost of calculating the additional minimum and maximum with atomics. It eventually pulls ahead of the baseline method, but never catches Half Z. However, this method's smaller depth ranges can still be useful if additional optimizations are implemented, as shown next.

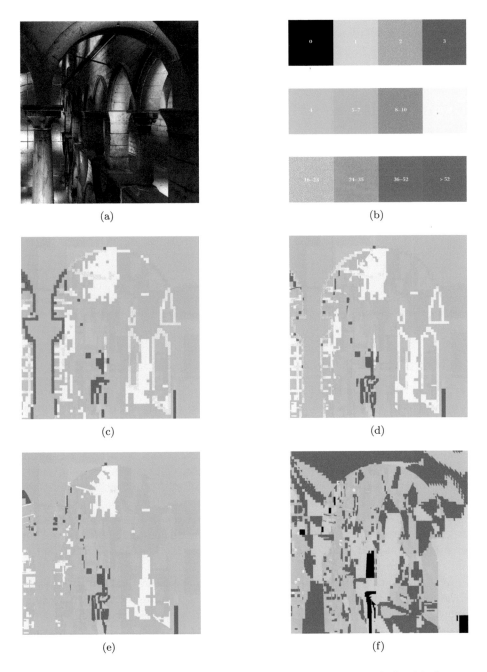

Figure 1.5. Tiled-culling optimization results using the companion code for this chapter. (a) Scene render. (b) Log scale lights-per-tile legend. (c) Baseline. (d) Half Z. (e) Modified Half Z. (f) Modified Half Z with AABBs.

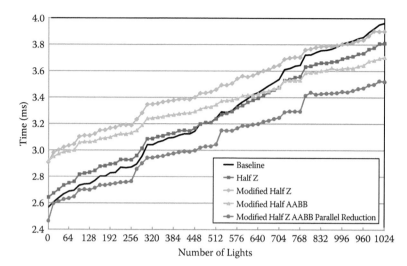

Figure 1.6. Tiled-culling optimizations. GPU execution time versus number of lights using the companion code for this chapter. The vertical axis represents the combined time for the tiled-culling compute shader and the forward pixel shader in Forward+ rendering at 1920×1080.

1.4.3   Frustum Planes versus AABBs

In our previous discussion of the results in Figure 1.5, one result was not mentioned. If view-space axis-aligned bounding boxes (AABBs) are used to bound the tile instead of frustum planes, per-tile light counts can be further reduced, as shown in Figure 1.5(f).

Testing intersection against a frustum using six planes is an approximation. As shown in Figure 1.7(a), the actual intersection volume has curved corners. Regions exist outside the curved corners that will still pass testing against the planes, resulting in false-positive intersections.

Fitting an AABB around the tile's frustum partition will also produce regions where false-positive intersections can occur, as illustrated in Figure 1.7(b). The key difference is that, as the depth range decreases (i.e., as Max Z gets closer to Min Z), these regions get smaller for AABBs, as shown in Figure 1.7(c).

Referring back to Figure 1.5(f), using AABBs with the smaller depth ranges of the Modified Half Z method results in a significant reduction in per-tile light counts. Whereas the previous results showed improvement primarily at depth discontinuities, this method shows an overall improvement. For small depth ranges, the AABB intersection volume nearly matches the true volume, resulting in tighter culling.

Referring back to Figure 1.6, the "Modified Half Z, AABB" curve still starts out at a deficit, due to the increased cost of finding the second minimum and max-

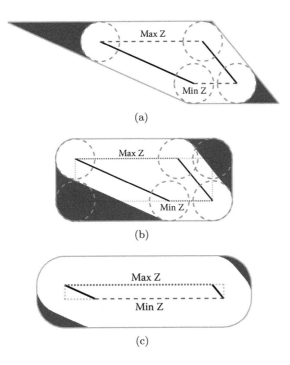

Figure 1.7. Frustum planes versus AABBs. False positive intersections will occur in the shaded regions. (a) Frustum intersection testing. (b) AABB intersection testing. (c) AABB intersection with a small depth range.

imum. However, it scales better as light count increases, eventually overtaking the Half Z method.

1.4.4 Parallel Reduction

Using AABBs with the smaller depth ranges of the Modified Half Z method produces good culling results, but the cost of the second minimum and maximum is significant. There is, however, another way to calculate the depth bounds: parallel reduction. Using the methods first outlined in [Harris 07], as well as the results from [Engel 14], an optimized parallel reduction implementation can be used to produce the smaller depth ranges of the Modified Half Z method, as shown in Listing 1.5.

```
1 Texture2D<float>    g_SceneDepthBuffer;
2 RWTexture2D<float4> g_DepthBounds;
3
4 #define TILE_RES 16
5 #define NUM_THREADS_1D (TILE_RES/2)
```

```
 6 #define NUM_THREADS (NUM_THREADS_1D*NUM_THREADS_1D)
 7
 8 // Thread Group Shared Memory (aka local data share, or LDS)
 9 groupshared float ldsZMin[NUM_THREADS];
10 groupshared float ldsZMax[NUM_THREADS];
11
12 // Convert a depth value from postprojection space
13 // into view space
14 float ConvertProjDepthToView( float z )
15 {
16   return (1.f/(z*g_mProjectionInv._34 + g_mProjectionInv._44));
17 }
18
19 [numthreads(NUM_THREADS_1D,NUM_THREADS_1D,1)]
20 void DepthBoundsCS( uint3 globalIdx : SV_DispatchThreadID,
21                     uint3 localIdx  : SV_GroupThreadID,
22                     uint3 groupIdx  : SV_GroupID )
23 {
24   uint2 sampleIdx = globalIdx.xy*2;
25
26   // Load four depth samples
27   float depth00 = g_SceneDepthBuffer.Load(uint3(sampleIdx.x,
28                                                 sampleIdx.y,0)).x;
29   float depth01 = g_SceneDepthBuffer.Load(uint3(sampleIdx.x,
30                                                 sampleIdx.y+1,0)).x;
31   float depth10 = g_SceneDepthBuffer.Load(uint3(sampleIdx.x+1,
32                                                 sampleIdx.y,0)).x;
33   float depth11 = g_SceneDepthBuffer.Load(uint3(sampleIdx.x+1,
34                                                 sampleIdx.y+1,0)).x;
35
36   float viewPosZ00 = ConvertProjDepthToView(depth00);
37   float viewPosZ01 = ConvertProjDepthToView(depth01);
38   float viewPosZ10 = ConvertProjDepthToView(depth10);
39   float viewPosZ11 = ConvertProjDepthToView(depth11);
40
41   uint threadNum = localIdx.x + localIdx.y*NUM_THREADS_1D;
42
43   // Use parallel reduction to calculate the depth bounds
44   {
45     // Parts of the depth buffer that were never written
46     // (e.g., the sky) will be zero (the companion code uses
47     // inverted 32-bit float depth for better precision).
48     float minZ00 = (depth00 != 0.f) ? viewPosZ00 : FLT_MAX;
49     float minZ01 = (depth01 != 0.f) ? viewPosZ01 : FLT_MAX;
50     float minZ10 = (depth10 != 0.f) ? viewPosZ10 : FLT_MAX;
51     float minZ11 = (depth11 != 0.f) ? viewPosZ11 : FLT_MAX;
52
53     float maxZ00 = (depth00 != 0.f) ? viewPosZ00 : 0.0f;
54     float maxZ01 = (depth01 != 0.f) ? viewPosZ01 : 0.0f;
55     float maxZ10 = (depth10 != 0.f) ? viewPosZ10 : 0.0f;
56     float maxZ11 = (depth11 != 0.f) ? viewPosZ11 : 0.0f;
57
58     // Initialize shared memory
59     ldsZMin[threadNum] = min(minZ00,min(minZ01,
60                                         min(minZ10,minZ11)));
61     ldsZMax[threadNum] = max(maxZ00,max(maxZ01,
62                                         max(maxZ10,maxZ11)));
63     GroupMemoryBarrierWithGroupSync();
64
65     // Minimum and maximum using parallel reduction, with the
66     // loop manually unrolled for 8x8 thread groups (64 threads
67     // per thread group)
68     if (threadNum < 32)
69     {
```

```
 70        ldsZMin[threadNum] = min(ldsZMin[threadNum],
 71                                 ldsZMin[threadNum+32]);
 72        ldsZMax[threadNum] = max(ldsZMax[threadNum],
 73                                 ldsZMax[threadNum+32]);
 74        ldsZMin[threadNum] = min(ldsZMin[threadNum],
 75                                 ldsZMin[threadNum+16]);
 76        ldsZMax[threadNum] = max(ldsZMax[threadNum],
 77                                 ldsZMax[threadNum+16]);
 78        ldsZMin[threadNum] = min(ldsZMin[threadNum],
 79                                 ldsZMin[threadNum+8]);
 80        ldsZMax[threadNum] = max(ldsZMax[threadNum],
 81                                 ldsZMax[threadNum+8]);
 82        ldsZMin[threadNum] = min(ldsZMin[threadNum],
 83                                 ldsZMin[threadNum+4]);
 84        ldsZMax[threadNum] = max(ldsZMax[threadNum],
 85                                 ldsZMax[threadNum+4]);
 86        ldsZMin[threadNum] = min(ldsZMin[threadNum],
 87                                 ldsZMin[threadNum+2]);
 88        ldsZMax[threadNum] = max(ldsZMax[threadNum],
 89                                 ldsZMax[threadNum+2]);
 90        ldsZMin[threadNum] = min(ldsZMin[threadNum],
 91                                 ldsZMin[threadNum+1]);
 92        ldsZMax[threadNum] = max(ldsZMax[threadNum],
 93                                 ldsZMax[threadNum+1]);
 94    }
 95  }
 96  GroupMemoryBarrierWithGroupSync();
 97
 98  float minZ = ldsZMin[0];
 99  float maxZ = ldsZMax[0];
100  float halfZ = 0.5f*(minZ + maxZ);
101
102  // Calculate a second set of depth values: the maximum
103  // on the near side of Half Z and the minimum on the far
104  // side of Half Z
105  {
106      // See the companion code for details
107      ...
108  }
109
110  // The first thread writes to the depth bounds texture
111  if(threadNum == 0)
112  {
113      float maxZ2 = ldsZMax[0];
114      float minZ2 = ldsZMin[0];
115      g_DepthBounds[groupIdx.xy] = float4(minZ,maxZ2,minZ2,maxZ);
116  }
117 }
```

Listing 1.5. Depth bounds using parallel reduction.

As noted in [Harris 07] and [Engel 14], an optimized parallel reduction implementation requires each thread to work on more than one source value. For the code in Listing 1.5, each thread loads four depth samples in a 2×2 grid instead of just a single sample. However, this requires the thread layout to be 8×8 for 16×16-pixel tiles. That is, the parallel reduction must be executed in a separate compute shader. However, even with the extra overhead of an additional pass, the four-samples-per-thread method is faster than keeping the parallel reduction in the culling compute shader but only loading a single sample per thread.

Referring back to Figure 1.6, the "Modified Half Z, AABB, Parallel Reduction" curve is the fastest method throughout. For 1024 lights, the baseline code executes in 3.97 ms, whereas this final optimized version takes 3.52 ms, a reduction of roughly half a millisecond. This represents an 11% decrease in execution time compared to the baseline.

1.5   Unreal Engine 4 Results

Results to this point have been gathered using the companion code for this chapter. This section presents results using the Unreal Engine 4 *Infiltrator* real-time demo. Unreal Engine 4 is a leading real-time rendering engine that implements the tiled-deferred technique. The *Infiltrator* demo allows results to be gathered using state-of-the-art visuals.

Figures 1.8 and 1.9 show two examples of the per-tile light count reduction achieved by using the Modified Half Z method with AABBs. Note the results for baseline tiled culling, which uses an implementation similar to Section 1.3. In each example, high-light-count areas appear along the silhouette of the infiltrator character, where the transition from foreground to background causes depth discontinuities. These areas are eliminated in the optimized version. In addition, the tighter tile bounding volumes from AABBs with small depth ranges reduce light counts overall.

Figure 1.10 shows the GPU execution time improvement of the optimized method (Modified Half Z with AABBs using parallel reduction for the depth ranges) compared to the baseline implementation similar to Section 1.3. For tiled deferred, the execution time includes the three parts of Algorithm 1.1 (depth bounds calculation, tile bounding volume construction, and intersection testing), as well as the lighting calculations. As shown in Figure 1.10, the optimized version is substantially faster over the entire *Infiltrator* demo. Average cost of the baseline implementation is 5.17 ms, whereas the optimized average cost is 3.74 ms, a reduction of 1.43 ms, or roughly 28% faster.

1.5.1   Standard Deferred versus Tiled Deferred

Unreal Engine 4 can apply lighting using either standard deferred or tiled deferred, offering the opportunity to compare the performance of the two methods. Figure 1.11 shows the GPU execution time improvement of the optimized tiled-deferred method compared to the standard-deferred method. Note that, while tiled deferred is usually faster in the demo, there are areas where standard deferred is faster (i.e., the negative values in the chart). Recall that the primary lighting performance concern with standard deferred is the extra bandwidth consumed when blending overlapping lights. In areas without much light overlap, the savings from tiled deferred's single-pass lighting might not outweigh the cost

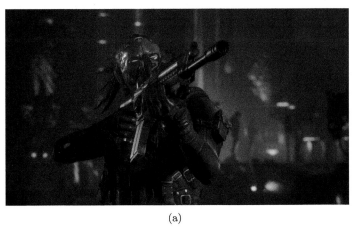

(a)

(b)

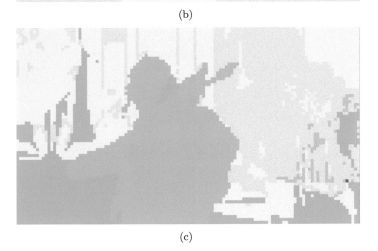

(c)

Figure 1.8. Unreal Engine 4 *Infiltrator* demo: Example 1. (a) Scene render. (b) Baseline tiled culling. (c) Modified Half Z with AABBs.

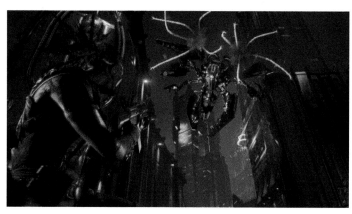

(a)

(b)

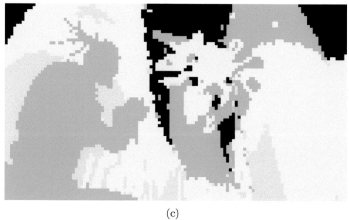

(c)

Figure 1.9. Unreal Engine 4 *Infiltrator* demo: Example 2. (a) Scene render. (b) Baseline tiled culling. (c) Modified Half Z with AABBs.

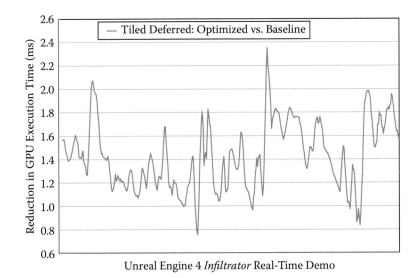

Figure 1.10. Unreal Engine 4 tiled-culling execution time improvement for the optimized version compared to the baseline implementation. Performance was measured over the entire *Infiltrator* demo at 1920×1080.

of calculating the depth bounds and performing the per-tile culling. However, averaged over the entire demo, tiled deferred is still faster overall. Specifically, the average cost of standard deferred is 4.28 ms, whereas the optimized tiled-deferred average cost is 3.74 ms, a reduction of 0.54 ms, or roughly 13% faster.

It is natural to wonder exactly how many lights are needed in a scene with "many lights" before tiled deferred is consistently faster than standard deferred. The answer will depend on several factors including the depth complexity of the scene and the amount of light overlap. For the *Infiltrator* demo, Figure 1.12 is a scatterplot of the data used to generate Figure 1.11 plotted against the number of lights processed during that particular frame. The demo uses a wide range of light counts, from a low of 7 to a high of 980. The average light count is 299 and the median is 218.

For high light counts (above 576), tiled deferred has either comparable or better performance, and is often significantly faster. For example, for counts above 640, tiled deferred is 1.65 ms faster on average. Conversely, for low light counts (below 64), standard deferred is faster. For light counts above 64 but below 576, the situation is less clear from just looking at the chart. Standard deferred values appear both above and below tiled deferred in this range. However, it is worth noting that tiled deferred comes out ahead on average over each interval on the "Number of Lights" axis (i.e., $[0, 64]$, $[64, 128]$, $[128, 192]$, etc.) except $[0, 64]$.

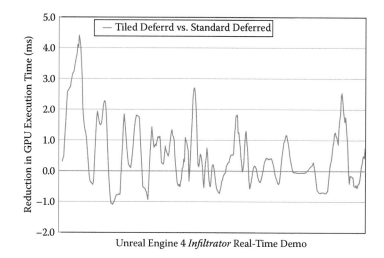

Figure 1.11. Unreal Engine 4 optimized tiled-deferred execution time improvement compared to standard deferred. Performance was measured over the entire *Infiltrator* demo using 1920×1080 screen resolution.

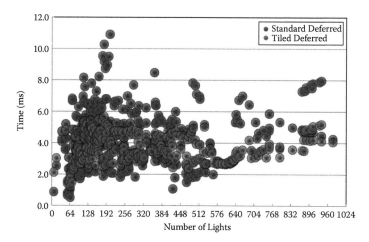

Figure 1.12. Unreal Engine 4 optimized tiled deferred versus standard deferred. GPU execution time versus number of lights. Performance was measured over the entire *Infiltrator* demo at 1920×1080.

To get a clearer picture of average performance, Figure 1.13 applies a moving average to the data in Figure 1.12. The data shows that, while standard deferred is 0.76 ms faster on average for light counts of 70 and below, tiled deferred is

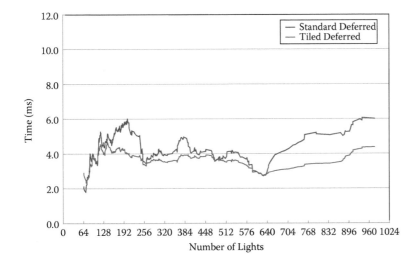

Figure 1.13. Unreal Engine 4 optimized tiled deferred versus standard deferred. GPU execution time versus number of lights. A moving average was applied to the data in Figure 1.12 to show overall trends.

on par with or faster than standard deferred for above 70 lights. Thus, for the particular case of the *Infiltrator* demo, 70 is the threshold for when tiled deferred is consistently faster than (or at least comparable to) standard deferred.

Referring back to Figure 1.12, another thing to note about the data is that the standard deviation is lower for tiled deferred. Specifically, the standard deviation is 1.79 ms for standard deferred and 0.90 ms for tiled deferred, a 50% reduction. Note that worst-case performance is also much better for tiled deferred, with no tiled deferred data point appearing above the 6.0 ms line. That is, in addition to getting faster performance on average, tiled deferred also offers more consistent performance, making it easier to achieve a smooth framerate.

1.6   Conclusion

This chapter presented an optimized compute-based tiled-culling implementation for scenes with many dynamic lights. The technique allows forward rendering to support such scenes with high performance. It also improves the performance of deferred rendering for these scenes by reducing the average cost to calculate lighting, as well as the worst-case cost and standard deviation. That is, it provides both faster performance (on average) and more consistent performance, avoiding the bandwidth bottleneck from blending overlapping lights. For more details, see the companion code.

1.7   Acknowledgments

Many thanks to the rendering engineers at Epic Games, specifically Brian Karis for the idea to use AABBs to bound the tiles and Martin Mittring for the initial implementation of AABBs and for the Modified Half Z method. Thanks also go out to Martin for providing feedback for this chapter. And thanks to the Epic rendering team and Epic Games in general for supporting this work.

The following are either registered trademarks or trademarks of the listed companies in the United States and/or other countries: AMD, Radeon, and combinations thereof are trademarks of Advanced Micro Devices, Inc.; Unreal is a registered trademark of Epic Games, Inc.; Xbox One is a trademark of Microsoft Corporation.; NVIDIA is a registered trademark of NVIDIA Corporation.; Playstation 4 is a trademark of Sony Computer Entertainment, Inc.

Bibliography

[Andersson 09] Johan Andersson. "Parallel Graphics in Frostbite—Current and Future." Beyond Programmable Shading, SIGGRAPH Course, New Orleans, LA, August 3–7, 2009.

[Engel 14] Wolfgang Engel. "Compute Shader Optimizations for AMD GPUs: Parallel Reduction." *Diary of a Graphics Programmer*, http://diaryofagraphicsprogrammer.blogspot.com/2014/03/compute-shader-optimizations-for-amd.html, March 26, 2014.

[Harada et al. 12] Takahiro Harada, Jay McKee, and Jason C.Yang. "Forward+: Bringing Deferred Lighting to the Next Level." Paper presented at Eurographics, Cagliari, Italy, May 13–18, 2012.

[Harris 07] Mark Harris. "Optimizing Parallel Reduction in CUDA." NVIDIA, http://developer.download.nvidia.com/compute/cuda/1.1-Beta/x86_website/projects/reduction/doc/reduction.pdf, 2007.

[Lauritzen 10] Andrew Lauritzen. "Deferred Rendering for Current and Future Rendering Pipelines." Beyond Programmable Shading, SIGGRAPH Course, Los Angeles, CA, July 25–29, 2010.

[Lauritzen 12] Andrew Lauritzen. "Intersecting Lights with Pixels: Reasoning about Forward and Deferred Rendering." Beyond Programmable Shading, SIGGRAPH Course, Los Angeles, CA, August 5–9, 2012.

[Saito and Takahashi 90] Takafumi Saito and Tokiichiro Takahashi. "Comprehensible Rendering of 3-D Shapes." *Computer Graphics: Proc. SIGGRAPH* 24:4 (1990), 197–206.

Rendering Vector Displacement-Mapped Surfaces in a GPU Ray Tracer
Takahiro Harada

2.1 Introduction

Ray tracing is an elegant solution to render high-quality images. By combining Monte Carlo integration with ray tracing, we can solve the rendering equation. However, a disadvantage of using ray tracing is its high computational cost, which makes render time long. To improve the performance, GPUs have been used. However, GPU ray tracers typically do not have as many features as CPU ray tracers. Vector displacement mapping is one of the features that we do not see much in GPU ray tracers. When vector displacement mapping is evaluated on the fly (i.e., without creating a large number of polygons in the preprocess and storing them in the memory), it allows us to render a highly geometric detailed scene from a simple mesh. Since geometric detail is an important factor for realism, vector displacement mapping is an important technique in ray tracing. In this chapter, we describe a method to render vector displacement-mapped surfaces in a GPU ray tracer.

2.2 Displacement Mapping

Displacement mapping is a technique to add geometric detail to a simple geometry. Although the goal is similar to normal mapping, it actually creates high-resolution geometries, as shown in Figure 2.1, from a low-resolution mesh (Figure 2.2), while normal mapping only changes the normal vector to add an illusion of having a geometric detail. There are two types of displacement mapping. The one we usually call displacement mapping uses textures storing scalar values, which are used as offsets for the displacement using the surface normal as the

Figure 2.1. The "Party" scene with vector displacement-mapped surfaces rendered using the proposed method. The rendering time is 77 ms/frame on an AMD FirePro W9100 GPU. Instancing is not used to stress the rendering algorithm. If pretessellated, the geometry requires 52 GB of memory.

Figure 2.2. The base mesh used for the "Party" scene.

displacement direction. We call this approach *scalar displacement mapping*. The other is *vector displacement mapping*, which uses a texture storing vector values that are used as the displacement vector of the surface. Because the displacement can be an arbitrary direction, it gives a lot of freedom for what we create from a simple geometry. For example, scalar displacement mapping cannot create an overhang as shown in Figure 2.3, but vector displacement mapping can.

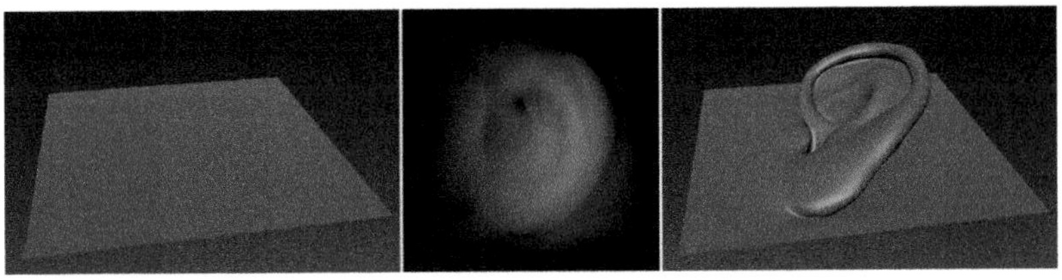

Figure 2.3. Illustration of vector displacement mapping. (a) Simple geometry (a quad). (b) A vector displacement map. (c) Surface after applying vector displacement.

This freedom in vector displacement mapping poses technical challenges when it is ray traced. Although we could use algorithms, such as the method proposed by [Smits et al. 00], for ray tracing a scalar displacement-mapped surface by utilizing the constraint in the displacement direction, we cannot apply it for a vector displacement-mapped surface because the assumption does not apply. In vector displacement mapping, there is no constraint in displacement direction. So when we check the intersection of a ray with a vector displacement patch (VD patch), we cannot avoid creating the detailed geometry by tessellating and displacing vertices and building a spatial acceleration structure for those.

2.3 Ray Tracing a Scene with Vector Displacement Maps

Ray tracing requires identifying a closest hit point for a ray with the scene, which is accelerated by using a spatial acceleration structure. Bounding volume hierarchies (BVHs) as acceleration structures are often employed. When we implement a ray tracer only for simple primitives such as triangles and quads, we compute the intersection to a primitive once we encounter it during BVH traversal. However, an intersection to a VD patch is much more expensive to compute than an intersection test with these simple primitives, especially when direct ray tracing is used (i.e., a VD patch is tessellated and displaced on the fly). To amortize the cost of tessellation and displacement, we want to gather all the rays intersecting the AABB of a VD patch and process them at once rather than subdividing and displacing a VD patch every time a ray hits its AABB, as studied by [Hanika et al. 10].

2.4 Ray Tracing a Vector Displacement Patch

This section focuses on the ray–VD patch intersection, although using it in a ray tracer requires additional changes, which are going to be discussed in Section 2.5. In this section, we first describe a single-threaded implementation of the intersection of a ray with a VD patch to simplify the explanation. We then extend it for a parallel implementation using OpenCL.

2.4.1   Single Ray

To intersect a ray with a VD patch, we first need to build the detailed geometry of the patch by tessellating it to generate vertices, which are then displaced by the value fetched from the vector displacement map. Although there are several ways to generate vertices, we simply generate them uniformly on the patch (i.e., all the generated vertices are on the plane of the patch) without geometry smoothing.

Data structure.   We could find the closest intersection by testing primitives in the scene one by one, but it is better to create a spatial acceleration structure to do this efficiently. As we build it on the fly, the build performance is as important as the intersection performance. Therefore, we employed a simple acceleration structure. A patch is split into four patches recursively to build a complete quad BVH. At the lowest level of the BVH, four vertex positions and texture coordinates are linearly interpolated from the values of the root patch. The displaced vertex position is then calculated by adding the displacement vector value, which is fetched from a texture using the interpolated texture coordinate. Next, the AABBs enclosing these four vertices are computed and used as the geometry at the leaves rather than a quad because we subdivide the patch smaller than a pixel size. This allows us not to store geometries (e.g., vertices), but only store the BVH. Thus, we can reduce the data size for a VD patch. A texture coordinate and normal vector are also computed and stored within a node. Once leaf nodes are computed, it ascends the tree level by level and builds the nodes of the inner level. It does this by computing the union of AABBs and averaging normal vectors and texture coordinates of the four child nodes. This process is repeated until it reaches the root node.

For better performance, the memory footprint for the BVH has to be reduced as much as possible. Thus, an AABB is compressed by quantizing the maximum and minimum values into 2 byte integers $(\max_q, \min_q)$ these as follows:

$$\max_q = 0xfff7 \times (\max_f - \min_{\text{root}})/\text{extent}_{\text{root}} + 1,$$
$$\min_q = 0xfff7 \times (\min_f - \min_{\text{root}})/\text{extent}_{\text{root}},$$
$$\text{extent}_{\text{root}} = \max_{\text{root}} - \min_{\text{root}}.$$

where $\max_f$ and $\min_f$ are uncompressed maximum and minimum values, respectively, of the AABB and $\max_{\text{root}}$ and $\min_{\text{root}}$ are values of the root AABB. We considered compressing them into 1-byte integers, but the accuracy was not high enough since the subdivision level can easily go higher than the resolution limit of 1-byte integers (i.e., eight levels). We also quantized texture coordinates and the normal vectors into 4 bytes each. Therefore, the total memory footprint for a node is 20 bytes (Figure 2.4).

We separate the hierarchy of the BVH from the node data (i.e., a node does not store links to other nodes such as children). This is to keep the memory footprint for nodes small. We only store one hierarchy data structure for all VD

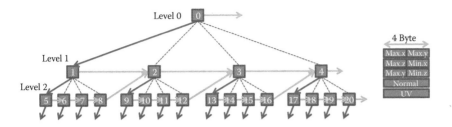

Figure 2.4. Quad BVH. Each node stores two links: one pointing to the first children (red), and one pointing to the skip node (green). To check if a node is a leaf of level i, the node index is compared to $(4^i - 1)/3$, e.g., leaf nodes of level 2 BVH are nodes whose index is greater than 5. Data layout in a node is shown on the left.

patches because we always create a complete quad BVH so that the hierarchy structure is the same for all the BVHs we construct. Although we build a BVH at different depths (i.e., levels), we only compute and store the hierarchy structure for the maximum level we might build. As nodes are stored in breadth-first order, leaf nodes can be identified easily by checking their index. Leaf nodes at the ith level are nodes with indices larger than $(4^i - 1)/3$, as shown in Figure 2.4.

We use stackless traversal for BVH traversal. Thus, a node in the hierarchy structure stores two indices of the first child and the skip node (Figure 2.4). These two indices are packed and stored in 4 bytes of data.

To summarize the data structure we have

- precomputed data for the hierarchy structure,

- BVH (array of nodes) built on the fly.

In Listing 2.1, they are denoted as **gNodes** and **gLinks**, respectively.

Traversal and intersection. The primary reason we employed a stackless traversal is to reduce the memory traffic and register pressure, which affects the performance. Moreover, since the data for the state of the ray is the index of the current node, we could easily shuffle rays to improve the performance, although we have not investigated this optimization yet.

As we have already built the BVH for the patch, the traversal is straightforward. Pseudocode is shown in Listing 2.1. An overview of the process is depicted in Figure 2.5.

2.4.2 OpenCL Implementation

To fully utilize the GPU, we have to parallelize the algorithm described in Section 2.4.1. We implemented our algorithm using OpenCL, and we used AMD GPUs; thus, we follow these respective terminologies in the next explanation.

```
__global Node* gNodes;
__global u32* gLinks;
float f;
u32 n, uv;
int o = getOffset( lodRes );
while( nodeIdx != breakIdx )
{
  Aabb node = NodeGetAabb( gNodes[nodeIdx] ); // reconstruct AABB
  float frac = AabbIntersect( node, &from, &to, &invRay );
  bool isLeaf = nodeIdx >= o;
  if( frac < f )
  {
    if( isLeaf )
    {
      f = frac;
      n = gNodes[nodeIdx].m_n;
      uv = gNodes[nodeIdx].m_uv;
      nodeIdx = LinkGetSkip( gLinks[nodeIdx] );
    }
    else
      nodeIdx = LinkGetChild( gLinks[nodeIdx] );
  }
  else
    nodeIdx = LinkGetSkip( gLinks[nodeIdx] );
}
```

Listing 2.1. Bottom-level hierarchy traversal.

Before we start intersecting rays with VD patches, we gather all the rays hitting the AABB of any VD patches. When a ray hits multiple VD patches, we store multiple hits. These hits are sorted by a VD patch index. This results in a list of VD patches, each of which has a list of rays.

We implemented a kernel doing both BVH build and its traversal. Work groups are launched with the number of work items optimal for the respective GPU architecture. We use AMD GPUs, which are 64-wide SIMD, so 64 work items are executed for a work group. A work group first fetches a VD patch from the list of unprocessed VD patches. This work group is responsible for the intersection of all rays hitting the AABBs of the root patch. First, we use work items executing in parallel for building the BVH. However, as we build a BVH for the patch that has to be stored somewhere, we need to allocate memory for it and therefore the question is where to allocate. The first candidate is in the local data share (LDS), but it is too small if we build a BVH with six levels (64×64 leaf nodes), which requires 108 KB (= 5400 nodes $\times$ 20 B). If we limit the number of levels to five (32×32 leaf nodes), we only require 26 KB. Although this is smaller than the maximum allocation size for the LDS (32 KB) for an AMD FirePro W9100 GPU, we can only schedule two work groups per compute unit. (A compute unit has 4 SIMD engines.) Thus, it cannot schedule enough work groups for a SIMD to hide latencies, which results in poor performance. Instead of storing it in the LDS, we store it in the global memory, whose access

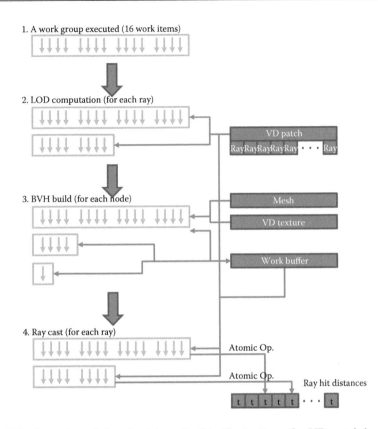

Figure 2.5. Overview of the algorithm. In this illustration, the VD patch has 24 rays intersecting the root AABB; it builds a BVH with depth 3.

latency is higher than the LDS, but we do not have such a restriction in the size for the global memory. Since we do not use the LDS for the storage of the BVH data in this approach, the LDS usage is not the limiting factor for concurrent work group execution in a SIMD. The limiting factor is now the usage of vector general purpose registers (VGPRs). Our current implementation allows us to schedule 12 work groups in a compute unit (CU), which is 3 per SIMD, as the kernel uses 72 VGPRs per SIMD lane.

Because we know the maximum number of work groups executed concurrently in a CU for this kernel, we can calculate the number of work groups executed in parallel on the GPU. We used an AMD FirePro W9100 GPU, which has 44 CUs. Thus, 528 work groups (44 CUs × 12 work groups) are launched for the kernel. A work group processes VD patches one after another and executes until no VD patch is left unprocessed. As we know the number of work groups executed, we allocate memory for the BVH storage in global memory before execution and assign each chunk of memory for a work group as a work buffer. In all the test cases, we limit the maximum subdivision level to 5, and thus a 13-MB (= 26 KB × 528) work buffer is allocated.

After work groups are launched and a VD patch is fetched, we first compute the required subdivision level for the patch by comparing the extent of the AABB of the root node to the area of a pixel at the distance from the camera. As we allow instancing for shapes with vector displacement maps (e.g., the same patch can be at multiple locations in the world), we need to compute the subdivision level for all the rays. Work items are used to process rays in parallel at this step. Once a subdivision level is computed for a ray, the maximum value is selected using an atomic operation to an LDS value.

Then, work items compute the node data, which is the AABB, texture coordinate, and normal vector of a leaf in parallel. If the number of leaf nodes is higher than the number of work items executed, a work item processes multiple nodes sequentially. Once the leaf level of the BVH is built, it ascends the hierarchy one step and computes nodes at the next level of the hierarchy. Work items are used to compute a node in parallel. Since we write node data to global memory at one level and then read it at the next level, we need to guarantee that the write and read order is kept. This is enforced by placing a global memory barrier, which guarantees the order in a work group only; thus, it can be used for this purpose. This process is repeated until it reaches the root of the hierarchy. Pseudocode for the parallel BVH build is shown in Listing 2.2.

```
int localIdx = GET_LOCAL_IDX;
int lIdx = localIdx%8;// Assuming 64 work items in a work group
int lIdy = localIdx/8;
// Compute leaf nodes
for(int jj=lIdy*nn; jj<(lIdy+1)*nn; jj++)
for(int ii=lIdx*nn; ii<(lIdx+1)*nn; ii++)
{
  Aabb aabb;
  for(int j=0; j<2; j++) for(int i=0; i<2; i++)
  {
    float2 w = make_float2( (ii+i)/(float)nSplit, (jj+j)/(float)↩
        nSplit );
    float2 uv = interpolateUv( uv0, uv1, uv2, uv3, w );
    float4 v = interpolateVertex( v0, v1, v2, v3, w );
    v += texture_fetch( gVDispMap[faceIdx], uv );// Apply ↩
        displacement
    AabbIncludePoint( &aabb, v );
  }
  int o = getOffset( tessLevel );
  __global GridCell* dst = &myCells[o + ii + jj*nSplit];
  dst->m_aabb = quantizeAabb( aabb );
  dst->m_n = compressF4( computeNormal(ii,jj) );
  dst->m_uv = compress( computeUv(ii,jj) );
}
GLOBAL_BARRIER;
// Computes internal nodes level by level
for(int level = tessLevel-1; level>=0; level--)
```

```
{
  int nc = (1<<level);
  int nf = (1<<(level+1));
  int oc = getOffset( level );
  int of = getOffset( level+1 );
  while( localIdx < nc*nc )
  {
    int ii = localIdx%nc;
    int jj = localIdx/nc;

    GridCell g  = myCells[ of + (2*ii)+(2*jj)*nf ];
    GridCell g1 = myCells[ of + (2*ii+1)+(2*jj+1)*nf ];
    GridCell g2 = myCells[ of + (2*ii+1)+(2*jj)*nf ];
    GridCell g3 = myCells[ of + (2*ii)+(2*jj+1)*nf ];
    myCells[ oc + ii + jj*nc ] = merge( g, g1, g2, g3 );
    localIdx += WG_SIZE*WG_SIZE;
  }
  GLOBAL_BARRIER;
}
```

Listing 2.2. BVH build, starting with the leaf-level build and then the upper-level build.

Once the hierarchy is built, we switch the work item usage from a work item for a node to a work item for a ray. A work item reads a ray from the list of rays hitting the AABB of the VD patch. A ray is then transformed to the object space of the model and traversed using the hierarchy information. If the current hit is closer than the last found hit, the hit distance, element index, normal vector, and texture coordinate at the hit point are updated. However, we cannot simply write this hit information because a ray can be processed by more than one work item in different work groups. The current OpenCL programming model does not have a mechanism to have a critical section, which would be necessary for our case.[1] Instead, we used 64-bit atomic operations, which are not optimal in terms of performance, but at least we avoided the write hazard. When the element index, quantized normal vector, and quantized texture coordinate are all 32 bit data, the hit distance is converted into a 32-bit integer and appended at the top of those 32 bits to create 64-bit integers. By using an atomic min operation, we can store the closest hit information (Figure 2.5).

Pseudocode for the entire kernel is shown in Algorithm 2.1.

2.5 Integration into an OpenCL Ray Tracer

Although ray tracing one mesh with a vector displacement map is simple, we want to use several meshes with vector displacement maps, together with other triangle meshes, as shown in Figure 2.1. This section describes how the ray tracing of a VD patch is integrated into our OpenCL ray tracer.

---

[1] Note that barrier (CLK_GLOBAL_MEM_FENCE) only guarantee synchronization of global memory access from a work group but not for different work groups.

```
while Unprocessed VD patch do
   {Max LOD level computation}
   for rays in parallel do
      level ← computeLODLevel(ray_i)
      maxLevel ← max(level)
   end for
   {Build BVH}
   for leaves in parallel do
      computeLeafNode(leaf_i)
   end for
   for lv = maxLevel − 1, lv > 0 do
      for nodes at level lv in parallel do
         computeNode(node_i)
      end for
   end for
   {BVH traversal and Ray VD patch intersection}
   for rays in parallel do
      level ← computeLODLevel(ray_i)
      hit ← rayCast(level)
      storeHit(ray_i, hit)
   end for
end while
```

Algorithm 2.1. Bottom-level hierarchy build and traversal kernel.

2.5.1 Scene Description

We could store all the primitives in the scene in a single spatial acceleration structure. However, this does not allow us to use techniques such as instancing, which is a powerful method to increase the scene complexity with small overhead. Therefore, we put meshes in the scene and build an acceleration structure storing meshes at leaves. A mesh is a triangle mesh, a quad mesh (some of which might be VD patches), or an instance of one of those with a world transformation. We then build another hierarchy for each mesh in which primitives (e.g., triangles, quads) are stored at leaf nodes. If a primitive is a VD patch, we build another hierarchy in a patch, as we discussed in Section 2.4. Therefore, we have a three-level hierarchy. (See Figure 2.6.) The top and middle stores meshes and primitives, and the bottom exists only for a VD patch, which is generated on the fly.

2.5.2 Preparation

Before rendering starts, we compute AABBs for primitives and build top- and middle-level BVHs. For VD patches, the computation of an accurate AABB is expensive as it requires tessellation and displacement. Instead, we compute the maximum displacement amount from a displacement texture and expand the

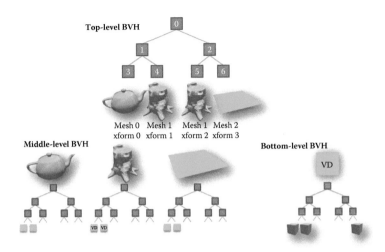

Figure 2.6. Three-level hierarchy. A leaf of the top-level BVH stores an object, which is a middle-level BVH and transform. A leaf of the middle-level BVH stores primitives such as a triangle, a quad, or a VD patch. There is a bottom-level BVH that is built on the fly during the rendering for a leaf storing a VD patch.

AABB of a quad using the value. Although this results in a loose-fitted AABB, which makes ray tracing less efficient than when tight AABBs are computed, it makes the preparation time short.

2.5.3 Hierarchy Traversal

We fused the traversal of top- and middle-level hierarchies into a traversal kernel. When a ray reaches a leaf of the top-level hierarchy, the ray is transformed into object space and starts traversing the middle-level hierarchy. Upon exiting the middle-level hierarchy, the ray is transformed back to world space. Once a ray hits a leaf node of the middle-level hierarchy, it computes a hit the primitive stored at the leaf node immediately if the primitive is a triangle or a quad. As discussed in Section 2.4, we do not compute the intersection of a ray with the VD patch on a visit to a leaf node. Instead, a primitive index and ray index are stored in a buffer for further processing. (Precisely, we also store the mesh index, which is necessary to get its transform.) An atomic operation is used to allocate space for a pair in the buffer. After the top- and middle-level hierarchy traversals, the computed hits are only those computed with triangles and quads. Thus, we need to determine if there are closer intersections with VD patches.

The primitive index and ray index are stored in random order. As we process patch by patch, these values are sorted by the primitive index using a radix sort [Harada and Howes 11], and the start and end indices of pairs for a primitive are computed. The buffer storing the start indices is used as a job queue.

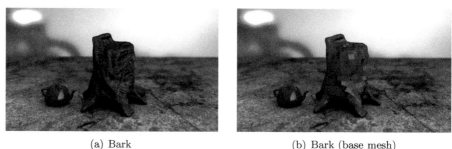

(a) Bark   (b) Bark (base mesh)

(c) Barks   (d) Barks (base mesh)

(e) Pumpkin   (f) Pumpkin (base mesh)

Figure 2.7. Some of our test scenes with and without vector displacement mapping.

We then execute a kernel described in Section 2.4, which computes the intersection with VD patches. The minimum number of work groups filling the GPU is executed and each work group fetches an unprocessed VD patch from the queue and then processes one after another.

2.6 Results and Discussion

We created models with vector displacement maps in Mudbox for evaluating the method. Base meshes and vector displacement maps are exported in object space. We created four test scenes with these models and models without vector displacement maps (Figures 2.1 and 2.7). To stress the renderer, we intentionally

Scene	Pretessellation	Direct Ray Tracing
Party	52 GB	16 MB
Bark	1.7 GB	0.47 MB
Barks	12 GB	3.3 MB
Pumpkin	380 MB	0.12 MB

Table 2.1. Memory usage for geometry and acceleration structure.

did not use instancing for these tests, although we could use it to improve the performance for a scene in which a same geometry has been placed several times. We used an AMD FirePro W9100 GPU for all the tests.

The biggest advantage of using vector displacement maps is their small memory footprints, as they create highly detailed geometry on the fly rather than preparing a high-resolution mesh. The memory usages with the proposed method and with pretessellation are shown in Table 2.1. The "Party" scene requires the most memory and does not fit into any existing GPU's memory with pretessellation. Even if we could store such a large scene in memory, it takes time to start the rendering because of the preprocess for rendering, such as IO and spatial acceleration structure build. This prevents a fast iteration of modeling and rendering. On the other hand, those overheads are low when direct ray tracing of vector displacement maps is used. The difference is noticeable, even for the simplest "Pumpkin" scene.

The advantage of the memory footprint is obvious, but the question is, "What is the cost at runtime, (i.e., the impact for the rendering speed)?" Despite its complexity in the ray-casting algorithm, direct ray tracing of vector displacement maps was faster for most of the experiments. We rendered direct illumination of the scene under an environment light (i.e., one primary ray cast and one shadow ray cast) and measured the breakdown of the rendering time, which is shown in Figure 2.8.[2] Pretessellation is faster only for the "Pumpkin" scene whose geometric complexity is the lowest among all tests. Pretessellation is slower for the "Bark" scene and it fails to render the other two larger scenes. This is interesting because direct ray tracing is doing more work than pretessellation. This performance came from less divergent computation of direct ray tracing (i.e.,the top- and middle-level hierarchies are relatively shallow, and we batch the rays intersecting with a VD patch).

To understand the ray-casting performance for direct ray tracing better, we analyzed the breakdown of each ray-cast operation for the scenes (Figure 2.9). These timings include kernel launch overhead, which is substantial especially for sorting that requires launching many kernels. Computation time for sorting is roughly proportional to the number of hit pairs, although it includes the overhead. Most of the time is spent on bottom-level BVH build and ray casting for

---

[2]The renderer is a progressive path tracer, and thus all screenshots are taken after it casts some samples per pixel.

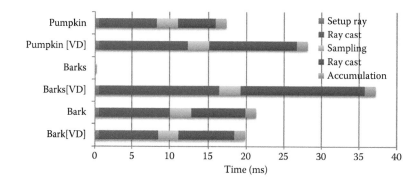

Figure 2.8. Breakdown of computational time for a frame. There are two graphs for each scene. One is with pretessellation and the other (VD) is with the proposed method. Barks cannot render without using instancing with VD patches.

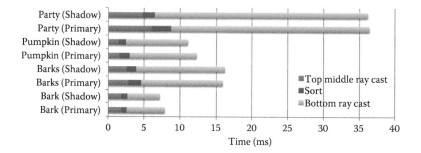

Figure 2.9. Time for top and middle ray casts, sort, and bottom ray cast.

VD patches. The time does not change much when we compare primary and shadow ray casts for the "Barks" scene, although the number of shadow rays is smaller than the number of primary rays. This indicates the weakness of the method, which is that the bottom-level BVH construction cost can be amortized when there are a large number of rays intersecting with a VD patch, but it cannot be amortized if this number is too low. This is why the ray casting for shadow rays in the "Pumpkin" scene is so slow compared to the time with pretessellation. The situation gets worse as the ray depth increases. We rendered indirect illumination with five ray bounces (depths) for the "Bark" scene (Figure 2.10). Figure 2.11 shows the ray casting time measured for each ray bounce. Although the number of active rays decreases as it goes deeper, the ray casting time did not decrease much. This can be improved by caching the generated bottom-level BVH, which is disposed and computed again for each ray casting operation. This is an opportunity for future research.

Figure 2.10. The "bark" scene rendered with five-bounce indirect illumination.

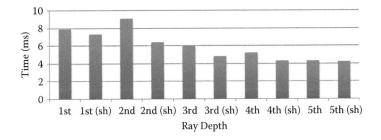

Figure 2.11. Ray casting time for each ray depth in indirect illumination computation. Those marked (sh) are ray casts for shadow rays.

2.7 Conclusion

In this chapter, we have presented a method to ray-trace vector displacement-mapped surfaces on the GPU. Our experiments show that direct ray tracing requires a small memory footprint only, and ray tracing performance is competitive or faster than ray tracing with pretessellation. The advantage gets stronger as there are more VD patches in the scene.

From the breakdown of the rendering time, we think that optimizing the BVH build for the scene and ray casting for simple geometries such as triangles and quads are not as important as optimizing the bottom-level hierarchy build and ray casting because the complexity of the bottom-level hierarchy easily becomes higher than the complexity of the top- and middle-level hierarchies once we start adding vector displacement to the scene.

Bibliography

[Hanika et al. 10] Johannes Hanika, Alexander Keller, and Hendrik P. A. Lensch. "Two-Level Ray Tracing with Reordering for Highly Complex Scenes." In *Proceedings of Graphics Interface 2010*, pp. 145–152. Toronto: Canadian Information Processing Society, 2010.

[Harada and Howes 11] T. Harada and L. Howes. "Introduction to GPU Radix Sort." Supplement to *Heterogeneous Computing with OpenCL*, edited by Benedict Gaster, Lee Howes, David R. Kaeli, Perhaad Mistry, and Dana Schaa. San Francisco: Morgan Kaufmann, 2011. Available at http://www.heterogeneouscompute.org/?page_id=7.

[Smits et al. 00] Brian E. Smits, Peter Shirley, and Michael M. Stark. "Direct Ray Tracing of Displacement Mapped Triangles." In *Proceedings of the Eurographics Workshop on Rendering Techniques*, pp. 307–318. Aire-la-Ville, Switzerland: Eurographics Association, 2000.

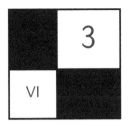

Smooth Probabilistic Ambient Occlusion for Volume Rendering

Thomas Kroes, Dirk Schut, and Elmar Eisemann

3.1 Introduction

Ambient occlusion [Zhukov et al. 98] is a compelling approach to improve depth and shape perception [Lindemann and Ropinski 11, Langer and Bülthoff 99], to give the illusion of global illumination, and to efficiently approximate low-frequency outdoor lighting. In principle, ambient occlusion computes the light accessibility of a point, i.e., it measures how much a point is exposed to its surrounding environment.

An efficient and often-used version of ambient occlusion is screen-space ambient occlusion [Kajalin 09]. It uses the depth buffer to compute an approximate visibility. This method is very appealing because its computational overhead is minimal. However, it cannot be applied to direct volume rendering (DVR) because voxels are typically semitransparent (defined via a transfer function). Consequently, a depth buffer would be ambiguous and is not useful in this context.

The first method to compute ambient occlusion in DVR, called *vicinity shading*, was developed by Steward [Stewart 03]. This method computes the ambient occlusion in each voxel by taking into account how much the neighboring voxels obscure it. The resulting illumination is stored in an additional volume, which needs to be recomputed after each scene modification. Similarly, Hernell et al. [Hernell et al. 10] computed ambient occlusion by ray tracing inside a small neighborhood around the voxel. Kroes et al. extended this method by taking the entire volume into account [Kroes et al. 12].

Our approach tries to avoid costly ray tracing and casts the problem into a filtering process. In this sense, it is similar in spirit to Penner and Mitchell's

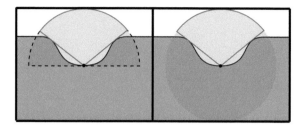

Figure 3.1. The hemisphere around a point that determines ambient occlusion (left). The blue part is unoccluded. Volumetric obscurance relies on a full sphere (right).

method [Penner and Mitchell 08], which uses statistical information about the neighborhood of the voxels to estimate ambient occlusion, as well as the method by Ropinski et al., which is similar and also adds color bleeding [Ropinski et al. 08]. Furthermore, our approach relates to Crassin et al.'s [Crassin et al. 10], which proposes the use of filtering for shadow and out-of-focus computations.

Our Smooth Probabilistic Ambient Occlusion (SPAO) is a novel and easy-to-implement solution for ambient occlusion in DVR. Instead of applying costly ray casting to determine the accessibility of a voxel, this technique employs a probabilistic heuristic in concert with 3D image filtering. In this way, ambient occlusion can be efficiently approximated and it is possible to interactively modify the transfer function, which is critical in many applications, such as medical and scientific DVR. Furthermore, our method offers various quality tradeoffs regarding memory, performance, and visual quality. Very few texture lookups are needed in comparison to ray-casting solutions, and the interpretation as a filtering process ensures a noise-free, smooth appearance.

3.2 Smooth Probabilistic Ambient Occlusion

There are various definitions for ambient occlusion. Here, we define it as the part of a point that is accessible from the outside world. A 2D example is given in Figure 3.1 and illustrates the ambient occlusion computation. More formally, the ambient-occlusion value $\mathcal{A}(p, n)$ is given by the integral of the visibility function over the hemisphere Ω centered around a point p in the direction of the normal n of that point:

$$\mathcal{A}(p, n) := \frac{1}{\pi} \int_{\Omega(n)} V(p, \omega) d\omega,$$

where V is the visibility function. In other words, V stems from the volume data itself after it was transformed by the transfer function. Note that $V(p, \omega)$ is 0 if the ray from point p in direction ω is blocked and 1 if it is unblocked; an intermediate value attenuates the ray. To simplify the description, we will use only the notion of blocked and unblocked rays in the following. Please notice that we can interpret intermediate values of V as a probability for a ray to be blocked. For example, if V returns a value of 0.5, there is a 50% chance for a ray to be blocked.

It is also possible to integrate the visibility function over the whole sphere around a point, making Ω a full sphere, instead of a hemisphere and making it independent of n. The result is called obscurance and denoted $\mathcal{A}(p)$, and it produces similar effects. Calculating obscurance instead of ambient occlusion has the advantage that it does not require a normal. However, this definition will lead to parts of the volume that are located behind the point to intervene in the computation. This property can be a disadvantage for standard scenes, as the result might become too dark, but in the context of DVR, it is sometimes even preferable, as it will unveil information below the surface, which is often desired.

Both ambient occlusion and obscurance only depend on the geometry of the volume. Therefore, they can be stored in an additional volume that is then used to modulate the original volume's illumination. The occlusion values can be calculated directly from the opacity of the original volume. Nonetheless, the values have to be recomputed when the original volume changes—for example, when the user changes the transfer function. This latter step can be very costly and makes it impossible to interact with transfer functions while maintaining a high visual fidelity. Our approach is fast to compute and enables a user to quickly apply such modifications without having to wait a long time for the result.

Initially, our solution will be explained in the context of obscurance, but in Section 3.3, we will extend our algorithm to approach ambient occlusion by making use of the normals to reduce the influence of the part of the volume below the surface.

3.2.1 Overview

To approximate obscurance at a certain point in the volume, we avoid ray casting. Instead, we introduce an approximation that is based on the probability of the rays being blocked by the volume. Instead of solving $\mathcal{A}(p)$ and its integral entirely, we consider a limited region around p, formed by volumes of increasing size. The volume between successive volumes forms a layer of voxels, a so-called shell (Figure 3.2). We will show how to derive the probability of a random ray to be blocked by a shell. From this result, we deduce an approximation of the integral $\mathcal{A}(p)$ assuming that the entire volume is represented by a single shell. Finally, the results for these various shells are combined heuristically to yield our occlusion approximation for the entire volume.

First, we consider shells being represented by a sphere with a one-voxel-wide boundary S. These shells are formed by a set of successive spheres, which each grow in radius by one voxel. In this situation, if we consider one independent shell, any random ray sent from its center will intersect exactly one voxel. If all

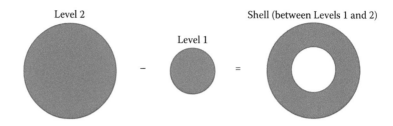

Figure 3.2. A shell is a layer of voxels formed by the difference between two differently sized volumes. By creating a cascade of these volumes, a set of shells is formed. For each shell, we approximate the probability of a ray to be blocked and combine these probabilities heuristically to form the final obscurance value.

directions are equally likely, the probability for a ray to be blocked then boils down to an average of all voxel values in the shell, $\text{average}_S(p)$. Looking carefully at this definition, it turns out that this probability is equivalent to solving for $\mathcal{A}$ in the presence of a single shell.

If we now decompose the volume into such a set of shells around a point, we can compute the probability of the rays to be blocked by each shell, but still need to combine all these blocking contributions together. In order to do so, we make use of a heuristic. We assume a statistical independence between the value distributions in the various shells. The probability of rays originating at p to be blocked by a set of n englobing shells $\{S_i\}_{i=1}^n$ ordered from small to large is then given by

$$\prod_{i=1}^{n}(1 - \text{average}_{S_i}(p)).$$

To understand this formula, it helps considering only two layers $\{S_1, S_2\}$. A random ray from p traverses S_1 with probability $(1 - \text{average}_{S_1}(p))$. If this ray passed S_1, it is again, potentially, stopped by S_2, this time with probability $(1 - \text{average}_{S_2}(p))$, yielding a total probability of $(1 - \text{average}_{S_1}(p))(1 - \text{average}_{S_2}(p))$. In the following, we will describe an efficient and GPU-friendly approach to compute an approximation of this solution.

3.2.2   Approximating Obscurance for Cube Shells

In practice, we will use box-shaped shells instead of spheres (Figure 3.3). We will show in the next section that this choice will allow us to benefit from GPU texture filtering to compute average_{S_i}, making the algorithm very efficient. The cubes are chosen to be of increasing size and centered at each point p of the volume. The shells are then defined by hollowing out these cubes by subtracting the next-smaller cube from its successor. In reality, these cubes will never have

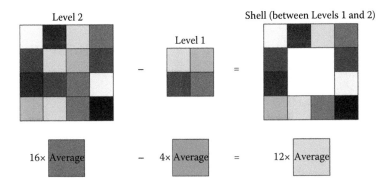

Figure 3.3. In this 2D illustration, the shell on the right is a one-voxel-thick hull that is formed by subtracting the average opacity from level 1 (in the middle) from level 2 (on the left).

Figure 3.4. Cube shells used to approximate obscurance.

to be constructed explicitly, but it is helpful to think of them for illustrative purposes. The process is illustrated in Figure 3.4.

Following the previously described steps, we need to deduce $average_{S_i}$ for each of the shells, which in our new situation corresponds to the average of all voxel values between two successive cubes. If we assume for now that we have a quick way of determining the average inside of a complete cube, we can rapidly determine $average_{S_i}$. To illustrate this computation, we will assume that we want to determine $average_S$ of a shell S defined by two cubes C_1 and C_2, with voxel-value averages A_1 and A_2 and number of voxels S_1, S_2 ($S_1 < S_2$), respectively. The solution is then given by

$$average_S = \frac{S_2 A_2 - S_1 A_1}{S_2 - S_1}. \tag{3.1}$$

In other words, we can subtract from the total voxel sum of one cube $S_2 A_2$ the total voxel sum of the next-smaller one ($S_2 A_2$) and normalize the result by the number of voxels in the shell between both (Figure 3.3, lower row).

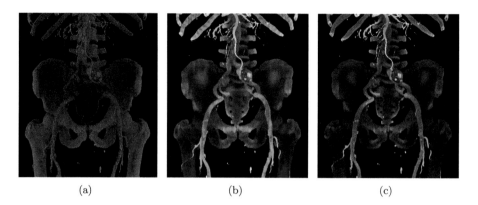

(a)   (b)   (c)

Figure 3.5. Volumetric obscurance using (a) ray tracing (256 rays/voxel), (b) mipmap filtering, and (c) N-buffer filtering.

Please note that Equation (3.1) can be rewritten as

$$\text{average}_S = \frac{1}{1 - \frac{S_1}{S_2}} \left(A_2 - \left(\frac{S_1}{S_2} \right) A_1 \right).$$

Consequently, only the average and the relative change in size (S_1/S_2) is needed to deduce average_S, which facilitates computations further. Imagine that each cube is obtained by doubling the length of each edge of the predecessor. Then, the ratio would be $1 : 8$, resulting in $\text{average}_S = \frac{8}{7}(A_2 - \frac{1}{8}A_1)$.

3.2.3 Fast Cube Averages

In the previous section, we assumed to have a quick method to determine the average inside of a cube. Here, we will propose two possible solutions to this problem. Our observation is that, for a given cube size, the averages are equivalent to a box filtering of the volume.

Determining averages of various kernel sizes is a common problem in computer graphics in the context of texture mapping. These techniques translate to corresponding operations in a 3D volume. The most common such approximation is mipmapping, but we will also present N-buffers [Décoret 05], which deliver higher-quality filtering at an additional cost.

As mipmaps are rather standard, we will only focus on N-buffers here. Like mipmaps, they consist of multiple levels l, each representing the average values of the original volume inside cubes of width 2^l. Unlike mipmaps, the resolution of an N-buffer is not reduced in each level. Consequently, it is possible to retrieve the exact filled part of a cube at every position in the volume, whereas for a mipmap linear interpolation can provide only an approximation based on the eight closest voxels, which reduces the quality (Figure 3.5).

```
                                                        0,0 0,0 0,0 0,0 0,0 0,0 0,0 0,0 0,0 0,0 0,0 0,0
                                                        0,0 0,1 0,1 0,1 0,1 0,0 0,0 0,0 0,0 0,0 0,0 0,0
                                0,0 0,0 0,0 0,0 0,0 0,0 0,0 0,0 0,0 0,0 0,0 0,0     0,0 0,1 0,1 0,1 0,1 0,0 0,1 0,1 0,0 0,0 0,0
0,0 0,0 0,0 0,0 0,0 0,1 0,0 0,0 0,0 0,0     0,0 0,3 0,3 0,0 0,0 0,1 0,1 0,0 0,0 0,0 0,0     0,0 0,2 0,3 0,3 0,4 0,3 0,2 0,2 0,1 0,1 0,0
0,0 1,0 0,0 0,0 0,1 0,1 0,1 0,0 0,0 0,0     0,0 0,5 0,5 0,0 0,1 0,2 0,2 0,1 0,0 0,0 0,0     0,0 0,3 0,4 0,5 0,6 0,5 0,4 0,3 0,2 0,1 0,1
0,0 1,0 0,0 0,0 0,1 0,3 0,1 0,0 0,0 0,0     0,0 0,5 0,8 0,5 0,5 0,4 0,3 0,2 0,1 0,0 0,0     0,1 0,3 0,4 0,6 0,8 0,6 0,5 0,4 0,3 0,2 0,1
0,0 1,0 1,0 1,0 1,0 0,3 0,3 0,3 0,1 0,0     0,1 0,6 1,0 1,0 1,0 0,7 0,4 0,3 0,3 0,1 0,0     0,1 0,3 0,4 0,7 0,9 0,8 0,7 0,6 0,4 0,3 0,1
0,5 1,0 1,0 1,0 1,0 0,5 0,3 0,3 0,3 0,1     0,3 0,6 0,8 0,9 1,0 0,8 0,4 0,3 0,3 0,2 0,1     0,0 0,1 0,2 0,3 0,5 0,5 0,6 0,5 0,4 0,2 0,1
0,5 0,5 0,5 1,0 1,0 0,5 0,3 0,3 0,3 0,1     0,1 0,4 0,5 0,8 1,0 0,8 0,6 0,5 0,3 0,1 0,0     0,0 0,1 0,1 0,2 0,3 0,3 0,4 0,4 0,3 0,2 0,0
0,0 0,5 0,5 1,0 1,0 0,5 1,0 0,3 0,1 0,0     0,0 0,3 0,4 0,4 0,8 0,9 0,9 0,6 0,1 0,0 0,0     0,0 0,0 0,0 0,0 0,1 0,1 0,2 0,2 0,2 0,1 0,0
0,0 0,5 0,0 0,0 1,0 1,0 1,0 0,1 0,0 0,0     0,0 0,1 0,1 0,0 0,3 0,6 0,7 0,4 0,0 0,0 0,0     0,0 0,0 0,0 0,0 0,0 0,0 0,0 0,0 0,0 0,0 0,0
0,0 0,0 0,0 0,0 0,0 0,3 0,3 0,0 0,0 0,0     0,0 0,0 0,0 0,0 0,0 0,1 0,2 0,1 0,0 0,0 0,0     0,0 0,0 0,0 0,0 0,0 0,0 0,0 0,0 0,0 0,0 0,0
0,0 0,0 0,0 0,0 0,0 0,0 0,0 0,0 0,0 0,0     0,0 0,0 0,0 0,0 0,0 0,0 0,0 0,0 0,0 0,0 0,0     0,0 0,0 0,0 0,0 0,0 0,0 0,0 0,0 0,0 0,0 0,0
```

Figure 3.6. A 2D example of how N-buffers are calculated. A dataset is shown on the left, with the first two N-buffer levels next to it. In each level, the average of four values of the previous level is combined into one value.

The N-buffer construction is efficient, as each new level can be computed from the previous using only eight lookups. A 2D example of the calculation is shown in Figure 3.6. Nonetheless, N-buffers result in higher memory consumption, so it can be useful to apply a few mipmap levels before processing the rest using N-buffers.

3.3 Approximating Ambient Occlusion

In Section 3.2, we explained that ambient occlusion in comparison with obscurance can provide cues that are closer to realistic lighting because voxels behind the point of interest are not taken into account. To reduce this effect, we can offset the lookup operations in the direction of the normal. When choosing the offset carefully, the increase in size of the cubes and the offset can be correlated to obtain shells that correspond now to hemispheres. This goal can be achieved by multiplying the normal vector by half the size of the box. An example with a shorter vector is illustrated in Figure 3.7.

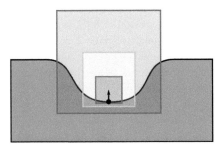

Figure 3.7. The lookups of the cubes from a point with a normal of length 0.75 in the upward direction.

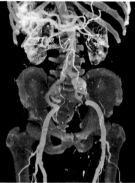
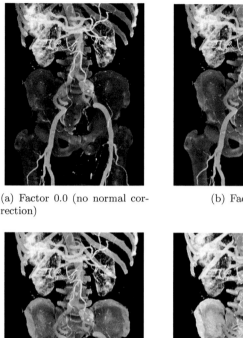
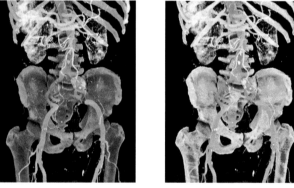

(a) Factor 0.0 (no normal correction)

(b) Factor 0.5

(c) Factor 1.0

(d) Factor 2.0

Figure 3.8. Effect of the normal factor

However, in DVR, a normal is not always clearly defined, e.g., inside a homogeneous semitransparent volume like jelly pudding. Similarly, between two different semitransparent voxels, it might be less clear how to define a normal at the interface between opaque and transparent materials. Consequently, we propose to scale the cube offset based on how strong the gradient is. Interestingly, while most techniques derive normals from the normalized gradient via central differences, we can use the gradient magnitude to determine if a normal is clearly defined. Hence, we propose to remove the normalization operation and instead normalize the voxel values themselves to the range [0,1], which will lead to the gradient becoming an appropriately scaled normal. Additionally, we allow the user to specify a global scale to either pronounce or reduce the impact of this ambient-occlusion approximation (Figure 3.8).

	N-buffers	Mipmaps	Ray trace, 512 rays
Level 0	30.93 ms	33.00 ms	-
Level 1	33.99 ms	4.58 ms	-
Level 2	40.13 ms	0.66 ms	-
Level 3	41.16 ms	0.17 ms	-
Level 4	42.69 ms	0.14 ms	-
Level 5	38.09 ms	0.13 ms	-
Level 6	41.91 ms	0.12 ms	-
Levels Total	268.90 ms	38.8 ms	-
AO Computation	63.24 ms	110.39 ms	425.36 sec
Total	332.14 ms	149.19 ms	425.36 sec

Table 3.1. Performance measurements for the Macoessix data set ($512 \times 512 \times 512$) for N-buffers and mipmap-based SPAO. For each technique we show the time it takes to compute the individual levels and to combine them into an ambient occlusion volume.

3.4 Results

Our method has been implemented in a CUDA-based stand-alone software program for DVR. The program and its source code are available under the original BSD license. It is shipped with sample datasets. The transfer function and, thus, the visual representation can be changed on the fly. Also, the user can select from three different methods of ambient occlusion computation: mipmaps, N-buffers, and ray tracing. Our program makes use of CUDA 3.0 texture objects and will not support lower CUDA versions.

We tested the performance of our technique using the publicly available Macoessix dataset from the Osirix website[1] (see Table 3.1). All tests were peformed on an Intel Xeon W3530 (2.80 GHz) workstation with 12 GB RAM and a GeForce GTX TITAN Graphics Card with 4 GB of RAM. N-buffers are slightly more costly than mipmaps, but both are orders of magnitude faster than a volumetric ambient-occlusion ray tracer. The latter takes more than four minutes, see Table 3.1.

Figure 3.9 shows some results of our approach on the Backpack and Manix datasets.

3.5 Conclusion

This chapter presents a novel approach to compute ambient occlusion for DVR. We demonstrate that by considering the ambient-occlusion computation as a filtering process, we can significantly improve efficiency and make it usable in a real-time DVR application. Such an approach is useful for medical visualization applications, where transfer functions are very often subject to change.

---

[1] http://www.osirix-viewer.com/datasets/

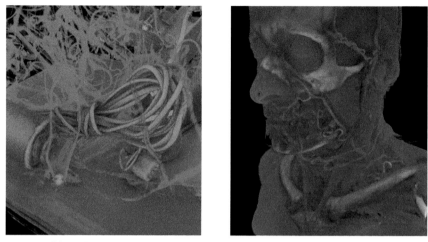

(a) Backpack data set   (b) Manix data set

Figure 3.9. SPAO applied to the Backpack ($512 \times 512 \times 461$) and Manix ($512 \times 512 \times 460$) data sets.

Our approach is efficient and simple to implement and leads to a very good quality/performance tradeoff. Nonetheless, we also experimented with more complex combinations of the shells, especially, as the assumption of independence of the occlusion probabilities is usually not true in most datasets. In practice, it turns out that our solution seems to be a good choice, and any increase in complexity also led to a significant performance impact. Nonetheless, this topic remains interesting for future work. Furthermore, we would like to investigate approximating physically plausible light transport, such as global illumination, with our filtering technique, which could further enhance the volume depiction.

Bibliography

[Crassin et al. 10] Cyril Crassin, Fabrice Neyret, Miguel Sainz, and Elmar Eisemann. "GPU Pro: Advanced Rendering Techniques." edited by Wolfgang Engel, Chapter Efficient Rendering of Highly Detailed Volumetric Scenes with GigaVoxels, pp. 643–676. Natick, MA: A K Peters, 2010.

[Décoret 05] Xavier Décoret. "N-Buffers for Efficient Depth Map Query." *Computer Graphics Forum* 24:3 (2005), 393–400.

[Hernell et al. 10] Frida Hernell, Patric Ljung, and Anders Ynnerman. "Local Ambient Occlusion in Direct Volume Rendering." *IEEE Transactions on Visualization and Computer Graphics* 16:4 (2010), 548–559.

[Kajalin 09] Vladimir Kajalin. "Screen Space Ambient Occlusion." In *ShaderX7*, edited by Wolfgang Engel, Chapter 6.1. Boston: Cengage Learning, 2009.

[Kroes et al. 12] Thomas Kroes, Frits H. Post, and Charl P. Botha. "Exposure Render: An Interactive Photo-realistic Volume Rendering Framework." *PLoS ONE* 7:7 (2012), e38586.

[Langer and Bülthoff 99] Michael S Langer and Heinrich H Bülthoff. "Depth Discrimination from Shading under DiffuseLighting." *Perception* 29:6 (1999), 649–660.

[Lindemann and Ropinski 11] Florian Lindemann and Timo Ropinski. "About the Influence of Illumination Models on Image Comprehension in Direct Volume Rendering." *IEEE Trans. Visualization and Computer Graphics: Vis Proceedings* 17:12 (2011), 1922–1931.

[Penner and Mitchell 08] Eric Penner and Ross Mitchell. "Isosurface Ambient Occlusion and Soft Shadows with Filterable Occlusion Maps." In *Proceedings of the Fifth Eurographics/IEEE VGTC Conference on Point-Based Graphics*, pp. 57–64. Aire-la-Ville, Switzerland: Eurographics Association, 2008.

[Ropinski et al. 08] Timo Ropinski, Jennis Meyer-Spradow, Stefan Diepenbrock, Jörg Mensmann, and Klaus Hinrichs. "Interactive Volume Rendering with Dynamic Ambient Occlusion and Color Bleeding." *Computer Graphics Forum* 27:2 (2008), 567–576.

[Stewart 03] A James Stewart. "Vicinity Shading for Enhanced Perception of Volumetric Data." In *Proceedings of the 14th IEEE Visualization 2003 (VIS'03)*, p. 47. Los Alamitos, CA: IEEE Computer Society, 2003.

[Zhukov et al. 98] Sergey Zhukov, Andrei Iones, and Grigorij Kronin. "An Ambient Light Illumination Model." In *Rendering Techniques 98*, pp. 45–55. New York: Springer, 1998.

3D Engine Design

Welcome to the 3D Engine Design section of this edition of *GPU Pro*. The selection of chapters you will find in here covers a range of engine design problems.

First, Holger Gruen examines the benefits of a block-wise linear memory layout for binary 3D grids in the chapter "Block-Wise Linear Binary Grids for Fast Ray-Casting Operations." This memory layout allows mapping a number of volumetric intersection algorithms to binary AND operations. Bulk-testing a subportion of the voxel grid against a volumetric stencil becomes possible. The chapter presents various use cases for this memory layout optimization.

Second, Michael Delva, Julien Hamaide, and Ramses Ladlani present the chapter "Semantic-Based Shader Generation Using Shader Shaker." This chapter offers one solution for developing and efficiently maintaining shader permutations across multiple target platforms. The proposed technique produces shaders automatically from a set of handwritten code fragments, each responsible for a single feature. This particular version of the proven divide-and-conquer methodology differs in the way the fragments are being linked together by using a path-finding algorithm to compute a complete data flow through shader fragments from the initial vertex attributes to the final pixel shader output.

Finally, Shannon Woods, Nicolas Capens, Jamie Madill, and Geoff Lang present the chapter "ANGLE: Bringing OpenGL ES to the Desktop." ANGLE is a portable, open-source, hardware-accelerated implementation of OpenGL ES 2.0 used by software like Google Chrome. The chapter provides a close insight on the Direct3D 11 backend implementation of ANGLE along with how certain challenges were handled, in addition to recommended practices for application developers using ANGLE.

I hope you enjoy this edition's selection, and I hope you find these chapters inspiring and enlightening to your rendering and engine development work.

Welcome!

—Wessam Bahnassi

Block-Wise Linear Binary Grids for Fast Ray-Casting Operations
Holger Gruen

1.1 Introduction

Binary grids only contain one bit of information per cell. Even reasonably high grid resolutions (e.g., $4096 \times 4096 \times 256$ amount to 512 MB of memory) still fit into GPU memory and are thus practical in real-time situations.

This chapter examines the benefits of a block-wise linear memory layout for binary 3D grids. This memory layout allows mapping a number of volumetric intersection algorithms to binary AND operations. Bulk-testing a subportion of the voxel grid against a volumetric stencil becomes possible. The number of arithmetic operations and the amount of memory words to be accessed is lower than for regular sampling schemes.

Below, techniques for rendering binary grids are discussed. The text then describes how to use block-wise linear grids to cast rays through the grid to detect occluded light sources in the context of an indirect illumination rendering technique as a real-world use case. Finally, various other use cases for using block-wise linear grids are discussed.

1.2 Overview

There is a wealth of work regarding the use of binary voxel grids in 3D graphics: [Eisemann and Décoret 06] lists various applications, specifically some from the area of shadowing; [Penmatsa et al. 10] describes a volumetric ambient occlusion algorithm; and [Kasik et al. 08] presents the use for precomputed visibility applications, to name a few.

The rendering of binary voxel grids (BVGs) is often realized by mapping the third axis (e.g., the z-axis) of the grid to the bits of the pixels of a multiple render target (MRT) setup. During rendering, voxels/bits along the z-axis are set using

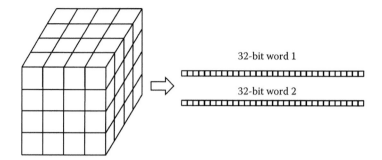

Figure 1.1. A $4 \times 4 \times 4$ voxel grid fits into two consecutive 32-bit words.

blending operations of the graphics hardware. A pixel/fragment shader computes which bit to set and computes the outputs accordingly.

Specifically, on more modern hardware and with modern graphics APIs, binary blend operations can be used to switch on specific bits in render targets using unsigned integer pixel formats.

The downside of this approach is that voxelization is only possible along one view direction per rendering pass.

With the use of scattering pixel/fragment shaders, this changes as one can now render along three view directions and scatter to the same binary grid using interlocked binary OR operations.

How to make use of the geometry shader stage to only render one geometry pass to voxelize a scene is described in [Crassin and Green 12].

1.3 Block-Wise Linear Memory Layout

Block-wise memory layouts are used in GPU architectures to improve cache coherency during texturing operations. The idea is to store a small 2D block of texels into a contiguous block of memory instead of using a scanline after scanline memory layout.

This idea extends into 3D textures and can also be applied to binary voxel grids.

Trivially, any portion of the binary voxel grid of size $2^N \times 2^N \times 2^N$ fits into $\frac{2^N \times 2^N \times 2^N}{32}$ 32-bit integer words.

Figure 1.1 depicts a simple example and shows the simple case of a $4 \times 4 \times 4$ subgrid being mapped to two 32-bit integer words.

Please note that the case of $2 \times 2 \times 2$ voxels is not considered here as the benefits of packing such a small part of the grid can be ignored in the context of this chapter.

Subgrids of size $4 \times 4 \times 4$ may seem small, but they can be used as the building blocks for compositing the storage pattern for bigger blocks.

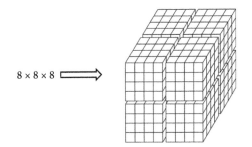

$8 \times 8 \times 8$

Figure 1.2. Here, $8 \times 8 \times 8$ voxels fit into eight $4 \times 4 \times 4$ blocks.

These bigger blocks store each of the $4 \times 4 \times 4$ subblocks—of which they are comprised—in two consecutive 32-bit integer locations. Figure 1.2 depicts this idea for a $8 \times 8 \times 8$ block that maps to sixteen 32-bit integer words.

In order for readers to start using the described memory layout, Listing 1.1 provides an implementation of a function that can be used to compute the buffer address and bit-value for a given grid size and block size.

Please note that the number of bits that are set in each $4 \times 4 \times 4$ portion of the grid can be used to compute a value for volumetric coverage. Modern GPUs have operations that can count the nonzero bits in integer values—thus mapping bits to coverage is efficient.

Another way to efficiently implement storing $4 \times 4 \times 4$ bits in a memory coherent way instead of using a 1D buffer of unsigned integer under Direct3D 11 can be the use of a `RWTexture3D<uint2>`. In this case, each texel can be used to encode a $4 \times 4 \times 4$ of the grid.

1.4 Rendering Block-Wise Linear Binary Voxel Grids

Assuming Direct3D 11 class hardware, a simplified version of voxelization can be implemented very similar to what is described in [Crassin and Green 12].

In the following description, a geometry shader is used during rendering in order to allow sending the voxelized geometry only once. The geometry shader projects each triangle in a way that maximizes its rasterized surface area or the number of pixels is covers. This is achieved by setting a per-triangle view matrix that looks along the normal of the triangle.

In this chapter, a geometry shader is used for convenience only. It is also possible to use a vertex shader (using ideas from [Gruen 12]) to get all the data for a triangle directly from the vertex buffer. Alternatively, all data necessary to set up the per-triangle view matrix can be stored per vertex, which also allows skipping the use of the geometry shader stage.

Please note that the following code doesn't implement a solid voxelization strategy. Only the voxels that intersect the plane of the triangle are set.

```
// Return the offset into the buffer in bytes in .x and the
// value to OR to the 32-bit integer to set the grid pos in .y
uint2 computeOffsetAndVal (float3 pos, // 3D pos in the grid
                           float GridSize, // size of the grid
                           float BlockRes) // block-size,
                                        // e.g., 8 to pack 8x8x8
{
    // Compute which of the BlockRes x BlockRes x BlockRes blocks
    // `pos' is in
    float3 block_pos = floor( floor( pos ) * (1.0f/BlockRes) );

    // Compute 3D position within subblock
    float3 sub_pos = floor( floor( pos ) % BlockRes );

    // Compute the size of a grid with grid cells each BlockRes wide
    float RGS = GridSize/BlockRes;

    // block size in bytes
    uint block_size = uint( BlockRes * BlockRes * BlockRes ) / 8;

    // byte offset to the BlockRes x BlockRes x BlockRes `pos' is in
    uint block_off = block_size * uint( block_pos.x +
                                block_pos.y * RGS +
                                block_pos.z * RGS * RGS );
    // Compute which of the final 4x4x4 blocks the voxel resides in
    float3 sub_block_pos = floor( sub_pos * 0.25f );

    // Compute the bit position inside the final 4x4x4 blocks
    float3 bit_pos = sub_pos % 4.0f;

    // Compute the size of a block in 4x4x4 units
    Float FBS = BlockRes * 0.25f;

    // Compute byte offset for final 4x4x4 subblock in the current
    // BlockRes x BlockRes x BlockRes block
    uint off = 8.0f * ( sub_block_pos.x +
                        sub_block_pos.y * FBS +
                        sub_block_pos.z * FBS * FBS );
    return uint2(
                // Add memory offsets and add final offset base on z
                block_off + off + ( bit_pos.z > 1.0f ? 0x4 : 0x0 ),

                // Compute bit position in 32-bit word
                0x1 << uint ( bit_pos.x + bit_pos.y * 4.0f +
                            ( bit_pos.z % 2.0f ) * 4.0f * 4.0f )
                );
}
```

Listing 1.1. Compute the offset and bit position for a position in a block-linearly stored binary grid.

Listing 1.2 shows shader fragments of such an implementation. Here, the assumption is that tessellation isn't enabled, as otherwise the domain shader needs to take the role of the vertex shader fragment given below.

Assuming a viewport with a resolution sufficient to deliver a reasonable number of pixels to the pixels shader is set, Algorithm 1.1 is used. Listing 1.2 provides the implementation details.

1. Set up a viewport with sufficient resolution to grant a dense enough rasterization of the triangles.

   - Experiments have shown that a resolution of two times the dimension of the grid is a good resolution.
   - The application passes the dimension as a constant in 'g_ViewportResolution' to the shaders.

2. Disable back-face culling and depth testing.

3. Set up the UAV for the 'RWByteAddressBuffer BinaryGrid' in the pixel shader (see Listing 1.2).

4. The vertex shader (see Listing 1.2), on-top of what it does for vertex processing, passes on the world-space position of each vertex.

5. The geometry shader sets up a viewing matrix that looks along the world-space normal of the triangle, maximizing its projected area, and passes grid-space positions to the pixel shader.

6. The pixel shader computes the offset into the grid buffer using the function from Listing 1.1. It then uses an interlocked operation to set the bit for the current grid position.

Algorithm 1.1. One-pass voxelization.

```
struct GS_RenderGridInput
{
    float3 f3WorldSpacePos : WSPos;
    ...
};
GS_RenderGridInput VS_BinaryGrid( VS_RenderSceneInput I )
{
    GS_RenderGridInput O;
    // Pass on world-space position — assuming WS is passed in
    O.f3WorldSpacePos = I.f3Position;
    // Compute/pass on additional stuff
    ...
    return O;
}
struct PS_RenderGridInput
{
    float4 f4Position : SV_POSITION;
    float3 f3GridPosition : GRIDPOS;
};
[maxvertexcount(3)]
void GS_BinaryGrid( triangle GS_RenderGridInput input[3],
                inout TriangleStream<PS_RenderGridInput> Triangles )
{
    PS_RenderGridInput output;
    // g_WorldSpaceGridSize contains the world-space size of the
    // grid
    float3 f3CellSize = g_WorldSpaceGridSize.xyz *
                            ( 1.0f / float(BINARY_GRID_RES).xxx );
```

```
float3 gv[3], v[3];

// Compute grid-space positions from world-space positions;
// g_SceneLBFbox contains the left, bottom, and front points
// of world-space bounding box of the grid
gv[0] = ( input[0].f3WorldSpacePos - g_SceneLBFbox.xyz ) /
          f3CellSize;

gv[1] = ( input[1].f3WorldSpacePos - g_SceneLBFbox.xyz ) /
          f3CellSize;

gv[2] = ( input[2].f3WorldSpacePos - g_SceneLBFbox.xyz ) /
          f3CellSize;

// Compute triangle edges
float3 d0 = gv[1] - gv[0];
float3 d1 = gv[2] - gv[0];

// Compute triangle normal
float3 N = normalize( cross( d0, d1 ) );
float3 C = ( 1.0f/3.0f ) * ( gv[0] + gv[1] + gv[2] );

// Move eye position to 1 unit away from the triangles center
float3 Eye = C - N;

// Set up view axis for looking along the triangle normal
float3 xaxis = normalize( d1 );
float3 yaxis = cross( N, xaxis );

// Set up view matrix for looking along the triangle normal
float4x4 ViewMatrix = {
                       xaxis.x, xaxis.y, xaxis.z, -dot( xaxis, Eye ),
                       yaxis.x, yaxis.y, yaxis.z, -dot( yaxis, Eye ),
                       N.x, N.y, N.z, -dot( N, Eye ),
                       0.0f , 0.0f , 0.0f , 1.0f
                       };

// Compute view-space positions
v[0] = mul( ViewMatrix, float4( gv[0], 1.0f ) ).xyz;
v[1] = mul( ViewMatrix, float4( gv[1], 1.0f ) ).xyz;
v[2] = mul( ViewMatrix, float4( gv[2], 1.0f ) ).xyz;

// Set up a projection matrix using a constant;
// g_ViewportResolution is a constant set by the application
float4x4 ProjMatrix =
{

    2.0f / g_ViewportResolution, 0.0f, 0.0f, 0.0f,
    0.0f, 2.0f / g_ViewportResolution, 0.0f, 0.0f,
    0.0f, 0.0f, 1.0f, -0.5f,
    0.0f, 0.0f, 0.0f, 1.0f
}

// Project vertices and pass on grid-space position
[unroll]for( int i = 0; i < 3; ++i )
{
    output.f4Position = mul( ProjMatrix, float4( v[i], 1.0f ) );
    output.f3GridPosition = gv[i];
    Triangles.Append( output );
}
    Triangles.RestartStrip();
}

RWByteAddressBuffer BinaryGrid :                       register( u0 );
```

```
void PS_BinaryGrid( PS_RenderGridInput I )
{
    uint old;
    // BINARY_GRID_RES holds the resolution/size of the binary grid
    float3 f3GridCoord = max( (0.0f).xxx,
                              min( ( BINARY_GRID_RES-1 ).xxx,
                                   floor( I.f3GridPosition ) ) );
    // Compute the offset and the values of the bit to manipulate
    uint2 off_val = computeOffsetAndVal( f3GridCoord );

    // Turn on the bit for the current grid position
    BinaryGrid.InterlockedOr( off_val.x, off_val.y, old );
}
```

Listing 1.2. Vertex and geometry shader fragments for one-pass voxelization under Direct3D 11.

1.5 Casting Rays through a Block-Wise Linear Grid

Algorithm 1.2 details one way to cast rays through the grid. It does it in a way that benefits from the memory layout of block-wise linear grids. It tests for intersections by building small ray segments in local registers holding grid-aligned $4 \times 4 \times 4$ test blocks. The actual intersection test only amounts to doing two binary AND operations. The memory cost for this ray intersection test is lower than performing four isolated load operations into a grid that has a "normal" memory layout.

1.6 Detecting Occlusions during Indirect Light Gathering

The article [Gruen 11] describes the implementation of a reflective shadow map (RSM)–based one-bounce indirect illumination algorithm (see [Dachsbacher and Stammminger 05]). An RSM, in a nutshell, is a G-buffer as seen from the point of the light and usually consists of the combination of a depth buffer, a buffer that contains surface normals, and a buffer that contains the colors of the lit scene.

In order to detect occluded RSM pixels, a grid of singly linked lists of triangles is build. A set of rays is cast through this grid trying to find blocked RSM pixels and to compute the color of the blocked indirect light. In a final pass, the blocked indirect light is subtracted from the indirect light that is the result of running a filter kernel over the RSM treating its pixels as virtual point lights (VPLs).

Replacing the grid of lists of triangles by a binary block-wise linear grid is straightforward. Instead of using a compute shader for rasterizing blocker triangles into the grid, the voxelization algorithm described in Algorithm 1.1 is used to create a binary 3D grid.

Using the freely available assets and shaders from [Gruen 11], the scenario was recreated using a block-wise linear binary grid for detecting occluded VPLs to estimate blocked indirect light.

For all voxels along the ray, start an iterator $V(I)$ at the start point of the ray.

1. Determine which $2^N \times 2^N \times 2^N$ block B that $V(I)$ sits in.

2. Determine which $4 \times 4 \times 4$ subblock S of B that $V(I)$ sits in.

3. Reserve two 32-bit integer registers $R[2]$ to hold a ray subsection.

4. Build a ray segment in R.

    (a) For all voxels v along the ray starting at $V(I)$ that are still inside S,

        i. set the bit in R to which v maps,

        ii. advance I by 1.

5. Load two 32-bit integer words $T[2]$ from the buffer holding G that contain S.

6. Perform the following bitwise AND operations:

    (a) $R[0]$ & $T[0]$,

    (b) $R[1]$ & $T[1]$,

7. If any of the tests in Steps 6(a) or 6(b) return a nonzero result, the ray has hit something.

Algorithm 1.2. Casting a ray in small segments.

Listing 1.3 provides the implementation details. In order to hide the fact that a discrete binary grid is used, the edges cast through the grid are randomized using pseudorandom numbers. Also, instead of computing unblocked and blocked indirect light separately, the shaders in Listing 1.3 cast a ray segment toward each VPL that is considered.

```
// Compute a long word sized offset into the grid for a grid
// position 'pos'
uint compute4x4x4BlockLWOffset( float3 pos, float GridRes, float
    BlockRes )
{
  float3 block_pos = floor( floor( pos ) * (1.0f/BlockRes) );
  //local address in block
  float3 sub_pos = floor( floor( pos ) % BlockRes );

  uint block_off = ( BINARY_BOCK_SIZE / 4 ) *
              uint( block_pos.x + block_pos.y * (GridRes/BlockRes)
                  + block_pos.z * (GridRes/BlockRes ) *
                  (GridRes/BlockRes));

  float3 sub_block_pos = floor( sub_pos * float(1.0f/4.0f) );

  uint off = 2.0f * ( sub_block_pos.x +
```

```
                                sub_block_pos.y * ( BlockRes * 0.25f ) +
                                sub_block_pos.z * ( BlockRes * 0.25f ) *
                                                 ( BlockRes * 0.25f ) );
   return block_off + off;
}

// Trace an edge through the binary grid in 4x4x4 blocks
float traceEdgeBinaryGrid( float3 f3CPos, // start pos of ray

                           float3 f3CN, // normal at start pos of ray
                           float3 f3D, // normalized direction of ray
                           float3 f3Pos, // end pos of ray/egde
                           float3 f3N ) // normal at end pos
{
   float fCount = 0.0f;

   // g_SceneBoxSize is the world-space size of the scene
   float3 f3CellSize = g_SceneBoxSize.xyz *
                          ( 1.0f / float(BINARY_GRID_RES).xxx );

   // Step along normal to get out of current cell
   // to prevent self-occlusion;
   // g_SceneLBFbox is the left, bottom, and front pos of the world box
   float3 f3GridPos = ( f3CPos + ( f3CN * f3CellSize ) --
                          g_SceneLBFbox.xyz ) / f3CellSize;
   float3 f3DstGridPos = ( f3Pos + ( f3N * f3CellSize ) --
                          g_SceneLBFbox.xyz ) / f3CellSize;

   // Clamp to the grid;
   // BINARY_GRID_RES holds the resolution/size of the binary grid
   float3 f3GridCoord = max( (0.0f).xxx, min( ( BINARY_GRID_RES-1 ).
                          xxx, floor( f3GridPos ) ) );

   float3 f3DstGridCoord = max( (0.0f).xxx, min((BINARY_GRID_RES-1).
                          xxx, floor( f3DstGridPos ) ) );

   // Compute position in a grid of 4x4x4 blocks
   float3 f3SubPos = f3GridCoord%4.0f;
   float3 f3Dg = f3DstGridCoord - f3GridCoord;
   float3 f3AbsD = abs( f3Dg );
   float fMaxD = max( max( f3AbsD.x, f3AbsD.y ), f3AbsD.z );

   // Scale step to step 1 pixel ahead
   f3Dg *= rcp(fMaxD);

   // Where do we step out of the local 4x4x4 grid?
   float3 f3LocalDest = ( f3Dg < 0.0f ? -1.0f : 4.0f );
   float fLoopCount = 0.0f;

   // Only step along two 4x4x4 segments
   while( fMaxD >= 0.0f && fLoopCount <= 2.0f )
   {
       float3 f3Steps = abs( ( f3LocalDest - f3SubPos ) / f3Dg );
       float fSteps    = floor( min( min( f3Steps.x, f3Steps.y ),
                          f3Steps.z ) );
       uint offset     = compute4x4x4BlockLWOffset( f3GridCoord,
                          BINARY_GRID_RES, BINARY_BLOCK_RES );
       uint2 lineseg   = uint2( 0,0 );
       uint2 grid;

       fLoopCount += 1.0f;

       // Load the local 4x4x4 grid
       grid.x = g_bufBinaryGrid[ offset++ ];
```

```
            grid.y = g_bufBinaryGrid[ offset ];

            // Build line mask for current 4x4x4 grid
            [unroll]for( int ss = 0; ss < 4; ++ss )
    {
            [flatten]if( fSteps > 0.5f )
            {
                uint bitpos = uint( f3SubPos.x + ( f3SubPos.y * 4.0f ) +
                                    ( ( f3SubPos.z % 2.0f ) * 16.0f ) );

                lineseg.x |= f3SubPos.z > 1.0f ? 0x0 : ( 0x1 << bitpos );
                lineseg.y |= f3SubPos.z < 2.0f ? 0x0 : ( 0x1 << bitpos );

                f3SubPos += f3Dg;
                f3GridCoord += f3Dg;
                fMaxD -= 1.0f;
                fSteps -= 1.0f;
            }
    }

    if( ( ( lineseg.x & grid.x ) | ( lineseg.y & grid.y)) != 0x0 )
    {
            fCount += 1.0f;
            break;
    }

    // Recompute sub pos
    f3SubPos = f3GridCoord%4.0f;

    }
    return fCount;
}

// publicly available pseudorandom number algorithm
uint rand_xorshift( uint uSeed )
{
  uint rng_state = uSeed;

  rng_state \ = (rng_state << 13);
  rng_state \ = (rng_state >> 17);
  rng_state \ = (rng_state << 5);

  return rng_state;
}

float computeFakeNoise( uint uSeed )
{
  uint uRand = rand_xorshift( uSeed );
  uRand = rand_xorshift( uRand );
  uRand = rand_xorshift( uRand );
  return float( uRand ) / 4294967295.0f;
}

// Compute the indirect light at f3CPosOrg casting rays to test
// for blocked VPLs
float3 computeIndirectLight(float2 tc, // RSM texture coord
                            float2 fc, // fractional texture coord
                            int2 i2Off,// offset for dithering
                            float3 f3CPosOrg, // current pos
                            float3 f3CN ) // normal at current pos
{
  float2 tmp;
  float3 f3IL = (0.0f).xxx;
  int3 adr;
```

```
    float3 f3CPos = f3CPosOrg;

    adr.z = 0;
    adr.y = int( tc.y * g_vRSMDimensions.y + (-LFS) + i2Off.y );

    // Loop over sparse VPL kernel
    for( float row = -LFS; row <= LFS; row += 6.0f, adr.y += 6 )
{
        adr.x = int( tc.x * g_vRSMDimensions.x + (-LFS) + i2Off.x );

        for( float col = -LFS; col <= LFS; col += 6.0f, adr.x += 6 )
        {
                float3 f3Pos, f3Col, f3N;

                // Unpack G-buffer data
                float3 f3Col, f3Pos, f3N;
                GetGBufferData( f3Col, f3Pos, f3N );

                // Compute indirect light contribution
                float3 f3D = f3Pos.xyz - f3CPosOrg.xyz;
                float fLen = length( f3D );
                float fInvLen = rcp( fLen );
                float fDot1 = dot( f3CN, f3D );
                float fDot2 = dot( f3N, -f3D );
                float fDistAtt = saturate( fInvLen * fInvLen );

                // Form factor like term
                fDistAtt *= saturate( fDot1 * fInvLen ) *
                                saturate( fDot2 * fInvLen );

                // Compute noise for casting a noisy ray
                float fNoise1 = 0.15f * computeFakeNoise( uint(adr.x
                                        + fc.x * 100));
                float fNoise2 = 0.15f * computeFakeNoise( uint(adr.y
                                        + fc.y * 100));

                f3Pos -= f3D * fInvLen * fNoise1;
                f3CPos += f3D * fInvLen * fNoise2;

                if( fDistAtt > 0.0f )
                {
                    f3IL += f3Col * fDistAtt * traceRayBinaryGrid
                        ( f3CPos.xyz, f3CN, f3D * fInvLen, f3Pos, f3N );
                }
        }
    }
    return f3IL;
}
```

Listing 1.3. Compute indirect light tracing rays through a binary grid for each VPL.

Please note that the noisy indirect light is computed at a reduced resolution, as described in [Gruen 11]. The resulting indirect light gets blurred bilaterally and is then up-sampled to the full resolution.

The screenshots in Figures 1.3, 1.4, and 1.5 have been generated with and without the detection of occluded VPLs.

Figure 1.3. Screenshot 1: the scene without indirect light.

1.7   Results

One goal of this chapter is to show that using block-wise binary grids does help to speed up ray casting through a binary voxel grid.

In order to prove this, a standard implementation of traversing the grid has been implemented as well.

Table 1.1 shows the performance of both methods on a $64 \times 64 \times 64$ grid on an NVIDIA GTX680 at 1024×768. In the final test, the standard implementation is also allowed to operate on a packed grid in order to show that just the ability to perform block-wise tests is already enough to generate a speedup.

In the test scene and the test application, block-wise tests allow for a speedup of around 20%.

1.8   Future Work

The following describes future work that has not been implemented yet. The algorithms are therefore not necessarily detailed enough to be directly implemented but are an outlook to what would be interesting to implement next.

1.8.1   Casting Cone Stencils

The algorithm for casting a cone through a block-linear BVG G is detailed in Algorithm 1.3. It performs intersections by intersecting small ray segments with

Figure 1.4. Screenshot 2: the scene with indirect light but without detecting occluded VPLs.

Figure 1.5. Screenshot 3: the scene with indirect light from only unoccluded VPLs.

Packed Grid + standard ray marching	~ 180 fps
Packed Grid + block-wise tests	~ 150 fps

Table 1.1. Performance comparison.

1. Determine which $4 \times 4 \times 4$ subblock S of G contains the position of the current pixel.

2. Take the world-space tangent at the current pixel and divide it by the world-space size of a $4 \times 4 \times 4$ subblock of $G \Rightarrow T$.

3. Take the world-space bi-tangent at the current pixel and divide it by the world-space size of a $4 \times 4 \times 4$ subblock of $G \Rightarrow BT$.

4. Iterate along points P on a ray segment starting at S (stepping from one $4 \times 4 \times 4$ block to the next).

   (a) Compute cone radius $r(P)$.

   (b) Divide r by the world-space size of a $4 \times 4 \times 4$ subblock.

   (c) Iterate points hp from $P + r \times (-T - BT)$ to $P + r \times (T - BT)$.

      i. Iterate points vp from hp to $hp + r \times BT$.

         A. Zero an array of two integer registers R.

         B. Set all bits in R (representing a $4 \times 4 \times 4$ block of G) for positions that intersect the original cone.

         C. Load the $4 \times 4 \times 4$ block at vp from G into registers $T[2]$.

         D. If $(R[0]$ AND $T[0])$ or $(R[1]$ AND $T[1])$, then the cone hits the grid; Exit the test.

Algorithm 1.3. Casting a cone through a block-linear BVG.

the voxel grid. If this is not intended, it is possible to change the code to test step by step. Please note that the coherency of memory accesses for this is still higher than performing texture lookups for each step along the ray.

1.8.2   Arbitrary Other Stencils

If possible, one should try to construct any stencil in $4 \times 4 \times 4$ subblocks in order to perform the intersection test in block-wise way for efficiency.

   If dynamic construction is not feasible, a number of stencils can be precomputed and stored in a buffer that is available to the GPU. This works especially well if the stencils can be defined in grid space and don't depend on data from the test origin—e.g., they don't depend on the per-pixel normal or other per pixel attributes.

1.8.3   Using Grid Mipmaps

It is possible to build mipmaps of a block-wise–linear binary grid. The most obvious way is to down-sample an $8 \times 8 \times 8$ block into a $4 \times 4 \times 4$ block. The strategies on how to down-sample each $2 \times 2 \times 2$ block into just one bit do vary depending on the application.

Similar in spirit to [Crassin et al. 11] one could switch to testing a lower mip for intersections after a certain distance when, e.g., testing ray segments. This would speed up the testing of longer rays.

1.9 External References

The assets and shaders used in [Gruen 11] are available in the "Downloads" section of the CRC Press webpage for *GPU Pro 2* at http://www.crcpress.com/product/isbn/9781568817187.

Bibliography

[Crassin and Green 12] Cyril Crassin and Simon Green. "Octree-Based Sparse Voxelization Using the GPU Hardware Rasterizer." In *OpenGL Insights*, edited by P. Cozzi and C. Riccio, pp. 259–278. Boca Raton, FL: CRC Press, 2012.

[Crassin et al. 11] Cyril Crassin, Fabrice Neyret, Miguel Sainz, Simon Green, and Elmar Eisemann. "Interactive Indirect Illumination Using Voxel Cone Tracing." In *Symposium on Interactive 3D Graphics and Games*, p. 207. New York: ACM, 2011.

[Dachsbacher and Stamminger 05] Carsten Dachsbacher and Marc Stamminger. "Reflective Shadow Maps." In *Proceedings of the 2005 Symposium on Interactive 3D Graphics and Games*, pp. 203–231. New York, ACM Press, 2005.

[Eisemann and Décoret 06] Elmar Eisemann and Xavier Décoret. "Fast Scene Voxelization and Applications." In *Proceedings of the 2006 Symposium on Interactive 3D Graphics and Games*, pp. 71–78. New York, ACM, 2006.

[Gruen 11] Holger Gruen. "Real-Time One-Bounce Indirect Illumination and Shadows using Ray Tracing." In *GPU Pro 2: Advanced Rendering Techniques*, edited by Wolfgang Engel, pp. 159–172. Natick, MA: A K Peters, 2011.

[Gruen 12] Holger Gruen. "Vertex Shader Tessellation." In *GPU Pro 3: Advanced Rendering Techniques*, edited by Wolfgang Engel, pp. 1–12. Boca Raton, FL: A K Peters/CRC Press, 2012.

[Kasik et al. 08] David Kasik, Andreas Dietrich, Enrico Gobbetti, Fabio Marton, Dinesh Manocha, Philipp Slusallek, Abe Stephens, and Sung-Eui Yoon. "Massive Model Visualization Techniques." SIGGRAPH course, Los Angeles, CA, August 12–14, 2008.

[Penmatsa et al. 10] Rajeev Penmatsa, Greg Nichols, and Chris Wyman. "Voxel-Space Ambient Occlusion." In *Proceedings of the 2010 ACM SIGGRAPH Symposium on Interactive 3D Graphics and Games*, Article No. 17. New York: ACM, 2010.

Semantic-Based Shader Generation Using Shader Shaker
Michael Delva, Julien Hamaide, and Ramses Ladlani

2.1 Introduction

Maintaining shaders in a production environment is hard, as programmers have to manage an always increasing number of rendering techniques and features, making the amount of shader permutations grow exponentially. As an example, allowing six basic features, such as vertex skinning, normal mapping, multitexturing, lighting, and color multiplying, already requires 64 shader permutations.

Supporting multiple platforms (e.g., HLSL, GLSL) does not help either. Keeping track of the changes made for a platform and manually applying them to the others is tedious and error prone.

This chapter describes our solution for developing and efficiently maintaining shader permutations across multiple target platforms. The proposed technique produces shaders automatically from a set of handwritten code fragments, each responsible for a single feature. This divide-and-conquer methodology was already proposed and used with success in the past, but our approach differs from the existing ones in the way the fragments are being *linked* together. From a list of fragments to use and thanks to user-defined semantics that are used to tag their inputs and outputs, we are using a pathfinding algorithm to compute the complete data flow from the initial vertex attributes to the final pixel shader output.

Our implementation of this algorithm is called Shader Shaker. It is used in production at Fishing Cactus on titles such as *Creatures Online* and is open source for you to enjoy.

2.2   Previous Work

As mentioned earlier, there are two main categories of issues graphic programmers may have to deal with at some point when it comes to shader maintenance: the (possibly high) number of feature permutations and the multiple backends to support (e.g., HLSL, GLSL).

2.2.1   The Permutation Hell Problem

The *permutation hell* problem is almost as old as the introduction of programmable shaders in the early 2000s. [Kime 08] categorizes the solutions to this problem into three main families (code reuse through includes, subtractive approaches, and additive approaches). To these categories, we added a fourth one that we will call *template-based approaches.*

Code reuse. This should be the solution that is the most familiar to programmers. It consists of implementing a library of utility functions that will be made available to the shaders thanks to an inclusion mechanism (e.g., include preprocessor directive) allowing code to be reused easily. The main function of the shader can then be written using calls to these functions and manually feeding the arguments. This is a natural way of editing shaders for programmers, but it gets difficult for the less tech savvy to author new permutations and still requires maintaining all permutations by hand.

   A related solution is the one described in [Väänänen 13], where the Python-based Mako templating engine is used to generate GLSL shaders.

Subtractive solutions. Über-shader solutions rely on one (or a few) mammoth shader(s) containing all the code for all features. The different permutations are generated using a preprocessor to select the relevant portions of code. This technique has proved to be a valid solution for a long time and has been used in countless productions. Nevertheless, its major drawback is that über-shaders are usually hard to maintain (because of their length and the lack of readability caused by the preprocessor directives), especially in a multilanguage environment. Another problem with this approach is that shader semantics can also be tricky to work with (their number is limited and they sometimes need to be sequentially numbered, making it hard to use them with a simple preprocessor).

Additive solutions. These work the other way around by defining a series of elementary *nodes* (or functions) to be aggregated later (either online or offline) to produce the shader. The aggregation is performed by wiring nodes' inputs and outputs together, either visually using a node-based graph editor or programmatically. This approach has seen lots of implementations [Epic Games Inc. 15, Holmér 15] largely because of its user friendliness, allowing artists to produce visually pleasing effects without touching a single line of code. Its main drawback remains the difficulty to control the efficiency of the generated shaders [Ericson 08, Engel 08b].

A complete system for generating shaders from HLSL fragments is described in [Hargreaves 04] in which each shader fragment is a text file containing shader code and an interface block describing its usage context. In this framework, fragments are combined without actually parsing the HLSL code itself. The system was flexible enough to support adaptive fragments, which could change their behavior depending on the context in which they were used, but lacked the support of a graph structure (i.e., the system was restricted to linear chain of operations). Tim Jones implemented this algorithm for XNA 4.0 in [Jones 10].

Trapp and Döllner have developed a system based on code fragments, typed by predefined semantics that can be combined at runtime to produce an über-shader [Trapp and Döllner 07].

In [Engel 08a], Wolfgang Engel proposes a shader workflow based on maintaining a library of files, each responsible for a single functionality (e.g., lighting.fxh, utility.fxh, normals.fxh, skinning.fxh), and a separate list of files responsible for stitching functions calls together (e.g., metal.fx, skin.fx, stone.fx, eyelashes.fx, eyes.fx). This is similar to the node-based approach, but it is targeted more at programmers. As will be shown later, our approach is based on the same idea but differs from it (and the other node-based solutions) by the fact that the wiring is done automatically based on user-defined semantics.

Template-based solutions. The last category finds its roots in the famous template method pattern [Wikipedia 15b], where the general structure of an algorithm (the program skeleton) is well defined but one is still allowed to redefine certain steps.

This is one of the higher-level techniques adopted by Unity (alongside the regular vertex and fragment shaders), which is itself borrowed from Renderman: the surface shader [Pranckevičius 14b]. By defining a clear interface (predefined function names, input and output structures), the surface shader approach allows the end user to concentrate on the surface properties alone, while all the more complex lighting computations (which are much more constant across a game title) remain the responsibility of the über-shader into which it will be injected. It should be noted that it would be possible to combine this with any of the previous three methods for handling permutations at the surface level only.

Taking the idea a bit further, [Yeung 12] describes his solution where he extends the system with interfaces to edit also the vertex data and the lighting formula. Unnecessary code is stripped by generating an abstract syntax tree and traversing it to obtain the variables' dependencies.

2.2.2 The Language Problem

Extensive reviews about the different techniques and tools available to maintain shaders across different languages are available in [Pranckevičius 10a, Pranckevičius 12, Pranckevičius 14a]. We refer the reader to these articles for more information, but we summarize the approaches to handling this problem into the following four families.

The manual way. This could eventually be performed with the help of macros where the languages do differ, but it does not scale well. It is still tricky because of subtle language differences and is hard to maintain.

Use another language. Use a language (eventually a graphical one) that will compile into the target shader language as output.

Cross-compile from one language to another. Lots of tools are available to translate from one language to the other at source code level. The problem can be considered as solved for DirectX 9–level shaders, but there is still work to do for supporting the new features that have appeared since then (e.g., compute, geometry, etc.).

Compile HLSL to bytecode and convert it to GLSL. This is easier to do than the previous technique but suffers from a partly closed tool chain that will run on Windows only.

2.3   Definitions

Our technique is based around the concepts of *fragments* and *user-defined semantics* (not to be confused with the computer graphics fragment used to generate a single pixel data).

- Fragment: In this context, a fragment is a single file written in HLSL that is responsible of implementing a single feature and that contains all the information required for its execution, including uniforms and samplers declarations, as well as code logic. A fragment example is provided in Listing 2.1.

- User-defined semantic: A user-defined semantic is a string literal used to tag a fragment input or output (e.g., `MeshSpacePosition`, `ProjectedPosition`). This tag will be used during shader generation to match a fragment's output to another one's input. User-defined semantics use the existing HLSL semantic feature, used for mapping input and output of shaders.

2.4   Overview

Shader Shaker, our shader generator, uses a new idea to generate the shader. User-defined semantics are added to intermediate variables, as shown in Listing 2.1. The generation algorithm uses those intermediate semantics to generate the list of call functions. The algorithm starts from expected output, e.g.,

```
float4x4 WvpXf;

void GetPosition(
    in float3 position : VertexPosition,
    out float4 projected_position : ProjectedPosition
    )
{
    projected_position = mul( float4( position, 1 ), WvpXf );
}
```

Listing 2.1. GetPosition fragment.

LitColor, and creates a graph of the function required to generate the semantic up to the vertex attributes.

To generate a shader, one has to provide the system with a list of fragments to use (vertex_skinning + projected_world_space_position + diffuse_texturing + normal_mapping + blinn_lighting, for example). Thanks to the semantics, it is possible to link the desired fragments together to produce the final output semantic required by the system (e.g., LitColor) and generate the corresponding complete shader.

Fragments are completely uncoupled; code can be written without consideration of where the data comes from. For example, for a fragment that declares a function that needs an **input** argument with a semantic of type VieSpaceNormal, the tool will search another fragment with a function that has an **output** argument of the very same semantic to link to this one. In deferred rendering, the fragment that provides this **output** argument with the semantic ViewSpaceNormal would read the geometry buffer to fetch that value, whereas in forward rendering, a function could, for example, just return the value of the view-space normal coming from the vertex shader. In any case, the fragment in the pixel shader that uses this ViewSpaceNormal is agnostic to where the data it needs comes from.

To achieve this, the code generator adopts a compiler architecture, going through separate phases:

- HLSL fragments are processed by Shader Shaker to generate for each of them an abstract syntax tree (AST).

- The ASTs are processed to create a final AST, which contains all the needed code (functions/uniforms/samplers). The algorithm (explained in detail in the following section) generates this final AST from the required output semantics (the output of the pixel shader), then goes upward to the input semantics, calling successively all functions whose output semantic match the input semantic of the previous function.

- Eventually, this final AST is converted to the expected output language (e.g., HLSL, GLSL, etc.).

As the concept has been introduced, let's dig into the algorithm.

```
struct FunctionDefinition
{
    set<string> InSemantic;
    set<string> OutSemantic;
    set<string> InOutSemantic;
};
```

Listing 2.2. FunctionDefinition structure.

2.5 Algorithm Explanation

The algorithm used to generate the shader is inspired by the A* path-finding algorithm [Wikipedia 15a]. The idea is to find a path from the required output semantic to the existing input semantics, i.e., the vertex attributes. The path is searched using open and closed semantic sets, in the same way as the open and closed node lists of the original algorithm. To successfully generate the code, the compiler must be provided the following information:

- the list of fragments to use, i.e., the feature list;

- the list of required output semantics (each of them will be mapped to a system semantic such as COLOR0; multiple render target code can be generated by defining multiple final output semantics);

- the list of available input semantics (this can change from mesh to mesh, creating tailored shaders for a given vertex format).

After the parsing of all fragments, the AST is inspected to extract the signature of functions. Each function that declares one or more semantics for its arguments is processed, others being considered as helper functions. A FunctionDef inition structure describing the function is filled up with these semantics information (see Listing 2.2). A fragment is then defined by a map of definitions addressed by function names. It's important to notice that inout function arguments are supported. It's useful when a fragment wants to contribute to a variable, like summing different lighting into a final lit color or when transforming a vertex position through several fragments. When processing an inout semantic, the semantic is kept in the open set. As each function can only be used once, another function outputting the semantic is required.

The code generation is done in two steps. The first step consists of the creation of the call graph. The algorithm is described in Listing 2.3. This algorithm generates a directed acyclic graph of all function calls from the output to the input. The second step consists of code generation from the call graph. As the graph represent the calls from the output, it must be traveled depth first. To

```
open = {required semantic}
closed = {}

repeat until open is empty
    for each fragment from last to first
        for each semantic in open
            if unused function with semantic
                            in OutSemantic exists
                add_function( function )
                restart
            end
        end
    end

    report error, semantics in open set do not resolve
end

add_function( f )
    node = { f, f.InSemantic, f.InOutSemantic}
    open -= f.InSemantic
    open += f.OutSemantic
    //Add inout semantic back in the open set
    open += f.InOutSemantic
    closed += f.InSemantic
    //Link node that required the semantic
    for each semantic in { f.OutSemantic, f.InOutSemantic }
        node[ semantic ].children.add( node )
    end

    //Report as requiring those semantics
    for each semantic in { f.InSemantic, f.InOutSemantic }
        node[ semantic ] = node
    end
    //Remove semantic provided by vertex
    open -= Vertex.AttributeSemantics;
end
```

Listing 2.3. Code generation.

simplify code generation and debugging, the semantic is used as the variable name. The code generation algorithm is described in Listing 2.4. Finally, a map of user semantics to system semantics is generated, information to be used in the engine to bind vertex attributes accordingly.

To illustrate this algorithm, a toy example will be executed step by step. The fragments are defined as shown in Listing 2.5, Listing 2.6, and Listing 2.7. The function definitions are created as shown in Listing 2.8. The required semantic is LitColor. The algorithm generates a graph as shown in Figure 2.1. One can see the open and closed set populated as the algorithm creates the graph. Finally, the graph is processed to create the code shown in Listing 2.9. It is important to notice that the code just uses functions declared in fragments. The final code aggregates all the fragments codes, only with semantic information removed. It's not the purpose of this module to prune unused code. This step can be left to further modules.

```
write function definition with required attributes/varyings
for each node in depth first order
    for each output variable
        if variable has not been encountered yet
            write variable declaration
        end
    end

    write function call

end
```

Listing 2.4. Code generation.

```
Texture DiffuseTexture;

sampler2D DiffuseTextureSampler
{
    Texture = <DiffuseTexture>;
};
void GetDiffuseColor( out float4 color : DiffuseColor,
    in float2 texcoord : DiffuseTexCoord
    )
{
    color = tex2D( DiffuseTextureSampler, texcoord );
}
```

Listing 2.5. Diffuse color from texture fragment.

```
void ComputeNormal( in float3 vertex_normal : VertexNormal,
    out float3 pixel_normal : PixelNormal )
{
    pixel_normal = normalize( vertex_normal );
}
```

Listing 2.6. Simple normal fragment.

```
float4 SomeLighting( in float4 color : DiffuseColor,
    in float3 normal : PixelNormal ) : LitColor
{
    return ( AmbientLight
        + ComputeLight( normal ) )* color;
}
```

Listing 2.7. Some lighting fragment.

```
GetDiffuseColor :
{
    InSemantic  : { "DiffuseTexCoord" }
    OutSemantic : { "DiffuseColor" }
}

ComputeNormal :
{
    InSemantic  : { "VertexNormal" }
    OutSemantic : { "PixelNormal" }
}

SomeLighting :
{
    InSemantic  : { "DiffuseColor" , "PixelNormal" }
    OutSemantic : { "LitColor" }
}
```

Listing 2.8. Function definition examples.

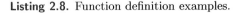

First Step : Open = {DiffuseColor, PixelNormal}

Closed = {LitColor}

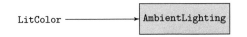

Second Step: Open = {DiffuseTexCoord, PixelNormal}

Closed = {LitColor, DiffuseColor}

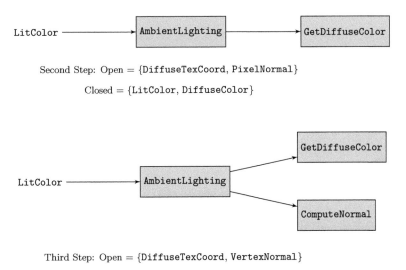

Third Step: Open = {DiffuseTexCoord, VertexNormal}

Closed = {LitColor, DiffuseColor, PixelNormal}

Figure 2.1. Graph generation process.

```
float4 main( in float3 VertexNormal : NORMAL,
    in float2 DiffuseTexCoord : TEXCOORD0 )
{
    float4 DiffuseColor;
    GetDiffuseColor(DiffuseColor, DiffuseTexCoord);
    float3 PixelNormal;
    ComputeNormal(VertexNormal,PixelNormal);
    float4 LitColor
        = SomeLighting(DiffuseColor, PixelNormal);
    return LitColor;
}
```

Listing 2.9. Generated code.

2.6   Error Reporting

2.6.1   Syntax Errors

Syntactic errors existing in fragments are reported as a shader compiler would. Each fragment should be a valid compilation-wise shader. This is detected when parsing the fragments.

2.6.2   Fragment Compliance

A fragment must comply to a list of rules:

- It must only output a given semantic once.

- It must define all constants and sampler it uses.

If either of these rules is broken, the generator reports the error and how to fix it.

2.6.3   Missing Semantics

If any semantic is not found while generating the call graph, the user is informed and the generation is stopped.

2.6.4   Graph Cycles

When a node is inserted in the graph, the graph is checked for cycles. If any are found, the semantics found in the cycle are output.

2.6.5   Mismatching Types for a Semantic

After graph generation, a sanity check is run to ensure all occurrences of a semantic are of the same type. No automatic casting is allowed (e.g., from `float3` to `float2`).

2.6.6 Target Code Restrictions

When targeting a specific platform, additional conditions are checked (e.g., sampler count, vertex attribute count, unsupported texture fetch in vertex shader, etc.)

2.7 Usage Discussions

On top of solving the permutation and the multiplatform problems mentioned earlier, this technique offers the ability to support some noteworthy tricks and features. This discussion lists how they can be leveraged to improve both programmers' and artists' experiences.

2.7.1 Fragments Variants

By using a system similar to [Frykholm 11], it becomes easy to allow your engine file system to choose among multiple variants of a given fragment (e.g., `lighting.fx`, `lighting.low.fx`). We exploit this feature for various purposes:

Platform-specific code. When dealing with multiple graphic platforms, it may happen that the default implementation of a fragment cannot be used natively because the resulting shader is not compatible with the rendering API, or the hardware (e.g., vertex texture fetch). This mechanism allows us to provide a platform-specific version of a given fragment.

Graphic quality. The same principle can be used to manage graphic quality settings. Depending on user settings or based on device capabilities, appropriate fragments can be selected to balance quality against performance.

2.7.2 Fragment Metadata

Each fragment can be associated with a metadata file to ease its integration into the tools. In our case, we chose to export this metadata automatically from the fragments themselves and in JSON format. The available information includes the list of uniforms, the list of textures, a description of what the fragment does, etc.

Thanks to this information, it is easy to populate a combo box from which the artists can select the fragment they want to add to the current material and then tweak the settings the newly added fragment offers.

Furthermore, this metadata also allows us to match the required attributes against the mesh vertex format. A missing component in the vertex format triggers an error, whereas unused data can be stripped safely.

2.7.3   Data-Driven Features

Adding a new rendering feature to the engine and the editor is as easy as adding a new fragment file to the fragment library. As the editor is data-driven, no intervention of a programmer is needed: reloading it is enough. Still, creating a new fragment requires an understanding of the underlying concept. It also requires knowledge of the set-defined semantic, as it could be project specific.

2.7.4   Programming

Accessing the metadata of generated shaders can be leveraged as a data-driven feature, e.g., binding the vertex attributes and the uniforms without using the rendering API to enumerate them. This is even more useful when the graphics API doesn't allow us to do so at all.

2.7.5   Debugging

Programmers can easily debug shaders that are generated by Shader Shaker. Indeed, the output semantics are provided as arguments to the generation process. If an issue is suspected at any level, the shader can be regenerated with an intermediate semantic as the output semantic. For example, if we want to display the view-space normal, the `ViewSpaceNormal` semantic is provided as the output semantic. If the semantic variable type is too small to output (e.g., `float2` while ouputs should be `float4`), a conversion code is inserted.

2.7.6   Choice of Semantics

Semantics are just considered links by the algorithm. Nevertheless, the choice of semantics is really important. If the set is not chosen correctly, new features might require redesigning it, which would require existing fragments' refactoring. The set should be documented precisely to remove any ambiguity on the usage.

2.8   What's Next

While Shader Shaker in its current form is already used with success in our games and tools, there is still room for improvements.

- Use custom semantics for uniforms and samplers. For now, the semantic resolution is only applied to functions and input/output arguments. Applying it to uniforms can be convenient, allowing some values to be passed either at the vertex level or as uniforms.

- The concept of semantic could be augmented. Semantics could have additional properties, such as default values, ranges, normalization, etc. On top of function calls, extra code would be emitted to answer extra specifications.

- Some improvements can be made to the error reporting. In case of an error when generating a shader, the exact position of the error in fragments could be provided with the line number. Also, currently the tool is not yet able to detect cycles in dependency between fragments. It will be of a great help to be able to detect those. Another improvement related to error reporting is a finer detection of grammar errors in the fragments.

- As said before, Shader Shaker does not do any optimizations over the generated shader. Converting Shader Shaker as a frontend to already existing modules, which could take care of those optimizations, would be an interesting improvement. In our toolchain at Fishing Cactus, we already execute the GLSL optimizer [Pranckevičius 10b, Pranckevičius 15] over the generated GLSL files produced by Shader Shaker. We could, for example, integrate LLVM [LLVM 15] at different steps of the generation to optimize the AST and/or the IR.

- We have designed Shader Shaker so that it's really easy to support new output shader languages. Currently, we only support output to HLSL and GLSL, but new languages could be easily supported.

2.9 Conclusion

This technique and its user-semantic linking algorithm brings a new ways of creating shaders. It provides a new way to manage the complexity and combinatory complexity. Each feature can be developped independently, depending only on the choice of semantics. Shader Shaker, our implementation, is distributed as open source software [Fishing Cactus 15].

Bibliography

[Engel 08a] Wolfgang Engel. "Shader Workflow." *Diary of a Graphics Programmer*, http://diaryofagraphicsprogrammer.blogspot.pt/2008/09/shader-workflow.html, September 10, 2008.

[Engel 08b] Wolfgang Engel. "Shader Workflow—Why Shader Generators are Bad." *Diary of a Graphics Programmer*, http://diaryofagraphicsprogrammer. blogspot.pt/2008/09/shader-workflow-why-shader-generators.html, September 21, 2008.

[Epic Games Inc. 15] Epic Games Inc. "Materials." *Unreal Engine 4 Documentation*, https://docs.unrealengine.com/latest/INT/Engine/Rendering/Materials/index.html, 2015.

[Ericson 08] Christer Ericson. "Graphical Shader Systems Are Bad." http://realtimecollisiondetection.net/blog/?p=73, August 2, 2008.

[Fishing Cactus 15] Fishing Cactus. "Shader Shaker." https://github.com/
    FishingCactus/ShaderShaker2, 2015.

[Frykholm 11] Niklas Frykholm. "Platform Specific Resources." http://www.
    altdev.co/2011/12/22/platform-specific-resources/, December 22, 2011.

[Hargreaves 04] Shawn Hargreaves. "Generating Shaders from HLSL Frag-
    ments." http://www.shawnhargreaves.com/hlsl_fragments/hlsl_fragments.
    html, 2004.

[Holmér 15] Joachim 'Acegikmo' Holmér. "Shader Forge." http://acegikmo.com/
    shaderforge/, accesssed April, 2015.

[Jones 10] Tim Jones. "Introducing StitchUp: 'Generating Shaders from HLSL
    Shader Fragments' Implemented in XNA 4.0." http://timjones.tw/blog/
    archive/2010/11/13/introducing-stitchup-generating-shaders-from-hlsl
    -shader-fragments, November 13, 2010.

[Kime 08] Shaun Kime. "Shader Permuations." http://shaunkime.wordpress.
    com/2008/06/25/shader-permutation/, June 25, 2008.

[LLVM 15] LLVM. "The LLVM Compiler Infrastructure." http://llvm.org/,
    2015.

[Pranckevičius 10a] Aras Pranckevičius. "Compiling HLSL into GLSL in 2010."
    http://aras-p.info/blog/2010/05/21/compiling-hlsl-into-glsl-in-2010/, May
    21, 2010.

[Pranckevičius 10b] Aras Pranckevičius. "GLSL Optimizer." http://aras-p.info/
    blog/2010/09/29/glsl-optimizer/, September 29, 2010.

[Pranckevičius 12] Aras Pranckevičius. "Cross Platform Shaders in 2012." http:
    //aras-p.info/blog/2012/10/01/cross-platform-shaders-in-2012/, October 1,
    2012.

[Pranckevičius 14a] Aras Pranckevičius. "Cross Platform Shaders in 2014." http:
    //aras-p.info/blog/2014/03/28/cross-platform-shaders-in-2014/, March 28,
    2014.

[Pranckevičius 14b] Aras Pranckevičius. "Shader Compilation in Unity 4.5."
    http://aras-p.info/blog/2014/05/05/shader-compilation-in-unity-4-dot-5/,
    May 5, 2014.

[Pranckevičius 15] Aras Pranckevičius. "GLSL Optimizer." *GitHub Repository*,
    https://github.com/aras-p/glsl-optimizer, 2015.

[Trapp and Döllner 07] Matthias Trapp and Jürgen Döllner. "Automated Combination of Real-Time Shader Programs." In *Proceedings of Eurographics 2007*, edited by P. Cignoni and J. Sochor, pp. 53–56. Eurographics, Aire-la-Ville, Switzerland: Eurographics Association, 2007.

[Väänänen 13] Pekka Väänänen. "Generating GLSL Shaders from Mako Templates." http://www.lofibucket.com/articles/mako_glsl_templates.html, October 28, 2013.

[Wikipedia 15a] Wikipedia. "A* Search Algorithm." http://en.wikipedia.org/wiki/A*_search_algorithm, 2015.

[Wikipedia 15b] Wikipedia. "Template Method Pattern." http://en.wikipedia.org/wiki/Template_method_pattern, 2015.

[Yeung 12] Simon Yeung. "Shader Generator." http://www.altdev.co/2012/08/01/shader-generator/, August 1, 2012.

3
VII

ANGLE: Bringing OpenGL ES to the Desktop

Shannon Woods, Nicolas Capens, Jamie Madill, and Geoff Lang

3.1 Introduction

The Almost Native Graphics Layer Engine (ANGLE) is a portable, open source, hardware-accelerated implementation of OpenGL ES 2.0 used by software like Google Chrome to allow application-level code to target a single 3D API, yet execute on platforms where native OpenGL ES support may not be present. As of this writing, ANGLE's OpenGL ES 3.0 implementation is under active development. Applications may choose among ANGLE's multiple rendering backends at runtime, targeting systems with varying levels of support. Eventually, ANGLE will target multiple operating systems.

ANGLE's original development was sponsored by Google for browser support of WebGL on Windows systems, which may not have reliable native OpenGL drivers. ANGLE is currently used in several browsers, including Google Chrome and Mozilla Firefox. Initially, ANGLE provided only an OpenGL ES 2.0 implementation, using Direct3D 9 as its rendering backend. D3D9 was a good initial target since it's supported in Windows systems running XP or newer for a very large range of deployed hardware.

Since that time, WebGL has been evolving, and ANGLE has evolved along with it. The WebGL community has drafted new extensions against the current WebGL specification, as well as draft specifications for WebGL 2.0. Some of the features contained within these, such as sRGB textures, pixel buffer objects, and 3D textures, go beyond the feature set available to ANGLE in Direct3D 9. For this reason, it was clear that we would need to use a more modern version of Direct3D to support these features on Windows systems, which led us to begin work on a Direct3D 11 rendering backend.

While we use the Direct3D 11 API in our implementation, we target the 10_0 feature level. A feature level in D3D groups a set of limitations and capabilities; see the D3D11 programming guide for more information [MSDN 14c]. All the features of OpenGL ES 2.0, most of the extensions we expose via OpenGL ES 2.0 contexts, and even most of the features of OpenGL ES 3.0 are available within 10_0. A few features of OpenGL ES 3.0, however, are only available in hardware at the 10_1 or 11_0 feature levels; we'll cover those in more detail later in the chapter.

We chose to implement the Direct3D 11 backend as an addition, not as a replacement, for the original renderer; runtime renderer selection allows the application to support new features when the hardware is available and fall back to previous feature sets on older hardware. The abstraction necessary to allow multiple backends to be easily swapped in and out would come with an additional benefit: it would be relatively easy to add further backends in the future.

Koch and Capens [Koch and Capens 12] have discussed some of prior ANGLE challenges in creating a conformant implementation of OpenGL ES 2.0 using Direct3D 9. Recreating this implementation using Direct3D 11 presented challenges of its own; while we found that the newer API reduced implementation complexity in some areas, it raised it in others. We'll discuss some of these differences below. We'll then discuss ANGLE's shader translator in Section 3.3, give some case studies of implementing OpenGL ES 3.0 features in Section 3.4, and discuss the future directions of ANGLE in Section 3.5. We close off with recommended practices for application developers in Section 3.6.

3.2   Direct3D 11

Of the API differences we encountered while implementing ANGLE's new Direct3D 11 backend, some were relatively minor. In the case of fragment coordinates, for example, Direct3D 11 more closely aligns with OpenGL ES and related APIs, in that pixel centers are now considered to be at half-pixel locations—i.e., $(0.5, 0.5)$—just as they are in OpenGL. This eliminates the need for half-pixel offsets to be applied to fragment coordinates as in our Direct3D 9 implementation. There are quite a few places, however, where Direct3D 11 differs from both Direct3D 9 and OpenGL, requiring ANGLE to find new workarounds for this rendering backend.

3.2.1   Primitives

Direct3D 9's available set of primitive types for draw calls is more limited than OpenGL's, and Direct3D 11's is reduced slightly further by removing triangle fans. ANGLE enables `GL_TRIANGLE_FAN` by rewriting the application-provided index buffer to express the same polygons as a list of discrete triangles. This is a similar tactic to the one we employed to support `GL_LINE_LOOP` in Direct3D 9 (and which is still necessary in Direct3D 11), although the modification required to index buffers for line loops is considerably simpler—we need only repeat the initial point to close the line loop.

Direct3D 11 also removes support for large points, commonly used for rendering point sprites. While point lists themselves are still supported, the size of points is no longer configurable. This is a less trivial problem for ANGLE to solve. Thankfully, Direct3D 11 also introduces geometry shaders, which allow us to expand each point into a billboarded quad, achieving the same effect without CPU overhead.

3.2.2 Texture Formats

One small change from Direct3D 9 to Direct3D 11 that provides a significant benefit to ANGLE is the addition of native support for RGBA formats. While Direct3D 9 had very limited support for texture and screen formats outside of BGRA, Direct3D 11 provides a wide range of supported formats, including RGBA. This reduces the amount of pixel-by-pixel copying and channel swizzling that ANGLE needs to do to get textures from user space to the GPU. Direct3D 11 does lose a couple of formats used by OpenGL ES, though: native support for luminance and luminance alpha textures is dropped, requiring ANGLE to support them by storing to RGBA textures. Compressed texture formats, specified by `ANGLE_texture_compression_dxt`, and immutable textures, as defined in `EXT_texture_storage`, continue to be supported as they were for Direct3D 9 [Koch and Capens 12].

3.2.3 Vertex Buffers

One of the most significant differences between Direct3D 9 and Direct3D 11 from the perspective of ANGLE is a change in the way that vertex and index buffers are declared. In Direct3D 9, it's necessary to specify whether a buffer will be used to store vertex or index data at creation time. OpenGL has no such restriction— it's perfectly valid for an application to generate a buffer, fill it with data, bind it for use as a vertex buffer in one draw call, and then rebind it as an index buffer for a subsequent draw call. In our Direct3D 9 implementation, this meant that we would need to cache the vertex data CPU-side until draw time, at which point we could create vertex and index buffers based on the current bindings.

Additionally, Direct3D 9 supports a much more limited set of vertex element types than OpenGL ES 2.0, which contributes significantly to the complexity of our implementation for that API and can influence performance, as we must interpret and convert application-provided vertex data on the CPU before uploading. Additionally, our Direct3D 9 implementation unpacks interleaved vertex data to avoid conversions on unused data in any given draw. For more information, refer to Koch and Capens's discussion of vertex data [Koch and Capens 12].

Direct3D 11 removes these restrictions to some degree, albeit with some caveats. It uses a single buffer class instead of specializations for index and vertex buffers. Additionally, Direct3D 11 provides native support for all OpenGL ES vertex formats. This frees ANGLE from its prior duty of expanding, converting, and/or de-interleaving application-provided vertex data in many cases; instead, we can forward this data directly to the GPU without manipulation.

One major exception to the automatic vertex format support in Direct3D 11 is unnormalized integer data. While supported in Direct3D 11, integer attributes are not automatically converted to floating points when sent to a vertex shader that accepts floating point inputs. This issue becomes moot in GLSL ES 3.00, which does provide nonfloat vertex attribute types, but *all* vertex data, regardless of how it is provided to the API, is accessed via floats in GLSL ES 1.00 shaders. ANGLE's initial Direct3D 11 implementation addressed this by converting vertex attributes with the CPU before upload. This imposed the same performance overhead that we'd seen in our Direct3D 9 implementation—but we could do better. We will discuss our solution in Section 3.3.7.

One other caveat about Direct3D 11's buffer handling became apparent after we deployed our initial implementation. While Direct3D 11 allows us to bind a vertex buffer as both a source for vertex and index data, some hardware would use the bind flags we provided as a hint for how the buffers should be stored and processed. When we were initially flagging all buffers with both `D3D11_BIND_VERTEX_BUFFER` and `D3D11_BIND_INDEX_BUFFER`, there was a clear performance penalty for some hardware and some drivers. To avoid dual-flagged buffers, we instead store application-provided vertex data in staging buffers until draw time. At draw time, we know if the buffer is being used for index or vertex data, and we can copy the data to an appropriately flagged buffer object. We found this extra copy overhead was preferable to the performance drag introduced by dual-flagging buffers.

What also caught us by surprise is that for Direct3D 11, a −1 in the index buffer (corresponding to 65535 or 0xFFFF for a 16-bit index format) is always interpreted as a triangle strip cut, also known as a primitive restart. In OpenGL ES 2.0 and Direct3D 9, this is a valid index value, so we were seeing geometric anomalies using the same index buffer data with Direct3D 11. We worked around it by promoting buffers that contain this index value to 32 bits.

3.2.4   Moving Forward

For the most part, Direct3D 11 provides an opportunity for ANGLE to support new features and improve performance. Old features that required emulation on Direct3D 9 can often utilize hardware features exposed by the newer API to keep the extra work on the GPU. Perhaps an even more interesting observation is that adding a Direct3D 11 backend caused us to start abstracting things in a way that opened the door for even more rendering backends in the future. This will turn ANGLE into a dependable implementation of OpenGL ES across multiple operating systems and graphics API generations. We'll discuss this vision and the architectural implications in more detail in Section 3.5.

3.3 Shader Translation

Shaders play a major role in modern graphics APIs, and their complexity makes translating between them challenging. Early on in ANGLE's development, it was decided that we should only translate between high-level shading languages and not attempt to compile them down to assembly shaders. This was largely motivated by the availability of Microsoft's HLSL compiler and the fact that unlike Direct3D 9, from Direct3D 10 onward there would no longer be assembly-level shader support. Source-to-source translation was also what Chrome needed for validating WebGL's variant of GLSL ES and translating it into OpenGL ES's GLSL or desktop GLSL and for applying security measures or driver bug workarounds.

This decision turned out to be a double-edged sword. The Direct3D 9 assembly shading language has many quirks and restrictions, and the HLSL compiler knows how to deal with those adequately, most of the time. This saved us from duplicating that effort, and we did not have to deal with optimizations. However, any shortcomings in the HLSL compiler turned out to be a bigger problem to us than to someone directly targeting Direct3D. That's because when a developer encounters an issue with HLSL, he or she will simply rewrite the shader, and the application that gets shipped will work on all the platforms it targets (often using precompiled shaders). With ANGLE, it's unacceptable to expect developers to adjust their shaders just because this one implementation on this one platform has a certain issue, no matter how understandable the limitation and no matter how easy it is to work around. So the ANGLE team had to identify problematic patterns and apply their workarounds as part of the ESSL-to-HLSL shader translator. We found out about most of the issues the hard way from bug reports, as there is no systematic way to discover them. We'll highlight some of the most challenging issues later in this section, but first we'll provide an overview of the translator's architecture and design.

3.3.1 Source-to-Source Translation

The general approach for source-to-source translation is to parse the input string(s) and build an abstract syntax tree (AST) intermediate representation, and then traverse the AST to systematically construct the output string. An example of how some code is parsed and represented as an AST is illustrated in Figure 3.1.

ANGLE's shader translator was founded on 3Dlab's open source GLSL compiler framework [3Dlabs 05]. Out of the box, this framework only supported desktop GLSL version 1.10, but its parser is generated by the Bison tool, which

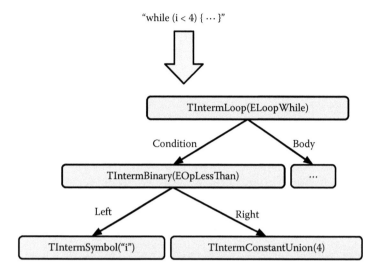

Figure 3.1. Example of parsing a string into an abstract syntax tree.

makes it relatively easy to update the grammar. The GLSL ES specification conveniently lists the entire grammar in its appendix. Also, 3DLab's code was clearly intended for assembly or binary output, but the AST traverser architecture is nicely object-oriented to allow for alternative implementations. The biggest change that was required for outputting a high-level language was to not just perform an implementation-dependent action before and after traversing a tree node's children (dubbed `PreVisit` and `PostVisit`), but also in between them (`InVisit`). This allows for the instance to put commas in between a list of arguments, or semicolons in between a sequence of statements.

We also defined new AST node types to preserve information from the GLSL source code that would not have been required for assembly output, for instance, predeclared functions. While traversing the AST to output the body of the HLSL code, we also keep track of information that should be added to the top. This gets written to the header stream and later prepended to the body. Examples of things that have to be in the header include intrinsic function definitions, which we'll cover later, and structure constructors. In GLSL, structures have an implicit constructor function that has the same name as the structure and takes the field types as parameters. This allows us to create nameless instantiations in the middle of an expression. HLSL does not support this directly. Instead, structures can only be initialized at declaration using an initializer list (similar to C). Therefore, we explicitly generate functions that act as a constructor by declaring and initializing a local variable of the required structure type and returning it.

When we commenced the work to support OpenGL ES 3.0, an architectural decision had to be made on how to deal with multiple input languages. Either we duplicated a large portion of the translator, or we somehow had to support both (significantly different) specifications while minimizing the entanglement. The latter turned out to be feasible through two elegant modifications. First, the lexer, which provides the parser with tokens from the input string, was adjusted to ensure that new keywords in ESSL 3.00 would still be recognized as identifier names for ESSL 1.00 input. Likewise, some keywords of ESSL 3.00 were already reserved for ESSL 1.00 and thus would generate an error or not depending on the specified shader version. To avoid cluttering the lexer specification itself, these decisions are delegated to a few functions that will return the proper token type.

The second major change to support ESSL 3.00 was made to the symbol table. The symbol table is essentially a map used by the parser to store previously encountered variable, structure, or function names and their corresponding types. This also includes predefined intrinsic function names, which greatly differ between ESSL 1.00 and 3.00. The symbol table has multiple layers to deal with variables that are redefined at a different scope or become unavailable by going out of scope. This led us to implement the difference between ESSL 1.00's and 3.00's intrinsics by defining a persistent symbol table layer specific to each specification, and a shared one for common intrinsics. When looking up an identifier for ESSL 3.00 input, we would first look for it in its own layer, skip the ESSL 1.00 layer, then check the common layer, and afterward look into the scoped layers for user-defined identifiers.

For the HLSL backend, no changes had to be made to deal with the two input specifications differently. That's because at this level the GLSL code is fully validated, so we just have to generate any HLSL code that properly implements each AST node, regardless of which version it originated from. ESSL 1.00 intermediate code can be translated into either Shader Model 3.0 or Shader Model 4.0 HLSL, which needed few changes (except for texture intrinsics, discussed below), while ESSL 3.00 constructs demand Shader Model 4.0 features, which we're targeting anyway for OpenGL ES 3.0, so the translator doesn't explicitly have to differentiate between anything at this level.

3.3.2 Shader Debugging

One of the added advantages of source-to-source compilation is that ANGLE's output is relatively easy to debug. Most shader constructs translate in a predictable way, and you can debug your application with Direct3D debugging tools. To assist with this, several features of ANGLE and Chrome help expose its implementation. First, Chrome can be launched with the `--gpu-startup-dialog` command line flag. This halts its execution right after creating the GPU process. This allows you to attach a debugger or other analysis tool to it before

```
var debugShaders = gl.getExtension('WEBGL_debug_shaders');
var hlsl = debugShaders.getTranslatedShaderSource(myShader);
```

Listing 3.1. WEBGL_debug_shaders extension usage.

continuing (which is especially useful when you've set your WebGL application as the startup page) or use `--new-window yoursite.com`. For HLSL compilation issues, you can set a breakpoint at `HLSLCompiler::compileToBinary()` (function name subject to change).

You can also retrieve the HLSL code from within WebGL through the `WEBGL_debug_shaders` extension, as in Listing 3.1. Note that the format returned by this extension is implementation specific.

You may notice that the original variable names have been replaced by hardly legible `_webgl_<hexadecimal>` names. This circumvents bugs in drivers that can't handle long variable names, but makes the HLSL difficult to debug. To disable this workaround, you can use Chrome's `--disable-glsl-translation` flag. Note that this merely disables Chrome's ESSL-to-ESSL translation, meant only for validation and driver workaround purposes, not ANGLE's ESSL-to-HLSL translation. This may change in the future as more of the validation becomes ANGLE's responsibility and duplicate translation is avoided. Even with the aforementioned flag, some variable names may have been modified to account for differences in scoping rules between GLSL and HLSL.

3.3.3   Semantic Differences

Source-to-source translation meant that many workarounds could be handled with some string manipulation. But what if the actual core semantics of the languages differ? This was encountered when it turned out that the ternary operator (e.g., `x = q ? a : b;`) evaluates differently between GLSL and HLSL. GLSL conforms to the C semantic specification by only evaluating the expression corresponding with the condition, while HLSL evaluates both sides before selecting the correct result. Similarly, the `||` and `&&` operators have short-circuiting behaviors in GLSL but not HLSL.

We actually did find a way to deal with this through mostly string operations. For each expression containing a ternary operator, we'd create a new temporary variable in HLSL to hold the ternary operator's result and outputted an `if...else` construct to evaluate only the desired result. Because ternary operators can be nested, we handle this substitution in a separate AST traverser, which can be called recursively, before the original statement, which contained the short-circuiting operators, is outputted with the corresponding temporary variables replacing the short-circuiting operators.

More recently, we've started dealing with these differences at the AST level itself instead of at the string output level. When a short-circuiting operator is encountered, we replace it with a temporary variable node and move the node representing the short-circuiting operator itself up through the tree before the most recent statement and turn it into an `if...else` node. When the child nodes are visited and they themselves contain short-circuiting operators, the same process takes place. So this approach takes advantage of the naturally recursive nature of AST traversal. This doesn't work at the string level because that would require inserting code into part of the string that has already been written.

3.3.4 Intrinsics Implementation and Emulation

Shading languages provide a large part of their built-in functionality that isn't basic arithmetic or flow control constructs through intrinsic functions. Examples include `min()`, `max()`, trigonometric functions, and, most notably, texture sampling operations. Intrinsic functions use the syntax of a function call but are compiled into just one or very few assembly instructions. For ESSL-to-HLSL translation, we had to implement intrinsics that don't have a direct equivalent as actual functions. This is fine because functions typically get inlined, so this typically doesn't have a performance impact compared to a native OpenGL implementation.

ANGLE implements all ESSL texture-sampling intrinsics as functions in HLSL. For ESSL 1.00, this was only a handful of intrinsics, so for each of them we had a handwritten HLSL equivalent. When Direct3D 11 and ESSL 3.00 support was added, there were so many variations of the intrinsics that this became impractical. For example, the ESSL 3.00 specification defines a `gsampler` virtual type to signify `sampler`, `isampler`, and `usampler` types, and most of these texture intrinsics also optionally take a `bias` parameter, resulting in six variants in HLSL for just a single definition in the specification (and there are several dozen definitions). To make this more manageable, we switched to generating the necessary HLSL functions on the fly. Also, to avoid code duplication for predeclaring them in the symbol table, we defined our own `gsampler` type, which causes the function declaration to be expanded into the three actual variants.

While most ESSL 3.00 texture intrinsics have close relatives in HLSL, we were surprised to find that HLSL has no support whatsoever for unnormalized integer format cube maps. Of course, one might also question why ESSL offers support for a feature for which no significant use case was found to make it a feature of HLSL. Whichever stance is taken, we were stuck having to pass the conformance tests for a feature for which there's fundamentally no support in Direct3D 11. The solution was to treat these cube maps as a six-element array texture and to manually compute which face of the cube should be sampled from. Fortunately, because unnormalized integers can't be filtered in any meaningful way and thus only point sampling is defined, we didn't have to deal with finding the closest neighboring texels (potentially across multiple faces)! In any case, it was an interesting exercise in software rendering on the GPU, and we expect to encounter more occurrences like this in the future as graphics APIs become more low level and the operations become more granular and software controlled.

3.3.5 HLSL Compiler Issues

Source-to-source compilation saved us from writing a compiler backend but made us very dependent on Microsoft's HLSL compiler. Bugs and intrinsic limitations require our constant attention and intricate workarounds. Early on, we discovered that for Direct3D 9, loops with more than 254 iterations would fail to compile. While most common uses of WebGL and OpenGL ES 2.0 don't require loops with more iterations, the Khronos conformance test suite includes shaders with 512 iterations to create references to compare trigonometric operations against! So, to obtain conformance certification, we needed a workaround. The solution was to split these loops into multiple loops each with a duplicated body that processes 254 or fewer iterations. Fortunately, the OpenGL ES 2.0 specification limits loops to have statically determinable iteration counts with a single iterator variable which cannot be modified within the loop. We also had to be careful to ensure that a `break`; statement in a prior (split) loop would cause subsequent loops to be skipped. Note that Direct3D 9's assembly instructions are limited to 255 iterations due to its encoding format (an 8-bit field for the iteration count), so a similar solution of splitting the loop would be required at the assembly level. It's just a low-level limitation the HLSL compiler doesn't abstract away at the high-level language.

Similarly, we hit several issues related to balancing the optimization level—not really to achieve better performance (we found that it has little effect, probably due to driver-level reoptimization), but to ensure that the optimizations try to keep the number of instructions and registers within the limits, while not making it take too long to compile. Chrome kills the GPU process after 10 seconds of no progress to prevent attacks where your system would be made unresponsive. Some optimization levels of the HLSL compiler appear to be very aggressive and take a long time to complete. Some shaders even appear to cause the compiler to get stuck in an infinite loop. These optimizations are probably aimed at being used for offline compilation only. Still, we need some optimization to get relatively poorly written ESSL shaders to fit the resource limits.

One particularly challenging issue is that of avoiding differential operations on discontinuous execution paths. This includes explicit differential operations like `dFdx` and `dFdy`, but also implicit ones for texture-sampling intrinsics to determine the mipmap level. The way these gradients are computed is based on how pixels are processed in 2×2 pixel quads in parallel and the value of the variable in question is compared (subtracted) between the neighboring pixels. This works as long as the code path executed by each pixel in the quad is the same. Any divergence caused by taking different branches may cause differentiated variables to not have meaningful values for some of the pixels, and thus there's an undefined discontinuity in the differentiation. GLSL deals with this by simply stating that the result is undefined, while for HLSL it causes a compilation error. You can either use a texture-sampling intrinsic with an explicitly specified LOD value or "flatten" the branches that contain texture sampling intrinsics. *Flattening* means that all pixels execute all code blocks and the desired results are selected afterward. Until recently, there was no control over the HLSL compiler's flattening behavior, and results depended on the presence of texture-sampling intrinsics, and the optimization levels. Nowadays, it can be controlled with the `[flatten]` attribute, but for ANGLE it is hard to determine for which branches it is needed. At the time of writing, we instead generate `Lod0` texture-sampling functions that always sample from the top-level mipmap, which is valid since GLSL defines the derivatives to be undefined.

The HLSL compiler continues to be a source of various issues, most of which are fairly small and affect few users. Ultimately, ANGLE has different design goals than those of applications that target Direct3D directly, which is mostly games with statically compiled shaders or shaders known to compile without issues for a certain HLSL compiler version and optimization flags. Still, we manage to isolate the user from these issues as much as possible, making ANGLE the de facto robust and conformant OpenGL ES implementation on Windows. In the future, we may have to resort to performing most optimizations at the AST level ourselves and outputting only very basic HLSL statements closely corresponding with assembly instructions.

3.3.6 Driver Bugs

We also encountered shader-related issues deeper into the graphics stack. A number of them are related to robustness. Some graphics drivers would, for example, attempt to compile shaders with arrays much larger than 4096 elements, even though that's a limit for many register resources in Direct3D 11, and they would end up choking on it. In the best case, it just exceeds the 10-second time limit of Chrome and the tab gets killed, but in the worst case the user-mode graphics driver crashes and the entire screen goes black until the driver resets itself. To prevent this, we had to limit the size of arrays within ANGLE. We settled on 65,536 for now because optimizations may cause shaders with such a large array to still fit within the actual resources, although it is low enough to avoid the crashes.

One specific driver bug was caused by wrong optimization of `if...else` statements on one brand of graphics cards, and only within vertex shaders. Values of a variable that could only be computed in one branch would pop up in the other branch. This was worked around by rewriting things as `if(x) {} if(!x) {}`. Avoiding re-evaluation of `x` and dealing with one or more `else if` statements makes this nontrivial. Although issues like these are eventually addressed by the graphics card vendors, it takes a while for these fixes to be deployed to all users, so thus far we've always left these kinds of workarounds enabled.

Driver bugs are even less under our control than HLSL compiler issues, but hopefully graphics APIs will continue to become more low level so that eventually we get access to the bare instructions and data. Just like on a CPU, the behavior of elementary operations is very tightly defined and verifiable so that compilers can generate code that produces dependable results.

3.3.7   Dynamic Shaders

Because ANGLE can only generate full HLSL programs after we know the signatures between the vertex and pixel stages, we cannot immediately call the Direct3D compiler at GL compile time. Moreover, we also might modify our shaders at draw time. For ESSL 1.00 shaders, which treat all vertex inputs as floating point, we insert conversion code to transform unnormalized integer vertex attributes in the shader preamble.

ANGLE is not the only program to do this kind of draw-time optimization. A common complaint from application developers is that draw calls sometimes perform very slowly due to dynamic shader re-compilation [AMD 14]. A future design direction for ANGLE, when targeting a more modern API, is to perform the vertex conversion in a separate shader pass, which would then be linked with another compiled shader.

3.4   Implementing ES3 on Feature Level 10

3.4.1   Lessons Learned

The degree of similarity or difference between GLES 3 and Direct3D 11 varies significantly depending on the graphics feature in question. ANGLE's task of implementing GLES 3 on top of Direct3D 11 feature level 10 ranged in difficulty accordingly. We might describe some aspects of our translation as "squashing a dog into a cat suit, and asking it to meow." In other cases, the implementation came naturally. Often the most challenging workarounds come from corner cases, the little sneaky cases, instead of the most common usage. In this section, we'll discuss three examples of some conflicting limitations and corner cases: uniform buffers, transform feedback, and pixel buffer objects.

In the future we might choose a simpler, more flexible approach. Instead of mapping one high-level feature onto another high-level feature, we might improve our lives by assembling the high-level features from simple compute shader components. ANGLE's stars align with the direction of many modern APIs, such as the recently announced (as of this writing) Direct3D 12 [McMullen 14], Apple's Metal [Apple 14], and AMD's Mantle [AMD 14]; with these modern APIs, ANGLE could use the features we discuss in this section as compute shaders.

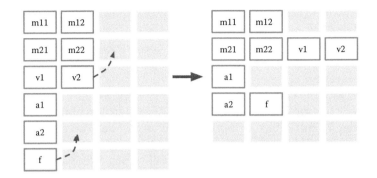

Figure 3.2. Example HLSL packing of a simple uniform block.

3.4.2 Uniform Buffers

Uniform buffer objects (UBOs) are a marquee feature of OpenGL ES3. UBOs give applications the ability to upload blocks of uniform data as typed, mappable buffer objects. UBOs are particularly useful for applications, such as skinning, that deal with large arrays of bone and joint matrices. Moreover, UBOs are a more complex part of the ESSL 3.00 specification. This complexity is due partially to the intricate packing and unpacking rules for getting data out of the buffer to the active vertex or fragment shader.

Here's a simple UBO with four members:

```
uniform sampleBlock
{
    mat2 m;
    vec2 v;
    float a[2];
    float f;
};
```

The GL API defines three layouts for unpacking data from UBOs to the shader. We treat the *packed* and *shared* layouts identically; in both, the details are left to the GL implementation. The *std140* layout, however, is defined precisely by the GL specification. Because it's an application, you can choose the simplicity of the standardized layout or the benefit of a memory-saving packed layout. With a GL implementation, you must at the very least support the std140 layout.

UBOs map relatively closely to Direct3D 11's concept of *constant buffers* [MSDN 14d]. We chose to implement UBOs on top of constant buffers and offer the memory-saving benefits of the packed layout, while maintaining the necessary std140 layout. In both cases, good performance is also a requirement. Unsurprisingly, HLSL's default unpacking scheme for constant buffers differs from the std140 layout; thus, we have two competing requirements.

The (somewhat undocumented) HLSL unpacking algorithm reads subsequent variables from the empty space left over from unpacking prior variables. See Figure 3.2, where the `vec2` is folded into the prior `mat2`, and the `float` is folded into the prior array.

Thus, to support both std140 and packed layouts, we insert invisible padding variables into the uniform block definition for std140 layouts. We leave packed blocks as the default HLSL definition. This works well, except for the case of nested structures. Nested structures, because they can be used in both std140 and other layouts, require us to create two internal struct definitions: one definition with the extra std140 padding and one without.[1] Nested structures also prevent us from using HLSL's register offset specifiers to specify the unpacking scheme.

While our implementation offers a choice between space and generality, both with good performance, it suffers from complexity. A future direction is to skip the specialized API for constant buffers entirely; we could opt to bind our UBOs as structured buffers and unpack the data manually in the shader preamble. Using a more modern feature level in Direct3D, or MANTLE or Metal, would give us access to the necessary tools.

3.4.3 Transform Feedback

GLES 3 adds a method for the application to capture the vertex data stream's output from the vertex shader stage. GLES calls this operation transform feedback, while Direct3D 11 has a very analogous operation called *Stream output* [MSDN 14e]. In both, the application can even skip rasterization completely. Vertex stream capture has a few notable use cases; inspecting vertex outputs for debugging is much easier by capturing streams directly. GPGPU applications, such as particle systems, often need to transform vertex data (particle position, velocity, etc.) in their update step.

Direct3D's stream output has many similarities, and some notable differences—particularly notable in their limitations on the number of active capture buffers. Under feature level 10, our low-specification feature set, we are limited to writing a single four-component vector output per stream-output buffer[2]. Feature level 10 also imposes a limit of no more than four Stream-Output buffers per draw call. These limits, fortunately enough, exactly match the minimum/maximum values in the GLES 3 Specification, Table 6.24 [Lipchak 13].

In the future, under more flexible APIs, we could implement GL's transform feedback from more general shaders. Instead of mapping to the high-level stream output, we could implement stream output in a compute shader kernel. This

---

[1] We also end up with two additional `struct` permutations to handle unpacking row-major and column-major matrices from nested `structs`.

[2] Note that the stream-output buffer at slot zero has a larger upper bound.

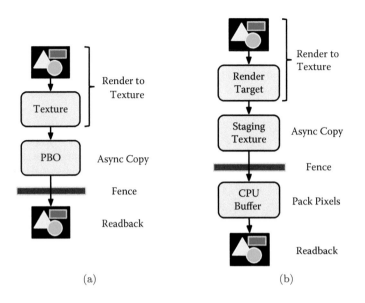

(a)   (b)

Figure 3.3. Asynchronous readback with PBOs: (a) Simple GL implementation. (b) ANGLE–Direct3D 11 implementation.

simple shader approach would fit naturally into a MANTLE/Metal-like API, or even with a higher feature level in Direct3D 11.

3.4.4 Pixel Pack Buffers

Pixel pack and unpack buffers, collectively known as *pixel buffer objects* (PBOs), round out the new data copying operations in GLES 3. Of particular interest to us are pack buffers, which are buffer objects that receive pixel data from a texture object. A primary use case for pack buffers is reading back texture data asynchronously. The application first triggers the pixel copy operation to the pack buffer without blocking the application layer. Next, it creates a fence sync object (see Section 5.2 of the OpenGL ES 3 specification [Lipchak 13]) to detect when the GPU is finished. The application then reads back the pixel data, while spending minimal time blocked waiting for the GPU. Figure 3.3(a) gives an example of asynchronous readback.

PBOs map to Direct3D 11's notion of staging resources [MSDN 14b]. Staging resources act as CPU-accessible memory; they proxy data to and from the GPU. They are not orthogonal; Direct3D places several limitations on staging (and also nonstaging) resources, making life for our PBO implementation a bit tougher.

First, Direct3D 11 does not allow direct copies between texture and buffer resources. Thus, when we implement a copy from a texture to a buffer, we can't rely on Direct3D 11's `CopyResource` methods. Another option might be stream output, as we described in Section 3.4.3, to capture texture data into a buffer using a vertex shader. Direct3D's constraints on stream output notably lack support for some data types, making this quite challenging. Compute shaders also offer a promising and elegant solution. Since we are limited to supporting Shader Model 4 as a minimum, we unfortunately couldn't rely on compute shaders in all cases.

More problems arise from the different requirements GL and Direct3D 11 both enforce on the data packing after the asynchronous copy step. GL gives a set of fine-grained pack parameters, which control how the pixel data packs into the pack buffer (see Table 4.4 of the OpenGL ES 3 specification [Lipchak 13]). Direct3D 11, on the other hand, packs pixels row by row with a gap at the end of each row, specified by a stride [MSDN 14a].

The intended use of staging buffers and pack buffers is to copy from CPU to GPU memory; this similarity makes the use of staging buffers a suitable starting point. The differences in details lead us to choose a simple, nonoptimal implementation. After copying back to the staging texture, we do an extra CPU-side packing step that requests the data, usually via a call to `glMapBufferRange`. We run the GL packing algorithm, resolving the GL pack parameters with the Direct3D 11 offsets, into a CPU memory buffer. This process is illustrated in Figure 3.3(b). The net result cleanly dresses up Direct3D in a GL suit, at the cost of a bit of extra work.

A compute shader could lead to a simple, preferable implementation; running the packing algorithm on the GPU give more work to the GPU. On feature level 11 or other modern APIs, such as Metal or MANTLE, we could make better use of compute shaders.

3.5   Future Directions: Moving to New Platforms

Since early 2014, the ANGLE team has been redesigning ANGLE to cover a broader scope and to provide a conformant and fast OpenGL ES 2/3 and EGL implementation across as many platforms as possible.

3.5.1   Creating a Cross-Platform OpenGL ES Driver

The last year has seen the announcements of at least three new major graphics APIs, most of them tied to specific hardware or platforms. The new APIs are typically very low level, attempting to abstract very little of the hardware, and are a great opportunity for graphics engines to write specialized code for targeted devices. For writing simple applications and games, this can be a big burden; ANGLE hopes to alleviate this by being able to provide a common API that can translate to the lower-level APIs without a significant performance impact. See Figure 3.4 for a high-level diagram of an application's interaction with ANGLE and the native graphics API.

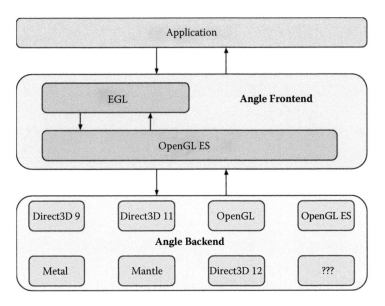

Figure 3.4. ANGLE–application interaction.

3.5.2 An Extensible Architecture

To easily support multiple rendering backends, ANGLE needed an architecture that did as much work as possible before sending work to the native renderer. The library has been split into three distinct layers to create the simplest possible interface that a new renderer must implement. See Figure 3.5 for a high-level diagram of ANGLE's architecture.

Layers. The layers are the following:

1. The *entry point/validation* layer exports all of the EGL and OpenGL ES entry point functions and handles validation of all paramters. All values passed to the layers below this are assumed to be valid.

2. The *object layer* contains C++ representations of all EGL and OpenGL ES objects and models their interactions. Each object contains a reference to a native implementation for forwarding actions to the native graphics API.

3. The *renderer layer* provides the implementation of the EGL and GL objects in the native graphics API; the interfaces are simplified to only *action* calls such as drawing, clearing, setting buffer data, or reading framebuffer data. All queries and validation are handled by the layers above.

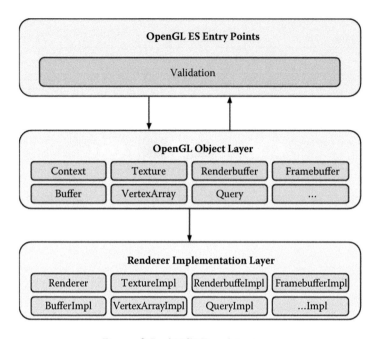

Figure 3.5. ANGLE architecture.

```
class BufferImpl
{
  public:
    virtual void setData(size_t size, void *data,
                         GLenum usage) = 0;
    virtual void setSubData(size_t offset, size_t size,
                            void *data) = 0;
    virtual void *map(GLenum access) = 0;
    virtual void unmap() = 0;
};
```

Listing 3.2. The `Buffer` interface.

The buffer object. A simple example of a renderer layer object that requires a native implementation is the OpenGL ES 3.0 `Buffer` (see Listing 3.2). ANGLE's Direct3D 9 implementation simply stores the supplied memory in CPU-side memory until the first use of the `Buffer` in a draw call when the data is uploaded to a `IDirect3DVertexBuffer9` or `IDirect3DIndexBuffer9`. The Direct3D 11 implementation stores the data in a `ID3D11Buffer` with the `D3D11_USAGE_STAGING` flag and will copy the buffer data lazily to one of several specialized buffers for use as an index buffer, vertex buffer, transform feedback buffer, or pixel buffer.

```
class Renderer
{
  public:
    virtual BufferImpl *createBuffer() = 0;
    virtual TextureImpl *createTexture() = 0;
    ...

    virtual void drawArrays(const gl::State &state, GLenum mode,
                            size_t first, size_t count) = 0;
    ...
    virtual void clear(const gl::State &state,
                       GLbitfield mask) = 0;
    ...
};
```

Listing 3.3. A snippet of the `Renderer` interface.

```
const char *ex = eglQueryString(EGL_NO_DISPLAY, EGL_EXTENSIONS);
if (strstr(ex, "EGL_ANGLE_platform_angle")     != NULL &&
    strstr(ex, "EGL_ANGLE_platform_angle_d3d") != NULL)
{
    EGLint renderer = EGL_PLATFORM_ANGLE_TYPE_D3D11_ANGLE;
    const EGLint attribs[] =
    {
        EGL_PLATFORM_ANGLE_TYPE_ANGLE, renderer,
        EGL_NONE,
    };
    display = eglGetPlatformDisplayEXT(EGL_PLATFORM_ANGLE_ANGLE,
                                       nativeDisplay, attribs);
}
```

Listing 3.4. Example ANGLE `Renderer` selection.

The renderer object. The `Renderer` object is the main interface between the object layer and the renderer layer. It handles the creation of all the native implementation objects and preforms the main actions, such as drawing, clearing, or blitting. See Listing 3.3 for a snippet of the `Renderer` interface.

Runtime renderer selection. Specific renderers can be selected in EGL by using the `EGL_ANGLE_platform_angle` extension. Each renderer implemented by ANGLE has an `enum` that can be passed to `eglGetDisplayEXT` or a default `enum` that can be used to allow ANGLE to select the best renderer for the specific platform it is running on. See Listing 3.4 for an example of selecting the Direct3D 11 renderer at runtime.

3.5.3 The Next Step: Creating an OpenGL Renderer

The first non-Direct3D renderer to be implemented by the ANGLE team will use desktop OpenGL. This will allow the project to quickly expand to other desktop platforms and allow users to write OpenGL ES applications that run on all mobile and desktop platforms.

Despite the ANGLE project originally being created to work around the poor quality of OpenGL drivers on the Windows desktop, the quality has improved enough over the last five years that offering an OpenGL renderer is viable. With having the Direct3D renderer fallback, ANGLE will be able to offer OpenGL renderers on driver versions that are known to be stable and fast with less CPU overhead than a Direct3D renderer.

Dealing with the enormous number of permutations of client version and extension availability in desktop OpenGL will be a complicated aspect of implementing an OpenGL renderer. Loading function pointers or using texture format enumerations may involve checking a client version and up to three extensions. For example, creating a framebuffer object could be done via `glGenFramebuffers`, `glGenFramebuffersEXT`, `glGenFramebuffersARB`, or `glGenFramebuffersOES` (when passing through to OpenGL ES), depending on the platform.

Driver bugs are notoriously common in OpenGL drivers, and working around them will be necessary. In order to promise a conformant OpenGL ES implementation, ANGLE will have to maintain a database of specific combinations of driver versions, video card models, and platform versions that have known conformance issues and attempt to work around these issues by avoiding the issue or manipulating inputs or outputs. In the worst case, when a driver bug cannot be hidden, EGL offers the `EGL_CONFORMANT` configuration field to warn the user that there are issues that cannot be fixed.

3.6   Recommended Practices

ANGLE is an important implementation of OpenGL ES for desktops and powers the majority of WebGL usage. So it pays off to try to take a few of its preferred and less preferred rendering practices into account.

- Avoid line loops and triangle fans. Instead try using line lists and triangle lists.

- Wide lines are not supported. Many native OpenGL implementations also don't support them, because there's no consensus on how to deal with corner cases (pun intended). Implement wide lines using triangles.

- Avoid having an index value of 0xFFFF in a 16-bit index buffer. Configure your tool chain to create triangle strips with a maximum index of 65534.

- Keep geometry that uses different vertex formats in separate buffers.

- Avoid using luminance and luminance-alpha texture formats. Try to use four-channel texture formats instead.

- Make use of the `EXT_texture_storage` extension (only applies to desktop applications).

- Avoid using texture-sampling intrinsics within control flow constructs (e.g., `if`, `else`, `switch`). Instead, sample the texture outside of these constructs.

- Test your WebGL application with early releases of Chrome (Beta, Dev, and Canary). It's the best way to catch bugs early, fix them, and create a conformance test for it so it will never affect your users.

Bibliography

[3Dlabs 05] 3Dlabs. "GLSL Demos and Source Code from the 3Dlabs OpenGL 2." http://mew.cx/glsl/, 2005.

[AMD 14] AMD. "AMD's Revolutionary Mantle." http://www.amd.com/en-us/innovations/software-technologies/mantle#overview, 2014.

[Apple 14] Apple. "Metal Programming Guide." *Apple Developer*, https://developer.apple.com/library/prerelease/ios/documentation/Miscellaneous/Conceptual/MTLProgGuide/, 2014.

[Koch and Capens 12] Daniel Koch and Nicolas Capens. "The ANGLE Project: Implementing OpenGL ES 2.0 on Direct3D." In *OpenGL Insights*, edited by Patrick Cozzi and Christophe Riccio, pp. 543–570. Boca Raton, FL: CRC Press, 2012.

[Lipchak 13] Benjamin Lipchak. "OpenGL ES Version 3.0.3." *Khronos Group*, http://www.khronos.org/registry/gles/specs/3.0/es_spec_3.0.3.pdf, 2013.

[McMullen 14] Max McMullen. "Direct3D 12 API Preview." *Channel 9*, http://channel9.msdn.com/Events/Build/2014/3-564, April 2, 2014.

[MSDN 14a] MSDN. "D3D11_MAPPED_SUBRESOURCE Structure." *Windows Dev Center*, http://msdn.microsoft.com/en-us/library/windows/desktop/ff476182(v=vs.85).aspx, 2014.

[MSDN 14b] MSDN. "D3D11_USAGE Enumeration." *Windows Dev Center*, http://msdn.microsoft.com/en-us/library/windows/desktop/ff476259(v=vs.85).aspx, 2014.

[MSDN 14c] MSDN. "Direct3D Feature Levels." *Windows Dev Center*, http://msdn.microsoft.com/en-us/library/windows/desktop/ff476876(v=vs.85).aspx, 2014.

[MSDN 14d] MSDN. "How to: Create a Constant Buffer." *Windows Dev Center*, http://msdn.microsoft.com/en-us/library/windows/desktop/ff476 896(v=vs.85).aspx, 2014.

[MSDN 14e] MSDN. "Stream-Output Stage." *Windows Dev Center*, http: //msdn.microsoft.com/en-us/library/windows/desktop/bb205121(v=vs.85) .aspx, 2014.

About the Editors

Marius Bjørge is a Graphics Research Engineer at ARM's office in Trondheim, Norway. Prior to ARM he worked in the games industry as part of Funcom's core engine team. He has presented research at SIGGRAPH, HPG, and GDC and is keenly interested in anything graphics-related. He's currently looking at new ways of enabling advanced real-time graphics on current and future mobile GPU technology.

Wessam Bahnassi is a software engineer and an architect (that is, for buildings not software). This combination drives Wessam's passion for 3D engine design. He has written and dealt with a variety of engines throughout a decade of game development. Currently, he is leading the programming effort at IN—Framez Technology, the indie game company he cofounded with his brother Homam. Their first game (*Hyper Void*) is a live shaders showcase (some of which have been featured previous *GPU Pro* volumes), and it is in the final development stages.

Carsten Dachsbacher is a full professor at the Karlsruhe Institute of Technology. Prior to joining KIT, he was an assistant professor at the Visualization Research Center (VISUS) of the University of Stuttgart, Germany, and postdoctoral fellow at REVES/INRIA Sophia-Antipolis, France. He received a MS in computer science from the University of Erlangen-Nuremberg, Germany, in 2002 and a PhD in computer science in 2006. His research focuses on real-time computer graphics, interactive global illumination, and perceptual rendering, on which he has published several articles at various conferences, including SIGGRAPH, I3D, EG, and EGSR. He has been a tutorial speaker at Eurographics, SIGGRAPH, and the Game Developers Conference and a reviewer for various conferences and journals.

Wolfgang Engel is the CEO of Confetti (www.conffx.com), a think tank for advanced real-time graphics for the game and movie industry. Previously he worked for more than four years in Rockstar's core technology group as the lead graphics programmer. His game credits can be found at http://www.mobygames.com/developer/sheet/view/developerId,158706/. He is the editor of the *ShaderX* and

GPU Pro book series, the author of many articles, and a regular speaker at computer graphics conferences worldwide. He is also a DirectX MVP (since 2006), teaches at UCSD, and is active in several advisory boards throughout the industry. You can find him on twitter at @wolfgangengel.

Christopher Oat is the Technical Director at Rockstar New England where he works on real-time rendering techniques and low-level optimizations for many of Rockstar's latest games. Previously, he was the Demo Team Lead for AMD's Game Computing Applications Group. Christopher has published his work in various books and journals and has presented at graphics and game developer conferences worldwide. Many of the projects that he has worked on can be found on his website: www.chrisoat.com.

Michal Valient leads the technology team at Guerrilla in Amsterdam. He spends his time working on the core engine technology powering the highly acclaimed *Killzone* games on Playstation 3 and Playstation 4 as well as some yet unannounced projects. Previously he worked as a programmer and a lead at Caligari where he developed the shader-based real-time rendering engine for Caligari trueSpace7. His interests include many aspects of light transfer, shadows, and parallel processing in general. He believes in sharing the knowledge, and he gave talks at GDC and SIGGRAPH and wrote graphics papers published in *ShaderX* books and conference journals.

About the Contributors

Abdul Bezrati is a senior engine programmer at Insomniac Games studio in Burbank, California. He is passionate about finding new real-time rendering techniques and sharing them with other game developers.

Vladimir Bondarev is a senior graphics programmer at Confetti Interactive Inc. He graduated with honors from NHTV Breda University of Applied Sciences. He worked on CPU optimizations for the new Futuremark Benchmark and GPU optimizations for *Dirt 4*, and he is currently working on Super Evil Megacorp's title *Vainglory*.

Jean-Normand Bucci is managing a multi-disciplinary team of seven engineers and two technical artists as the director of Labs, Eidos-Montrèal's research-and-development department. The team's mandate is to work on innovation for the portfolio of all the western studios of Square-Enix Europe: Eidos-Montrèal, Io Interactive, and Crystal Dynamics. Prior to Labs, Jean-Normand, technical art director at the time, shipped *Thief* for both past and present generations of consoles. He worked in close collaboration with the lead 3D and programming director in finding the best visual improvements for the game given the constraints. With ten years of experience working on major AAA games at both Ubisoft Montrèal and Eidos-Montrèal, Jean-Normand feels comfortable and performs well in pipeline, feature, and tool brainstorming/creation roles.

Nicolas Capens is a member of Google's Chrome GPU team and a contributor to Android graphics tools. He is passionate about making 3D graphics more widely available and less restricted. His work on the ANGLE project helped create reliable WebGL support for Chrome on Windows. As the lead developer of SwiftShader, he enabled WebGL on systems with blacklisted GPUs or drivers. Through innovative multi-threading, wide vectorization, and dynamic code specialization, he continues to drive the convergence between CPU and GPU capabilities. Nicolas received his MSciEng degree in computer science from Ghent University in 2007.

Amir Chohan is a software developer in the financial industry. He graduated from the University of Bristol with an MEng in mathematics and computer science in

2014, and he developed the prototype of the HDR computational photography pipeline as part of his final-year project.

Dan Curran is a researcher in the HPC group at the University of Bristol, where his work focuses on the development of efficient algorithms for many-core computer architectures. He has worked on a range of different applications, including computational fluid dynamics, de-dispersion for the SKA, lattice Boltzmann, and computational photography. He is an expert in GPU computing, with a particular focus on OpenCL. Dan graduated with an MEng in computer science in 2012.

Samuel Delmont is a graphics programmer at Eidos Montrèal. He graduated in computer science at ESIEE Paris in 2007, and he worked in the game industry on several engines as an R&D programmer. In 2013 he joined Eidos Montrèal to work on *Thief* and is now a research programmer in Eidos Montrèal's Labs, an R&D group dedicated to new graphic technologies.

Michael Delva always thought he would be a sports teacher until he realized after his studies that his way was in programming. He learned C++ by himself, and he created his own company to develop and sell a basketball video and statistical analysis software, until he had to end this great period four years later. Then, he worked for a few years at NeuroTV, where he participated in the development of real-time 3D solutions and interactive applications for the broadcast industry. He is now happy to be able to mix his passion for programming and video games at Fishing Cactus, where he works as an engine/gameplay programmer.

Daniele Di Donato is a senior software engineer in the ARM Demo Team. In his daily job he develops demos for ARM Mali GPU-based devices to showcase the latest OpenGL ES features available on mobile. He obtained an MEng in computer science from the University of Bologna in 2012.

Hawar Doghramachi studied dental medicine at the Semmelweis University in Budapest and received in 2003 the doctor of dental medicine (DMD) title. After working for a while as a dentist, he decided to turn his lifetime passion for programming into his profession. After he studied 3D programming at the Games Academy in Frankfurt, from 2010 he worked as an Engine-Programmer in the Vision team of Havok. Currently he is working as a Graphics-Programmer in the R&D team of Eidos Montreal. He is particularly interested in finding solutions for common real-time rendering problems in modern computer games.

Uriel Doyon is a 3D programmer at Eidos Montreal. He studied computer engineering at Ecole Polytechnique de Montreal, during which he made several internships at Matrox Graphics. He joined Ubisoft Montreal in 2004 as a 3D programmer and worked on several titles on the GameCube, Wii, and Playstation

3. In 2009, he started working at Eidos Montreal as the lead 3D programmer on *Thief*. He is currently working in Labs, which is an R&D group dedicated to new graphic technologies.

Michał Drobot is a principal rendering engineer at Infinity Ward, Activision. He most recently helped design and optimize the 3D renderer in *Far Cry 4* at Ubisoft Montreal. Prior to that, he worked at Guerrilla Games, designing and optimizing the rendering pipeline for the Playstation 4 launch title *Killzone: Shadow Fall*. He likes sharing his work at conferences as well as spending time writing publications about art and technology. He finds fast and pretty pixels exciting.

Alex Dunn, as a developer technology engineer for NVIDIA, spends his days passionately working toward advancing real-time visual effects in games. A former graduate of Abertay University's Games Technology Course, Alex got his first taste of graphics programming on the consoles. Now working for NVIDIA, his time is spent working on developing cutting-edge programming techniques to ensure the highest quality and best player experience possible is achieved.

Elmar Eisemann is a professor at Delft University of Technology (TU Delft), heading the Computer Graphics and Visualization Group. Before, he was an associated professor at Telecom ParisTech (until 2012) and a senior scientist heading a research group in the Cluster of Excellence (Saarland University / MPI Informatik) (until 2009). His interests include real-time and perceptual rendering, alternative representations, shadow algorithms, global illumination, and GPU acceleration techniques. He coauthored the book *Real-Time Shadows* and participated in various committees and editorial boards. He was local organizer of EGSR 2010, EGSR 2012, and HPG 2012, as well as co-paper chair for HPG2015, and he was honored with the Eurographics Young Researcher Award in 2011.

Andrew Girdler is a real-time rendering specialist in the graphics demo team at Imagination Technologies, where he works on developing new real-time techniques for embedded graphics platforms. He was an integral part of developing the team's new in-house engine and rendering technologies, including the shell-based fur rendering technique outlined in this book. Andrew is graduating with a degree in computer science from the University of Bath in 2015.

Holger Gruen ventured into creating real-time 3D technology over 20 years ago writing fast software rasterizers. Since then he has worked for games middleware vendors, game developers, simulation companies, and independent hardware vendors in various engineering roles. In his current role as a developer technology engineer at NVIDIA, he works with games developers to get the best out of NVIDIA's GPUs.

Julien Hamaide is an experienced programmer and technical director of Fishing Cactus. His main interest is sharing his accumulated knowledge with his team while learning more every day. Previously senior and lead programmer in a scrumm-based team at 10Tacle Studio Belgium, he decided to launch Fishing Cactus with Bruno Urbain and Ramses Ladlani. Always looking to increase overall knowledge, he contributed five articles to the *Game Programming Gems* series, one to *AI Programming Wisdom 4*, and one to *Game Engine Gems 2*. He also presented two lectures at the GDC 2008 and 2009. Owning an engineering degree in electricity and signal processing, he has a complete scientific background. By working in small studios, he had the chance to work on lots of different topics, running from low-level console programming to AI passing through multithreading.

Dongsoo Han works as a researcher in AMD's GPU Tech Initiatives Group. At AMD, he focuses on developing physics simulations such as rigid body, fluid, cloth, hair, and grass for real-time applications. His research focuses on parallelizing physics simulation algorithms on GPUs. His hair simulation technique is a part of TressFX and has been used for several games and demos. He earned his master's degree in computer science at University of Pennsylvania, where he focused on various fluid simulation methods.

Takahiro Harada is a researcher in AMD's office of the CTO, where he is exploring the possibility of GPU computing. Currently he is spending most of his time on research and development of physics simulation and rendering algorithms. Before joining AMD, he engaged in research and development on real-time physics simulation on PC and game consoles at Havok. Before coming to industry, he was in academics as an assistant professor at the University of Tokyo, where he also earned his PhD in engineering.

Viktor Heisenberger is a software engineer at GRAPHISOFT, working on CAD software for the AEC industry. He graduated with a master's degree in information technology engineering at Budapest University of Technology and Economics. His professional interests include computer graphics and web development. In his free time, he enjoys photography and various sports.

John Huelin is a graphics programmer at Ubisoft Montreal, where he has worked mostly on the *Assassin's Creed* games developing and optimizing a variety of 3D technologies. He earned his master's degree in computer science at University of Technology of Belfort-Montbeliard (UTBM), where he focused on image and 3D.

James L. Jones graduated with a degree in computer science from Cardiff University and works on real-time graphics demos in the demo team at Imagination Technologies. He is currently focused on physically based rendering techniques for modern embedded graphics platforms and research for demos with Imagination's real-time ray-tracing technology.

Benjamin Keinert is a PhD candidate in the DFG-funded Research Training Group "Heterogeneous Image Systems" at the University of Erlangen-Nuremberg, Germany. He received his MSc degree from the same university in 2013 after completing his thesis about "Dynamic Attributes for Hardware Tessellated Meshes." His current research involves real-time rendering techniques as well as interactive global illumination approaches.

Thomas Kroes is a PhD student in computer science at Delft University of Technology (TU Delft). He has a bachelor's degree in mechanical engineering and a master's in industrial design engineering. He is interested in medical visualization, in particular real-time photo-realistic volume visualization. He is the author of Exposure Render, an interactive photo-realistic volume rendering framework.

Ramses Ladlani is lead engine programmer at Fishing Cactus, the video game company he co-founded in 2008 with three former colleagues from 10tacle Studios Belgium (a.k.a. Elsewhere Entertainment). When he is not working on the next feature of Mojito, Fishing Cactus's in-house cross-platform engine, he can be found playing rugby or learning his new role as a father. He received his master's degree in computer engineering from Université Libre de Bruxelles.

Geoff Lang is a software engineer at Google on the Chrome graphics team. He is currently working on bringing ANGLE and OpenGL ES to as many platforms as possible to make the lives of graphics developers easier. In his spare time, he creates indie video games.

Hongwei Li received his PhD in computer science from Hong Kong University of Science and Technology. He was a researcher in AMD advanced graphics research group, focusing on real-time rendering and GPGPU applications. He is also very active in the open source community and is the main contributor of a rendering engine for mobile platforms.

Anton Lokhmotov has been working in the area of programming languages and tools for 15 years, both as a researcher and engineer, primarily focussing on productivity, efficiency, and portability of programming techniques for heterogeneous systems. In 2015, Anton founded dividiti to pursue his vision of efficient and reliable computing everywhere. In 2010–2015, Antonled development of GPU Compute programming technologies for the ARM Mali GPU series, including production (OpenCL, RenderScript) and research (EU-funded project CARP) compilers. He was actively involved in educating academic and professional developers, engaging with partners and customers, and contributing to open source projects and standardization efforts. In 2008–2009, Anton investigated heterogeneous programming as a research associate at Imperial College London. He received a PhD in computer science from the University of Cambridge in 2008 and an MSc in applied mathematics and physics (summa cum laude) from the Moscow Institute for Physics and Technology in 2004.

Jamie Madill works on Google Chrome's GPU team to help Chrome's OpenGL backend work uniformly across every device and API, via ANGLE. His background is in simulation and rendering, with which he still tinkers in his spare time. He graduated with a master's degree in computer science from Carleton University in 2012.

Hugh Malan is a principle tech programmer at Guerrilla Games. Previously, he worked for CCP on Dust 514, and before that at Realtime Worlds, as graphics lead on *Crackdown*. He developed the "Realworldz" real-time procedurally-generated planet demo for 3Dlabs. He has an MSc in computer graphics from Otago University, New Zealand, and a BSc in physics with honors in mathematics from Victoria University, New Zealand.

Simon McIntosh-Smith leads the HPC research group at the University of Bristol in the UK. His background is in microprocessor architecture, with a 15-year career in industry at companies including Inmos, STMicroelectronics, Pixelfusion, and ClearSpeed. Simon co-founded ClearSpeed in 2002 where, as director of architecture and applications, he co-developed the first modern many-core HPC accelerators. In 2003 he led the development of the first accelerated BLAS/LAPACK and FFT libraries, leading to the creation of the first modern accelerated Top500 system, TSUBAME-1.0, at Tokyo Tech in 2006. He joined the University of Bristol in 2009, where his research focuses on efficient algorithms for heterogeneous many-core architectures and performance portability. He is a joint recipient of an R&D 100 award for his contribution to Sandia's Mantevo benchmark suite, and in 2014 he was awarded the first Intel Parallel Computing Center in the UK. Simon actively contributes to the Khronos OpenCL heterogeneous many-core programming standard.

Doug McNabb is currently a game developer's voice inside Intel. He's currently creating new technologies to help advance the state of the art in visual computing. He was previously the CTO and rendering system architect at 2XL Games and the rendering system architect at Rainbow Studios. He contributed to more than a dozen games, with the most-recent being *Baja: Edge of Control*. You can find him on twitter @mcnabbd.

Gareth Morgan has been involved in games and 3D graphics since 1999, starting at Silicon Graphics followed by several games companies including Activision and BAM Studios. Since 2008 he has been a leading software engineer at Imagination

Technologies specializing in researching sophisticated rendering techniques using Imagination's ray-tracing technology.

Matthias Nießner is a visiting assistant professor at Stanford University affiliated with the Max Planck Center for Visual Computing and Communication. Previous to his appointment at Stanford, he earned his PhD from the University of Erlangen-Nuremberg, Germany, under the supervision of Günther Greiner. His research focuses on different fields of computer graphics and computer vision, including real-time rendering, reconstruction of 3D scene environments, and semantic scene understanding.

Gustavo Bastos Nunes is a graphics engineer in the Engine team at Microsoft Turn 10 Studios. He received his BSc in computer engineering and MSc in computer graphics from Pontifícia Universidade Católica do Rio de Janeiro, Brazil. He has several articles published in the computer graphics field. He is passionate about everything graphics related. Gustavo was part of the teams that shipped Microsoft Office 2013, Xbox One, and *Forza Motorsport 5*.

David Pangerl is the CEO of Actalogic, where he is working as a lead researcher and engine architecture designer. He has been involved in computer graphics and engine research for over a decade.

João Lucas Guberman Raza is a program manager at Microsoft's 343 Industries, where he works in the services cloud compute systems. Previously he was in the Windows Phone division, where he helped ship the SDK for game developers. An avid gamer, he has worked in the game industry for over five years. He holds a bachelor of computer science from Universidade Federal de São Carlos (UFSCar). He runs the blog www.versus-software.com, where he writes about his main interests in graphics, networking, and game design.

Benjamin Rouveyrol has been working in the game industry for the past ten years, working on the *Far Cry* and *Assassin's Creed* series. He is currently working at Ubisoft Montreal on *Rainbow Six Siege*, making pixel faster and prettier.

Henry Schäfer is currently working toward a PhD degree in computer graphics at the University of Erlangen-Nuremberg. His research interests include realistic image synthesis, data-compression techniques, and real-time rendering.

Dirk Schut is a student at Delft University of Technology. He worked on the chapter as part of the honors track of his bachelor's degree in computer science. Now he is doing a master's degree in computer science, focussing on computer graphics and signal processing. Before he started studying, he programmed computer graphics techniques for fun.

Peter Sikachev graduated from Lomonosov Moscow State University in 2009, majoring in applied mathematics and computer science. He started his career in academia, defending his thesis in gemstone rendering. After graduation, he moved to Vienna University of Technology, changing his research interests to scientific visualization. In 2011 he decided to switch to game development and joined Mail.Ru Games as a graphics programmer. He contributed to a range of rendering features of the *Skyforge* next-generation MMORPG. In 2013 he moved to Eidos Montreal as a research-and-development graphics programmer, finding a perfect balance between pure research and pure industry. As well as looking at emerging technologies and creating prototypes, he works closely with the game teams, contributing to the rendering engines of *Thief* and *Deus Ex: Universe*. He is a principal author of four publications in peer-reviewed international conference proceedings.

Ivan Spogreev is a rendering software engineer at EA Canada working on *FIFA* for Xbox One, Playstation 4, and PC. He started his career in the game industry in 2007 and has always been passionate about 3D graphics technology and visuals. He has previously worked at Ubisoft and HB Studios on various projects including *Madden*, *Assassin's Creed 2*, and *Splinter Cell: Conviction*. His main focus is making games look as realistic as possible.

Marc Stamminger is a professor for computer graphics at the University of Erlangen-Nuremberg, Germany, since 2002. After finishing his PhD thesis on finite element methods for global illumination in 1999, he was a post doctorate at MPI Informatics in Saarbrücken, Germany, and at the INRIA Sophia-Antipolis, France. In his research he investigates novel algorithms to exploit the power of current graphics hardware for rendering, geometry processing, and medical visualization. He participates in the program committees of all major computer graphics conferences and was program co-chair of Eurographics 2009 and the Eurographics Rendering Symposium 2010. Since 2012, he is head of the DFG-funded Research Training Group "Heterogeneous Image Systems."

Jason Stewart is a developer technology engineer at AMD. He studied computer science and computer graphics at the University of North Carolina at Chapel Hill. Prior to joining the developer technology team at AMD, he worked in the game industry for eight years, developing and optimizing graphics features for several major titles. He previously worked at Electronic Arts and Red Storm Entertainment, shipping games on original Xbox, Xbox 360, Playstation 2, Playstation 3, Wii, 3DS, and iOS. Prior to his game industry work, he worked as a hardware and real-time embedded software engineer. In his roll at AMD, he works with professional game developers to integrate technologies and optimize performance on AMD graphics hardware.

Márton Tamás is currently studying computer engineering at Budapest University of Technology and Economics. His interests include real-time rendering, GPU programming, and engine development. Follow him on twitter @0martint.

Shannon Woods is the project lead for ANGLE at Google. Prior to her current work, she explored other corners of the 3D graphics world, developing software for game portability and real-time distributed simulation. She is a graduate of the University of Maryland and enjoys close specification analysis, music, and teapots.

Bartłomiej Wroński is a senior staff programmer at Sony Computer Entertainment America. He started his career at the Polish game development studio CD Projekt RED in Warsaw, working as an engine and graphics programmer for *The Witcher 2* and later leading the technical side of the porting process for *The Witcher 2: Enhanced Edition* for Xbox 360. After conducting R&D activities and developing new rendering and lighting techniques for upcoming titles *The Witcher 3: Wild Hunt* and *Cyberpunk 2077*, he joined the Ubisoft Montreal studio. He worked there on next-generation visual effects for critically acclaimed AAA video game titles including *Assassin's Creed IV: Black Flag* and *Far Cry 4*. Recently, Bart joined Sony Computer Entertainment America at the Santa Monica Studio to continue his work on novel real-time algorithms for the Sony Playstation console platform. He runs a graphics- and photography-oriented blog at www.bartwronski.com. His hobbies include digital and film photography, electronic music synthesis and sound processing, strength sports, and traveling.

Egor Yusov is a senior graphics software engineer in Visual Computing Engineering group at Intel, where he has worked on a variety of 3D technologies including deformable terrain, physically based water rendering, shadows, and volumetric and postprocess effects. He received his PhD in computer science from Nizhny Novgorod State Technical University, Russia, in 2011. His research interests include real-time visualization and rendering, data compression, GPU-based algorithms, and shader programming.

Index